Constraints on Learning

Constraints on Learning

Limitations and Predispositions

Based on a conference sponsored by
St. John's College, Cambridge, England

Edited by

R. A. HINDE

and

J. STEVENSON-HINDE

1973

ACADEMIC PRESS · LONDON · NEW YORK

ACADEMIC PRESS INC. (LONDON) LTD.
24/28 Oval Road
London NW1

United States Edition published by
ACADEMIC PRESS INC.
111 Fifth Avenue
New York, New York 10003

Library of Congress Catalog Card Number: 72–12271
ISBN: 0–12–349150–9

PRINTED IN GREAT BRITAIN BY
COX & WYMAN LTD
LONDON, FAKENHAM AND READING

List of Participants

*G. P. BAERENDS *Zoologisch Laboratorium, Der Rijksuniversiteit te Groningen, Kerklaan 30, Haren, The Netherlands.*

R. BAMBROUGH *St. John's College, University of Cambridge, Cambridge, England.*

*P. P. G. BATESON *Sub-Department of Animal Behaviour, University of Cambridge, Madingley, Cambridge, England.*

*C. BLAKEMORE *The Physiological Laboratory, University of Cambridge, Downing Street, Cambridge, England.*

*P. E. BRYANT *Department of Experimental Psychology, University of Oxford, South Parks Road, Oxford, England.*

D. F. CHANTREY *Sub-Department of Animal Behaviour, University of Cambridge, Madingley, Cambridge, England.*

*K. J. CONNOLLY *Department of Psychology, Motor Development Research Unit, University of Sheffield, Sheffield, England.*

*A. S. ETIENNE *Sub-Department of Animal Behaviour, University of Cambridge, Madingley, Cambridge, England. (Now at: École de Psychologie et des Sciences de l'Éducation, University of Geneva, Palais Wilson, CH–1200 Geneva, Switzerland).*

*B. M. FOSS *Bedford College, University of London, Regent's Park, London, N.W.1, London.*

*S. E. GLICKMAN *Department of Psychology, University of California, Berkeley, California, U.S.A.*

*R. A. HINDE *MRC Unit on the Development and Integration of Behaviour, University of Cambridge, Madingley, Cambridge, England.*

*J. A. HOGAN *Department of Psychology, University of Toronto, Toronto 181, Canada (Visitor to the Sub-Department of Animal Behaviour, University of Cambridge, Madingley, Cambridge, England. 1971–1972).*

---

* Participants who contributed papers.

L. Hogan–Warburg *Department of Psychology, University of Toronto, Toronto 181, Canada.*

†W. K. Honig *Department of Psychology, Dalhousie University, Halifax, N.S., Canada.*

G. Horn *Department of Anatomy, University of Cambridge, Downing Street, Cambridge, England.*

†N. K. Humphrey *Sub-Department of Animal Behaviour, University of Cambridge, Madingley, Cambridge, England.*

†S. J. Hutt *Human Development Research Unit, University of Oxford, Park Hospital for Children, Headington, Oxford, England.*

P. S. Jackson *Sub-Department of Animal Behaviour, University of Cambridge, Madingley, Cambridge, England.*

*H. M. Jenkins *Department of Psychology, McMaster University, Hamilton, Ontario, Canada.*

*J. Kruijt *Zoologisch Laboratorium, Der Rijksuniversiteit te Groningen, Kerklaan 30, Haren, The Netherlands.*

S. E. G. Lea *Department of Experimental Psychology, University of Cambridge, Downing Street, Cambridge, England.*

N. R. Liley *Department of Zoology, University of British Columbia, Vancouver, Canada (Visitor to the Sub-Department of Animal Behaviour, University of Cambridge, Madingley, Cambridge, England. 1971–1972).*

*N. J. Mackintosh *Department of Psychology, Dalhousie University, Halifax, N.S., Canada (From 1973 at: Laboratory of Experimental Psychology, University of Sussex, Falmer, Brighton, England).*

*D. J. McFarland *Department of Experimental Psychology, University of Oxford, South Parks Road, Oxford, England.*

*J. C. Marshall *MRC Speech and Communication Research Unit, University of Edinburgh, Buccleuch Place, Edinburgh, Scotland.*

*B. R. Moore *Department of Psychology, Dalhousie University, Halifax, N.S., Canada.*

M. J. Morgan *Department of Experimental Psychology, University of Cambridge, Downing Street, Cambridge, England.*

T. J. Roper *Department of Experimental Psychology, University of Cambridge, Downing, Street, Cambridge, England.*

*J. Ryan *Unit for Research on Medical Application of Psychology, University of Cambridge, Salisbury Villas, Station Road, Cambridge, England.*

---

* Participants who contributed papers.
† Discussion leaders.

*H. R. SCHAFFER *Department of Psychology, University of Strathclyde, Richmond Street, Glasgow, Scotland.*

*P. SEVENSTER *Zoologisch Laboratorium, Der Rijksuniversiteit te Leiden, Kaiserstraat 63, Leiden, The Netherlands.*

*S. J. SHETTLEWORTH *Department of Psychology, University of Toronto, Toronto 181, Canada.*

E. SIQUELAND *Department of Psychology, Brown University, Providence, Rhode Island, U.S.A. (Visitor to the Behaviour Development Research Unit, London, England, 1972).*

*H. SINCLAIR *École de Psychologie et des Sciences de l'Éducation, University of Geneva, Palais Wilson, CH-1200 Geneva, Switzerland.*

†J. STEVENSON-HINDE *Sub-Department of Animal Behaviour, University of Cambridge, Madingley, Cambridge and Department of Experimental Psychology, University of Cambridge, Downing Street, Cambridge, England.*

W. H. THORPE *Sub-Department of Animal Behaviour, University of Cambridge, Madingley, Cambridge, England.*

C. ULDAL *Sub-Department of Animal Behaviour, University of Cambridge, Madingley, Cambridge, England.*

---

* Participants who contributed papers.
† Discussion leaders.

Preface

Specification of the conditions under which learning occurs has been a major goal of experimental psychology since its birth as a natural science. An impressive literature has accumulated, and a great deal is now known about the determinants of learning in rats, pigeons and, though to a lesser extent, primates including man. In much of this work it has been assumed that laws of learning could be found which, with some manipulation of the constants, would be applicable in all situations and to all species. On this view differences between species in particular situations, and between the learning performances of the same species in different situations, were explicable in terms of quantitative differences in such characters as "generalization gradients" and "memory capacity".

During the last decade there has been increasing discontent with this view. This has come in part from the learning theory approach itself. In nearly all the early work the conventional reinforcers of food, water and escape from painful or frightening stimuli were used. When it became clear that reinforcing properties were associated with a much wider range of stimuli it became necessary, in order to escape circularity, to predict in advance what stimuli would and would not have reinforcing properties. As more species were studied in more situations, it became apparent that such predictions could not be made without taking into account both species and situation. This was, of course, especially the case when attempts were made to interpret the complex learning that occurs in real-life situations in terms of the processes studied in laboratory animals. In addition, close observation of behaviour during learning in laboratory experiments revealed previously unsuspected complexities. For these and other reasons a growing number of experimental psychologists have come to feel that the traditional learning theory approach requires at least some qualification if it is to cope with the range of phenomena now being studied.

At the same time biologists, trained to focus on species differences, found that some species would learn when related species would not, and that what was learned in one situation could not be accounted for in terms of generalizations about the capacity of the species for learning in all situations. Indeed the sterility of attempts to divide behaviour into that which is "innate" and that which is "learned" came to be accepted in part because of evidence that organisms were predisposed to learn some things and not others.

The new view has an importance extending beyond the need to qualify generalizations about learning. For example it has profound educational implications in that the predispositions of man to learn certain things at certain times in certain ways (but not in others) must be taken into account in planning curricula. And, on a wider basis, it bids us reflect whether the increasing pace of cultural change is requiring man to modify his behaviour in ways contrary to his biologically adapted predispositions.

Because of the importance of these problems we approached St. John's College, Cambridge, with a request that they should sponsor a conference which would draw together some of the current work. The College agreed, and the meeting was further underwritten by the Nuffield Foundation. The conference, attended by 37 participants, was held in the College between April 4th and 7th, 1972.

A few lines about the procedure we adopted are necessary. Chapter 1 was precirculated to all speakers, and invited discussants each received in addition a selection of manuscripts before the meeting. These discussants were asked to draw the papers together at intervals during the meeting. Participants who asked questions, raised issues or provided additional data after the main contributions were asked to put their points in writing both to the contributors in question and to the editors. After the meeting the contributors were asked to revise their manuscripts in the light of these comments, which many did, or to answer them directly. To this extent the whole book can be regarded as a cooperative enterprise of those who attended the meeting. Any outstanding issues we have taken up, using such editorial devices—additional comments appended to chapters, cross-references and "editorials" interspersed throughout the book—as seemed appropriate: for these we must take full responsibility.

Finally, on behalf of ourselves and all the participants, we would like to thank St. John's College, Cambridge for the generous support it provided, and the Nuffield Foundation for offering to supplement it.

We are also grateful to those within the College, especially Dr. C. M. P. Johnson, Mr. A. C. Crook, 'Mr. A. M. P. Brookes and Dr. W. D. Armstrong, for their help with the arrangements. We are greatly indebted to T. J. Roper for undertaking the onerous task of preparing the subject index. We would like to express our special gratitude to Carole Perkis for the help she gave with administrative matters at all stages from the early planning to the submission of the manuscript: her conscientious and cheerful attention to detail did much for the success of the enterprise.

R.A.H.
J.S.-H.

January 1973
MRC Unit on the Development and Integration of Behaviour
Madingley, Cambridge, England.

Contents

1
Constraints on Learning – An Introduction to the Problems

by R. A. Hinde

Introduction

During the thirties and forties psychology passed through a period of heroic optimism, characterised by a belief in the possibility of constructing a comprehensive theory of behaviour. Amongst learning theorists, Tolman (1932) was concerned with all non-reflex behaviour of all organisms. Skinner (1938) was interested in setting up a science of behaviour where "behaviour is that part of the functioning of an organism which is engaged upon or having commerce with the outside world". Hull (1943) hoped that his system would be extended to provide a "systematic theory of all social sciences". All three derived their primary data from rats, or later pigeons, in restricted situations: all three hoped that a system so based would have almost limitless applicability.

There were doubts even in the early days of learning theory (e.g. Thorndike—see Seligman, 1970), and with the growth of knowledge and sophistication a number of learning theorists came to regard such grandiose attempts as naive. In part because of the explicitness for its formulation, in part because of its nature, Hull's system came most readily under attack. Hull had tried to establish a set of principles from which "it should be possible to deduce . . . an extensive logical hierarchy of secondary principles which will exactly parallel all of the objectively observable behaviour of higher organisms". In his 1954 discussion of Hullian theory Koch wrote "In the present state of our ignorance, no one can *seriously* believe that a comprehensive, quantitative, hypothetico-deductive theory of behaviour is possible"; and in 1959, in the course of an evaluation of the Hull-Spence approach, Logan wrote "most of the difficulties encountered by it have arisen when one leaves the simpler situations with which it was originally concerned". Miller (1959), although developing Hullian methodology, went further to argue that it is not necessary to have one all-embracing theory: "Although different theories should not be scrambled together in one grand eclectic hash, there is nothing to prevent the scientist from using entirely different models to deal with different aspects of his theoretical and practical problems".

Tolman's system was more loosely constructed: in a late paper (1959) he coupled a charming disclaimer ("I have not the type of mind that can remember which were my axioms and which were my deductions") with a strong condemnation of the method ("To attempt to build psychology on the analogy of a closed mathematical or logical system seems to me a 'bad error' "). The intellectually stimulating attempt by MacCorquodale and Meehl (1954) to set out the theory more rigidly has proved only moderately productive, and Tolman (l.c.) himself remarked "I think the days of such grandiose, all-covering systems in psychology as mine attempted to be are, at least for the present, pretty much passé".

For Skinner the laws were reached inductively from the data, and his system does not stand or fall on their logical consistency or independence. For the most part the basic concepts were established with rats or pigeons, and then the experimental procedures, terminology, and relationships between variables transferred to other situations by analogy: where possible, the analogy was subsequently tested by experiment (Verplanck, 1954). Skinner, therefore, has been concerned primarily with generalizations, initially of limited scope, whose validity elsewhere can then be tested— though perhaps not all the claims in his writings are quite so modest as this.

However, even a system of this sort can be misused, and the laws of learning that it provides are easily assumed to have a generality which has not been empirically justified. For example, to take up a quite general issue, the systems of both Hull and Skinner assume learning to be of one or two basic types. This is no place to enter the lists on this issue (see e.g. Chapters 8, 9 and 13), which in any case is partly semantic and depends on the level of analysis and on what is meant by "type". But it must be said that a system based on types of learning necessarily assumes, within each type, that learning is (or is not) always similarly dependent on events which can be labelled as reinforcers, and that the time relations between stimulus, response and reinforcement are always within certain limits. Furthermore, amongst examples of each type, assumptions must be made concerning the extent to which different stimuli, responses and reinforcements are interchangeable. But, as we shall see later in this volume, there is a growing body of empirical data which contradicts the assumptions that have been made for the limited number of learning types specified by the theorists.

The view that laws of learning of considerable generality and precision could be found was so firmly established that those experimental psychologists who questioned it did so in the teeth of their own training. For biologists, however, the reverse has been the case. Until recently, at any rate, all biology students were subjected to a review of the animal kingdom. Although such courses often required the memorization of a vast assemblage of facts, they had one outstanding advantage—they brought the student immediately face to face with diversity. This included not only the diversity of organisms, but also the diversity of mechanisms within organisms. The student learnt, for instance, that animals may respire through gills, lungs, skin, mouth, gut or rectum, and that one animal may respire by more than one of these mechanisms. He learnt, furthermore, that this is not just random diversity: each species is adaptive to a particular way of life, and its various characteristics are inter-related with each other to form an adaptive complex. Thus birds have a highly efficient system of respiration involving ventilation through lungs from air sacs: this is associated with an active mode of life, flight, high body temperature, low body weight and so on. Frogs may breathe through skin, oral cavity, or lungs, or through combinations of these, in accordance with the different media in which they live, and these mechanisms are associated with a wide variety of other adaptations, such as the position of the external nares on the head permitting them to breathe air when nearly submerged, and the functioning of the hyoid apparatus as a respiratory pump. The significance of each character can be seen only in relation to the others, and evolutionary change in one is likely to have repercussions through the whole complex.

Of course biologists inevitably assimilate some envy for the physicists who can say $e = mc^2$ in every contingency, and they have indeed had two good breaks themselves with the theory of evolution by natural selection and the unravelling of the genetic code. But by and large they are still sufficiently impressed by diversity to be suspicious of such assumptions as "all behaviour of the individuals of a given species and that of all species of mammals, including man, occurs according to the same set of primary laws" (Hull, 1945). Although in other contexts they have often enough been guilty of over-generalization or over-simplification, biologists have been quick to stress that learning may be closely adapted to the species' way of life (e.g. Tinbergen, 1951; Lorenz, 1937, 1965). In this area they have (with some notable exceptions) preferred to proceed not only inductively but cautiously, establishing generalizations on the basis of firm data and then gradually determining their range of applicability. And in so doing they are aware that the broader the generalizations, the more superficial they are likely to be.

However, although the possibility of establishing general laws of learning that have sufficient precision to be meaningful is being called into question from all sides (see e.g. Kling & Riggs, 1971), the issue is by no means closed. Furthermore, at the strategic level, we must decide how to proceed. It is not clear whether we should do better to seek for generalizations about learning in real life which differ *in kind* from those which can be made about learning in mazes and Skinner boxes, or whether we should merely tinker with the constants. Must we accept a multiplicity of principles, as Shettleworth (1972) advocates, or can we formulate new and general laws of learning by introducing new dimensions like "preparedness" (Seligman, 1970), and cut the circularity of the concept of reinforcement with the views that reinforcing agents are those which elicit species-characteristic responses, and that they may be classified as positive or negative according to whether they promote approach or withdrawal sequences (Glickman & Schiff, 1967)?

A first step toward answering these questions must involve an examination of just where the traditional learning theorist's approach breaks down. In this introductory chapter I shall mention briefly the principal issues as a framework for the more detailed discussion of these and other points in later chapters. In doing so I must of course acknowledge my indebtedness to many who have previously discussed these problems, including especially Tingergen (1951), Lorenz (1965), Breland and Breland (1961), Glickman and Schiff (1967), Seligman (1970) and especially Shettleworth (1972).

In what follows, I shall not be concerned with questions of learning ability, though these become an important issue later in the volume. For the moment, we may merely note that the mastery of a particular problem (e.g. maze running) to a given criterion by different species *may* involve *qualitatively* distinct processes (e.g. Schneirla, 1959; *see also* Razran, 1971). And at no point do I wish to imply that learning theorists cannot cope with the issues raised, only that they have been neglected and do rather complicate the problem. In principle, they can be met by an inductive approach.

Two Issues With Learning Theories

(i) *Intervening variables*

This is not the place to examine the variables used by learning theorists, but one point must be made. Any theory which depends either on a general drive variable, or on a limited number of unitary drives, will inevitably lack generality. The difficulties which accrue from the use of such concepts as analysis proceeds have been discussed elsewhere (Hinde, 1959), and only three points need to be made here:

(a) Within one functional category of behaviour, appetitive or instrumental behaviour may have considerable independence from the consummatory behaviour to which it leads. The evidence for this view comes from a variety of sources including observational material on the hunting behaviour of carnivores (Lorenz, 1937; Leyhausen, 1956) and birds (Hinde, 1953); evidence for the reinforcing effectiveness of the performance of appetitive acts (King & Weisman, 1964; Roberts and Carey, 1965); and studies of the differential effects on instrumental and consummatory behaviour of both physiological interference (e.g. Davis et al., 1967; McFarland, 1969) and extinction procedures (Morgan, in prep.).

(b) The probability that an animal will continued in a particular functional category of behaviour may be lowered by stimulus changes external or internal to the animal, by the performance of particular activities, or by changes internal to the nervous system itself. The relative importance of these differs between the various functional categories of behaviour. For example, the feeding behaviour of mammals (reviewed Grossman, 1967) and the sexual behaviour of the three-spined stickleback *Gasterosteus aculeatus* (Sevenster-Bol, 1962) are brought to an end by stimuli encountered as a result of the behaviour. By contrast, when a rat encounters a strange object the exploratory or investigatory behaviour elicited ceases not as a result of any change in the external stimulus situation, but of (presumably) the internal changes which occur as the object becomes familiar.

(c) The same functional category of behaviour may be controlled in quite different ways in different species. Compare, for instance, feeding in a mammal with that in a blowfly (Dethier, 1969) or a blood-sucking bug (Bennet-Clark, 1963): the only generalizations that are possible are, for most purposes, trivial.

For reasons such as these, generalizations that depend on drive variables with similar properties for different types of behaviour and different species are likely to run into difficulties.

(ii) *How episodic is learning?*

The point to be made here concerns merely a matter of emphasis in some traditional approaches to learning, but it is one which has had considerable repercussions. So long as the learning theorist defines learning in terms of a change in behaviour, he is likely to omit from discussion effects of experience not apparent in immediate changes in behaviour. Furthermore, by assessing the conditions under which a change in behaviour (performance) occurs, he may imply that learning occurs on certain occasions when there is a suitable concatenation of events, and not at other times. A broader approach, however, suggests that learning is not episodic, but is occurring more continuously, though not necessarily affecting behaviour immediately.

The data to be considered here are of several types:

(a) *The ubiquity of habituation.* The ongoing behaviour of higher organisms is always influenced by the environment. If the environment is unfamiliar, various types of exploratory behaviour are either shown exclusively or interfere intermittently with other types of behaviour. So-called normal behaviour occurs only when habituation has occurred—i.e. when the animal is in a familiar environment. In practice every learning experiment is preceded by a period of habituation to the experimental apparatus, but habituation is often disregarded by learning theorists.

(b) *Imprinting.* The learning involved in the processes whereby the filial responses of nidifugous birds become attached to a parent figure have been studied in the context of "imprinting". It is now clear that familiarity with the parent object *per se* plays a large role. For instance Bateson (1964) has shown that day-old chicks will avoid models painted like the pens in which they had previously been reared less, and follow them more, than models painted differently. The early exposure affected later performance (see Chapter 5).

(c) *Early experience in song-learning.* There are many other contexts in which early experience affects later performance, but song-learning in some birds is of particular interest. The finding of relevance in the present context is that in some species the song developed in the first breeding season may be affected by the songs that the bird had heard earlier, weeks or months before it started to sing itself. Learning in fact seems to involve first learning what to sing, and then learning how to sing it (Thorpe, 1961; Marler, 1970; Konishi & Nottebohm, 1969; Hinde, 1969).

These examples of learning that occurs as a result of mere exposure may well involve processes similar to those involved in perceptual learning (e.g. Gibson, 1969), the acquired distinctiveness of cues (Lawrence, 1949, 1950), latent learning (reviewed MacCorquodale & Meehl, 1954), and even two-stage discrimination learning (e.g. Sutherland, 1959; Sutherland & Mackintosh, 1971). A related issue is discussed in Chapter 4 of this volume. It is not suggested here that learning theorists cannot cope with such phenomena. Tolman's system encompassed the facts of latent learning and Hull (1951) amended his to cope with them: Deutsch's (1960) model also embraces the facts of exposure learning. The point at issue is that, while its importance is now coming to be recognized (e.g. Razran, 1971; Kling, 1971), in the past most learning theorists have tended to treat such exposure learning as of secondary importance, while some biologists have regarded it as primary (e.g. Thorpe, 1963). Indeed other processes such as sensitization, pseudo-conditioning (e.g. Razran, 1971), sensory preconditioning (Seidel, 1959) and priming (Noirot, 1973) which appear to come within most formal definitions of learning but are disregarded by many learning theorists, may well also be important outside the laboratory.

Limitations within and Differences Between Species in Learning in Particular Contexts

(i) *Constraints on what is learned within a species.*

Many of the examples cited in subsequent sections involve a failure to learn in one context by animals which possess the appropriate perceptual and motor apparatus, and whose learning ability in other contexts seems well developed. Here we shall cite only two classic examples from Tinbergen's (1953) work on the herring gull (*Larus argentatus*):

(a) *Egg-rolling.* The herring gull, like many other ground nesting birds, retrieves an egg that has rolled out of its nest by placing its beak beyond the egg and pulling it towards its breast. Since the beak is narrow and the egg asymmetrical, the performance is clumsy and inefficient. Although the egg could be more efficiently retrieved with a sweep of the half extended wing, or by being pushed with the webbed foot, the bird never learns to use these other effectors.

(b) *Lack of differential responding to own eggs.* There is considerable individual variation in the background colour and degree of speckling of herring gulls' eggs. In spite of this, tests in which incubating birds were confronted with two clutches adjacent to their nest site showed that they had little or no tendency to choose their own. In other contexts gulls learn to respond individually to their mates, and they respond differentially to their own chicks within a few days of hatching. Apparently, natural selection has not operated to produce differential responsiveness to eggs in the natural situation (see Chapter 2).

(ii) *Preparedness to learn*

The converse to cases in which learning does not occur, even though the perceptual and effector mechanisms are present and learning occurs adequately in other contexts, involves cases in which learning occurs with exceptional rapidity. A number of cases studied by Russian investigators are cited by Razran (1971). For example, a hare's running response to a moving object plus a tactile stimulus on its neck was readily conditioned to a sound resembling the animal's lip-smacking, and could not be extinguished one-and-a-half years later in 300 non-reinforced trials. The same response could be conditioned to a metronome only in hundreds of trials, and was then readily extinguished (Biryukov, 1960, cited by Razran, 1971).

While few detailed analyses are yet available, it is probable that many naturally occurring sequences of behaviour depend on such predispositions to learn (Lorenz, 1965). For example, a turkey hen (*Meleagris* sp.) at first attacks all objects moving within the nest, unless they utter the particular note emitted by turkey chicks. Any stuffed animal fitted with a loud-speaker emitting these notes is treated as a chick. A deaf hen invariably kills her progeny unless she is carefully habituated to them, and even then she does not behave maternally to them. A normal hen's maternal behaviour rapidly becomes conditioned to the other characteristics of the chick so that, after a few hours, she will brood them even when they are silent. The successful rearing of the chicks thus depends on the ready conditionability of the hen to other characteristics of the chicks associated with this particular sound signal (Schleidt et al., 1960). Many of the descriptions of the development of behaviour in young animals, such as that by Craig (1912) of drinking doves, imply similar rapid learning.

Other examples are given by Seligman (1970), and lead him to propose the dimension of "preparedness". He pointed out that, in most learning studies of rats and pigeons, the problems that had to be learnt were deliberately arbitrary, because it was hoped that, by virtue of this arbitrariness, features would be found in the animal's behaviour that could be generalized to real-life instrumental situations. Seligman suggests that the laws of learning hold only for such "unprepared" associations, and that we must study also the learning of prepared and contraprepared associations: it will then be an empirical issue whether differences in learning vary systematically with the dimension of preparedness. The ways in which associations may be "prepared" or "contraprepared" are of course diverse, and some will be mentioned in subsequent sections (see especially Chapters 5, 6, 11, 13 and 14).

In addition to cases involving increases in response strength, there is suggestive evidence that there are also marked differences in the rapidity with which responses extinguish or habituate. Orienting responses to potential predators, for example, often seem to habituate very much more slowly than those to potential sources of food (e.g. Melzack, 1961; Lorenz, 1965): again, this makes adaptive sense.

(iii) *Species differences in what is learned*.

Of particular interest are cases in which closely related species differ in the extent to which learning occurs in similar functional contexts.

(a) *Egg recognition*. While the herring gull does not learn to respond differentially to its own eggs (see above), the guillemot (*Uria aalge*) does (Tschanz, 1959). This difference between the two species seems to be adaptive: while herring gulls' nests are usually some yards apart, guillemots nest close together on narrow ledges. (The possibility that herring gulls would learn to recognize their eggs if they laid in conditions similar to those in which guillemots lay their eggs cannot be tested experimentally, but seems improbable.)

(b) *Species recognition.* Species differ markedly in the extent to which learning is necessary for recognition of other members of their species. For example, a greylag gosling (*Anser anser*) hatched in an incubator will readily learn to direct its filial responses to a human foster parent, but curlew (*Numenius*) or godwit (*Limosa*) chicks are much less ready to do so (Lorenz, 1935).

(c) *Song development.* While some species of passerine birds sing something very close to the species characteristic song even if reared from the egg in acoustic isolation (Mulligan, 1966) and do not imitate sounds that they hear, others have to be exposed to the song in order to sing it (e.g. Konishi & Nottebohm, 1969), while yet others are able to imitate a wide variety of sounds (e.g. mynahs, *Gracula religiosa*, Bertram, 1970).

(d) *"Tool-using".* There are a number of scattered instances of the use of objects as functional extensions of mouth, beak or paw (van Lawick-Goodall, 1970). Sometimes one species regularly uses a tool, while closely related species do not (e.g. woodpecker finch, *Cactospiza pallida*, Lack, 1947; Eygptian vulture, *Neophron percnopterus*, van Lawick-Goodall, 1970). In such cases the development of the behaviour is unlikely to depend on a sophisticated learning ability absent in closely related species. Such evidence as is available suggests both that experience plays an important part in the development of tool-using, and that the occurrence of learning depends in part on the performance of species characteristic movement patterns which come to form part of the tool-using sequence (e.g. Eibl-Eibesfeldt, 1967).

(e) *Orientation in fish.* Braemer & Schwassmann (cited by Lorenz, 1965) studied sun orientation in sunfish (*Centrachidae*) which are found only in the northern hemisphere, and the *cichlid aequidens portalegrensis* whose range spans the equator. The former, after rearing in artificial light, can orient by the sun at their first exposure provided the sun moves from left to right, but they cannot adjust to a sun moving as it would in the southern hemisphere. The cichlid, by contrast, can orient by either a northern or a southern sun, depending only on the way the sun was moving when first seen.

(f) *Bee orientation.* Lauer & Lindauer (1971) have even demonstrated a difference between two races of the same species. In experiments on the abilities of honey bees to learn the locations of sources of food, they found that two European races showed closely similar learning curves when the food was placed on a feeding tray in an open field, but markedly different ones when the tray was near a tree or other striking landmark. The difference in the latter situation persisted even when both races were members of the same colony. It thus seems clear that there was a genetically based difference between the two races in their ability to use landmarks.

(g) *Language development.* However one assesses the achievements of the Gardners (1972) or Premack (1972) in teaching young chimpanzees to use signs, there is clearly a vast difference in the ease with which chimpanzees and young humans learn something approximating to human language (see Chapters 19, 21 and 22).

These examples are of course heterogeneous. Such inter-species differences could have a variety of bases, such as differences in learning ability *per se*, differences in predispositions to form particular associations, differences in the availability of motor patterns, or differences in relationships between stimulus, response and reinforcer. Some of these will be discussed in subsequent sections.

Some Mechanisms Whereby Learning is Constrained

(i) *Constraints on the stimuli which become associated.*

That responsiveness to stimuli is selective, and that selectivity may both differ between species and depend in subtle ways on experience, is well established (see e.g. Chapters 2, 4 and 7). This may affect learning in a number of ways:

(a) *Non-availability for learning.* At least one case is known where the organism is known to be responsive to a particular category of stimuli, but apparently cannot use it for learning. *Octopus* compensates appropriately for the weight of objects it picks up, but is unable to learn to distinguish objects differing only in weight (Wells, 1961).

(b) *"General" stimulus preferences.* In some cases preferences for stimuli in one modality over another, or for particular types of stimuli within one modality, may affect performance in a wide variety of learning situations. Most of the evidence here comes from studies in which an animal learns to discriminate between two stimulus complexes and is then tested with individual stimulus components absent. Such tests show that monkeys tend to use primarily cues they can touch, though colour is also important, within the visual modality rats tend to rely on the orientation of visual features, and so on (review by Cowey, 1968). The extent to which such stimulus preferences are general is however by no means firmly established (Gilbert, 1969). In any case Mackintosh (Chapter 4) stresses that they may be markedly influenced by previous experience.

(c) *Response-specific stimulus preferences.* In other cases animals will learn to respond to a particular stimulus parameter in one context, but not in another. Some examples from the feeding behaviour of honey bees may be cited. Bees can be trained to come to feeding places marked by olfactory or colour cues, or by particular patterns. The ease with which learning occurs differs: it occurs most rapidly for olfactory cues, next for colour, and most slowly for patterns. Within each of these categories, different stimuli produce different learning curves, but the readiness with which the stimuli are learned is not related to their "effectiveness" as measured physiologically. Thus bees learn to approach some stimuli more readily than others (Lindauer, pers. comm., 1970); Menzel, 1967, 1968; Kriston, 1971). When bees are learning to approach a food source, conditioning does not occur equally all the time to all stimuli asscociated with feeding. Opfinger (1931) arranged that bees should see different colours under a food bowl when they were approaching it, feeding from it, and leaving it. When they next returned the bees went to the colour which had been exposed when they previously approached, rather than that exposed when they were feeding or leaving. More refined experiments showed that learning was confined to the period between two seconds before the bee started to feed and one second afterwards (Menzel, 1967).

Studies of song learning in birds have recently provided examples of species differences in the way in which stimulus patterns are selected for learning. The chaffinch is a species which must hear the species characteristic song in order subsequently to develop it. However, although chaffinches' subsongs show that they are able to sing a much wider variety of notes than appears in the full song, they will not reproduce, in the full song, any auditory patterns that they hear: since they will learn a chaffinch song with the end displaced into the middle, but will not learn the songs of related species, it seems likely that the constraint depends on a responsiveness selective to the structure of the notes (Thorpe, 1961). The song learning of bullfinches (*Pyrrhula pyrrhula*, Nicolai, 1956), zebra finches (Immelmann, 1969) and parasitic weaver finches (*Viduinae*, Nicolai, 1964) is restricted in another way: they learn the song of the individual that reared them, and in the first two cases this occurs even if they can hear the song of their own species.

To cite a quite different type of example, Dobrzecka *et al.* (1966) used dogs in instrumental differentiation problems involving either the quality of an auditory stimulus (metronome versus buzzer) or the direction of its source (in front or behind). When the task involved a left leg – right leg differentiation (S_1—R_1, S_2—R_2), the dogs used exclusively directional cues and were unable to learn when only quality cues were available. When confronted with a go – no go task (S_1–R_1, S_2–no R), however, they usually learned on quality cues but had difficulty with locational ones.

(d) *Reinforcement-specific stimulus preferences.* The stimulus preferences discussed so far have been related to the response being trained. Sometimes, however, the reinforcement seems to determine which stimuli are associated. Examples are provided by the work of Garcia and his colleagues (Revusky & Garcia, 1970) on avoidance of poisons (see Chapter 7).

(ii) *Constraints on the response*

It is usually assumed that the rate of any operant response can be increased by suitable reinforcement. In fact some responses are extremely difficult to train. For instance, although Hogan (1964) was successful in training pigeons to preen for food reinforcement, the preening was perfunctory and accompanied by other irrelevant movements. Konorski (1967) had a similar difficulty with yawning: his dog learnt to open its mouth but not to yawn. This implies that what was being conditioned was not preening or yawning as such, but some of their components. One possible explanation is that reinforcement sometimes came before the movement was complete: Konorski, in conditioning ear scratching, found that the movement tended to become incomplete unless reinforced only after it was completed (see also Chapter 11).

Some cases of contraints on the response may be based on the principles mentioned in section (iv).

(iii) *Species and sex differences in reinforcing effects.*

That food and water are reinforcing to a rat is not an intrinsic property of the stimuli, but of the animal. Stimuli which are reinforcing to one species are not necessarily reinforcing to another: which stimuli can act as reinforcers to a particular species, and when, is a matter determined in the first instance by natural selection (Lorenz, 1965). Even within one species, stimuli that are reinforcing to one sex are not necessarily reinforcing to the other. All this is obvious enough, but it becomes of paramount importance when learning is studied in situations other than the conventional laboratory ones, and when the reinforcing properties of stimuli other than food and water are investigated. For instance it was not predicted, from studies using food or water as a reinforcer, that stimuli eliciting components of aggressive display would be reinforcing (Thompson, 1963; Hogan, 1967). Again, for a chaffinch (*Fringilla coelebs*), the species song is positively, and a particular call notes negatively, reinforcing (Stevenson, 1969; Thompson, 1969): this makes sense when considered in relation to the occasions when these sounds are heard in nature (Stevenson-Hinde, 1972). Indeed it is becoming likely that much of the confusion that exists in studies of the reinforcing effects of illumination changes (Kavanau, 1967) and other sensory reinforcers (Stevenson, 1969) could have been avoided if their relationship to the natural situation had been considered (see also Chapters 10, 11, 12 and 13).

(iv) *Response/reinforcer interactions.*

When operant responses like bar-pressing are used, they are often assumed to be neutral with respect to the learning task. Experiments on auto-shaping (see Chapters 8 and 9) have shown this not to be the case. In the natural situation factors relevant to the operant may play an even more important role. In some cases the operant response may share causal factors with the consummatory behaviour, and thus have a high probability of occurrence, rendering learning relatively easy. Rats readily learn to run or jump to escape electric shock, but can be trained only with difficulty to press a lever: Bolles (1970) suggests that aversive stimulation elicits a variety of species-specific defence reactions, which are thus available for conditioning, but suppresses other types of behaviour, which thus are not (see Chapters 10–13).

A similar principle probably operates with many naturally occurring sequences, such as the nest-building of birds. Although the integration of the various patterns of behaviour involved in nest-building into a functional sequence depends on learning, this learning is almost inevitable because the various activities share causal (e.g. hormonal) factors (Hinde & Stevenson, 1969) and because the performance of some (at least) of them is itself reinforcing (Hinde & Steel, 1972). Similar principals probably operate in the head-turning/nipple-grasping/sucking sequence of the human newborn (e.g. Prechtl, 1958; Gunther, 1955).

In other cases motivational factors relevant to the operant may affect its nature independently of the reinforcement contingencies. If a hungry pigeon is reinforced with food when it pecks another pigeon, it comes also to show other aspects of aggressive behaviour such as vocalization and display (Azrin & Hutchinson, 1967; see also (vi) below). This case differs from the preening case cited above, where only certain aspects of the movement become conditioned, in that here the whole motivational complex becomes involved.

(v) *Diversity of reinforcing effects*

It is not necessarily the case that a reinforcer effective in influencing the rate of one operant will be effective also for another (Meehl, 1950). As noted in the previous section, a reinforcer may be effective for some responses but not others. In any case, the effectiveness of even a primary reinforcer may depend on experience.

In addition, the assumption that all reinforcers act in the same way must be questioned. For example it is usually found that as a fixed ratio schedule of reinforcement is increased, the rate of a food reinforced operant increases in such a manner that the frequency of reinforcement is maintained until finally the behaviour breaks down. By contrast the operant behaviour of fighting fish (*Betta splendens*) reinforced by the opportunity to behave aggressively (Hogan, *et al.*, 1970), and that of zebra finches (Stevenson-Hinde & Uldal, in prep.) reinforced with nest material, do not increase markedly in frequency as the ratio of responses to reinforcements is increased, so that the frequency of reinforcement declines (Chapters 10, 11 and 13).

(vi) *Interference by behaviour elicited by aspects of the situation not relevant to the learning task or not specifically reinforced.*

The importance in studies of learning of pre-experimental habituation to the apparatus has already been stressed. That behaviour other than fear or exploration may interfere with the course of a learning task, or even with the performance of a task already learned, has been stressed by Breland & Breland (1961). For example, they attempted to teach a racoon to pick up coins and deposit them in a metal box for food reinforcement. When the racoon was required to pick up and deposit two coins he often dipped them briefly into the container without letting go, and spent long periods rubbing the two coins together. This behaviour, although not reinforced, became so persistent that it disrupted the training. In this and other cases cited by the Brelands the interference came from responses naturally associated with conditions in the testing situation or the reinforcer (see also Chapter 12).

(vii) *Age changes in what is learned.*

Learning does not occur equally easily at all stages in the life cycle. Two examples of cases where it is dramatically limited may be cited.

(a) *Song learning.* To develop the species characteristic song pattern, a chaffinch (*Fringilla coelebs*) must be exposed to it before the season in which it comes into full song (Thorpe, 1961). In the white-crowned sparrow (Marler, 1970) the sensitive period is much more restricted than in the chaffinch, and is over when the birds are 2 to 4 months old. Males reared in isolation from a few days of age and exposed to two song dialects, one during their first 2 months and the second between 3 and 10 months, learn only the former. In this species, therefore, the sensitive period is over before the bird itself starts to sing. In the zebra finch (*Taeniopygia guttata*) there is evidence that different features of the song are acquired at different ages. In this species song is first heard at 35–40 days of age, and is fully developed at 80 days. The elements of the song can be acquired either before the bird itself starts to sing, or in the early stages of song development. The length, sequence and rhythm of the song elements, however, are fixed during song development. After 80 days of age the song can be modified by example to only a very limited extent (Immelmann, 1969).

(b) *Imprinting*. As we have seen already, the young of many nidifugous birds readily come to direct their filial responses to a foster parent. In particular, they will learn to follow a novel model with little resemblance to their natural parent. The age during which this is possible is, however, limited to a sensitive period extending from shortly after hatching to a few days of age—the precise limits varying with the species, conditions of rearing and testing, and other factors (e.g. Bateson, 1966). In this case the end of the sensitive period is related to the development of fear responses to strange objects, "strangeness" demanding an acquired background of the familiar before it is effective (see Chapter 5). In some species the learning of the characteristics of the sex partner depends on learning that is similarly limited to a sensitive period, though rather later in development.

In these cases the period during which learning can occur is fairly clearly defined, though as research has proceeded it has become clear that the limitations on the sensitive period are determined in part by preceding experience. The effect of experience at one stage in development on subsequent learning ability is of course quite general. Although learning theorists were formerly concerned primarily with adult organisms, many investigators, largely through Hebb's (1949) initiative, have been concerned with the influence of earlier experience on adult performance in discrimination and problem-solving tasks. This issue is of course of crucial importance in the understanding of human development (see Chapters 15–23).

Acknowledgements

I am grateful to A. Etienne, J. Hogan and N. K. Humphrey for their critical comments.

References

Azrin, N. H. and Hutchinson, R. R. (1967). Conditioning of the aggressive behaviour of pigeons by a fixed-interval schedule of reinforcement. *J. exp. Anal. Behav.* **10**, 395–402.

Bateson, P. P. G. (1964). Effect of similarity between rearing and testing conditions on chicks' following and avoidance responses. *J. comp. physiol. Psychol.* **57**, 100–103.

Bateson, P. P. G. (1966). The characteristics and context of imprinting. *Biol. Rev.* **41**, 177–220.

Bennet-Clark, H. C. (1963). The control of meal size in the bloodsucking bug, *Rhodnius prolixus. J. exp. Biol.* **40**, 741–750.

Bertram, B. (1970). The vocal behaviour of the Indian Hill Mynah, *Gracula religiosa. Anim. Behav. Mono.* **3**, Pt. 2.

Biryukov, D. A. (1960). "Ecological Physiology of Higher Nervous Activity." Medgiz, Leningrad.

Bolles, R. C. (1970). Species-specific defense reactions and avoidance learning. *Psychol. Rev.* **77**, 32–48.

Breland, K. and Breland, M. (1961). The misbehavior of organisms. *Am. Psychol.* **16**, 681–684.

Cowey, A. (1968). Discrimination. *In* "Analysis of Behavioural Change" (L. Weiskrantz, 1968 ed.). Harper & Row, New York.

Craig, W. (1912). Observations on doves learning to drink. *J. Anim. Behav.* **2**, 273–279.

Davis, J. D., Gallagher, R. L. and Ladove, R. (1967). Food intake controlled by a blood factor. *Science* **156**, 1247–1248.

Dethier, V. G. (1969). Feeding behaviour of the blowfly. *In* "Advances in the Study of Behaviour" Vol. 2. (D. S. Lehrman, R. A. Hinde, and E. Shaw, eds.) Academic Press, New York.

Deutsch, J. A. (1960). "The Structural Basis of Behaviour." Cambridge Univ. Press, London & University of Chicago.

Dobrzecka, C., Szwejkowska, G. and Konorski, J. (1966). Qualitative versus directional cues in two forms of differentiation. *Science* **153**, 87–89.

Eibl-Eibesfeldt, I. (1967). Concepts of ethology and their significance in the study of human behaviour. *In* "Early Behaviour" (H. W. Stevenson, E. H. Hess, and H. L. Rheingold, eds.) Wiley, New York.

Estes, W. K., Koch, S., MacCorquodale, K., Meehl, P. E., Mueller, C. G., Schoenfeld, W. N. and Verplanck, W. S. (1954). "Modern Learning Theory." Appleton-Century-Crofts, New York.

Gardner, B. T. and Gardner, R. A. (1972). Two-way communication with an infant chimpanzee. *In* "Behaviour of Nonhuman Primates Vol. 4." (A. M. Schrier, and F. Stollnitz, eds.). Academic Press, New York.

Gibson, E. J. (1969). "Principles of Perceptual Learning and Development." Appleton-Century-Crofts, New York.

Gilbert, R. M. (1969). Discrimination learning. *In* "Animal Discrimination Learning" (R. M. Gilbert, and N. S. Sutherland, (eds.). Academic Press, London & New York.

Glickman, S. E. and Schiff, B. B. (1967). A biological theory of reinforcement. *Psychol. Rev.* **74**, 81–109.

Grossman, S. P. (1967), "Physiological Psychology." Wiley, New York.

Gunther, M. (1955). Instinct and the nursing couple. *Lancet* **1955**, 575–578.

Hebb, D. O. (1949). "The Organization of Behaviour." Wiley, New York.

Hinde, R. A. (1953). A possible explanation of paper-tearing behaviour in birds. *Brit. Birds* **46**, 21–23.

Hinde, R. A. (1959). Unitary drives. *Anim. Behav.* **7**, 130–141.

Hinde, R. A. (Ed.) (1969). "Bird Vocalizations: Their Relation to Current Problems in Biology and Psychology." Cambridge Univ. Press.

Hinde, R. A. and Steel, E. A. (1972). Reinforcing events in the integration of canary nest-building. *Anim. Behav.* **20**, in proof.

Hinde, R. A. and Stevenson, J. G. (1969). Sequences of behavior. *In* "Advances in the Study of Behavior" Vol. 2, (D. S. Lehrman ,R. A. Hinde, and E. Shaw, eds.). Academic Press, New York.

Hogan, J. A. (1964). Operant control of preening in pigeons. *J. exp anal. Behav.* **7**, 351–352.

Hogan, J. A. (1967). Fighting and reinforcement in the Siamese fighting fish (*Betta splendens*). *J. comp. physiol. Psychol.* **64**, 356–359.

Hogan, J. A., Kleist, S. and Hutchings, C. S. L. (1970). Display and food as reinforcers in the Siamese fighting fish (*Betta splendens*). *J. comp. physiol. Psychol.* **70**, 351–357.

Hull, C. L. (1943). "Principles of Behavior." Appleton-Century-Crofts, New York.

Hull, C. L. (1945). The place of innate individual and species differences in a natural-science theory of behavior. *Psychol. Rev.* **52**, 55–60.

Hull, C. L. (1951). "Essentials of Behavior." Yale Univ. Press, New Haven.

Immelmann, K. (1969). Song development in the zebra finch and other Estrildid finches, *In* Hinde (1969).

Kavanau, J. L. (1967). Behavior of captive white-footed mice. *Science* **155**, 1623–1639.

King, J. A. and Weisman, R. G. (1964). Sand digging contingent upon bar pressing in deermice (*Peromyscus*). *Anim. Behav.* **12**, 446–450.

Kling, J. W. (1971). Learning: introductory survey. *In* "Experimental Psychology" 3rd Ed, (J. W. Kling, and L. A. Riggs, eds.). Holt, Rinehart and Winston, New York.

Kling, J. W. and Riggs, L. A. (Eds.) (1971). "Experimental Psychology" 3rd ed. Holt, Rinehart and Winston, New York.

Koch, S. (1954). Clark L. Hull. In Estes, *et. al.* (1954).

Koch, S. (Ed.) (1959). "Psychology: A Study of a Science." McGraw-Hill, New York.

Konishi, M. and Nottebohm, F. (1969). Experimental studies in the ontogeny of avian vocalizations. *In* Hinde (1969).

Konorski, J. (1967). "Integrative Activity of the Brain." Univ. Chicago Press, Chicago, Illinois.

Kriston, I. (1971). Zum Problem des Lernverhaltens von *Apis mellifica L.* gegenüber verschiedenen Duftstoffen. *Z. vergl. Physiol.* **74**, 169–189.

Lack, D. (1947). "Darwin's Finches." Cambridge Univ. Press, London.

Lauer, J. and Lindauer, M. (1971). Genetisch fixierte Lerndispositionen bei der Honigbiene. *Abh. Akad. der Wissenschaften und der Literatur* **1**.

Lawick-Goodall, J. van. (1970). Tool-using in primates and other vertebrates. *In* "Advances in the Study of Behavior" Vol. 3. (D. S. Lehrman, R. A. Hinde and E. Shaw, eds.). Academic Press, New York.

Lawrence, D. H. (1949). Acquired distinctiveness of cues: I. Transfer between discriminations on the basis of familiarity with the stimulus. *J. exp. Psychol.* **39**, 770–784.

Lawrence, D. H. (1950). Acquired distinctiveness of cues: II. Selective association in a constant stimulus situation. *J. exp. Psychol.* **40**, 175–188.

Leyhausen, P. (1956). Verhaltensstudien bei Katzen. *Z. Tierpsychol., Beiheft*, **2**.

Lindauer, M. (1970). Lernen und gedächtnis—Versuche an der Honigbiene. *Naturwissenschaften* **57**, 463–467.

Logan, F. A. (1959). The Hull-Spence approach. *In* Koch (1959).

Lorenz, K. (1935). Der Kumpan in der Umwelt des Vogels. *J.f. Ornith.* **83**, 137–213, and 289–413.

Lorenz, K. (1937). Uber die Bildung des Instinktbegriffes. *Naturwiss.* 25, 289–300, 307–318, 324–331.

Lorenz, K. (1965). "Evolution and Modification of Behavior." Univ. of Chicago.

MacCorquodale, K. and Meehl, P. E. (1954). Edward C. Tolman. *In* Estes, *et al.*, (1954).

McFarland, D. J. (1969). Separation of satiating and rewarding consequences of drinking. *Physiol. & Behav.* 4, 987–989.

Marler, P. (1970). A comparative approach to vocal learning. *J. comp. physiol. Psychol.*, 7, Mono., 1–25.

Meehl, P. E. (1950). On the circularity of the law of effert. *Psychol. Rev.* 52, 324–332.

Melzack, R. (1961). On the survival of mallard ducks after "habituation" to the hawk-shaped figure. *Behaviour* 17, 9–16.

Menzel, R. (1967). Untersuchungen zum Erlernen von Spektralfarben durch die Honigbiene. *Z. vgl. Phys.* 56, 22–62.

Menzel, R. (1968). Das Gedächtnis der Honigbiene für Spektralfarben. *Z. vgl. Phys.* 57.

Miller, N. E. (1959). Liberalization of basic S-R concepts: extensions to conflict behavior, motivation and social learning. *In* Koch (1959).

Morgan, M. (in prep.). Resistance to satiation.

Mulligan, J. A. (1966). Singing behaviour and its development in the song sparrow, *Melospiza melodia. University of California Publ, Zool.* 81, 1–75.

Nicolai, J. (1956). Zur Biologie und Ethologie des Gimpels (*Pyrrhula pyrrhula L.*). *Z. Tierpsychol.* 13, 93–132.

Nicolai, J. (1964). Der Brutparasitismus der Viduinae als ethologisches Problem. *Z. Tierpsychol.* 21, 129–204.

Noirot, E. (1972). The onset of maternal behaviour in rats, hamsters, and mice. *In* "Advances in the Study of Behavior" Vol. 4, (D. S. Lehrman, R. A. Hinde, and E. Shaw. eds.). Academic Press, New York.

Opfinger, E. (1931). Über die Orientierung der Biene an der Futterquelle. *Z. vergl. Physiol.*, 15, 431–487.

Prechtl, H. F. R. (1958). The directed head turning response and allied movements of the human baby. *Behaviour* 13, 212–242.

Premack, D. (1972). The assessment of language competence in the chimpanzee. *In* "Behavior of Nonhuman Primates" Vol. 4, (A. M. Schrier and F. Stollnitz eds.). Academic Press, New York.

Razran, G. (1971). "Mind in Evolution: An East-West Synthesis of Learned Behavior and Cognition." Houghton Mifflin, Boston.

Revusky, S. H. and Garcia, J. (1970). Learned associations over long delays. *In* "The Psychology of Learning and Motivation", (G. H. Bower, ed.). Academic Press, New York.

Roberts, W. W. and Carey, R. J. (1965). Rewarding effect of performance of gnawing aroused by hypothalamic stimulation in the rat. *J. comp. physiol. Psychol.* 59, 317–324.

Schleidt, W. M., Schleidt, M. and Magg, M. (1960). Störund der Mutter-Kind-Beziehung bei Truthuhern durch Gehörverlust. *Behaviour* 16, 254–260.

Schneirla, T. C. (1959). An evolutionary and developmental theory of biphasic processes underlying approach and withdrawal. *In* "Nebraska Symposium on Motivation". Univ. of Nebraska Press, Lincoln.

Seidel, R. J. (1959). A review of sensory preconditioning. *Psych. Bull.* 56, 58–73.

Seligman, M. E. P. (1970). On the generality of the laws of learning. *Psychol. Rev.* 77, 406–418.

Sevenster-Bol, A. C. A. (1962). On the causation of drive reduction after a consummatory act. *Arch. néerl. Zool.* **15**, 175–236.

Shettleworth, S. J. (1972). Constraints on learning. *In* "Advances in the Study of Behavior" Vol. 4, (D. S. Lehrman, R. A. Hinde and E. Shaw, eds.). Academic Press, New York.

Skinner, B. F. (1938). "The Behavior of Organisms: an Experimental Analysis." Appleton-Century-Crofts, New York.

Stevenson, J. G. (1969). Song as a reinforcer. *In* Hinde (1969).

Stevenson-Hinde, J. G. (1972). Effects of early experience and testosterone on song as a reinforcer. *Anim. Behav.* **23**, 430–435.

Stevenson-Hinde, J. G. and Uldal, C. (in prep.). Reinforcing effects of nest-material.

Sutherland, N. S. (1959). Stimulus analysing mechanisms. *In* "Proc. Sym. Mechanization of Thought Processes." Her Majesty's Stationery Office, London, 575–609.

Sutherland, N. S. and Mackintosh, N. J. (Eds.) (1971). "Mechanisms of Animal Discrimination Learning." Academic Press, New York.

Thompson, T. I. (1963). Visual reinforcement in Siamese fighting fish. *Science* **141**, 55–57.

Thompson, T. I. (1969). Conditioned avoidance of the mobbing call by chaffinches. *Anim. Behav.* **17**, 517–522.

Thorpe, W. H. (1961). "Bird-song." Cambridge Univ. Press, London.

Thorpe, W. H. (1963). "Learning and Instinct in Animals." (1st Ed. 1956), Methuen, London.

Tinbergen, N. (1951). "The Study of Instinct." Clarendon Press, Oxford.

Tinbergen, N. (1953). "The Herring Gull's World." Collins, London.

Tolman, E. C. (1932). "Purposive Behavior in Animals and Man." Appleton-Century-Crofts, New York.

Tolman, E. C. (1959). Principles of purposive behavior. *In* Koch (1959).

Tschanz, B. (1959). Zur Brutbiologie der Trottellumme (*Uria aalge aalge* Pont). *Behaviour* **14**, 1–100.

Verplanck, W. S. (1954). Burrhus F. Skinner. In Estes, *et al.*, (1954).

Wells, M. J. (1961). Weight discrimination by *Octopus*. *J. exp. Biol. et al.*, **38**, 127–133.

Editorial: 1

At every moment an animal's sense organs are being bombarded by physical energy in many forms. To this chiaroscuro it responds selectively. The selectivity in its responsiveness must influence what it can learn.

Of the ways in which this selectivity may arise, biologists have emphasized mainly three. First, and mundanely, selectivity may be a consequence of the nature of the sense organs with which the animal is equipped: to some physical changes it is simply not responsive. Second, selectivity may be a consequence of sensory-perceptual mechanisms whereby some stimulus arrays are more effective than others for a wide range of responses—as, for example, circular shapes are more conspicuous than irregular ones, and objects are seen more readily when moving than when stationary. Or third, selectivity may be peculiar to one or to a small group of responses.

In their studies of the responses of gulls to eggs, Baerends and Kruijt (Chapter 2) are concerned with selective responsiveness to a variety of features of the stimulus object. In some cases at least, the effective characters of the eggs vary with the response studied: selectivity is thus response-specific. Their analysis reveals how the various features interact to influence response strength, and permit them to specify, in general terms, the point in the processing of the sensory input at which response specificity operates.

Baerends and Kruijt argue that, for many of the features with which they are principally concerned, either a direct influence of learning can be excluded, or learning can be shown merely to affect a previous bias. However they also point out that some of the features they found to be effective are clearly related to properties of the gull's sensory/perceptual systems. Even where the effectiveness of particular stimulus characters do not depend on previous experience with the natural object, the relevant properties of the sensory/perceptual systems may themselves depend on less specific experience at an earlier stage. Blakemore's chapter takes up this

21

issue. It has been shown that cells in the visual system of mammals are selectively responsive to certain features of the visual input: study of such cells is revealing in considerable detail how the visual input is processed and the mechanisms by which some features of the visual world are more effective than other. The question arises, are the properties of such cells pre-determined, or do they arise as a result of visual experience? Blakemore's experiments demonstrate how some of the properties of cells in the visual cortex of kittens can be influenced by experience.

Experimental psychologists have been interested in selectivity primarily in learning stiuations—more specifically in why some stimuli more readily become effective elicitors of a response than others. Where one aspect of a complex array is selected, it has been argued that the necessity for selection is imposed on the animal by limitations in its ability to process information. It is then necessary to suggest further reasons why particular features are selected and not others. Mackintosh (Chapter 4) suggests that the importance of such limitations in channel capacity has been exaggerated, and that many of these cases of stimulus selection can be understood as the results of previous experience. In particular his own experiments demonstrate something hitherto insufficiently appreciated—that animals may learn to ignore irrelevant uninformative stimuli. "Exposure to a given stimulus in the absense of any reinforcing event may reduce the associability of that stimulus with any reinforcer." Speaking colloquially, we are unwilling to treat as significant stimuli that we have become accustomed to as being insignificant. On this view, then, prior experience plays a large role in the constraints on learning imposed by stimulus selection.

Mere exposure to a stimulus also plays a role in imprinting. Bateson (Chapter 5) shows how exposure to a stimulus complex may increase both the probability that a chick will subsequently address social responses to it, and the readiness with which the chick learns to respond or avoid it in a discrimination situation. While on Mackintosh's paradigm exposure without significant consequences decreases "attentiveness" to the stimulus, in Bateson's situation the opposite occurs. There are, however, many differences between the situations: Bateson's work is concerned with young animals of very limited experience; in imprinting (as in perceptual learning in other contexts) "conspicuousness" is an important parameter of the stimulus, and the stimulus itself has reinforcing properties. Bateson's own data reveal a surprising complexity in the consequences of exposure to a stimulus, which clearly merits further study. However of primary interest in the present context is the manner in which his chapter demonstrates, in a naturally occurring learning situation, the multiple constraints that determine the course of learning, and shows how these are adapted to the context.

2
Stimulus Selection

by G. P. Baerends and J. P. Kruijt

Stimulus selection is defined here as the phenomenon whereby the various physical stimuli activating the receptors of an organism are not quantitatively equivalent with regard to their controlling effect on a particular behaviour pattern. Such stimuli can in fact be ranked in order of effectiveness.

The phenomenon has been recognized, probably independently, in ethology and experimental psychology. In ethology it was an essential element in Von Uexküll's "Umweltlehre" (Von Uexküll, 1934). Lorenz (1935) used it to explain the development in the course of evolution of those conspicuous morphological and behavioural characters of an organism whose function is to elicit in another organism a response which is in some way favourable to the actor ("Auslöser", social releasers, signals). The production of stimuli high in the rank order for the control of the response (sign or key stimuli) would be strongly selected for, and thus we would expect an evolutionary trend for their elaboration. Because of the species-specificity of signals, ethologists originally used to consider the corresponding rank order of the stimuli in the receiver as a genetically fixed characteristic and consequently called the mechanism ("receptive correlate") responsible for stimulus selection, the 'innate releasing mechanism" (I.R.M.). But even in 1935 Lorenz had stated that the receptive correlate often becomes extended through learning. Schleidt (1962) has discussed the ways in which this might occur. He proposed to classify within the category "releasing mechanism" (R.M.), not only the "innate releasing mechanism" (I.R.M.), but also the "innate releasing mechanism modified by experience" (I.R.M.E.) and the "acquired releasing mechanism" (A.R.M.). We strongly doubt whether it will in principle be possible to pigeonhole the entire releasing mechanism serving a particular response in such a neat way. We prefer to leave the possibility open that such a mechanism will turn out to consist of several links, each of which may be differently influenced by an interplay of genetic and environmental factors.

Experimental psychologists found stimulus selection in operant and in classical conditioning experiments with a number of species, including man (D'Amato, 1970; Thomas, 1970). In subjects conditioned to a compound cue (e.g. a shape superimposed on a colour, or light superimposed on sound) one component was found to "overshadow" the other. Such preferences can be specific as well as individual, and they may have developed through experience (Sutherland, 1969).

Specific selectivity for certain stimulus categories has been extensively demonstrated for the conditioning of digger wasps to landmarks near their nest and of the honey bee to landmarks around a food source. In the bee-hunting wasp *Philanthus*, Tinbergen and Kruijt (1938) found the preference for landmark characteristics to decrease in the order: solid and dented—solid and smooth—flat and chequered—flat and plain. The preference for solid was shown to be not for real three-dimensionality, but only for objects standing out above the ground. In contrast Van Iersel *et al.* (Van Iersel, 1951; Van Iersel and Van den Assem, 1965) found in the related fly-hunting wasp *Bembex* a preference for flat beacons; their effectiveness for orientation increased with their surface. When honey bees (*Apis mellifica*) learn to locate a food source the learning speed for a violet landmark exceeds that for other colours and particularly for blue-green (Menzel, 1967). The learning speed also varies for different odours: it is fast for flower scents and slow for fatty acids (Kriston, 1971). Conditioning to flower scents is quicker than to colours while conditioning on two-dimensional patterns is slowest. Lauer and Lindauer (1971) found ecologically adaptive differences between honey-bee races in some preferences for landmark characteristics (see Chapter 1).

Ethologists usually study the relative value of the various components of a stimulus situation by means of dummies in which certain characteristics of the adequate object have been changed (omitted, reduced, enhanced) or to which new characteristics have been added. Such experiments have shown that—provided the subject is internally sufficiently motivated—dummies from which effective features are missing can nevertheless release a response. The frequency and intensity of the response depends on the summated value of all the stimuli present which are effective for this response (rule of heterogeneous summation, Seitz, 1940). This suggests that the releasing mechanism for each response must at least comprise units for the evaluation of the different perceptible aspects of the stimulus situation, as well as a unit into which these partial evaluations are fed and in which they are transformed into a single output to the motor mechanism of the response. This leads to a model as depicted in Fig. 1.

In a number of cases (e.g. Prechtl, 1953; Hinde, 1954, 1970; Schleidt, 1954; Eikmanns, 1955; Noirot, 1965) the effectiveness of a stimulus for the release of a particular response was found to decrease with repeated presentation. This seems to indicate that the evaluation process is not constant, but can be modified. Further, in a few cases (Tinbergen *et al.*, 1943; Drees, 1952; Baerends, 1957, 1964, 1972) motivational differences were found to influence the effectiveness of a stimulus situation, but these data can also be interpreted without assuming an effect on the evaluation unit (see below).

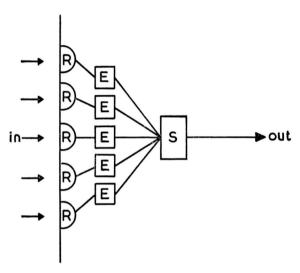

Fig. 1. Model of the releasing mechanism. R = receptor, E = evaluation unit, S = summation unit. After Baerends (1971).

According to the classical definition of the releasing mechanism (see Schleidt, 1962), each response has its own R.M. Particularly in insects, strong evidence supporting this view has been obtained. For instance, whereas Von Hess (1913) showed that honey bees could not be taught to use colour as a cue to escape from confinement, Von Frisch (1914) demonstrated their marked ability to use colour as cues in feeding behaviour. In the butterfly *Eumenes semele*, Tinbergen *et al.* (1943) could elicit selective visits to yellow and blue among a range of coloured papers by stimulating the insects with odour, but the authors found that colour played no role in releasing and directing the sexual flight of these butterflies. In these examples the control of a response by a particular stimulus was considered to be either present or absent, in an all-or-none way. Below we shall deal with cases in which one type of stimulus controls different responses with different strengths. On the present model this implies that each response has its own evaluation unit for these stimuli. It is conceivable, however, that different responses might also share evaluation units, but this possibility is still insufficiently investigated.

The releasing mechanism concept should be used in a functional sense only. The underlying physiological machinery and morphological structures are likely to vary between cases; the same probably applies to the degree of complexity. Evidence is available (Schneirla, 1952; Marler, 1961; Schleidt, 1962, 1964) that the evaluation, or filtering, of stimuli may sometimes take place in the receptor, but more centrally situated afferent mechanisms can also be involved. Studies of the decrements after repeated presentation of a constant stimulus can be used as a tool to detect stages in the way along which the information is passed to the motor mechanisms, but such stages need not necessarily be identical with the filters that are thought to present on the basis of other experiments (e.g. Prechtl, 1953).

Sutherland (1959, 1964) has developed a theoretical model to describe a number of aspects of discrimination learning, including stimulus selection and attention. In this model the input is assumed to go into a number of "analysers" which can themselves send an output to different responses (Fig. 2). Each analyser is thought to evaluate the variation of a particular

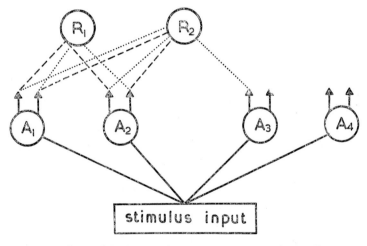

Fig. 2. Sutherland's model. A = analyser, R = response, darker lines are strong response attachments, dotted lines represent possible further response attachments. After Sutherland (1964).

stimulus along one dimension. The outputs of the different analysers become combined in the response mechanisms. As the experimental animals could usually be trained to each of the stimulus dimensions used (although to some better than to others), the possibility for novel attachments between any analysers and any response is included in the model.

Analysers can be switched on or off, and Sutherland particularly emphasizes that this can be learned. Switching in need not be an all-or-none process, so that a number of analysers can be at work simultaneously, possibly to different extents. However, in many cases the more strongly one analyser is activated, the less strongly are others switched in.

The independently developed ethological and experimental psychological models strongly resemble each other, particularly with respect to the intervening elements postulated for evaluation or as analysers. However, the arguments which lead to this postulation differed considerably between the two disciplines. Moreover, whereas experimental psychologists emphasize the importance of learning processes, particularly in the establishment of linkages between analysers and responses, and in the switching in of analysers, ethologists have thought about these information processing mechanisms chiefly in terms of characteristics more stable with respect to experience.

The importance of further investigations on the nature of the conceptual units represented in the models will certainly be enhanced by a combination of both types of approach. Up till now the different questions have been asked in different cases and with different subjects. As a result the available evidence mostly concerns unrelated scraps from the behaviour repertoire of different systematic groups of animals, and thus can hardly be linked together. We know of only one group of studies providing relevant information sufficient to serve as a factual basis for a discussion of our aims and as a core for suggesting a further working programme. We refer here to the studies that have been made about egg and parent recognition in Charadriiform birds, especially gulls, terns and guillemots. These studies originated from the I.R.M. concept mentioned above; they were aimed at testing various aspects of this concept and at developing it further.

One case, in which the existence of a rank order between different physical stimuli controlling a response was investigated, involves aspects of incubation behaviour in the herring gull (*Larus argentatus*) (Baerends, 1957, 1959). Two responses were considered: settling on a clutch and retrieving an egg placed on the nest rim. Since experiments are technically easier for retrieving than for settling, the majority of the data available were obtained with the former response. Whenever the effect of stimuli on both responses was studied the results turned out to be identical.*

* We like to acknowledge the enthusiastic help of many of our students in carrying out over 10,000 tests used in this study. In addition we want to thank Miss G. J. Blokzijl for her important contribution to the planning and organisation of the field work and Dr. R. H. Drent for his assistance (financially made possible by a grant from the Netherlands Organisation for the Advancement of Pure Research) in working out the data and for his very constructive criticism.

When herring gulls were given three-dimensional wooden dummies, in which features of size, colour, speckling or shape of the natural egg had been changed in various ways, they nearly always accepted them whether they were presented singly on the nest rim or as a clutch of three in the nest bowl. Full responses were readily given to objects lacking many of the physical stimuli present in the real egg and perceptible to the birds. Transparent dummies, made from plastic or glass, and two-dimensional dummies were usually ignored. Thus, a great variety of three-dimensional opaque objects was found to release the retrieving and settling responses, but—as shown by experiments in which the nest structure was moved—only when the nest was intact and correctly localized with respect to various landmarks.

By contrast, when the bird was given a choice between two different dummy clutches (in two artificial nests, close together on the original nest spot—an experiment only feasible in an area poor in landmarks), or two different dummies on the nest rim, and was thus forced to make a choice, consistent preferences for certain egg features became apparent. Simultaneous presentation of dummies is therefore a more sensitive method than successive presentation. The latter method tends to demonstrate characters of high rank only and may thus erroneously give the impression that no other features are being used. However, in choice experiments it is difficult to decide whether preferences concern only the orientation of the response or also its release (Franck, 1966). In our experiments, the latency with which the bird returned tended to decrease with an increase of the value of at least one of the models presented: this suggests that the preferences applied not only to orientation but also to release.

When dummies of different size (a series of models varying from half to twice all linear dimensions of the normal egg) were presented in pairs on the nest rim, the birds retrieved the larger model first in a significant majority of tests (1087 as against 592). As in all choice experiments, position preference may obscure preference for a model. Therefore the outcome of the test was, as often as possible, controlled by another test with the same bird but with the dummies of the pair in the reversed positions. From these controls one may conclude that 428 choices for the larger and 434 for the smaller dummy of a pair were due to position preference. Thus 659 choices for the larger and 158 choices for the smaller should be considered as real consistent preferences: we shall call them majority and minority choices respectively. We shall deal with the majority choices first; the very interesting minority choices, which may occur from time to time in any bird, will be discussed later.

The majority results show that size plays a part in the visual control of the retrieving response, but that for this function the normal size is not the optimal one. While with dummies below the normal size, the readiness to retrieve an "undersized" model dropped quickly, the readiness to retrieve increased in the range of "oversized" eggs, at least as far as the upper limit we have been using. The preference for larger than normal size seemed to be "open-ended".

Speckled models were preferred to those without speckles. A greater number of speckles was preferred to fewer, smaller speckles to larger, and darker and more contrasting speckles were preferred to lighter and less contrasting ones (Kruijt, 1958). Thus, the preferences along several dimensions of speckling also seem to be open-ended.

The role of colour was studied with a series of models painted red, yellow, green, blue, khaki and three shades of grey, all with black speckles. We attempted to make these different paints look to the human eye as saturated and brilliant as the average natural egg. Again the models were presented in pairs in all possible combinations. Table 1 shows the percentage of tests in which each model presented was preferred by a bird. Green evidently had the highest stimulus value, while the blue, red and

TABLE I

Relative effectiveness of colours in eliciting various responses from gulls.

Experiments	Blue	Green	Yellow	Red	Khaki	Greys (average)	Unit used	Authors
Egg retrieval	45	87	62	31	46	40	% of total presentations	Baerends et al. (unpubl.)
Nest attendance	50	83	75	20	67	—	% of total presentations	Baerends et al. (unpubl.)
Food recovery	21	53	46	36	49	43	% of total presentations	Mudde, (unpubl.)
Egg robbing	—	3	10	12	21	—	% of total presentations	Baerends et al. (unpubl.)
Approach (hungry)	39	21	31	42	—	—	no./100 chicks	Impekoven (1969)
Approach (cold)	41	22	16	36	—	—	no./100 chicks	Impekoven (1969)
Begging	44	4	28	40	—	—	no./min.	Hailman (1967)
Shell removal	27	18	33	37	25	—	% of total presentations	Tinbergen et al. (1962a)
Approach (alarm)	33	31	13	25	—	—	no./100 chicks	Impekoven (1969)

grey models ranked lowest. The fact that all grey dummies scored lower than any coloured dummy permits the conclusion that wavelength plays a part in controlling the retrieval response. It is interesting that the green colour preferred is to the human eye not the best match with the natural colouration of the egg. We have done no experiments on the role of dimensions within a spectral band, such as saturation or intensity; it would be interesting to check whether the preference would also be open-ended.

Dummies of various shape (rounded and sharp edged blocks, cylinders, prisms, elongated and compressed egg shapes, all of equal volume) were paired with egg shaped models, as well as with each other. The results made it clear that the gulls discriminated at least between normal and abnormal egg shapes, but the very high percentage of position rather than model preferences among the test results suggest that characteristics of shape are relatively unimportant in controlling the retrieval response. Models with rounded edges were slightly preferred to those with sharp-edges; roundness is probably the only characteristic of shape which allows exaggeration in a physical sense and, thus, for which an open-ended preference would be expected.

The results given above show that the four categories of features tested are all used, but suggest that they are of differing importance in controlling the manipulations of eggs. However, to establish a real dominance order, we need a scale of reference, a measuring stick.

Our experiments with the size series showed position preference to be a quantitative phenomenon. A first choice for the smaller egg in the preferred position can always be overcome by increasing the size of the model in the non-preferred position. With our series of models gradually increasing in size it was possible to identify stepwise, in successive tests with the same bird (Fig. 3), the minimum size of a model required to overcome position preference, when in competition with a dummy of smaller size in the preferred position. Thus, through this "titration", a model was found the value of which, in combination with that of the non-preferred site, could just outweigh the combined values of the smaller model and the preferred site. Empirically it turned out that the birds were acting in accordance with the ratios between the surfaces of the maximal projections (maximal shadows when turned around in a beam of parallel light) of the models. Different pairs of models, matching each other with respect to other parameters tried (e.g. volume), or equal with regard to the difference instead of the ratio in the parameters used, proved to be unequal in counteracting position preference. The ratio between sites often remained constant for a couple of hours, and within that period the relative value of dummies with any kind of stimulus combination could be measured and expressed with reference to the standard size series (Fig. 3).

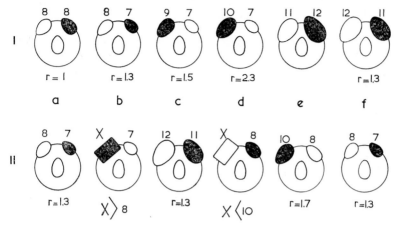

Fig. 3. The "titration" method for determining the value of an egg dummy. The circle represents the nest with one egg in the nest bowl and two dummies on the rim. The code numbers 7, 8, 9, 10, 11, 12 refer to the dummies of the size series (R) shown in Fig. 4; X is the model to be measured; r is the ratio between maximal projection surfaces of the dummies on the nest rim. The black dummy is always the preferred one.

I. Determination of the value of the position preference. Ia shows that the right site is preferred. This preference remains when dummy 8 is replaced by the smaller dummy 7 (Ib) but can then be overcome by replacing 8 by 9 (Ic); this sequence shows that the value of the position preference lies between $r = 1.3$ *and* $r = 1.5$: this conclusion holds when another pair of dummies with the same ratio is used (If). Control test Ie shows that the size optimum for this gull exceeds size 11.

II. Determination of the value of model X. Tests IIa, IIc and IIf show that the position preference has remained unchanged. Test IIb and IId indicate, in combination with the preceding and succeeding tests, that the value of X is between those of the models 8 and 10 of the reference size series.

A full description of the methods will be given elsewhere (Baerends and Drent, in prep.)

Our results have been depicted in Fig. 4. It shows how the value of a dummy with respect to the size series is affected by certain changes in features, viz. (1) changing the egg shapes into a round edged block shape; (2) omitting the speckling pattern on standard brown dummies; (3) changing the standard brown background for a green one; and (4) adding a speckling pattern to the green dummies. All changes were carried out on dummies of different sizes. The exactitude of the method should not be overestimated. First, it is limited by the sizes of the steps used in our "titration" series. Second, there is considerable spread between the results of individual tests, and the method we used to calculate the average values for each dummy indicated in the figure is not infallible. However, we may conclude from the figure that various combinations of stimuli, all incomplete if compared with the real egg, are able to control the retrieval response. The quantitative impact of a combination on the response depends on which features are present and to what extent. Each feature adds its specific quantitative contribution which is independent of the contribution of other features (e.g. the shift of a dummy after changing its form or its

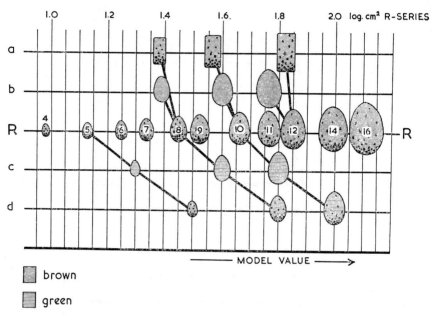

Fig. 4. The average values found for various dummies with respect to the reference size series *R*. The position of different types of dummies (brown, speckled, block-shaped; brown, unspeckled, egg-shaped; green, unspeckled, egg-shaped; green, speckled, egg-shaped) each in different sizes was determined with the method described in the legend of Fig. 3. The code numbers 4 to 16 stand for, respectively, 4/8 to 16/8 of the linear dimensions of the normal egg size (8 = 8/8). The maximal projection surfaces of the eggs of the reference series have been plotted (egg centres) along the logarithmic scale (cm²) of the abscissa. Equal distances between points on this scale imply equal ratio values.

background colour with respect to the scale is independent of its size). This means that the rule of heterogeneous summation applies. More important for our purpose, however, is the possibility of reading from Fig. 4 the effect of a number of physical changes in the egg dummies on the control of retrieving. The change of the standard brown background for the optimal green one is dominant over the addition of the standard speckle pattern to a plain standard brown egg.* Changing of a round edged block shape for an egg shape is probably of least relative importance.

How much of the R.M. concept do we need to explain these results? This mechanism was actually postulated to account for the recognition of the typical features of an external stimulus situation. Our analysis has shown that not all physical stimuli coming from the egg are equally effective. But a high value was found for green that is never shown by a real herring gull egg (whereas the apparently more similar khaki, blue and grey hues had lower values), and a relatively low value was found for the very characteristic egg shape (which can nevertheless be distinguished by the bird from other shapes). The adaptedness of these preferences is not impressive. Even less adapted to the appearance of the normal egg are the apparently unlimited preferences for larger egg size and for smaller, more conspicuous speckles.† These observations seem to justify an attempt to relate these phenomena to consequences of the physiology of the receptor.

The photopic spectral sensitivity of the bird's eye follows an optimum curve with a maximum for green and minima for the ends of the visible spectrum (Thompson, 1971). For this reason one would expect green dummies to stimulate the gulls more strongly than dummies of other colours. Further, Schneirla (1952) has suggested that a higher responsiveness to patterned than to plain surfaces might be due to an effect of flicker on elements of the retina. One would expect this effect to increase with the number of speckles and with their contrast to the background. Moreover, small speckles when moving over the retina will probably stimulate more elements per unit time than larger patches. Thus our results on the character speckling appear to fit Schneirla's interpretation. Finally, our finding that the birds compare models of different size by means of the ratios between their projected surfaces, the value of a model increasing with its projection, suggests that the impact of the stimulus on the receptor cells is of paramount importance in the evaluation process.

Consequently, we must assume the presence of a mechanism for determining the total amount of stimulation of each of the different types of

---

* The value of the speckling pattern on green exceeds that on a standard brown background because the speckles contrasted more with the bright green than with the rather dark brown of the standard dummies, which was different from the khaki used in the colour series.

† Tinbergen, *et al.* (1962a) have demonstrated the camouflage value of the speckling pattern of the eggs. Although it has not yet been checked experimentally, it is likely that better cryptic protection is given by the approximately 5 mm, not highly contrasting and irregularly distributed speckles of the natural egg than by the 3 mm black and equally distributed speckles on some of the highly effective dummies. Moreover, the natural speckling consists of a mixture of dark brownish and somewhat ligher greyish speckles, by which depth is suggested.

D

detector units present in the receptor. However, on the evidence discussed so far there is no need to postulate in addition special evaluation units. This would be necessary only if one kind of stimulus could be shown to have a different value in controlling another response of the same kind of animal. It is, therefore, interesting to investigate how far other responses to eggs may be controlled by different characters or, if controlled by the same characters, whether these form a different rank order.

First, the influence of egg characters on readiness to attend to the nest was studied by replacing normal clutches with wooden dummy eggs and by checking at intervals during the breeding season whether these nests were incubated. Red clutches were the most frequently abandoned, blue clutches came next and for green and yellow clutches the percentages of deserted nests were lowest (Table 1).

Second, the herring gull's habit of robbing each other's eggs gave an opportunity to study which physical features of the egg release and direct the behaviour of the bird when it is motivated to feed. To this end real eggs and several kinds of dummy eggs were distributed, either in the territories of gulls or in areas near the colony where great numbers of gulls passed on their way to their feeding areas. Table 1 gives a summary of the relative frequencies of attempts to feed on different types of objects. Of the colour-dummies used, the red ones elicited most feeding responses, the green dummies fewest. Both kinds of dummies appeared to us equally conspicuous against the sandy background. Blue dummies have not yet been used in these experiments, which are still in progress.

Third, stimulus selection was investigated in a totally different feeding situation in gulls kept in the laboratory (Mudde, unpubl.). After these gulls had been trained to obtain food by removing with their bills grey covers from pots dug into the ground, they were given a choice between two pots placed beside each other and each covered by a differently coloured lid, measuring 20×20 cm. The same colours were used as in the experiments on egg retrieving and egg robbing. Each choice was rewarded, but the bird was allowed to choose only once for each combination; this choice was taken to indicate a preference for the colour of the lid. Despite a considerable amount of variation between birds and between sessions, for plain coloured covers a rank order, green-yellow-red-blue, could be established (Table 1). Khaki was about equal to green, and one shade of grey (reflection 44%) scored in between green and yellow. Darker greys obtained less responses than blue, and the lightest grey (33%) released no feeding but only a few spontaneous drinking responses. The data suggest that the birds in this situation mainly reacted to subjective brightness, in contrast to the results of the egg rolling and egg robbing experiments.

Similar experiments in which covers with big speckles or with small speckles, in each case with either a high density or a low density of speckles, were presented in pairs did not give conclusive results, but the data suggest that, in contrast to our findings in egg retrieval, lids with big speckles and lids with relatively few speckles were more frequently taken first.

Fourth, another behaviour pattern directed at eggs, the carrying away of empty eggs shells, has been studied: unfortunately for us the work concerned not the herring gull but the black-headed gull (*Larus ridibundus*) (Tinbergen, *et al.,* 1962, 1962b). The authors presented differently coloured and differently shaped dummies of egg shells on the nest rim. White and khaki (a paint prepared to match the natural egg colour) objects proved to have high releasing values for the shell removal activity, the response to green was lowest and that to blue, yellow and red intermediate. The presence or absence of a speckling pattern had no effect on the value of a model. The shape of the dummy was found to play a role; a rank order (egg shells—cylindrical rings—angles) was found.

We are not sure whether a comparison of these data with those on egg-retrieval, nest-attendance and egg-eating in the herring gull is permissible. Although the egg colour of both species looks practically the same, for the black-headed gull comparable data are not available. However, the study of Tinbergen, Kruuk and Paillette (1962b) contains some information indicating that in the black-headed gull also, green might have a high value for egg-retrieval.

A further source of information comes from studies of the stimulus situation releasing and directing the begging response of gull and tern chicks. This response involves pecking directed at the bill of the parent, and was first studied by Tinbergen and Perdeck (1950). They found the begging response to be controlled by some characteristics of the shape, position and movement of the parental bill and by a contrasting patch on the lower mandible, which was most effective when coloured red. Similar studies, sometimes with more refined techniques, have been made with related species, viz. Weidmann and Weidmann (1958), Weidmann (1961) and Impekoven (1969) in the black-headed gull, Cullen (1962) in the Wideawake tern (*Sterna fuscata*), Quine and Cullen (1964) in the Arctic tern (*Sterna macrura*) and Hailman (1967, 1968, 1969, 1970) in the laughing gull (*Larus atricilla*). Essentially the results for all these species agree: all showed that red was most effective in releasing the begging response, that blue also had a relatively high value, but that green scored lowest (Table 1). Thompson (1971) has determined the spectral sensitivity in juvenile and adult herring gulls. The small differences she found cannot account for the difference in the rank orders of the colours between juvenile food-begging and adult egg-retrieving.

Finally Impekoven (1969) has studied in the black-headed gull the approach responses of a chick towards differently coloured models of the parent, and also towards differently coloured hiding boxes in alarm (Table 1). The colour preferences when approaching the parent were roughly the same as those for the begging response. When alarmed the chicks responded to subjective brightness only, with a preference for darkness.

Although the data referred to above include some response-specific differences in preference for characters of shape (egg retrieval and egg shell removal) and speckling (preference for many small speckles in egg retrieval, for few and big speckles in the food recovery response and indifference to this character in egg shell removal) the data on the effect of colour in controlling different responses are the most suitable for a discussion of the postulate that each response has its own R.M., or in other words that stimulus selection is response-specific. The relative effectiveness of five different colours in releasing and directing different responses can be deduced from Table 1 and Fig. 5. Because of the great differences in the techniques and in the parameters used for each response, comparison between responses should not concern the absolute values of the figures, but rather the position of the maxima and minima for each response. Then three responses (approach, begging and egg-robbing) show a minimum for green and maxima for red and blue. Two other responses for which the control by wavelength was demonstrated (nest-attendance, egg retrieval) show a maximum for green and a minimum for red and blue. Although the same type of preference was shown in the food recovery response, the relatively high value of one shade of grey in these experiments suggests that brightness rather than colour was controlling this response. The alarm responses of black-headed gull chicks were without doubt controlled by subjective brightness.

The fact that the rank order of the effectiveness of control by colours differs for different responses compels us to postulate a mechanism through which the information received by the receptors can be differentially used. The similarity of the rank order for a number of different responses indicates that such a mechanism can be used in common. As the rank order for one group of responses appears to be the mirror image of that for the other, it is parsimonious to assume that both groups of responses use the same mechanism, but with opposite sign. This idea was first suggested by Hailman (1967, 1970) when he explained the relation between the readiness of the gull chick to peck, and the colour of the releasing object, on the basis of the spectral transmission of the oil droplets in the cones (see also Thompson, 1971). His interaction hypothesis predicts that the birds can code either a red-blue or a yellow-green preference; the evidence collected here appears to substantiate this view (Fig. 5). For switching from one code to the other an evaluation unit or analyser in the sense discussed above is needed.

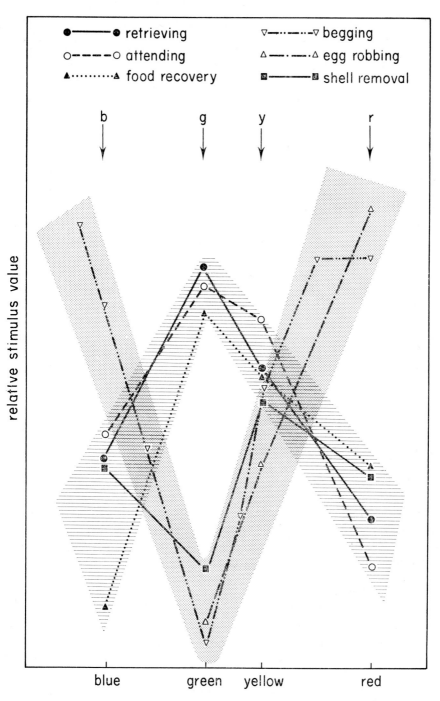

Fig. 5. Relative responsiveness to four colours (paints, not spectral bands) for six different activities. The data from Table 1 have been used; the curves were matched by suitable contraction or expansion of their ordinates.

The physiological possibility to switch in either the red-blue or the yellow-green preference has been exploited in the development of the stimulus-response attachments for approaching, begging and eating on the one side and for retrieving and nest-attendance on the other. In this way a reduction of redundant stimulation and a rough adaptation to the natural stimulus situation, the colours of the egg shell and of the throat of the parent respectively, is achieved. In correspondence with this red preference of the chick, some gulls and terns have evolved social releasers which stimulate and direct the pecking response (red bill or red patch on the bill).

The fact that use has been made of this existing switch mechanism accounts for the imperfections of the adaptation, e.g. the preference for such an unnatural shade of green and the puzzling blue preferences in the begging responses of juvenile gulls and terns. For terns Quine and Cullen (1964) suggest that this blue preference might be an adaptation to bluish fish in the bill of the parent, but this functional explanation can hardly hold for those gulls that usually feed their chicks with a predigested amorphous brownish coloured mass. The low value for green in feeding situations can very well be an adaptation in these non-herbivorous birds, the more so because Kear (1964) found the reverse (viz. a yellow-green preference) in several plant-eating species of Anatidae (ducks) and Phasianidae (pheasants). A yellow preference during food pecking has also been found for naïve domestic chicks (Hess, 1956), whereas Schaeffer and Hess (1959) have shown that the red-blue code is used in the following response of naïve chicks of the same breed. Thus each of the codes is used in the appropriate functional situation: the ability to switch them in on the right occasion must be attached to the causal system activated in that context and may differ between systematic groups (i.e. in gulls the red-blue code when feeding is activated, but the yellow-green code during incubation; on the other hand, in herbivorous birds, the yellow-green code when feeding, but the red-blue code when following). The data of some of the studies referred to above, e.g. those on egg shell removal, do not fit into this simple model. The high value for yellow is incompatible with the red-blue analyser and the low value for green does not fit with the yellow-green code. Similarly, Hess (1956) found a high value for yellow during food pecking of domestic chicks, but a low one for green. These deviations could be explained by postulating an additional filter to the yellow-green analyser. We shall return to this suggestion below.

The model as developed so far implies that a definite physical value of a stimulus would always have the same quantitative effect on a particular response. Observations made on the value of green for egg retrieval in gull JK8 ♂ during a period of four days, show that this is not true (Fig. 6). On

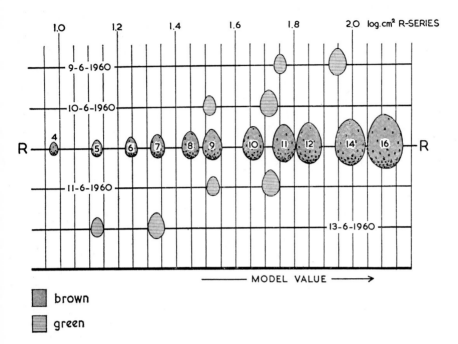

Fig. 6. The value of green for gull JK8 ♂ on different days. Control tests with brown dummies showed that the value of other characters had not changed.

June 12 and 13 green had a value not significantly different from the average we found for all birds. However, on June 9, the first day this bird was confronted with a green model, the value was exceptionally high. In the light of other observations we are inclined to interpret this temporary high value as an effect of novelty. On June 13, on the contrary, the value of green was exceptionally low. On the first presentation of green that day, just at the moment when the gull first touched the dummy with its bill, it was frightened by a diving jet plane and flew up. After this the value of green remained low for the rest of that day. If these interpretations are correct, novelty and conditioning, and probably also other factors not recognized, can modify the value of an output from a receptor element.

More information on the influence of motivational factors on the effect of a stimulus was obtained in a thorough analysis of the minority cases (see p. 28) in which a gull consistently preferred the smaller dummy of a pair. Actually the preference of these birds showed a size optimum, which was in some cases situated around model no. 10, in others around the natural size no. 8 and in few cases around the undersized no. 6. The behaviour of the birds before, during and after the choice in the 20 minute tests had been carefully watched and qualitatively and quantitatively recorded. Comparison between tests with minority choices and tests with majority results revealed a number of differences. In tests with minority choices it took the birds on average more time to return to the nest after the test situation had been changed than when majority choices were made. Short bouts of preening corresponded more often with minority than with majority choices; and in the former the bird sat more often upright with a long neck and sleeked plumage, while in the latter the bird's overall contour tended to be rounded. As Baerends and his collaborators have shown (Baerends, 1970; Baerends *et al.*, 1970), these differences indicate that during the minority choices the birds must have had a relatively high tendency to flee from the nest. In these cases this tendency was activated by the abnormal position of the eggs outside the nestbowl, and probably in addition also by the unnatural appearance of several of the models. The higher the scores for these behavioural indications of fright, the lower was the size preferred during the minority tests.

Conversely it follows from these data that the frightening effect of a dummy on the nest rim increases with increasing size; we have similar evidence that green models and models with a conspicuous speckling pattern are potentially more frightening than models of standard colour. We must therefore conclude that the strength of the fright response caused by the dummies is determined by the same stimulus characteristics as the incubation responses. However, in addition its strength depends on the degree to which the escape system is activated. The conflicting tendencies to incubate and to leave the nest are not fully incompatible. At relatively low levels both may simultaneously influence behaviour. Many of the minority choices can be understood on the assumption that when the escape and the incubation systems are both active the tendency to retrieve the larger egg is counteracted by the tendency to avoid it, and the bird compromises with a shift of the preference optimum down the scale. This shift might therefore be considered as due to an approach-withdrawal conflict in Schneirla's (1959) sense.

So far we have hardly touched upon the questions of where and to what extent learning processes may be involved in the development and use of an evaluation unit or analyser.

Since the experiments on the pecking preferences of gull chicks were carried out with naïve chicks, their preferences for colour and contrast cannot have been learned from experience with the parent bird. Hailman (1967) raised his chicks in the dark, and it is therefore unlikely that the preferences could have originated from experience, even with inadequate objects. Kear's (1964) results on green preferences in ducks were also obtained with inexperienced birds. We can take it, therefore, that in these cases the attachment of the red-blue or the yellow-green analyser to the proper response was not learned.

The incubating birds we experimented with in the field were of course all experienced. To test the possibility that they might have been conditioned to features of the egg, we made use of the occasional occurrence of completely albinistic eggs, which are light blue and lack speckles. Gulls incubating a fully albinistic clutch were given the choice between a plain blue and a plain brown model: they showed a significant preference for blue. As seen above, blue had a low value with birds sitting on normal clutches.

Tinbergen *et al.* (1962b) experimented with black-headed gulls which had been allowed to sit on clutches painted solid green or solid black. Although both groups retrieved a higher percentage of normal eggs than of plain coloured models when these were presented on the nest rim, birds which had been sitting on black eggs retrieved relatively more black egg dummies, and those with green clutches more green dummies, than birds of the other experimental groups or than control birds sitting on normal clutches. The scores for green in birds sitting on green eggs were far greater than those for black in birds on black eggs; this indicates the presence of a non-learnt bias for green which we have already mentioned. In both experimental groups the preference for real eggs equalled that of the controls. We conclude that conditioning to the background colour of the eggs the gull has been incubating is possible, but such a learnt preference can apparently be counteracted by preferences not dependent on learning.

The latter is still more evident from the results of further experiments with herring gulls which had incubated albinistic eggs for at least one season. Confronted with a speckled and an unspeckled model (or real, even their own, eggs) on the nest rim, these gulls showed significant preferences for the speckled egg. The learning was evidently not able to overcome the non-learnt preference for speckles.

In the egg shell removal experiments by Tinbergen *et al.* (1962b) gulls that had been sitting on black eggs showed an increased responsiveness to black shell dummies, and those that had been forced to incubate green eggs removed a higher percentage of green than of otherwise coloured shells. Correspondingly the high releasing value of khaki (=naturally coloured) shell dummies and, perhaps also the high score for yellow (as an appreciable amount of yellow was present in khaki), in birds incubating normal clutches can be attributed to learning. The authors do not believe that the low responsiveness to green and the high responsiveness to white should be attributed to learning during incubation, but they admit that more information is needed for a full evaluation of the part experience can play.

Herring and black-headed gulls find the way back to their nest by a very detailed knowledge of the landmarks (even rather distant ones): these enable them to localize the nest spot, often to within one meter, when the nest structure has been removed. The nest structure is conspicuous so that the birds do not need markings from the eggs to recognize their clutches. However, they should be potentially able to learn individual characteristics of the eggs just as they learn to distinguish their own chicks on detailed differences in the head pattern (Tinbergen, 1953).

The related guillemots (Fam. Alcidae), who nest on ledges of rocky coasts, make no nest structure but keep their single egg on the webs of the feet. Tschanz (1959) showed that, apart from localizing the "nest" area by means of landmarks, each guillemot recognizes its own egg; birds do not normally incubate eggs of other pairs. Egg features are learned within half an hour after egg-laying, and the engram is adjusted when eggs get covered with faeces. The individual eggs vary in size, shape, colour and speckling pattern, but the only features used in the learning process are colour and speckling pattern. Whereas relatively slight differences in colour and pattern made the birds refuse their own eggs, they readily accepted very abnormally shaped dummies on which the right colour and pattern had been carefully painted. Reactions to colour and pattern followed the rule of heterogeneous summation, colour proving to be dominant over pattern, just as we found in the herring gull.

We conclude that in this case, where conditioning to the bird's own egg is highly adaptive because of the lack of a nest bowl and nest material, the bird learns those features of the egg that in the herring gull showed a high value for the retrieving and settling responses. Shape was low in the rank order for non-learnt as well as for learnt retrieval attachments. The learning mechanism evidently makes use of "strong" stimulus outputs in preference to weak ones.

We have already mentioned that herring gulls rob each other's eggs. Sometimes a gull seems to specialize for some time on this kind of food. We have some evidence that such gulls approach and take real eggs more readily than more conspicuous dummy eggs. In the feeding experiment described above, the normal eggs got the second highest score (14%), the red dummies being most effective. Further, in an experiment primarily set up for other purposes, we made a great number of artificial nests in an area near the colony, not occupied by gull territories but often frequented by the birds. In 69 of these nests we put one real unchanged herring gull egg, and in the others gull eggs painted khaki, in 129 nests without and in 129 with speckles. At regular intervals the number of nests robbed was determined, the whole procedure being followed by telescope from a distance. It appeared that only a few gulls took part in the robbery. The painted eggs, whether or not they bore speckles, disappeared at a lower rate than the natural eggs which were less conspicuous than the painted ones. On the basis of direct observations of the behaviour of gulls with painted eggs we believe that these eggs were more frightening to the birds than the familiar real eggs, which they seemed to know in sufficient detail to distinguish them from the painted ones.*

We have already seen that stimuli of a strongly evaluated category can be made still more powerful by changing their magnitude. The extent of such effects seemed to be unlimited (open-ended) for the response considered, unless other conflicting behaviour patterns were simultaneously aroused by the same stimuli, in which case by way of compromise a limit (optimum) was set. For instance, the speckling pattern gained in value when the number and/or the contrast of the speckles was increased, and/or the size reduced. This principle is responsible for the fact that stimulus situations can be made supernormal.

To investigate whether this principle as well as the rule of heterogeneous summation would apply also to cases of stimulus-response attachments brought about by conditioning, Baerends, Bril and Bult (1965) trained a pigtail monkey in a "Wisconsin Test Apparatus" to look for food under a piece of cardboard bearing a complicated pattern in two shades of grey. After the monkey had been conditioned the relative releasing value for the food seeking act of incomplete designs was investigated in choice trials, in a manner essentially similar to that followed in the study of egg recognition in the gulls. Incomplete models were found always to have some releasing value, the value increasing with the degree of completeness of the design. A rank order existed among the different features and the rule of heterogeneous summation applied. But, in spite of several attempts, no design could be developed that turned out to be supernormal.

Also when specific characters of the bird's own eggs were learned (background colour in gulls and guillemots, speckling pattern only in guillemots), it was not a stimulus category as such, but a very definite dimension of it, with equal but limited possibilities for variations on all sides, which proved to have been learned.

However, phenomena similar to supernormality have been found in other learning situations. For example, Hanson (1959) trained pigeons on the key pecking response with food as reinforcement and monochromatic

---

* The fact that robbing gulls appear to have no greater difficulties in finding the cryptic natural eggs than the more conspicuous painted eggs does not argue against the survival value of the camouflage pattern, particularly as a defense against less specialised predators (see also footnote on page 33).

illumination of the response key as the positive discriminative stimulus. In extinction these pigeons showed a symmetrical generalization gradient with a peak of responding in the presence of the wavelength that had acted as the positive stimulus and decreased response rates in the presence of longer and shorter wavelengths. Experimental groups that had been subjected to successive discrimination training in which one wavelength was the positive stimulus and another the negative, did not show a peak of responding in the presence of the positive stimulus during extinction; instead, highest responding was shifted away from the positive stimulus, to the side opposite to that of the negative stimulus. A similar peak shift can occur with more complex stimuli. Hogan, Kruijt and Frijlink (in prep.) using the same technique, found no peak shift with pigeons trained on a pattern of 37 speckles projected on the window of the key as the positive stimulus, and a white window as the negative, when patterns with a higher and lower number of speckles were presented in extinction. The peak of responding occurred at the pattern of 37 speckles. However, pigeons first trained with successive presentations to discriminate between a pattern of 37 speckles as the positive and one of 21 speckles as the negative stimulus showed in extinction a peak shift towards a pattern with more than 37 speckles.

In similar experiments in which pigeons pecked a key illuminated with light of different wavelengths, Terrace (1968) analysed the conditions under which a peak shift occurs, namely when there is "a reduction in the rate of responding to one of two alternating discriminative stimuli" (p. 737). Following such training, the conditions of testing for a shift have little effect on its occurrence (Stevenson, 1966). From a series of related experiments, Terrace argues that during the training which does produce a shift, the animal has learned to respond to the positive stimulus and to withhold responses to the negative stimulus. On the other hand, during training conditions which do not produce a shift, the animal has learned to respond to the positive stimulus and not to its absence; no stimulus control seems to be established by the negative stimulus.

It remains to be investigated whether and to what extent supernormality in natural situations can be explained by learning processes similar to those supposed to underly a peak shift in the learning experiments described. It is difficult to believe that the conditions mentioned by Terrace are fulfilled in the case of, for example, egg retrieving. As far as we know, the gulls do not attempt to retrieve objects other than their own eggs outside experimental situations. That is, they do not seem to respond to any "negative stimulus" situation.

However, a strict discrimination of a particular point on a stimulus dimension is required in the case of feed-back stimulation from situations maintaining a response. Baerends *et al.* (1970) have shown that definite tactile and thermal stimuli are necessary for the incubation of a herring gull to continue. Learning may play a role in matching the feedback response, since herring gulls that have lost one egg from their clutch of three, habituate to the resulting deficiency of the feedback information. On the other hand Beer (1965) found in black-billed gulls (*Larus bulleri*), which normally had a clutch of two, that addition of a third egg (this gull has, just like the other gulls, three brood patches) decreases the frequency with which incubation is interrupted. It is unlikely that the rule of heterogeneous summation could apply for the evaluation of a stimulus situation maintaining a response; it would not be functional, for instance, if the deficient tactile stimulation from an undersized egg could be compensated by an increase in its temperature.

Conclusion

The above comparison in gulls of the relative value of various components of the stimulus situations releasing and directing a number of different responses thus confirms the original idea in the I.R.M. concept that physically identical stimuli may be evaluated differently by an animal, according to the activity they are controlling. The evidence suggests that this evaluation takes place in a series of steps. The first concerns the receptivity of the sensory cells; in further steps, located more centrally in the sensory pathways but not necessarily all outside the receptor organ, the output of the receptors is processed in analysers or evaluating units. Finally, heterogeneous summation of the outputs of these units takes place before the motor mechanisms are triggered.

As shown especially by the data on colour, an analyser (i.e. the yellow-green code or its mirror image the red-blue code) can be used by different responses. This suggests that it is not the information processing units themselves, but the pathway through which the relevant information flows, that is specific for the response.

The common use of analysers for incompatible responses implies that conflicts are possible when the internal factors facilitating these responses are simultaneously activated. Simultaneous activation of the tendencies to incubate and to flee led to a compromise in which incubation responses were directed towards objects suboptimal to both responses.

A relatively rough adaptation of the responsiveness to important environmental stimulation can be achieved by an appropriate use and linkage of analysing units. Where and to what extent learning processes play a role in the establishment of the analysing units and of their attachments is likely to be primarily under genetic control. For some cases a direct influence of learning could be experimentally excluded.

In the case studied the rule of heterogeneous summation was found to apply independently of whether the stimulus-response attachment perceived was learnt or not. The phenomenon of supernormality occurred in cases where no influence of learning on the stimulus-response attachments has been found. So far the open-ended shift of the preference peak characterizing this phenomenon could be achieved through learning only in a few cases, and then with a procedure not very likely to be followed under natural conditions.

References

Baerends, G. P. (1957). The ethological concept "releasing mechanisms" illustrated by a study of the stimuli eliciting egg-retrieving in the Herring Gull. *Anat. Rec.* **128**, 518–519.

Baerends, G. P. (1959). The ethological analysis of incubation behaviour. *Ibis* **101**, 357–368.

Baerends, G. P. (1964). La réconnaissance de l'oeuf par le Goéland argenté. *Bull. Soc. Scient. de Bretagne* **37**, 193–208.

Baerends, G. P. (1970). A model of the functional organisation of incubation behaviour in the Herring Gull. *In* "The Herring Gull and its Egg" (G. P. Baerends and R. H. Drent, eds.). *Behaviour* Suppl. **17**, 261–312.

Baerends, G. P. (1971). The ethological analysis of fish behavior. *In* "Fish Physiology", Vol. 6, (W. S. Hoar and D. J. Randall, eds.), pp. 279–370. Academic Press, New York.

Baerends, G. P. (1972). Moderne Methoden und Ergebnisse der Verhaltensforschung bei Tieren. Veröff. der Rheinisch-Westfälische Akademie (in press).

Baerends, G. P., Bril, K. A. and Bult, P. (1965). Versuche zur Analyse einer erlernten Reizsituation bei einem Schweinsaffen (*Macaca nemestrina*). *Z. Tierpsycol.* **22**, 394–411.

Baerends, G. P., Drent, R. H., Glas, P. and Groenewold, H. (1970). An ethological analysis of incubation behaviour in the Herring Gull. *In* "The Herring Gull and its Egg". (G. P. Baerends and R. H. Drent, eds.). *Behaviour*, Suppl. **17**, 135–235.

Baerends, G. P. and Drent, R. H. The Herring Gull and its Egg. Part II. *Behaviour* Suppl. (in prep.).

Beer, C. G. (1965). Clutch size and incubation behaviour in Black-billed Gulls (*Larus bulleri*). *Auk* **82**, 1–18.

Cullen, J. M. (1962). The pecking response of young Wideawake Terns (*Sterna fuscata*). *Ibis* **103b**, 162–170.

D'Amato, M. R. (1970). "Experimental Psychology." McGraw-Hill, New York.

Drees, O. (1952). Untersuchungen über die angeborenen Verhaltensweisen bei Springspinnen (Salticidae). *Z.f. Tierpsychol.* **9**, 169–207.

Eikmanns, K. H. (1955). Verhaltensphysiologische Untersuchungen über den Beutefang und das Bewegungssehen der Erdkröte (*Bufo bufo* L.). *Z.f. Tierpsychol.* **12**, 229–253.

Franck, D. (1966). Möglichkeiten zur vergleichenden Analyse auslösender und richtender Reize mit Hilfe des Attrappenversuchs, ein Vergleich der Successiv- und Simultanmethode. *Behaviour* **27**, 150–159.

Hailman, J. P. (1967). The ontogeny of an instinct. The pecking response in chicks of the laughing gull (*Larus atricilla* L.) and related species. *Behaviour*, Suppl. 15, 159 pp.

Hailman, J. P. (1968). Spectral reflectance of gull's bill: physiological and evolutionary implications for animal communication. *Science* **162**, 139.

Hailman, J. P. (1969). Spectral pecking preference in gull chicks: possible resolution of a species difference. *J. comp. physiol. Psychol.* **67**, 465–467.

Hailman, J. P. (1970). Comments on the coding of releasing stimuli. In "Development and Evolution of Behaviour". (L. R. Aronson, E. Tobach, D. S. Lehrman and J. S. Rosenblatt, eds.). W. H. Freeman, San Francisco.

Hanson, A. M. (1959). Effects of discrimination training on stimulus generalization. *J. exp. Psychol.* **58**, 321–334.

Hess, E. H. (1956). Natural preferences of chicks and ducks for objects of different color. *Psychol. Reports* **2**, 477–483.

Hinde, R. A. (1954). Changes in response to a constant stimulus. *Brit. J. Anim. Behav.* **2**, 41–55.

Hinde, R. A. (1970). "Animal Behaviour", 2nd Ed. McGraw-Hill, New York.

Hogan, J. A., Kruijt, J. P. and Frijlink, J. H. (in prep.). "Supernormality" in a learning situation.

Impekoven, M. (1969). Motivationally controlled stimulus preference in chicks of the black-headed gull (*Larus ridibundus* L.). *Anim. Behav.* **17**, 252–270.

Kear, J. (1964). Colour preference in young Anatidae. *Ibis* **106**, 361–369.

Kriston, I. (1971). Zum Problem des Lernverhaltens von Apis mellifica L. gegenüber verschiedenen Duftstoffen. *Z. vergl. Physiol.* **74**, 169–189.

Kruijt, J. P. (1958). Speckling of the herring gull egg in relation to brooding-behaviour. *Arch. Néerl. Zool.* **12**, 565–567.

Lauer, J. and Lindauer, M. (1971). Genetisch fixierte Lerndispositionen bei der Honigbiene. *Abh. Akad. der Wissenschaften und der Literatur, Mainz, Mathematik Naturw. Tech.* 1–87.

Lorenz, K. (1935). Der Kumpan in der Umwelt des Vogels. *J.f.Ornith.*, **83**, 137–213, 289–413.

Marler, P. (1961). The filtering of external stimuli during instinctive behaviour. In "Current Problems in Animal Behaviour", (W. H. Thorpe, and O. Zangwill, eds.). pp. 150–166. Cambridge University Press.

Menzel, R. (1967). Untersuchungen zum Erlernen von Spektralfarben durch die Honigbiene (*Apis mellifica*). *Z. vergl. Physiol.* **56**, 22–62.

Noirot, E. (1965). Changes in responsiveness to young in the adult mouse. III. The effect of immediately preceding performances. *Behaviour* **24**, 318–325.

Prechtl. H. F. R. (1953). Zur Physiologie der angeborenen auslösenden Mechanismen: I. Quantitative Untersuchungen über die Sperrbewegungen junger Singvögel. *Behaviour* **5**, 32–50.

Quine, D. A. and Cullen, J. M. (1964). The pecking response of young Arctic Terns (Sterna macrura) and the adaptiveness of the "releasing mechanism". *Ibis* **106**, 145–173.

Schaeffer, H. H. and Hess, E. H. (1959). Color preferences in imprinting objects. *Z.f.Tierpsychol.* **16**, 161–172.

Schleidt, M. (1954). Untersuchungen über die Auslösung des Kollern beim Truthahn (*Meleagus gallopavo*). *Z.f.Tierpsychol.* **11**, 417–535.

Schleidt, W. (1962). Die historische Entwicklung der Begriffe "Angeborenes auslösendes Schema" und "Angeborener Auslösemechanismus" in der Ethologie. *Z.f.Tierpsychol.* **19**, 697–722.

Schleidt, W. (1964). Wirkungen äusserer Faktoren auf das Verhalten. *Fortschr. Zooi.* **16**, 469–499.

Schneirla, T. C. (1952). A consideration of some conceptual trends in comparative psychology. *Psychol. Bull.* **49**, 559–597.

Schneirla, T. C. (1959). An evolutionary and developmental theory of biphasic processes underlying approach and withdrawal. *In* "Nebraska Symposium on Motivation", (M. R. Jones, ed.), pp. 1–42. Univ. Nebraska Press, Lincoln.

Seitz, A. (1940). Die Paarbildung bei einigen Cichliden. I. *Astatotilapia strigigenia* Pfeffer. *Z.f. Tierpsychol.* **4**, 40–84.

Stevenson, J. G. (1966). Stimulus generalization: the ordering and spacing of test stimuli. *J. exp. Analysis Behav.*, **9**, 457–460.

Sutherland, N. S. (1959). Stimulus analysing mechanisms. *In* "Proc. Symp. Mechanization of Thought Processes", **2**, 575. H.M.S.O., London.

Sutherland, N. S. (1964). The learning of discrimination by animals. *Endeavour* **23**, 148–152.

Sutherland, N. S. (1969). Outlines of a theory of visual pattern recognition in animals and man. *In* "Animal Discrimination Learning", (R. M. Gilbert and N. S. Sutherland, eds.), pp. 385–411. Academic Press, London.

Terrace, H. S. (1968). Discrimination learning, the peak shift, and behavioral contrast. *J. exp. Analysis. Behav.*, **11**, 727–741.

Thomas, D. R. (1970). Stimulus selection, attention, and related matters. *In* "Current issues in animal learning", (J. H. Reynierse, ed.) Univ. Nebraska Press, Lincoln. 311–356.

Thompson, G. (1971). The photopic spectral sensitivity of gulls measured by electro-retinographic and pupillometric methods. *Vision Rec.* **11**, 719–731.

Tinbergen, N. (1953). "The Herring Gull's World." Collins, London.

Tinbergen, N., Broekhuysen, G. J., Feekes, F., Houghton, J. C. W., Kruuk, H. and Szule, E. (1962a). Egg shell removal by the black-headed gull, *Larus ridibundus L.*; a behaviour component of camouflage. *Behaviour* **19**, 74–117.

Tinbergen, N., Kruuk, H. and Paillette, M. (1962b). Egg shell removal by the black-headed gull, *Larus r. ridibundus*. II. *Bird study* **9**, 123–131.

Tinbergen, N. and Kruijt, W. (1938). Ueber die Orientierung des Bienenwolfes (*Philanthus triangulum* Fabr.) III. Die Bevorzugung bestimmter Wegmarken. *Z. vergl. Physiol.*, **25**, 292–334.

Tinbergen, N., Meeuse, B. J. D., Boerema, L. K. and Varossieau, W. N. (1943). Die Balz des Samtfalters, *Eumenis* (= *Satyrus*) *semele* (L.). *Z.f.Tierpsychol.* **5**, 182–226.

Tinbergen, N. and Perdeck, A. C. (1950). On the stimulus situation releasing the begging response in the newly hatched herring gull chick (*Larus a. argentatus* Pont.). *Behaviour* **3**, 1–39.

Tschanz, B. (1959). Zur Biologie der Trottellume (*Uria a. aalge* Pont.). *Behaviour* **14**, 1–100.

Van Iersel, J. J. A. (1951). On the orientation of *Bembex rostrata* L. *Trans. 9th Int. Congress Entomol.* Amsterdam, Vol. 1, 384–393.

Van Iersel, J. J. A. and Van den Assem, J. (1965). Aspects of orientation in the digger wasp *Bembix rostrata*. *In* "Learning and Associated Phenomena in Vertebrates". *Behaviour, Suppl.*, **1**, 154–162.

Von Frisch, K. (1914). Der Farbensinn und Formensinn der Biene. *Zool. Jahrb. Allg. Zool. Physiol.* **35**, 1–188.

Von Hess, C. (1913). Experimentelle Untersuchungen über den angeblichen Farbensinn der Bienen. *Zool. Jahrb. Allg. Zool. Physiol.*, **34**, 81–106.
Von Uexküll, J. (1934). Streifzüge durch die Umwelten von Tieren und Menschen.
Springer, Berlin. *Translated in* "Instructive Behaviour", (C. H. Schiller, ed.)
(1957). Methuen, London.
Weidmann, R. and Weidmann, U. (1958). An analysis of the stimulus situation
releasing food-begging in the black-headed gull. *Anim. Behav.*, **6**, 114.
Weidmann, U. (1961). The stimuli eliciting begging in gulls and terns. *Anim. Behav.*
9, 115–116.

Comments

1. Bateson pointed out that the ethological model of a releasing mechanism presupposes a summation process between the components of a stimulus complex. However, simple addition cannot be all that is involved in those cases where the pattern of stimulation is important.

This issue is related to that of what constitutes an element of stimulation—how far does the experimenter analyse the stimulus complex before assessing the relations between the components? There is of course a danger in regarding that which an experimenter chooses to vary as elemental.

In any case the question of how different stimulus components interact to influence response strength is inseparable from that of how response strength is measured: a combination that appears to be multiplicative would have been additive if a logarithmic scale had been used.

2. Cases in which the effectiveness of stimuli that are relevant to only one response is determined by known properties of the sensory/perceptual apparatus are known in a number of other animals. Hutt cited the example of the newly hatched crow, whose food-begging response is elicited by the adult's "caw" vocalization. Neurobiological analysis of the basilar membrane of the hatchling's cochlea reveals that only those parts which resonate to the frequencies of the "caw" are functionally mature (Anokhin, 1964).

Other well analysed cases include the dependence of the specificity in responsiveness to particular pheromones shown by some moths on specificity in the sensory cells (Schneider, 1963), and the demonstration by Capranica (e.g. 1965) and his co-workers that specificity in responsiveness to the species-characteristic mating call of frogs is mediated by the peripheral auditory system.

3. Hutt commented further as follows: "Once colour is accounted for, I wonder whether a fairly simple subcortical mechanism might be sufficient to account for the gulls' responses to other parameters of their eggs. Weiskrantz (1963) demonstrated that a monkey with bilateral removal of the striate cortex could make accurate discriminations between figures containing different amounts of "edginess", i.e. number of light-dark gradients. Similarly, Humphrey (1970) has demonstrated that, over a somewhat limited range of values, there is a monotonic relationship between probability of reaching

towards, and relative size of, a figure. Other factors which have been shown to facilitate discrimination are relative brightness (Humphrey, idem), and movement (Humphrey and Weiskrantz, 1967). Changes in any of these four factors—edginess, size, brightness and movement—would produce a change in what Weiskrantz (1963) called "the integral of all retinal ganglionic activity". From Baerends' experiments, it looks as though over a certain range there is increasing preference for objects that produce increasing amounts of retinal activity (differential preferences amongst shapes can be accounted for in the same way). At a certain point however, at which the greatest intensity of retinal activity would theoretically be obtained, the animals begin to show fear responses. It thus appears that the relationship between total retinal activity and preference is an inverted U. The facts probably could be accounted for fairly parsimoniously by Schneirla's (1965) model of biphasic processes underlying approach-withdrawal."

It may be noted that many now believe the "integral of all retinal ganglionic activity" to be an over-simple notion.

References

Anokhin, P. K. (1964). Systemogenesis as a general regulator of brain development. *In* "Progress in Brain Research". IX, (W. A. and H. E. Himwich, eds.). Elsevier, Amsterdam.

Capranica, R. E. (1965). "The evoked vocal response of the Bullfrog." M.I.T. Press, Cambridge, Mass.

Humphrey, N. K. (1970). What the frog's eye tells the monkey's brain. *Brain Behav. Evol.* **3**, 324–337.

Humphrey, N. K. and Weiskrantz, L. (1967). Vision in monkeys after removal of the striate cortex. *Nature* **215**.

Schneider, D. (1963). Electrophysiological investigation of insect olfaction. *In* "Olfaction and Tastes", (Y. Zotterman, ed.), pp. 85–103. Macmillan, New York

Schneirla, T. C. (1965). Aspect of stimulation and organization in approach/ withdrawal processes underlying vertebrate behavioural development. *In* "Advances in the Study of Behavior". Vol. I. (D. S. Lehrman, R. A. Hinde and E. Shaw, eds.). Academic Press, New York.

Weiskrantz, L. (1963). Contour discrimination in a young monkey with striate cortex ablation. *Neuropsychologia* **1**, 145–164.

3

Environmental Constraints on Development in the Visual System

by Colin Blakemore

Censorship in Visual Messages

Nowadays we look upon visual perception as a piecemeal affair: our seemingly unified view of the world around us is really only a plausible hypothesis about reality put to us by our brains on the basis of fragmentary evidence. The transformations that go on in the retinae and visual pathways of animals are not merely reproductions, in high fidelity, of the visual image. At every stage a censor is at work, cutting with its scissors, and deleting with a red pencil, the unwanted visual messages. This neural censor, however, does not protect the brain from visual titillation or dangerous knowledge: just the contrary, in fact. The fundamental process occurring in the visual system is elimination of trivial signals and the preservation of only the spiciest parts of the message.

What exactly is a spicy visual signal? It is one with high information content; one in which redundancy has been eliminated. Barlow (1961) has made a strong point that certain features in a visual image, such as the edges of patterns and moving objects, carry much information. One mechanism whereby such features are especially effective in producing activity in the visual system is that of *lateral inhibition*. This is a process in which ganglion cells, excited by light falling on one group of receptors, are inhibited by light on a neighbouring group. Illumination of all the receptors at once produces rather little response, but if a dark-light contour falls on the receptors, ganglion cells become very active. To the behaviourist the important point is that, when an animal looks at the world, the uniform areas of sky or grass do not clog up its visual pathways with trivial signals. But the hawk in the sky or the mouse in the field is a very exciting event.

Another good example of common-sense in sensory systems is the universal property of neuronal adaptation. Even if a ganglion cell looks at a contour on the right part of the retina, its vigorous response is short-lived. It produces an initial discharge of impulses but the torrent soon subsides to a mere trickle. Again, the function seems to be, at least in part, to rid the optic nerve of old news, to signal only the changes in sensory stimulation. So if lateral inhibition reduces spatial redundancy, adaptation decreases temporal redundancy.

These are easy examples, but there is a fundamental barrier to this sort of argument: the criteria for what is biologically important are not universal. We must weigh our estimates of what is important by considering the animal's behavioural repertoire and its environmental context. What is information to one animal is redundancy to another. For a primitive creature whose entire visual capacity is a simple phototropism, knowledge of absolute, uniform illumination is essential. Even for the control of the diameter of our pupils it is clear that we need more than an awareness merely of borders in the visual field. In fact, in this regard, it is interesting to note that there are indeed a small number of ganglion cells in the cat's retina that break the rules and signal tonically the mean illumination of their receptive fields. Perhaps these cells provide messages for the regulation of the pupil (Barlow and Levick, 1969).

Species-Specific Visual Information

We must expect, then, to find that the feature-detecting neurones in an animal's visual system are sensitive to just those features of the visual environment that possess high information content for that particular animal. Recent neurophysiological investigations of the stimulus-specific properties of single neurones in various animals' visual systems have shown them to have much in common, but also to have some differences. For example, pigeons (Maturana and Frenk, 1963), rabbits (Levick, 1967), ground squirrels (Michael, 1968, 1970), cats (Hubel and Wiesel, 1962) and monkeys (Hubel and Wiesel, 1968) all have visual neurones that respond selectively to the orientation of edges or to the direction of movement of objects, as well as having contrast-detecting cells with simple inhibitory surrounds. These feature-detecting neurones are not found in the same part of the visual pathway for different animals: in cats and monkeys they are in the visual cortex and the superior colliculus, but in the species that lack binocular vision the ganglion cells in the retina themselves have these complicated properties.

As well as the detectors of fundamental visual events (edge, orientation and movement), each species has some uniquely specialized neurones of its own; curvature detectors in pigeons, very fast movement detectors in rabbits, corner detectors in cats and specific colour-contrast detectors in ground squirrels and monkeys. In fact all these animals live in rather similar environmental contexts: perhaps we should expect to see even more species-specific information extraction if we were to explore among animals with more singular visual adaptations to unusual environments. Similarly, neurones very deep in the visual pathway of any animal might be expected to detect certain behaviourally significant combinations of encoded features. A provocative hint of this possibility comes from the description by Gross *et al.* (1972) of neurones in the monkey's inferotemporal cortex that responded optimally to the shape of a monkey's hand.

Strategies for Building a Visual System

If we admit that environmental information is somehow impressed on an animal's visual neurones (it is hard to avoid the word "imprinted"), then how is this process achieved? In the extreme this question reduces to the old issue of Nature versus Nurture, but the possible mechanisms number more than two.

(1) The feature-detecting properties of visual neurones could be entirely functional at birth, each animal coming into the visual world brandishing a set of detectors for spotting its own environmental information and deleting its own environmental redundancy.

(2) The neurones might be entirely pre-determined at birth but not fully responsive. After a period of passive maturation the full properties could appear, quite independently of post-natal experience.

(3) The detectors could be completely specified (or merely pre-determined) at birth but require interaction with the appropriate environmental features before they become validated.

(4) They could be partially genetically specified but capable of modification or sharpening by environmental experience.

(5) Unspecified cells might be chiselled by the environment into detectors for any conceivable feature. Genetics would play no part except supplying the eyes and the naked neurones.

Different rules must surely determine the mechanism of specification in different species and even in different parts of the visual system, but some possibilities can probably be eliminated altogether, simply on logical grounds. For example, it is patently implausible that the connexions of every neurone should be totally defined by genetic information. Likewise it is unlikely that the rest of the brain could handle signals from detectors whose entire coding properties were unpredictable and forced on them by environmental pressures. Surely the most likely arrangement is that crudely pre-determined detectors are tuned-up or modified by the environment (Hypothesis 4).

The cat's visual cortex as a developmental model

To take a very particular case, consider the visual system of cats, which is not so different from that of monkeys, nor probably from our own. The majority of ganglion cells in the cat's retina have straightforward round receptive fields with inhibitory interaction between the centre and the surround (Kuffler, 1953): they are merely detectors of local contrast. At the synapse in the lateral geniculate nucleus there is rather little change in the message and the receptive fields of geniculate cells are also mainly concentric (Hubel and Wiesel, 1961). However, in the adult cat's cortex virtually every neurone is an orientation-detector. A specific set of afferent fibres contacts each neurone and gives it a receptive field that demands a long black or white bar, or a black-white edge of a particular angle, to make it respond (Hubel and Wiesel, 1962). These orientation-detectors come in all shapes and sizes of receptive field and every possible orientation is equally represented amongst the whole population of detectors (Fig. 10A).

Fig. 1 illustrates responses from a typical neurone in the cat's primary

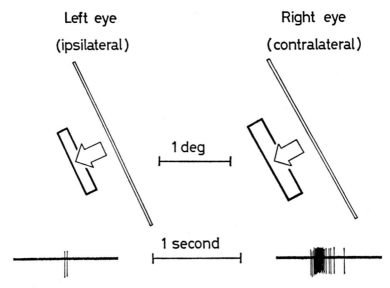

Fig. 1. Responses from a binocular cortical cell from the cat's visual cortex. This neurone responded to a diagonal bright bar moving to the left. The action potentials, photographed from an oscilloscope, are shown below for stimuli presented to each eye in turn. (Reproduced, by permission, from Blakemore and Pettigrew, 1970.)

visual cortex. The cell responded to slow movement of a thin diagonal slit of light across the screen in front of the animal. The records of action potentials from the neurone, photographed from an oscilloscope, are shown below a plot of the receptive field. The cell obviously responded to the same sort of target shown to each eye separately, although it was much more sensitive to stimuli in the right eye. In fact the microelectrode was in this cat's left hemisphere, so the right eye was contralateral to this cell.

About 85% of cat cortical cells are binocular with clear excitatory inputs from both eyes. However, like the cell described by Fig. 1, they are not necessarily equally driven by both of them. Hubel and Wiesel (1962)

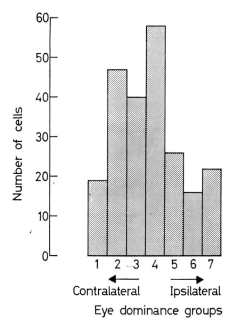

Fig. 2. Ocular dominance histogram for 228 cells from normal adult cats. The eye dominance groups are defined in the text. (Reproduced, by permission, from Blakemore and Pettigrew, 1970.)

have suggested a simple system for classifying the eye-dominance of these cells, by sorting them into seven groups. In Fig. 2 there is a histogram of eye-dominance for 228 cortical neurones (Blakemore and Pettigrew, 1970). Groups 1 and 7 are monocular, having excitatory input from only the contralateral or the ipsilateral eye respectively. Group 4 neurones are equally sensitive to both eyes. So Groups 4 to 7 have increasing ipsilateral dominance, Groups 4 to 1 increasing contralateral dominance. Notice that about twice as many neurones are contralaterally dominated (Groups 1, 2, and 3) as are ipsilaterally (Groups 5, 6 and 7).

The *trigger feature*, then, for most cortical cells of an adult cat is the image of the edge of an object falling simultaneously on the receptive field in both retinae. Indeed the response of these cells is usually greatly facilitated by stimulating both eyes at the same time. This means that for any particular fixed position of the eyes each neurone demands that its object be placed at a particular *distance* from the eyes in order for the images to fall on the two receptive fields. By virtue of the horizontal separation of the two eyes, objects closer, or more distant, than the fixation point have their images on relatively different, non-corresponding points in the two retinae. The receptive fields of binocular cells are laid out with a considerable range of disparity between the positions of the fields in the two eyes. For those binocular cells all connected to one particular spot in one eye, the receptive fields can be in a wide variety of different positions in the other eye. So different neurones will respond to objects at different distances (Barlow, Blakemore and Pettigrew, 1967; Bishop, 1970). Fig. 3 shows a simple model of this neural mechanism, which must surely be involved in stereoscopic depth perception.

So the contours of objects at particular distances have high information content for the adult cat's cortex. Let us ask how these neurones are specified and how their response properties become so tightly constrained.

The Naïve Kitten's Cortex

The obvious experiment to answer this question is to record cellular activity from the inexperienced kitten's cortex, preferably as soon as its eyes are open. This has been done by two groups of workers, unfortunately with rather different results. First of all Hubel and Wiesel themselves (1963), who first discovered orientation detectors in the adult, examined a small number of cells in an eight-day-old kitten, just as the eyes were about to open, and others in a slightly older kitten whose eyes had been covered with translucent occluders from the moment they opened. To them the picture was clear: after all their vast experience with normal cats they were prepared to say that responses of cortical cells in these kittens were "strikingly similar to those of adult cats". There were subtle differences, to be sure (lower spontaneous activity, sluggish responses with rapid habituation for repetitive presentations of the stimulus, less well-defined optimal orientations), but in general the gospel was transparently evident. Nature had won the day !

Only very recently, however, Nurture has re-entered the battle. In California, Barlow and Pettigrew (1971) have looked again at the visually

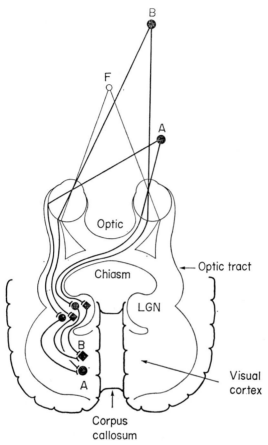

Fig. 3. A simple neural model for binocular depth discrimination (stereopsis). The eyes are fixating point F and the two objects, A and B, not at the same distance as F, have disparate retinal images, not on corresponding points in the two eyes. The four cells shown in the lateral geniculate nucleus (LGN) each have excitatory input from only one of the eyes. The cells shown as diamonds have their receptive fields under the two images of B and those shown as circles detect the images of A. The two binocular cells, A and B, in the visual cortex have input from the appropriate pairs of LGN cells, so that they respond uniquely to the two objects A and B respectively.

inexperienced kitten's cortex and their results are somewhat at odds with those of Hubel and Wiesel. They find that before patterned visual experience, cortical neurones are largely unspecified. They usually respond to patterns of light, but the receptive fields are diffuse and certainly the responses habituate quickly. None of the cells is orientation-selective in the manner of those in the adult cortex. Most will fire, although weakly, to a moving edge of any orientation. Even those that seem to prefer one angle

of contour would be better called direction-selective, rather than orientation selective, because they respond for any sort of moving pattern travelling in one direction but not for motion in the reverse direction. Movement
along an axis orthogonal to this preferred-null axis causes an equal response in both directions. This is totally different from the adult cat where
usually only long edges are effective and the response is completely
abolished by a small change in orientation.

There is no simple resolution of this momentous debate; probably no
trivial explanation in terms of different anaesthetics or different procedures. Let us at least consider the points on which both groups agree.
First, kitten neurones are certainly much less specific in their feature-
detection than adult cells and they respond very weakly. So something at
least must be added by age or experience. Second, both groups find that
the majority of kitten cells are binocular with the normal sort of eye-
dominance distribution (Fig. 5A), although Barlow and Pettigrew tested
the way that the neurones respond to images at different retinal disparities
and found that they are not at all specific for the stereoscopic distance of
the target, unlike normal cells in the cat. So experience may have some
important part to play in honing down the binocular response characteristics of the neurones too.

With these somewhat conflicting results in mind let us now move on to
see how experimental manipulation of visual experience can influence the
final organization of the cortex.

Binocular Deprivation of Patterned Vision

If cortical cells merely mature automatically, or if they are specified at
birth and need no environmental validation, we should expect that de-
priving a kitten totally of patterned vision might not interfere with the
ultimate organization of its cortex. On the other hand, if experience plays
any part in specification, binocular deprivation should be disastrous.

Wiesel and Hubel (1965) sutured both eyelids closed (which allows some
diffuse light but not pattern to reach the retina) and opened them for
recording experiments at ages from $2\frac{1}{2}$ to $4\frac{1}{2}$ months. Only about one
third of the neurones were normal, by their definitions, in terms of orient-
ation-selectivity and responsiveness. One third were responsive but very
sluggish and abnormal, and about one third were spontaneously active but
could not be persuaded to respond to visual stimuli at all. Of course, it is
quite likely that there were many other unresponsive cells that had no
spontaneous discharge and hence were missed altogether. Barlow and Pettigrew (1971) disagree. Their binocularly deprived cats are just like their
newborn kittens; there are no totally specified cells.

Everyone agrees, however, that binocular deprivation does nothing to the distribution of eye-dominance. Neurones that respond at all usually still do so through both eyes, and, just as in the normal adult, the contralateral eye on average is more influential (Fig. 4). This certainly seems

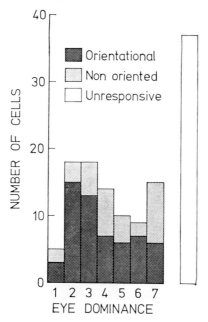

Fig. 4. Eye dominance histogram for 126 cells from four kittens binocularly deprived of vision from about 8 days to $2\frac{1}{2}$ to $4\frac{1}{2}$ months. Normal orientation selective cells, abnormal cells with no orientational preferencc and completely unresponsive neurones are shown separately, as described by the inset code. (Redrawn from Wiesel and Hubel, 1965.)

to point to hard-wired binocular connexions that are not under environmental control. Nothing is further from the truth!

Monocular Deprivation

If binocular connexions are beyond the touch of visual experience, then covering one eye rather than both should also leave them undisturbed, but it certainly does not. Hubel and Wiesel (1970) have sutured just one eyelid for various periods of time after birth and afterwards looked at the eye dominance distributions of cortical cells. The results of these painstaking experiments are summarized in Fig. 5. They deprived the right eye and recorded in the left visual cortex, thus pitting any reduction in effectiveness of the deprived eye against the natural contralateral dominance.

Amazingly, monocular eye-closure for as little as three or four days during the fourth and fifth weeks leaves the cortex virtually totally disconnected from that eye. The experience silences great patches of cortical tissue, leaving isolated clumps of neurones that are almost all monocular and, although normal in their orientational properties, can only be driven through the experienced left eye. This drastic environmental modification can occur

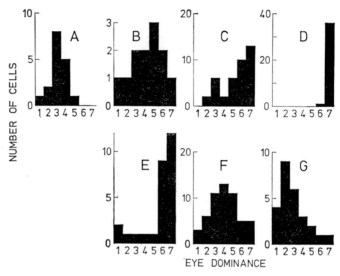

Fig. 5. A series of eye dominance histograms from Hubel and Wiesel's (1963, 1970) experiments defining a critical period for monocular deprivation of patterned vision. A. Two normal, very young, visually inexperienced kittens, one 8 days old, one 16 days, but with no previous patterned vision in either eye. B. Monocular deprivation from 9 to 19 days. In this kitten the right eye was covered by a translucent occluder. C. Monocular deprivation from 10 to 31 days. In this kitten, as in D to G, the right eyelids were sutured and the cells recorded in the left hemisphere after the end of the period of deprivation. D. Monocular deprivation from 23 to 29 days. E. Monocular deprivation from 2 to 3 months. F. Monocular deprivation from 4 to 7 months. G. A previously normal adult cat monocularly deprived for 3 months.

only within a fairly well defined *sensitive or critical period* from about three to twelve weeks of age. Monocular deprivation from nine to nineteen days (Fig. 5B) and from about three-and-a-half to six-and-a-half months (Fig. 5F) has no detectable effect whatever on binocularity.

    How can one reconcile these dire consequences of monocular deprivation with the retention of binocular cells when both eyes are covered? Wiesel and Hubel (1965) think of afferent fibres from the two eyes competing for synaptic sites on cortical cells. As long as both eyes are normal, or equally abnormal, the status quo is maintained, but reducing the input from one eye lets the other get the upper hand.

Alternating Monocular Occlusion

If this simple competitive theory is true we can gain an idea of the speed of this take-over by one eye by alternately covering the two eyes. Hubel and Wiesel (1965) did this by covering only the left eye with a translucent occluder, then the next day only the right eye and so on, from ten days to ten weeks of age. They found in these kittens that about 90% of all cells were purely monocular with roughly equal numbers driven by each of the eyes (Fig. 6). So the crucial point is that a lack of synchronous binocular in-

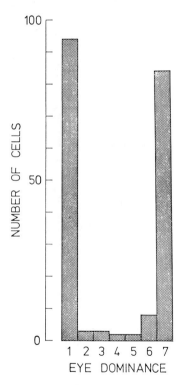

Fig. 6. Eye dominance histograms from two 10-week-old kittens raised with a translucent occluder covering one eye one day, the other eye the next. (Redrawn from Hubel and Wiesel, 1965.)

put to a cell disrupts the synaptic arrangement and leads to capture by one of the eyes, presumably the one that was originally dominant for the cell.

Artificial Squint

There is even a condition in which both eyes can be open all the time any yet binocularity is lost. Hubel and Wiesel (1965) induced an artificial divergent squint by cutting the medial rectus muscle of the right eyeball so that the eye deviated laterally (Fig. 8B). They did this at about nine days of age and recorded from the kitten's cortex at three months or one year. The picture was very similar to that for alternating monocular occlusion: very few binocular cells remained but each eye drove a roughly equal number of monocular cells (Fig. 7).

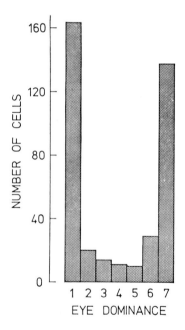

Fig. 7. Eye dominance for 384 cells from four kittens raised with an artificial divergent squint until 3 months or 1 year of age. (Redrawn from Hubel & Wiesel, 1965.)

In this case each eye had quite a normal view and both were open at the same time. The only problem is that any particular binocular neurone was very unlikely to find an identical target on its receptive fields in both eyes, because the two eyes were simply not pointing in the same direction. As the eyes moved back and forth each cell would often be bombarded by signals from its initially dominant eye and at other times receive weaker messages from the other eye. So conditions would exist for the loss of binocularity: the afferents from the two eyes would never fire synchronously and competition could take place.

Fig. 8 is a diagram of these changes that occur in a squinting kitten and it may point out the possible biological value of this whole modifiable binocular system. In the normal animal (8A) the maps of the visual world are, in a sense, congruent on the cortex, each region of visual space projecting to a particular area through both eyes. Indeed, as I have pointed out, this is the mechanism by which binocular fusion and stereoscopic

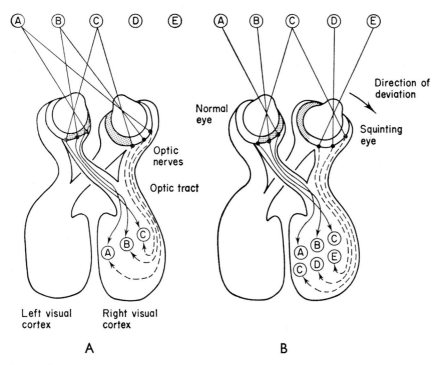

Fig. 8. **A.** A simplified diagram of the binocular input to the visual cortex in the normal cat. B. After the creation of an artificial divergent squint in the right eye, neurones in the visual cortex become monocular and there are essentially two independent maps of the one visual world in the cortex. (Reproduced, by permission, from Blakemore, 1971.)

vision are achieved. In the squint situation (8B), however, the misalignment of the visual axes leaves the maps from the two eyes totally out of register, in terms of projections from particular points in space to particular parts of the cortex.

The fact that the neurones become monocular means that each map is handled by a completely independent set of neurones. Presumably the messages from each eye can be interpreted unambiguously. Imagine what would happen if the original binocular arrangement were retained. The message of every neurone would be logically ambiguous as to the position of the stimulus in the total visual field. The brain could not know whether a message was coming from an image in one eye, or an image in a totally different part of the visual world from the other eye.

In fact it is very pertinent to mention that these squinting kittens, and those with alternating monocular occlusion, have apparently quite normal vision and localization through each eye alone, whereas after monocular eye closure, the deprived eye is virtually blind.

What looks like the crudest possible form of environmental control of the developing cortex could, then, have a beneficial function. If for any reason the kitten does not normally encounter simultaneous, corresponding signals from both eyes during the critical period, it abandons all hope of setting up a sophisticated system for binocular depth discrimination and single vision, and opts instead for the next best thing—independent visual systems for the two eyes. The sorts of situations that could produce this binocular discrepancy are squint (strabismus), difference in magnification (aniseikonia) and difference in refactive error (anisometropia) in the two eyes; just the conditions that often lead to a loss of stereoscopic vision in human infants.

Plastic Trigger Features

If binocularity is modifiable then it seems reasonable to ask whether orientation selectivity itself is under some sort of environmental influence. The newborn kitten's neurones are either completely non-specific or very broadly tuned for orientation so, either way, something must happen to them early in life. It could be merely maturation or it could be dependent on visual experience.

Hirsch and Spinelli (1971) invented a technique for combining binocular incongruence with selective patterned experience. They fitted masks on to their kittens with a simple trans-illuminated pattern of three black stripes visible to each eye. For one eye they were vertical stripes, for the other horizontal. The kittens wore these masks for several hours each day and at other times they were kept in the dark. Certainly their binocular neurones never received simultaneous congruent input, so one might expect them to have become monocular. But in addition the range of orientations experienced was restricted in each eye.

In fact their results are rather hard to compare with those of the conventional receptive field plotters because they used an automated method for analysing the responses to moving spots and thus for determining the shape of the receptive field. Most visual cortical neurones will hardly respond at all to a small spot, so they were able to plot rather few elongated receptive fields that would obviously respond best to an oriented edge or bar. But of the cells with oriented receptive fields that they could find, all were monocular and all but one had a receptive field orientation that closely matched the angle of the lines seen by that eye. Perhaps this is not so surprising, because any primordial vertical detector would only have been stimulated through one eye and according to the competition hypothesis would therefore have lost contact with the other. The hint that something more than this is involved comes from their failure to find any diagonally oriented receptive fields, binocular or monocular. Something else, not explicable on the basis of binocular competition, must have happened to all the potential diagonal detectors which were essentially binocularly deprived in Hirsch and Spinelli's experiment.

Blakemore and Cooper (1970), independently of Hirsch and Spinelli, did a closely related experiment. We decided to raise kittens in a fairly natural situation in which their visual experience, through both eyes, was restricted almost exclusively to edges of one orientation. The apparatus we used was a tall plastic tube painted with horizontal or vertical black and white stripes on the inside and with a glass platform suspended in the middle (Fig. 9): the tube was illuminated from above. Our kittens were housed in the dark except for about four or five hours each day when each one was put on the glass platform in one of these tubes. The kitten wore a collar around its neck to prevent it from seeing its own body, so its visual experience was almost wholly restricted to edges of one orientation. The kitten was quite free to rotate its head, which might have upset our experiments. However, observation through a peephole showed us that they did not, in fact, tilt their heads through large angles.

Our first two animals were exposed from two weeks to five and a half months of age. Then we brought them into a normal room for a few hours each week, spread over two months, to look at their visual behaviour. To be brief, they were initially almost blind: they had no startle response for a rapidly approaching object, no following head movements, no "visual placing" response to reach out for a surface over which they were held, and no depth perception. But they very soon recovered from these preliminary problems—perhaps they were visuomotor difficulties rather than strictly visual deficits, since the kittens had never before been required to interact with visual stimuli: this condition is known to cause temporary blindness (Held and Hein, 1963).

After the initial recovery they were left with subtle visual impediments. In short, they could not respond to edges of an orientation perpendicular to that which they had experienced. Probably the best test was to watch the way that the kittens reacted to a thin rod held and shaken by

F

the experimenter. If it was held vertically the kitten raised in verticals would orient to it, run to it and play with it, while its fellow kitten was completely disinterested. If the rod was now turned horizontally the first kitten behaved as if it had disappeared and the horizontally experienced kitten would now come to play.

Fig. 9. Apparatus to rear kittens in an environment of vertical strips. (Reproduced, by permission, from Blakemore and Cooper, 1970.)

When we recorded from the cortex of these first two kittens at seven-and-a-half months we found that in every way but one the cells were almost completely normal. There were no unresponsive cells, the receptive fields were quite normal in size and binocularity. But there were simply no neurones sensitive to the orientation orthogonal to that which the kitten had experienced when young, or indeed within almost ± 45 deg. of it. Fig. 10A is the distribution of preferred orientations for a sample of cortical

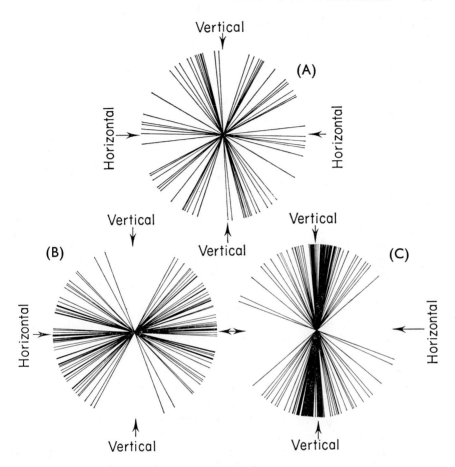

Fig. 10. A. A polar diagram of the range of preferred orientations for 34 neurones from a normal adult cat. Each line represents the optimal orientation for one cell. B. A kitten reared in horizontal stripes from 2 weeks to 5½ months, then allowed a little normal vision spread over 2 months. C. A kitten like that in B, but reared in vertical stripes.

neurones from a normal adult cat. Every line is the optimal orientation of a moving edge or bar for one neurone. Statistically, all angles are equally represented. The other two polar histograms (10B and 10C) are from the first kittens, reared in horizontals and verticals respectively.

Orientation selectivity as well as binocularity is, then, under environmental control. It probably cannot mean simply that busy cells are validated and unused ones degenerate, because we certainly found no regions of silent cortex, and no decrease in the density of neurones. Every cell encountered was responsive and all responded to much the same orientation. So this is no passive validation or selection of specified cells by the environment. The neurones are actually all being modified to match the probability of occurrence of features in the visual world.

At first this observation seems totally contradictory to the binocular competition hypothesis. Since in a vertically experienced kitten all the potential horizontal detectors are binocularly deprived they should mainly survive. To interpret these results one has to consider the possibility that there is also competition for synaptic sites by different sets of afferents even from the same eye, so that any neurone can adopt whatever orientation it is most commonly subject to.

A Sensitive Period

Knowing that monocular eye closure is only influential early in life it is reasonable to ask whether orientational modification too has a sensitive or critical period. I have recently been trying to sort out this question (Blakemore, in prep.) and the picture is already quite clear. I kept my kittens, as before, in the dark, except during their exposure to stripes, which was limited to certain periods of early life. After the end of the exposure the kittens were continuously housed in the dark and I performed the neurophysiological experiments as soon as possible, without any period of prolonged normal vision.

Fig. 11 shows polar diagrams for the neurones from nine animals in the current series. The times of exposure are described in the legend. Evidently even short periods of presentation can modify the whole visual cortex, but again there is a distinct critical period from before four weeks to about twelve weeks outside which no amount of exposure will bias the distribution of preferred orientations. The kitten exposed from three to five months (Fig. 11H) and the adult kept in verticals for four months (Fig. 11I) had equal representation of all angles.

Not surprisingly, those kittens that had already spent a considerable proportion of the sensitive period in the dark before seeing anything had a lot of rather unusual cells, some non-orientational, most showing rapid habituation, some purely direction selective. The very fact, though, that the kitten that was in horizontals from three to five months (11H) certainly had some truly orientation selective cells, including some for vertical edges, raises an interesting issue. If Barlow and Pettigrew (1971) are correct, then where did this kitten get its vertical detectors from (let alone its horizontal ones)? Perhaps there is some natural spontaneous maturation (subject to environmental modification) or possibly the few seconds of light each day for the feeding of the kittens in their home cages was enough to set up some orientation detectors at all angles. It is certainly remarkable to find that as little as 33 hours of exposure to stripes can modify every neurone. (Fig. 11C): one must wonder whether even a few minutes is enough.

Retrospect

Now we are in a position to reconsider the alternative strategies for constructing feature detecting neurones. Alternative 4 seems to be the only tenable one: visual cortical cells can be manipulated by the environment within a particular set of genetic constraints. I suppose there is still a possibility that a completely different type of feature detector could be synthesized by a suitably restricted environment. Perhaps a kitten reared in curved lines would develop curvature detectors, or if reared in an array of random dots would find itself with dot detectors. Somehow this just seems patently implausible because with total randomness in the nature of the coding properties it is difficult to understand how the next stage in the pathway could cope with the inherently unpredictable messages from such a system. However, only future experiments will settle this point, one way or the other.

The mechanism is certainly a beautiful way of matching central visual processing to the specific demands of the environment. It seems that these feature detectors are simply set up on the basis of the probability of stimulus features in the kitten's visual world.

With neural changes so total but so fast, it is difficult to avoid thinking that whatever synaptic re-arrangement is happening it may have properties in common with processes involved in learning and memory. Hopefully it will be feasible to use this plasticity as a paradigm for studying rapid synaptic modification at a physiological and an anatomical level.

There is another obvious analogy—with imprinting (see Chapter 5). We have seen that in cats too there can be a change in visual behaviour (with a known neural substrate) as a result of interaction with environmental features during a sensitive period early in life. It is possible that common synaptic mechanisms underlie the process of imprinting; even that enigmatic phenomenon may yield a little to the microelectrode in the next few years.

Finally, to return to my first point, we must conclude that the behavioural repertoire of an adult animal is restricted by not only the immediate environmental context and the species-specific information within it, but also the environmental context in which the animal grew up. If we take these experiments as a serious indication of the role of early visual experience in human infants (perhaps over a much longer critical period) then the lesson is straightforward. We may live in a world con-

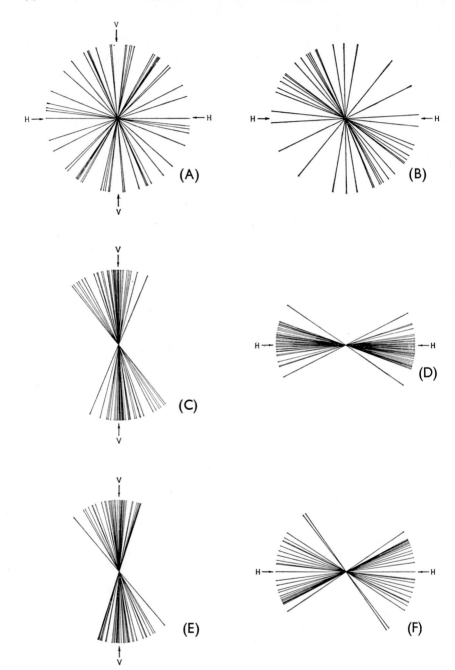

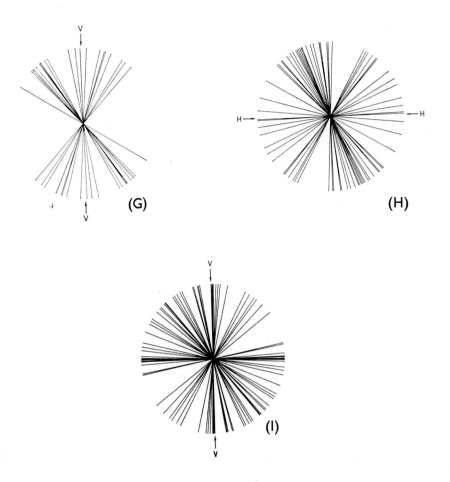

Fig. 11. A series of polar diagrams of preferred orientations to illustrate the critical period for environmental modification of cortical cells. The experimental animals were kept in the dark at all times when they were not being exposed to stripes. A. A normal kitten of about 3 months of age. B. A kitten reared in horizontals for a total of about 15 hours from 10 to 20 days. C. Verticals for a total of about 33 hours from 4 to 5 weeks. D. Horizontals from 6 to 9 weeks. E. Verticals from 6 to 9 weeks. F. Horizontals from 9 to 12 weeks. G. Verticals from 10 to 13 weeks. H. Horizontals from 3 to 5 months. I. A normal adult exposed to verticals for 4 months.

strained by our own early environment, and our adult capabilities, not only visual, may be fundamentally confined within the context of our experience as infants.

Acknowledgements

The Medical Research Council, London, has given supporting grants for this project on visual development. I am very grateful to Ron Loewenbein and Janet Dormer for their excellent technical help.

References

Barlow, H. B. (1961). Possible principles underlying the transformations of sensory messages. *In* "Sensory Communication", (W. A. Rosenblith, ed.), pp. 217–234. M.I.T. Press, Cambridge, Mass.

Barlow, H. B. and Levick, W. R. (1969). Changes in the maintained discharge with adaptation level in the cat retina. *J. Physiol.* **202**, 699–718.

Barlow, H. B. and Pettigrew, J. D. (1971). Lack of specificity of neurones in the visual cortex of young kittens. *J. Physiol.* **218**, 98–100p.

Barlow, H. B., Blakemore, C. and Pettigrew, J. D. (1967). The neural mechanism of binocular depth discrimination. *J. Physiol.* **193**, 327–342.

Bishop, P. O. (1970). Beginning of form perception and binocular depth discrimination in cortex. *In* "The Neurosciences: Second Study Program", (F. O. Schmitt, ed.), pp. 471–485. New York. N.Y.: Rockefeller University Press.

Blakemore, C. (1971). Why we see what we see. *New Scientist* **51**, 614–617.

Blakemore, C. and Cooper, G. F. (1970). Development of the brain depends on the visual environment. *Nature* **228**, 477–478.

Blakemore, C. and Pettigrew, J. D. (1970). Eye dominance in the visual cortex. *Nature* **225**, 426–429.

Gross, C. G., Rocha-Miranda, C. E. and Bender, D. B. (1972). Visual properties of neurons in inferotemporal cortex of the macaque. *J. Neurophysiol.* **35**, 96–111.

Held, R. and Hein, A. (1963). Movement-produced stimulation in the development of visually guided behavior. *J. comp. physiol. Psychol.*, **56**, 872–876.

Hirsch, H. V. B. and Spinelli, D. N. (1971). Modification of the distribution of receptive field orientation in cats by selective visual exposure during development. *Expl. Brain Res.*, **12**, 509–527.

Hubel, D. H. and Wiesel, T. N. (1961). Integrative action in the cat's lateral geniculate body. *J. Physiol.* **155**, 385–398.

Hubel, D. H. and Wiesel, T. N. (1962). Receptive fields, binocular interaction and functional architecture in the cat's visual cortex. *J. Physiol.* **160**, 106–154.

Hubel, D. H. and Wiesel, T. N. (1963). Receptive fields of cells in striate cortex of very young, visually inexperienced kittens. *J. Neurophysiol.* **26**, 994–1002.

Hubel, D. H. and Wiesel, T. N. (1965). Binocular interaction in striate cortex of kittens reared with artificial squint. *J. Neurophysiol.* **28**, 1041–1059.

Hubel, D. H. and Wiesel, T. N. (1968). Receptive fields and functional architecture of monkey striate cortex. *J. Physiol.* **195**, 215–243.

Hubel, D. H. and Wiesel, T. N. (1970). The period of susceptibility to the physiological effects of unilateral eye closure in kittens. *J. Physiol.* **206**, 419–436.

Kuffler, S. W. (1953). Discharge patterns and functional organization of mammalian retina. *J. Neurophysiol.* **16**, 37–68.

Levick, W. R. (1967). Receptive fields and trigger features of ganglion cells in the visual streak of the rabbit's retina. *J. Physiol.* **188**, 285–307.

Maturana, H. R. and Frenk, S. (1963). Directional movement and horizontal edge detectors in the pigeon retina. *Science* **142**, 977–979.

Michael, C. R. (1968). Receptive fields of single optic nerve fibers in a mammal with an all-cone retina. II: Directionally selective units. *J. Neurophysiol.* **31**, 257–267.

Michael, C. R. (1970). Integration of retinal and cortical information in the superior colliculus of the ground squirrel. *Brain, Behav. Evolutn.* **3**, 205–209.

Wiesel, T. N. and Hubel, D. H. (1965). Comparison of the effects of unilateral and bilateral eye closure on cortical unit responses in kittens. *J. Neurophysiol.* **28**, 1029–1040.

Comments

Sevenster asked about the significance of the changes brought about by rearing in vertical (or horizontal) environments for development in a natural environment. If the kitten develops in an environment in which lines are oriented at random, what determines the selectivity of each particular cell? Is genetical determination important here?

Blakemore: This is, of course, the fundamental issue, but there is no certain answer. I have suggested that this mechanism of neuronal plasticity may permit an animal to manufacture those detector neurones that it needs to cope with its immediate environment, but that is very difficult to prove. Moreover, if all visual cortical cells were equipotential with respect to orientational preference, then unless the environmental specification were to occur literally in a second or two, during a single fixation, the constant bombardment of the receptive fields by different patterns during head and eye movements should preclude any simple environmental influence. Alternatively, one could propose that the cells have a strong in-built predisposition to acquire a particular preference and if given normal experience will do so. Only under the strange circumstances of an experimental environment might their plasticity become evident. But in this case what purpose would the modifiability serve? One possibility, which I find attractive, is that orientational modifiability must be present to ensure that each cell acquires virtually identical preferred orientations in the two eyes, an essential feature for the role of these neurones in stereoscopic vision.

4

Stimulus Selection: Learning to Ignore Stimuli that Predict no Change in Reinforcement

by N. J. Mackintosh

Introduction

Phenomena suggesting the operation of some principle of stimulus selection have been described by ethologists and animal psychologists with ever increasing frequency for the past 25 years. It is now generally accepted, to the point of platitude, that in any situation we must distinguish between the potential and the effective stimuli—between those changes in physical energy impinging on an animal that the animal's sensory apparatus is capable of detecting, and those which do in fact exert significant control over behaviour in that situation. Ethologists, as the chapter by Baerends illustrates, have typically studied the extent to which different categories of behaviour are controlled or released by different features of a complex stimulus object, or by different values of a given stimulus dimension. Psychologists have typically studied the conditions determining which features or elements of a compound stimulus display will become associated with the delivery of such reinforcing events as food, water or shock in laboratory experiments on learning. (The term "reinforcement" is used here with reference to classical as well as operant conditioning.)

The simplest experimental situation for studying how stimuli become associated with reinforcement (become signals for reinforcement) probably remains the classical conditioning experiment; and conditioning experiments have, since the time of Pavlov, provided evidence that the probability of a particular stimulus becoming an effective signal for reinforcement is affected not only by its own intensity or salience, past history, and current schedule of reinforcement, but also the nature of the other stimuli impinging on the animal at the same time. To employ

Pavlov's terminology, it is clear that other simultaneously presented stimuli may "overshadow" a given stimulus, i.e., reduce its effectiveness as a signal for reinforcement. Three kinds of overshadowing effects have been observed in classical conditioning experiments. First, a relatively weak stimulus (e.g., a tone of low intensity) may be readily conditioned when paired with reinforcement by itself, but when paired with reinforcement only in conjunction with another more intense stimulus (e.g. a bright light), the weaker or less salient stimulus may be overshadowed by the stronger or more salient stimulus, and little or no conditioning may be detected when it is presented alone (e.g. Pavlov, 1927, p. 141; Kamin, 1969; Mackintosh, 1971). Overshadowing of this sort seems to occur only when one of the stimuli is relatively intense, and the other considerably less intense.

Secondly, when two stimuli of roughly comparable intensity are paired with reinforcement, one may overshadow the other if it is a more reliable predictor of reinforcement. For example, if reinforcement is delivered only some of the time when a compound stimulus is presented, then both elements of the compound may become signals for reinforcement; but if one of the elements is turned into a more reliable signal for reinforcement by being consistently reinforced when presented on its own, it may completely overshadow the other element of the compound (e.g. Egger and Miller, 1962; Wagner, Logan, Haberlandt and Price, 1968; Wagner, 1969).

Finally, in a case which clearly has parallels with this second type of result, prior establishment of one element of a compound stimulus as a reliable signal for reinforcement may overshadow or block conditioning to the other element during subsequent reinforcement of the compound (e.g. Kamin, 1969; Mackintosh, 1971).

The empirical generalization suggested by this series of experiments is, as I have suggested, by now a matter of general acceptance. Not unsurprisingly, this is rather more than can be said for the theoretical interpretation of such data. Several different theories have been proposed to explain some or all of these findings. But most of these theories have relied, in one way or another, on the idea that instances of stimulus selection are due to competition between stimuli for some limited resource. The constraint involved is a constraint on the organism's capacity to analyse, process, or store information. Theories of selective attention, for example, have suggested that an animal occupied attending to one stimulus will be less likely to attend to another, and have formalized this notion by postulating an inverse relationship between the probabilities or strengths of attending to different events (Zeaman and House, 1963; Lovejoy, 1968; Sutherland and Mackintosh, 1971). The rationale underlying this assumption seems to have been derived from the idea popularized by information theory—that animals have a limited channel capacity for processing incoming information, and that this prevents the simultaneous analysis of an indefinite number of events (Broadbent, 1961).

Experiments on Blocking and Latent Inhibition

I do not want to argue that this theoretical consensus is by any means completely mistaken. It is reasonable enough to suggest that animals exposed for brief, controlled intervals to a complex stimulus array may not be able to analyse all elements in the array, and some recent studies of matching-to-sample by pigeons have shown exactly such an effect (Maki and Leuin, 1972; Turner, personal communication). But it is a far cry from this sort of situation to many of those in which stimulus selection has been observed. Consider, for example, the experiments on blocking reported by Kamin (1969). Here, a rat is given a number of conditioning trials on which a three-minute period of white noise (the CS) precedes a brief, inescapable electric shock (the UCS), and is then given further training with a light added to the noise to form a compound CS (i.e., noise + light is followed by shock). When the animal is tested with the light alone, it may be virtually impossible to detect evidence that significant conditioning has occurred to the light. Once the noise has become a reliable signal for shock, it may completely block conditioning to the light. In this experiment, the rat is in a sparse, familiar environment; the stimuli in question are a moderately loud white noise signal, and a bright overhead light which diffusely illuminates the entire chamber. It is hard to believe that the channel capacity of the rat is so limited that it is unable to attend to both of these stimuli in a single, three-minute trial (nor, it should be pointed out, did Broadbent, 1961, ever suppose so: his argument was, in fact, that overshadowing effects, which he supposed would be due to limitations on channel capacity, were only to be expected in complex situations, where many different stimuli were competing for control of behaviour).

This initial dissatisfaction is made more acute by a consideration of the results of further experiments reported by Kamin. It appears that failure to learn about the light is critically dependent on the fact that the noise-light compound signals the same reinforcement as did the noise alone. If the shock is increased in intensity at the same time that the light is added, then the light becomes an entirely effective signal for shock; if the shock is omitted at the same time that the light is added, then the light becomes a safety signal (a Pavlovian conditioned inhibitor). It is difficult (although perhaps not impossible) to accept that rats fail to learn about the light when noise-light signals the original shock, simply because they are fully occupied attending to the noise, but at the same time are perfectly capable of learning about the light if reinforcement is changed. Perhaps a more natural interpretation would be to say that the light fails to become a signal for reinforcement when it is not correlated with any change in reinforcement. When the introduction of the light is correlated with an increase or decrease in the intensity or probability of reinforcement, then animals learn the relationship between change in visual stimulation and change in reinforcement, and a relatively straightforward test procedure is adequate to detect such learning. However, instead of saying that animals failed to learn about the light when its introduction signalled no change in reinforcement, perhaps we should say that they did learn about the light under these conditions, but that what they learned is precisely that it signalled no change in reinforcement.

If such learning did occur, it would not have been detected by the test procedure employed in Kamin's experiments. A more likely way of seeing whether an animal has learned that a given stimulus signals no change in reinforcement, is to see whether exposure to the conditions presumed to be responsible for such learning produces interference when the animal is subsequently asked to learn that this stimulus does signal a change in reinforcement. The process being invoked here, and the procedure for measuring its effect, are the same as those involved in studies on the (misnamed) phenomenon of "latent inhibition" (Lubow and Moore, 1959). In these experiments, animals are pre-exposed, in the absence of any reinforcement, to a stimulus that is later to be used as the CS in a series of conditioning trials. The effect of this pre-exposure is to retard subsequent conditioning to that CS. The effect is a pervasive one, having been observed with a variety of conditioning procedures, e.g., with conditioned suppression in rats (Carlton and Vogel, 1967), and eyelid conditioning in rabbits (Siegel, 1969), as well as flexion conditioning in sheep and goats (Lubow and Moore, 1959). It is reasonable to suggest that during such pre-exposure, animals learn that the stimulus in question signals no change in the probability of reinforcement, and that such learning interferes with the subsequent formation of an association between the stimulus and reinforcement.

In order to see whether similar learning would produce similar interference with later conditioning in the context of Kamin's experiments on blocking, we undertook an experiment whose design is shown in Table 1 (Mackintosh and Turner, 1971). The basic idea was to see whether the excitatory or inhibitory conditioning to light observed by Kamin, when a noise-light compound signalled an increase or decrease from the shock signalled by noise alone, would be interfered with by exposing animals, after conditioning to noise alone and before the eventual change in shock, to a small number of trials during which the noise-light compound signalled exactly the same shock as that previously signalled by noise alone.

TABLE 1

Experimental Design of Mackintosh and Turner (1971)

Condition	Group	Stage 1	Stage 2	Test
INHIBITORY	Control	24N→Shock plus 8T→Shock	10NL→No Shock plus 10T→Shock	4TL plus 4T
	Experimental	24N→Shock plus 8T→Shock followed by 4NL→Shock		
EXCITATORY	Control	24N→Shock	4NL→SHOCK	4L
	Experimental	24N→Shock followed by 4NL→Shock		

N = white noise; T = tone; L = light; Shock = 1mA shock; SHOCK = 4mA shock.

Would exposure to noise-light and unchanged shock teach animals that light signalled no change in shock, and would such learning be detected as a failure to condition to the light when the noise-light compound did signal a change in shock?

The experiment was divided into two main parts.* In the inhibitory condition, animals initially received 24 conditioning trials to a noise, and eight trials to a tone CS. The control group then received 10 trials on which a noise-light compound signalled no shock, alternated with 10 shock trials to the tone. In the test phase, inhibitory conditioning to the light was assessed by comparing suppression to the tone alone with suppression to the tone-light compound: if the light has become an effective signal for the omission of shock, its addition to the tone should reduce the amount of suppression produced by the tone presented on its own. The experimental group was treated exactly the same as the control group, except that they received four trials with the noise-light compound signalling the original shock, before being exposed to noise-light and no shock. In the excitatory condition, all subjects first received 24 conditioning trials with noise as the CS. The control group then received four trials on which the noise-light compound signalled a much more intense shock, and was finally tested for suppression to the light. The experimental group was treated in exactly the same way, except that they received four additional trials on which noise-light signalled the original shock before they were exposed to noise-light and the more intense shock.

The results for both inhibitory and excitory conditions are shown in Fig. 1. The control groups were treated in much the same way as were the groups in Kamin's original experiments, and they gave similar results. In the inhibitory condition, it can be seen that the control group is much less suppressed to the tone-light compound than to tone alone; thus significant inhibitory conditioning had occurred to the light. In the excitatory condition, the control group showed almost complete suppression when tested with the light alone. But it is clear that the treatment given to the experimental groups markedly interfered with this conditioning. In the inhibitory condition, the experimental group was just as strongly suppressed to the tone-light compound as to tone alone; in the excitatory condition,

---

* The general experimental procedure was similar to that employed by Kamin: rats were initially trained to press a lever for food on a variable interval schedule; conditioning trials consisted of presenting a one-minute stimulus (white noise, tone, or light) followed by a half-second shock to the grid floor of the chamber. In this procedure, conditioning is assessed by the extent to which the presentation of the CS results in a suppression of lever-pressing, and is usually measured by calculating a suppression ratio of the form $a/(a+b)$, where $a =$ the number of lever presses during the CS, and $b =$ the number of presses in an equal interval of time immediately preceding the CS. A suppression ratio of 0.00, therefore, indicates no responding during the CS, i.e., complete suppression, and one of 0.50 indicates equal responding before and during the CS, i.e., no suppression.

the experimental group showed relatively little suppression to the light. In the former case, therefore, there is no evidence that the light had become a signal for the omission of shock; in the latter case, the light had certainly not become a very good signal for the increase in intensity of shock.

The results seem entirely clear. Animals learned about the light when it was presented in conjunction with the noise, provided that the noise-light compound signalled an increase or decrease in shock (additional control groups, not shown in Table 1, established that no conditioning occurred to the light when noise-light signalled the same shock as had been previously

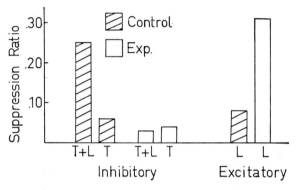

Fig. 1. Group mean suppression ratios over the first two test trials to the tone-light compound and the first two test trials to tone alone in the Inhibitory condition; in the Excitatory condition, the results are for the first test trial to the light (Mackintosh and Turner, 1971).

signalled by noise alone). However, this learning about the light could be markedly attenuated if, on its initial introduction in conjunction with the noise, the light signalled no change in reinforcement. The implication is not that animals fail to attend to the light because they are fully occupied attending to the noise; on the contrary, they do attend to the light, but what they learn is that it is redundant.

There is one, apparent serious, objection to this account of Kamin's experiments. If animals learn that light is redundant when a noise-light compound signals the same reinforcement as noise alone, then subsequent conditioning to light should, presumably, always be retarded. Although this is, in effect, what we found in our experiment, Kamin (1969) has reported that if rats are given noise-shock trials followed by trials with noise and light signalling the same shock, then subsequently conditioning to the light alone (signalling the same shock), so far from being retarded, may actually be slightly facilitated. This clearly raises problems for our analysis. We have undertaken a number of (as yet unpublished) experiments to see

G

if we can resolve this discrepancy. Although we are still uncertain as to the conditions responsible for the difference in outcome, our own studies have generally found rather little evidence of the savings effect reported by Kamin. Under some conditions, indeed, we have observed marginal retardation of conditioning to the light after a noise-light compound has signalled the same reinforcement as noise alone.

It should be stressed, however, that this effect has, at best, been of marginal significance, not at all comparable to the magnitude of the interference effect observed in Mackintosh and Turner's study. One explanation for this difference is that the two sets of experiments utilized different procedures for producing conditioning to the light. In Mackintosh and Turner's experiment, exposure to noise-light and unchanged reinforcement substantially interfered with learning about the light when the noise-light compound subsequently signalled changed reinforcement. In these other experiments, subsequent conditioning to light, presented on its own, was at best only slightly affected by exposure to noise-light and unchanged reinforcement. Perhaps this is because animals learn that a light accompanied by a noise signals no change in reinforcement, but transfer this learning only imperfectly to the case where light it presented on its own.

If the processes underlying learned irrelevance are similar to those studied in experiments on habituation, then there is already good evidence for this supposition. It is well known that habituation is extremely sensitive to any change in the habituated stimulus (cf. Hinde, 1970, p. 290), and Engen and Lipsitt (1965), for example, have shown that newborn babies habituated to a compound olfactory stimulus may show nearly complete recovery of the habituated response when tested with one of the elements of the compound in isolation. In order to see whether such an effect would occur in the type of situation we are concerned with here, we undertook a simple experiment on latent inhibition in conditioned suppression. Three groups of rats were trained to press a lever for food; during this preliminary training, one group received a series of 16 latent inhibition trials to a one-minute light; a second group received 16 presentations of a one-minute noise-light compound; while the third group served as a control, receiving no stimulus presentations. All three groups finally received eight conditioning trials on which a one-minute light CS was followed by a brief shock. Fig. 2 shows the suppression ratios for each group on each trial of conditioning. The group pre-exposed to the light alone was clearly slower to condition to the light than was the control group ($p < 0.01$); but animals pre-exposed to the noise-light compound conditioned significantly more rapidly than those pre-exposed to the light alone ($p < 0.01$) and were only marginally slower to condition than the control group ($p < 0.10$). It is

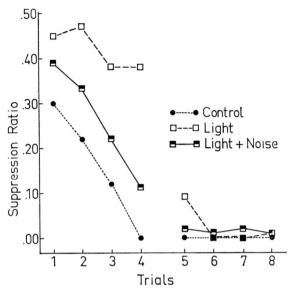

Fig. 2. Acquisition of conditioned suppression to a light (group mean suppression ratios) following latent inhibition to the light alone or to a noise-light compound.

clear, therefore, that exposure for a small number of trials to a noise-light compound signalling no change in reinforcement produces relatively little interference when animals are subsequently required to associate the light alone with reinforcement. It seems reasonable to suppose that this is one reason why Kamin's basic blocking procedure does not significantly retard subsequent conditioning to the blocked element presented in isolation.

Experiments on Latent Inhibition and Reinforcement-Specific Irrelevance

Although my argument, up to this point, has stressed the parallel between experiments on blocking and those on latent inhibition, it is time to point to one, possibly important, difference between the two. In experiments on latent inhibition, animals are exposed to a given stimulus in the absence of all (obvious) reinforcement; in experiments on blocking, animals are exposed to a given stimulus in the absence of any change in one particular reinforcer. It is conceivable that in the first case animals learn that the stimulus predicts nothing, while in the second case they learn that it predicts no change in one, specific, reinforcer. Perhaps some of the effects of learned irrelevance are general and not specific to any one reinforcer, but this does not rule out the possibility that there is a reinforcer-specific effect over and above that studied in experiments on latent inhibition.

In order to test this suggestion, we need a procedure, similar to latent inhibition in that the subject is repeatedly exposed to a stimulus later to be used as a CS, but different from latent inhibition in providing the subject with the opportunity to learn that the stimulus predicts nothing about one particular reinforcer. The obvious candidate is the so-called "random control" procedure, in which the presentation of a particular stimulus is randomly interspersed with presentations of a reinforcer, with the probability of one occurring at any given moment being entirely independent of the occurrence of the other. This random presentation of CS and UCS was first suggested by Prokasy (1965) and Rescorla (1967) as a suitable control condition for obtaining a neutral baseline from which to assess both excitatory and inhibitory conditioning; but some recent studies have, in fact, suggested that exposure to such a procedure profoundly retards subsequent conditioning with that CS and UCS (Gamzu and Williams, 1971; Kremer, 1971). Our next experiment, therefore, was designed to provide a direct comparison of the effects on subsequent conditioning of simple, unreinforced exposure to a particular stimulus and of exposure to random presentations of that stimulus and the reinforcer later to be used in conditioning.

As a change from studying conditioned suppression in rats, the procedure employed in this experiment was conditioned key-pecking ("autoshaping") in pigeons. As the chapters by Moore and Jenkins document, if the key-light in a pigeon chamber is illuminated for a few seconds before the food magazine is operated, a hungry pigeon will, within a few trials, start pecking the key. Moore and Jenkins argue convincingly that both the procedures and the processes underlying autoshaping are those of classical conditioning; pecking at the key, therefore, may be taken as an indicator that the key light has become a signal for food reinforcement. The purpose of the experiment, then, was to see whether the acquisition of key-pecking would be retarded by prior exposure to the key-light alone, and yet further retarded by prior exposure to random presentations of key-light and food.

Thirty-two pigeons were initially trained to eat from the magazine of a conventional pigeon chamber, and then assigned to one of four equal groups. For the next four days, each bird was placed in the chamber for a 45-minute session each day. During these sessions, Group CS-only received 40 presentations of the CS (illumination of the response-key with a green light for a five-second period); Group CS/Food received similar exposure to the CS, but also received 40 presentations of food (a five-second operation of the magazine) semi-randomly distributed throughout each session;* Group Food-only received 40 presentations of food in each session;

* The scheduling of events in the random CS/UCS groups in this and the following experiment differed from that usually employed in random control groups. Since the performance of CS/UCS groups in later conditioning was to be compared with that of CS-only

and finally, the Control Group was simply placed in the apparatus without any scheduled events. In the second, conditioning phase of the experiment, all birds received 40 trials in each of eight, daily 45-minute sessions, with each trial consisting of a five-second CS (illumination of the key with a green light) followed by a five-second UCS (operation of the food magazine). The inter-trial interval ranged from 40 to 80 seconds, averaging about 60 seconds (the same as the interval between CS presentations during the first phase of the experiment).

No subject pecked on the key more than a few times during the first phase of the experiment. The results of the eight days of conditioning are shown in Fig. 3. It is apparent that although pre-exposure to CS only did retard conditioning, the effect was confined to the first two sessions; exposure to random presentations of CS and food, however, had a much more profound, long-lasting effect (indeed, for reasons which remain obscure, the effect was not particularly apparent during the first two or three sessions). This difference cannot simply be attributed to the additional effect of exposure to food, since the Food-only group conditioned at much the same rate as the control group. Statistical analyses (two-tailed t-tests) tended to confirm these impressions, although significant differences were hard to find owing to the amount of variability in the data (each group had at least one subject that showed little sign of conditioning). Group CS-only pecked the key somewhat less than the control group on Days 1 and 2 ($p < 0.10$); but over the eight days of conditioning the only significant effect was that Group CS/Food differed from each of the other groups ($p < 0.10$), none of whom differed from each other.

Even if we accept results of such borderline significance, they are open to one quite trival interpretation. It is conceivable that the pigeons in the CS only group, exposed during Phase 1 to repetitive presentation of the CS, went quietly to sleep in a corner of the box, and were therefore not effectively exposed to as many presentations of the CS as were the birds in the CS/Food group, who were kept awake by the occasional presentations

---

and UCS-only groups, it was obviously desirable to maintain, as far as possible, comparable intervals between CSs and between UCSs in all three groups, and to keep these intervals roughly comparable to the intertrial interval used in subsequent conditioning. Accordingly, the scheduling of events for the CS/Food group in this experiment maintained a distribution of intervals between successive CSs that was virtually the same as that employed in the CS-only group; and food presentations were then scheduled so as to ensure an equal probability of food being presented in each five-second interval following a CS, with the following restrictions. Food was never delivered in the same five-second interval as a CS (on the assumption that the pigeon would have its head in the food magazine and therefore not see the CS); in each interval between successive CSs (ranging from 40 to 80 seconds) between zero and two presentations of food might occur; there was at least a 20-second interval between successive presentations of food. For the Food-only group, food was presented in accordance with the same schedule as that used for the CS/Food group.

of food. According to this interpretation, the delivery of food simply served an arousal function. The more interesting interpretation is that the random presentations of CS and food specifically taught the subjects that changes in the key-light and changes in food reinforcement were uncorrelated. One reason for thinking this the more interesting possibility is

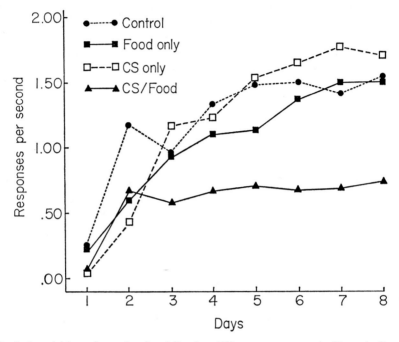

Fig. 3. Acquisition of autoshaping following different treatments in Phase 1. Group means of the number of responses per second during the CS, corrected for intertrial interval responses.

that it implies if a stimulus signals no change in the probability of one reinforcer, then subsequent association between that stimulus and that reinforcer will be severely impaired, whereas subsequent association between that stimulus and a *different* reinforcer would be only slightly affected. Our final experiment was designed to test this possibility.

The question at issue is whether random presentations of a given CS and UCS exert an effect on subsequent conditioning specific to that UCS. This required an experimental preparation in which the same stimulus could be used as a CS with two different reinforcers, each of which would produce a different pattern of conditioned behaviour. After some preliminary work, we settled on the following procedures. The subjects were thirsty rats, the apparatus a small chamber with a water tube protruding through one wall, from which water could be delivered via a solenoid operated valve (the apparatus is described in more detail in Mackintosh, 1971). The CS was a 20-second tone delivered through a speaker mounted in the wall above the water tube. Conditioning sessions consisted of eight trials presented in a 30-minute session with an intertrial interval ranging from two to four minutes. The UCS was either the delivery of water for the last 15 seconds of the CS, or a 0.5 second 0.4 mA electric shock delivered at the end of the CS to the grid floor of the chamber. When water was used as the reinforcer, conditioning was measured as an increase in licking responses on the tube during the first five seconds of the CS (before water was delivered) compared to licking that occurred in the five seconds preceding the CS. When shock was used, the subjects received five-second presentations of water on a variable interval 30-second schedule, a procedure which maintained a relatively steady rate of licking at the tube throughout each session. Conditioning was now measured as a suppression of licking during the 20-second presentation of each tone compared to a 20-second period immediately preceding the CS. The particular parameters chosen succeeded in producing relatively comparable rates of conditioning with the two reinforcers.

TABLE 2

Design of Experiment on the Relevance of Conditioned Stimuli to Unconditioned Stimuli

| Conditioning to Water | | Conditioning to Shock | |
Phase 1	Phase 2	Phase 1	Phase 2
Control		Control	
Tone only		Tone only	
Water only	Tone→Water	Shock only	Tone→Shock
Tone/Water		Tone/Shock	
Tone/Shock		Tone/Water	

The design of the experiment is shown in Table 2. There were two major groups in the experiment—animals given conditioning with water as the UCS, and those given conditioning with shock as the UCS. Within each of these two groups, different sub-groups received a variety of treatments in the first phase of the experiment. These treatments involved exposure to: the CS alone; the appropriate UCS alone; random presentations of the CS and the appropriate UCS; random presentations of the CS and the opposite UCS; and, finally, simple exposure to the apparatus*.

* Scheduling of events in Phase 1 was carried out in the same general way as in the preceding experiment. The intervals between CSs varied between two and four minutes, and the probability of a UCS was equal in each five-second interval following the onset of a CS. The only difference was that coincidence of CS and UCS presentations was permitted in this experiment.

Phase 1 lasted for eight days with one 30-minute session per day during which eight CSs and/or eight UCSs were delivered (except for the control groups); except for animals receiving water UCSs during this phase, the water tube was withdrawn from the chamber. All animals received a preliminary 15-minute session before the start of Phase 1 in which water was delivered on a VI-30 second schedule, and all animals given shock during Phase 1 received a 30-minute recovery session after Phase 1 when water was again delivered on a VI-30 second schedule. There were eight rats per sub-group.

The results of the conditioning phase are shown in Figure 4 for groups

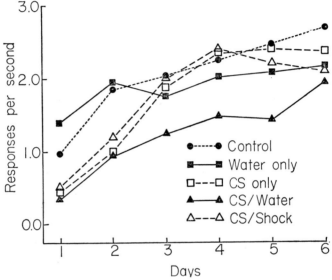

Fig. 4. Acquisition of conditioned licking following different treatments in Phase 1. Group means of the number of responses per second during the CS minus the number of responses per second in the five seconds preceding each CS.

conditioned to water, and in Figure 5 for groups conditioned to shock. The impression gained from these two figures is that in each case all but one group conditioned at approximately the same rate, and in each case the exception was the group exposed to random presentations of the CS and UCS used in conditioning. The results for animals conditioned to water are particularly clear-cut. Group CS-only and Group CS/Shock conditioned at very much the same rate: both showed some latent inhibition effect over the first two days of conditioning, i.e. gave fewer conditioned responses than the control group ($p < 0.05$). When performance was examined over the entire six days of conditioning, Group CS/Water differed from every other group at the 0.05 confidence-level or better, while none of the remaining groups differed from each other ($p > 0.10$).

The results from the groups conditioned to shock were similar, although complicated by the fact that (as has been observed before, for example by Annau and Kamin, 1961) conditioned suppression with the relatively weak shock showed some sign of diminishing as training continued. On Day 1, Groups CS-only and CS/Water showed a latent inhibition effect

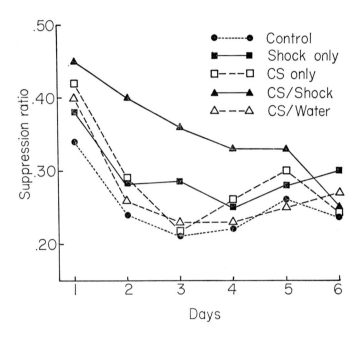

Fig. 5. Acquisition of conditioned suppression (group mean suppression ratios) following different treatments in Phase 1.

by comparison with the control group ($p < 0.05$); the only difference in mean suppression ratios over all six days of conditioning was between Group CS/Shock and the control group ($p < 0.01$). Over the first four days of conditioning, however, Group CS/Shock differed from each of the other groups at 0.05 confidence-level or better, while none of the remaining groups differed from each other (p > 0.10). It is reasonable to conclude that random presentations of a given CS and UCS specifically retard the subsequent formation of an association between the two.

Conclusions

We began with the notion that attention was selective because of a limitation on channel capacity. This is a plausible assumption, clearly applicable to cases where subjects are briefly exposed to complex arrays of stimuli. At least some cases of overshadowing in animal learning should probably be attributed to the operation of this sort of selective processing. When, for example, an animal is presented with a compound CS consisting of one salient and one relatively weak element, the stronger element can be shown to overshadow the weaker from the very first trial of conditioning (Mackintosh, 1971). In this case, at any rate, it seems reasonable to talk of perceptual competition between stimuli. But even here it is possible that, as training continues, the subject learns that reinforcement is predicted by the occurrence of the more salient stimulus, and therefore learns that the less salient stimulus is redundant; and where overshadowing occurs because, of two equally salient stimuli, one is better correlated with reinforcement than the other (as in the experiment of Wagner *et al.*, 1968), it seems reasonable to talk of animals learning the relationship between stimuli and reinforcing events, and specifically learning that one of the stimuli is a less reliable predictor of reinforcement. Finally, as we have seen, when blocking of a newly added stimulus occurs because the subject has learned that reinforcement is fully predictable on the basis of an old stimulus, there is good evidence that animals learn that the redundant stimulus predicts no change in reinforcement.

Traditional theories of selective attention (even if too recent to be described as traditional), such as those of Zeaman and House (1963), Lovejoy (1968) and Sutherland and Mackintosh (1971), have not placed any emphasis on the possibility that animals might learn to ignore irrelevant or uninformative stimuli. In all these models, subjects are assumed to learn to attend to relevant stimuli, and this is represented by saying that the probability or strength of relevant analysers or observing responses increases. Since there is a reciprocal relationship between different analysers, it follows that as attention to relevant stimuli increases, so attention to irrelevant stimuli will decrease. But there is no independent mechanism for decreasing attention to irrelevant stimuli (as opposed to extinguishing attention to a formerly relevant set of stimuli if they subsequently become irrelevant). There is no way, therefore, for such theories to explain why pre-exposure to a stimulus should retard subsequent conditioning to that stimulus, let alone the more complicated finding that exposure to random presentations of a stimulus and a reinforcer specifically retards the formation of a subsequent association between the two.

The procedures employed in the present experiments were as contrived and artificial as the procedures employed by experimental psychologists usually are. One general justification for the artificial simplicity of psychological experiments is that only by such methods is it possible to study the operations of a single, potentially important process, uncontaminated by simultaneous variations in numerous other factors. It is perhaps worth illustrating this in the present context, by comparing some of the present results with those of other experiments involving stimulus pre-exposure. Studies of latent inhibition in classical conditioning deliberately use simple, obvious stimuli such as tones and lights, and a relatively straightforward measure of the rate at which those stimuli subsequently enter into associations with other events. Under these conditions, it is possible to measure the effects of a process that is akin to habituation, but, in one sense at least, of more general importance: animals may learn that a particular stimulus signals nothing of consequence, and this learning may not only underly current changes in the behaviour elicited by that stimulus (as in habituation), but may also affect subsequent learning about the relationship between that stimulus and other events. Such a process, if it is of any generality, must presumably occur under other, more complicated conditions, but here its effects may be masked by the added complexities. For example, if rats are exposed to two visual patterns over a long period of time, without any correlation between either stimulus and reinforcement, they may (sometimes) learn a discrimination between the two stimuli more rapidly than a control group (Gibson and Walk, 1956; cf. Gibson, 1969, p. 258). The effect is discussed in the context of related work on young chicks in the chapter by Bateson in this volume. It is reasonable to suppose that one decisive difference between these experiments and those on latent inhibition in classical conditioning lies in the complexity of the stimuli the animals are required to discriminate (it is also possible that for the young chicks, stimuli themselves acquire reinforcing properties). The learning measured by an experiment on latent inhibition is a simple reduction in the associability of a given stimulus with reinforcement. The outcome of such experiments in no way precludes the possibility that during prolonged exposure to more complex stimuli, animals may come to learn the characteristics of those stimuli (build up complex analysers for them) and that this effect may override any reduction in associability with reinforcement. The point is, of course, that had experiments been undertaken only with more complex stimuli (and these have actually given extremely conflicting results), the process underlying latent inhibition might never have been recognized.

The second major empirical generalization that can be drawn from the presents series of experiments is that unreinforced pre-exposure to a particular stimulus, although reliably retarding subsequent conditioning to that stimulus, does not have anything like the same effect as random presentations of that stimulus and the reinforcer later to be used in conditioning. Random presentation of a CS and UCS was originally designed as a procedure for obtaining a true baseline of responsiveness to that CS from which to assess excitatory or inhibitory conditioning (e.g., Rescorla, 1967). Although the present results do not call this conclusion into question, they do quite strikingly show that exposure to random presentations of a CS and UCS does not leave an animal unaffected, but may in fact have a profound effect on the animal's later ability to associate the two. It is tempting to conclude that animals are able to learn that the two events are uncorrelated, and it is this learning that later interferes with learning that they are correlated. One interesting implication is the light this throws on some recent controversies about the nature of conditioning. Rescorla (1967) originally seemed to be suggesting that what was learned during a series of conditioning trials was not simply that CS and UCS were paired, but that there was a positive contingency between the two events. The problem with this contingency view of conditioning is that it seems to postulate a subject capable of calculating a running correlation coefficient between two events, and Rescorla (1969) later put forward some theoretical ideas (developed by Rescorla and Wagner, 1972) which showed how a more simple and traditional contiguity view of conditioning could explain the apparently problematic finding that the occasional pairings of CS and UCS occurring in a random control procedure are not sufficient to produce any conditioning. This analysis assumes that no learning about the relation between CS and UCS occurs during random presentation of the two. The present results suggest, on the contrary, that animals learn a great deal about this relationship during random presentations: they learn that the two events are uncorrelated. This seems to imply that there is more to be said for a contingency view of conditioning than has recently been thought.

The final point to be made may help to relate the present chapter to some of the main themes of this volume. My main argument has been that constraints of stimulus selection may not always be a consequence of current limits on capacity, but of a past history of exposure to certain relationships between stimuli and reinforcing events. Exposure to a given stimulus in the absence of any reinforcing event may reduce the associability of that stimulus with any reinforcer; exposure to a given stimulus in the context of random occurrences of a particular reinforcer may specifically reduce the associability of that stimulus with that reinforcer. Is not hard to see the application of these observations to some of the special principles sometimes invoked to explain apparent constraints on learning.

The concept of an "attending hierarchy" was proposed by Baron (1965), and has been accepted by others, as an explanation of the finding that different animal groups respond selectively to different stimuli from a complex stimulus array. Pigeons, for example, are more likely to respond to the wavelength of light projected onto a key than to the tilt of a line on the key, and this is said to be because a wavelength analyser has a higher position in the pigeon's attending hierarchy than an orientation analyser. This has all the marks of a redundant explanation. In the first place, it is probable that many differences in probabilities of attending to different dimensions can be reduced to differences in the discriminability of the various values of the different dimensions that are used: a pigeon that learns more about colour than about line-tilt when trained to discriminate between a vertical line on a 500 nm background and a horizontal line on a 550 nm background, will certainly reverse this preference if the two backgrounds are changed to 500 and 505 nm. If there is anything left to the concept once this has been controlled, i.e., if we could demonstrate different probabilities of control by equally discriminable stimuli from different dimensions (a nice problem in experimental design), it seems reasonable to suggest that the subject's past experience may have something to do with this. An extension of the principle of latent inhibition would be quite sufficient to account for any current preference for some classes of stimuli over others.

A second, more dramatic, and much better documented example of a constraint on stimulus selection is the stimulus-reinforcer specificity of tastes to poisoning demonstrated by Garcia, Revusky, and Rozin, and discussed in McFarland's chapter in this volume. A rat given a particular food substance will associate the visual characteristics of the food with subsequent external reinforcing events (e.g., shock), but the taste of the food with subsequent poisoning. This striking specificity of stimulus to reinforcer has been attributed to a principle of "relevance" or "belongingness". When we consider the results of the final experiment reported here, however, a different explanation may seem equally plausible. In this experiment, the treatment given in Phase 1 produced some rats prepared to associate tones with water but not with shock, and other rats prepared to associate the same tone with shock but not with water. It is tempting to suggest that if these results have any generality, they imply that animals may learn that variations in a specific class of stimuli are unrelated to variations in a specific class of reinforcer; hence, a tendency for an animal now to associate only certain stimuli with a given reinforcer might possibly be (at least in part) a consequence of a past history in which *other* classes of stimuli have varied without predicting variations in the reinforcer in question. Tastes are now readily associated with internal changes because the adult rat has a lifetime's experience of such changes not being correlated with changes in external stimuli.

It is clear that if this idea has any merit, it must at least face up to the well-documented fact that birds which prey on insects associate the *visual* characteristics of their prey, rather than its taste, with subsequent poisoning (Brower, 1971; given the results reported by Wilcoxon, Dragoin & Kral, 1971, for quail, this tendency to associate the visual characteristics of food with poisoning may not be confined to predatory birds). Whether this difference between rats and birds, however, is due to innate differences in sensory *capacity*, or to innate differences in the relevance of particular stimuli to particular reinforcers, or whether it is a consequence of a different past history, is not at all clear. One thing that is apparent from some data reported by Hogan in this volume is that, in at least one case, very young animals are not at all efficient at associating the characteristics of what they eat with later internal consequences.

It is indeed possible that different animals have evolved diverse and specialized learning mechanisms particularly appropriate to the problems that they are confronted with in their natural environment. But there is a danger that too enthusiastic an acceptance of this possibility will result in the postulation of a myriad of new principles to cover any newly discovered speciality. It is at least worth stopping to question the necessity of such a proliferation. How far do the phenomena associated with avoidance of poisononous foods by rats really require the postulation of new principles of learning? Although the association between a taste and a poison occurs over an unusually long delay, Revusky (1971) has suggested that this may be (in part) because such associations are subject to unusually little interference. This is because, by the principle of "relevance", only tastes are readily associated with subsequent poisoning. What I am suggesting, in a much more sketchy fashion, is that the principle of relevance may be (in part) an instance of a much more general phenomenon of associative learning.

Acknowledgements

This research was supported by Grant APA 259 from the National Research Council of Canada. I am grateful to Janet Lord and Ann Cauty for experiment assistance, and to Robert Moore for the design of apparatus.

References

Annau, Z. and Kamin, L. J. (1961). The conditioned emotional response as a function of intensity of the US. *J. comp. physiol. Psychol.* **54**, 428–432.
Baron, M. R. (1965). The stimulus, stimulus control, and stimulus generalization. *In* "Stimulus Generalization", (D. I. Mostofsky, ed.), pp. 62–71. Stanford University Press, Stanford.
Broadbent, D. E. (1961). Human perception and animal learning. *In* "Current

Problems in Animal Behaviour", (W. H. Thorpe and O. L. Zangwill, eds.), pp. 248–272. University Press, Cambridge.

Brower, L. P. (1971). Prey coloration and predator behavior. In "Topics in Animal Behavior", pp. 66–76. Harper & Row, New York.

Carlton, P. L. and Vogel, J. R. (1967). Habituation and conditioning. *J. comp. physiol. Psychol.* **63**, 348–351.

Egger, M. D. and Miller, N. E. (1961). Secondary reinforcement in rats as a function of information value and reliability of the stimulus. *J. exp. Psychol.* **64**, 97–104.

Engen, T. and Lipsitt, L. P. (1965). Decrement and recovery of responses to olfactory stimuli in the human neonate. *J. comp. physiol. Psychol.* **59**, 312–316.

Gamzu, E. and Williams, D. R. (1971). Classical conditioning of a complex skeletal response *Science* **171**, 923–925.

Gibson, E. J. (1969). "Principles of Perceptual Learning and Development." Appleton-Century-Crofts, New York.

Gibson, E. J. and Walk, R. D. (1956). The effect of prolonged exposure to visually presented patterns on learning to discriminate them. *J. comp. physiol. Psychol.* **49**, 239–242.

Hinde, R. A. (1970). "Animal Behaviour." McGraw-Hill, New York.

Kamin, L. J. (1969). Predictability, surprise, attention and conditioning. In "Punishment and Aversive Behavior", (B. Campbell and R. Church, eds.), pp. 279–296. Appleton-Century-Crofts, New York.

Kremer, E. F. (1971). Truly random and traditional control procedures in CER conditioning in the rat. *J. comp. physiol. Psychol.* **76**, 441–448.

Lovejoy, E. (1968). "Attention on Discrimination Learning." Holden-Day Inc., San Francisco.

Lubow, R. E. and Moore, A. U. (1959). Latent inhibition: the effect of non-reinforced preexposure to the conditioned stimulus. *J. comp. physiol. Psychol.* **52**, 415–419.

Mackintosh, N. J. (1971). An analysis of overshadowing and blocking. *Q. Jl. ex. Psychol.* **23**, 118–125.

Mackintosh, N. J. and Turner, C. (1971). Blocking as a function of novelty of CS and predictability of UCS. *Q. Jl. exp. Psychol.* **23**, 359–366.

Maki, W. S. and Leuin, T. C. (1972). Information processing by pigeons. *Science* **176**, 535–536.

Pavlov, I. P. (1927). "Conditioned Reflexes." Oxford University Press, Oxford.

Prokasy, W. F. (1965). Classical eyelid conditioning: Experimenter operations, task demands, and response shaping. In "Classical Conditioning: a Symposium", (W. F. Prokasy, ed.), pp. 208–225. Appleton-Century-Crofts, New York.

Rescorla, R. A. (1967). Pavlovian conditioning and its proper control procedures. *Psychol. Rev.* **74**, 71–80.

Rescorla, R. A. (1969). Conditioned inhibition of fear. In "Fundamental Issues in Associative Learning", (N. J. Mackintosh and W. J. Honig, eds.), pp. 65–89. Dalhousie University Press, Halifax.

Rescorla, R. A. and Wagner, A. R. (1972). A theory of Pavlovian conditioning: Variations in the effectiveness of reinforcement and nonreinforcement. In "Classical Conditioning II", (A. Black and W. F. Prokasy, eds.), pp. 64–99. Appleton-Century-Crofts, New York.

Revusky, S. (1971). The role of interference in association over a delay. In "Animal Memory", (W. K. Honig and P. H. R., James, eds.), pp. 155–213. Academic Press, New York.

Siegel, S. (1969). Effect of CS habituation on eyelid conditioning. *J. comp. physiol. Psychol.* **68**, 245–248.

Sutherland, N. S. and Mackintosh, N. J. (1971). "Mechanisms of Animal Discrimination Learning." Academic Press, New York.

Wagner, A. R. (1969). Stimulus validity and stimulus selection in associative learning. *In* "Fundamental Issues in Associative Learning", (N. J. Mackintosh and W. K. Honig, eds.) pp. 90–122. Dalhousie University Press. Halifax.

Wagner, A. R., Logan, F. A., Haberlandt, K. and Price, T. (1968). Stimulus selection in animal discrimination learning. *J. exp. Psychol.* **76**, 171–180.

Wilcoxon, H. C., Dragoin, W. B. and Kral, P. A. (1971). Illness-induced aversions in rat and quail: relative salience of visual and gustatory cues. *Science* **171**, 826–828.

Zeaman, D. and House, B. J. (1963). The role of attention in retardate discrimination learning. *In* "Handbook of Mental Deficiency: Psychological Theory and Research", (N. R. Ellis, ed.) pp. 159–223. McGraw-Hill, New York.

Comments

1. *Honig wrote as follows:*

"In support of his distinction between potential and effective control over behaviour by stimuli, Mackintosh concentrates upon three learning situations where this difference is experimentally induced. In overshadowing, a "weak" stimulus is compounded with a "strong" or "more salient" stimulus, and the latter can be shown to prevent the acquisition of conditioning or stimulus control by the former (Miles and Jenkins, in press). The potential effectiveness of the "weak" stimulus is assessed by a control condition in which it is presented alone in training. A second kind of overshadowing can be observed if two stimuli are presented, of which one is a better predictor of reinforcement than the other. The better predictor acquires stimulus control at the expense of the poorer (Wagner *et al.*, 1968). Finally, Mackintosh discusses blocking in some detail, where the acquisition of control by one stimulus prevents a second stimulus from doing so when it is redundantly added in training (Kamin, 1968).

"Mackintosh does not discuss another common group of instances in which potential stimuli are not immediately effective. These are the many cases where certain stimuli do not acquire control over behaviour even in the absence of any experimental procedures designed to prevent them from doing so. As a classic example, we may cite the study by Jenkins and Harrison (1960). Pigeons were taught to peck a key for intermittent food reinforcement in the presence of a pure tone at 1000 Hz. (The tone was interrupted every second or so to preclude sensory adaptation.) After training, a generalization test was administered in which various auditory frequencies were presented. There was only a slight response decrement in the presence of the test stimuli other than 1000 Hz. Jenkins and Harrison then trained birds to distinguish between the training tone and its absence, i.e. the ambient noise level. After this training, a very steep generalization gradient on the dimension of auditory frequency was obtained. Clearly, we can distinguish here between pure auditory stimuli as potential and effective stimuli. Initially, their effect on behaviour was minimal. After training which did not even involve two different frequencies, their effect was very marked.

"What is the explanation for this kind of finding, which seems to represent a marked constraint in many learning situations? Why are some animals inattentive to potentially effective stimuli? It hardly seems adequate to appeal to the "saliency" of certain dimensions, or the "strength" of certain stimuli; such words are little more than shorthand to describe the observed facts. Recent work by Ronald Van Houten and Robert Rudolph at Dalhousie University suggests that the reason such initially "weak" stimuli are ineffective is that they are overshadowed in the training situation.

"In his doctoral dissertation, Van Houten (1972) describes a number of studies on airflow as a discriminative stimulus for pigeons in an operant situation. Pigeons pecked at a key in front of a source of airflow that blew at the subject at calibrated velocities (Van Houten et al., 1972). While the velocity of the airflow could acquire stimulus control over key pecking following discrimination training, this dimension appeared to exert little "natural" control following simple acquisition of responding. Van Houten studied the role of visual stimuli in the experimental situation as follows: three groups of pigeons were trained to peck a key in front of a source of airflow that entered the experimental chamber at 30 mph. For one group the key was illuminated in the usual fashion with a white light; for the second group, the key was not illuminated, but the houselight was on, and the key was clearly visible. The third group was also trained with the houselight on, but after the first session, the light was faded out so that the pigeon ended up pecking in the dark after 3 sessions. After ten sessions of training, all groups were given a generalization test with a variety of values on the dimension of airflow velocity, ranging from 0 to 30 mph. The obtained gradients were relatively flat for the groups trained with the key light or houselight throughout, but they were steep for those subjects who ended up pecking the key in the dark. Thus it appears that the presence of the visual cues overshadowed the airflow; only when the former were removed did the latter come to control behaviour. Without this demonstration one might conclude that airflow was not a "salient" dimension, and that discrimination training on this dimension would be necessary for it to acquire stimulus control.

"In the second experiment, Van Houten investigated the speed of acquisition of a discrimination between two airflow velocities. One group was trained with the key-light on, while the other was trained after it had been faded out, so that the animals were pecking in the dark. The birds run in the dark learned the discrimination much more quickly, after showing a greater initial generalization decrement between the positive value presented in pretraining and the negative stimulus when it was first introduced. All animals run in the dark reached a criterion of 90% correct responses after ten sessions; none of the other pigeons came close to this value within that time.

"The implications of this research were then applied by Rudolph and Van Houten to the situation first studied by Jenkins and Harrison. Two groups of

H

pigeons were trained to peck at a lighted key in the presence of a tone of 1000 Hz. For one group, the key light was faded out, so that the animals again had to end up pecking in the dark. The key light stayed at full strength for the other group. A generalization test on the dimension of auditory frequency provided a much steeper gradient for the dark-trained group; the other pigeons provided the sort of flat gradient obtained by Jenkins and Harrison. Then Rudolph and Van Houten gave discrimination training between 1500 Hz as S+ and 670 Hz at S—. These two values had governed approximately equal numbers of responses during the generalization test. Again, the group trained in the dark learned the problem more quickly than the group trained with the key light on.

"It appears, then, that failures to obtain stimulus control after simple acquisition in past experiments have often been due to the presence of overshadowing stimuli in the situation. This represents a kind of constraint on learning that may not be noticed in many studies, where the difficulty of the problem is attributed to some special insensitivity of the subject to the dimension in question. The subject may in fact be sensitive to the dimension, but simply distracted by the presence of more powerful cues. The fact that some cues are more powerful than others—in other words, that they command attention without the intervention of any special experimental procedure—still needs to be explained. Clearly, the results cited here do not explain overshadowing. They merely provide an interpretation for the failure of association that has been observed in some experiments, and they dispel some of the mystery that has long surrounded these observations.

"There is always the possibility in work of this kind that the failure of stimulus control is not due to a failure of association in training, but to the overshadowing by a stronger cue during testing. Evidence for this comes from experiments in "cue utilization", where subjects are trained in the presence of compounded "weak" and "strong" stimuli, and tested in the presence of the weak stimulus. For example, Newman and Benefield (1968) trained pigeons in the presence of a white vertical line on a green background, and then tested one group on the dimension of line orientation in the presence of the background, while for the other group the background was removed. The latter group provided a sharp gradient on the orientation dimension, while the former did not. This showed that the animals had indeed learned about the orientation of the line in the presence of the stronger stimulus, and that the green background had merely prevented control by orientation during the generalization test. Freeman and Thomas (1967) obtained similar results. For a fuller discussion, see Honig (1970, pp. 196–203).

"It is possible that differences in cue utilization are responsible for the results described above. Thus, the steep gradient obtained by Rudolph and Van Houten on the dimension of auditory frequency may have been due to the absence of a key light during the test rather than during training. These experimenters are currently carrying out work to assess this possibility. Overshadowing in the traditional sense is not a "test effect"; in fact, it is specifically observed as a failure of the weak stimulus to control responding when the stronger is removed. In order to support the interpretation presented here—that a stimulus or a dimension to which the subject appears "insensitive" is in fact only being overshadowed by a more salient cue—it is particularly important to distinguish experimentally between cue utilization and overshadowing.

2. McFarland suggested that if animals do learn zero correlations between stimuli and reinforcers, they could not learn all possible such correlations. The concept would thus seem to be useful only when one can specify the conditions under which zero correlations are learned.

3. Chantrey emphasized that animals may learn not only the predictive value of an event, but also its characteristics. Chantry's own work (see Bateson, this volume; Bateson and Chantrey, 1972; Chantrey, in press), like other studies mentioned briefly by Mackintosh in this chapter, involves pre-exposure of animals to stimuli predicting no change in the probability of any event. Under such circumstances, learning of the characteristics of the stimulus is the conspicuous consequence. No doubt the question asked by the experimenter determines which process is made apparent by the results.

4. Mackintosh's findings go one further than mere habituation; exposure to a stimulus does not just lead to a diminution in response, but also diminishes the probability that that stimulus will control behaviour in another context. But a parallel may exist in studies of habituation: Russian workers (e.g. Sokolov, 1960) have stressed how, with stimulus repetition, a "generalized orienting response" becomes changed to a "localized orienting response" limited to the modality in question, and this to an "adaptive response" which tends to reduce specifically the stimulus features that elicited the initial response.

References

Bateson, P. P. G. and Chantrey, D. F. (1972). Retardation of discrimination learning in monkeys and chicks previously exposed to both stimuli. *Nature* **237**, 173–174.

Chantrey, D. F. (in press). Enhancement and retardation of discrimination learning in chicks after exposure to the discriminanda. *J. comp. physiol. Psychol.*

Freeman, F. and Thomas, D. R. (1967). Attention vs. cue utilization in generalization testing. Paper presented at the meetings of the Midwestern Psychological Association.

Honig, W. K. (1970). Attention and the modulation of stimulus control. *In* "Attention: Contemporary Theory and Analysis", (D. Mostofsky, ed.) pp. 193–238. Appleton-Century-Crofts, New York.

Jenkins, H. M. and Harrison, R. H. (1960). Effect of discrimination training on auditory generalization. *J. exp. Psychol.* **59**, 246–253.

Kamin, L. J. (1968). "Attention-like" processes in classical conditioning. *In* "Miami Symposium on the Prediction of Behavior: Aversive Stimulation", (M. R. Jones, ed.), pp. 9–33. University of Miami Press, Miami.

Miles, C. G. and Jenkins. H. M. (In press). Overshadowing in operant conditioning as a function of discriminability. *Learning and Motivation.*

Newman, F. L. and Benefield, R. L. (1968). Stimulus control, cue utilization, and attention: effects of discrimination training. *J. comp. physiol. Psychol.*, **66**, 101–104.

Sokolov, E. N. (1960). Neuronal models and the orienting reflex. *In* "The Central Nervous System and Behavior", (M. A. B. Brazier, ed.). Macy Foundation, New York.

Van Houten, R. (1972). Overshadowing and stimulus control. Unpublished Ph.D. thesis, Dalhousie University.

Van Houten, R., Seraginian, P. and Rudolph, R. L. (1972). Airflow as a discriminative stimulus. *J. exp. Analysis Behav.* **17**, 99–105.

Wagner, A. R., Logan, F. A., Haberlandt, K. and Price, T. (1968). Stimulus selection in animal discrimination learning. *J. exp. Psychol.* **76**, 171–180.

5

Internal Influences on Early Learning in Birds

by P. P. G. Bateson

As is now well known, many of the birds which are feathered and active shortly after hatching will, at an early age, respond socially to a surprising range of visual stimuli. They will approach, and attempt to nestle against, animals that look nothing like adults of their own species and, even more remarkably, will behave in a similar way towards moving boxes, flashing lights and much else besides. As the result of experience with one object, the young bird comes to prefer this to others, and eventually may direct social behaviour exclusively towards the familiar object. This process by which young birds form a social attachment early in their lives is known as "imprinting" (reviews in Smith, 1969; Sluckin, 1972). It provides a striking example of the way in which a particular experience has a specific effect only when the animal is at a certain stage of behavioural development. Indeed, the constraints and controls on imprinting predispose many species of bird to learn the characteristics of their parents at what would appear to be the biologically appropriate time in their life-cycles.

The influences on the learning process appear to be so exquisitely adated to the biological requirements of the species that imprinting has frequently been taken as the example, *par excellence*, of ways in which learning processes are themselves genetically determined (e.g. Eibl-Eibesfeldt, 1970). Whether or not the various influences on imprinting are necessarily so exclusively genetic in origin is a matter of active research at the moment. But the question of what determines the influences does not bear directly on the problem with which I shall be primarily concerned, which is to specify those influences. I shall first review the evidence for the major constraints and do so quite briefly since I have recently gone over the same ground elsewhere (Bateson, 1971, 1972). "Constraints on learning" implies that internal limits are set on the extent to which events in the external environment control behaviour. An analysis of such limits lies comfortably within a stimulus-response framework and is obviously a legitimate line of inquiry. Nevertheless, I do not feel that it would adequately encompass all the influences that operate on learning processes. In particular it would leave out the active behavioural processes that predispose learning to occur in a particular context. For this reason I shall deal at some length with the activities that increase the probability of the young bird presenting itself with specific stimuli which it then goes on to learn. Finally, since I wish to emphasize that internal influences on learning can be environmentally determined, I shall deal with some of the consequences of imprinting on discrimination learning occurring later in life.

Selective Responsiveness

Even though birds like domestic chicks and mallard ducklings, the species most commonly used in studies of imprinting, respond to a wide range of objects before they have formed an attachment, they do respond much more strongly to some things than to others. Their selective responsiveness is unequivocally a major constraint on what is readily learnt in the imprinting situation. The characteristics of the stimuli which are most effective in eliciting social behaviour in naïve birds vary from species to species. But even in the most extensively studied species no single or simple feature is of paramount importance. At one time movement was regarded as essential in eliciting the following response, and hence in initiating the imprinting process. It is now clear, however, that the effectiveness of the many visual stimuli used in the imprinting situation depends on such properties as shape and the intensity of light they emit or reflect. Moreover, the rates at which these variables change are also important; hence the effectiveness of movement and flicker. In very general terms the more conspicuous the stimulus is to the human eye, the more effective it is in the imprinting situation. Nevertheless, two important qualifications have to be made to this generalization. First, size is a very important variable. In domestic chicks objects about 10 cm in diameter are most effective in eliciting approach (Schulman, et al., 1970). Ducklings tend to treat objects smaller than the size a match box as potential food (Fabricius and Boyd, 1954). The second point is that the effectiveness of the stimulus depends very much on the wavelength of light coming from it. Considerable evidence suggests that light at the red end of the spectrum is most effective (Bateson, 1966) and recently Kovach (1971) has found that chicks are remarkably unresponsive to green light. Chicks exposed to a green flashing light were much less likely to approach it in a subsequent test than chicks exposed to blue, yellow, red or indeed, white flashing lights.

The cluster of physical characteristics making up the optimal stimulus for use in the imprinting situation is not easily defined. Nevertheless, it is already obvious that the pattern of stimulation to which the young birds are exposed markedly affects how they respond and, what is more central to the present discussion, how much they will learn of its characteristics.

Sensitive Period

One of the most striking features of imprinting is its apparent restriction to a brief period early in life. The evidence for a sensitive period is obtained by taking birds at different stages after hatching, exposing them for a certain amount of time to a conspicuous object, and then some time later measuring how many of the birds have developed a preference for it. In general the proportion of birds that approach preferentially the object to which they have been exposed initially increases with age of exposure and then declines. The supposition has been that the extent of a bird's preference for the object to which it was previously exposed is a measure of the extent to which it has learned the characteristics of that object. Admittedly, the beautiful clear-cut results shown in many text books have not been replicated. Nevertheless, a great many studies have suggested that an optimal period for learning the characteristics of a specific object in a short period of time is found roughly in the second half of the first day for chicks and ducklings.

Undoubtedly the factors which give rise to the sensitive period are major constraints on what a young bird learns while being exposed to a particular stimulus. But, just because the sensitive period is in general terms dependent on age, it was often assumed that a unitary explanation could be offered for those factors. This thinking stemmed in large part from Lorenz (1935), who drew a vivid analogy between embryological induction and imprinting. The idea was that endogenous changes, rather than specific forms of experience, were the determinants of both the beginning and the end of the optimal period for imprinting. It was as though a window opened on the external world and then closed again. While the window was open the young animal was affected by certain types of experience, at other times it was not. This attractive interpretation did not, however, necessarily follow from the evidence, since specific types of experience affecting the behaviour of the bird can, and indeed do, vary with developmental age. So attempts should have been made to break the correlation before a strong hypothesis was advanced. In the case of the optimal period of imprinting, analyses revealed different causes underlying its onset and termination. Maturational changes, occurring independently of specific experience, have been strongly implicated in the onset. The evidence here comes largely from the work of Gottlieb (1961, 1971), who made use of the fact that birds hatch at different stages of embryonic development. This makes it possible to have birds of the same developmental age, but with different amounts of post-hatch experience; it is also possible to have birds of the same post-hatch age which have hatched at different stages of embryonic development. Gottlieb found that the sensitive period for imprinting in mallard ducklings is not so well marked if age is measured from hatching as it is if age is measured from the beginning of embryonic development. This suggests that experience after hatching has relatively little effect on the onset of the sensitive period. Now a number of changes, all of which are likely to influence the attachment process, take place at the same time as the onset of the sensitive period. The visual system becomes more highly organized (e.g. Paulson, 1965), the birds are better able to move about (e.g. Hess, 1959b), and there appear to be general biochemical changes taking place in the brain. For example, in chicks RNA synthesis, as measured by the incorporation of radio-actively labelled uracil into acid insoluble substances, increases significantly from 21 days to $21\frac{1}{2}$ days after the beginning of embryonic development. Over the same period the time elapsing before a chick approaches a flashing light significantly decreases (Bateson, Rose and Horn unpublished). Cor-

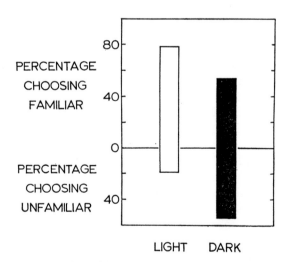

Fig. 1. The percentage number of day-old chicks approaching familiar or unfamiliar flashing lights in a choice test. One group (open bar) was exposed to a constant overhead light for 30 minutes before training for 45 minutes, and the other group (solid bar) was kept in the dark before training (from Bateson and Wainwright, 1972).

relations of this type tend to suggest that the timing of the sensitive period is dependent on endogenous changes. However, the developing animal is by no means totally buffered from environmental influences, which may very well contribute to the maturational process. Indeed, some evidence suggests that imprinting can occur at an earlier age in visually stimulated birds than in those which have been kept in the dark (e.g. Adam and Dimond, 1971; Dimond, 1968; Haywood and Zimmerman, 1964). Moreover, Bateson and Wainwright (1972) have found that day-old chicks exposed to the light for 30 minutes, then trained with a flashing light for 45 minutes, are more likely to prefer the familiar flashing light when given a choice than chicks which were not exposed to light before training (Fig. 1).

It is likely that exposure to light has a general effect on the visual pathways rather than specifically affecting the onset of the sensitive period for imprinting. Nevertheless, this result emphasizes how misleading it can be to think of maturation as being purely influenced by endogenous events.

The factors responsible for the end of the sensitive period have proved to be different from those implicated in its onset. For many years the offset was attributed to the development of fear occurring independently of specific experience (e.g. Hess 1959a). To be sure, a great deal of evidence shows that, on the second day after hatching, naïve domestic chicks and ducklings are much more likely to avoid a strange moving object than on the first day after hatching (see Bateson, 1966). However, a number of authors have demonstrated that rearing conditions have a marked effect on the age at which avoidance of novel objects first occurs (Guiton, 1959; Moltz and Stettner, 1961; Sluckin and Salzen, 1961). Moreover, I found that chicks isolated for three days following hatching avoided a moving object that resembled in pattern their home pens much less than one that differed in pattern (Bateson, 1964a). This suggests the birds had learnt the characteristics of their home pens and avoided objects that they could detect as being different. Thus the sensitive period seems to be brought to an end by a very specific type of experience. Its end, as defined under any given set of experimental conditions, does not necessarily mark the point at which learning is complete; it merely marks the point at which the young bird is able to discriminate between stimuli which it has already experienced and the object used by the experimenter for training purposes.

It would seem easy to test the hypothesis that familiarity with a particular input is solely responsible for determining the end of the sensitive period. In practice, however, it is difficult to prevent a bird from receiving some visual input, for even darkness constitutes an environment in which the retinal receptors discharge in a characteristic way. In an attempt to overcome this difficulty MacDonald (1968) has attempted to reduce visual experience in chicks through the injection of sodium pentobarbital during the first four days after hatching. The drug effectively anaesthetizes the birds. When tested on day 5, these chicks showed considerably more social responsiveness to a strange moving object than control birds. Here, of course, there is no evidence for the view that endogenous factors are even partly responsible for the termination of the sensitive period. On the contrary, MacDonald's data support the view that specific experience is the primary cause. Thus the strongest hypothesis is that birds become familiar with their immediate environment whether this be their mother, other chicks, or the walls of their isolation cage, and come to discriminate between such stimuli and moving objects used by the experimenter. When they can make a discrimination they avoid the strange object and subsequently show no evidence of having developed a preference for it.

The analysis of the factors responsible for the sensitive period, although far from complete, has shown quite clearly that the increase is not brought about by the same processes as are responsible for the decrease. Furthermore, the so-called "end" of the sensitive period is not determined absolutely and does not necessarily mark the end of lability in the process of attachment.

Considerable evidence suggests that changes take place in chicks' social preferences after they have first shown signs of being attached to a familiar object (Bateson, 1972; Connolly, 1968). Furthermore their preferences can be radically changed for several days after they have initially become attached to one object (Salzen and Meyer, 1968). So the sensitive period should not be taken to have all-or-nothing properties.

Analysis of the sensitive period for imprinting has suggested that constraints on what can be learned in a particular situation can be traced back to both internal and external factors and that the onset and offset are controlled by different mechanisms. Descriptive evidence for a sensitive period does not, therefore, imply a unitary process. Without very good supporting evidence, the sensitive period should not be referred to in an explanatory sense as though its timing provides a single constraint on what can be learned.

Behavioural Influences on Acquisition

The stimuli whose characteristics are readily learnt by young birds elicit "social behaviour". This category may involve a number of components like begging for food and calling in a characteristic way, and will differ from species to species. But in the species that leave the nest shortly after they have hatched, the most characteristic response is approaching the conspicuous object and following it if it moves away. When birds like domestic chicks are very young and are not able to regulate their body temperature, having approached an object they attempt to nestle underneath it. The activities of approaching and nestling against the mother are a form of constraint on the rate at which they can learn her characteristics, because they curtail their visual experience for as long as they stay underneath her. Another point is that a strong tendency to approach a stimulus will make it very difficult for the young bird to learn a detour problem in which the parent is the goal. Indeed, Scholes (1965) has found that chicks are unable to take a detour in order to approach their siblings until they are five or six days old. His results can be explained in terms of their approach movements effectively preventing side-to-side exploratory activities which would enable them to learn the detour problem. While these aspects of the young birds' behaviour can certainly be regarded as constraints, there are others aspects which strongly suggest that the course of learning is not merely constrained but is more positively controlled by their own activities.

When a young mallard duckling, which has been sitting quietly in a dark incubator, is removed and placed in a bare alley at room temperature, it soon begins to move about. Before long it starts "distress" calling, and it shuffles about in disorientated fashion with its neck extended. If a conspicuous visual stimulus is now presented to the duckling, it orientates towards the stimulus and its "distress" calling stops. In many ways, its behaviour resembles that of an older duckling that has become separated from its mother, vigorously searches for her, and then regains contact with her. Such an observation suggests that even before they have been imprinted, ducklings will behave in a way that increase the likelihood of their making visual contact with a conspicuous object. If stimuli that are highly effective in the imprinting situation do bring such appetitive behaviour to an end, and are thereby consummatory, they might be expected to reward the young bird. A considerable body of evidence has been built up over the years demonstrating that domestic chicks and ducklings which have already formed a social attachment can be rewarded with the presentation of the familiar object. Of special importance was the discovery by Hoffman et al. (1966) that ducklings exposed to a toy train one day after hatching could subsequently be trained to peck at a pole by running the train past them immediately after they had pecked, whereas ducklings exposed at a later stage in development could not be rewarded in the same way. In other words, they demonstrated that events occurring within the sensitive period determined the subsequent reinforcing properties of the object. Therefore, they linked the reinforcing properties of the familiar object fairly and squarely with the imprinting process. This evidence could be interpreted in two ways. Moltz (1960, 1963) has plausibly argued that the reinforcing properties of the familiar object are a consequence of imprinting since experienced birds avoid unfamiliar objects and show marked signs of distress when separated from the familiar object. The alternative view that imprinting narrows down the range of stimuli which have reinforcing properties is supported by some studies done by Ellen Reese and myself. Day-old domestic chicks and wild mallard ducklings taken from a dark incubator quickly learned to operate a pedal that turned on a flashing light (Bateson and Reese, 1968). Prior exposure to the flashing light, which in itself was a highly effective imprinting stimulus, far from increasing the rate of their learning to press a pedal, slowed up acquisition.

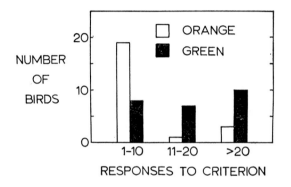

Fig. 2. The number of responses of day-old chicks to reach an arbitrary criterion of learning in an operant conditioning situation. Half the chicks were required to press a pedal which turned on an orange flashing light, the other half were required to press a pedal which turned on a green flashing light (from Bateson and Reese, 1969). The orange flashing light is strongly preferred to the green light when naïve day-old chicks are given a choice between them.

Now it can be argued that our results could have been produced by any sensory change. However, a close correspondence was found between the factors affecting the reinforcing properties of the flashing light and those affecting elicitation of social behaviour by a social stimulus. Age, and prior experience, affected the ability of domestic chicks to learn the pedal-pressing task in the same way as they affect the imprinting process. Particularly striking were the results showing that an orange flashing light, approached preferentially by naïve day-old chicks in a choice test, was a more effective reinforcer than a green flashing light (Fig. 2). Furthermore, Bateson and Reese (1969) showed that in the course of learning to work for a flashing light, day-old chicks also learned its characteristics and preferred it to a different flashing light when given a choice.

So strong are the links between the imprinting situation and the one in which a flashing light was used as a reinforcer, that it seems valueless to attribute the reinforcing effects to non-specific stimulus change. Indeed, I should like to go further and argue that before imprinting occurs the bird shows specific appetitive behaviour which can be terminated by any one of the broad class of effective imprinting objects. The relevance of this conclusion to a discussion of influences on learning is that the animal is playing an active part in determining the kinds of things that it will learn.

I had thought that once a bird locks onto an appropriate stimulus, the role which that animal plays in the subsequent learning process was a reactive one. Recently, however, I have obtained some evidence suggesting that chicks continue to play an active part in determining what they learn even after the imprinting process is under way. For example, with some new apparatus we have been able to obtain a quantitative measure of a bird's preference when given a choice between familiar and unfamiliar stimuli (Bateson and Wainwright, 1972). In one experiment we exposed day-old chicks to a constant light for 30 minutes, and then trained them with a flashing light for 45 minutes, and finally gave each chick a choice between the familiar and an unfamiliar flashing light. Subsequently we related the approach scores of the chicks while they were being trained to their performance in the choice test, and obtained a surprising result (Fig. 3). If the birds are divided into four equal groups according to their approach activity during training, it is apparent that the relationship is U-shaped.

On the face of it, this result is paradoxical because some previous work had suggested that, in general, the more active a bird is during the period of training, the more likely it is to prefer the familiar object when subsequently tested (Hess, 1959a). Since we suspect that our results may reflect subtle changes taking place during the learning process, we have systematically varied chicks exposure to a flashing light and studied their preferences in a choice test. The relationship between length of exposure and preference for the familiar is not monotonic (Bateson and Jaeckel, unpublished). At first the birds show an increasing preference for the familiar, then this trend is reversed so that some birds may actually prefer the unfamiliar. Finally after very considerable exposure to a particular flashing light the birds show a strong preference for it. In other words a biphasic relationship is found between strength of preference for the familiar and length of exposure. The data in Fig. 3 can be explained in terms of such a biphasic curve if, as seems likely, approach activity during exposure is correlated with maintenance of visual contact and hence with how much is learned. Those birds in the third group, that quite actively approached during the period of training, may, after 45 minutes, have reached the phase in learning when they are likely to show a preference for a novel stimulus. The birds which approached less actively may not have reached this phase and the birds which approached more actively may have passed through it.

If birds will work for slightly novel objects during the attachment process their behaviour would be an important influence on what is learnt under natural conditions. To clarify the point, I should first like to suggest a functional explanation for what is probably going on and then propose a simple model.

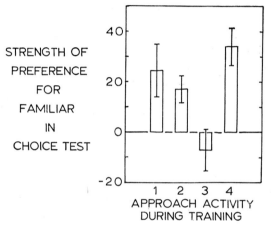

Fig. 3. The relationship between the strength of preference for the familiar object in a choice test and activity during prior training with that familiar object in day-old chicks ($N = 47$). The scores for approach activity during training have been ranked and divided into equal groups with the exception of the least active birds in which $N = 11$. The strength of preferences for which means and standard errors are given, is obtained by the method described in Bateson and Wainwright (1972). Briefly the strength of preference is the maximum distance travelled in centimetres from the mid-point between the familiar and unfamiliar stimuli in a 5 minutes test. The chick is placed in a specially geared wheel in which its movements carry it away from the stimulus it is attempting to approach. When a chick has been carried sufficiently close to the less preferred stimulus, it usually turns round and attempts to approach that one. A negative score means that a chick attempted to approach the unfamiliar stimulus.

The ability to recognize a parent from all likely angles surely requires considerably more information than can possibly be acquired as the result of learning the characteristics of a single view of that parent. The transformations from front view to side view, and from side view to back view, could not easily be accomplished by mechanisms ordinarily understood as being involved in perceptual constancy. In other words, it is doubtful that the bird could predict what the back view of its mother is like from knowledge of its front view. If birds which have formed an attachment to an individual can respond selectively to that individual regardless of its orientation with respect to them (and it must be admitted that the evidence that they can do so is not yet available), then the bird must have been exposed to all those views of the parent which it can subsequently identify. It has, I suggest, built up a composite picture of its parent's characteristics. In the normal course of events, the mother will probably present many different aspects of herself during the attachment process while the young are learning her characteristics. Nevertheless, assurance would be made doubly sure if, after learning a certain amount about her, the young actively work to present themselves with a different view. Thus a plausible functional explanation for the process producing a biphasic curve is that it enables the young bird to learn as much as possible about its mother and, indeed, its siblings. The active element in the young bird's behaviour makes the attachment process much more flexible and adaptive than it would have been if the bird simply locked on to the first thing it saw and attempted to maintain contact with that and nothing else.

The model which I should like to propose for this active working for the slightly novel presupposes what is now widely accepted—namely, that as attachment occurs the range of objects to which the birds respond socially is narrowed down. If a stimulus continuum is used, the generalization gradient along it steepens as a function of exposure. Now, I suggest that superimposed on the stready restriction of the bird's preferences is another phenomenon which leads the birds to respond increasingly to stimuli differing slightly from the ones to which they were exposed. This is a version of the discrepancy hypothesis (see Thomas, 1971) but with the added feature that as the animals come to prefer the discrepant stimulation, the exact amount of the discrepancy that is optimally attractive will be inversely related to the length of exposure. In other words, as the birds learn more about the familiar, objects that are detected by them as being slightly novel will in reality resemble more and more closely the familiar object. These hypothetical changes can be represented in a three-dimensional diagram (Fig. 4).

I am aware that with three variables it is possible to describe virtually anything, but this model does have one major advantage—it predicts the form of the curves which should be obtained if the difference between familiar and unfamiliar stimuli used in a choice test were changed. It can be seen from Fig. 4 that the shape of the biphasic curve will be altered as the difference between the familiar and the novel test stimuli is reduced. We are currently testing this hypothesis.

Whether or not the functional and causal explanations that I have offered have any value or power, I believe it is much more difficult to regard a young bird as passively learning the characteristics of a suitable object during the attachement process. The evidence suggests increasingly that internally controlled processes actively direct the course of learning by affecting the stimulation that the bird receives.

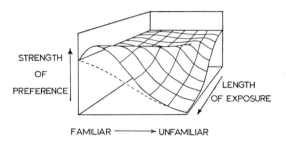

Fig. 4. The hypothetical relationship between lengths of exposure in the imprinting situation, strength of preference for a test stimulus and the difference between the familiar object and the test stimulus. Superimposed on a steady steepening of the generalization gradient as training proceeds, which is shown by the dashed line, is another phenomenon which leads the young bird to prefer increasingly a slightly novel stimulus. Furthermore, as training proceeds, what the bird detects as being slightly novel increasingly resembles the familiar.

Consequences of the Attachment Process

The development of a preference restricts the range of objects to which an animal will respond. And, inasmuch as such a restriction places limits on what will subsequently be experienced, the consequences of this attachment process provides a marked constraint on what is subsequently learnt. The constraints that derive from specific preferences are further buttressed by two other aspects of the young animal's behaviour. One is that they search for the familiar object in its absence in the sense that they behave in ways that increase the probability of encountering the familiar object, and they cease to behave in this way when they have found it. Secondly, they avoid objects which differ markedly in characteristics from the ones to which they were exposed. Such canalizing effects of early experience provides a powerful explanation for a variety of types of selective responsiveness found later in development.

The specific effects of imprinting on discrimination learning occurring in other contexts have been fairly extensively studied. Four separate studies have shown, for example, that when chicks are exposed to an object in the imprinting situation and subsequently a familiar object is used as one of the discriminanda in a food-rewarded discrimination-learning task they learn the discrimination much more quickly than the control group which has seen neither of the stimuli before (Bateson, 1964b; Kovach, *et al.*, 1966; Polt, 1969; Chantrey, 1972). Furthermore, they do so both when a familiar stimulus is the rewarded one *and* when it is the unrewarded one. In these cases previous experience is not a constraint on learning, it *facilitates* subsequent discrimination learning when there is a possibility of transfer of training.

However, the relationship between early learning and subsequent learning processes is not always as simple as this. When rhesus monkeys and domestic chicks were required to discriminate between two stimuli—both of which they had seen before, they took much longer to learn the discrimination than control groups which had seen neither stimuli before (Bateson and Chantrey, 1972). Chantrey (unpublished) has found that this retarding effect of previous experience with the two discriminanda in the imprinting situation was obtained only if the stimuli were presented in rapid alternation. When he trained them with one stimulus for half-an-hour followed by the other stimulus for half-an-hour and so on, the chicks' ability to discriminate between the two stimuli in a food rewarded situation was greater than that of a control group. Just what the retarding effect is due to is not yet clear. Nevertheless, it is very unlikely that it can be explained in terms of habituation. Possibly two stimuli, which have been experienced within a short time of each other in the same context, are given the same value and in a sense are classified together. They share the same identity. This could be an integral part of the imprinting situation where the young animal has to build up a composite picture of its parents as it obtains the opportunity to view the parent at various angles. The advantage of doing this are not restricted to the attachment process. Classification together of physically different stimuli may well be necessary for some of the more complex examples of "concept formation" (e.g. Herrnstein and Loveland, 1964), even though abstraction of common features of different stimuli and generalization from familiar to novel stimuli are also likely to be involved. The process may also play a larger part in human perception than personal experience suggests—introspection being a poor guide to the distinctions which we ignore in our own classifications.

Conclusions

The study of early perceptual development in birds has highlighted two general points. First, it is clear that the internal influences on what can be learned are diverse. Some of these, such as selective responsiveness to particular stimuli, set limits on what can be learned and can be described

I

unambiguously as constraints. Others, such as the birds' active working for stimuli of a certain type before and during the attachment process, suggest that the course of perceptual learning is, in part, *controlled* by events occurring inside the animal.

The second general issue brought out by the work on imprinting is that an internal influence is not necessarily and exclusively genetically determined. Admittedly it seems likely (although not yet established) that the initial preferences and the specific form of the initial behaviour shown by the young birds are determined only by genetic factors even though non-specific environmental influences play a part in the development of the preference and the patterning of social and appetitive behaviour. However, the consequences of experience in the imprinting situation undoubtedly have a major effect on subsequent learning processes. What is more, the specific experience interacts with the pre-existing organization of the animal's behaviour and can produce unexpected outcomes. Simple additive models are no more satisfactory in explaining the ontogeny of behaviour than they are in explaining chemical reactions. It would be a delusion to pretend that the relationship between the internal influences on learning and the processes involved in their development is straightforward. The lesson is, then, that the issue of what constrains and controls learning should not be confused with the question of how those constraints and controls were specified earlier in development.

References

Adam, J. and Dimond, S. J. (1971). The effect of visual stimulation of embryonic development on approach behaviour. *Anim. Behav.* **19**, 51–54.

Bateson, P. P. G. (1964a). Effect of similarity between rearing and testing conditions on chicks' following and avoidance response. *J. comp. physiol. Psychol.* **57**, 100–103.

Bateson, P. P. G. (1964b). An effect of imprinting on the perceptual development of domestic chicks. *Nature, Lond.* **202**, 421–422.

Bateson, P. P. G. (1966). The characteristics and context of imprinting. *Biol. Rev.* **41**, 177–220.

Bateson, P. P. G. (1971). "Imprinting." *In* "Ontogeny of Vertebrate Behavior", (H. Moltz, ed.), pp. 369–387. Academic Press, New York.

Bateson, P. P. G. (1972). The formation of social attachments in young birds. *Proc. XV Int. Ornithol. Congr.* 303–315.

Bateson, P. P. G. and Chantrey, D. F. (1972). Retardation of discrimination learning in monkeys and chicks previously exposed to both stimuli. *Nature, Lond.* **237**, 173–174.

Bateson, P. P. G. and Reese, E. P. (1968). Reinforcing properties of conspicuous objects before imprinting has occurred. *Psychon. Sci.* **10**, 379–380.

Bateson, P. P. G. and Reese, E. P. (1969). Reinforcing properties of conspicuous stimuli in the imprinting situation. *Anim. Behav.* **17**, 692–699.

Bateson, P. P. G. and Wainwright, A. A. P. (1972). The effects of prior exposure to light on the imprinting process in domestic chicks. *Behaviour* **42**, 279–290.

Chantrey, D. F. (1972). Enhancement and retardation of discrimination learning in chicks after exposure to the discriminanda. *J. comp. physiol. Psychol.* **81**, 256–261.

Connolly, K. (1968). Imprinting and the following response as functions of amount of training in domestic chicks. *Brit. J. Psychol.* **59**, 453–460.

Dimond, S. J. (1968). Effects of photic stimulation before hatching on the development of fear in chicks. *J. comp. physiol. Psychol.* **65**, 320–324.

Eibl-Eibesfeldt, I. (1970). "Ethology: The Biology of Behavior." Holt, Rinehart & Winston, New York.

Fabricius, E. and Boyd, H. (1954). Experiments on the following reactions of ducklings. *Wildfowl Trust Ann. Rep.* 1952–53, 84–89.

Gottlieb, G. (1961). Developmental age as a baseline for determination of the critical period in imprinting. *J. comp. physiol. Psychol.* **54**, 422–427.

Gottlieb, G. (1971). "Development of Species Identification in Birds." Univ. of Chicago Press, Chicago.

Guiton, P. (1959). Socialization and imprinting in Brown Leghorn chicks. *Anim. Behav.* **7**, 26–34.

Haywood, H. C. and Zimmerman, D. W. (1964). Effects of early environmental complexity in the following responses in chicks. *Percept. Motor Skills.* **18**, 653–658.

Herrnstein, R. J. and Loveland, D. H. (1964). Complex visual concept in the pigeon. *Science* **146**, 549–551.

Hess, E. H. (1959a). Imprinting. *Science* **130**, 133–141.

Hess, E. H. (1959b), Two conditions limiting critical age for imprinting. *J. comp. physiol. Psychol.* **52**, 515–518.

Hoffman, H. S., Searle, J., Toffey, S. and Kozman, F. (1966). Behavioral control by an imprinted stimulus. *J. exp. Analysis. Behav.* **9**, 177–189.

Kovach, J. K. (1971). Effectiveness of different colors in the elicitation and development of approach behavior in chicks. *Behaviour* **38**, 154–168.

Kovach, J. K., Fabricius, E. and Fält, L. (1966). Relationships between imprinting and perceptual learning. *J. comp. physiol. Psychol.* **61**, 449–454.

Lorenz, K. (1935). Der Kumpan in der Umwelt des Vogels. *J. Ornithol.* **83**, 137–213, 289–413.

MacDonald, G. (1968). Imprinting: drug-produced isolation and the sensitive period. *Nature. Lond.* **217**, 1158–1159.

Moltz, H. (1960). Imprinting: empirical basis and theoretical significance. *Psychol. Bull.* **57**, 291–314.

Moltz H. (1963). Imprinting: an epigenetic approach. *Psychol. Rev.* **70**, 123–128.

Moltz, H. and Stettner, L. J. (1961). The influence of patterned-light deprivation on the critical period for imprinting. *J. comp. physiol. Psychol.* **54**, 279–283.

Paulson, G. W. (1965). Maturation of evoked responses in the duckling. *Exp. Neurology.* **11**, 324–333.

Polt. J. M. (1969). Effect of imprinting experience on discrimination learning in chicks. *J. comp. physiol. Psychol.* **69**, 514–518.

Salzen, E. A. and Meyer, C. C. (1968). Reversibility of imprinting. *J. comp. physiol. Psychol.* **66**, 269–275.

Scholes, N. W. (1965). Detour learning and development in the domestic chick. *J. comp. physiol. Psychol.* **60**, 114–116.

Schulman, A. H., Hale, E. B. and Graves, H. B. (1970). Visual stimulus characteristics for initial approach response in chicks (*Gallus domesticus*). *Anim. Behav.* **18**, 461–466.

Sluckin, W. (1972). "Imprinting and Early Learning", 2nd Edit. Methuen, London.

Sluckin, W. and Salzen, E. A. (1961). Imprinting and perceptual learning. *Q. J. exp. Psychol.* **13**, 65–77.

Smith, F. V. (1969). "Attachment of the Young: Imprinting and Other Developments." Oliver & Boyd, Edinburgh.

Thomas, H. (1971). Discrepancy hypothesis: methodological and theoretical considerations. *Psychol. Rev.* **78**, 249–259.

Editorial: 2

The preceding chapter, by Bateson, was based on an analysis of the manner in which newly hatched chicks come to limit much of their social behaviour to their mothers. He showed that the course of learning is channelled by a number of limitations and predispositions such that an adaptive result is normally attained. The progressive analysis of a natural learning situation revealed the variety of constraints that operate.

Newly hatched chicks must not only form a social attachment to their mother, they must also learn what to eat. This is discussed by Hogan (Chapter 6). Just as the approach response studied by Bateson is first elicited by a wide, though not unlimited, range of stimulus objects, so also is pecking. And with pecking, also, the range of adequate simuli becomes narrowed through experience. One factor operating here is in fact the social attachment to the mother: the chick tends to peck where she pecks. This, however, is only one of the ways in which selectivity is achieved. The constraints that operate are more complex than appear at first sight: they involve a delayed effect of ingestion on pecking rate and, under some circumstances, on selectivity between potential food items. Indeed the effect may not be manifest at all for half an hour or longer after ingestion. Such a delayed effect is remarkable in that most previous experimental studies have shown that a reinforcer must follow the response closely to be effective. However, as mentioned by Mackintosh (Chapter 4), a somewhat similar phenomena has been known for some time in rats: rats will learn to avoid a food item if they become ill after ingesting it, and in some circumstances will learn to take foods that contain a dietary item of which they are deficient.

This work on rats is summarized by McFarland in Chapter 7. A major problem is how the rats manage to associate the taste of food with the subsequent toxic effects, when a long interval may separate the one from the other: there are, one might think, many other events with which the ill-effects could be associated. Some constraints must operate on the stimuli that become linked with the physiological consequences. In the terms of earlier chapters, the problem here is one of stimulus selection: why does the rat select, from all the stimuli to which it has recently been exposed, taste stimuli as the ones to be avoided. McFarland supports an answer in terms of "stimulus relevance"—some stimuli apparently being more readily associated with such adverse physiological consequences than others. As Rozin and Kalat (1971) point out, one characteristic of the stimuli selected is that they are "eating-related": it will be recalled that Mackintosh (Chapter 4) suggested that the readiness with which internal changes are associated with tastes by adult rats stems from a lifetime's experience of their not being correlated with changes in stimuli other than taste. McFarland also discusses the further issue of why some "eating-related" cues should be selected in preference to others.

A second problem concerns whether an animal can learn what is good for it as well as what is harmful. McFarland suggests that both learning to prefer substances that lead to an improved physiological state and learning to avoid substances that lead to sickness are due to learned aversions to inadequate or harmful foods. The applicability of this learned aversion hypothesis to the data on the development of pecking in chicks is discussed by Hogan.

References

Rozin, P. and Kalat, J. W. (1971). Specific hungers and poison avoidance as adaptive specializations of learning. *Psychol. Rev.* **78**, 459–486.

6

How Young Chicks Learn to Recognize Food

by Jerry A. Hogan

Many of the papers in this book are concerned with a particular kind of constraint on learning. This paper, however, considers various constraints placed on a newly-hatched chick that must solve a specific problem: learning quickly to recognize food. A review of the available evidence in 1896 led C. Lloyd Morgan to the following conclusion: "It seems, therefore, that . . . there is no instinctive discrimination; that what shall be selected for eating and what rejected is a matter of individual experience; and that, by repetition of the selective process, the eating of certain materials, and not of others, passes into a more or less fixed habit." (p. 55).

The purpose of this paper is threefold. Firstly, the evidence that has accumulated in the past 76 years on the kinds of experience that affect the development of the discrimination between food and non-food items in young chicks will be reviewed, including much evidence that has been obtained from experiments recently carried out in my laboratory. Secondly, the results from the chick studies will be compared with results from similar studies using rats. Finally, several kinds of constraints on learning implied by these studies will be considered including critical periods, delay of reinforcement, and the interrelationships among stimulus, response, and reinforcer.

Pecking in Chicks

Pecking in young chicks is controlled by many factors, both internal and external. One group of these factors can loosely be called motivational in that they control the rate or total amount of pecking. These factors include pecking drive (Hogan, 1971, p. 145ff), hunger, stimulus change, amount of stimulus present, colour and intensity of illumination, and the behaviour of conspecific companions (Bayer, 1929; Beck, 1930; Collias, 1952;

Shreck, Sterritt, Smith and Stilton, 1963; Tolman, 1968; Hogan, 1971; see also Katz, 1937; Wood-Gush, 1971). Ingestion is controlled by some of these same factors, but other factors such as taste and touch also play a role.

Another group of factors control the direction of pecking: these factors determine which among several possible stimuli will be pecked*. In naïve chicks, certain colours (Hess, 1956) and certain sizes and shapes (Fantz, 1957; Goodwin and Hess, 1969) are preferred. With experience, however, pecking preferences may change. For example, 1-day-old Junglefowl chicks peck slightly more often at sand than at commercial chick crumbs; by 3 days of age, they peck more at the food than at the sand, and this preference for food increases still more in the next few days (Hogan, 1971).

There are several kinds of experience that could influence the motivation and/or direction of pecking. Three kinds of experience will be considered below: (1) the behaviour of a mother-hen; (2) immediate effects—primarily gustatory and tactual—of pecking at, mandibulating, and/or swallowing objects; (3) longer-term effects—primarily metabolic—of ingesting particular objects. Other kinds of experience may also play a role in controlling pecking and ingestion. For example, with respect to the approach response of young chicks, it has been shown that early perceptual experience with patterns and colours can influence the stimuli most readily approached (Bateson, 1964; Kovach, 1971). Visual perceptual experience may also be important in affecting pecking in young chicks, but this and other experience will not be considered any further in this paper.

The role of the mother-hen

Under natural conditions, the first food normally eaten by a newly-hatched chick will be food offered to it by its mother-hen. When a mother-hen discovers food, she makes a special food call which attracts and greatly activates the chicks. While making her food-call, the hen pecks at, and picks up and drops pieces of food which the young chicks peck at and frequently pick up and swallow. It seems clear that one effect of the hen's behaviour is directive: that is, the chicks peck more at the stimuli pecked at and mandibulated by the hen than at alternative stimuli which are also readily available; and this pecking seems to generalize to stimuli of the same kind.

Turner (1964) measured the number of pecks that 1-day-old chicks

* This distinction points to two separate problems in the analysis of pecking: absolute number of responses and relative number of responses to different stimuli. Any particular stimulus will generally be a source of both motivational and directing factors. This distinction is similar to the distinction between the releasing and directing functions of a stimulus—see the recent discussion by R. Dawkins and Impekoven, 1969.

directed towards equal numbers of orange and green grains. When a very rough cut-out model of a hen behind some wire mesh was made to "peck" at similar grains, the chicks pecked about twice as much at the colour which the model "pecked" at. Casual observations suggest that chicks react similarly to the behaviour of a real hen. Before it is possible to assess the role of this experience with the hen, however, it will be necessary to see whether chicks continue to prefer the stimuli selected by the hen when they are retested in her absence. It would also be desirable to see whether the behaviour of a hen or hen-model can override preferences that would develop in chicks without such experience.

Immediate effects of pecking and swallowing

Young chicks can be observed to pick up and mandibulate many different small objects. In some cases the object is swallowed, while in other cases it is dropped. If the object is dropped, it may be pecked up one or more times again until it is swallowed or finally rejected. The factor determining whether the object is swallowed or not could be gustatory, tactual, or both. Frequently, objects quickly come to be accepted or rejected on the basis of sight alone. Gustatory and/or tactual feedback clearly must have provided sufficient conditions for learning in many of these cases.

Chicks can show very strong reactions to stimuli on the basis of taste*. For example, day old chicks show clear signs of disgust when they peck at fresh droppings; their reaction includes head shaking with the mouth open, bill wiping, and retreat from the offending stimulus. Similar behaviour was observed by Morgan (1896) when he presented newly hatched chicks with distasteful cinnabar caterpillars (*Euchelia jacobiae*). In both cases, after just one such experience, a chick may avoid all further contact with the object. Not infrequently a chick makes an intention peck towards a previously experienced, distasteful object, but does not touch it; it may then retreat one or two steps and make a trill call, shake its head, or even wipe its bill—"a memory of the nasty taste being apparently suggested by association at sight of the [object]." (Morgan, 1896, p. 41). Strong positive reactions to gustatory stimuli are also seen. Young chicks often show clear avoidance reactions to mealworms (*Tenebrio* larvae), and can only be induced to accept the first mealworm with much effort; yet, in

* Histological studies (Lindenmaier and Kare, 1959) show that newly-hatched chicks have about 8 taste buds in the mouth (adult fowl have about 24), and electrophysiological studies (Kitchell, *et al.*, 1959) show that these receptors respond to bitter, sour, and salty substances and to water, but not to sugars. Halpern (1962) recorded electrophysiological responses to various sugars, but only in very high concentrations; he also discusses some of the problems involved in generalizing from physiological data to behaviour. See also Wood-Gush, 1971, pp. 13–15.

most cases, after eating just one mealworm, a chick accepts the second and later mealworms almost unhesitatingly (Hogan, 1966).

Tactual stimuli are presumably responsible for other cases of object selection, although direct experimental evidence is generally lacking. Hellwald (1931), for example, presented newly-hatched chicks with a wide variety of objects on a floor covered with soil. The objects included chick crumbs, sago, glass pearls, small steel balls, small stones, and pieces of straw and wood. The proportion swallowed of each object varied widely: about 40% of the sago pecked at was swallowed, about 8% of the glass pearls, and less than 1% of the steel balls. Although taste may have played a role in determining which objects were swallowed, the nature of the stimuli makes it likely that the tactual qualities of the objects were primarily responsible for the selection in many cases. More direct evidence has been collected by Hogan-Warburg (personal communication). She observed chicks pecking at chick crumbs, sand, and small stones. Initially all three stimuli were pecked at and swallowed. After swallowing a few of the stones, however, stones were clearly avoided, while both the food and the sand continued to be swallowed. The behaviour of the chicks suggested that swallowing a stone is uncomfortable. The basis of rejection would be tactual feedback from the throat. Chicks sometimes show similar signs of discomfort when swallowing a mealworm for the first time. The fact that chicks continue to eat mealworms indicates that the taste of the mealworm almost always overrides these negative tactual effects. Chicks that show such negative reactions, however, do show some hesitation before accepting another mealworm (Hogan, 1966).

It may have been noted that many of the examples cited above demonstrate that discrimination learning can occur very rapidly in young chicks, often in just one or two trials. In general, this rapid learning would seem to be beneficial to the chicks, though sometimes it leads to disastrous results, as when some chicks become so fond of mealworms that they reject other less palatable food completely until they ultimately perish of starvation (Hogan, 1971, p. 191). Not all food recognition takes place so rapidly, however; nor does it all depend on the immediate effects of ingestion. Some other mechanisms are considered in the next section.

Delayed effects of ingestion

Young Junglefowl chicks change their pecking preference from sand to food during the first three days after hatching (Hogan, 1971). The time course of this change suggests that the immediate effects of pecking and ingestion discussed above are not sufficient to explain the change. The immediate effects of pecking and ingestion are also insufficient to explain preferences for particular foods that develop in chickens (Dove, 1935) and the behaviour of chickens when deprived of necessary substances in their diets (Hellwald, 1931; Hughes and Wood-Gush, 1971). I have recently carried out a number of experiments which investigate the role played by longer-term effects of ingestion in changing the pecking preferences of young chicks.

In one experiment (Hogan, 1973a, Experiment 2), chicks ranging in age from 6 hours to 72 hours were allowed to peck either at sand or at commercial chick food for 10 minutes. In order to test for delayed effects of ingestion, each chick was retested on the same stimulus for 2 minutes about $1\frac{1}{2}$ hours later. All chicks were tested on only one day and with only one stimulus. The change in pecking rate between the test and the retest is shown for each group of chicks in Fig. 1. The solid circles are data from

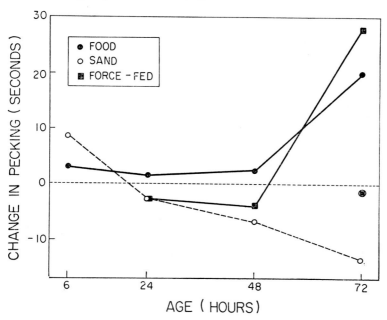

Fig. 1. Delayed effects of pecking as a function of age. Each data point represents the mean of a separate group of 10 or 20 chicks.

chicks tested on food; the open circles are data from chicks tested on sand. (The solid squares will be discussed later.) In this figure, positive changes (above the dotted line) mean that chicks pecked at a higher rate in the 2-minute retest than they did in the original 10-minute test; negative changes mean that chicks pecked at a lower rate in the retest.

Looking first at the results for chicks tested on food, it can be seen that for chicks up to 48 hours of age, the pecking rate in the retest was approximately the same as the pecking rate in the original test. For the 3-day-old chicks, however, a very large and significant increase in pecking occurred during the retest. The results for sand are very different: pecking at sand for 10 minutes led to larger and larger decreases in pecking during the retest as a function of the increasing age of the chicks (the decreases at 48 and 72 hours were both statistically significant).

The increase in pecking as a result of experience with food on day 3 is especially interesting. One interpretation of this result is that chicks do not ingest enough food to have any effects on behaviour until they are about 3 days old. This interpretation is quite plausible: the time spent pecking in the 10-minute test did increase as the chicks grew older, and previous results showed that chicks actually ingest very little of what they peck before 3 days of age (Hogan, 1971, p. 147). In order to test this hypothesis, another experiment was designed in which chicks varying from 24 to 72 hours of age were allowed to peck at sand for 10 minutes, and then were immediately force-fed a mixture of food and water (Hogan, 1973a, Experiment 5). In this experiment, therefore, chicks of all ages ingested the same amount of food. The chicks were retested on sand about $1\frac{1}{2}$ hours later for 2 minutes. The change in pecking rate between the test and the retest for each group of chicks is plotted as solid squares in Fig. 1. It can be seen that the results are the same as for the chicks that pecked food in the previous experiment: at 24 and 48 hours, ingestion of food has no effect on subsequent pecking; whereas at 72 hours, ingestion of food leads to a large and significant increase in pecking $1\frac{1}{2}$ hours later.

These two experiments show that food ingestion is ineffective in influencing pecking behaviour before day 3. The increase in pecking that does occur on day 3, however, might be due to several causes. For example, it might be merely a consequence of the nutriment provided by the food (yolk sac reserves are reduced by more than half by day 3 (Parker, 1929)); or it might depend on the association between pecking and food ingestion. The first alternative could be considered a motivational interpretation of the increase in pecking as opposed to the learning interpretation of the second alternative. In order to choose between these two interpretations, a control group was included in the forced-feeding experiment described above. This group of 3-day-old chicks was allowed to peck at sand for 10 minutes. Two hours elapsed before the chicks were force-fed the food-water mixture, and $1\frac{1}{2}$ hours later the chicks were retested for 2 minutes. The change in pecking rate between the test and retest is shown as an encircled solid square in Fig. 1. It can be seen that force-feeding, *per se*, has no effect upon pecking rate. It follows that the increase in pecking seen on day 3 is the result of the association of pecking with food ingestion; that is, the increase in pecking is a learning phenomenon.

The foregoing experiments show that food ingestion on day 3, when associated with pecking, has a delayed effect on subsequent pecking, but they do not give much information on the length of delay involved. A further set of experiments was undertaken to determine the length of the delay (Hogan, 1973b, Experiment 1). Six groups of 3-day-old chicks were allowed to peck at food for 10 minutes. After delays ranging from 20 minutes to 2 hours, the chicks were retested for 2 minutes. The differences in pecking rate between the test and retest are plotted in Fig. 2. It can be

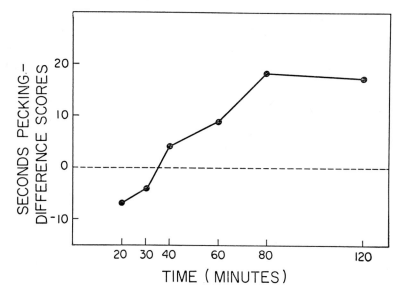

Fig. 2. Delayed effects of pecking food as a function of the length of delay. Each data point represents the mean of a separate group of 10 chicks.

seen that there is a slight depression of pecking rate for about half an hour after food is first ingested; but, by 40 minutes after ingestion, pecking rate has increased over its original level; pecking rate continues to increase until it reaches an asymptote at an interval of about 80 minutes.

Several additional experiments were performed in order to determine the reason for the delayed appearance of increased pecking. One possible reason is that the chicks become satiated as they eat the food in the 10-minute test, and that it takes about an hour before they become hungry again and demonstrate increased pecking. This hypothesis was tested by manipulating the amount of food the chicks ingested in their first exposure to food (Hogan, 1973b, Experiment 2). Some chicks received only 4 minutes exposure to food in the first test, and other chicks received 10 minutes exposure to food followed immediately by force-feeding. Chicks with both kinds of experience were then tested 20, 40, 60, or 80 minutes later for 2 minutes. There were no significant differences between these results and the results already presented in Fig. 2. It can be concluded that a fourfold variation in the amount of food ingested has no effect on the delayed appearance of increased pecking. This means that the satiation-hunger hypothesis is not supported. Further evidence against the satiation-hunger hypothesis comes from an experiment using chicks that had had food available within a few hours after hatching (Hogan, 1973b, Experiment 3). These chicks were deprived of food from 67 to 72 hours, given food again for 10 minutes, and then retested 20, 40, or 80 minutes later for 2 minutes. There was a small decrease in pecking rate after an interval of 20 minutes, but by 80 minutes the pecking rate had returned to the original level; that is, the increase seen before did not occur in the experienced chicks. Some implications of these results will be discussed at the end of this paper.

The results presented to this point demonstrate that ingestion of food has delayed effects, but they do not demonstrate what role these delayed effects play in the development of food recognition. One experiment was designed to investigate this problem (Hogan, 1973a, Experiment 3). Three-day-old naïve chicks were exposed to either food or sand for 10 minutes. About $1\frac{1}{2}$ hours later, half the chicks tested on food were retested on food for 2 minutes, and half were retested on sand. Likewise, half the chicks tested on sand were retested on sand and half were retested on food. Thus, chicks had experience with only stimulus at a time, but half the chicks had successive experience with both stimuli, while the other half had successive experience with the same stimulus. Somewhat surprisingly, whether chicks were retested on food or sand made no difference: chicks with their original test on food showed a large and significant increase in pecking to both food *and* sand in the retest, whereas chicks with their original test on sand showed a small, though not significant, decrease in pecking to both food and sand. This result is unexpected because it appears to mean that ingestion of food, in association with pecking, leads to an increase in the occurrence of the act of pecking, but does not support discrimination learning.

A number of further studies have recently been carried out in order to see under what conditions the delayed effects of food ingestion may provide the basis for the development of food recognition. Some of these studies have not yet been replicated, but the results seem fairly clear in most cases. A summary of some of the findings will be presented here; a complete report will be published elsewhere.

One reason the chicks in the previous experiment may not have discriminated between food and sand is that they never had an opportunity to compare food and sand at the same time. Franck (1966), for example, has presented evidence that a choice method may provide a more sensitive measure of discrimination than a one-stimulus method (cf. Dawkins and Impekoven, 1969); though it should be noted that there is little, if any, evidence that a simultaneous procedure is more effective than a successive procedure for the *development* of a discrimination (N. J. Mackintosh, personal communication). An additional reason is that the original 10-minute exposure to the stimuli may not have been long enough to establish a discrimination (though it should be recalled that a 4-minute exposure to food was sufficient for a large increase in pecking to appear $1\frac{1}{2}$ hours later). Therefore, 3-day-old chicks were given $1\frac{1}{2}$ hours experience on either food or sand and were retested $1\frac{1}{2}$ hours later. Some chicks were tested on only one stimulus (successive discrimination), while others were tested on a floor containing separate piles of both food and sand (simultaneous discrimination). The results for the chicks given the successive choice task were exactly the same as reported above when the chicks had only 10 minutes of prior exposure: chicks originally exposed to food showed much higher pecking rates than chicks originally exposed to sand; but whether sand or food was used as the test stimulus made no difference at all to the pecking rates. The chicks given the simultaneous discrimination task were no better at discriminating: although some individual chicks pecked almost exclusively at food while others pecked almost exclusively at sand, the chicks' previous experience had no significant effect on stimulus choice during the test. Chicks in the simultaneous discrimination groups were actually given 10-minute tests (as opposed to 2-minute tests which had been used in the previous experiments), and the data were broken down into pecks given in each 2-minute interval. No preferences for either sand or food developed during the 10-minute test. These results suggest that the delayed effects of ingestion may, in fact, not be able to support discrimination learning.

Still other experiments have investigated what effects quite long exposures to the food and sand stimuli might have. In one such experiment, chicks lived on either an empty floor, a food-covered floor, or a sand-covered floor from the time they were removed from the incubator at 6 hours until they were 67 hours old. All chicks then lived on an empty floor for 5 hours. At 72 hours of age, chicks were tested either on food or on sand for 10 minutes. The control chicks, raised on the empty floor, showed typical levels of pecking to both sand and food, and there were no differences in pecking between the two stimuli. The chicks raised on food showed elevated rates of pecking to both stimuli during the first 2 minutes of the test; during the remaining 8 minutes, pecking at food remained at the same high level, while pecking at sand dropped quite rapidly until it was less than half the initial rate. The chicks raised on sand showed initial rates of pecking that were about half the rate of the control birds to both stimuli; by the end of the test, pecking food had increased slightly, while pecking sand dropped off still further until the chicks almost stopped. Thus, prolonged experience with either food or sand leads to discrimination within 10 minutes.

One final experiment will be mentioned which may give some insight into a possible mechanism responsible for this discrimination. In this experiment, all chicks were raised on an empty floor, but half the chicks received a total of 15 mealworms on days 2 and 3. At 72 hours, chicks were tested for 10 minutes on either sand or food. In chicks raised on the empty floor only, there were no differences between pecking food and sand, and no changes in pecking rate over the 10-minute test. Chicks that had been fed mealworms showed equal initial rates of pecking to both stimuli—at the same absolute level as the control chicks; but by the end of the 10-minute test, pecking at sand had been reduced to about 60% of the initial level, while pecking at food showed no reduction at all. This experiment seems to indicate that experience with nutritious objects facilitates later recognition of other nutritious objects; since the physical properties of mealworms and chick crumbs are so different it seems most likely that this facilitation is mediated at a metabolic level. It may be that food in the stomach "primes" (cf. Noirot, 1969) the chicks in some way such that subsequently ingested food provides quicker feedback than the food that was originally ingested. One possible mechanism for such an effect involves the development of active sugar transport in the chick intestine (Bogner, Braham, and McLain, 1966): ingestion of food affects the rate at which the sugar transport mechanism develops in newly-hatched chicks.

Comparisons with Diet Selection by Rats

The problems faced by young chicks learning to recognize food are similar in many ways to the problems faced by rats that must decide which food made them better if their previous diet was lacking essential nutrients or which food poisoned them. In all these cases the animal is in a situation where the effects of ingestion become apparent only some time after ingestion has occurred, and where there is frequently a choice among several alternatives. The problems of specific hungers and poison avoidance in rats have recently received considerable experimental attention, and much of this work has been reviewed by Rozin and Kalat (1971). In this section of the paper, I will consider two of the mechanisms that have been proposed to account for the results of experiments on specific hungers and then see how far similar mechanisms can be used to explain the behaviour of the chicks.

Learned aversions

A rat that has been deprived of thiamine for several days begins to lose both weight and its appetite. Following ingestion of thiamine the rat shows clear signs of recovery within a few hours. If thiamine is offered to a thiamine-deficient rat in one of two or more foods, most rats come to prefer the food containing the thiamine within the first few days. This situation is almost exactly analogous to the young chick placed in the midst of food crumbs and sand. Rozin (1967) was able to show that many of the problems involved in understanding the rat's behaviour became clearer when specific hungers were interpreted as a learned aversion to the deficient diet. Preference for a thiamine-rich diet could then be understood as a preference for novel foods by deficient rats (Rodgers, 1967).

A learned aversion interpretation can also be applied to some of the chick results described above. Naïve chicks that are given sand for 10 minutes and then are retested $1\frac{1}{2}$ hours later show increasingly large decreases in pecking as a function of age (see Fig. 1). A large amount of sand in a chick's stomach is presumably aversive; and since the chicks peck more as they grow older, it follows that increasing aversion to sand would be expected in the older chicks. A similar explanation could be applied to the low rate of pecking and to the discrimination between food and sand that appeared in chicks that had lived on sand for $2\frac{1}{2}$ days. When those chicks were presented with sand, pecking fell off very rapidly during the 10-minute session; but pecking at food showed no decline at all.

Results of other investigators who have studied changes in pecking preferences in chicks can also be explained in terms of learned aversions. Capretta (1961) associated the eating of red or green food with crop-injection of either sweetened milk, water, or strong salt solution; the positive and neutral consequences had no effect on subsequent preference, but the strong salt solution led to avoidance of the associated colour. R. Dawkins (1968) investigated the development of a pecking preference for solid, as opposed to flat, objects. In his study the waning of pecking with experience was strongly stimulus-specific. He suggests that the "increase in the strength of the solidity preference is caused by generalized waning of responsiveness to flat objects, as a result of unrewarded pecking at the flat walls of the living boxes". It has been shown that hens prefer pecking, and peck longer, at grains on a soft as opposed to a hard surface (Bayer, 1929). Thus, in the absence of reward, pecking at hard, flat objects may be aversive. In the other chick studies, chicks could pick up and mandibulate the stimuli; this may be sufficient reward to maintain pecking behaviour.

One problem with applying the learned aversion hypothesis to the chick results is that an opportunity to peck at sand does not always lead to a discrimination. Thus 3-day-old chicks that peck at sand for 10 minutes show the same pecking rate to both food and sand $1\frac{1}{2}$ hours later. And in the simultaneous discrimination study, chicks with $1\frac{1}{2}$ hours of experience on sand showed no sign of a discrimination when tested later for 10 minutes with both food and sand present at the same time. In both these cases, the absolute level of pecking was reduced, but it was reduced equally to both stimuli. These results suggest that the delayed effects of pecking at sand affect behaviour in more than one way. This problem will be considered again in the concluding section.

Finally, learned aversions can not explain the preference for food over sand that develops after long exposure to food or after ingestion of meal-worms. As suggested above, a priming mechanism could explain these results.

Feeding patterns

A second mechanism that operates to help rats solve the specific hunger problem is a rat's natural behaviour with respect to a choice among a number of new foods. In such a choice situation, vitamin-deficient rats (and to some extent normal rats as well) tend to restrict their meals to one food. Since meals are generally isolated in time, this feeding pattern allows the rat to associate each food with the consequences of ingesting it (Rozin, 1969b).

Chicks also tend to eat in meals. Observations in the laboratory indicate that, during the first week, chicks generally follow a cyclical pattern that begins with pecking and swallowing, followed by a period of general exploration (walking, looking, pecking), followed by quiet sitting and preening, followed by sleep. The whole cycle takes a quarter-hour or longer, depending on the age of the chick. A similar cycle is seen when the chicks live with a mother-hen. This pattern changes as the chicks grow older. But, at least up to 4 months of age, chicks continue to eat in meals which occur about twice an hour, on the average, during the light period (Jensen, Merrill, Reddy, and McGinnis, 1962; Duncan, Horne, Hughes, and Wood-Gush, 1970).

On the other hand, young chicks do not seem to restrict their meals to one stimulus. In an experiment not yet reported, naïve chicks were tested for 10 minutes on a floor covered half with food and half with sand. Each chick was given three such tests on day 3 (each test was separated from the next by 2 hours) and a fourth test on the morning of day 4. The data were broken down into five 2-minute intervals for each test. In the first two minutes, 23 of 30 chicks had pecked at least once at each stimulus; by the fourth minute of the test, 29 of the chicks had pecked at both stimuli. In fact, all 30 chicks pecked at both stimuli in each of the first three tests; and 29 chicks pecked at both stimuli in the fourth test. It is thus not surprising that the chicks did not learn to discriminate between food and sand under the conditions of this experiment. Four of the chicks preferred food on all tests and 9 chicks preferred sand on all tests. The other 17 chicks changed their preference during the course of the experiment; 9 of these preferred food on the last test, and 8 preferred sand.

It is possible that chicks might exhibit feeding patterns that would lead them to discriminate between sand and food more quickly if the experimental conditions were less restricted. M. Dawkins (1971) has shown, for example, that young chicks peck at green and orange rice grains in runs of pecks to one colour that depart markedly from a random order. Observations on the pecking patterns of newly-hatched chicks to chick crumbs and sand over a period of several hours might uncover high correlations between particular pecking patterns and the rapid development of discrimination. Recent experiments by Hogan-Warburg (personal communication) have demonstrated that separate 15-minute experiences with sand and chick crumbs are sufficient to establish very strong preferences for the food when the chicks are given a choice test an hour or two later. These results imply that chicks do learn to discriminate if they have an opportunity to associate each stimulus with the consequences of ingesting it.

Conclusion

The experiments on development of food recognition in chicks have brought to light a number of results that are difficult to explain in terms of traditional learning theory. These include the fact that ingestion of food does not affect pecking rate before the chicks are three days old; that ingestion of food does not affect the pecking rate in 3-day-old chicks until about an hour after ingestion; and that ingestion of food or sand, in many cases, does not affect subsequent discrimination between these stimuli even though there are large effects on pecking rate. These results will be discussed in turn under the headings: critical periods; long-delay learning; and interrelationships among stimulus, response, and reinforcer.

Critical periods

Ingestion of food has no effect on pecking rate until chicks are 3 days old. This finding implies a notable constraint on learning in 1- and 2-day-old chicks. Possibly related to this finding is the report by Hess (1962, 1964) that food reinforcement supports long-term discrimination learning in domestic chicks between 3 and 5 days of age, but is not effective either before or after this period. He suggests, in fact, that "there is a definite 'critical period' during which food reinforcement is most effective in modifying innate preferences for pecking at certain objects". (Hess, 1964, p. 1136.) Other studies on several species of birds have also provided some evidence that early experience with particular foods may influence later food preferences (Rabinowitch, 1968; Capretta, 1969) and that this experience may be most effective during a certain sensitive period (Rabinowitch, 1969).

Unfortunately, in my experiments, ingesting food does not seem to modify pecking preferences for food and sand. For example, in the simultaneous discrimination experiment described above, $1\frac{1}{2}$ hours experience pecking food on day 3 had no influence on pecking preference in a 10-minute choice test $1\frac{1}{2}$ hours later. A possible explanation of this apparent discrepancy will be considered later. Further, my experiments were not carried out for long enough to provide evidence concerning the end of a critical period, such as that proposed by Hess. It should also be noted that the age at which experience affects pecking rate may be unrelated to the age at which experience affects discrimination learning.

It is natural to inquire why food ingestion does not appear to support learning before day 3, and one reason frequently put forward is that the changing effectiveness of food is associated with the absorption of the yolk sac. In discussing other examples of critical or sensitive periods, Hinde (1970, ch. 23) has pointed out that numerous factors may all play a role in setting limits on sensitive periods for learning—and the present case is no exception. In a functional sense, absorption of the yolk sac may be the reason why chicks do not *need* to react to food before day 3, but there are several reasons for believing that changes in the yolk sac are not responsible, in a causal sense, for the changing effectiveness of food. On the one hand, yolk absorption is a gradual process that is not complete until chicks are more than 6 days old (Parker, 1929), yet changes in the effects of food appear rather abruptly between days 2 and 3. On the other hand, many changes are still taking place in the anatomy and physiology of the chick's digestive system during the first few days after hatching, as mentioned above (Bogner *et al.*, 1966). Any one (or more) of these changes could be responsible for the changing effectiveness of food.

Long-delay learning

The pecking rate of 3-day-old chicks increases markedly between 40 and 80 minutes after the chicks have ingested their first food; and this increase in pecking occurs only if pecking and food ingestion are closely associated in time. Whenever a response increases as a result of the contingency between that response and a particular stimulus change, it is conventional to speak of that stimulus change as a reinforcer. In the present case, use of the concept of reinforcement raises several problems, but there is no obvious alternative formulation. Two closely related problems— identification of the reinforcer and the time factors involved in the response-reinforcer contingency—are discussed in this section.

One way to pose the question is this: Is reinforcement immediate and its effect delayed, or is reinforcement delayed and its effect immediate? The former alternative implies that ingesting food has a positive reinforcing effect on pecking that is somehow counterbalanced by a negative motivational effect; the motivational effect presumably dissipates with a time course of about one hour. In experiments described above, varying the amount of food ingested had no effect on the time when increased pecking appeared, and chicks that had prior experience with food did not show an increase in pecking. These results suggest that satiation and hunger are not responsible for the delayed increase in pecking. Other motivational effects that are independent of the amount eaten might be invoked to explain these findings. However, on the initial exposure, a chick's behaviour towards food is very similar to its behaviour towards sand for at least several minutes; it is thus difficult to argue that the immediate motivational effects of ingesting food are so different from the effects of ingesting sand the first time a chick experiences either stimulus.

Careful consideration of the forced-feeding experiments described above also poses problems for an immediate reinforcement interpretation of the results. In these experiments chicks were allowed to peck at sand for 10 minutes. In fact, many of the chicks hardly pecked at all during the last two minutes of the test; a conservative estimate (assuming a random distribution of pecking throughout the interval) is that 7 seconds elapsed between a chick's last peck and the end of the test. An estimated 3 to 5 seconds then elapsed before the chick was picked up and brought to the food container for forced feeding. Thus, there was an average minimum of 10 to 12 seconds between the last peck at sand and food ingestion. In a traditional learning theory framework, these data mean that after 150 unreinforced pecks, a chick is reinforced for the first time in its life *once* with a delay of more than 10 seconds; the chick then shows a 50% increase in pecking rate $1\frac{1}{2}$ hours later! Further, the data suggest that it is inappropriate to consider food in the mouth as the reinforcer, at least in naïve chicks, since any tactual or gustatory differences between food and sand are not reflected in a chick's behaviour for at least several minutes. Thus, the delay in reinforcement must be considerably longer than 10 seconds.

A look at the available physiological evidence does not help much in deciding how long reinforcement is delayed. For example, an early study determined that within 5 minutes after ingestion of a starchy meal, the blood-sugar level of deprived, adult fowl rose distinctly (Henry *et al.*,

1933). More recently, Steffens (1969a, b) has developed a method for measuring the blood-glucose level in the rat using blood samples from unanaesthetized, undisturbed animals. He has found that blood-glucose level rises sharply within *two minutes* after the start of a carbohydrate-rich meal. By using radioactive ^{14}C-glucose in the test meal, Steffens showed that the rapid rise was due entirely to absorption of glucose from the intestinal tract. Very recently, Hall (1971) has shown that injection of glucose solution into the crop of 3- and 4-day-old chicks leads to behavioural effects within seconds. One of these effects is increased pecking. These data all suggest that internal changes occurring within a few seconds or minutes of food ingestion might be the source of reinforcement.

Other considerations, however, suggest that it is probably premature to identify reinforcement with internal changes that occur shortly after food ingestion. In the first place, although blood-sugar level shows a significant increase within two minutes of ingestion, the level continues to rise for at least half an hour in rats, and even longer in adult fowl. A certain level, or change in level, may be necessary before reinforcement effects are seen. Second, studies on glucose metabolism in newly hatched chicks, already mentioned above (Bogner, *et al.*, 1966), show that intestinal active sugar transport mechanisms are still developing during the first few days after hatching. It is therefore unwise to generalize from results on adult fowl. (It should be noted that Hall's chicks had already eaten food before crop loading of glucose solution began, cf. p. 128.) Finally, metabolic factors, other than blood-sugar, may determine whether or not reinforcement occurs.

This example of learning with a long delay of reinforcement is similar to previously-analysed examples in some ways, but there are also differences. Like previous examples, the present case involves the feeding system and learning occurs very rapidly, often in one trial (for reviews see Revusky and Garcia, 1970; Rozin and Kalat, 1971). Most previous evidence, however, involves rats learning to avoid certain substances that have been followed by sickness sometime later (e.g. Garcia, *et al.*, 1966; Rozin, 1969a). A number of studies have now shown that learned associations over long delays also occur when behaviour has positive consequences, though the effects are usually of smaller magnitude and take longer to develop (e.g. Garcia, *et al.*, 1967; Rozin 1969b; Revusky and Garcia, 1970; Green and Garcia, 1971). Unlike all these studies, however, the chicks do not seem to be associating a particular stimulus with the consequences of food ingestion, since they show an equal increase in pecking at both food and sand regardless of which stimulus they were pecking prior to food ingestion.

Interrelationships among stimulus, response, and reinforcer

Ingestion of food or sand in limited amounts does not affect subsequent discrimination between these stimuli even though ingestion of the same limited amounts leads to large changes in pecking rate. This finding implies that the delayed consequences of pecking are specific to the act of pecking itself. A similar relationship between pecking and food ingestion has also turned up in a very different kind of experiment by Sterritt and Smith (1965). These investigators gave 3-day-old domestic chicks visual discrimination training in a Y-maze. Separate groups of chicks received one of four consequences for making a correct choice: (1) nothing; (2) an opportunity to peck at immovable objects; (3) injection of liquid food directly into the oesophagus; (4) an opportunity to peck plus injection of food. The only group in which most of the chicks learned the discrimination was the last: the group that pecked and received food in the goal box. Only 4 of 10 chicks in the food-only group learned the discrimination; and in this group there was a significant positive correlation between amount of pecking in the goal box and efficiency in learning. Only 1 of 19 chicks in the other two groups learned the discrimination. These results suggest that neither pecking nor food ingestion by itself is sufficient to provide reinforcement, but rather a special interaction between them is necessary.

It has been seen that ingestion of food reinforces the response of pecking, but one further implication of my results and those of Sterritt and Smith is that ingestion of food does not reinforce other responses. My results also suggest that ingestion of sand has similar, but opposite effects: that is, ingestion of sand acts as a punishment for pecking, but does not affect other responses. Once the association between pecking and food ingestion is established, pecking food objects can serve to reinforce other behaviour.

Of course, the results of Sterritt and Smith apparently provide other difficulties in interpreting the chick results I have obtained, in that some of their 3-day-old chicks learned a visual discrimination in as few as 4 trials. Likewise, the results of Hess (1962, 1964) mentioned earlier provide further evidence that 3-day-old chicks can learn a visual discrimination at a very high level with only two hours experience. A very important difference between their situation and mine, however, is that their chicks were learning about a stimulus, in the presence of which pecking was reinforced. My chicks were learning about which stimulus they should peck.

One resolution of these apparently contradictory findings is provided by a reinterpretation of Hess's results. It may be that Hess's results do not demonstrate food imprinting, but rather demonstrate imprinting to a situation in which food is to be found. Three-day-old chicks may, indeed, be especially sensitive to learning about where in the environment they should peck. As long as the objects they ingest do not have any adverse effects, they do *not* learn immediately which particular objects to peck. If one considers that chicks, under natural conditions (including the barnyard), eat many different kinds of food, it would be highly disadvantageous to stop trying out new foods as soon as one food was found. Chicks mentioned above, that became mealworm specialists on day 3, in fact died of starvation before they were a week old! If the objects a chick ingests are not nutritious (e.g. sand), it tends to stop pecking and to move elsewhere. Previous results show that young chicks observed on a sand-covered floor do show more locomotion than chicks on a food-covered or empty floor (Hogan, 1971, p. 140). These mechanisms function to allow chicks to ingest the wide variety of foods that is necessary to provide all their nutritional requirements. The preference for particular foods that does develop with continued exposure could be based upon learned aversions and on occurrences of long runs of pecking at a single stimulus, as well as on the immediate effects of pecking and ingestion discussed in the first section.

The story of how newly hatched chicks learn to recognize food is still incomplete, yet at least two general principles seem to emerge from the data. First, many of the mechanisms that lead the chick to its goal appear to be specially adapted to the conditions encountered by a newly-hatched chick, and these mechanisms frequently seem to defy some of the laws of traditional learning theory. Thus, critical or sensitive periods, associations over long delays, and reinforcement of the pecking response with no concomitant discrimination of the object being pecked, all play a role in the development of food recognition. Second, the very numerosity of mechanisms involved in leading the chick to its goal brings to mind Waddington's (1966) concept of canalization of development. This concept refers to the tendency of a developing (embryological) system to attain its normal end result even when one or more of the normal casual factors in development is upset. The development of food recognition provides a good example of post-embryological canalization: neither the behaviour of a mother-hen nor the immediate effects of pecking and ingestion nor the delayed effects of ingestion is necessary for the development of food recognition, and all these factors can partially compensate for disturbances that occur when one or more of these factors malfunctions.

Acknowledgements

This paper was written at the Sub-Department of Animal Behaviour, University of Cambridge while I was on sabbatical leave from the University of Toronto. I am grateful for the facilities which have been made available to me during my stay, and would like to thank the members of the Sub-Department and especially R. A. Hinde for their kind hospitality. I would also like to thank R. A. Hinde, A. J. Hogan-Warburg, J. Stevenson-Hinde, and J. M. Daly for helpful comments on the manuscript. The research reported in this paper was supported by a grant from the National Research Council of Canada.

References

Bateson, P. P. G. (1964). Effect of similarity between rearing and testing conditions on chicks' following and avoidance responses. *J. comp. physiol. Psychol.* **57**, 100–103.

Bayer, E. (1929). Beiträge zur Zweikomponententheorie des Hungers (Versuche mit Hühnern). *Z. Psychol.* **112**, 1–54.

Beck, G. (1930). Neue Beiträge zur Zweikomponententheorie des Hungers (Versuche mit Hühnern). *Z. Psychol.* **118**, 283–349.

Bogner, P. H., Braham, A. H., and McLain, P. L. (1966). Glucose metabolism during ontogeny of intestinal active sugar transport in the chick. *J. Physiol.* **187**, 307–321.

Capretta, P. J. (1961). An experimental modification of food preference in chickens. *J. comp. physiol. Psychol.* **54**, 238–242.

Capretta, P. J. (1969). The establishment of food preferences in chicks *Gallus gallus*. *Anim. Behav.* **17**, 229–231.

Collias, N. E. (1952). The development of social behavior in birds. *Auk.* **69**, 127–159.

Dawkins, M. (1971). Shifts of 'attention' in chicks during feeding. *Anim. Behav.* **19**, 575–582.

Dawkins, R. (1968). The ontogeny of a pecking preference in domestic chicks. *Z. Tierpsychol.* **25**, 170–186.

Dawkins, R. and Impekoven, M. (1969). The 'peck/no-peck decision-maker' in the black-headed gull chick. *Anim. Behav.* **17**, 243–251.

Dove, W. F. (1935). A study of individuality in the nutritive instincts and of the causes and effects of variations in the selection of food. *Amer. Naturalist* **69**, 469–544.

Duncan, I. J. H., Horne, A. R., Hughes, B. O. and Wood-Gush, D. G. M. (1970). The pattern of food intake in female Brown Leghorn fowls as recorded in a Skinner box. *Anim. Behav.* **18**, 245–255.

Fantz, R. L. (1957). Form preferences in newly hatched chicks. *J. comp. physiol. Psychol.* **50**, 422–430.

Franck, D. (1966). Möglichkeiten zur vergleichenden Analyse auslösender und richtender Reize mit Hilfe des Attrappenversuchs, ein Vergleich der Successiv- und Simultanmethode. *Behaviour* **27**, 150–159.

Garcia, J., Ervin, F. R. and Koelling, R. A. (1966). Learning with prolonged delay of reinforcement. *Psychon. Sci.* **5**, 121–122.

Garcia, J., Ervin, F. R., Yorke, C. H. and Koelling, R. A. (1967). Conditioning with delayed vitamin injection. *Science* **155**, 716–718.

Goodwin, E. B. and Hess, E. H. (1969). Innate visual form preferences in the pecking behavior of young chicks. *Behaviour* **34**, 223–237.

Green, K. F. and Garcia, J. (1971). Recuperation from illness: flavor enchancement for rats. *Science* **173**, 749–751.

Hall, T. J. (1971). Effects on feeding, aggression and copulation of sugars given intracranially or enterally. Unpublished Ph.D. thesis, Univ. of Sussex.

Halpern, B. P. (1962). Gustatory nerve response in the chicken. *Am. J. Physiol.* **203**, 541–544.

Hellwald, H. (1931). Untersuchungen über Triebstärken bei Tieren. *Z. Psychol.* **123**, 94–141.

Henry, K. M. Macdonald, A. J. and Magee, H. W. (1933). Observations on the functions of the alimentary canal in fowls, *J. exper. Biol.* **10**, 153–171.

Hess, E. H. (1956). Natural preferences of chicks and ducklings for objects of different colors. *Psychol. Reports* **2**, 477–483.

Hess, E. H. (1962). Imprinting and the "critical period" concept. *In* "Roots of Behavior", (Bliss, E. L., ed.). Harper, New York.

Hess. E. H. (1964). Imprinting in birds. *Science* **146**, 1128–1139.

Hinde, R. A. (1970). "Animal Behaviour", 2nd Ed. McGraw-Hill, New York.

Hogan, J. A. (1966). An experimental study of conflict and fear: an analysis of behavior of young chicks toward a mealworm. II. The behavior of chicks which eat the mealworm. *Behaviour.* **27**, 273–289.

Hogan, J. A. (1971). The development of a hunger system in young chicks. *Behaviour.* **39**, 128–201.

Hogan, J. A. (1973a). The development of food recognition in young chicks: I. Maturation and nutrition. *J. comp. physiol. Psychol.* (in press).

Hogan, J. A. (1973b). The development of food recognition in young chicks: II. Learned associations over long delays. *J. comp. physiol. Psychol.* (in press).

Hughes, B. O. and Wood-Gush, D. G. M. (1971). A specific appetite for calcium in domestic chickens. *Anim. Behav.* **19**, 490–499.

Jensen, L. S., Merrill, L. H., Reddy, C. V., and McGinnis, J. (1962). Observations on eating patterns and rate of food passage of birds fed pelleted and unpelleted diets. *Poultry Science* **41**, 1414–1419.

Katz, D. (1937). "Animals and Men: Studies in Comparative Psychology." Longmans, Green, London.

Kitchell, R. L., Ström, L. and Zotterman, Y. (1959). Electrophysiological studies of thermal and taste reception in chickens and pigeons. *Acta Physiol. Scand.* **46**, 133–151.

Kovach, J. K. (1971). Interaction of innate and acquired: color preferences and early exposure learning in chicks. *J. comp. physiol. Psychol.* **75**, 386–398.

Lindenmaier, P. and Kare, M. R. (1959). The taste end-organs of the chicken. *Poultry Science* **38**, 545–550.

Morgan, C. L. (1896). "Habit and Instinct." Arnold, London.

Noirot, E. (1969). Changes in responsiveness to young in the adult mouse: V. Priming. *Anim. Behav.* **17**, 542–546.

Parker, S. L. (1929). Effects of early handicaps on chickens as measured by yolk absorption and body weight to twenty days of age. *Hilgardia.* **4**, 1–56.

Rabinowitch, V. E. (1968). The role of experience in the development of food preferences in gull chicks. *Anim. Behav.* **16**, 425–428.

Rabinowitch, V. E. (1969). The role of experience in the development and retention of seed preferences in zebra finches. *Behav.* **33**, 222–236.

Revusky, S. H. and Garcia, J. (1970). Learned associations over long delays. *In* "The Psychology of Learning and Motivation", Vol. 4, (G. H. Bower, ed.). Academic Press, New York.

Rodgers, W. L. (1967). Specificity of specific hungers. *J. comp. physiol. Psychol.* **64**, 49–58.

Rozin, P. (1967). Specific aversions as a component of specific hungers. *J. comp. physiol. Psychol.* **64**, 237–242.

Rozin, P. (1969a). Central or peripheral mediation of learning with long CS-US intervals in the feeding system. *J. comp. physiol. Psychol.* **67**, 421–429.

Rozin, P. (1969b). Adaptive food sampling patterns in vitamin deficient rats. *J. comp. physiol. Psychol.* **69**, 126–132.

Rozin, P. and Kalat, J. W. (1971). Specific hungers and poison avoidance as adaptive specializations of learning. *Psychol. Rev.* **78**, 459–486.

Shreck, P. K., Sterritt, G. M., Smith, M. P. and Stilton, D. W. (1963). Environmental factors in the development of eating in chicks. *Anim. Behav.* **11**, 306–309.

Steffens, A. B. (1969a). Rapid absorption of glucose in the intestinal tract of the rat after ingestion of a meal. *Physiol. Behav.* **4**, 829–832.

Steffens, A. B. (1969b). A method for frequent sampling of blood and continuous infusion of fluids in the rat without disturbing the animal. *Physiol. Behav.* **4**, 833–836.

Sterritt, G. M. and Smith, M. P. (1965). Reinforcement effects of specific components of feeding in young Leghorn chicks. *J. comp. physiol. Psychol.* **59**, 171–175.

Tolman, C. W. (1968). The varieties of social stimulation in the feeding behaviour of domestic chicks. *Behaviour* **30**, 275–286.

Turner, E. R. A. (1964). Social feeding in birds. *Behaviour* **15**, 284–318.

Waddington, C. H. (1966). "Principles of Development and Differentiation". Macmillan, New York.

Wood-Gush, D. G. M. (1971). "The Behaviour of the Domestic Fowl." Heinemann, London.

7

Stimulus Relevance and Homeostasis

by D. J. McFarland

It is now widely recognized that there are important behavioural links in homeostatic mechanisms, and that much behaviour is ultimately concerned with the maintenance of an optimal *milieu intérieur*. In particular, hunger and thirst differ from some other aspects of homeostasis in that appropriate behaviour is essential for maintenance of the *status quo*. The deprived animal cannot compensate for loss of water or energy, it can only reduce the rate of loss. In my experience, it is easier to train an animal to obtain a reward by operant means when the reward is relevant to an homeostatic system in which appetitive behaviour normally plays an important role. For example, Barbary doves (*Streptopelia risoria*) seem to have poor energy conservation, and are very easy to train to work for food rewards. They have quite good water conservation mechanisms, and are harder to train to peck for water rewards. They have extremely effective temperature regulation (McFarland and Budgell, 1970), and it is very difficult indeed to train them to regulate environmental temperature by operant means (Budgell, 1971). Thus there may be constraints on learning corresponding to the weighting given to behavioural aspects of homeostasis within a particular system. In addition, it seems likely that the relationship between the animal's normal behavioural repertoire and the operant response required by the experimenter may constrain learning (Chapters 8 to 13). Pecking is presumably a more relevant response for a dove in a feeding situation than in a temperature regulation situation.

There may not always be a one-to-one relationship between a particular activity and its physiological consequences. Thus in behavioural thermoregulation the animal may associate a particular activity with a one-dimensional (univalent) consequence, namely a change in body temperature. Feeding activity, however, has multi-dimensional consequences relating to the many nutrients involved. These consequences will be ambivalent when a particular food has a number of components.

If we ask what principles are involved in the execution, by the animal, of the behaviour patterns that are required to achieve certain physiological consequences, the answer that has traditionally been given is fairly clear. The behaviour is governed by a conventional type of negative feedback mechanism, by which the physiological consequences of behaviour, or their short-term neurological representatives, progressively reduce the level of motivation as the animal becomes more satiated. This is the type of thinking that underlies Cannon's (1932) concept of homeostasis and governs much current research into physiological (e.g. Cross, 1964) and behavioural (McFarland, 1970) aspects of regulation. However, the simple negative feedback model is not adequate to account for the complexity of the situation that arises in nature. Even the introduction of refinements to the classical regulatory model, such as positive feedback and feed-forward (McFarland, 1970), does little to account for possible ambivalent consequences of ingestion, or for changes in the constitution of available food.

McFarland and Sibly (1972) have considered some theoretical problems that arise when the consequences of behaviour are ambivalent. Their main point is that constraints may be set up such that the animal cannot satisfy its needs in the face of environmental ambivalence. This poses serious problems for the stability of physiological state (Sibly and McFarland, 1973), and it appears that there must be some sort of "adaptive control" (McFarland, 1971) by which the animal is able to change the properties of its regulatory mechanisms to suit environmental circumstances. The adaptive control can occur, either through the medium of physiological acclimatization, or by means of changes in behavioural strategy. The manner in which these two mechanisms interact poses interesting problems (Sibly and McFarland, 1973).

Adaptive control is necessary to cope with changes in the constitution of available food. A simple case is discussed by McFarland (1971). Barbary doves (*Streptopelia risoria*), that habitually drink distilled water, are able to regulate very accurately when allowed a single drinking session per day. When given 0.5% saline, which they cannot distinguish by taste, they drink it as if it were distilled water, presumably because their short-term satiation mechanisms are calibrated to distilled water. However, in terms of physiological consequences, saline is much less hydrating than water and much more is needed to satisfy thirst. It is possible to show that the doves can adapt to drinking saline, and this appears to be achieved by recalibration of the short-term satiation mechanisms; a true instance of adaptive control. Generalizing from this example, it seems obvious that an animal that relies on short-term satiation mechanisms to tell it how much to eat or drink at a particular time, must be able to recalibrate those mechanisms in relation to the ultimate physiological consequences of ingestion. Although animals may sometimes be able to detect changes in the constitution of food by taste, this could account for only a few of the many changes that are possible. It seems more probable that animals learn how much to eat as a result of experiencing the physiological consequences of eating particular foods.

In addition to learning how much to eat, animals also have to learn what to eat. As Rozin and Kalat (1971) point out, "it is hard to believe that the rat comes equipped with prewired recognition systems for each of the many substances for which it can show a specific hunger".

Evidence for the importance of learning was available at quite an early stage of research into specific hungers. Scott and Verney (1947) offered a distinctively flavoured vitamin supplemented food and an unflavoured vitamin deficient food to vitamin deficient rats. After a preference had developed for the flavoured food, the flavour was switched to the deficient food, but the rats continued to prefer the flavoured, now deficient, food. The main problem in interpreting this type of result was the long delay between the ingestive behaviour and its physiological, and presumably reinforcing, consequences. In terms of traditional learning theory, learning is not possible under such conditions, and many attempts were made to bypass the problem by postulating short-term feedback provided by an enhanced ability to taste the substance responsible for the deficiency; or by postulating some mediation process, such as a prolonged aftertaste resulting from feeding. Many of these objections were dispensed with by means of an innovation introduced by Garcia et al. (1955) who fed rats a harmless substance and then produced a physiological aftereffect by an independent means. Gamma radiation was used in this study, and the results showed that the rats developed an aversion to previously preferred saccharin-flavoured water. Garcia et al., (1961) pointed out the possible importance of this type of effect, and cited nine confirmatory studies, but learning theorists persisted in ignoring the phenomenon. The situation was eventually remedied by the publication of admirable reviews by Revusky and Garcia (1970) and by Rozin and Kalat (1971). These have received widespread attention, and deservedly so, since they provide convincing evidence on the generality of the phenomenon, disposed effectively of numerous conceivable artefacts, and provide a reasonable explanation for the occurrence of bait shyness and specific hungers.

The following paradigm case is presented by Revusky and Garcia (1970), "An animal is made to consume a flavoured substance, such as saccharin solution, and is later subjected to toxic after effects produced by such independent means as injection of poison or X-irradiation. After it has recovered from the toxicosis, the animal will avoid consuming the flavoured substance. The animal behaves as though it thinks that consumption of the substance made it sick. This specific aversion will not develop if toxicosis occurs in the absence of previous consumption, or if consumption occurs without being followed by toxicosis. It differs from the types of learning usually investigated in that it can occur after a single pairing even when the interval between ingestion and toxicosis is a number of hours."

An important step in the solution to these problems is the realization that the development of specific aversions has much in common with the development of specific hungers. As Rozin and Kalat (1971) point out, a vitamin deficient diet is a slowly acting poison. It is unreasonable to hold that rats show innate aversions to man-made poisons, and it is unlikely that they have innate aversions to dietary deficiencies. Somehow the rat must learn to associate eating a particular food with delayed physiological consequences. For this to happen, there must be distinctive markers for the two events. Let us consider these two types of marker in turn.

Stimulus Relevance as an Ingestion Marker

The problem here is that there are ostensibly many possible candidates which a rat could associate with physiological disturbance. During the interval between eating a poisoned food and suffering toxic effects, there will generally be numerous events, including a number of meals, with which the toxicosis could be associated. This problem has generally been met by the introduction of such concepts as "preparedness" (Seligman, 1970), "belongingness" (Garcia and Koelling, 1966), and "stimulus relevance" (Capretta, 1961). "Stimulus relevance" refers to the principle that the associative strength of a cue with some consequence depends, in part, on the nature of the consequence (Dietz and Capretta, 1967). Revusky and Garcia (1970) claim that the "relevance principle responsible for association of delayed physiological consequences with flavours is that flavour has a high associative strength relative to physiological consequence, while an exteroceptive stimulus has low associative strength (at least in the mammal). If the consequence is an event which normally emanates from the environment, such as shock or receipt of a pellet of food, the converse is true." The evidence in favour of this view is impressive. In their "bright, noisy, water" experiment, Garcia and Koelling (1966) provided light, sound and taste cues simultaneously with either electric shock or poisoning, in different groups of animals. The shocked animals avoided the light and sound, but not the taste cue. The poisoned animals avoided the taste, but not the light or sound. Garcia et al. (1968)

used two sizes of Purina Chow pellet, coated with flour or powdered sugar, or uncoated. The design of their experiment is summarised in Table I.

TABLE 1

Plan of the experiment by Garcia *et al.*, (1968) and the results expected on the basis of stimulus relevance.

Type of Stimulus	Type of Stimulus	Expected Result
Size of pellet	Shock	Aversion
Size of pellet	Toxicosis	No aversion
Flavour	Toxicosis	Aversion
Flavour	Shock	No aversion

That is, rats ate pellets differing in size, or in flavour, and were concurrently punished with electric shock, or with X-irradiation. The results indicate that eating pellets distinguishable by flavour was markedly suppressed by irradiation, but not by shock. Conversely, eating pellets differing in size was suppressed by shock, but not by toxicosis. Thus the result expected on the basis of stimulus relevance (Table I) was confirmed.

Rozin and Kalat (1971) suggest that part of the weakness of exteroceptive cues in relation to toxicosis derives from a very rapid decay of their associability with time. Rozin obtained rapid learning of aversion to the location and shape of the drinking vessel when apomorphine was injected during drinking from the appropriate vessel but not when injection was delayed by 30 minutes. A number of experiments by Brower (1969) indicated that birds can readily learn aversions to the sight of food, and experiments by Wilcoxon *et al.*, (1971) indicated that Japanese quail, in contrast to rats, learn poison-based aversions more rapidly to the colour than to the taste of a solution. Rozin and Kalat (1971) propose that the critical dimension of poison-based aversion learning may be "eating-related cues versus other cues", and that the relevant cues would vary from species to species.

Rozin and Kalat (1971) also claim evidence for "intramodality belongingness", which they call "salience". Kalat and Rozin (1970) found that rats tend to associate poisoning with some novel solutions more than others. "Rats drank one novel solution briefly, 15 minutes later drank a second novel solution, and another 15 minutes later were poisoned. The following day the rats were offered both solutions simultaneously. Under these conditions, certain solutions, which we describe as highly salient, became more aversive than others. The salience of a solution proved to be

L

a more potent predictor of amount of acquired aversion than temporal proximity to poisoning. It was found possible to rank novel solutions in a stable, transitive "salience" hierarchy, such that each solution proved more salient (associable with poisoning) than all solutions lower on the list. It is not clear to me how the concept of salience has different explanatory power to the concept of relevance, since both are defined in terms of associability with poisoning, or its equivalent. Nevertheless, it is clear that novelty does play an important role in determining which food is relevant.

Rodgers and Rozin (1966) found that thiamine deficient rats show an immediate marked preference for new foods, even when the new food is thiamine deficient and the old food has thiamine supplement. The preference reverses in a few days. Rodgers (1967) failed to obtain a specific hunger to thiamine when deficient rats were offered a choice of a deficient novel diet, or the same novel diet supplemented with thiamine. Moreover, separate groups of thiamine deficient rats and pyridoxine deficient rats showed no preference when offered their basal diet in two forms; one supplemented with thiamine, the other with pyridoxine. However, Rozin (1968) found that rats suffering from dietary deficiency, or from effects of poisoning, and faced with a choice among a familiar safe diet, a familiar aversive diet, and new diet, showed a preference for the familiar safe food. There were no significant differences between deficient and poisoned groups of rats, supporting the view that we can consider specific hungers as parallel to poisoning. In the view of Rozin and Kalat (1971), the rat learns to avoid the deficient food when it is the only diet available. Because of this learned aversion, rats show an immediate preference for a novel food, thus making it possible to learn about its consequences. In addition, the rat's feeding pattern maximizes the possibility of associating each diet with its physiological consequences, since meals tend to be separated in time and to consist of a single food (Rozin, 1969). This behaviour, together with the rat's sensitivity to changes in available food, probably does much to mark out the particular meal which is most likely to be responsible for subsequent illness, or recover from dietary deficiency. It is the relevance of the stimuli characteristic of each meal that serves as a marker for association with subsequent physiological changes.

Since both "relevance" and "salience" serve the same function, it seems unnecessary to separate them. The Dietz and Capretta (1967) definition of stimulus relevance, favoured by Revusky and Garcia (1970), is sufficiently general to embrace the arguments of Rozin and Kalat (1971). Thus we could define the *degree of stimulus relevance* in relation to ingestion, as the heterogeneous sum of ingestion-related cues, including both inter- and intra-modality effects.

Sickness as a Marker for Physiological State

Most workers are agreed that, with the exception of certain specific factors such as sodium and water content, the characteristic of physiological state that is important in this type of problem is a general state of "sickness" or "wellbeing", rather than specific information concerning the nature of dietary deficiency or toxicosis. Harris et al., (1933) offered deficient rats a choice among a large variety of foods with only one containing B vitamins in significant amounts. They found that the rats were unable to select the vitamin enriched food, and this type of finding has been well substantiated. This type of inability suggests that information concerning the consequences of ingestion is general rather than specific. In order to obtain a well-defined concept of this type of general physiological indicator, it may be worthwhile to define precisely what is meant by physiological state.

The internal environment of an animal can be viewed as a system of interacting variables, which is subject to influences resulting from changes in the animal's behaviour. The state of any biological system can in principle be characterized in terms of the state variables of the system, the minimal number of state variables necessary for a complete description of the system being the same as the number of degrees of freedom of the system (McFarland, 1971; Milsum, 1966; Rosen, 1970). The state of the internal environment can thus be represented in terms of a finite number of physiological state variables, each of which can be represented as an axis of an n dimensional hyperspace. The state at any time can thus be represented in terms of a vector [z] (Sibly and McFarland, 1973). In terms of this definition, the degree of sickness is a state function, where "A state function is any scalar function of the state variables, and possible time, whose value at any instant of time is completely determined by the values of the state variables at that instant and the time itself" (Schultz and Melsa, 1967). Thus the state function Z might be a simple sum of the elements of [z], viz:

$$Z = z_1 + z_2 + z_3 \ldots + z_n,$$

or it might be a more complex function, viz:

$$Z = z_1^2 + z_2^2 + z_3^2 \ldots + z_n^2.$$

For the present purpose, it is sufficient to suppose that Z is a specific function of [z], so that degree of sickness, for example, might be representable as the sum of the deviations of each of the physiological state variables from its optimal value. The theory would then say that the degree of stimulus relevance R is associated with some function of Z. The question of what function of Z is an important one.

Firstly, it is clear that the association cannot be with Z itself, because the strength of association must be related to degree of improvement, which is independent of the initial condition of Z. Direct association with Z would mean that the absolute value of Z following ingestion of a distinctively flavoured food would be the prime influence of the strength of association. Clearly, it must be changes in Z that are important. In other words, the derivative of $Z = dZ/dt = \dot{Z}$ should appear in the association function. A second point concerns the question of whether changes in Z in both directions are effective in determining association between ingestion and physiological consequences.

Rozin and Kalat (1971) consider the question "are there learned preferences as well as learned aversions?". Their answer seems to be somewhat equivocal. They note that "Much of the evidence which appears to demonstrate positive preferences can be reinterpreted in terms of learned aversions." Both Rozin and Kalat (1971) and Revusky and Garcia (1970) note that positive preference effects are both small and difficult to obtain in comparison with learned aversions. On the other hand, Rozin and Kalat (1971) note some recent experiments which present "serious challenges to a pure aversion model". Garcia et al. (1967) and Campbell (1969) found that thiamine deficient rats show an increase in their absolute intake of a flavoured solution which has been paired with recovery from deficiency. Zahorik and Maier (1969) found that rats prefer the taste associated with recovery to both the taste associated with deficiency and a novel taste.

To my mind, the problem can be resolved in common sense terms. Considering the frame of reference within which the problem is at present conceived, it is impossible for an animal both to learn to prefer flavoured substances on the basis of improved physiological state, and to avoid them on the opposite basis. The two processes will simply cancel each other out. For example, an animal that learns to avoid a flavour because of subsequent sickness must also learn to approach the same flavour when it recovers from the sickness. This view can be made more explicit by reference to Fig. 1.

This figure illustrates a hypothetical case, in which a rat ingests a distinctively flavoured food (R) and receives an injection (I) some time later. The flavoured food produces a large peak in the degree of stimulus relevance. The injection, marked with an arrow, produces no such change (graph iii). Two cases are considered: (1) The rat is on a deficient diet, and therefore suffers a progressively increasing level of Z up to the time of injection (graph i). (2) The rat is on a normal diet and suffers no increase in Z up to the time of injection (graph v). In case (1), the rat receives an injection which provides the deficient substance, and the level of Z consequently falls (graph i). In case (2), the rat receives an injection of a toxic substance, which causes Z to rise temporarily (graph v).

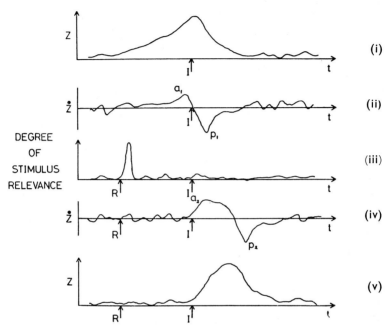

Fig. 1. A unidirectional rate sensitivity hypothesis relating to a specific hungers and poison avoidance. (i) Sickness state function Z as a function of time during development and recovery of a specific hunger. I indicates the time of injection of the deficient or toxic substance; (ii) First derivative of top graph; a_1 = peak of sickness rate, p_1 is peak of improvement; (iii) Degree of a stimulus relevance as a function of time; R indicates time that a highly relevant food (e.g. novel flavour) is introduced; (iv) First derivative of bottom graph; a_2 = peak of sickness rate, $p2$ = peak of improvement; (v) X as a function of time during sickness induced by injection I.

According to preference theory, the rat in case (1) (graphs i and ii) associates the peak following R with the rapid improvement in Z following the injection; that is, with the negative peak in $\dot{Z}$, marked p_1. According to aversion theory, the rat in case (2) (graphs iv and v) associates the peak following R with the increase in Z following the injection; that is, with the positive peak in $\dot{Z}$, marked a_2. However, according to preference theory, the rat should also associate the peak following R with the negative peak p_2, which characterizes recovery from sickness. Clearly, in case (2) the preference and aversion theories are mutually incompatible, and a similar situation can be argued for case (1). An alternative theory is that the peak following R is associated only with positive values of $\dot{Z}$, or only with negative values. This could be an example of "unidirectional rate sensitivity" (Clynes, 1961), a well documented biological phenomenon (Milsum, 1966; McFarland, 1971). If the rat were sensitive only to positive values of $\dot{Z}$, then in case (1) it would not associate the peak following R with the decrease in $\dot{Z}$ following injection. The rat would reject the deficient diet, but would not actively prefer a normal diet. This implies that there is some level of relevance of the deficient diet that becomes associated with a. It would show an apparent preference for the flavoured food, when given a choice between the flavoured food and the food to which it had developed an aversion. In case (2) the rat would develop an aversion for the flavoured food by associating the peak following R with the increase in $\dot{Z}$ following injection. Thus according to this "aversion only" theory, a rat on a deficient diet develops an aversion to this diet, and prefers a novel food by contrast. A rat becoming sick after exposure to a novel diet develops an aversion to it in contrast to the familiar safe diet.

Evidence in favour of this view comes from Rozin's (1967) observations on the feeding behaviour of rats on a thiamine-deficient diet. He noted that the rats appeared to be reluctant to eat the food, showing excessive spillage and redirected feeding. When a new deficient diet was provided the rats ate avidly, suggesting that an aversion had developed to the familiar food. This aversion could be demonstrated even after the rats had recovered from the deficiency. Revusky and Garcia (1970) note that anorexia is considered a clinical symptom of radiation sickness, and this has been confirmed in the rat. However, if a novel food substance is presented during radiation sickness, it is readily consumed by the rat, suggesting that an aversion specific to the normal diet had developed by association with the radiation sickness. Rozin and Kalat (1971) argue "It seems reasonable to assume that the anorexia characteristic of most vitamin deficiencies reflects, at least in part, a learned aversion to the deficient food. This is dramatically clear in the case of thiamine deficiency, where the anorexia symptom disappears precipitously when a new diet is offered. On the other hand there is relatively little anorexia in vitamin D or vitamin A deficiency, and in both cases there has *not* been a clear demonstration of a specific hunger."

Against these arguments for an explanation of specific hungers purely in terms of aversion learning are the studies cited above, which seem to show that deficient rats prefer tastes that have been associated with recovery from deficiency (Garcia *et al.*, 1967; Campbell, 1969; Zahorik and Maier, 1969). The problem is that these studies do not give the rat a fair choice. Zahorik and Maier (1969) gave their rats a choice among a taste associated with recovery, a taste associated with deficiency, and a novel taste. But they did not offer them food with a familiar safe taste. The requisite experiment has since been done by Maier (personal communication), who found that the rats showed no preference for the taste associated with recovery over the taste of a safe familiar food. The implication of this experiment is that the apparent preference for the taste associated with recovery found in previous experiments appears only in contrast to rats' aversion for the taste associated with deficiency, and for novel food. Rats prefer a familiar safe food to a novel food (Rozin, 1968).

In an attempt to show that food with clear positive consequences would be preferred to food with neutral consequences, Revusky (1967) fed rats on nutrient solution while hungry, and a different one while satiated. He found a significant preference in a two-bottle test for the solution drunk while deprived. This result suggests that the taste of the solution drunk while deprived had greater reward value, but has it anything to do with associations between ingestion and delayed physiological consequences? No one doubts that rats are capable of acquiring preferences, but the question of the role of such preferences requires careful consideration.

One important difference, between recovery from deprivation and recovery from dietary deficiency or sickness, is that there is a close temporal association between ingestive cues and recovery cues in the former case, which is absent in the latter. In recovery from deprivation there is short-term feedback of information which could be directly associated with flavours. In such cases the incompatibility between aversion and preference mechanisms need not arise, because the problem can be overcome by means of a short-term primacy effect. That is, the animal could learn to approach or avoid food on the basis of the first change in physiological consequences following ingestion, provided that the primacy effect decays rapidly so as to permit subsequent learning. Thus an animal could learn to approach or avoid certain flavours, depending upon the sign of the subsequent change in physiological state, or its neurological representative. However, such a mechanism would work only in those cases, such as recovery from deprivation, where the physiological change occurs soon after the ingestive behaviour. When the relevant change in physiological state is delayed, as in recovery from dietary deficiency, the primacy indicator will decay either too rapidly or too slowly, depending upon the period of the delay of physiological change. Thus the reason why a primacy effect is not possible in such cases is that delayed consequences of ingestion are, by their very nature, variable. To avoid contradiction within such systems there has to be unidirectional rate sensitivity.

Clearly, the question of flavour preferences, established in association with recovery from deprivation, requires further investigation. Would a rat prefer a flavour associated with recovery to a familiar safe flavour not association with satiation? Would a rat made sick during ingestion of a particular flavoured food in recovery from deprivation, learn to avoid that flavour because sickness was the prime consequence? The theoretical speculations outlined above are open to experimental disproof, but by the same token the case for active preferences for flavours associated with recovery from sickness remains unproven.

Acknowledgements

This paper was written as part of a project on behavioural systems analysis, supported by the Science Research Council. The author is grateful to R. Dantzer for his helpful criticism of the manuscript.

References

Brower, L. P. (1969). Ecological chemistry. *Scient. Am.* **220**, 22–29.
Budgell, P. (1971). Behavioural thermoregulation in the Barbary dove (*Streptopelia risoria*). *Anim. Behav.* **19**, 524–531.
Cannon, W. B. (1932). "The Wisdom of the Body." Norton, New York.
Campbell, C. (1969). Development of specific preferences in thiamine-deficient rats: evidence against mediation by aftertastes. Unpublished master's thesis, Library of the University of Illinois at Chicago Circle.
Capretta, P. J. (1961). An experimental modification of food preference in chickens. *J. comp. physiol. Psychol.* **54**, 238–242.
Clynes, M. (1961). Unidirectional rate sensitivity. A biocybernetic law of reflex and humoral systems as physiological channels of control and communication. *Ann. N.Y. Acad. Sci.* **93**, 946–969.
Cross, B. A. (1964). The hypothalamus in mammalian homeostasis. *Symp. Soc. Exp. Biol.* XVIII. 157–193.
Dietz, M. N. and Capretta, P. J. (1967). Modification of sugar and sugar-saccharin preference in rats as a function of electrical shock to the mouth. *Proc. 75th a. Conv. Am. Psychol. Assoc.* 161–162.
Garcia, J., Green, K. F. and McGowan, B. K. (1969). X-ray as an olfactory stimulus. *In* "Taste and Olfaction", Vol. III, (C. Pfaffman, ed.), pp. 299–309. Rockefeller University Press, New York.
Garcia, J., Ervin, F. R., Yorke, C. H. and Koelling, R. A. (1967). Conditioning with delayed vitamin injection. *Science* **155**, 716–718.
Garcia, J., Kimeldorf, D. J. and Hunt, E. L. (1961). The use of ionizing radiation as a motivating stimulus. *Psychol. Rev.* **68**, 383–385.
Garcia, J., Kimeldorf, D. J. and Koelling, R. A. (1955). Conditioned aversion to saccharin resulting from exposure to gamma radiation. *Science* **122**, 157–158.
Garcia, J. and Koelling, R. A. (1966). Relation of cue to consequence in avoidance learning. *Psychon. Sci.* **4**, 123–124.
Garcia, J., McGowan, B. K., Ervin, F. R. and Koelling, R. A. (1968). Cues: their effectiveness as a function of the reinforcer. *Science* **160**, 794–795.

Harris, L. J., Clay, J. Hargreaves, F. and Ward, A. (1933). Appetite and choice of diet. The ability of the vitamin B deficient rat to discriminate between diets containing and lacking the vitamin. *Proc. R. Soc. Lond. (Series B)* **113**, 161–190.

Kalat, J. W. and Rozin, P. (1970). "Salience": a factor which can override temporal continuity in taste-aversion learning. *J. comp. physiol. Psychol.* **71**, 192–197.

McFarland, D. J. (1970). Recent developments in the study of feeding and drinking in animals. *J. psychosom. Res.* **14**, 229–237.

McFarland, D. J. (1971). "Feedback Mechanisms in Animal Behaviour." Academic Press; London.

McFarland, D. J. and Budgell, P. (1970). The thermoregulatory role of feather movements in the Barbary dove (*Streptopelia risoria*). *Physiol. Behav.* **5**, 763–771.

McFarland, D. J. and Sibly, R. (1972). "Unitary drives" revisited. *Anim. Behav.* (in press).

Milsum, J. H. (1966). "Biological Control Systems Analysis." McGraw-Hill, New York.

Revusky, S. H. (1967). Hunger level during food consumption: effects on subsequent preference. *Psychon. Sci.* **7**, 109–110.

Revusky, S. and Garcia, J. (1970). Learned associations over long delays. *In* "Psychology of Learning and Motivation", Vol. 4, (G. H. Bower, ed.) pp. 1–83. Academic Press, New York.

Rodgers, W. L. (1967). Specificity of specific hungers. *J. comp. physiol. Psychol.* **64**, 49–58.

Rodgers, W. and Rozin, P. (1966). Novel food preferences in thiamine-deficient rats. *J. comp. physiol. Psychol.* **61**, 1–4.

Rosen, R. (1970). "Dynamical System Theory in Biology", Vol. 1. Wiley, New York.

Rozin, P. (1967). Specific aversions as a component of specific hungers. *J. comp. physiol. Psychol.* **64**, 237–242.

Rozin, P. (1968). Specific aversions and neophobia as a consequence of vitamin deficiency and/or poisoning in half-wild and domestic rats. *J. comp. physiol. Psychol.* **66**, 82–88.

Rozin, P. (1969). Adaptive food sampling patterns in vitamin deficient rats. *J. comp. physiol. Psychol.* **69**, 126–132.

Rozin, P. and Kalat, J. W. (1971). Specific hungers and poison avoidance as adaptive specializations of learning. *Psychol. Rev.* **78**, 459–486.

Schultz, D. G. and Melsa, J. L. (1967). "State Functions and Linear Control Systems." McGraw-Hill, New York.

Scott, E. M. and Verney, E. L. (1947). Self selection of diet. VI. The nature of appetites for B vitamins. *J. Nutr.* **34**, 471–480.

Seligman, M. E. P. (1970). On the generality of the laws of learning. *Psychol. Rev.* **77**, 406–418.

Sibly, R. and McFarland, D. J. (In press). A state-space approach to motivation. *In* "Methods of Motivational Control Systems Analysis", (D. J. McFarland, ed.). Academic Press.

Wilcoxon, H. C., Dragoin, W. B. and Kral, P. A. (1971). Illness-induced aversions in rat and quail: relative salience of visual and gustatory cues. *Science* **171**, 826–828.

Zahorik, D. M. and Maier, S. F. (1969). Appetite conditioning with recovery from thiamine deficiency as the unconditioned stimulus. *Psychon. Sci.* **17**, 309–310.

Comments

1. *Mackintosh wrote:*

"The argument is that rats would not associate tastes both with sickness and with recovery from sickness (deficiency), because any increase in sickness must be followed by a recovery, and a taste that preceded both would be associated with both. This is like saying that rats would not associate an auditory signal with both an increase and a decrease in pain (e.g. produced by electric shock), because if a tone were paired with shock onset, it would also (eventually) signal shock offset (all shocks come to an end), and the tone would now be treated as a signal for both. But in fact, rats can learn, under appropriate conditions, that one tone signals shock onset, and another signals shock offset. They associate the tone with the first change that follows the tone. A similar primacy principle would serve to allow rats to associate a taste with the first change—for the better or for the worse—that followed ingestion of that taste.

"One objection to this primacy principle is to point out that in experiments where normal eating of a meal intervenes between a novel taste and subsequent poisoning, the first internal change to follow the novel taste is the normal consequence of eating. According to a primacy principle, it would be this change that became associated with the novel taste. The counter-argument to this objection is that the normal consequences of eating a meal are already predicted by the taste of the meal; hence the taste of the meal will block any association being formed between the initial novel taste and the consequences of the meal, leaving the novel taste free to be associated with subsequent poisoning."

McFarland replied:

"I certainly agree that rats are capable of learning both to approach and to avoid certain stimuli, but I think that stimuli associated with eating constitute a special case. When a rat eats a deficient or poisoned food in nature, there will always be some improvement in Z due to the nutrient properties of the food. If this food has a novel flavour, it cannot be claimed that 'the normal consequences of eating a meal are already predicted by the taste of the meal'. In the case of a familiar but deficient food, every meal is followed by some improvement, due to the nutrient properties of the diet, but the improvement is not complete because of the deficiency. By a primary principle, it is this improvement that should be associated with eating, in which case the animal could never develop an association with deficient food that was different from its associations with non-deficient food.

"Not only is there likely to be an improvement in Z following meals with high stimulus relevance, but there may be other meals prior to the development of sickness. Thus Garcia, Green and McGowan (1969) reported that an aversion to hydrochloric acid solution can be induced by X-irradiation with a one hour delay interval even if the rat consumes a meal during the interval.

Similarly, Revusky and Garcia (1970) cite experiments in which consumption of familiar substances during such intervals produced no interference, and novel substances only partial interference, with the association between a particular eating bout and delayed toxicosis. As such intervening meals must produce considerable improvement in Z, but do not affect the association, it is difficult to see how a primacy hypothesis is tenable."

2. Hogan wrote:

"With respect to the upper two panels of the graph: thiamine deficiency develops over a course of weeks—recovering within three hours. The derivative is therefore almost zero and flat until ingestion of the recovery diet. Thus there is no real a_1."

McFarland replied:

"This question relates to the acceleration in Z during dietary deficiency, illustrated in the Figure. I think that this is a correct representation. Rozin (1967) points out that it is likely that the metabolism of most food requires thiamine. Thus a thiamine deficient diet has a double effect on Z: there is an increase in Z due to the deficiency itself, and a further progressive increase due to failure to utilize the nutrients in the diet. Another process producing acceleration in Z is the anorexia that often accompanies aversion to deficient diets. Thus once an animal becomes slightly aversive to a diet, it eats less, thus accentuating the process which is responsible for the aversion. As noted in the text, specific hungers do not appear to develop in those cases of deficiency that do not produce anorexia. It is probably true, as illustrated in the Figure, that the negative peak in Z may be smaller during deficiency (a_1) than it is during sickness (a_2), but this is concordant with the well-known fact that associations are harder to establish with deficient diets than with poisons."

References

Garcia, J., Green, K. F. and McGowan, B. K. (1969). X-ray as an olfactory stimulus. *In* "Taste and Olfaction", Vol. III, (C. Pfaffmann, ed.), pp. 299–309. Rockefeller Univ. Press, New York.

Revusky, S. and Garcia, J. (1970). Learned associations over long delays. *In* "Psychology of Learning and Motivation", Vol. 4, (G. H. Bower, ed.), pp. 1–83. Academic Press, New York.

Rozin, P. (1967). Specific aversions as a component of specific hungers. *J. comp. physiol. Psychol.* **64**, 237–242.

Editorial: 3

Within each of the previous four chapters, the concept of reinforcement has arisen. In the six which follow, it is the central issue. One's opinion about the role of reinforcement in learning is related to how learning phenomena are categorized. Some have argued that all learning can be reduced to one basic type: if one accepts that view, our present knowledge of the range of learning phenomena makes it difficult to hold that reinforcement is always necessary. If one recognizes several types, then reinforcement can be necessary for some but not others.

Now, procedurally at least, it is clear that the operations of presenting an unconditioned stimulus or a reinforcer are necessary to obtain learning in a Pavlovian or operant situation. There has also been some agreement, again on procedural grounds, that a basic distinction can be made between these two types of conditioning. In the next chapters, by Moore and by Jenkins, doubt is thrown even on this distinction through the phenomenon of "autoshaping". This involves shaping an operant response by the Pavlovian procedure of presenting a to-be-conditioned stimulus, which must be localized, with an unconditioned stimulus. If, for example, illumination of a response key (CS) is followed by presentation of food (US), a hungry pigeon will come to peck the key even though the food presentation is not dependent upon this response. This important finding raises the question of what role Pavlovian conditioning usually plays in the control of operant responses. Moore presents a case for a considerable role. Jenkins is more cautious, making a distinction between selected and unselected responses: a *selected* response "in an unambiguous example, would not occur as the natural consequence of arranging for the temporal pairing of the discriminative stimulus with the reinforcer. In the Pavlovian experiment, on the other hand, the conditioned response is a natural consequence of the stimulus-reinforcer pairing and is in that sense *unselected*" (Chapter 9, p. 190). A selected response appears to be especially sensitive to the response-reinforcer relation, and an unselected response to the stimulus-reinforcer relation. Jenkins argues that experimental comparisons of the role of response-reinforcer and stimulus-reinforcer relations in controlling selected and unselected responses will be a fruitful approach towards an understanding of simple learning.

The phenomenon of auto-shaping is possible only if the reinforcer (US) elicits a response (UR). Glickman argues that most reinforcing stimuli do in fact elicit some response. This correlation, although not a perfect one, between eliciting and reinforcing effects, can help predict which stimuli will act as reinforcers. At a physiological level, most CNS sites which elicit some behaviour pattern are also sites at which electrical stimulation is reinforcing. Glickman's chapter is a critical review of the implications of brain stimulation research for a response-oriented theory of reinforcement.

The relation between the operant response and reinforcer is considered in the chapters by Shettleworth and by Sevenster. In her study of hamsters Shettleworth, using one reinforcer (food), compares the consequences of making it contingent upon a number of different operant responses. The finding that they do not all vary similarly indicates that response-reinforcer relations impose a constraint on the ease with which learning occurs: just why some responses are more effective than others is a further issue. Sevenster compares the use of two reinforcers for two operant responses and shows that, with one pairing, a low level of operant responding can be related to inhibitory relations between consummatory behaviour and subsequent operant responding. These results throw doubt upon the generality of many formulations about the control of conventional operants (bar press or key peck) by conventional reinforcers (food or water). Yet no simple generalizations emerge, and the chapter by Stevenson-Hinde attempts to categorize the various constraints that have been demonstrated.

8

The Role of Directed Pavlovian Reactions in Simple Instrumental Learning in the Pigeon*

by Bruce R. Moore

When food reward is used, it is very easy to train pigeons to peck keys. With aversive reinforcement, pecking is difficult to establish, but other, more appropriate responses can be conditioned readily. The instrumental-learning process appears to work very well, or very badly, for particular combinations of response and reinforcer.

The pecking response which food-rewarded pigeons so rapidly learn is a rather stereotyped reaction, and not easily modified. According to oper-ant-conditioning theory, response topographies are determined by re-inforcement contingencies, and can be modified simply by changing these contingencies. However, attempts to demonstrate such response differentiation in the pigeon often fail. When one tries to condition the "normal" key-pecking response, the instrumental-learning process appears to work; when one tries to condition some variant of this response, the process often seems not to work, or to work very slowly or indirectly.

Pigeons may also fail to learn, or they may learn slowly or indirectly, in what Breland and Breland (1966) called the "cross-drive conditioning" situation. That is, it is difficult to use a reinforcer belonging to one instinc-tive or motivational system to strengthen a response pattern appropriate to another such system. Here again, the *Law of Effect* appears not to hold for certain combinations of response and reinforcer.

Upon examination of these data it becomes clear that the pigeon's in-strumental learning differs in quite fundamental ways from the process

* Dedicated to the late Dr. C. J. Brimer, who contributed to this work in many ways. This chapter is based on a doctoral dissertation submitted to Stanford University. I am grateful to Drs. W. K. Estes, R. C. Atkinson and E. E. Smith who served as the thesis com-mittee, and also to Drs. H. M. Jenkins, P. J. Dunham and N. J. Mackintosh and to Betty Moore for comments on early drafts of the manuscript.

described by Skinner's very influential (1938) theory. This paper will examine the discrepancies between theory and data and will end by offering a new explanation for much of the pigeon's simplest instrumental learning. The key to the new explanation is provided by the phenomenon which Brown and Jenkins (1968) called "auto-shaping". It is worthwhile to pause here to examine that phenomenon, for we shall need to refer to it at many points.

Auto-Shaping

Briefly, Brown and Jenkins found that when pigeons were exposed to repeated temporal pairings of a lighted key and food, the animals began to peck the key. This was potentially important because it showed that *Pavlovian* procedures could generate the key-pecking response so often utilized in *operant* conditioning research. The behaviour of the pigeons conformed precisely to Pavlov's definition of conditioning (Pavlov, 1941, pp. 47, 62, 120, 150; Moore, 1971; Jenkins and Moore, in press). The lighted key was paired with grain, and the pigeons pecked it as if it were grain. However, the fact that both the procedure and the outcome were Pavlovian did not guarantee that the pecking was in fact due to the Pavlovian process.

It should be stressed that auto-shaped key pecks look identical to those seen in operant conditioning experiments and arise through a similar progression of stages. The following passages describe the emergence of auto-shaped reactions.

> First, pigeons tended to orient toward the front of the chamber nearly all of the time. Second, the Ss tended to move their entire body to the side of the chamber which contained the key they were looking at. Finally, the Ss tended to stand within a few inches of the key they were viewing. . . .
>
> *Brown, 1968, p. 140*
>
> Direct observation and a study of motion pictures made of pigeons that were not part of the present group showed the following gross stages in the emergence of the key-peck : first, a general increase of activity, particularly during the trial-on period; second, a progressive centering of movements around the area of the key when lighted; and, finally, pecking movements in the direction of the key.
>
> *Brown and Jenkins, 1968, p. 3*

These passages might easily have been written to describe the progression of stages seen when pecking is shaped by operant-conditioning techniques, i.e., by the method of successive approximations (Ferster and Skinner, 1957). Because of the striking similarities, it is reasonable to suspect that auto-shaped key pecking and instrumental key pecking might arise from the same process. In particular, it would seem possible that auto-shaping might be due to a hidden instrumental-learning process, or that instrumental pecking might be due to a hidden Pavlovian process.

Let us begin by examining the first possibility. There have been several series of experiments testing the Pavlovian and instrumental-learning explanations of auto-shaping. One way to test the Pavlovian interpretation is to perform the auto-shaping experiment with water, rather than food, reinforcement. Obviously, the Pavlovian process should cause water-reinforced birds to drink, rather than peck, the key; and that is precisely what happens. Jenkins and Moore (in press) made films of key responses auto-shaped with food and with water reinforcement. Student judges were able to distinguish between filmed food and water reactions with 87% accuracy. "Blind" procedures were of course used, and the food and water reactions were screened in random order. The judges characterized the food responses as sharp, vigorous pecks, whereas the birds auto-shaped with water were said to make slower, more sustained contact with the key, often accompanied by swallowing movements. With water reinforcement, the bird's beak is typically closed, or almost so, as shown in Fig. 1a. With food reinforcement, however, the beak typically springs open just before contact with the key, as shown in Fig. 1b. Wolin (1948) has described food- and water-reinforced instrumental responses in similar terms.

The fact that the auto-shaped responses were of appropriate consummatory form supported the Pavlovian interpretation of the phenomenon, but there remained the possibility that these response topographies were artifacts of the animals' deprivation states or of reinforcement aftereffects rather than expressions of Pavlovian conditioning. To control these factors, other pigeons were run under compound food and water deprivation (Jenkins and Moore, Experiments 4, 5). These birds were concurrently auto-shaped to two stimuli; one stimulus was paired with food and the other was paired with water. To balance reinforcement aftereffects, the food and water auto-shaping trials were intermixed in random order. The phenomenon survived these controls. The birds pecked at the food stimuli and made drinking responses to the water stimuli, indicating that the response topographies were indeed due to associate learning.

In a sequel to the food and water experiments, Rackham (1971) has exposed pigeons to repeated pairings of a stimulus light and a sexual reinforcer. He obtained what might be called conditioned fetish behaviour in the pigeon. Four mated pairs of birds were used. The male and female of each pair were housed in adjacent halves of a large chamber, separated by a sliding door. Once each day the stimulus light was turned on;

M

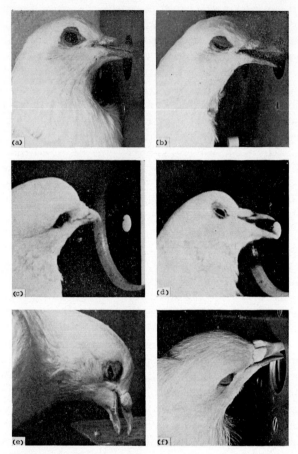

Fig. 1. (a) and (b) show the consummatory topographies obtained when key responses are auto-shaped with water (a) and food (b) reinforcement. (c) and (d) (from Blough, 1961) show a food-reinforced instrumental response. The spot of light is a discriminative stimulus. (Reproduced with permission of *Scientific American*). (e) shows the consummatory reaction which often arises even when very different forms of lever pressing have been reinforced. When presses are reinforced only in the presence of some positive cue, the cue itself may elicit consummatory reactions, as shown in (f).

the sliding door was then removed, allowing the male to initiate the courtship ritual.

The male subjects began to make conditioned responses within five to ten trials. The first reactions to appear were approach to the CS, nodding and bowing. Then, cooing, strutting and pirouetting began to occur intermittently. Conditioned nest calls appeared midway through the study and were elicited by 60% of all CS presentations from trial 80 onward. Rack-ham's thesis contains sonograms which show objectively the similarity of the conditioned and unconditioned vocalizations. The courtship reactions, like auto-shaped eating and drinking, were directed towards the con-ditioned stimulus itself.

Elsewhere, Rachlin (1969) obtained key pecking in an aversive-re-inforcement experiment which contained elements of auto-shaping. He stressed that the pecking resembled that seen when pigeons are auto-shaped with food. However, it is well known that shock may elicit aggressive behaviour, and pecking is an important reaction in the pigeon's agonistic repertoire. It is likely that the pecks which Rachlin obtained were aggressive reactions, for a photograph of one of his subjects reveals that as the animal pecked, one wing was raised high in the species-specific threat posture. This is, of course, a highly stereotyped intention movement and therefore easily identified. Only one of Rachlin's three relevant photo-graphs shows this posture, but McFarland and Baher (1968) found that, at any given distance, a threatening object was more likely to elicit pecking than the raised-wing response. Thus Rachlin's data are not, as they had seemed, an embarrassment to the Pavlovian interpretation of auto-shap-ing. Quite the contrary.

In other relevant experiments, Williams and Williams (1969) and Kirby (1968) used Sheffield's (1965) omission-training technique to ensure that key-pecking was never adventitiously reinforced. Their procedures were identical to those used in simple auto-shaping, except that reinforcement was withheld whenever a subject pecked the key. That is, the subject received food after each presentation of the light *if* it refrained from peck-ing the light. If the pigeon's behaviour in this situation were controlled by the Law of Effect, the bird would of course refrain from pecking. If the auto-shaping phenomenon were Pavlovian, however, the bird should peck; omission training would merely weaken the tendency to respond by introducing Pavlovian partial reinforcement. The results of these studies supported the Pavlovian hypothesis. Many of the animals reacted to the key for hundreds of trials in spite of the negative instrumental con-tingency.

Another way to test between the Pavlovian and the adventitious-oper-ant interpretation of auto-shaping is to make the occurrence of the key-pecking response physically impossible during the training period. Making the lighted key inaccessible during otherwise-normal auto-shaping sessions would obviously preclude the possibility of any adventitious reinforcement of key pecking. Kirby, Muir and I have run nine subjects in this situation. After extended training, the animals were given access to the key during a series of unreinforced test trials. The outcome of the tests was unequivocally Pavlovian: when the key was first illuminated, eight of the nine animals approached and pecked it within seconds.

Thus, the inaccessible key studies, like the omission-training experiments, indicate that the auto-shaping effect cannot be explained in terms of adventitious reinforcement of the response of pecking the key. Further, the food, water, shock, and courtship studies show that the form of auto-shaped behaviour varies with the nature of the reinforcing stimulus as required by the Pavlovian hypothesis. Finally, the effect survives all normal controls for non-associative factors (Brown, 1968; Brown and Jenkins, 1968; Kirby, 1968). Altogether, the data leave no reason to doubt that auto-shaping in the pigeon is a simple Pavlovian phenomenon.

Instrumental Response Topographies

The Pavlovian explanation of auto-shaping is potentially important because pigeons similar to those of Brown and Jenkins, pecking similar keys for similar grain, have generated much of the literature of operant conditioning.

The behaviour obtained in operant situations very closely resembles that seen in auto-shaping. In a paper presented in 1948, but not published until 1968, Wolin pointed out the resemblance of food- and water-reinforced instrumental responses to actual eating and drinking. Food-reinforced pecks, like eating reactions, were characterized as "rapid, short powerful thrusts of the head with the beak open". Water-reinforced instrumental responses, like drinking reactions, were said to involve "slow, long, easy pushing motion[s] with the beak almost closed".

A very detailed analysis of the topography of the food-reinforced instrumental peck is found in a dissertation by Smith (1967). Smith relied primarily upon 200-frame-per-second photographs taken with a kymograph camera and stroboscopic light. These films were supplemented by still photographs taken at the moment of key contact. Additionally, Smith sometimes monitored key displacements or velocities during responding. He obtained some records of response forces, and he analysed inter-response times. When data from these sources were correlated, the following description of the food-reward operant emerged.

> (1) the beak begins to open about 20–25 msec before contact with the key, (2) the upper bill encounters the key at an upward angle while the lower bill remains roughly horizontal (i.e., perpendicular to the key), (3) beak opening continues for about 10 msec on the key, (4) the beak remains open for about 5–10 msec, (5) beak closure, on the key, requires about 10–15 msec, and is produced by the downward movement of the upper bill and (6) retraction follows closure almost immediately and is

accompanied by a slight downward tilt of the head. In a number of such sequences, the estimated time from key contact to beak closure was usually 30–40 msec.

Smith, 1967, pp. 10–11

Thus, the beak springs open just before contact with the key. It begins to close some 25 milliseconds after contact, and the head is retracted about 20 milliseconds later. The spring opening, followed by bite and retraction, clearly suggests an eating response.

Breland and Breland (1966, p. 104) report that chickens, too, often peck operant manipulanda with open beaks. They add that photographs often show that the amount by which the beak is opened is determined by the size of some target stimulus. Photographs published by Blough (1961) appear to show exactly this effect with pigeons. They are reproduced in the centre of Fig. 1. The circular spot of light was a discriminative stimulus. The pigeon's aim is not always so precise, but pecks of this sort are not uncommon.

It is obvious that the pigeon's "operant" response topography is quite intimately related both to the consummatory reaction elicited by grain and to the Pavlovian reaction so easily auto-shaped with that reinforcer.

Response Differentiation

Now let us see what happens when one tries to modify these instrumental response forms. According to Skinner's (1938) system, the topography of a true operant response is determined by implicit and explicit reinforcement contingencies. The following passage describes the theoretical effect of implicit contingencies upon response form.

Concurrent Negative Reinforcement. The execution of a response may supply negative reinforcing stimulation tending to reduce the net reinforcing effect. 'Difficulty' and 'awkwardness' may be expressed in terms of the negatively reinforcing stimulation automatically produced by a response. If the various members of an inductive group of responses differ in awkwardness or difficulty, there will be a resulting differential effect of the reinforcement. The simplest and easiest form prevails, because it receives a positive reinforcement without emotional depressant effect.

Skinner, 1938, pp. 309–310

If a response is awkward, then intrinsic negative reinforcement is supposed to shape the animal towards more comfortable response forms. One would suppose that this process would be especially rapid if one response were painful, and if a simple variant of that response were not painful. However, when Hefferline *et al.* (1961) attempted to measure response forces with an unyielding key, the pigeons pecked so vigourously that their beaks began to bleed, and they then ceased responding. The conditions of this experiment seem perfect for rapid differentiation, but it did not occur. The animals were able to peck or to cease pecking, but gave no evidence of learning to peck gentlly.

Cole (1965) tried explicitly to shape the force of the pecking response. He rewarded pigeons only for those pecks which exceeded some force criterion. The effort failed. Whenever the force requirement was raised, the birds simply earned fewer reinforcers. As a consequence, they pecked *less* forcefully. This negative-feedback process continued until, in Cole's words, "The bird[s] invariably spiraled into extinction" (1965, p. 241). In his principal experiment, Cole ran four groups of pigeons for about one thousand trials but found no evidence that response impact was modified by differential reinforcement.

Skinner has also reinforced high-impact pecks, and claims to have been more successful.

> We built a gauge to measure the force with which a pigeon pecked a horizontal block, and by differentially reinforcing harder pecks we built up such forceful blows that the base of the pigeon's beak quickly became inflamed.
>
> *Skinner, 1958, p. 94*

Unfortunately, Skinner's paper gives no other details of that experiment. Since we now know that beak injuries sometimes arise from "normal" pecks, and since we do not know whether Skinner had this control condition, and do not know what force levels his birds achieved, it is difficult to evaluate his findings.

In the same paper, Skinner described the shaping of a different beak response.

> The pigeon was to send a wooden ball down a miniature alley towards a set of toy pins by swiping the ball with a sharp sideward movement of the beak. . . . The result amazed us. . . . The spectacle so impressed Keller Breland that he gave up a promising career in psychology and went into the commercial production of behaviour.
>
> *Skinner, 1958, p. 94*

If this response were of arbitrary form, it might be said to demonstrate differentiation, or at least true operant shaping. However, it is not an arbitrary response.

> In loose friable earth, leaf-mould, chaff, etc., pigeons (all species of *Columba* and *Streptopelia* whose feeding behaviour is known as well as

the present species) will search for buried seeds by turning over the substrate with their bills. The bird uses a quick sideways flicking movement of the head, whereby some of the loose earth is thrown to one side.

Goodwin, 1954, p. 201

In the laboratory, pigeons often use this reaction to toss aside grit and gain access to grain. Thus, the rapidly-learned responses of Skinner's "bowling" pigeons appear to have come from the reinforcement-appropriate instinctive repertoire.

A brief note by Bullock (1960) does appear to show differentiation of the *duration* of the pecking response. He reported that when three pigeons with several years of prior experimental training were placed on a 26-second fixed interval reinforcement schedule, they learned eventually to hold down the key as the end of the interval approached. Since no pulse former had been used in the circuit, this allowed them to receive reward at the earliest possible moment. Unfortunately, we do not know what these responses looked like. Auto-shaped animals occasionally bite (or tear at) the opening through which the lighted key is seen. Two of Kirby's (1968) birds bit at the edge of the key opening in such a way as to operate the micro-switch for several seconds at a time. While biting, these subjects wedged one mandible between the key and the rear of the intelligence panel. Their mean response durations during the first session were 500 and 640 milliseconds. The responses often continued until interrupted by food presentations. It is possible that Bullock's birds were doing something analogous to this rather than making prolonged pecks.

A more systematic effort to obtain duration shaping was made in an unpublished study by James Warren. Twelve previously auto-shaped pigeons served as subjects. Half were rewarded for long-duration and half for short-duration responses. Factorially, half were run with food and half with water reward. A single-response, fixed-trial procedure was used. A laboratory computer timed each response duration to the nearest 0.1 millisecond and kept track of each bird's ten most recent times. It calculated a reinforcement criterion for each subject on each trial, always requiring it to do better than it had on eight of the ten preceding trials. The programme thus raised the criterion at every sign of improvement, lowered it when necessary, and generally maintained pressure in the desired direction. Warren's data are shown in Fig. 2. The animals which received water reinforcement for long duration responses learned to prolong their reactions by a factor of five or six after 5000 trials. The prolonged contact responses were in no sense abnormal; pigeons often take much longer drinks of water. Thus the conditioned behaviour was simply more fully expressed after 5000 trials of differential reinforcement. The response durations of the corresponding food-reinforced group changed by a factor of two or three during the same period. Most of the effect came when one subject learned to initiate its pecks from a point above and to the right of the key, and near the wall. Normal pecks initiated from that point necessarily struck the key obliquely, thus the old response was merely measured from a new angle. Conceivably, the key seen from point B had become associated with a higher reinforcement density than the key seen from point A.

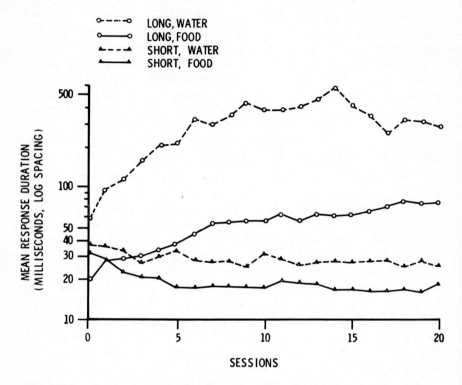

Fig. 2. Mean learning curves from Warren's duration-shaping experiment. The initial point on each curve is based upon trials 1–25 of the first session. Subsequent points are means of entire (250-trial) sessions.

Birds receiving food or water for short-duration responses gave some evidence of learning. One of the water subjects learned to direct some drinking responses towards the inside rim of the key opening. Normal drinking reactions made there occasionally brushed the key in such a way as to close the switch momentarily. Again, the bird had simply re-directed the normal response. Note that this sort of instrumental learning might arise through a purely Pavlovian process if, after one or more generalized responses, the rim became associated with a high reinforcement density. Bindra (1972) has hypothesized precisely this sort of *stimulus-differentiation* mechanism.

Statistically, Warren's treatments and treatment-by-session interactions were all significant ($p < 0.05$). The statistical analysis was necessary because most of the subjects in three of the four groups showed little evidence of learning. Water-reinforced birds proved well able to make prolonged drinking responses. In the other groups, however, only two out of nine subjects' response durations changed by more than 50% during the entire 5000 trials of computer shaping. Thus, in spite of the learning curves, the data did not demonstrate strong operant differentiation. In most groups, the results were weak, nil, or attributable to mere shifts in response direction.

Schwartz (1971) also attempted to shape the durations of food-reinforced pecks. The selective reinforcement of long-duration responses led to an increase in their frequency. However, long-durations also became more frequent when *short* durations were selectively reinforced. Adjustment of the reinforcement criterion produced some recovery, but the extent of the effect is hard to ascertain, and the data are difficult to interpret.

The preceding studies collectively show that while the pigeon's response topographies are sometimes modifiable, they are more often highly resistant to differentiation. The mere nature of the reinforcer typically affects at once countless dimensions of response topography. Implicit and explicit reward contingencies, by contrast, are less likely to prove effective, and when effective, they often act slowly or weakly and affect single topographic dimensions. When changes are obtained, they often arise because the animal has begun to direct the old response pattern towards some new stimulus. When real topographic changes occur, the pigeon has often merely shifted from one to another species-specific pattern.

Cross-Drive Conditioning

The data so far suggest that pigeons in instrumental-learning situations tend to utilize reinforcement-appropriate species-specific response patterns. Now let us see what happens when one tries to condition species-specific patterns *not* appropriate to the reinforcer being used. This is the "cross-drive conditioning" situation.

Reynolds *et al.* (1963) described an attempt to use food reinforcement to strengthen the pigeon's aggressive behaviour. They did obtain fighting, but through an interesting two-stage process.

Successive frames from motion pictures show that the pigeon attacked with closed eyes and open beak, just as in pecking a standard wall key. The feathers on the aggressor's neck occasionally fluffed (pennerection) before an attack (Skinner, 1959) though reinforcement was never specifically contingent on this behavior. Fluffing was most common when the aggressee tended to return the attack or to ward it off vigorously. Some aggressors did not fluff.

When the aggressee returned the attack, fighting occurred in the stereotyped pattern characteristic of pigeons (Levi, 1959; Smith & Hosking, 1955). The birds clasped beaks, wrestled, and flapped violently around the cage, often cooing loudly. . . .

However, conditioned and unconditioned aggression have different topographies. The aggression shaped by the experimenter does not take on the characteristics of the instinctive pattern. It simply brings the bird into a situation which may release unconditioned fighting.

Reynolds, Catania and Skinner, 1963, pp. 73–74

The analysis offered by Reynolds *et al.* is quite compatible with ethological data and with the ideas advanced in this paper. The close proximity of conspecifics is sufficient to release aggression in pigeons (Willis, 1966) as in many other species (Marler and Hamilton, 1966, pp. 166 ff.). Hungry animals may be less likely to avoid one another and are, therefore, more likely to be drawn into fights, especially near localized food sites (Marler and Hamilton, 1966, pp. 167, 176). Thus, it appears that the direct effect of food reward was not to strengthen fighting but, rather, to strengthen an approach reaction. If this were treated as a food-appropriate appetitive response, the learning might be explicable in purely Pavlovian terms. A similar analysis might be applied to the fighting conditioned by Azrin and Hutchinson (1967).

In a cross-drive study by Hogan (1964), food reward was used in an attempt to condition the pigeon's preening response. During ten sessions of continuous reinforcement the birds learned to touch their feathers with their beaks, but the reaction bore little resemblance to the naturally-occurring pattern. When reinforcement was then given according to a variable-interval schedule, the naturally-occurring topography appeared. It should be noted, however, that birds preen as a displacement activity in a great variety of conflict situations (Armstrong, 1965). Intermittent reinforcement, or non-reinforcement, might well evoke the response. This interpretation of the data is supported by the fact that when the animals were returned to continuous reinforcement, the natural topography disappeared. When they were then put on extinction, it reappeared. Obviously, non-reinforcement played some critical role. Some sort of instrumental learning may also have been important in an indirect way. Tinbergen (1952) briefly discusses the possibility that "the posture in which an animal finds itself when a drive is thwarted may decide which [displacement] activity will be used as an outlet". He attributes this idea to Baerends and describes several possible instances of such postural facilitation (see also Lind, 1959). Quite possibly, the postures and movements carried over from periods of continuous reinforcement made displacement preening the most likely reaction to non-reinforcement in Hogan's very interesting study.

A variation of the cross-drive design involves establishing a response with one reinforcer and then shifting to another. Wolin (1948) did this with pigeons, changing from food reward to water, and from water to food, and Jenkins and Moore (in press) have shifted these reinforcers in the auto-shaping situation. In each case, the response topography shifted slowly towards the newly-appropriate form although adventitious re-inforcement (Skinner, 1948) might have been expected to preserve the established behaviour. A more powerful design would make presentation of the new reinforcer contingent upon some critical aspect of the old topography.

The differentiation and cross-drive studies together suggest that direct instrumental learning proceeds most rapidly when the pigeon is rewarded for performing a *reinforcement-appropriate*, species-specific reaction. This is true not only with positive reinforcers but also with aversive ones.

Escape and Avoidance Conditioning

It is possible, but notoriously difficult, to train pigeons to peck to avoid or escape shock. Hoffman and Fleshler, who first called attention to the problem, gave the following account of their efforts to use shock offset (negative reinforcement) to train pigeons to approach and peck keys.

After a few such reinforcements, the bird usually was to be found in the vicinity of the key shortly after shock was turned on. At this point the E would withhold reinforcement until the bird had emitted a response which approximated the desired key peck.

Invariably, the results of such hand shaping were disappointing. Either the behavior would become superstitious, or responses would cease to be emitted. Thus, a bird might learn to place its beak within millimeters of the key; but if it were not reinforced consistently for this behavior, it would lose the response completely. On the other hand, repeated reinforcement strengthened only the behavior of placing the beak near the key, so that even when operant pecks occurred and were reinforced, the increment in response strength would be insufficient to change the previously acquired topography (placing beak up to key).

Hoffman and Fleshler, 1959, pp. 213–214

The authors pointed to two sources of difficulty in this situation. The first was the presence of a number of elicited reactions (unconditioned responses) which competed with the desired response pattern. The second was the birds' tendency to cease responding altogether during prolonged shock trains. But this, too, might be treated as a competing respondent.

The negative reinforcement of approach to some object necessarily creates a place of refuge or safety. The rest of the environment is associated with shock; the manipulandum is not, or is associated with a lower shock density. Hoffman and Fleshler's pigeons learned within "a few" (perhaps 20–40) trials to approach a safe place, but, once there, they did not learn to peck.

Smith and Keller (1970) described similar difficulties. "While some avoidance pecking was shaped, the response rapidly dropped out and was replaced by wing flapping and jumping against the panel containing the keys." This behaviour occasionally operated the keys, but was "generally ineffective".

The pigeon's wing-flapping reaction is often elicited by shock. The jumping behaviour was quite possibly aggressive charging.

The Mourning Dove shares with many other pigeons, including the Blond Ring-Dove, a habit of charging upon other individuals.... In charging, the bird often gives a great leap, or even a series of leaps. . . .

Craig, 1911, pp. 400–401

Maintaining an attack posture, the dove often runs or rushes at the opponent. At times the dove will fly toward the opponent but cage conditions tend to inhibit a rush by flying.

Miller and Miller, 1958, p. 6

While attempts to condition pecking with negative reinforcement usually fail, the effect can sometimes be obtained if special techniques are used. Azrin (1959) reported very briefly that difficulties produced by shock-elicited behaviour could be avoided "by continuously varying the shock intensity (via a potentiometer) in accordance with the subject's behavior at each moment . . ." More recent work by Rachlin and Hineline (1967), Hineline and Rachlin (1969) and Rachlin (1969) has shown that pigeons can learn to peck to escape shock if, during each trial, the shock is introduced at sub-threshold intensity and gradually increased. This technique would be related to Azrin's if the gradual introduction of shock served to minimize the elicitation of competing responses—or to maximize elicitation of the desired response. For shock can, of course, elicit aggression; and we saw earlier that the pecking of Rachlin's (1969) birds was sometimes accompanied by the raised-wing reaction.

Perhaps the reason that even aggressive pecking is so difficult to obtain is that pigeons are not very brave, and enemies as formidable as shock generators usually elicit other behaviour patterns. Attempts to condition more appropriate behaviour have been more successful. Thus, Hoffman and Fleshler (1959) were able to strengthen, very slowly, a head-lifting response which had appeared occasionally "in rudimentary form" during shock. Graf and Bitterman (1963) obtained Sidman avoidance (Sidman, 1953) with a presumably-elicited activity response. McPhail (1968) found pigeons able to learn shuttle-box avoidance, and Bedford and Anger (1968; described in Smith and Keller, 1970) trained them to fly from perch to perch. Smith and Keller's animals readily learned a treadle response "compatible with . . . aspects of the UCR, such as jumping and wing flapping" (1970, p. 212). Foree and LoLordo (1970) also obtained treadle avoidance. Wing flaps could not operate their manipulandum, but it lent itself to other appropriate behaviour.

> For all birds, except AV-5 responses occurred in bursts even when no shock was received. Often such bursts were due to walking along the length of the lever. . . .
>
> *Foree and LoLordo, 1970, p. 286*

Some birds learned to stand poised to step upon the lever. At other times,

> the avoidance response consisted of a sudden lunge and rapid depression of the lever after the bird had been motionless for 6 to 10 sec. Pigeons that received higher shock rates often remained on the lever after a response, and released the lever only when the next shock occurred. In no case did a pigeon depress the lever by other than a stepping movement.
>
> *Foree and LoLordo, 1970, p. 287*

The treadle used in Foree and LoLordo's study was 8 inches long and was mounted 1.2 inches above floor level. The avoidance contingency ensured that it would become the place associated with lowest shock density. The animals learned to run along it, step onto it, or perch upon it. The authors stressed that treadle responses were likely to occur in the presence of shock.

Most of the recent contributors to this literature have pointed out that pigeons are best able to learn avoidance responding when the required behaviour is compatible with appropriate species-specific responses (see also Breland and Breland, 1966). Bolles (1970) has, of course, stressed this same point with reference to mammalian avoidance learning. It is scarcely necessary to add that these species-specific reactions include, by definition, the set of possible Pavlovian CRs and URs.

In general, the literature of escape and avoidance conditioning simply reinforces the ideas which emerged from many of the differentiation and cross-drive experiments and from examination of the topographies of food- and water-rewarded responses. In instrumental learning situations, the pigeon seems ordinarily to utilize the sorts of responses which Pavlov called URs and CRs and which Skinner (1938) called *respondents*.

> With the discovery of the stimulus and the collection of a large number of specific relationships of stimulus and response, it came to be assumed by many writers that all behavior could be accounted for in this way. . . . The brightest hope of establishing the generality of the eliciting stimulus was provided by Pavlov's demonstration. . . .
> But an event may occur without any observed antecedent event and still be dealt with adequately in a descriptive science. . . . This kind of behavior might be said to be *emitted* by the organism. . . .
> Differences between the two kinds of behavior will accumulate throughout the book. . . . The kind of behavior that is correlated with specific eliciting stimuli may be called *respondent* behavior. . . . Such behavior as is not under this kind of control I shall call *operant*. . . .
>
> *Skinner, 1938, pp. 19–20*

The passage is unambiguous. If the instrumental responses which pigeons ordinarily utilize in food-, water-, and aversive-reinforcement situations are basically the same as reactions elicited by those reinforcers—and they are—then they are not operants but respondents, according to Skinner's definitions.

Skinner's system describes organisms which are distinguished by their ability to transcend the limitations of elicited responses and to utilize operants of arbitrary form. The pigeon cannot conceivably be described in such terms. It is distinctly inferior to, and often appears to be the antithesis of, the theoretical organism of Skinner's (1938) system.

The Acquisition of Instrumental Pecking

The pigeon's reliance upon respondent behaviour in so many situations strengthens the suspicion raised by the auto-shaping studies. The data force us to examine the possibility that the birds' simplest instrumental responses might be nothing more than Pavlovian CRs.

We have seen that the instrumental key response resembles both the consummatory response to grain and the Pavlovian reaction so readily auto-shaped with grain. But we have not looked to see why Pavlovian conditioning should occur in instrumental learning situations. So let us examine the procedures by which pigeons are trained to peck keys.

Once a bird has been taught to react quickly to food presentations, there are at least six ways to establish the pecking response. The simplest, but slowest, way (Ferster and Skinner, 1957, p. 31; Neuringer, 1970) is to withhold all further reinforcement until the bird actually operates the key. This may involve hours of waiting, but if the response finally occurs, the technique usually works. This is consistent with Pavlovian, as well as instrumental learning, assumptions. If the response does occur, it leads at once to the presentation of grain. This will be the first reinforcer to have been received in a very long time, and it will come immediately after a very close look at the key.

The reinforcer is thus paired closely with the sight of the key at a time when other associations would have been weakened by prolonged non-reinforcement. As a consequence, the key might elicit one or more Pavlovian responses; these would be reinforced, and the Pavlovian association further strengthened. This could lead to even more reinforced responses, and an even stronger Pavlovian association. It is obviously a self-energizing or positive-feedback process: a Pavlovian trapping mechanism, which leads to instrumental learning. Bindra (1972) has independently hypothesized just such a mechanism.*

A second way to train pigeons to peck keys is to utilize an efficient prompting technique.

> Where the process of acquisition is not important, a small grain of corn can be attached to the key with Scotch tape. . . . The pigeon will quickly peck at the grain, and the magazine will open. When conditioning to the key has taken place, the grain can then be removed. . . .
> *Ferster and Skinner, 1957, p. 31*

Reid, French and Pollard (1969) explored a similar technique. Again, the Pavlovian interpretation is obvious.

A third procedure was brought to my attention by Peter Seraganian. During magazine training, the reinforcement site becomes associated with food, and the pigeon may peck in its vicinity. The experimenter can take

---

* Bindra's (1972) theory contains, explicitly or implicitly, many of the ideas presented in the present paper. His conclusions are given in a much broader frame of reference, and he has not needed specifically to analyze the pigeon's instrumental learning. But the principles which emerge from this species' behaviour and those which Bindra has deduced from other considerations are alike at many points.

advantage of this and simply reinforce the bird for pecking further from the magazine, and nearer to the key. The consummatory response is thus re-directed, perhaps by shifting the region of strongest Pavlovian association towards and onto the manipulandum.

A fourth way to condition pecking is to shape the response by the method of successive approximations. In a typical sequence, the animal might first be rewarded for facing the key. As that behaviour emerged, reward might be withheld until the bird approached the key. Next, reward might be delivered only when the bird's head was in front of the key, then only when the bird pecked towards it, then the pecks might have to touch the key, and finally the pecks would have to operate the key.

The shaping process is said to depend upon the direct operant strengthening of the reinforced movements, the "successive approximations" to pecking. However, we have seen that the same progression occurs without selective reinforcement; auto-shaped birds, too, tend first to begin to face the key, then to begin to approach it, then to peck towards it, and so forth. Apparently, successive approximations to key pecking can arise through the mere strengthening of a Pavlovian association between the key and grain. This is really quite reasonable. It means that a weak association might evoke only the beginning links of a species-specific sequence, and that with a stronger association, the sequence might be more fully expressed. Additionally, we have seen that attempts to shape other response topographies usually fail. Thus the end product of response shaping, the familiar peck, typically arises under favourable response contingencies (operant shaping), unfavourable ones (differentiation studies; omission training), or none at all (auto-shaping).

It is quite possible that the success of operant shaping techniques in this situation is due to stimulus-reinforcement, rather than response-reinforcement, pairings. Note that the reinforcer is at first given when the pigeon is facing the key; stimuli in that area are thus paired with food, and should begin to attract the animal. The bird is then reinforced only when nearer the key; peripheral cues are thus extinguished, and those nearer the key are more strongly paired with the reinforcer. Through successive approximations, the Pavlovian association would be further strengthened, and the set of conditioned stimuli concurrently narrowed and finally limited to the key and immediately surrounding cues.

The fifth way to train pigeons to peck keys was developed by Ferster and Skinner. It involves the use of a training panel which they called a "punch board". The normal response panel contains one to three plastic response keys, each mounted behind a circular hole. The "punch-board" training panel contains many such holes. Tissue paper is stretched behind the panel. Thus, the bird sees many white paper discs, each resembling a response key. Behind each disc is a small pocket of grain. Some of the discs are torn open so that the grain can be seen. Others are torn only slightly or not at all. This of course elicits consummatory pecking, and creates an association between the paper discs and grain. The association transfers almost perfectly to plastic response keys. Most of the subjects used in Ferster and Skinner's research were trained by *this* technique (1957, p. 32). The respondent origin of their "operants" is obvious.

The sixth way to train pigeons to peck keys is to utilize auto-shaping.

In summary, the pecking response can be prompted by the punch-board technique or by taping grain to the key; it can be awaited and reinforced or shaped through successive approximations; it can be re-directed from the food site; it can be auto-shaped. In every case both the acquisition and maintenance of the response follow at once from Pavlovian principles. In every case, the Pavlovian process accounts for both the form and direction of the learned behaviour. The operant principle, by contrast, is in some cases patently irrelevant, and in all cases unnecessary. For these reasons, it seems parsimonious to interpret the pigeon's simple instrumental peck as a Pavlovian conditioned response.

Related Situations

The Pavlovian mechanism could produce instrumental learning with certain other combinations of response and reinforcer. A bird given water for "drinking" a key might return to the key and drink, for Pavlovian reasons. One might instrumentally condition the male pigeon's courtship behaviour if the reinforcer were a female pigeon, or strengthen aggressive responses if the reinforcer were a male conspecific. Escape reactions might be reinforced by the cessation of shock, and so forth.

The process could also work with delayed instrumental reward, although some efficiency might be lost due to trace-conditioning decrements, or through the direct strengthening of competing Pavlovian associations. (With immediate reward, competing associations could arise only through trace conditioning, and even this source of interference could be minimized by insuring repeated exposures to the manipulandum—perhaps by using ratio schedules of reinforcement.)

In many situations, the Pavlovian mechanism could lead to the strengthening of appetitive reactions. These, however, might prove temporary if the manipulandum or some other cue became so strongly conditioned as to elicit consummatory reactions. For example, the bird shown in Fig. 1e was trained to operate the lever by stepping on it, but after extended training the walking response was abandoned and the bird began to peck the lever (cf. Breland and Breland, 1961; Reynolds, Catania and Skinner, 1963).

N

One water-reinforced animal abandoned a stepping response and began to make drinking reactions to the lever, a behaviour so inefficient that it sometimes postponed reinforcement for several minutes.

Other pigeons in the same exploratory study operated the lever with appetitive or consummatory reactions which were directed at background stimuli. One bird learned to use the lever as a step while climbing towards a corner of the ceiling, or so it appeared. A water-reinforced animal learned to bar press with its tail, but even that was not an arbitrary operant. The bird had begun to direct classic drinking responses to the normally-dry underside of the water dispenser. To reach the chosen spot required contortions which almost inevitably brought the animal's tail to bear on the lever.

Conditionally-Effective Cues

Pavlov's animals were often conditioned to react to stimulus A only in the presence (or absence) of stimulus B. The conditions necessary for the formation of such discriminations are implicit in most instrumental-learning situations. Reinforcement sites, manipulanda, and various background cues are typically experienced in conjunction with reinforcement only under certain conditions. Within limits, the pigeon's behaviour should reflect these implicit Pavlovian contingencies.

The process is illustrated by a simple observation reported by Staddon and Simmelhag (1971). When their pigeons received free reinforcement every twelve seconds, the birds soon began to stand with their heads in the food magazine, or to peck the magazine wall. These reactions were at first continuous, persisting both when reinforcement was imminent and when it was not. Later, the appropriate temporal discrimination emerged. The animals reacted to the food site only towards the end of each twelve-second interval, as if a conditional discrimination had been formed; the food site appeared to function as a conditionally-effective CS. The same process might occur when key pecking is reinforced on a fixed-interval schedule. The key would be most closely associated with food towards the end of each interval, and should best elicit pecking at such times.

Similarly, if exposure to the reinforcement site or to the key were followed by grain only in the presence of an auditory signal, the object should eventually tend to elicit conditioned behaviour primarily in the presence of that signal. This seems to occur both for reinforcement sites (Farthing, 1971) and response keys (Jenkins and Harrison, 1962). The behaviour of Jenkins' photocell-pecking subjects (Chapter 9) also conforms to this paradigm.

Of course, the signal would itself become associated with the reinforcer and would sometimes compete with the conditionally-attractive object for control of the animal's behaviour. This happens occasionally when the signal is auditory (Farthing, 1971) and often when it is visual. An obvious example is the usual auto-shaping situation where the pigeon's behaviour is directed towards the lighted key instead of the food magazine. After extended training however, auto-shaped subjects occasionally abandon the key to peck down the wall to the conditionally-attractive reinforcement site (Moore, 1971).

Note that Pavlovian reactions directed towards the reinforcement site (or towards any background stimulus) would avoid the omission-training contingency described earlier. An adventitious association between a background stimulus and grain could be consistently reinforced in the presence of the lighted key. Further, movements towards the key would produce stimuli associated with nonreinforcement; this might well cause the animal not to peck, or the reaction might be weak or incomplete. Thus, Pavlovian conditional discriminations might eventually weaken or extinguish key-directed pecking and strengthen the tendency to peck at other, conditionally-attractive objects. This is consistent with Kirby's (1968) observation that most of the pecks of her omission-trained subjects either landed upon the panel alongside the response key or stopped short of the panel or key. "Short" pecks or weak ones would often be recorded as brief-duration events, but they should *not* be interpreted as differing in kind from normally auto-shaped responses (Schwartz, 1971).

After extended training, some subjects do seem to learn to cope with the omission-training contingency, perhaps through the conditional-discrimination process; others, however, show little such learning even after a thousand or more trials (Williams and Williams, 1969; Kirby, 1968).

Conditional discriminations were also important in the exploratory study mentioned earlier in which pigeons were trained to bar press for food.* The levers were effectively paired with grain only in the presence of visual discriminative stimuli. Horizontal and vertical stripe patterns were projected onto standard response keys six inches above the levers. It has been noted that the pigeons at first operated the levers with appetitive reactions, but that after further training some subjects began to peck them. These birds continued to walk upon the levers during intertrial intervals but shifted abruptly to pecking whenever the discriminative stimuli were turned on. Thus, the tendency of the levers to elicit consummatory behaviour was conditional upon the presence of discriminative cues.

With further training, the signalling cues themselves began to elicit consummatory reactions. So long as the animals were responding equally often to the correct and incorrect levers, that did not occur; but at the

---

* I am grateful to Darwin Muir for several contributions to this work.

point at which an animal began to discriminate between the levers, it began also to approach and peck the discriminative stimuli, as shown in Fig. 1f. The birds were not required to make such responses, and had never been rewarded for pecking keys. The cue-elicited reactions could be taken for instrumental observing responses (Wyckoff, 1952, 1959; also cf. Polidora and Thompson, 1965); however, it is obvious that they might have been Pavlovian reactions to stimuli associated with food. No attempt has been made to test between these interpretations. However, Jenkins (in press) has thoroughly investigated the origins of cue-directed pecking in the related "feature-positive" situation and has found that those reactions depend upon stimulus-reinforcement, rather than response-reinforcement, pairings. Also, photographs of our subjects showed that most of the "observing" responses were made with *closed eyes* and opened beaks.

Cue-directed reactions of this sort might be mere by-products of the Pavlovian process. They are far from maladaptive, however. They not only increase the animal's exposure to relevant cues; they also draw it into a position from which it could more readily discriminate between correct and incorrect levers. In effect, the "observing responses" would tend to channel the organism in the right direction.

The conditional-discrimination process would add enormously to the adaptiveness of the Pavlovian mechanism, and it has one further implication which has yet to be examined. Because it permits the organism to react to a given stimulus only under certain discriminable circumstances, the process has obvious relevance to the sequential organization of behaviour.

Pavlovian Chaining

Response chaining is ordinarily thought of as an operant conditioning phenomenon. For the sake of simplicity, operant chains are customarily described in terms of discrete component reactions. These are said to be linked by stimuli which serve both discriminative and reinforcing functions. For purposes of illustration, we may imagine a hypothetical organism which pecks a key until a reinforcement-indicator light signals the availability of water. An operant chain of the following sort should be possible:

$$S_1 \text{ (key)} - R_1 \text{ (peck)}$$
$$S_2 \text{ (light)} - R_2 \text{ (approach water)}$$
$$S_3 \text{ (water)} - R_3 \text{ (drink)}$$

where R_1 and R_2 are operants and R_3 is a respondent; S_1 is a discriminative stimulus and a potentially effective conditioned reinforcer; S_2 is a discriminative stimulus for R_2 and a conditioned reinforcer which strengthens R_1; S_3 is a reinforcing stimulus which elicits R_3 and reinforces R_2.

The pigeons used in Warren's duration-shaping study (described earlier) did not conform to this model. First, of course, R_1 was neither a peck nor an arbitrary operant but a drinking reaction. Second, when the indicator light came on, the birds usually approached and "drank" it before proceding to the water, which was available and clearly visible an inch below the light. A third problem is that having assumed that S_1 and S_2 are Pavlovian CSs (otherwise they would not be conditioned reinforcers), it is not reasonable to deny them the properties of CSs (*viz.*, the ability to release and direct CRs). Once that has been corrected, the chain is entirely explained; there is no need to make further assumptions about response-reinforcement mechanisms *or* operant chaining.

The behaviour of Warren's birds might be analyzed in Pavlovian terms:

$$S_1 \text{ (key)} - R_1 \text{ (approach and drink key)}$$
$$S_2 \text{ (light)} - R_2 \text{ (approach light, perhaps drink)}$$
$$S_3 \text{ (water)} - R_3 \text{ (approach and drink water)}$$

In effect, the three stimuli *channel* the pigeon into contact with the reinforcer. The sequential organization of this chain is imposed by obvious factors: the key light is the first stimulus to be presented; the water light is more visible from a distance than is water; the stimuli most closely paired with reinforcement ordinarily become most strongly conditioned.

More complex Pavlovian chains are made possible by conditional discriminations; the process is isomorphic to operant chaining theory. The operant model explains the occurrence of a particular response at some discriminable point in a chain by noting that the response has been, in that situation, followed by a reinforcing stimulus. In a Pavlovian chain, the response is simply *elicited by stimuli* which have been, in that situation, followed by reinforcement.

Thus the Pavlovian process which has sometimes been thought irrelevant to skeletal behaviour can in principle generate response chains of great complexity.

Concluding Remarks

There are many factors which might prevent one from recognizing that an instrumental response had been caused, directly or indirectly, by the Pavlovian process. It is evident that such a response would not always resemble the reaction elicited by the reinforcer. Even in traditional

Pavlovian situations, conditioned and unconditioned responses are sometimes very different. The form of the conditioned behaviour depends upon the nature of the reinforcer, but also upon other factors, including the conditioned and unconditioned properties of the nominal CS, the reinforcement site, and various environmental cues. When Pavlovian reactions arise from response-contingent reinforcement, response selection may be greatly affected by the stimulus-differentiation mechanism described earlier. It is critical that the observer be able to recognize any species-specific response patterns used by the subject. But it is obvious that our knowledge of the pigeon's behaviour is far from complete, and that the many facts which are available have not received maximum exposure. The *Cumulative Reference Index* for the first ten volumes of the *Journal of the Experimental Analysis of Behavior* (1967) shows not a single reference to the classical works of C. O. Whitman or Wallace Craig. It should also be recalled that the pigeons used in most psychological research (Levi, 1963) differ experientially and genetically from feral animals; their reactions may differ in some situations. There are additional complications. The expression of an identifiable response may be prevented by lack of optimal stimulation or environmental support (cf. von Holst and von St. Paul, 1962, 1963). Stimuli, postures, or movements produced by the beginning of one reaction may release other, unrelated response patterns (Tinbergen, 1952; Lind, 1959). Displacement reactions may differ so greatly from their "examples" as to be almost unrecognizable in some situations (Tinbergen, 1952). The conditioning chamber may prevent the expression of normal reactions and facilitate abnormal forms, perhaps including stereotyped reactions induced by locomotion or by appetitive "searching" within a small, confined space. Further, it should be realized that the apparatus and procedures used in instrumental-learning laboratories have themselves evolved through the selection of features which maximized the incidence of desired reactions or suppressed the occurrence of "disruptive" ones; unfortunately, this is not a minor consideration.

All things considered, the Pavlovian mechanism may prove able to account for an appreciable part of the pigeon's instrumental learning. But it can scarcely be expected to account for everything; it is a primitive process, and explains primitive sorts of learning. The pigeon is decidedly inferior to the theoretical operant organism, but that does not mean that it is capable of nothing more than classical conditioning.

It is not possible in this paper to examine the importance of the Pavlovian mechanism in animals other than pigeons. But for examples of its generality, one need only turn to Sevenster's very interesting work with sticklebacks (Chapter 12), or read Sutherland's (1963, p. 182) graphic description of response topographies in the mollusc, *Octopus vulgaris*. In mammals, the mechanism is probably sufficient to account for the simplest sorts of runway and maze learning obtained with positive or negative reinforcement and the simplest discrimination learning obtained in jumping stands, mazes (see especially Bauer and Lawrence, 1953), and similar apparatus. Azrin, Hutchinson and Hake (1967) have observed that lever-pressing responses used by monkeys in avoidance situations are sometimes vestigial components of shock-elicited aggressive reactions. The marked facilitation of avoidance learning by separation of stimulus and response sites (Biederman et al. 1964), the equally-powerful but opposite effect obtained with positive reinforcement (Meyer et al., 1965), and the overt "observing responses" which often emerge in the latter situation (Polidora and Thompson, 1965), may all be Pavlovian in origin. Finally, the dramatic self-punitive behaviour observed when restrained monkeys are shocked for struggling (Morse et al., 1967) illustrates the extent to which the Pavlovian trapping mechanism can strengthen maladaptive behaviour in unusual circumstances.

The Pavlovian mechanism would be highly adaptive in most natural situations. It would cause the animal to return to places, or objects, or substances, or organisms in the presence of which it was likely to encounter the sorts of unconditioned stimuli which elicit approach reactions. Symmetrically, it would cause the animal to avoid many situations in which escape behaviour might otherwise have been evoked. Since unconditioned approach reactions are elicited primarily by beneficial agents, and escape reactions by harmful ones, the learned responses would often be highly adaptive. Further, since the physiological states which raise or lower the thresholds of unconditioned reactions have similar effects upon classically-conditioned responses, the animal would tend to react selectively to the environmental conditioned stimuli most relevant to its immediate needs. The sorts of proactive inhibition phenomena described by Mackintosh (Chapter 4) would tend to retard the formation of invalid associations, and the extinction process would tend to efface those which were no longer valid. In short, the instrumental behaviour produced by the Pavlovian mechanism would be attuned to the habitat, experience, and immediate biological needs of the individual organism. The process would be non-adaptive or seriously maladaptive in particular circumstances, but the effect upon a population of animals could scarcely fail to be positive.

One can easily imagine other instrumental learning processes which would be more perfectly adaptive than this primitive Pavlovian mechanism, but it is hard to imagine a superior process which would not entail far greater biological complexity. The striking simplicity of the Pavlovian process, and the economy with which it utilizes the instinctive mechanisms already present in primitive organisms, would have given it an initial evolutionary advantage of considerable magnitude. That is not to say that nothing else has evolved, either independently or from Pavlovian sources. It is quite possible that the primitive Pavlovian mechanism is most important at intermediate phylogenetic levels, and that superior processes begin to appear as one proceeds towards the more recent classes, *Aves* and, especially, *Mammalia*.

References

Armstrong, E. A. (1965). "Bird Display and Behaviour." Dover, New York.

Azrin, N. H. (1959). Some notes on punishment and avoidance. *J. exp. Analysis Behav.* **2**, 260.

Azrin, N. H. and Hutchinson, R. R. (1967). Conditioning of the aggressive behavior of pigeons by a fixed-interval schedule of reinforcement. *J. exp. Analysis Behav.* **10**, 395–402.

Azrin, N. H., Hutchinson, R. R. and Hake, D. F. (1967). Attack, avoidance, and escape reactions to aversive shock. *J. exp. Analysis Behav.* **10**, 131–148.

Bauer, F. J., and Lawrence, D. H. (1953). Influence of similarity of choice-point and goal cues on discrimination learning. *J. comp. physiol. Psychol.* **46**, 241–252.

Bedford, J. A. and Anger, D. (1968). Flight as an avoidance response in pigeons. Paper read at the annual meeting of the Midwestern Psychological Association, Chicago.

Biederman, G. B., D'Amato, M. R. and Keller, D. M. (1964). Facilitation of discriminated avoidance learning by dissociation of CS and manipulandum. *Psychon. Sci.* **1**, 229–230.

Bindra, D. (1972). A unified account of classical conditioning and operant training. *In* "Classical Conditioning II: Current Research and Theory", (A. H. Black and W. F. Prokasy, eds.). Appleton-Century-Crofts, New York.

Blough, D. S. (1961). Experiments in animal psychophysics. *Scient. Am.* **205**, (1), 113–122.

Bolles, R. C. (1970). Species-specific defense reactions and avoidance learning. *Psychol. Rev.* **77**, 32–48.

Breland, K. and Breland, M. (1961). The misbehavior of organisms. *Am. Psychol.* **16**, 681–684.

Breland, K. and Breland, M. (1966). "Animal Behavior." Macmillan, New York.

Brown, P. L. (1968). Auto-shaping and observing responses (R_o) in the pigeon. *Proc. 76th Conv. Am. Psychol. Assoc.* 139–140.

Brown, P. L. and Jenkins, H. M. (1968). Auto-shaping of the pigeon's key peck. *J. exp. Analysis Behav.* **11**, 1–8.

Bullock, D. H. (1960). Note on key-holding behavior in the pigeon. *J. exp. Analysis Behav.* **3**, 274.

Cole, J. L. (1965). Force gradients in stimulus generalization. *J. exp. Analysis Behav.* **8**, 231–241.

Craig, W. (1911). The expressions of emotion in the pigeons. II. The mourning dove (*Zenaidura macroura* Linn.) *Auk* **28**, 398–407.

Farthing, G. W. (1971). Effect of a signal previously paired with free food on operant response rate in pigeons. *Psychon. Sci.* **23**, 343–344.

Ferster, C. B. and Skinner, B. F. (1957). "Schedules of Reinforcement." Appleton-Century-Crofts, New York.

Foree, D. D. and LoLordo, V. M. (1970). Signalled and unsignalled free-operant avoidance in the pigeon. *J. exp. Analysis Behav.* **13**, 283–290.

Goodwin, D. (1954). Notes on feral pigeons. *Avicult. Mag.* **60**, 190–213.

Graf, V. and Bitterman, M. E. (1963). General activity as instrumental: application to avoidance training. *J. exp. Analysis Behav.* **6**, 301–306.

Hefferline, R. F., Birch, J. D. and Gentry, T. (1961). Simple transducers to detect or record operant amplitude. *J. exp. Analysis Behav.* **4**, 257–261.

Hineline, P. N. and Rachlin, H. (1969). Escape and avoidance of shock by pigeons pecking a key. *J. exp. Analysis Behav.* **12**, 533–538.

Hoffman, H. S. and Fleshler, M. (1959). Aversive control with the pigeon. *J. exp. Analysis Behav.* **2**, 213–218.

Hogan, J. A. (1964), Operant control of preening in pigeons. *J. exp. Analysis Behav.* **7**, 351–354.

von Holst, E. and von St. Paul, U. (1962). Electrically controlled behavior. *Scient. Am.* **206** (3), 50–59.

von Holst, E. and von St. Paul, U. (1963). On the functional organisation of drives. *Anim. Behav.* **11**, 1–20.

Jenkins, H. M. (In press). Noticing and responding in a discrimination based on a distinguishing element. *Learning and Motivation.*

Jenkins, H. M. and Harrison, R. H. (1962). Generalization gradients of inhibition following auditory discrimination learning. *J. exp. Analysis Behav.* **5**, 435–441.

Jenkins, H. M. and Moore, B. R. (In press). The form of the auto-shaped response with food or water reinforcers. *J. exp. Analysis Behav.*

Kirby, A. J. (1968). Explorations of the Brown-Jenkins auto-shaping phenomenon. Unpublished M.A. thesis, Dalhousie University.

Levi, W. M. (1963). "The Pigeon." Author, Sumter, South Carolina.

Lind, H. (1959), The activation of an instinct caused by a "transitional action". *Behaviour* **14**, 123–135.

McFarland, D. J. and Baher, E. (1968). Factors affecting feather posture in the barbary dove. *Anim. Behav.* **16**, 171–177.

Macphail, E. M. (1968). Avoidance responding in pigeons. *J. exp. Analysis Behav.* **11**, 629–632.

Marler, P. R. and Hamilton, W. J. (1966). "Mechanisms of Animal Behavior." Wiley, New York.

Meyer, D. R., Treichler, F. R. and Meyer, P. M. (1965). Discrete-trial training techniques and stimulus variables. *In* "Behavior of Non-Human Primates". (A. M. Schrier, H. Harlow and F. Stollnitz, eds.). Academic Press, New York.

Miller, W. J. and Miller, L. S. (1958). Synopsis of behavioural traits of the ring neck dove. *Anim. Behav.* **6**, 3–8.

Moore, B. R. (1971). On directed respondents. (Doctoral dissertation, Stanford University), Ann Arbor, Michigan: University Microfilms, Number 72–11, 623.

Morse, W. H., Mead, R. M. and Kelleher, R. T. (1967). Modulation of elicited behavior by a fixed-interval schedule of electric shock presentation. *Science* **157**, 215–217.

Neuringer, A. J. (1970). Superstitious key pecking after three peck-produced reinforcements. *J. exp. Analysis Behav.* **13**, 127–134.

Pavlov, I. P. (1941), "Lectures on Conditioned Reflexes", Vol. 2. Conditioned reflexes and psychiatry. (Translated by W. H. Gantt), International, New York.

Polidora, V. J. and Thompson, W. J. (1965). Orienting behavior and the S-R spatial discontiguity effect in monkeys. *J. comp. physiol. Psychol.* **59**, 240–245.

Rachlin, H. (1969). Autoshaping of key pecking in pigeons with negative reinforcement. *J. exp. Analysis Behav.* **12**, 521–531.

Rachlin, H. and Hineline, P. N. (1967). Training and maintenence of keypecking in the pigeon by negative reinforcement. *Science* **157**, 954–955.

Rackham, D. W. (1971). Conditioning of the pigeon's courtship and aggressive behavior. Unpublished M.A. thesis, Dalhousie University.

Reid, R. L., French, A. and Pollard, J. S. (1969). Priming the pecking response in pigeons. *Psychon. Sci.* **14**, 227–229.

Reynolds, G. S., Catania, A. C. and Skinner, B. F. (1963). Conditioned and unconditioned aggression in pigeons. *J. exp. Analysis Behav.* **6**, 73–74.

Schwartz, B. (1971), Two different kinds of key-peck in the pigeon: Some properties of responses maintained by a negative response-reinforcer contingency. Paper read at the annual meeting of the Eastern Psychological Association, New York.

Sheffield, F. D. (1965). Relation between classical conditioning and instrumental learning. *In* "Classical Conditioning", (W. F. Prokasy, ed.). Appleton-Century-Crofts, New York.

Sidman, M. (1953). Avoidance conditioning with brief shock and no exteroceptive warning signal. *Science* **118**, 157–158.

Skinner, B. F. (1938). "The Behavior of Organisms." Appleton-Century-Crofts, New York.

Skinner, B. F. (1948). "Superstition" in the pigeon. *J. exp. Psychol.* **38**, 168–172.

Skinner, B. F. (1958). Reinforcement today. *Am. Psychol.* **13**, 94–99.

Smith, R. F. (1967). Behavioral events other than key striking which are counted as responses during pigeon pecking. (Doctoral dissertation, Indiana University), Ann Arbor, Michigan: University Microfilms, Number 68=7225.

Smith, R. F. and Keller, F. R. (1970). Free-operant avoidance in the pigeon using a treadle response. *J. exp. Analysis Behav.* **13**, 211–214.

Staddon, J. E. R. and Simmelhag, V. L. (1971). The "superstition" experiment. *Psychol. Rev.* **78**, 3–43.

Sutherland, N. S. (1963). The shape-discrimination of stationary shapes by octopuses. *Am. J. Psychol.* **76**, 177–190.

Tinbergen, N. (1952). "Derived" activities; their causation, biological significance, origin, and emancipation during evolution. *Q. Rev. Biol.* **27**, 1–32.

Whitman, C. O. (1919). Posthumous works of Charles Otis Whitman. *In* "The Behavior of Pigeons", Vol. 3, (H. A. Carr, ed.). Carnegie Institution, Washington.

Williams, D. R. and Williams H. (1969). Auto-maintenance in the pigeon: sustained pecking despite contingent non-reinforcement. *J. exp. Analysis Behav.* **12**, 511–520.

Willis, F. N. (1966). Fighting in pigeons relative to available space. *Psychon. Sci.* **4**, 315–316.

Wolin, B. R. (1968). Difference in manner of pecking a key between pigeons reinforced with food and with water. Paper read at Conference on the Experimental Analysis of Behavior, 1948. *Reprinted in* "Contemporary Research in Operant Behavior", (A. C. Catania, ed.). Scott, Foresman, Glenview, Ill.

Wyckoff, L. B., Jr. (1952). The role of observing responses in discrimination learning: Part I. *Psychol. Rev.* **59**, 431–442.

Wyckoff, L. B., Jr. (1959). Toward a quantitative theory of secondary reinforcement. *Psychol. Rev.* **66**, 68–78.

Comments

1. *McFarland wrote:*

"I am disturbed by the fact that all studies of autoshaping *per se* are with pigeons. Is it possible that pigeons are in some ways a special case?

In this respect, it may be of interest to note that, in doves, oral factors are essential for reinforcement of drinking, while crop loading has no effect. Conversely, crop loading is essential for satiation, but oral factors contribute nothing (McFarland, 1969). When the beak of doves is partly denervated by central lesions, doves become aphagic, being unable to swallow grain. They are still motivated to eat, and will approach grain and peck at it. However, doves trained to peck a key for food will not peck after such lesions. The integrity of beak innervation seems to be important in the operant response (Wright, 1968)."

Moore replied:

"There have been a few studies with other species, e.g. Gardner's (1969) experiments with quail, and Squier's (1969) with fish (*Tilapia*). Sidman and Fletcher (1968) reported what seemed to be auto-shaping in the rhesus monkey, but there was a superimposed operant contingency which left several things uncertain. Because of that, Dr. David Likely and I have just done the experiment again, using purely Pavlovian procedures, and controlling for non-associative artifact. There were no real problems. The animals conditioned, and their responses were of appropriate form; they grasped and bit the key as if it were food.

I thought for a long time that rats did not auto-shape. I tried the experiment five years ago in response to Breland and Breland (1961) and failed. Then Jenkins gave a colloquium which left no doubt as to who had the better preparation, so I switched to pigeons. But I did run two or three further exploratory studies with rats. A few animals approached and chewed the CS; others learned apparently superstitious rituals, and still others made anticipatory responses. Recently research by Gail Peterson at Indiana University seems to have found the combination for autoshaping rats. His animals consistently behave in that fashion, and the studies are properly controlled. We should now explore the differences between his procedures and ours, to find out what variables cause the different outcomes."

2. A further comment is printed after the next chapter.

References

Breland, K. and Breland, M. (1961). The misbehavior of organisms. *Am. Psychol.* **16**, 681–684.

Gardner, W. M. (1969). Auto-shaping in bobwhite quail. *J. exp. Analysis Behav.* **12**, 279–281.

McFarland, D. J. (1969). Separation of satiating and rewarding consequences of drinking. *Physiol. Behav.* **4**, 987–989.

Sidman, M. and Fletcher, F. G. (1968). A demonstration of auto-shaping in the monkey. *J. exp. Anal. Behav.* **11**, 307–309.

Squier, L. H. (1969). Autoshaping key responses with fish. *Psychon. Sci.* **17**, 177–178.

Wright, P. (1968). Hypothalamic lesions and food/water intake in the Barbary dove. *Psychon. Sci.* **13**, 133–134.

9
Effects of the Stimulus-Reinforcer Relation on Selected and Unselected Responses

by H. M. Jenkins

A central problem for behaviour theory is to develop an adequate account of how a stimulus becomes a signal for action. Contemporary thinking about the process is still dominated by two conceptions. The one is Pavlovian and it holds that a stimulus becomes a signal for action by being presented together with another stimulus that already evokes action. The other is Skinnerian and it holds that a stimulus becomes a signal for action by being present when that action is reinforced.

These conceptions of the learning process are not based on a deep knowledge of how learning occurs. Rather, they are conceptions based on and closely tied to the experimental arrangements that generated them. In the Pavlovian experiment, one arranges response-independent pairings of a stimulus (CS) with a reinforcer (UCS) and observes the behaviour that develops in the interval between the CS, or signalling stimulus, and the reinforcer. In the simplest operant experiment, one arranges for some responses and not others to be followed by a reinforcer and observes progressive increases in the frequency of reinforced responses (shaping). In order to place the operant under the control of a discriminative stimulus, the reinforcement of the response is made to depend on the presence of the stimulus. The result is a three-termed sequence: stimulus (S^D or S^+), operant response, and reinforcer.

The three terms of the operant sequence have their parallel in the Pavlovian experiment. The Pavlovian CS may be coordinated to the operant S^+, the Pavlovian CR (conditioned response) to the operant response, and the Pavlovian UCS to the operant reinforcer. The principle distinction is in the procedure or operations used to establish the sequence. The discriminated operant involves a response *selected* by the experimenter through shaping. This response, in an unambiguous example, would not occur as the natural consequence of arranging for the temporal pairing of the discriminative stimulus with the reinforcer. In the Pavlovian experiment, on the other hand, the conditioned response is a natural consequence of the stimulus-reinforcer pairing and is in that sense *unselected.*

The Pavlovian and operant arrangements do not, however, segregate clearly the kinds of relations that occur among the three terms of the sequence. Consider the relation between classical conditioning with food as the UCS and operant conditioning with food as the reinforcer. The discriminated operant brings the discriminative stimulus in close temporal conjunction with the reinforcing stimulus, so there is a stimulus-reinforcer pairing here as well as in the Pavlovian experiment. It is true that the pairing of S^+ with the reinforcing stimulus depends on the occurrence of the required operant, but there is no reason to think that the effect of the pairing is thereby nullified. Conversely, the Pavlovian experiment typically entails the essential feature of operant conditioning; the close temporal conjunction between a response and a reinforcing stimulus. Although the reinforcing stimulus in the Pavlovian experiment does not depend on the responses that occur prior to the reinforcing stimulus, the law of effect has always been stated in terms of temporal conjunction, not dependency. The treatment of superstitious conditioning as a corollary of principles of operant reinforcement (Herrnstein, 1966) reflects the assumption that a reinforcer always reinforces some response whether or not that response produced the reinforcer. Making the reinforcer depend on certain responses will have an important effect on the eventual outcome of a conditioning regime, but it has always been assumed that the function of the dependency is simply to govern or to constrain the type of response that can occur in temporal conjunction with the reinforcer. In short, the Pavlovian experiment arranges a stimulus-reinforcer relation but brings some response into temporal conjunction with the reinforcer. The discriminated operant experiment arranges a response-reinforcer relation in the presence of a certain stimulus but thereby brings that stimulus into temporal conjunction with the reinforcer. Since the same temporal sequence of stimulus, response, and reinforcer can arise from either procedure, it is almost inconceivable that the operational distinction would segregate two distinct, non-overlapping, learning processes.

The auto-shaping experiment obviously involves both a stimulus-reinforcer and a response-reinforcer relation. The procedure is Pavlovian. It consists of response-independent pairings of a signalling stimulus with a positive reinforcer such as food. When the signal is a localized visual stimulus, pigeons and a variety of other animals, learn to approach and contact the source of the signal (Chapter 8). Skeletal movements of the kind involved in approach and contact are certainly subject to selective strengthening by arranging for a positive reinforcer to follow their occurrence. We are, therefore, confronted with a Pavlovian procedure leading to behaviour that differs in no obvious way from the kind of behaviour that can be selected by response contingent reinforcement. Because auto-shaping forces one to consider the joint action of stimulus-reinforcer and response-reinforcer relations, it may help to break the hold of the operant-classical dichotomy on our thinking and lead to a more organic treatment of simple learning.

In what follows, several facts about auto-shaping in pigeons with food or water as the reinforcer are stated and subsequently discussed briefly. We then consider in what particulars these facts require a treatment that exceeds the scope of the concept of the discriminated operant. The results of this exercise will be to conclude that the stimulus-reinforcer relation produces certain effects that cannot be accommodated even by a liberalized version of the operant reinforcement principle. The last section of the paper considers the possibility that some of these effects may also be found in the case of shaped or selected responses under stimulus control.

Some Facts About Auto-Shaping

1. A high percentage of pigeons exposed to the auto-shaping procedure end up regularly approaching and contacting the source of the signal.

2. The very first contact with the signalling stimulus is not an accident. The pairing of stimulus with reinforcer is instrumental in bringing about the initial contact.

3. Stimulus-reinforcer pairings presented to a bird restrained from reaching the stimulus source result in the later appearance of a complete approach and contact when the restraining barrier is removed.

4. In a hungry bird being auto-shaped with grain as the reinforcer, the contact response resembles pecking at grain. In a thirsty bird being auto-shaped with water as the reinforcer, the contact response resembles drinking.

5. In a hungry and thirsty bird auto-shaped with one stimulus signalling grain and another signalling water, the contact response resembles the consummatory response appropriate to the reinforcer being signalled.

6. Pecks will shift from a less predictive to a more predictive signal of food even when the reinforcer is produced only by a response to the less predictive signal.

7. The contingency between the stimulus and the reinforcer, not just the pairing of stimulus and reinforcer, is important in auto-shaping. Removal of the stimulus-reinforcer contingency by presenting the reinforcer during

stimulus-off periods at the same rate as during stimulus-on periods prevents acquisition and results in the loss of a previously acquired auto-shaped response.

Many of the above-mentioned facts about auto-shaping have been reviewed by Moore (Chapter 8), but some are less familiar and require further comment.

The fact that the (contingent) pairing of the signalling stimulus with the reinforcer is effective in bringing about the first response is important for its bearing on the possibility of an operant account of auto-shaping. Brown and Jenkins (1968) showed that the forward pairing of stimulus with reinforcer yielded the first contact (peck) in fewer trials than did backward pairing in which the stimulus followed the reinforcer. Brown (1968) examined auto-shaping in a two-key arrangement. The lighting of one key signalled the reinforcer while the lighting of the other key was uncorrelated with the reinforcer. Each of the six pigeons exposed to these conditions made their first peck at the key light which served as a signal of the reinforcer rather than to the uncorrelated key light. An unpublished experiment by Ronald Black of McMaster University also used two keys, the lighting of one serving as the signal of the reinforcer, while the lighting of the other was uncorrelated with the reinforcer. In this case, however, the keys were located at opposite ends of a rectangular enclosure almost six feet in length. The food tray was mounted midway between the keys. Seven pigeons were exposed to these conditions. One did not leave the vicinity of the food tray. The remaining six all became strongly auto-shaped to the predictive signal, and were still approaching and pecking it on virtually every trial in the last of the ten sessions that were run. It is of interest that because the key-light was located almost three feet from the grain dispenser, which remained in the up position for only four seconds, the behaviour of pecking at the lighted key until it went off caused a substantial loss in the amount of grain received. In addition to demonstrating auto-shaping to a remote signal, the experiment provides further evidence of the role of the signalling function of the stimulus in bringing about the very first contact since, of the six subjects that auto-shaped, five made their first peck to the predictive stimulus. The other subject made a single peck to the non-predictive key the very first time it appeared, but subsequently began pecking the predictive key. Finally, the experiment by Williams and Williams (1969) showed that the stimulus-reinforcer relation was capable of maintaining responses to the lighted key on a substantial number of trials even when responses precluded the delivery of the reinforcer on that trial (negative contingency). The evidence on the role of the stimulus-reinforcer relation in bringing about the first contact and in maintaining contact despite a negative contingency between the response and reinforcer leads to the generalization that the pairing of stimulus and reinforcer on trials during which a complete approach with contact does not occur increases the subsequent tendency to make a complete approach and contact.

Facts three, four, and five have been discussed by Moore. The sixth fact, that pecks shift from a less to a more predictive signal of the reinforcer even when the reinforcer is produced only by a response to the less predictive signal, comes from an experiment on the learning of a go/no-go discrimination between displays consisting of discrete elements.

The experiment grew out of experiments previously reported by Jenkins and Sainsbury (1969) and it made use of a similar method. The displays to be discriminated consist of a common element, say a green dot, and a distinguishing element, say a red dot. The displays are presented successively on a single pecking key which is divided into square quadrants in order to allow the recording of peck location. Only one element can appear in a quadrant, and the location of elements is shifted irregularly from trial to trial. Initial training consists of reinforced trials with only the common element, the green dot, present. The equipment is set so that a single peck on any quadrant will be reinforced, but in practise the pecks are confined to whatever quadrant contains the element on that trial. Following preliminary training on the common feature alone, discrimination training begins. In the so-called feature positive case, a peck to the display containing both the green dot and the distinguishing red dot is reinforced while a peck to the display containing only the green dot is non-reinforced. In the feature negative case, the positive and negative displays are interchanged.

The results in each of several experiments showed that when the distinguishing element is on the positive trial, the peck location gradually shifts, in the present example, from the common green dot to the distinguishing red dot. The response tracks the distinguishing element even though a peck anywhere on the positive display produces the reinforcer. The shift in peck location to the red dot is followed by the cessation of responding on negative trials where only the green dot appears. In the feature negative case, on the other hand, the pecks continue to be made to the common, green dot and the successive discrimination fails to develop within the limits of an amount of training that is sufficient to produce a clear discrimination in the feature-positive case.

In the experiment which now concerns us (Jenkins, in press), an attempt was made to learn whether the shift from the common to the distinguishing element was facilitated by a perception of the relation between that element and the reinforcer apart from the temporal conjunction of a peck to the distinguishing element and the reinforcer. For that purpose, the

o

feature-positive arrangement was modified by introducing a negative contingency on pecks to the distinguishing element. A peck to the positive display was reinforced unless the peck was made on the quadrant containing the distinguishing element. The distinguishing element served as the more predictive signal of the reinforcer, but the reinforcer was actually obtained by a peck to the common feature on the same display.

Despite the contingent loss of the reinforcer, pecks to the distinguishing element increased in frequency during the course of training. In some cases, more than half of the available reinforcers were lost as the result of pecks to the distinguishing element. The predictive or signalling function of the distinguishing element was an important factor in producing the shift to that element since in the feature-negative arrangement, in which the red dot signalled the absence of a reinforcer, no shift to that element occurred. It is concluded that perceiving the signalling function of an element produces a strong tendency to peck that element even when the reinforcer results from a peck to a different element.

The importance of stimulus-reinforcer contingency in auto-shaping, the last fact listed, was demonstrated in an experiment by Gamzu and Williams (1971). They showed that if the reinforcer was presented at the same average rate during the intertrial, or stimulus-off periods, as during the stimulus-on periods, thereby removing any contingency between stimulus and reinforcer, auto-shaped key pecking did not develop. Furthermore, if the contingency was removed by introducing intertrial reinforcers after acquisition, the auto-shaped response was lost. Restoring the contingency by eliminating the intertrial reinforcers restored the key-peck.

An Operant Account of Auto-shaping

The principle underlying the development of a discriminated operant may be stated as follows. The increased response strength resulting from the conjunction of a movement and reinforcer is greater in the stimulus conditions accompanying the reinforced movement than in other stimulus conditions. I would like to consider in what particulars the phenomena of auto-shaping in the pigeon are outside the reach of this very general operant principle.

The first fact, simply that auto-shaping occurs, does no apparent violence to the principle. Assume some "operant level" probability of a peck to the key when lighted. The pairing of the key-light with the reinforcer guarantees that a peck to the key when lighted will be followed directly by the reinforcer while pecks to an unlighted key will go unreinforced. Now, it is true that any other response the bird might make while the key is lighted will also be followed by the reinforcer, which leaves the question of why pecking should be the favoured response. An answer consistent with the principle, although *ad hoc*, is that other behaviours such as turning, pacing, bobbing, neck stretching, moving towards the tray and so on, which can also occur while the key is lighted, are less sharply controlled by the light than is a peck at the lighted key. That means that these other behaviours appear frequently when the key is not lighted and are, therefore, subject to extinction. If the key light gains especially strong control of a peck, perhaps because the peck is directed at the lighted disc, pecking will occur infrequently in the between-trial, light-off periods, and hence will be less subject to extinction than the other behaviours.

Although the plain fact that auto-shaping occurs can be accommodated to the operant principle, the second fact, that the pairing of stimulus with reinforcer contributes to the appearance of the very first complete approach and contact cannot be accommodated. On the trials prior to the first complete approach and peck some response other than the complete approach and peck is occurring. According to the operant reinforcement principle these incomplete responses should be strengthened, not the complete approach with contact that consistently emerges. The same problem with the operant reinforcement principle is made apparent by the maintenance of auto-shaped responding despite a negative contingency between the response and the reinforcer.

In auto-shaping, the delivery of the reinforcer following trials on which the animal's movements do not bring it into contact with the signalling stimulus leads systematically to something other than the "noncontact" movements that were in progress on those trials. Since the auto-shaping procedure contains no response-reinforcer contingency that could impose a progressive selection or shaping of the response towards a complete approach with contact, the nonaccidental emergence of the first contact response and its subsequent maintenance under negative contingency cannot be accommodated to the operant reinforcement principle.

A Modified Operant Account of Auto-shaping

It is of interest to consider how the operant principle might be modified to make it consistent with the development of the auto-shaped response. Rather than having the reinforcer operate to increase the probability of a movement, it would seem necessary to think of the reinforcer as operating on a partial expression of an action pattern to bring out a more complete expression of that pattern. In the specific case of auto-shaping, one might suppose that an incipient fragment of the action pattern, "peck lighted disc", occurs on early trials. The conjunction of this incipient fragment with the reinforcer eventuates in the appearance of the complete pattern.

The concept is related to that of intention movements: incomplete or preparatory movements which may occur several times before the complete action pattern appears. The flight-intention movement is a frequently cited example. Before springing into flight some birds show a characteristic pattern involving a crouch with head withdrawn and tail raised. This preparatory movement can appear without the follow-through. It is supposed that the reinforcement of a preparatory movement of this kind would lead to the complete pattern involved in taking flight.

This liberalized account of the operant reinforcement principle could be part of an explanation of how stimulus-reinforcer pairings lead to a complete approach and contact. It could also explain the failure of the negative contingency to eliminate the auto-shaped key-peck in the experiment by Williams and Williams (1969). Although the reinforcer is precluded by a complete peck, the reinforcer will appear on occasions when an approach-peck sequence to the lighted key is initiated but not completed. According to the present view, the effect would be to increase the likelihood of a complete sequence on a subsequent trial. The resulting omission of the reinforcer would again lead to an incomplete sequence, thereby restoring the reinforcer, and so on.

The third fact, that a complete approach and contact to a stimulus that was out of reach during the stimulus-reinforcer pairings may appear when the barrier is removed, is clearly consistent with the present view that reinforcers convert intention movements into action patterns since in that experiment (Kirby, cited by Moore, Chapter 8) the pigeons were clearly attempting to peck the lighted key through the wire screen that served as the barrier before the barrier was removed.

We are, however, left with a large gap. How does the intention movement related to the approach and peck pattern arise? Brown and Jenkins (1968) offered one suggestion. They supposed that looking at a lighted key is part of a sequence that tends to be completed by pecking if looking is followed by a reinforcer. The notion that orientation towards an object is an incipient segment of an approach-peck pattern would not, however, account for the fourth fact, that a hungry bird receiving food as the reinforcer contacts the key with a grain-pecking motion while a thirsty bird receiving water as the reinforcer contacts the key with a drinking motion. In order to accommodate this fact, it might be supposed that the dominant drive state, and/or the repeated occurrence of one action pattern (eating or drinking) in the experimental space, primes the reinforcer-related action pattern so that the intention movement is partly a consummatory action from the outset. The account is, then, that an intention movement related to the dominant drive and reinforcer occurs to the lighting of the key. It is followed by the reinforcer and that eventually yields a complete approach and contact sequence with the contact movement resembling the consummatory pattern.

Inadequacy of the Modified Operant Principle

Despite the freedom which has been exercised in modifying the operant principle to accommodate certain characteristics of auto-shaping, even this liberalized principle fails to account for each of the remaining facts. Consider the fifth fact, that concurrent auto-shaping with a bird that is both hungry and thirsty produces contact movements to the separate stimuli resembling the consummatory action patterns to the reinforcers which are being signalled. This is a critical observation because it shows that the stimulus-reinforcer pairing is itself capable of setting the form of the contact movement when the dominance of a drive state and the prior activation of a consummatory pattern are ruled out. According to the operant principle, the function of the discriminative stimulus is merely to serve as an occasion for (or to control) the reinforced responses that occur in its presence. The demonstrated function of the stimulus-reinforcer relation in determining the form of the contact response clearly exceeds the bounds of an operant account.

The modified operant principle also appears inadequate to deal with the sixth fact: the shift in peck location from a less to a more predictive signal of the reinforcer when the reinforcer is actually produced by a response to the less predictive signal. One might assume an intention movement towards the more predictive signal, but a completed peck towards the less predictive signal must still appear after the intention movement and before the reinforcer. The action in closer temporal conjunction with the reinforcer is, therefore, the peck at the less predictive, common stimulus. Even the modified operant principle would have the immediately reinforced, complete action of pecking the common stimulus strengthened more than the hypothesized intention movement preceding the complete action. It would not, therefore, predict the shift to the more predictive signal.

Finally, we have the seventh fact. When the signalling function of the stimulus (contingency between stimulus and reinforcer) is removed by presenting the reinforcer at the same frequency with the stimulus present or absent, the auto-shaped response is not acquired, and an already acquired response is lost. This fact also appears to be beyond the scope of an operant principle. Since the stimulus is still paired with the reinforcer, approach to and contact with the stimulus are still followed by the reinforcer. The response should, therefore, persist when the stimulus and reinforcer contingency is removed. While it is possible to construct alternative accounts that might preserve the operant principle (e.g. interference from other, superstitiously reinforced behaviour) the most parsimonious account is that the approach and contact response is primarily controlled by the function of the stimulus as a signal of the reinforcer rather than by the action of the reinforcer on responses occurring while the signal is on.

Implications of the Failure of the Operant Principle

At the outset, an operational distinction was drawn between selected or shaped responses and unselected responses, of which the auto-shaped response is an example. The basic assumptions made by Skinner about the process by which a selected response is developed and placed under the control of a prior stimulus were expressed in the principle of the discriminated operant. We have seen that even when this principle is liberalized it fails to account for a number of facts about the auto-shaped response of the pigeon to a localized visual stimulus. What are the implications of these findings for an understanding of learning?

At this point, some caution is needed. We have identified certain properties of an unselected response that are not encompassed by the principle of the discriminated operant. But we have not shown that each of these properties is peculiar to unselected responses. It is entirely possible that some of the demonstrated properties of unselected responses are shared by selected responses under stimulus control even though these properties go beyond anything that follows from the principle of the discriminated operant. It would be rash to suppose that the principle of the discriminated operant, which ascribes no direct function to the stimulus-reinforcer relation, provides an adequate summary of the functions of stimulus, response, and reinforcer in the case of selected responses. Direct experimental comparisons are needed between selected and unselected responses in order to establish the properties they have in common and those that differentiate between them.

Two properties of the auto-shaped response are of special interest for comparison with a selected response under stimulus control. The auto-shaped response appears to be especially sensitive to the stimulus-reinforcer relation and especially insensitive to the response-reinforcer relation. But, perhaps a selected response under stimulus control, although established by operations different from those used in developing the unselected response, becomes sensitive to the stimulus-reinforcer relation, and relatively insensitive to the response-reinforcer relation. Gamzu and Williams (1971) have argued from their demonstration of the importance of the stimulus-reinforcer contingency in auto-shaping that the response is classically conditioned. This argument apparently assumes that the maintenance of a selected response under stimulus control is less dependent on the stimulus-reinforcer contingency.

Comparing the Properties of Selected and Unselected Responses

The category—selected behaviour under stimulus control—is probably too broad to be useful for comparison with an auto-shaped response. Without pretending to completeness, the following distinctions among types of selected behaviour are recognized.

A contact response directed to a normally nonpreferred signalling stimulus.

For example, suppose a food reinforcer is signalled by two, simultaneously-presented stimuli; a bright red and a dim green dot. Pigeons normally direct their contact response almost exclusively to the bright red dot. However, the response can be shifted to the less preferred stimulus by making the reinforcer depend on responding to that stimulus. A selected response of this type involves only a small departure from an unselected approach and contact response.

A contact response directed to a constant stimulus but under the control of a signalling stimulus

For example, the reinforcer can be made to depend on a response directed at a constantly-lighted key when a sound is on. As the result of discriminative training, the sound comes to serve as a signal for the response. The nature of the signalling stimulus, whether visual or auditory, diffuse or localized, may be an important consideration.

A noncontact response under the control of a signalling stimulus

For example, the pigeon may be trained to turn in a circle, to stretch its neck, to bow, etc., when a signalling stimulus is present. Although one can ensure that a selected response does not involve contact with a stimulus it is not a simple matter to decide whether a response is or is not directed to a stimulus. Moore (Chapter 8) has suggested that much of what passes for shaping through control of the response-reinforcer relation can be better understood as resulting from a stimulus-reinforcer relation. In this case, the stimulus "presentation" is thought to be mediated by the animal's orientation to certain features of the environment just prior to the delivery of the reinforcer. It would seem, however, that movements like bobbing, turning and head waving, which do not entail a single approach to any one part of the environment, should be regarded for the present as in a different class from movements involving direct approach and contact.

Consider now, the general plan of an experiment to compare the effects of introducing a negative contingency between response and reinforcer on a selected response and on an auto-shaped response. Some animals would receive their initial training with the standard auto-shaping procedure. Others would receive training to establish stimulus control over the selected response. To fix ideas, assume a selected response consisting of a peck to a constantly lighted disc under the discriminative control of an auditory signal. The auto-shaped response is, of course, also a peck, but to the momentary lighting of the disc. One group of birds would receive training to establish the selected response and place it under precise stimulus control while the other would receive an approximately equal amount of auto-shaping. Some animals in both groups would then be placed on a negative response-contingency. In the case of the selected response, the sound would be followed by the reinforcer provided no contact response occurred to the constantly-lighted disc while the sound was on. Similarly, with the auto-shaped response the reinforcer would now follow the lighting of the disc provided no contact response occurred.

The simple comparison of the persistence of the two forms of behaviour under the negative contingency would be of some interest, but other comparisons would be needed. One would also want to know the persistence of the two behaviours under simple extinction (complete removal of food), and under extinction produced by uncorrelated presentations of the reinforcer. Experiments of this kind should help us to identify the features of behaviour under stimulus control that make the behaviour sensitive or insensitive to the response-reinforcer relation.

Another property of the unselected approach and contact response is its strong dependence on the stimulus-reinforcer contingency which underlies the signalling function of the stimulus. We have completed an experiment in which a parallel set of manipulations was carried out with a selected response. Naïve adult white King pigeons were used. The response was defined by the interruption of a photocell beam. The light source and the photosensitive element were contained in posts that projected 10 centimetres out from the wall containing the grain-tray opening. The posts were 8.5 centimetres apart. The height of the posts was raised in several steps for the purpose of shaping. The final height was 31.5 centimetres above the floor of the box. The response of interrupting the beam was regularly reinforced by 3 seconds of access to the grain tray. The response was then placed under the discriminative control of an auditory stimulus, a white noise of 80 decibels, by reinforcing only while the sound was on. The duration of the sound-on, or trial periods was set at 8 seconds with an average intertrial interval of 30 seconds. Reinforcement was then made intermittent and progressively reduced in probability, although still contingent on interrupting the beam, until the obtained rate of reinforcement was approximately equal to the response-independent rate of reinforcement used by Gamzu and Williams. The rate was such that about 13 reinforcements were received over the 50 8-second trials that constituted a daily session. Training under these conditions continued for all subjects for 12 sessions.

At this point the subjects were divided into two groups. In both groups, the delivery of the reinforcer was made entirely independent of the response so that the conditions during the trial were formally the same as in auto-shaping. The rate of reinforcement remained as before. One group ($N=4$) continued to receive reinforcers only during the trial so that the stimulus-reinforcer contingency was maintained. The other group ($N=4$) now received reinforcers at the same rate between trials as during the trial so that the stimulus-reinforcer contingency was destroyed. After 9 sessions, the conditions were interchanged by restoring the stimulus-reinforcer contingency in one group while removing it in the other.

The experiment was intended to produce a noncontact response under stimulus control but it did not succeed in this respect. By the end of the common phase of training, all birds were directing pecks at the photocell light source, at the receptive element, or at the wall between the posts, on some or all of the trials. These pecks served to interrupt the beam about as efficiently as the neck stretching and head waving responses that developed first. Pecks were, however, under clear discriminative control by the auditory signal. Response rate in the interstimulus period averaged about 0.05 responses per second as compared with an average of about 0.96 per second while the sound was on. In effect, the selected response was a contact response to a constant stimulus under the control of the signalling stimulus.

The response was clearly a selected response. To be sure of that, a group of 4 control birds was exposed to the same stimulus conditions without the response-reinforcer contingency. None of these birds interrupted the raised photocell beam in any manner.

The principle results are shown in Fig. 1. In the group in which the stimulus-reinforcer contingency remained, the removal of the response-reinforcer contingency resulted in a reduction in the rate of responding (photocell interruptions by whatever means) but the response was still occurring at a substantial rate and at a surprisingly steady rate after 9 sessions. On the other hand, in the group in which both the stimulus-reinforcer and response-reinforcer contingencies were removed, the response rate very quickly dropped to an extremely low level. The reduction

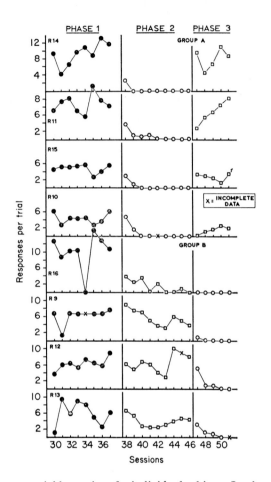

Fig. 1. Responses per trial by sessions for individual subjects. In phase 1 both groups received reinforcers contingent on responding and on the discriminative stimulus of an 8-second noise. The contingency on responses was removed in phases 2 and 3 for both groups. For Group A (first four *S*s), the stimulus-reinforcer contingency was removed in phase 2 and restored in phase 3. For Group B, the stimulus-reinforcer contingency remained in phase 2 but was removed in phase 3.

is not explained by satiation resulting from the additional reinforcers because it was just as apparent at the beginning of sessions, when all subjects were at approximately 80 percent of *ad lib* body weight, as later in the session.

A surprising result was that restoring the stimulus-reinforcer contingency by removal of the interstimulus reinforcers resulted in the reappearance of the response despite the continued absence of a response-reinforcer contingency. The removal of the stimulus-reinforcer contingency in the other group resulted in the virtual elimination of the response.

This preliminary experiment lacks a direct, internal comparison, with an auto-shaped response. It does show, however, a surprisingly strong role of the stimulus-reinforcer contingency on a selected response. At least qualitatively, the results parallel those reported by Gamzu and Williams for the unselected approach and contact response. These findings show that it is an error to regard the demonstration that some behaviour depends on the signalling function of the stimulus as symptomatic that the behaviour is classically conditioned.

I am encouraged by these results to think that a systematic comparison of the role of stimulus-reinforcer and response-reinforcer relations in unselected and selected behaviour sequences of different types will lead to a more organic treatment of simple learning.

References

Brown, P. L. (1968). Auto-shaping and observing responses (R_o) in the pigeon. *Proc. 76th Ann. Conv. APA*, 139–140.

Brown, P. L. and Jenkins, H. M. (1968). Auto-shaping of the pigeon's key-peck. *J. exp. Analysis Behav.* **11**, 1–8.

Gamzu, E. and Williams, D. R. (1971). Classical conditioning of a complex skeletal response. *Science* **171**, 923–925.

Herrnstein, R. J. (1966). Superstition: a corollary of the principles of operant conditioning. *In* "Operant Behavior: Areas of Research and Application", (W. K. Honig, ed.). Appleton, New York.

Jenkins. H. M. (In press). Noticing and responding in a discrimination based on a distinguishing element. *Learning and Motivation*.

Jenkins, H. M. and Sainsbury, R. S. (1969). The development of stimulus control through differential reinforcement. *In* "Fundamental Issues in Associative Learning", (N. J. Mackintosh and W. K. Honig, eds.), pp. 123–161. Dalhousie University Press, Halifax.

Williams, D. R. and Williams H. (1969). Auto-maintenence in the pigeon: sustained pecking despite contingent non-reinforcement. *J. exp. Analysis Behav.* **12**, 511–520.

Comment

Honig wrote as follows concerning the chapters by Moore and by Jenkins:

"The discovery of auto-shaping has initiated a very valuable set of inquiries on the development of 'unselected' responses in instrumental learning (cf. Jenkins) and 'directed respondents' (cf. Moore). There is no question that the classical-instrumental distinction, that has been accepted for so many years, must be reviewed on the basis of the work reported by Jenkins and by Moore. The most critical evidence militating against this distinction is the observation that portions of the consummatory act enter into the topography of instrumental behaviours, both selected and unselected. Furthermore, such responses come 'spontaneously' to be directed at features of the environment that are associated with the reinforcement.

"Confirming evidence on the latter point has been obtained in our laboratory in the course of research on concept attainment, with visual stimuli in the pigeon. In this work, pictures are displayed on a panel, and the pigeon has to learn to peck only in the presence of those which contain the positive cue (Siegel and Honig, 1970). (Displays in which the cue is not present are correlated with extinction.) In a doctoral dissertation, Siegel (1970) divided the display into four quadrants. The positive feature, which was all or part of a picture of a human being, was presented in only one quadrant. The other three quadrants contained the balance of the photograph. The pigeons had to peck at the display for a food reward. In the course of learning the concept, the pigeons gave about 50% of their responses to the quadrant containing the human, although responses to any of the four quadrants could be reinforced. Thus, they did not distribute the direction of the responses at random. The location of the human was of course balanced among the four quadrants. A second group of pigeons, which was specifically reinforced only for pecking at the quadrant containing the feature, learned to do so, to the extent of concentrating about 90% of the responses upon it.

"Even stronger evidence comes from studies in which the display is separate from a key at which the bird has to peck to obtain food. In this case, the display is located (for the sake of convenience) at right angles to the food key; it actually comprises the observation window of the pigeon's chamber. We have found that pigeons who acquire a concept tend to bang at the display with their beaks, directing the peck at the position of the positive feature. They alternate this behaviour with pecks at the food key, even though such behaviour normally results in a modest delay of reinforcement. We have observed this not only when the displays were pictures projected upon the window in question, but also in one case where the bird looked through the window at a three-dimensional display. Furthermore, this behaviour is correlated with good discrimination performance. When banging at the display does not develop the discrimination tends to remain poor.

"As Moore and Jenkins would agree, we should not assume that the above evidence applies to all aspects of instrumental learning. We should remember that in the research reported in these chapters, fairly specific, biologically important rewards were presented to which the animals typically respond with very stereotyped behaviour patterns. The appearance of components of these behaviour patterns in the instrumental responses may be due to the great strength of these patterns in the consummatory behaviour, and the proximity of the instrumental response to the reward. It is not a foregone conclusion that other species working for less powerful rewards will show the influence of consummatory behaviour patterns to a similar degree.

"One class of rewards that has been studied extensively, although they may not be very powerful, are sensory or perceptual. In such cases, the nature of the consummatory response is not always clear; presumably it involves the behaviour of attending to the stimuli, or observing them. When organisms are trained to work for such rewards, the required response is usually something quite different. A particularly interesting example comes from recent research by Siqueland and De Lucia (1969), who has shown that very young babies can be taught to modify ongoing sucking behaviour in order to obtain visual or auditory stimuli. Since sucking is normally a component of eating, its use as an arbitrary instrumental response is intriguing.

"In 1965 Premack made the challenging suggestion that instrumental and consummatory responses are often reversible: their roles depend on their relative probabilities. This also indicates a need for flexibility in thinking about the relationships between their topographies. Premack has shown that a rat deprived of exercise will learn to drink in order to run in a wheel, while a thirsty rat will run in a wheel in order to be able to drink. Now it is reasonable to suppose that running is a preliminary component of drinking, since drinking is normally preceded by locomotion to water. But the reverse is much harder to justify.

"Finally, we may observe that a large proportion of instrumental behaviour is emitted not with the prospect of immediate (or even slightly delayed) reward, but rather to provide an optimum distribution of the subject's time in contact with stimuli that are differentially associated with reward contingencies. Much of the work on concurrent schedules (Catania, 1966) supports this general statement. In some cases two opportunities for instrumental responding are simultaneously available, and it may well be that the directed choice with respect to each is a component of approaches to the primary reward when that is presented. In other cases, only one opportunity is available at a time, and the behaviour of changing between concurrent schedules is made explicit through a change-over response. Even here, one might say that the response contains elements of the consummatory behaviour in question. For example, pigeons are usually required to peck a 'change-over key' to alternate two schedules, and the key peck may be related to eating grain. (It would be interesting to determine whether, if schedules involving different reinforcers were concurrently available, the change-over response would differ in its topography depending on the direction of the animal's choice—whether he was switching from food to water reward or vice versa.) But in an experiment by Baum and Rachlin (1969) pigeons could choose between two schedules of food reward simply by standing in different parts of the chamber. No explicit response was required to obtain the reward, and the animal could alternate between schedules simply by moving about. It was found that pigeons would divide their time between the two locations (and associated schedules) in proportion to the relative rates of reinforcement, a rule that was originally established by Herrnstein (1961) and has often been confirmed since then. It does seem that animals are quite clever about 'managing' their relations to behavioural contingencies by putting themselves into the presence of appropriate stimuli. It would be reasonable to suppose that the behaviour involved in making such decisions has rather little to do with the very specific responses that immediately precede reward."

References

Baum, W. M. and Rachlin, H. C. (1969). Choice as time allocation. *J. exp. Analysis Behav.* **12**, 861–874.

Catania, A. C. (1966). Concurrent operants. *In* "Operant Behavior: Areas of Research and Application", (Honig, W. K., ed.), pp. 213–270. Appleton-Century-Crofts, New York.

Herrnstein, R. J. (1961). Relative and absolute strength of response as a function of frequency of reinforcement. *J. exp. Analysis Behav.* **4**, 267–272.

Premack, D. (1965). Reinforcement theory. *In* "*Nebraska Symposium on Motivation*", (Levine, ed.), pp. 123–180. Nebraska University Press, Lincoln.

Siegel, R. K. (1970). Discrimination learning between and within complex displays. Unpublished Ph.D. thesis, Dalhousie University.

Siegel, R. K. and Honig, W. K. (1970). Pigeon concept formation: successive and simultaneous acquisition. *J. exp. Analysis Behav.* **13**, 385–390.

Siqueland, E. R. and De Lucia, C. A. (1969). Visual reinforcement of non-nutritive sucking in human infants. *Science* **165**, 1144–1146.

10
Responses and Reinforcement*

by Stephen E. Glickman

At a minimum, reinforcing stimuli constrain what animals learn by controlling what they do. This is readily apparent in classical conditioning paradigms where the US—UR relation bears a clear connection with the CS—CR linkage established as the result of appropriate pairing. As Jenkins and Moore have indicated elsewhere in this volume, similar constraints on learning produced by the nature of the reinforcing stimulus may appear also in operant conditioning situations. In this chapter I shall concentrate on a set of properties supposedly common to most reinforcing stimuli and on a limited range of behavioural and physiological studies which are related to this categorization.

What reinforcers do

Most stimuli designated as rewarding or reinforcing have diverse effects on behaviour. By definition, they change the probability of emission of operant or conditioned responses when the proper temporal contingencies are arranged between response and reinforcement. Reinforcing stimuli also generally produce orienting movements which can often be classified as approach or avoidance behaviours. Finally, they elicit and maintain species-characteristic response patterns (sometimes designated as consummatory activities). Although there may be some reinforcing stimuli that control operant activities without noticeably eliciting approach movements or producing species-characteristic behaviour patterns (e.g. Stevenson, 1969), these are the exception rather than the rule. The "fact" of pure sensory reinforcement may render an exhaustive definition of reinforcing stimuli in terms of common response-evoking characteristics uncomfortable, if not impossible, but there are virtues in emphasizing the response-evoking qualities of most reinforcing stimuli. From a naïve evolutionary vantage point, stimuli that evoke vigorous consummatory activi-

* The research from our laboratory, and the writing of the literature review, were supported by grants (MH-13253 and MH-16649) from the U.S.P.H.S.

ties *should* also produce approach or withdrawal behaviour and, in a plastic organism, *should* also have the capability of modifying the probability of an arbitrary operant. Most response-oriented theories of reinforcement (Glickman and Schiff, 1967; Premack, 1965; Sheffield, 1966; Tinbergen, 1951) carry the implication that one can move from one type of situation to the next with predictable "trans-situational generality" (Meehl, 1950), partially avoiding the logical circularity inherent in such definitions of reinforcement and (hopefully) strengthening what Meehl has called the Weak Law of Effect.

Why reinforcers work

It is no accident that many reinforcement theorists began work at a behavioural level only to succumb to the temptations of physiology (e.g. Berlyne, 1967; Bindra, 1968; Miller, 1963). Although it is logically possible to arrive at a purely behavioural description of reinforcement, categorizations of reinforcers in terms of "tension-reduction" or "optimal levels of arousal" have always carried excess physiological baggage and it is difficult to resist the urge to find out whether the postulated mechanism really exists. Moreover, as we shall see, modern physiological procedures should enable (and occasionally do enable) just this kind of dissection of the reward situation.

As I have indicated, the emphasis in this paper is on response-oriented views of reinforcement. At a behavioural level, those experiments which have become identified with this kind of theorizing are generally studies in which an animal performs an operant response for the privilege of emitting a species-characteristic sequence which is not intuitively tension-reducing. The experiments of Sheffield and his co-workers on the rewarding effects of non-nutritive sweet substances (Sheffield and Roby, 1950), or incomplete copulatory behaviour (Sheffield *et al.*, 1951) are classic examples. However, in terms of mechanisms, it is apparent that these kinds of studies do not really define the critical reinforcing event(s). Wherever a response is emitted, sensory stimulation is changed both in terms of feedback from the musculature and due to new stimuli impinging on the organism. Analysis of the reinforcement process at this level of analysis would seem to require direct physiological specification and measurement. In fact, the very success of ingenious molar theorists (e.g. Brown, 1961; Schneirla, 1965) in maintaining their categorizations of reinforcement against all onslaughts can be taken as a persuasive argument for physiologizing.

In terms of physiology, the primary impetus for response-oriented views of reinforcement came from (a) the demonstration that diverse species-characteristic behaviour sequences could be elicited through electrical stimulation of the mammalian brainstem, and (b) the fact that animals would frequently "self-stimulate" for electrical pulses in these areas. Although the complete behaviour sequences did not appear in the typical self-stimulation situation (which lacked appropriate environmental "support"), the inference that motor paths are facilitated seemed plausible. The coincidence of hypothalamic sites from which elicited feeding could be obtained, with those from which self-stimulation could be supported (Hoebel and Teitelbaum, 1962; Margules and Olds, 1962) was probably the first direct evidence of this kind, although many additional reports have appeared since—some supporting the linkage, others not.

Some personal research strategy

Several years ago, we embarked on a research programme designed to explore the implications of response-oriented theorizing about the reinforcement process. The basic idea was to develop a complete-as-possible map of the characteristic behaviour patterns of a single species, and to be able to specify sets of stimulus conditions which would call forth one or another of those patterns. Armed with a description of the conditions necessary for the evocation of particular species-characteristic sequences, we should have been in a good position to predict approach or preference behaviours and to reinforce arbitrarily selected operants. With a reasonable understanding of the behavioural repertoire of our subjects, we should also have been able to evaluate the correspondence between the brain sites from which one could elicit special-characteristic activities and the ability of electrical stimulation at those sites to reinforce an arbitrary operant, i.e. self-stimulation.

Much of the research reported in this paper concerns Mongolian gerbils (*Meriones unguiculatus*). These small burrowing rodents from the semi-arid regions of Northern Asia exhibit a rich variety of species-characteristic behaviour patterns in captivity. They are busy active animals who acquire a passive avoidance response more slowly (Walters and Abel, 1971), and an active avoidance response more rapidly, than laboratory rats (Powell, 1971). A typical distribution of afternoon activity for 28 adult male gerbils, individually housed in 12 × 12 × 24 inch wood and glass cages, is presented in Table 1. It can be seen that the commonest activity under these conditions is shredding nest materials. The shredding percentage in the table is undoubtedly inflated because we had presented our gerbils with the cardboard used for shredding during the 30 minutes preceding the test. Nevertheless, shredding is an extremely potent pattern of behaviour in the gerbil: it is common to both male and female, and is very difficult to satiate or otherwise "turn-off" (Baran, 1968; Glickman, Fried and Morrison, 1967).

Gerbils are normally communal animals (Bannikov, 1954; Tanimoto,

P

1943) and they exhibit a relatively stereotyped set of patterns following the intrusion of a conspecific visitor into their laboratory cage. Many high-frequency solitary activities are replaced by social-investigatory reactions directed towards the visitor (Table 1). In addition, some moderately common solitary behaviours increase in frequency (e.g. self-grooming), and several patterns appear that are rare in the stable solitary condition: ventral rubbing and foot-thumping. In the former the ventral abdominal

TABLE 1

Distribution of Home-Cage Activities for 28 Male Gerbils[a]

Behaviour Patterns	Conditions		
	Solitary	Male Visitor	Female Visitor
Shredding	20.8	3.0[b]	1.2[b]
Sleeping	18.6	0.0[b]	0.0[b]
Crouching/alert	17.6	9.3[b]	18.7
Lying	14.7	2.4[c]	0.6[c]
Rearing	10.7	13.0	14.5[c]
Sniffing	10.0	12.3	13.2
Eating	11.1	1.3[c]	0.0[b]
Locomoting	7.8	6.1	4.5[c]
Burrowing	7.6	2.1[c]	1.4[b]
Grooming	4.3	9.2[b]	8.8[b]
Nest-building	6.0	0.2[c]	0.4[c]
Ventral-rubbing	0.2	3.1[b]	3.8[b]
Foot-thumping	0.0	9.9[b]	17.7[b]
Running-to-visitor	—	15.9	15.1
Sniffing visitor	—	32.1	31.7
Grooming visitor	—	13.5	8.1[d]
Side-by-side with visitor	—	6.3	3.1[d]
Fighting/boxing	—	1.5	3.9[d]

[a] Mean number of 5-second periods in which pattern was observed during a 10-minute test session. Social behaviour was recorded during minutes 1–5 and 11–15 of each encounter and more than one behaviour could be recorded during a given 5-second interval.

[b] $p < 0.01$. [c] $p < 0.05$. (changes from solitary condition by Wilcoxon signed ranks.

[d] $p < 0.05$ (differential interaction with male and female visitors by Wilcoxon signed ranks).

surface, which contains a sebaceous gland in the midline, is rubbed against the substrate: in the natural habitat, the sebum deposited presumably has some sort of signalling effect, on colony mates or potential intruders, or perhaps on the resident animal himself. In the male gerbil this response is androgen dependent (Thiessen et al., 1968; Thiessen and Yahr, 1970), and normally requires input from the olfactory system for its elicitation

(Baran and Glickman, 1970; Thiessen *et al.*, 1970; Wallen and Glickman, in press).

Foot-thumping is a rapid rhythmic drumming of the hindlegs against the floor of the cage. It is aroused by a great variety of situations including peripheral electric shock to the feet (Routtenberg and Kramis, 1967), experimenter handling and dropping into the home cage (Spatz and Granger, 1970), and copulatory behaviour, when the male gerbil foot-thumps after intromission and prior to pursuit of the female (Kuehn and Zucker, 1968).

In the sections that follow, I shall attempt to integrate our own gerbil data with a selective literature review. This survey has two broad divisions: the first concerned with the implications of recent brain stimulation research, and the second with the relevance of behavioural studies for response-oriented views of the reinforcement process.

Electrically Elicited Behaviour and Self-Stimulation

Elicited behaviour and self-stimulation:the basic correlation

It is now clear that there are sites in the hyothalamus from which one can both elicit species-characteristic behaviour patterns and reward arbitrary operant responses. In the rat, this has been demonstrated for sites facilitating feeding (Hoebel and Teitelbaum, 1962; Margules and Olds, 1962), drinking (Mogenson and Stevenson, 1966) and copulatory activity (Caggiula and Hoebel, 1966; Caggiula, 1970; Malsbury, 1971). There is some controversy over both the mechanisms involved in stimulus-bound copulatory behaviour and over the anatomical localization of the phenomenon. For example, Stephan *et al.* (1971) have noted that the "locking-in" of copulatory activity to the stimulus period may result from post-stimulatory inhibition of copulatory behaviour. They have also challenged Caggiula's contention that the anatomical concentration of loci yielding elicited copulation are predominantly in the posterior hypothalamus, while the sites from which elicited feeding is obtained are located in the lateral hypothalamic area. Although these are interesting issues in their own right, they are not crucial for the correlation under discussion here. Even in the Stephan *et al.* experiment, there are some sites where stimulation produces not just stimulus-bound sex, but shortens the post-ejaculatory interval thereby producing more sex per unit time (an effect not simply attributable to post-stimulation inhibition). Moreover, in the Malsbury (1971) study there were increments in both mounting and ejaculatory frequency when the medial preoptic area was electrically stimulated. In addition, there were significant correlations between the magnitude of facilitation of mounting or ejaculatory behaviour and self-stimulation rates at the same loci. Self-stimulation, but not facilitation of sexual activity, was obtained from the lateral preoptic area. This suggests at least some anatomical localization of the elicited behaviour. Unfortunately we do not know whether other elicited activities could be obtained from stimulation of the lateral preoptic area electrodes. Huston (1971) has also computed correlations across animals, comparing the thresholds necessary to sustain self-stimulation with the thresholds for elicited feeding, drinking and copulatory behaviour. He again found a significant correlation ($r=0.65$; $p < 0.01$) when analysing the data from 15 subjects from whom he had obtained elicited behaviour and self-stimulation. Both Malsbury and Huston interpret their data as supporting a hypothesis linking the response-organizing systems of the ventral diencephalon with reinforcement systems in those areas.

In the last few years there have also been a variety of studies attempting to specify the relation between the neural loci from which aggression can be elicited and the reinforcing properties of stimulation at those sites. These data are somewhat more complex, probably because many varieties of attack behaviour have all been called aggression. In general, sites where stimulation produces "affective" attack seem to be part of a negative reinforcement system; whether the subjects are rhesus monkeys—tested with a variety of conspecifics and other objects—(Plotnick et al., 1968); squirrel monkeys examined for hose-biting behaviour (Renfrew, 1969); or rats engaged in mouse killing (Panksepp and Trowill, 1969). However, stimulation of sites where mouse-killing behaviour is facilitated is not always negatively reinforcing for rats. King and Hoebel (1968) reported mixed results: most mouse-killing rats they tested pressed a lever to escape 3-second trains of electrical stimulation, but one subject also pressed to obtain 0.5 second trains of stimulation at a rate of more than 3000 presses/hour. Finally, Woodworth (1971) has studied extensively elicited attack behaviour in the rat, with careful anatomical mapping, detailed description of the behavioural patterns, and the provision of a variety of stimulus objects. Self-stimulation tests were carried out at 12 sites from which elicited attack was obtained, and positively reinforcing effects were observed at 10 of the 12 loci (mean response: 37.1/min.). Woodworth suggests that the discrepancy between his results and those of Panksepp and Trowill, with regard to self-stimulation, may be the result of the more anterior placement of electrodes in the latter study. In general, the selectivity of attack observed by Woodworth (i.e. live mice were attacked more readily than dead mice, and mice more readily than adult rats or guinea pigs), and the general behavioural description, suggested that this research was more often dealing with something akin to "stalking" or "predatory" attack than was the Panksepp and Trowill experiment. Certainly one might expect that systems involved in predatory/stalking attack behaviour would be less equivocal as regards positive reinforcement than sites concerned with the mediation of affective or aversive attack.

From our present vantage point, one weakness of many studies relating elicited behaviour and self-stimulation has been their failure thoroughly to explore the potential range of responses which can be elicited at a single hypothalamic site. A variety of activities may appear when a single hypothalamic point is stimulated, which actually appears depending upon stimulus parameters and the test situation, and which is recorded depending upon the particular interest of the experimenter. For example, it is apparent that testing an animal with only food pellets present, in an otherwise barren cage, and recording only elicited feeding, can severely limit the kinds of relations between elicited behaviour and self-stimulation that are detected. However, a number of investigators have made a systematic effort to explore the range of potential elicited activities and to correlate these with self-stimulation behaviour at the same anatomical loci.

In one such study, involving rhesus monkeys, high self-stimulation rates were associated with erections, food and object intake, and lip-licking; while lower self-stimulation rates were correlated with elicited defecation, urination and chair-shaking (Plutchik et al., 1966). Apparently, even those sites yielding these latter, seemingly aversive, reactions supported self-stimulation. However, the authors note that the majority of sites also elicited escape responses when long trains of current were delivered, and it seems likely that the positive results were obtained in the self-stimulation situation because of the brief (0.5 sec.) train duration employed in that phase of the research. Although latencies to produce the various elicited behaviours are not presented, escape latencies were longest at sites where stimulation induced chair-shaking behaviour.

Christopher and Butter (1968) carried out an extensive survey of the correlation between self-stimulation and elicited behaviour in the laboratory rat. Their most striking finding was a link between locomotor exploratory behaviour and positive reinforcement effects. Locomotor exploration was elicited at all 28 self-stimulation points that they studied and was absent at 24 non-self-stimulation sites. Biting and gnawing responses were also associated with self-stimulation activity, while undirected chewing movements tended to occur more frequently at non-self-stimulation sites. Elicited grooming, observed at 23 of 50 anatomical sites, was uncorrelated with self-stimulation although there was a tendency towards greater association of this elicited behaviour with non-self-stimulation sites. This is coincident with the similar failure of Hopkins (1970) to find positive self-stimulation at sites where grooming was elicited in the rat,

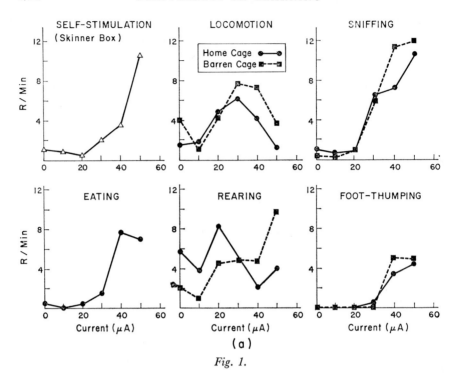

Fig. 1.

even when the train durations in reinforcement tests were increased through use of a shuttlebox procedure. Although one can produce *ad hoc* explanations of this "anomaly" based, for instance, on the mediation of some peripheral itch, it nevertheless points out a serious limitation in the ability of response-oriented explanations of the self-stimulation phenomenon to make accurate predictions about the approach-withdrawal characteristics of particular species-characteristic behaviour patterns.

In yet another attempt to carry out a broadly-based survey of the self-stimulation/elicited-behaviour correlation, Glickman and Higgins (1968) studied the responses of 15 adult male gerbils to stimulation at a total of 33 sites in the ventral diencephalon and basal forebrain. All subjects were tested at a variety of current levels both in their home cages (which provided food, water, nest materials, wooden blocks and a gravel substrate in which to burrow) and in an indentical cage with a barren interior. The latter was included in an effort to determine something of the nature of "substitute" behaviours, i.e. those behaviours which emerge in the absence of a crucial goal object. The responses of two representative animals to applied 60 cycle sine wave current are depicted in Fig. 1. Elicited behaviour was quantified by dividing each minute into 12 5-second periods

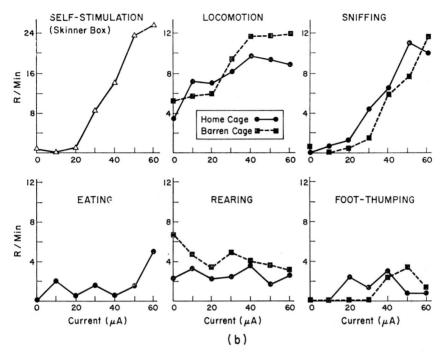

Fig. 1. Self-stimulation rate, and the frequency of emission of selected behaviour patterns as a function of current intensity for two gerbils. (a) shows the results of stimulation of the H_2 field of Forel (equivalent to level 40 in the Konig and Klippel rat atlas); (b) shows results from stimulation of the lateral preoptic area (equivalent to level 19 in the Konig and Klippel rat atlas).

and noting the ongoing activities on a prepared scoring sheet. A minimum of four such one-minute time samples was obtained at each current level in both the home cage and barren-cage conditions. Both subjects exhibited stimulus bound locomotion, sniffing and foot-thumping in home-cage and barren-cage conditions. However, the subject in the upper graphs showed a relative decrement in locomotion at the 40 and 50 microamp. levels in the home cage and at the 50 microamp. level in the barren cage. Presumably, these decrements occurred because of the emergence of feeding and of foot-thumping in the barren cage. In a sense, rearing was the kind of "substitute" behaviour we were looking for in the barren environment; however, there was no consistent pattern of substitution from one gerbil to the next; sniffing, locomotion, rearing, and burrowing all appeared as "substitute" activities. These graphs also show that a great variety of behavioural modifications, commonly result from stimulation of hypothalamic sites in the gerbil, with the particular patterns determined by an interaction between the test apparatus and the parameters of stimulation.

In the self-stimulation tests, the same current levels were explored as in the elicited behaviour tests, but each bar-press produced a brief (0.2—0.4 sec.) train of 60 cycle current. As Ball (1968) has indicated, this makes direct comparisons of thresholds for elicited behaviour and self-stimulation impossible. However, reference to Fig. 1 suggests that at the crude increments within which we were increasing current levels there was a correspondence between thresholds for elicited effects and those for self-stimulation. Positive self-stimulation was observed at 22 of the 33 sites stimulated in this study, with rates ranging from 8.5 to 101.5 per minute.

TABLE 2

Relation of Elicited Behaviour to Self-Stimulation
in the Mongolian gerbil[a]

Elicited Behaviours	Self-Stimulation Sites (N = 22)	Non-Self-Stimulation Sites (N = 11)
Foot-thumping	19	7
Post-stimulation foot-thumping	19	5
Sniffing	18	2
Locomotion	8	1
Oral activities:		
Feeding, gnawing, shredding	7	0

[a] Data taken from Glickman and Higgins (1968)

The remaining eleven subjects did not produce rates significantly higher than their operant levels. Some modification which could be characterized as elicited behaviour was observed at all but one of the twenty-two self-stimulation sites. On the other hand, elicited activities were also frequent accompaniments of sites which did not support self-stimulation. Table 2 shows that post-stimulation foot-thumping, sniffing, locomotion, and a category of oral behaviour (feeding, shredding and gnawing) were each predictive of self-stimulation. However, with the exception of the oral behaviour category, there were also negative cases in which the elicited behaviour did not invariably predict positive self-stimulation at that locus. Perhaps this imperfect correlation is an inevitable accompaniment of the wide range of behaviours which are elicited from most electrode points. However, it is safer to conclude simply that although reinforcement is significantly correlated with the ability to evoke particular patterns of response from the lateral hypothalamic area of the gerbil, the mere elicitation of some species-characteristic behaviour gives no assurance of concomitant self-stimulation at the same site.

In summary, the available data suggest a reasonable correlation between the ability to elicit species-characteristic behaviours through brain stimulation and the ability to reinforce behaviour at those same neural loci. However, there are a number of problems in the interpretation of this correlation. Some elicited behaviour patterns, e.g. grooming, have proved to be either uncorrelated with reinforcement (Christopher and Butter, 1968) or negatively reinforcing (Hopkins, 1970). In the case of elicited attack behaviour, the adequate classification of aggression remains a difficult problem and results in the literature are at least somewhat contradictory. In addition, investigators have generally biased their studies towards stimulation of areas known to result in elicited behaviour patterns. There are areas like the hippocampus in the rat that support self-stimulation (Ursin et al., 1966) but are not noted for producing much beyond seizure activity on direct stimulation (although post-stimulation eating has been reported by Milgram, 1968). This emphasis on sites-likely-to-produce-elicited-behaviour can obscure the probable existence of brain regions where positive reinforcement is obtained in the absence of overt elicited effects, other than a cessation of movement. Finally, there is the crucial issue of the mechanisms underlying the self-stimulation/elicited-behaviour correlation in those cases where this correlation has been observed. Is there some anatomical "accident" which has resulted in the intimate juxtaposition of motor pathways and reinforcement pathways, with brain stimulation generally activating both systems? Or is there really some causal link between the elicited activity and the reinforcing properties of the stimulation? Arguments can be advanced on both sides of this question.

The dissociation of elicited behaviour from reinforcement

If the reinforcing effects of electrical stimulation could be split from the behaviour-eliciting effects of stimulation at the same anatomical site, that could be taken as evidence against the single-mechanism view of response facilitation and reinforcement. Such evidence certainly exists. Threshold determinations have probably provided the simplest techniques for this kind of differentiation. Mendelson (1967), Coons and Cruce (1968) and Huston (1971) have all shown that elicited drinking or feeding can be obtained at lower thresholds than are needed to sustain self-stimulation *per se*. Mendelson (1967) and Coons and Cruce (1968) have further utilized this split to demonstrate that current levels which do not support self-stimulation in an empty Skinner box, have positively reinforcing effects if food or water is present and the subject is given the chance to perform the appropriate consummatory response following the bar-press (but during the period when current is still being delivered to the hypothalamus).

There are numerous ways of interpreting such information. It fits nicely into the kind of drive-reinforcement framework originally proposed by Deutsch and recently elaborated by Gallistel and others (Deutsch and Howarth, 1963; Gallistel, 1969b; Gallistel et al., 1969). On this view there are two separable neurological systems which mediate performance of learned behaviour patterns: a drive system and a reinforcement system. In the Mendelson (1967) and Coons and Cruce (1968) experiments, we might assume that the drive system was activated at a lower threshold than the reinforcement system, that this in turn resulted in feeding or drinking, and that the combination of brain stimulation and sensory input from the consummatory activity provided adequate reinforcement to sustain the lever-pressing response. However, the existence of separable drive systems activated by brain stimulation is still a controversial area (Panksepp et al., 1969). It is also possible to avoid postulating activation of separate systems and merely hypothesize that it takes more reinforcement, i.e. a greater incentive (Mendelson, 1970) to sustain an "arduous", newly acquired, arbitrary operant (such as lever pressing), then the consummatory activity whose acquired components necessitate less effort and are highly over-learned.

Pharmacological differentiation of the elicited behaviour and self-stimulation systems has also been described. Mogenson (1968) reported that amphetamine suppressed elicited drinking and enhanced self-stimulation at the same electrode sites. However, the effect of brain stimulation on other elicited activities was not reported. Pilot work in our laboratory suggested that although amphetamine suppressed elicited feeding, it actually enhanced elicited investigatory behaviour in gerbils. Thus any conclusions about the reported dissociation between elicited behaviour and self-stimulation must be limited to the drinking-self-stimulation correlation. In contrast to the amphetamine result, intraperitoneal adrenaline reduced both elicited feeding and self-stimulation rate at feeding sites (Mogenson et al., 1969). Again, it would be interesting to know whether other elicited activities were also suppressed by the adrenaline injections.

Stark et al. (1968) reported that intraperitoneal injections of the anti-cholinesterase physostigmine decreased the threshold for elicited feeding in rats, while increasing the threshold for self-stimulation. Although these results certainly suggest differentiation of the feeding and self-stimulation systems in the hypothalamus, conclusions must still be circumspect. Elicited behaviours other than feeding were not reported and, once again, it seems possible that the differentiation is not between reinforcement system and drive system, but rather between the effects of a drug on an arbitrary operant (in the case of self-stimulation) and the effects of the same drug on a consummatory pattern. Ideally, elicited feeding in this study should have been made dependent upon the same kind of response (lever-pressing) as self-stimulation.

Finally, Schiff (personal communication) has found that lesions of the reticular formation which markedly attenuate self-stimulation, do not reduce locomotor activity or sniffing resulting from stimulation of the lateral hypothalamic area of the rat. This result inevitably suggests that the very strong correlation between such elicited activities and self-stimulation reported by Christopher and Butter (1968) for the rat and Glickman and Higgins (1968) in the gerbil do not represent a causal connection. We had previously suggested, from a varied assortment of anatomical evidence, that extrapyramidal motor pathways passing through the mesencephalic regions were crucial for the maintenance of normal reinforcing effects (Glickman and Schiff, 1967). Routtenberg (*in press*) has assembled neuro-anatomical and electrophysiological evidence which implicates these (and other) extrapyramidal routes in the mediation of self-stimulation behaviour. Thus the data recently obtained by Schiff are not necessarily devastating for a motor-facilitation view of reinforcement.

Although *ad hoc* "explanations" for the varied data on dissociation of elicited behaviour and reinforcement pathways are possible, the line of research is impressive. The question of the interdependence of mechanisms necessary to account for elicited behaviour and reinforcement phenomena is still open, but should be solvable given the proper combinations of electrical, lesion-induction and pharmacological procedures.

Reinforcement: interaction of central and peripheral stimuli

Although the ultimate nature of the reinforcement mechanism (or mechanisms) is still obscure, the data generally suggest that a combination of central and peripheral stimulation which results in activation of some consummatory response system will be more reinforcing than either the central or peripheral alone. This was first clearly demonstrated in the studies of Roberts and Kiess (1964) on elicited attack behaviour in cats, and by Roberts and Carey (1965) on elicited gnawing in the rat. In both of these experiments, subjects learned to choose the correct arm of a Y-maze when reinforced with access to "relevant" stimuli (permitting emergence of the appropriate consummatory act). However, in these studies electrical stimulation was delivered in all portions of the maze from start box to goal box. In a subsequent investigation, Mendelson (1966) clearly demonstrated that in this kind of paradigm the stimulation need not be on until the subject reached the goal box. In Mendelson's experiment rats had electrodes implanted at sites in the hypothalamus where stimulation resulted in elicited feeding. These subjects learned to run in a T-maze to the goal box, where they received both the electrical stimulation and had access to food, in   preference to a goal box where they received only the hypothalamic stimulation. It was therefore shown that satiated rats would run "in order to eat", without invoking either physiological or electrically produced "drive" to get the animal out of the start box and running towards the goal.

This line of research was supported by the subsequent studies of Morgan and Mogenson (1966), Coons and Cruce (1968) and Mendelson (1967), who demonstrated enhancement of self-stimulation effects at sites yielding elicited drinking or feeding, when water or food was available in the test chamber. Phillips and Mogenson (1968) and Poschel (1968) refined the peripheral-central interactions still further by showing that the magnitude of reinforcing effects of stimulation at "feeding" or "drinking" sites in the hypothalamus of the rat interacted with the taste qualities of gustatory stimuli available . Access to sweet substances in the test chamber markedly enhanced the reinforcing properties of electrical stimulation, while the presence of bitter solutions depressed reinforcement effects below the water "control" level.

The shuttle-box provides yet another technique for combining central and peripheral stimuli in the assessment of reinforcing effects. In these experiments the subject can regulate the duration of a train of stimulating current by movement between two sides of a platform, with current available continuously on one side. Mendelson (1969) found that stimulus-bound "feeders", "drinkers", and "gnawers" would opt for longer train durations if the opportunity to feed, drink or gnaw was provided on the "hot" side of the box. In a similar vein, Schiff et al. (1971) found that rats, with electrodes in a variety of hypothalamic reinforcing points, would opt for longer train durations when stimulation occurred in a larger compartment, or when male or female conspecifics were housed in adjacent enclosures where they could be seen and smelled during the stimulus train. Since the most common accompaniment of stimulation of these areas in the rat is a motor pattern associated with locomotor exploratory behaviour (Christopher and Butter, 1968), the authors have shown that increasing the novel stimulation available in the environment apparently enhances the positively reinforcing characteristics of the central stimulation. Schiff et al. ultimately interpret their data in a very general "ecological" manner which they suggest may be applicable to the shuttlebox study of Phillips et al. (1969). In this experiment, rats with hypothalamic electrodes reduced their time on the current-delivering side of a shuttlebox when an assortment of small edible and inedible objects were provided in the test chamber. With the objects present in the shuttlebox, subjects ran to the "hot" side, picked up an object in the mouth, rapidly ran to the off side, deposited the object, ran back to the "hot" side, picked up another object, and so forth. Phillips and his colleagues emphasize the species-characteristic nature of this carrying response for the rat and speculate that it may represent an attempt to move objects from an open field to a home area as defined by some central state. In a later paper, Valenstein *et al.* (1970) note that guinea pigs who live in natural enclosures rather than constructed nests do not show this kind of carrying behaviour during brain stimulation.

All these studies emphasize the interaction between central and peripheral stimulation in determining the reinforcing properties of stimulation. They still do not identify the nature of the reinforcement mechanism, in the sense of enabling some choice among the alternatives of motor facilitation, the varied forms of sensory feedback from the response, and perhaps some arousal-activated reinforcement system (Routtenberg, 1968). However, they do emphasize an aspect of the elicited behaviour-reinforcement relation which has become a major focus of current research.

Plasticity and the reinforcing characteristics of response performance

One of the major discoveries of recent brain-stimulation work was the demonstration by Valenstein *et al.* (1968) that the responses elicited by brain stimulation are capable of substantial modification by appropriate arrangement of environmental contingencies. Thus, animals that initially fed, drank, or gnawed when electrically stimulated, were switched to one of the remaining alternative behaviours by removal of the first preferred goal object (e.g. water) and repeated central stimulation in the presence of the remaining two objects (e.g. food and wood). In this manner, a stimulation-bound "drinker" could be transformed into a "feeder" or a "gnawer", although considerably greater difficulty may then be encountered in switching the behaviour again to yet a third goal object (Roberts, 1969). The limits of this plasticity remain to be defined. As we shall see later, mammals with varied diets may have to learn what to eat and nourishment may be provided equally by chewing movements or through lapping movements of the tongue. It is therefore not surprising that if appropriate central feedback is provided coincident with performance of an elicited response, the normal tendency of the response to habituate may be counteracted and an apparently new oral response may appear linked with a new stimulus.

Valenstein *et al.* (1970) have used this demonstration of plasticity, in conjunction with detailed examination of anatomical correlates of elicited behaviour patterns and observation of discrepancies between electrically elicited and "normally" produced behaviour patterns, to argue that elicited activities may not be due to stimulation of discrete motivational pathways in the brainstem. Although the specific pathway views still have their adherents (Devor *et al.*, 1970; Roberts, 1969; Woodworth, 1971), the fact of plasticity is established in the literature and current research must be directed at exploring its properties (e.g. Mogenson, 1971).

The research of Valenstein and his colleagues has emphasized the importance of the reinforcement process in establishing a pattern of elicited behaviour. This is made particularly clear in a recent study (Valenstein, 1971) where repeated elicitation of a particular response (e.g. feeding) made it more difficult to switch to a second response at a later time. It is a kind of overlearning effect and, in his theorizing, Valenstein (1969) has suggested that elicitation of the consummatory response, through the interaction of central and environmental stimulation, contains the essence of the reinforcing effect. In this sense, Valenstein supports a view of the reinforcement process which emphasizes response evocation. However, there is another feature of this plasticity research which may lead to a more detailed perspective on the neural substrate.

Arousal and the "prepotency" hypothesis

As an alternative to the specific pathway interpretation of elicited behaviour, Valenstein *et al* (1970) have proposed a "prepotency" hypothesis. It is as if one were not eliciting the response directly at the point of stimulation, but rather creating a more generalized state within the organism to which each subject responds, partially on the basis of individual predisposition, and partly on the basis of a species predilection. A major weakness of this formulation has been the difficulty encountered in independently manipulating initial prepotencies, as opposed to inferring them from the results of stimulation.

However, disparate research findings are to some extent linked by assuming that many elicited behaviour patterns are really a byproduct of increased states of central arousal which are capable of facilitating any number of response sequences depending on the stimuli present in the test environment (see e.g. Wayner, 1970). On this view, the response would be facilitated by a relatively non-specific state of central arousal produced by brain stimulation interacting with the stimuli in the test chamber. "Reinforcement" could, in turn, result from the subsequent evocation of these responses.

A provocative body of evidence can be gathered around this theme. As Jacobs and Farel (1971) have noted, techniques presumed to produce moderately intense states of central arousal facilitate a wide variety of species-characteristic behaviour patterns. Electric shock, or low doses of pentobarbital, can facilitate copulatory behaviour (Barfield and Sachs, 1968; Caggiula and Eibergen, 1969), feeding (Siegel and Brantley, 1951; Jacobs and Farel, 1971); drinking (Siegel and Siegel, 1949) and aggression (Jacobs and Farel, 1971). Moreover, priming with electric shock facilitates self-stimulation behaviour in rats (Macdougall and Bevan, 1968) much as does direct intra-cranial priming at a variety of brain sites (Gallistel, 1969).

It is worth examining the foot-thumping behaviour of the gerbil in this context. As previously noted, this response is elicited by a wide variety of environmental conditions, which seem to have as their common component an excitatory or arousing effect. That this was the most commonly elicited behaviour obtained from stimulation of the gerbil hypothalamic region is coincident with a view of foot-thumping as an arousal-mediated behaviour. The latter would also be expected if the response were attached to a very diverse set of specific drive systems. However, the frequent occurrence of the behaviour in the absence of any concomitantly elicited traditional "consummatory" activity seems to argue against such an interpretation. Finally, Spatz, Leavitt, Ellisman and I have consistently elicited foot-thumping by chemical stimulation of these same hypothalamic regions with carbachol, which produces drinking at a great variety of brain loci in rats (Fisher and Coury, 1962).

A somewhat different hindleg thump is produced in rabbits by stimulation at a diverse set of neural loci (Black and Vanderwolf, 1969). Given (a) the wide range of situations which elicit foot-thumping; (b) the ubiquity of its appearance as an accompaniment of brain stimulation in the gerbil; and (c) the diversity of anatomical sites from which the behaviour can be elicited, it is tempting to conclude that we are dealing with a prototypical arousal-mediated behaviour. The relative invariance of the interthump interval (0.1 sec.) would even be coincident with the hypothesis that this behaviour results from the facilitation of a relatively primitive reflex-like mechanism.

In our study (Glickman and Higgins, 1968), the occurrence of post-stimulation foot-thumping was highly correlated with self-stimulation behaviour. The latter correlation was also reported by Routtenberg and Kramis (1967), although they interpreted the data in a rather different manner. Black and Vanderwolf (1969) observed a possibly related link between elicited foot-thumping behaviour and reinforcement effects in the rabbit. The authors emphasized the ambivalent quality of the reinforcement, i.e. that the rabbit would both initiate the current and terminate it after a suitable train duration. However, such an initiation—termination effect is common to many hypothalamic sites commonly classed as positively reinforcing.

Although this basic correlation between an elicited behaviour and self-stimulation could be taken as general support for the kind of response-oriented reinforcement theory advanced by Schiff and myself, it seems intuitively uncomfortable. That the same behaviour, foot-thumping, can be associated with both positively and negatively reinforcing situations emphasizes the impossibility of predicting the nature of reinforcing effects from knowledge of the elicited behaviour *per se*. In addition, this kind of relation between an arousal-mediated response and reinforcement is easily compatible with the many optimal-level-of-arousal formulations of reinforcement (Berlyne, 1967); or even with the dual pathway, drive-reinforcement hypotheses of Deutsch and Howarth (1963). In the latter case foot-thumping becomes an index of drive and stimulation would be expected usually to activate both the drive and reinforcement pathways, but might occasionally either stimulate only the drive system, or possibly some sort of aversive reinforcement mechanism.

I have not intended to argue that all, or even most, centrally elicited behaviour patterns are "accidental" byproducts of some state of central arousal. The research of Flynn (1967) on the elicited attack behaviour of the cat, and of Roberts *et al.* (1967) on the localization of diverse species-characteristic behaviour patterns in the opossum, is convincing evidence to the contrary. However, whereas I was recently only willing to contemplate the difficulties of "arousal" formulations (Glickman and Schiff, 1967), some consideration of arousal functions now seems required by a reasonable body of literature. The ultimate role that arousal mechanisms will play in accounting for elicited behaviour and reinforcement would seem to be a viable issue, if difficult to investigate.

Olfactory mediation of reinforcement

In this largely rodent-obsessed survey of the brain-stimulation literature, a final note on the role of the olfactory system is necessary. Both in the Christopher and Butter (1968) rat study and in our own gerbil research (Glickman and Higgins, 1968), sniffing was a prominent accompaniment of sites which supported self-stimulation. More recently, Clarke and Trowill (1971) have employed a much more sophisticated technique for the study of sniffing behaviour (involving the placement of a thermistor in the nasal cavity). They report that sniffing often accompanies both self-stimulation and also bar-pressing for saccharin reinforcement. Moreover, a detailed temporal analysis of their data suggests that the sniffing in both cases becomes anticipatory, i.e. there is an increase in sniffing rate as the animal approaches the lever during the course of habit acquisition. This is presumed to be a conditioned effect demonstrating incentive motivation, although its similarity to the beak movement phenomenon described by B. R. Moore in chapter 8 is intriguing.

That sniffing is so intimately associated with self-stimulation could be made to jigsaw with a considerable body of data suggesting that positive self-stimulation sites are concentrated in the medial forebrain bundle and associated limbic structures with olfactory connections (Olds and Olds, 1963). Again, several crucial questions remain about the nature of specific mechanisms. Is the reinforcement associated with the sensory consequences of sniffing (the odour), with the motor act of sniffing, or with some combination of these? Also, to what extent is this correlation between sniffing and self-stimulation a causal or dependent relation?

There seems little question that olfactory stimuli can interact with brain stimulation to modify reinforcement effects, although the effects appear to be less general than one might have predicted. A. G. Phillips (1970) observed that self-stimulation in the olfactory bulb increased when the odour of amyl acetate or peppermint was present. Self-stimulation rates in this region were depressed by the presence of evil smelling quinoline. Finally, self-stimulation rates at several other sites in and around the hypothalamus were unaffected by the presence of these odours (despite the fact that one would have expected elicited sniffing to have occurred as an accompaniment to self-stimulation in these latter areas as well). Perhaps the use of more biologically relevant odours would have resulted in a wider range of sites yielding central-peripheral interactions.

The available data suggest that: (a) elicited sniffing accompanies hypothalamic self-stimulation, and (b) that interactions between environmental odours and intracranial stimulation occur, but may be relatively limited. Some recent data obtained by M. I. Phillips (1972) further implicate the olfactory system in self-stimulation behaviour. He found that bilateral removal of the olfactory bulbs drastically reduces self-stimulation rates in the lateral hypothalamic area. We know from Welker (1964) that such bulbectomy reduces, but does not eliminate, spontaneous sniffing, but we still do not know the effects of bulbectomy on centrally elicited sniffing. Also, bulbectomy does much more than merely eliminate olfactory input; it is a CNS lesion with consequences far removed from the site of tissue destruction. Preliminary results from four rats in our laboratory suggest that self-stimulation in the lateral hypothalamic area survives peripheral anosmia produced by zinc sulphate treatment (Alberts and Galef, 1971). However, we can expect to see some concentrated research efforts in this area during the next few years. Phillips' finding seems to offer a rare opportunity to dissect the components of the reinforcement process as they are tied to a sensory system which is of critical importance for motivated behaviour in rodents.

Q

Species-Characteristic Behaviour Patterns and Reinforcement

The preceding sections have been concerned with the implications of brain stimulation research for response-oriented views of the reinforcement process. However, a parallel literature has been developing at a purely behavioural level. In fact, one of the primary virtues of the consummatory response views presented by Sheffield and his co-workers in the early 1950s was the implicit prediction that any stimulus that elicited a consummatory response would also serve to reinforce arbitrarily selected instrumental behaviour. There has been ample testimony elsewhere in this volume (see the chapters by Sevenster and Shettleworth) to the constraints placed on the response-reinforcer relation by the nature of the species. However, the consummatory response categorization of reinforcing stimuli played a major role in generating a search for "new" reinforcers ("new" can be taken to read: other than food, water or electric shock). The sections that follow review briefly this work and its implications for the categorization and mode of action of reinforcing stimuli. In addition, certain aspects of the relation between the operation of a given reinforcer in traditional operant situations and the effectiveness of that reinforcer in preference or consummatory situations are re-examined.

The reinforcement of arbitrary operants

Male rats have been shown to run mazes for access to female rats in oestrous (Kagan, 1955), and female rats in oestrous will press levers for access to male rats with whom they can copulate (Bermant, 1961; Peirce and Nuttall, 1961). Female rats (Wilsoncroft, 1969) and mice (Van Hemel, 1970) will bar press for the privilege of retrieving pups; and rats (Oley and Slotnick, 1970) and hamsters (Jansen et al., 1969) will emit appropriate instrumental responses to gain access to strips of paper which are used for nest-building. Sand-digging, potentially functional in burrow construction, is an effective reinforcer in the deermouse (*Peromyscus leucopus*) (King and Weisman, 1964), and Fantino and Cole (1968) have noted that sand-digging requires no "extra" reinforcers for its maintenance in laboratory mice.

In addition to the "constructive" acts which function as reinforcers in the situations noted above, some laboratory rats will run through a maze (Myer and White, 1965) or press a lever (Van Hemel, 1972) to obtain access to a mouse, which is then killed with an appropriately directed bite. Laboratory mice will, in turn, run mazes for the opportunity of fighting with conspecifics in the goalbox (Lagerspetz, 1964; Tellegen et al., 1969). These latter findings relate to the prior research of Thompson (1963, 1964) who showed that the emission of an arbitrary operant by Siamese fighting fish, or roosters, could be reinforced with stimuli eliciting aggressive displays. Finally, Azrin *et al.* (1965) found that squirrel monkeys receiving electric shock will pull a chain to gain access to a ball that they can then bite; while Cole and Parker (1971) reported that pigeons working for food on FR schedules preferred to peck a target which produced access to another pigeon (who was subject to pecking attack), than a target which merely produced food. Although there are controls that might be asked for in some of the preceding studies, the evidence suggests that many varieties of aggression can reinforce operant behaviour.

Investigatory behaviour, sensory reinforcement and the reliability of reinforcers

The presence of novel stimulus objects or enclosures evokes species-characteristic investigatory responses in many mammals (Glickman and Hartz, 1964; Glickman and Sroges, 1966). The demonstration that rats would learn a maze for the opportunity to explore a new maze (Montgomery, 1954; Montgomery and Segall, 1955) can therefore be reasonably encompassed within response-oriented categorizations of reinforcing stimuli. However, the demonstration of sensory reinforcing effects (see Fowler, 1971, for review), which apparently involve either no overt responses, or simple orienting reactions, do pose difficulties for such categorizations. This situation is particularly telling with stimuli of supposed biological significance for the organism. To the human observer, the sounds of foot-thumping arouse little more than a typical orienting response in "listening" gerbils (be they male or female); but anoestrous female gerbils appear to avoid this sound (preferring equal intensity white noise), while male gerbils show no consistent preference in a shuttlebox situation (data obtained by Spatz and Glickman; see Table 3). In a situation which provided her subjects with more options, Stevenson (1969) was able to demonstrate positive reinforcing effects of a tape recording of chaffinch song, although it appeared that this effect was very sensitive to the conditions of testing and the hormonal state of the bird. In fact, several investigators working with sensory reinforcers (Stevenson, 1969; Tapp and Simpson, 1966) have commented on the relative instability of such stimuli for the effective control of behaviour. Is this because of the lack of vigorous consummatory responses, or possibly because of the absence of the kinds of internal or external mechanisms which normally serve to cue the initiation of the operant response?

Shredding of nest materials and response-oriented views of reinforcement: what the theorists didn't tell you

We have mentioned the extraordinary vigour with which gerbils shred

TABLE 3

Preference Behaviour of Adult Gerbils for Different Stimulus Conditions

"Reinforcing" Stimulus	Subjects	Test Duration	Test Apparatus	Percent Time	
				"Reinforcing" Side	Control Side
Sound of foot-thumping[a]	10 male	10 min	Shuttlebox	46.3	53.7
Sound of foot-thumping[b]	9 female	10 min	Shuttlebox	47.3	52.7
Plastic blocks for ventral-rubbing[c]	9 male	20 min	Shuttlebox	50.1	49.9
Index cards for shredding[d]	8 male	10 min	Home cage	78.5	21.5

[a], [b] In these tests, the "reinforcing" side delivered a tape recording of gerbil's foot-thumping, while control side occupancy resulted in delivery of a continuous train of white noise at an equivalent sound level (68–71 decibels). Six of 10 males and 8 of 9 females "preferred" the control side.

[c] Subjects emitted an average of 13.8 rubs on the "reinforcing" side and 0.0 rubs on the control side; but only 4 of 9 subjects "preferred" the side with the rubbing blocks. These data were collected by Ann Johnson.

[d] All 8 subjects "preferred" the side of the cage containing the index cards; even when time spent actually shredding was deducted from the total time spent on the side with the stimulus cards.

nest materials. Because of its dominant position in the gerbil repertoire (see Table 1), any reasonable response-oriented theorist (e.g. Premack, 1965; Glickman and Schiff, 1967) should have predicted that shredding would be an exceptionally efficient reward, capable of consistently reinforcing any selected operant and maintaining a high level of performance. Given this bias, Ray Blatt, a graduate student in my laboratory, was cajoled into building a machine which delivered an adjustable length of adding machine tape each time the gerbil pressed a lever. Four gerbils were tested in this apparatus, while they lived for 24 hours per day with access to two levers, one of which delivered a preset quantity of paper tape, and the other small pellets of food. Gerbils will indeed bar-press for paper tape, thus verifying the weakest form of the theory: shredding can be used to reinforce lever-pressing. However, the character of this reinforcement differed markedly from the accompanying food reinforcement. Each gerbil pressed 111–133 times per day on the food lever. Pressing on the paper lever gave mean rates varying from 8 per day to 562 per day per subject, and the day-to-day variation was also substantial. Gerbils will press for paper, but not with the consistency exhibited in pressing for food. Recently, Oley and Slotnick (1970) trained two female rats to press for paper strips during prepartum and postpartum periods. Rates during the prepartum period were relatively low and the ratios employed during this time were limited to FR2 and FR5. During the postpartum period, these ratios were increased to FR20 for one of the subjects. In their description of the use of nesting material as a reinforcement for the hamster, Jansen *et al.* (1969) emphasize that they were ultimately able to produce consistently strong reinforcing effects. However, it seemed to require considerable manipulation of the test situation.

Although the data are both sparse and difficult to obtain, there are a number of cases in which reinforcers are statistically effective, but give very variable results when schedules are manipulated or test conditions changed. In one case, involving brain stimulation as a reinforcer, there is an ongoing controversy involving just this issue (Gallistel, 1969*a*; Panksepp *et al.* 1969). However, the controversy exists because a theoretical issue is at stake and because there are active experimenters on both sides. In general, such oddities of the reinforcement process are played down for several plausible reasons. First, in the early stages of theorizing, people are more interested in "demonstrating" a phenomenon than exploring its limits. There is a tendency to disregard quantitative effects and concentrate on manipulation of the test situation to maximize stimulus control and produce the effects that should appear. Certainly positive demonstrations are more convincing than failures. But, in the end, this biases the literature and prevents the accumulation of the kind of data that would illuminate the differences between reinforcers. Some years ago, I tried to train chinchillas to run a maze for the reward of sandbathing in a tray of Fuller's earth. This is a very vigorous response necessary for proper maintenance of the coat, and Stern and Merari (1969) have shown an orderly relation between deprivation of opportunity to sandbathe and the magnitude of subsequent sandbathing behaviour. My attempt to train chinchillas was a failure, although I am convinced that with proper ingenuity such training would be possible. I do not seriously advocate publishing an assortment of such trivial failures, but it would help if experimental reports of successful manipulation also contained more information in problems encountered.

Reinforcing stimuli: operants, preferences and consummatory responses

In an operant situation, the operant response can be separated from the consummatory response. In a preference situation, the distinction is less clear and depends on the conditions of the test situation (whether it is an acceptance-rejection, or a true two-choice test) and the mode of preference assessment: intake measures involve some combination of "choice" and the ability of stimuli to maintain ingestive behaviour, while a digital choice measure will usually permit some inference of learning. For example, the satiated laboratory rat exhibits a clear "preference" for saline solutions of 0.9% concentration; he will both imbibe more of this solution than water in a two-choice situation, and will also approach the saline bottle more frequently (Chiang and Wilson, 1963). The latter implies that the appearance of the saline spout has acquired motivating properties sufficient to produce a set of locomotor approach movements in the limited cage area. However, this does not apparently guarantee that saline will function as an effective reinforcer for other operant responses, even when the same basic motor requirements are involved. Pfaffmann (1969) emphasizes the difficulty experienced in training rats to run in a maze situation for saline reward (unless some special need state is induced by, e.g. adrenalectomy). On the other hand, Fisher (1965) has succeeded in training rats to lick at one drinking tube in order to gain access to a second tube containing saline, and Borer (1968) managed to train rats in a Skinner box to press for saline, although this was apparently accomplished in experienced animals who had previously worked for other reinforcement in the Skinner box and were then transferred to the saline reinforcer.

We have recently tried a variety of preference tests in gerbils, involving situations designed to elicit either ventral-rubbing or shredding of nest material. Essentially, we asked whether gerbils would prefer to enter into, and remain within, an area where marking or shredding will be elicited by appropriate environmental stimuli. Although these studies are still in their preliminary stages, the results thus far have not been encouraging for a simple consummatory-response view of the reinforcement process. As one might have expected, gerbils did prefer to spend their time on the side of their cage where index cards were available for shredding (Table 3). This was true even if one subtracted the time actually spent engaged in the consummatory act. On the other hand, gerbils showed no significant preference for the side of a shuttlebox where six plastic blocks had been affixed to the floor, despite the fact that they marked vigorously in this area and not at all on the opposite side of the box (Table 3). In another situation, the subject could enter either side of a field separated by a partition, with the rubbing blocks again placed on one side of the field and not the other. Despite marking 36 times in 15 minutes on the block-side and not at all on the empty side, our "champion" marker divided his entries evenly in terms of choice and actually spent more time investigating the empty area. There is always the possibility that with sufficient persistence and ingenuity, we will find some technique for demonstrating a preference for areas that elicit marking. However, it would be wrong to ignore the limitations and negative results. For these constraints on reinforcement are as important in defining the conditions of performance as are positive demonstrations of preference.

Habitat   demand   and   reinforcement: a   very   tentative hypothesis

In the course of the preceding review, I have described a number of species-characteristic response systems in the gerbil: sniffing, ventral-rubbing, foot-thumping and shredding. My theoretical idiosyncrasies led me to expect that evocation of any one of these responses would be sufficient to reinforce an arbitrary operant. Indeed, I could be encouraged by the fact that all of these responses can be elicited from the gerbil brain and, with the exception of ventral-rubbing, self-stimulation is likely to be obtained from neural loci at which these behaviours are elicited. However, careful examination of our own and other data suggests that there is surely more to the elicited behaviour-self-stimulation correlation than a single motor-facilitation mechanism. Very frequently correlations have appeared (e.g. involving elicited foot-thumping in the gerbil) which are accommodated equally, and perhaps better, by other formulations.

There are also interesting difficulties apparent at a behaviour level of analysis. Some stimuli (i.e. blocks eliciting ventral-rubbing) are very effective in eliciting consummatory behaviour, but cannot be used to maintain at least one simple kind of preference behaviour. Other stimuli (index cards) are powerful elicitors of consummatory acts (shredding) and efficient determinants of preference behaviour, but are relatively unreliable as determinants of reinforcement in a situation requiring an arbitrary operant. Finally, there is the kind of situation described by Pfaffmann (1969), where a stimulus (0.9% saline solution) evokes consummatory activity, and preference behaviour, but does not always seem capable of providing sufficient "incentive" to control behaviour when the sequence has to be initiated at a point spatially and temporally removed from the goal stimulus.

In a sense, the preceding is analogous to the experiments on the regulation of hamster behaviour described by Shettleworth (this volume), but whereas she was concerned with the difficulty of reinforcing different operants with a constant reinforcement, we have been asking about the ability of a variety of potential reinforcers to mediate both preference behaviours and learned operants.

Is there any way of characterizing the differences among the various stimuli that have been discussed in a manner that would enable predictions about as yet untested reinforcers and situations? Perhaps we should start with an examination of the situations in the habitat that call for the emission of each response sequence.

As we have seen, food was a very reliable reward for gerbils in an operant situation. Since food is required by gerbils at regular intervals, we must assume that internal cues have evolved that trigger the investigatory activity resulting in food acquisition, and gerbils may well learn pathways that lead from the burrow to good food sources. This latter would certainly be compatible with the fact that during the spring and summer gerbils accumulate huge stores of seeds which are utilized the following winter (Tanimoto, 1943). On the other hand, although gerbils have been found to line their nests with finely shredded plant materials, we have no indication that daily shredding is either necessary for the gerbil's health, or in any way internally cued. Some minimal nest seems necessary for adequate maintenance of the coat and young. We have lost several litters in the course of trying to breed animals without access to nest materials. However, given the presence of a minimal nest, the mechanism seems to operate much more with the instruction, shred-if-you-have-the-opportunity, than would be the case with a feeding system.

Finally, gerbils may never leave their nests/burrows in-order-to-rub. That is, emergence from the burrow is in search of food, mates, or nest materials. Finding good rubbing places would not terminate the expedition and send them scurrying for the burrow. What does seem to be critical is marking when a stimulus of appropriate configuration and novelty appears. Seen in this light, it is perhaps not surprising that gerbils do not go somewhere in order to mark, particularly given the neutral nature of our test situations. Perhaps in socially competitive arrangements of the type studied by Thiessen *et al.* (1971), where marking may be necessary to maintain the social order, we could demonstrate that stimuli eliciting marking possessed attractive properties, beyond basic evocation of the consummatory response. This latter suggestion is actually the key to making the preceding story useful in a scientific context. Until we can use this line of reasoning to make predictions about the interactions between test situations and reinforcing effects of, e.g. aggression-provoking stimuli, or about techniques for increasing the reward potency of shredding stimuli (such as making them visible to the gerbil), we are in possession of nothing more than a tempting fable, which alleges, in the worst evolutionary tradition, that all is for the best in the best of all possible worlds.

A final note on terminology and ontogenetic studies

Throughout this paper we have employed the term "consummatory response" as if its meaning were clear. I expect that this is a serious error. The terminology involved arose in an attempt to distinguish between relatively invariant species-characteristic activities and individually idiosyncratic appetitive or searching behaviours directed towards location of the consummatory stimuli. However, much more is implied. In various contexts, consummatory responses are viewed as being (a) species-characteristic, (b) independent of specific prior learning and (c) the terminal portions of a behavioural sequence. In regard to the latter, confusion is readily apparent. The studies of incomplete copulatory behaviour were originally viewed as supporting a consummatory response theory of reinforcement; yet mounts, or even intromissions, are surely not the terminal responses in the copulatory sequence of the rat. In addition, the searching or investigatory patterns of most animals are fully as species-characteristic as many so-called consummatory patterns, and it can be plausibly argued that investigatory responses are often an end-in-themselves, i.e. that they are consummatory.

Finally, the independence of most consummatory responses from specific prior learning is highly questionable. Certainly there are aspects of the feeding response pattern, in some species, which are apparently independent of prior specific learning. It seems highly likely that the preference for sweet substances exhibited by many rodents is in this category (Jacobs, 1967), although this preference is not as universal as is sometimes supposed (Kare, 1967). Similarly, Burghardt's (1967, 1970) demonstration of the responses of naïve garter snakes to olfactory cues is convincing in demonstrating a UCS–UCR relation that does not require prior learning.

However, the above cases are far removed from the situation commonly studied by psychologists in which rats approach some carefully concocted artificial food pellet, pick it up in the forepaws, and proceed to bite off small chunks, chew them and finally swallow them. Probably this represents an operant chain 'reinforced' in the prior history of the experimental animal, much as chicks learn to discriminate between grain and sand (Hogan, Chapter 6).

Some years ago, Dan Baran and I tested some young opossums (*Didelphis virginiana*) who had been taken from their mother and laboratory reared on a diet of milk and dog food. At one point, we examined the responses of four subjects in an olfactory preference apparatus in which steel mesh covered fluid-filled receptacles. During each test, a subject was confronted with two mesh-covered bottles, one of which contained water, and the other some aromatic compound. Although there were individual differences in magnitude of response and preference order, all of our subjects consistently bit violently at the steel mesh whether it covered a bottle of Xylene, Ethanol, or Benzyl Alcohol. Unlike Burghardt's snakes, these young opossums seemed to have been programmed on a much wider instruction: if it smells, bite it. They also showed intra- and intersession decrements in biting, and there may be some age-specificity since we were not able to elicit the same kind of behaviour in adult animals.

Although the opossum may be unusual among mammals in the vigour and range of the olfaction-bite linkage, it must be common for a variety of stimuli to evoke approach, biting, and even ingestion—with the commonly observed adult patterns dependent upon experience with a combination of oropharyngeal sensation and post-ingestive effects. Such experiential effects were investigated in a subsequent set of studies carried out by Sydney Reisbick with neonatal guinea pigs. These experiments were concerned with the ability of guinea pigs to recognize food during the first nine days of life. Two foods were presented: lettuce and rat pellets. Ten-minute sessions were run during which the infant guinea pigs either had access to rat pellets, wooden blocks or plastic blocks; or lettuce, paper and plastic. Thus, the subjects were required to make discriminations in situations which permitted simultaneous access to a nutritionally valuable food source and two objects of roughly similar contour whose dietary value was certainly very limited. The basic results of the first experiment in her series are presented in Fig. 2. Normal guinea pigs learned to make this discrimination with individual 10-minute periods of exposure on each of the first nine days after birth. As is usual in this type of study, there is an interaction between maturation and experience, with exposure on days 5, 7 and 9, being much more efficient than exposure on days 1, 3 and 5. However, clear evidence of the importance of the learned component of this recognition process can be seen in the comparatively poor performance of animals started on day 5, with those who have already had experience on days 1, 2, 3 and 4. In data gathered by Mrs. Reisbick, but not shown in the graph, it was found that inter-trial intervals of 4 to 8 hours were necessary for learning to occur with this kind of paradigm; even when testing was initiated between days 5 and 9. Evidently there is some sort of post-in-gestive mechanism which has to take time to operate (cf. Chapter 6).

The moral of this kind of research has a familiar cast to the followers of the developmental arguments offered by Schneirla (1966): simply because a stimulus is an effective reinforcer for an adult animal, one cannot con-clude that the efficacy of this reinforcement is not dependent upon prior

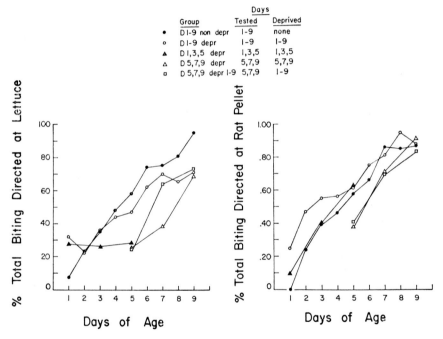

Fig. 2. Development of preferences for foods of dietary value in neonatal guinea pigs, as the result of repeated brief (10-min.) exposure to a situation requiring simul-taneous discriminatory ability. Subjects given similar experience, but with only one hour between sessions, failed to learn whether begun on days 1, 5, or 9. (Un-published data of Sydney Reisbick from the University of California, Berkeley).

learning. When the presentation of laboratory chow "elicits" a feeding response in an adult guinea pig, the varied components of this commonly designated "consummatory activity" are appearing only as the result of prior learning and are dependent upon post-ingestive effects which were, and are, operating following deglutition. I do not believe that the effects of reinforcing stimuli on so-called consummatory patterns are fundamentally different from the effects of such stimuli on so-called appetitive patterns. It is along other, much more finely graded distinctions, that we shall have to look if we are to understand how reinforcing stimuli control behaviour.

References

Alberts, J. and Galef, J. (1971). Acute anosmia in the rat: a behavioral test of peripherally induced olfactory deficit. *Physiol. Behav.* **6**, 619–621.

Azrin, N. H., Hutchinson, R. R. and McLaughlin, R. (1965). The opportunity for aggression as an operant reinforcer during aversive stimulation. *J. exp. Analysis Behav.* **8**, 171–180.

Ball, G. G. (1968). Electrically elicited eating and electrical self-stimulation of the brain—a comparison. *Commun. Behav. Biol.* Pt. A, **1**, 299–303.

Bannikov, A. G. (1954). "Mammals of the Mongolian Peoples Republic." U.S.S.R. Academy of Sciences. (Translated by Dr. Douglas Lay and distributed by Tumble-brook Farm, Brant Lake, New York.)

Baran, D. (1968). Shredding of nesting materials in the gerbil: effects of odor, temperature and drugs. Paper delivered at the meeting of the Eastern Psychological Association, Washington, D.C., April, 1968.

Baran, D. and Glickman, S. E. (1970). "Territorial marking" in the Mongolian gerbil: a study of sensory control and function. *J. comp. physiol. Psychol.* **71**, 237–245.

Barfield, R. J. and Sachs, B. D. (1968). Sexual behavior: stimulation by painful electric shock to skin in male rats. *Science* **161**, 292–294.

Berlyne, D. E. (1967). Arousal and reinforcement. *In* "Nebraska Symposium on Motivation", (D. Levine, ed.). University of Nebraska Press, Lincoln.

Bermant, G. (1961). Response latencies of female rats during sexual intercourse. *Science* **133**, 1771–1773.

Bindra, D. (1968). Neuropsychological interpretation on general activity and instrumental behavior. *Psychol. Rev.* **75**, 1–22.

Black, S. L. and Vanderwolf, C. H. (1969). Thumping behavior in the rabbit. *Physiol. Behav.* **4**, 445–449.

Borer, K. T. (1968). Disappearance of preferences and aversions for sapid solutions in rats ingesting untasted fluids. *J. comp. physiol. Psychol.* **65**, 213–221.

Brown, J. S. (1961). "The Motivation of Behavior." McGraw-Hill, New York.

Burghardt, G. M. (1967). Chemical-cue preferences of inexperienced snakes: comparative aspects. *Science* **157**, 718–721.

Burghardt, G. M. (1970). Intraspecific geographical variations in chemical food cue preferences of newborn garter snakes (*Thamnophis sirtalis*). *Behaviour* **36**, 246–257.

Caggiula, A. R. (1970). Analysis of the copulation-reward properties of posterior hypothalamic stimulation in male rats. *J. comp. physiol. Psychol.* **70**, 399–412.

Caggiula, A. R. and Eibergen, R. (1969). Copulation of virgin male rats evoked by painful peripheral stimulation. *J. comp. physiol. Psychol.* **69**, 414–419.

Caggiula, A. R. and Hoebel, B. G. (1966). "Copulation reward site" in the posterior hypothalamus. *Science* **153**, 1284–1285.

Chiang, H. and Wilson, W. A., Jr. (1963). Some tests of the diluted water hypothesis of saline consumption in rats. *J. comp. physiol. Psychol.* **63**, 24–27.

Christopher, Sister Mary and Butter, C. M. (1968). Consummatory behaviors and locomotor exploration evoked from self-stimulation sites in rats. *J. comp. physiol. Psychol.* **66**, 335–339.

Clarke, S. and Trowill, J. A. (1971). Sniffing and motivated behavior in the rat. *Physiol. Behav.* **6**, 49–52.

Cole, J. M. and Parker, B. K. (1971). Schedule-induced aggression: access to an attackable target bird as a positive reinforcer. *Psychonom. Sci.* **22**, 33–35.

Coons, E. E. and Cruce, J. A. F. (1968). Lateral hypothalamus: food and current intensity in maintaining self-stimulation of "hunger". *Science* **159**, 1117–1119.

Deutsch, J. A. and Howarth, C. I. (1963). Some tests of a theory of intracranial self-stimulation. *Psychol. Rev.* **70**, 444–460.

Devor, M., Wise, R., Milgram, N. W. and Hoebel, B. G. (1970). Physiological control of hypothalamically elicited feeding and drinking. *J. comp. physiol. Psychol.* **73**, 226–232.

Fantino, E. and Cole, M. (1968). Sand-digging in mice: functional autonomy? *Psychonom. Sci.* **10**, 20–30.

Fisher, A. E. and Coury, J. N. (1962). Cholinergic tracing of a central neutral circuit underlying the thirst drive. *Science* **138**, 691–693.

Fisher, G. L. (1965). Saline preference in rats determined by contingent licking. *J. exp. Analysis Behav.* **8**, 295–303.

Flynn, J. P. (1967). The neural basis of aggression in cats. *In* "Neurophysiology and Emotion", (J. P. Flynn, ed.). Rockefeller University Press, New York.

Fowler, H. (1971). Implications of sensory reinforcement. *In* "The Nature of Reinforcement", (R. Glaser, ed.) pp. 151–195. Academic Press, New York.

Gallistel, C. R. (1969a). Comments on Panksepp et al. *Psychonom. Sci.* **16**, 25–26.

Gallistel, C. R. (1969b). Self-stimulation: failure of pretrial stimulation to affect rats' electrode preference. *J. comp. physiol. Psychol.* **69**, 722–729.

Gallistel, C. R., Rolls, E. and Greene, D. (1969). Neuron function inferred from behavioral and electrophysiological estimates of refractory period. *Science* **166**, 1028–1029.

Glickman, S. E., Fried, L. and Morrison, B. A. (1967). Shredding of nesting material in the Mongolian gerbil. *Percept. Mot. Skills* **24**, 474–474.

Glickman, S. E. and Hartz, K. E. (1964). Exploratory behavior in several species of rodents. *J. comp. physiol. Psychol.* **58**, 101–104.

Glickman, S. E. and Higgins, T. M. (1968). Elicited behavior and reinforcement in the Mongolian gerbil. Paper delivered at the meeting of the Eastern Psychological Association, Washington, D.C., April, 1968.

Glickman, S. E. and Schiff, B. B. (1967). A biological theory of reinforcement. *Psychol. Rev.* **74**, 81–109.

Glickman, S. E. and Sroges, R. W. (1966). Curiosity in zoo animals. *Behaviour* **26**, 151–188.

Hoebel, B. and Teitelbaum, P. (1962). Hypothalamic control of feeding and self-stimulation. *Science* **135**, 375–377.

Hopkins, D. A. (1970). The neural basis of grooming behavior in the rat. Unpublished doctoral dissertation. McMaster University.

Huston, J. P. (1971). Relationship between motivating and rewarding stimulation of the lateral hypothalamus. *Physiol. Behav.* **6**, 711–716.

Jacobs, B. L. and Farel, P. B. (1971). Motivated behaviors produced by increased arousal in the presence of goal objects. *Physiol. Behav.* **6**, 473–476.

Jacobs, H. L. (1967). Taste and the role of experience in the regulation of food intake. *In* "The Chemical Senses and Nutrition", (M. Kare and O. Maller, eds.) pp. 187–200. The Johns Hopkins University Press, Baltimore.

Jansen, P. E., Goodman, E. D., Jowaisas, D. and Bunnell, B. N. (1969). Paper as a positive reinforcer for acquisition of a bar-press response by the golden hamster. *Psychonom. Sci.* **16**, 113–114.

Kagan, J. (1955). Differential reward value of incomplete and complete sexual behavior. *J. comp. physiol. Psychol.* **48**, 59–64.

Kare, M. (1967). Comments on Jacobs' paper. *In* "The Chemical Senses and Nutrition", (M. Kare, and O. Maller, eds.), pp. 197–199. The Johns Hopkins University Press, Baltimore.

King, M. B. and Hoebel, B. G. (1968). Killing elicited by brain stimulation in rats. *Commun. Behav. Biol.* Pt. A, **2**, 173–177.

King, J. A. and Weisman, R. G. (1964). Sand digging contingent upon bar pressing in deermice (*Peromyscus*). *Anim. Behav.* **12**, 446–450.

Kuehn, R. E. and Zucker, I. (1968). Reproductive behavior in the Mongolian gerbil. *J. comp. physiol. Psychol.* **66**, 747–752.

Lagerspetz, K. (1964). "Studies on the Aggressive Behavior of Mice." Suomalainen Tudeakatemia, Helsinki.

Macdougall, J. and Bevan, W. (1968). Influence of pretest shock upon rate of electrical self-stimulation of the brain. *J. comp. physiol. Psychol.* **65**, 261–264.

Malsbury, C. W. (1971). Facilitation of male rat copulatory behavior by electrical stimulation of the medial preoptic area. *Physiol. Behav.* **7**, 797–805.

Margules, D. L. and Olds, J. (1962). Identical "feeding" and "rewarding" systems in the lateral hypothalamus of rats. *Science* **135**, 374–375.

Meehl, P. E. (1950). On the circularity of the law of effect. *Psychol. Bull.* **47**, 52–75.

Mendelson, J. (1966). Role of hunger in T-maze learning for food by rats. *J. comp. physiol. Psychol.* **62**, 341–349.

Mendelson, J. (1967). Lateral hypothalamic stimulation in satiated rats: the rewarding effects of self-induced drinking. *Science* **157**, 1077–1079.

Mendelson, J. (1969). Lateral hypothalamic stimulation: Inhibition of aversive effects of feeding, drinking and gnawing. *Science* **166**, 1431–1433.

Mendelson, J. (1970). Self-induced drinking in rats: the qualitative identity of drive and reward systems in the lateral hypothalamus. *Physiol. Behav.* **5**, 925–930.

Milgram, W. (1968). Eating elicited by hippocampal self-stimulation. Paper delivered at the meeting of the Eastern Psychological Association, Washington, D.C., April, 1968.

Miller, N. E. (1963). Some reflections on the law of effect produce a new alternative to drive reduction. *In* "Nebraska Symposium on Motivation", (M. R. Jones, ed.), pp. 65–112. University of Nebraska Press, Lincoln.

Mogenson, G. J. (1968). Effects of amphetamine on self-stimulation and induced drinking. *Physiol. Behav.* **3**, 133–136.

Mogenson, G. J. (1971). Stability and modification of consummatory behaviors elicited by electrical stimulation of the hypothalamus. *Physiol. Behav.* **6**, 255–260.

Mogenson, G. J., Russek, M. and Stevenson, J. A. F. (1969). The effect of adrenaline on bar-pressing for food and for self-stimulation. *Physiol. Behav.* **4**, 91–94.

Mogenson, G. J. and Stevenson, J. A. F. (1966). Drinking and self-stimulation with electrical stimulation of the lateral hypothalamus. *Physiol. Behav.* **1**, 151–154.

Montgomery, K. C. (1954). The role of the exploratory drive in learning. *J. comp. physiol. Psychol.* **47**, 60–64.

Montgomery, K. C. and Segall, M. (1955). Discrimination learning based upon the exploratory drive. *J. comp. physiol. Psychol.* **48**, 225–228.

Morgan, C. W. and Mogenson, G. J. (1966). Preference of water deprived rats for stimulation of the lateral hypothalamus rather than water. *Psychonom. Sci.* **6**, 337–338.

Myer, J. S. and White, R. T. (1965). Aggressive motivation in the rat. *Anim. Behav.* **13**, 430–433.

Olds, M. E. and Olds, J. (1963). Approach-avoidance analysis of rat diencephalon. *J. comp. Neurol.* **120**, 259–295.

Oley, N. N. and Slotnick, B. M. (1970). Nesting material as a reinforcement for operant behavior in the rat. *Psychonom. Sci.* **21**, 41–43.

Panksepp, J., Gandelman, R. and Trowill, J. A. (1969). Reply to Gallistel. *Psychonom. Sci.* **16**, 26–27.

Panksepp, J. and Trowill, J. A. (1969). Electrically induced affective attack from the hypothalamus of the albino rat. *Psychonom. Sci.* **16**, 118–119.

Peirce, J. T. and Nuttall, R. L. (1961). Self-paced sexual behavior in the female rat. *J. comp. physiol. Psychol.* **54**, 310–313.

Pfaffmann, C. (1969). Taste preference and reinforcement. *In* "Reinforcement and Behavior", (J. T. Tapp. ed.), pp. 215–241. Academic Press, New York.

Phillips, A. G. (1970). Enhancement and inhibition of olfactory bulb self-stimulation by odours. *Physiol. Behav.* **5**, 1127–1131.

Phillips, A. G., Cox, V. C., Kakolewski, J. W. and Valenstein, E. S. (1969). Object-carrying by rats: an approach to the behavior produced by brain stimulation. *Science* **166**, 903–905.

Phillips, A. G. and Mogenson, G. J. (1968). Effects of taste on self-stimulation and induced drinking. *J. comp. physiol. Psychol.* **66**, 654–660.

Phillips, M. I. (1972). Olfactory bulb removal blocks self-stimulation. Paper delivered at the meeting of the American Psychological Association, Honolulu, Ha., September, 1972.

Plotnick, R., Mir, D. and Delgado, J. M. R. (1968). Aggression, noxiousness and brain stimulation in unrestricted rhesus monkeys. Paper delivered at the meeting of the *Amer. Assoc. Advance. Sci.*, Dallas, Texas, 1968.

Plutchik, R., McFarland, W. L. and Robinson, B. W. (1966). Relationships between current intensity, self-stimulation rates, escape latencies, and evoked behavior in rhesus monkeys. *J. comp. physiol. Psychol.* **61**, 181–188.

Poschel, B. P. H. (1968). Do biological reinforcers act via the self-stimulation areas of the brain? *Physiol. Behav.* **3**, 53–60.

Powell, R. W. (1971). Acquisition of free-operant (Sidman) avoidance in Mongolian gerbils (*Meriones unguiculatus*) and albino rats. *Psychonom. Sci.* **22**, 279–281.

Premack, D. (1965). Reinforcement theory. *In* "Nebraska Symposium on Motivation", (D. Levine, ed.), pp. 123–180. University of Nebraska Press, Lincoln.

Renfrew, J. W. (1969). The intensity function and reinforcing properties of brain stimulation that elicits attack. *Physiol. Behav.* **4**, 509–515.

Roberts, W. W. (1969). Are hypothalamic motivational mechanisms functionally and anatomically specific? *Brain Behav. Evolut.* **2**, 317–342.

Roberts, W. W. and Carey, R. J. (1965). Rewarding effect of performance of gnawing aroused by hypothalamic stimulation in the rat. *J. comp. physiol. Psychol.* **59**, 317–324.

Roberts, W. W. and Kiess, H. O. (1964). Motivational properties of hypothalamic aggression in cats. *J. comp. physiol. Psychol.* **58**, 187–193.

Roberts, W. W., Steinberg, M. I. and Means, L. W. (1967). Hypothalamic mechanisms for sexual, aggressive, and other motivational behaviors in the opossum, *Didelphis virginiana. J. comp. physiol. Psychol.* **64**, 1–15.

Routtenberg, A. (1968). The two-arousal hypothesis: reticular formation and limbic system. *Psychol. Rev.* **75**, 51–80.

Routtenberg, A. (In press). Intracranial self-stimulation pathways as substrate for stimulus-response integration. *In* "Efferent Organization and Integrative Behavior", (J. Maser, ed.). Academic Press, New York.

Routtenberg, A. and Kramis, R. C. (1967). "Foot-stomping" in the gerbil: rewarding brain stimulation, sexual behaviour, and foot-shock. *Nature* **214**, 173–174.

Schiff, B. B., Rusak, B. and Block, R. (1971). The termination of reinforcing hypothalamic stimulation: an ecological approach. *Physiol. Behav.* **7**, 215–220.

Schneirla, T. C. (1965). Aspects of stimulation and organisation in approach/withdrawal processes underlying vertebrate behavioural development. *In* "Advances in the study of behavior", Vol. 1. (D. S. Lehrman, R. A. Hinde and E. Shaw, eds.) pp. 1–74. Academic Press, New York.

Schneirla, T. C. (1966). Behavioural development and comparative psychology. *Quart. Rev. Biol.* **41**, 283–302.

Sheffield, F. D. (1966). A drive-induction theory of reinforcement. *In* "Current Research in Motivation", (R. N. Haber, ed.), pp. 98–111. Holt, Rinehart, New York.

Sheffield, F. D. and Roby, T. B. (1950). Reward value of a non-nutritive sweet taste. *J. comp. physiol. Psychol.* **43**, 471–481.

Sheffield, F. D., Wulff, J. J. and Backer, R. (1951). Reward value of copulation without sex drive reduction. *J. comp. physiol. Psychol.* **44**, 3–8.

Siegel, P. S. and Brantley, J. J. (1951). The relationship of emotionality to the consummatory response of eating. *J. exptl. Psychol.* **42**, 304–306.

Siegel, P. S. and Siegel, H. S. (1949). The effect of emotionality on the water intake of the rat. *J. comp. physiol. Psychol.* **42**, 12–16.

Spatz, C. and Granger, W. R. (1970). Foot-thumping in the gerbil: the effect of establishing a home cage. *Psychonom. Sci.* **19**, 53–54.

Stark, P., Totty, C. W., Turk, J. A. and Henderson, J. K. (1968). A possible role of a cholinergic system affecting hypothalamic-elicited eating. *Amer. J. Physiol.* **214**, 463–468.

Stephan, F. K., Valenstein, E. S. and Zucker, I. (1971). Copulation and eating during electrical stimulation of the rat hypothalamus. *Physiol. Behav.* **7**, 587–593.

Stern, J. J. and Merari, A. (1969). The bathing behavior of the chinchilla: effects of deprivation. *Psychonom. Sci.* **14**, 115.

Stevenson, J. G. (1969). Song as a reinforcer. *In* "Bird Vocalizations in Relation to Current Problems in Biology and Psychology", (R. A. Hinde, ed.), pp. 49–60. Cambridge University Press, Cambridge.

Tanimoto, K. (1943). An ecological report on several plague-carrying animals in Northeast China: 3. *Dobutsugaku Zasshi* (*Zoological Magazine*) **55**, 117–128.

Tapp, J. T. and Simpson, L. L. (1966). Motivational and response factors as determinants of the reinforcing value of light onset. *J. comp. physiol. Psychol.* **62**, 143–146.

Tellegen, A., Horn, J. M. and Legrand, R. G. (1969). Opportunity for aggression as a reinforcer in mice. *Psychonom. Sci.* **14**, 104–105.

Thiessen, D. D., Friend, H. C. and Lindzey, G. (1968). Androgen control of territorial marking in the Mongolian gerbil. *Science* **160**, 432–434.

Thiessen, D. D., Lindzey, G. and Nyby, J. (1970). The effects of olfactory deprivation and hormones on territorial marking in the male Mongolian gerbil (*Meriones unguiculatus*). *Horm. Behav.* **1**, 315–325.

Thiessen, D. D., Owen, K. and Lindzey, G. (1971). Mechanisms of territorial marking in the male and female Mongolian gerbil (*Meriones unguiculatus*). *J. comp. physiol. Psychol.* **77**, 38–47.

Thiessen, D. D. and Yahr. P. (1970). Central control of territorial marking in the Mongolian gerbil. *Physiol. Behav.* **5**, 275–278.

Thompson, T. I. (1963). Visual reinforcement in Siamese fighting fish. *Science* **141**, 55–57.

Thompson, T. I. (1964). Visual reinforcement in fighting cocks. *J. exptl. anal. Behav.* **7**, 45–49.

Tinbergen, N. (1951). "The Study of Instinct." Oxford University Press, London.

Ursin, R., Ursin, H. and Olds, J. (1966). Self-stimulation of hippocampus in rats. *J. comp. physiol. Psychol.* **61**, 353–359.

Valenstein, E. S. (1969). Behavior elicited by hypothalamic stimulation. *Brain Behav. Evolut.* **2**, 295–316.

Valenstein, E. S. (1971). Channeling of responses elicited by hypothalamic stimulation. *J. psychiat. Res.* **8**, 335–344.

Valenstein, E. S., Cox, V. C. and Kakolewski, J. W. (1968). Modification of motivated behavior elicited by electrical stimulation of the hypothalamus. *Science* **159**, 1119–1121.

Valenstein, E. S., Cox, V. C. and Kakolewski, J. W. (1970). Re-examination of the role of the hypothalamus in motivation. *Psychol. Rev.* **77**, 16–31.

Van Hemel, P. E. (1972). Aggression as a reinforcer: operant behavior in the mouse-killing rat. *J. exp. Analysis Behav.* **17**, 237–245.

Van Hemel, S. B. (1970). Retrieving as a reinforcer in nulliparous mice. Unpublished doctoral dissertation. The Johns Hopkins University.

Wallen, K. and Glickman, S. E. (In press). Effect of peripheral anosmia on ventral rubbing in the gerbil. *Behav. Biol.*

Walters, G. C. and Abel. E. L. (1971). Passive avoidance learning in rats, mice, gerbils and hamsters. *Psychonom. Sci.* **22**, 269–270.

Wayner. M. J. (1970). Motor control functions of the lateral hypothalamus and adjunctive behavior. *Physiol. Behav.* **5**, 1319–1325.

Welker, W. I. (1964). Analysis of sniffing in the albino rat. *Behaviour.* **22**, 223–244.

Wilsoncroft. W. E. (1969). Babies by bar-press: maternal behavior in the rat. *Behav. Resch. meth. Instrument.* **1**, 229–230.

Woodworth, C. H. (1971). Attack elicited in rats by electrical stimulation of the lateral hypothalamus. *Physiol. Behav.* **6**, 345–353.

R

11

Food Reinforcement and the Organization of Behaviour in Golden Hamsters

by Sara J. Shettleworth

Introduction

Not everything an animal does can be modified equally readily by reinforcement. There seem to be constraints on at least the performance of some elements of behaviour as operants, if not on their reinforceability, i.e. on learning *per se*. The existence of such constraints raises the question whether there is some way to classify responses *a priori* according to whether or how they will be affected by reinforcement.

A number of dichotomous schemes for classifying responses have been suggested in the past. All of them implicitly recognize that not all identifiable responses can be conditioned using operant methods, but most of them have been effectively undermined by evidence that at least one member of the "not conditionable" class can be conditioned. For example, Miller's (1969) work has forced abandonment of the notion that autonomic responses cannot be operantly conditioned while skeletal responses can. Skinner's (1938) classification in terms of emitted and elicited responses, that in terms of voluntary and involuntary responses (Vanderwolf, 1971), and others have had similar fates (Black and Young, 1972). Nevertheless, there remains a small body of evidence (reviewed by Shettleworth, 1972) that reward or punishment do not have the same effects on all responses. The frequency of some responses may not be modifiable at all, and the frequency of others may be modifiable only with some reinforcers or only to a limited extent. This evidence comes mainly from attempts to use operant techniques to condition the spontaneously occurring action patterns of various animals.

The first attempt to reinforce something other than an "arbitrary operant" seems to have been made by Thorndike (1911), who put a domestic chick into a box and allowed it to rejoin its companions whenever it preened itself. He also released cats from boxes whenever they licked or scratched themselves. Unlike topographically novel responses such as bar-pressing, which can never have had any role in the animal's pre-experimental life, such responses are already being performed by the animal "for other reasons", with some definite function or potential function. It would not be surprising to find that there are limits on the extent to which such units of behaviour can be altered in frequency or intensity by consequences that may have little relationship to their normal function or causation. And in fact the scattered reports of experiments on various species in which such responses have been rewarded or punished do contain some rather strange findings.

For example, one recurrent observation is that rewarded action patterns may become quite minimal in form even as they increase in frequency (e.g. Thorndike, 1911; Hogan, 1964; Konorski, 1967). Thorndike's cats and chicks, for example, eventually gave only the merest suggestion of the rewarded lick, scratch, or preening movement and did not always repeat the response immediately if reward was withheld. However, these responses may have become so perfunctory as a direct result of the reinforcement contingencies and not because of their special nature. If the animal is reinforced each time it begins to engage in some behaviour, it will never have a chance to perform or to be reinforced for more than a minimal form of it. In support of this explanation is Hogan's (1964) finding that although pigeons reinforced with food for preening did show rather abnormal preening behaviour when they were reinforced for each preening movement, preening became less abnormal when reinforcement was given on a variable interval schedule and in extinction.

Contrasting with these reports that minimal responses develop are a number of reports that a reinforced action pattern develops into a high-intensity form exceeding what is required for reinforcement. This has been reported several times for the operant conditioning of fighting behaviour in pigeons for food (Skinner, 1959; Reynolds et al., 1963; Azrin and Hutchinson, 1967) and also for fighting in rats for water reward (Ulrich et al., 1963). In such experiments, a minimal form of attack, such as exerting a given force against a conspecific, often develops into full-blown fighting including many movements other than that originally reinforced. The subjects may even fight to the extent that they fail to collect reinforcements. Nevertheless, at least in pigeons, fighting is still under the control of the reinforcement schedule (Azrin and Hutchinson, 1967). Similar behaviour in excess of the requirements of reinforcement contingencies was observed also by Breland and Breland (1966) in some situations. In the case of conditioned aggressive behaviour it may appear simply because the shaping procedure brings the animal into contact with stimuli eliciting unconditioned aggression (Reynolds *et al.*, 1963; Azrin and Hutchinson, 1967).

Surprisingly, a survey of the rather limited literature (cf. Shettleworth, 1972) reveals few outright failures of reinforcement to affect the frequency of a species-typical action pattern on which it was made contingent. It may be instructive that such failures have been reported more with negative reinforcers (i.e. in escape, avoidance, or punishment paradigms) than with positive reinforcers. Indeed, it has been observed quite often that an avoidance contingency which is demonstrably effective with some responses is quite ineffective with others, even responses which can be affected by other reinforcement contingencies. Findings of this sort have inspired an account of avoidance learning (Bolles, 1970) which states that the only readily acquired avoidance responses are those that are species-specific defence reactions or slight modifications of such responses.

Although reinforcement may almost always have some effect, its effect on some responses can be quite limited. In all the literature in this area, two of the most thoroughly analysed examples (Black and Young, 1972; Sevenster, 1968 and Chapter 12) seem to reveal a constraint purely on the performance of a reinforced response. Both of them show that to understand what happens when reinforcement is made contingent on performance of a species-typical action pattern it may be necessary to take into account the relationship of the normal causal factors for the reinforced response to the conditions present in the learning situation. Although reinforcement may bring it under the control of new causal factors, a response may remain under the control of its original ones as well. This can lead to apparent failures of reinforcement or apparent response-reinforcer interactions when the learning situation itself contains factors that normally inhibit the response. The internal state necessary to make the reinforcer effective and presentation of the reinforcer *per se* seem to be particularly important among such factors.

Black and Young, as well as Sevenster, suggest that it may be impossible for reinforcement to overcome factors inhibiting the reinforced response, and Black and Young were able to show this directly for drinking as an avoidance response in rats. They trained rats to drink water to avoid shocks in the presence of one discriminative stimulus and to press a lever to avoid shocks in the presence of a second stimulus. If the rats were water-deprived or if the water was sweetened, lever pressing and drinking were under stimulus control, and the rats avoided most of the shocks. But when the same rats were satiated and required to drink tap water to avoid, they responded only at a low rate in the presence of the stimulus signalling that drinking should avoid shocks. The constraint on conditioning here, and in the similar example reported by Sevenster, thus seems to be not a constraint on learning in the sense of failure of the to-be-conditioned response to be reinforced, but rather a failure of reinforcement to overcome other, specifically motivational, factors in the situation.

In contrast to these examples of continued control of a response by its normal causal factors, Konorski (1967) describes some results which seem to indicate that a response may be gradually weaned away from the control of its original eliciting factors. There may be a continuum of such effects (cf. Black and Young, 1972), since the sorts of cumulative records presented by Skinner (1938) show that a relatively "neutral" response like bar-pressing can be brought under the control of experimental factors almost immediately, in that it is performed at a nearly maximum rate as soon as it has been reinforced a few times. However, there may also be important differences between learning to perform a response in the absence of its original eliciting factors and performing it in the presence of inhibitory factors.

Although many of the anomalous results of reinforcing species-typical action patterns can be accounted for in terms of motivational factors like those already discussed (Shettleworth, 1972), in most cases there has not been enough experimental analysis to rule out other possibilities. For example, there may be responses which are refractory to all kinds of reward or punishment, as Konorski (1967) suggests, or to particular ones. Analysis might be helped in some cases by considering the normal consequences as well as the normal cause of a to-be-conditioned response in relation to the reinforcer. And something might be learned by considering how the response develops in the normal behaviour of the species in question.

A fairly comprehensive study of what happens when various elements of a single species' behaviour are reinforced with various reinforcers might be expected to show what, if anything, responses that are difficult or impossible to condition have in common in other respects. Thus it might help to show why conditionability may be limited. To make it possible to examine the role of purely motivational factors, such an investigation should include observations of the direct, as opposed to contingent, effects of the reinforcers. I will describe here the first stages of a programme of this sort using golden hamsters (*Mesocricetus auratus*). The experiments so far have dealt with the effects of reinforcement with food. The first one I shall describe provides background data on the effects of hunger and the presentation of food on the behaviour of hamsters in an open field, and the second deals with the effects of food reinforcement on several behaviour patterns the hamsters display in the open field.

Effects of Food and Hunger on the Behaviour of Hamsters in an Open Field

General method. The subjects in all the work to be reported were adult golden hamsters of both sexes, born and reared in the laboratory and at least three months old at the start of an experiment. They were observed in an open field, a two-foot square topless plywood box with one Plexiglas side, sides 18 inches high and sawdust about $\frac{1}{2}$ inch deep on the metal floor. A standard Gerbrands lever for rats and a dipper for delivering food pellets were close together on one wall. The hamsters lived under a reversed light cycle and were observed during the last hour of light or the first four hours of darkness.

All the data to be reported are based on 20-minute once-daily observation sessions during which a hamster's behaviour was recorded continuously in 18 mutually exclusive categories on a keyboard. This was attached to relay circuitry in another room which was programmed to record the number of one-second intervals in which each behaviour occurred. For some behaviours, this measure was recorded separately for each four-minute interval and the number of times the key was pressed (i.e. the number of continuous bouts) was also recorded.

The behaviours which will be of concern here are the following: grooming face and head with forepaws; grooming belly or sides with mouth and/or forepaws; scratching with a hind leg; scent marking; digging; rearing in the open ("open rearing"); rearing with forepaw(s) against the metal panel holding the feeder and lever, including times when the lever was being pressed; and scrabbling, a behaviour in which the hamster claws at the wall, often hopping up and down and moving along the wall as if trying to climb out. Depressions of the lever sufficient to activate a microswitch (about 23g force) and presentations of food pellets were recorded automatically.

Method: effects of food and hunger. A preliminary experiment, the "baseline experiment", was done to find out what hamsters did in the open field, how their behaviour changed with repeated experience there, and how hunger and/or the availability of food in the open field changed what they did. Thus it provided basic data against which to evaluate the effects of reinforcement with food, particularly because it included a group that received food periodically no matter what they did. Four groups of five experimentally naïve hamsters that were either hungry or not and either received no food in the open field or received 45 milligrammes of food pellets on a VI 30-second schedule were observed for nine 20-minute sessions. The food-deprived hamsters were also observed for an additional two sessions, during which those that had been receiving food in the open field no longer received it, and those that had not been receiving food did receive it, again on a VI 30-second schedule independently of their behaviour. A tone sounded whenever and for as long as a pellet was available in the dipper. "Hunger" in these experiments refers to a condition in which the hamster was gradually reduced to 80–85% of its weight and kept there by being given a measured amount of food one to two hours after the daily session. The undeprived animals were also handled and weighed daily.

Results. Food-restricted hamsters are more active than hamsters that are not food-restricted, as Mrosovsky (1964) found using a running wheel. In the open field, they not only moved about more, and generally more rapidly, but, as Prescott (1970) found for rats, specific activities involving active sampling of environmental stimuli (e.g. rearing, scrabbling) tended to increase while other types of activities (e.g. grooming, scent marking) tended to decrease. The hungry hamsters receiving food came to spend about half the session rearing at the panel containing the feeder, but the presence or absence of food had no apparent effect on the over-all distribution of behaviour in the undeprived animals. Different responses changed in various ways over days and the differences between deprived and undeprived hamsters appeared to increase over days, but on the whole the effect of sessions did not approach statistical significance. Further details of the results are discussed where they are relevant to interpreting the effects of reinforcing various behaviours with food.

Effect of Food Reinforcement on Bar-Pressing and Six Action Patterns

Bar-Pressing, open rearing, scrabbling, digging, and face-washing reinforced with food

Initially, bar-pressing and four action patterns were chosen for reinforcement with food. The four reinforced action patterns were face-washing (grooming face or head with forepaws), open rearing, scrabbling, and digging. All the action patterns were performed by hungry hamsters receiving food in the baseline experiment on an average of between 3 and 10 percent of the one-second intervals, and all typically had bout lengths in excess of one second. Since it is not possible to reinforce successive approximations to (i.e. shape) such responses as one would shape bar-pressing, it seemed important to avoid, at least initially, responses with operant levels so low as possibly to limit reinforceability in and of themselves. These five responses were affected in various ways by hunger in the baseline experiment: open rearing and scrabbling tended to be increased by hunger; face-washing, decreased; and digging and bar-pressing, not changed.

The procedure for reinforcing these responses was designed to avoid specifically reinforcing a form of the response so perfunctory and minimal as to be almost unrecognizable. It also included a minimum number of sessions with continuous reinforcement so that behaviour would be interrupted with food presentation no more than necessary to maintain the reinforced response and so that it would be possible to observe excessive forms of the response that might develop, including increases in behaviours related to the reinforced response.

Method. Accordingly, the procedure was as follows: 15 naïve food-deprived hamsters, about the same ages as those in the first experiment, were observed in the same way for ten sessions in the open field. Each of the five responses was reinforced in three different hamsters. During the first two sessions animals were given food on a VI 30-second schedule so that they would learn to approach the feeder when a pellet was presented. For the animals to be reinforced for bar-pressing, the next two sessions consisted of a small amount of shaping followed by continuous reinforcement for pressing the bar. They then had reinforcement on a VI 20-second schedule for four sessions and two sessions of extinction. During the first session of reinforcement for the hamsters reinforced for scrabbling, digging, open rearing, or face-washing, the recording device was wired so that a food pellet would be delivered whenever the selected response had occurred for 0.2 seconds, i.e. essentially as soon as it began. For the second session of continuous reinforcement and the four sessions on VI 20-second reinforcement that followed, the response requirement was 0.5 seconds. (It was possible to record responses shorter than this.) The six sessions of reinforcement were followed by two sessions of extinction, as in the case of bar-pressing. Throughout all of the sessions with reinforcement, each food pellet remained available until the hamster collected it, unless he did not immediately orient towards the feeder after performing the reinforced response.

Results. Fig. 1 shows the rate of bar-pressing and the number of one-second intervals in which the other reinforced responses occurred for each of the three hamsters reinforced for each of the five responses. While bar-pressing, digging, scrabbling, and open rearing increased almost immediately to rather high levels, face-washing increased only slightly and gradually. (Since face-washing was so sporadic the VI schedule was virtually equivalent to continuous reinforcement for this response.)

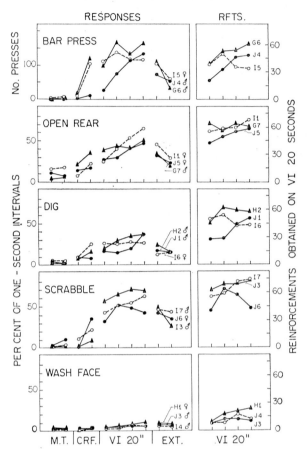

Fig. 1. Session-by-session response rates and numbers of reinforcements earned for the individual hamsters reinforced with food for bar-pressing, open rearing, digging, scrabbling, or face-washing. M.T., magazine training; CRF, continuous reinforcement; EXT, extinction. The maximum number of reinforcements that could be obtained during each session on VI 20-seconds was about sixty.

Although there are some obvious differences among the other responses in the proportion of the session they came to occupy, these differences are probably not very meaningful, since the responses differed in how near the feeder they were usually performed and thus in how much time was taken up in such things as going to the feeder between bouts of responding.* It was usually the case that after not much more than one session of

* Animals nearly always ran over and collected the food pellet immediately after performing the reinforced response, but the responses could have differed slightly in the time from response *initiation* to collection of the reinforcer. The method by which the present data were recorded did not permit this to be analysed.

reinforcement of any of these responses, almost all the experimental session was taken up with performing the reinforced response, eating, rearing at the feeder, and sniffing/walking. The steadiness with which digging, open rearing, scrabbling, and bar-pressing were performed when reinforced is evident in the fact that most of the animals in these groups earned nearly all of the approximately sixty reinforcements that were made available during each session on VI 20-seconds (Fig. 1, right panels). All five of the reinforced responses decreased in extinction, although to varying degrees. Any meaningful comparisons of rate of extinction are difficult if not impossible to make because of the differences in the final reinforced levels and in the effect of food withdrawal *per se* on the various responses.

It should be noted that although the responses did differ in unreinforced, or operant, level, the operant level of face-washing was no lower than that of other responses that exhibited large and immediate effects of food reinforcement (see Fig. 1). The within- and between-response relationships depicted in Fig. 1 are also evident if number of bouts of a response is considered instead of number of one-second intervals in which it was performed.

Instances of reinforced digging, open rearing, or scrabbling were clearly identical to instances of these action patterns in hamsters not reinforced for performing them. However, when they were being reinforced, these behaviours were usually performed in a rather stereotyped way and in the same location in the box, most often near the feeder. For example, a hamster reinforced for open rearing might collect a pellet, sniff/walk about three inches from the feeder, rear facing away from the feeder, then turn around and dash back to the feeder. Reinforced scrabbling nearly always consisted of clawing and hopping at the panel containing the feeder, which probably accounts for the large proportion of time it could occupy compared to the other responses.

The three action patterns which came to be performed a large proportion of the time when reinforced also, if anything, increased in bout length both within and between sessions. This was particularly clear in the case of digging. Although digging in the open field could be of the intense, sustained sort seen in hamsters burrowing in earth, unreinforced digging more often consisted of a few desultory scrapes in the sawdust with the forepaws. This latter form of digging was usually first to be reinforced, but by the second or third session many of the digging sequences consisted of rapid scraping with the forepaws followed by kicking with the hind legs. This could happen even when the hamster had already scraped most of the sawdust away from the area where it was digging so, as Daly (1971) concluded from other sorts of observations, hind-kicking is probably not just elicited by a pile of dug-up material accumulating under the animal's

belly. However, in spite of the apparent intensity of these reinforced behaviours, an animal only seldom became so "carried away" with performing them that it failed to collect reinforcements. But this might
happen if longer training and/or an interval schedule providing less frequent reinforcement were tried.

In contrast, not only was the frequency of face-washing much lower
than that of the other reinforced responses, but also most of the face-
washing was quite minimal in form. The hungry hamsters in the baseline
experiment would rear and face-wash from time to time. This usually
began with putting the paws briefly to the mouth and then rubbing them
back and forth along the sides of the nose with increasing amplitude until
the ears and back of the head were included in the area being rubbed. This
was often followed by turning to one side to bite and scratch at the fur on
the flank, and then by more face-washing. Occasionally very short bouts of
face-washing alone were also seen, but rather infrequently, and in the
hamsters reinforced for face-washing the first reinforcements were usually
given for bouts of face-washing and grooming belly or sides together.
Animals seldom interrupted such a bout to collect the food, so the response
followed by food was actually a rather elaborate, though short, grooming
sequence. Nevertheless, the increases in grooming after several sessions of
reinforcement were almost entirely composed of very short grooming bouts
in which the hamster reared and waved its forepaws a few times on either
side of its nose, sometimes hardly appearing to touch the nose at all. Unlike
the examples of minimal forms of reinforced responses described in the
introduction, these short face-washing bouts were seldom reinforced since
most of them did not meet the half-second criterion.

The increasing predominance of face-washing bouts too short to be
reinforced appears especially strikingly in the data for four additional
hamsters that had up to five sessions of continuous reinforcement for face-
washing. In all these animals the number of seconds during which face-
washing occurred and the number of face-washing bouts increased steadily
over the reinforced sessions but the number of bouts that were long enough
to be reinforced increased little if at all. Data from one of these animals
that eventually performed some face-washing on slightly less than 20% of
the one-second intervals are displayed in Fig 2.

When face-washing was reinforced the two other kinds of grooming
movements also tended to become more frequent. The levels of all types of
grooming in the three naïve animals reinforced for face-washing are
portrayed in Fig. 3, where they are compared to data from the two hungry
groups in the baseline experiment and from the groups reinforced for other
responses. The increase in grooming belly or sides might be expected since
this movement was normally associated with prolonged bouts of face-

washing. That it increased proportionally less than did face-washing would be expected from the fact that most of the face-washing took the form of very short bouts. On the other hand, scratching with the hind leg usually occurred in the open field at times other than face-washing, although in the home cage it often forms part of long bouts including all three types of grooming movements (Daly, 1971; personal observations). Yet when face-washing was reinforced, scratching with the hind leg grad-

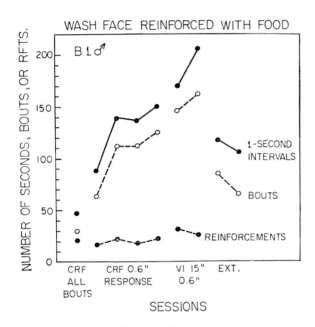

Fig. 2. Number of seconds in which face-washing occurred, number of face-washing bouts, and number of reinforcements earned for a typical one of four hamsters given several sessions of continuous reinforcement for face-washing.

ually increased to a level significantly above that shown by the hungry hamsters in the first experiment. An animal that had just been reinforced for face-washing would sometimes run back to the place where it had face-washed and scratch its side vigorously with its hind leg. For the various reasons suggested above, this cannot be regarded as the completion of a grooming bout that had been interrupted by food presentation.

Discussion. The relevance of the foregoing observations to understanding why reinforcement had such a small effect on face-washing is still obscure. The increases in all types of grooming when face-washing was reinforced may reflect the same processes as those in the cats Konorski (1967) reinforced for scratching their ears. He elicited the to-be-reinforced response at first by placing a wad of cotton in an animal's ear and sometimes saw other responses the cat might use to get the cotton out, even when some conditioning had taken place and the cotton was no longer there. Such findings are what would be expected if what is being reinforced or strengthened is not the response *per se* but some representation of the stimulus or state that normally elicits it (cf. Konorski, 1967). This

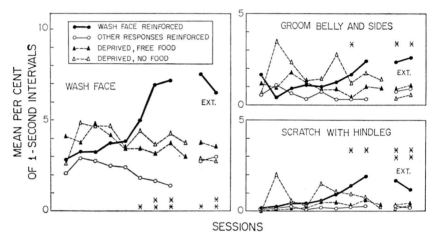

Fig. 3. Mean per cent of one-second intervals per session during which each type of grooming movement occurred for groups of hamsters reinforced with food for face-washing ($n = 3$), reinforced for other responses ($n = 12$), and for the food-deprived groups in the first experiment ($n = 5$). During the sessions marked EXT. the reinforced groups were extinguished, the deprived group given free food no longer received it, and the deprived group previously given no food in the open field did receive it. Stars indicate a significant difference in rate of the given response between the group reinforced for face-washing and one or both of the unreinforced deprived groups (Mann-Whitney U Test, $p < 0.05$).

generalization could also apply to the excessive responses discussed in the introduction. The increase in other causally and functionally related responses may have been peculiar to face-washing in these experiments partly because no other operant with other responses so closely related to it was studied. A similar phenomenon might have been observed if digging with the forepaws and kicking with the hind legs had been recorded and reinforced as separate responses.

Face-washing differs from the other reinforced action patterns and from bar-pressing, which is topographically a rearing response, in several ways that might be relevant to understanding why it increases so much less. It is the only one whose normal function does not seem directly relevant to obtaining food. All the others involve sampling environmental stimuli (cf. Prescott, 1970) in some way and could normally be part of a variety of appetitive sequences. A second difference between face-washing and the other four reinforced responses is that face-washing is apparently a displacement activity in the open field. Not only is it functionally irrelevant to exploring the open field, but also all types of grooming bouts in the open field are generally much shorter and composed of movements that appear more stereotyped and rapid than those performed by hamsters in their home cages. (Dieterlen, 1959, describes displacement grooming in hamsters similarly.) Finally, face-washing is the only one of the reinforced responses that was decreased by hunger in the baseline experiment.

Scent marking and scratching with a hind leg reinforced with food

Various other things the hamsters do in the open field share some or all of the characteristics that distinguish face-washing from the other reinforced responses. Attempts to modify the frequencies of some of these responses with food reinforcement might show if any of these characteristics of face-washing is related to the constraint on its conditioning. Therefore, two of these responses, scratching with a hind leg and scent marking, were reinforced with food. Scratching with a hind leg is a topographically dissimilar form of grooming which is like face-washing in not normally being used to obtain food and in being a displacement activity in the open field, but is unlike it in not being affected by hunger in the open field. Scent marking, a distinctive movement in which the hamster rubs the scent gland in its flank against a wall, is similar to grooming in not normally functioning as appetitive behaviour for food. It was also decreased somewhat by hunger in the first experiment. However, it is primarily social in function (Ewer, 1968; Ralls, 1971) and, unlike grooming, probably cannot be regarded as a displacement activity in a novel environment like the open field. Because these action patterns are performed seldom or not at all by hungry hamsters in the open field, it is necessary either to select subjects to be reinforced for them on the basis of their previous behaviour in the open field or to manipulate their frequencies directly.

Method. Three hamsters, previously reinforced and extinguished for digging, open rearing, and bar-pressing respectively, were selected to be reinforced for scratching with a hind leg because they performed this response sometime during most of their previous experimental sessions. Two animals, previously reinforced and extinguished for face-washing and scrabbing respectively, were selected in a similar way to be reinforced for scent marking.* Separate magazine training sessions were not necessary for any of these animals. Otherwise, the procedure for reinforcing scent marking or scratching with a hind leg was the same as the reinforcement procedure already described except that there were five rather than four sessions of VI 20-second reinforcement for scratching with a hind leg and that the response criterion for marking was always 0.2 seconds because this response was typically very brief when not reinforced.

Results. Like face-washing, and unlike scrabbling, digging, open rearing, or bar-pressing, scratching with a hind leg and scent marking increased little or not at all when they were followed by food. Each of these two responses had pecularities of its own during reinforcement.

Fig. 4 depicts the performance of the three individual hamsters reinforced for scratching with a hind leg. Although all these animals began

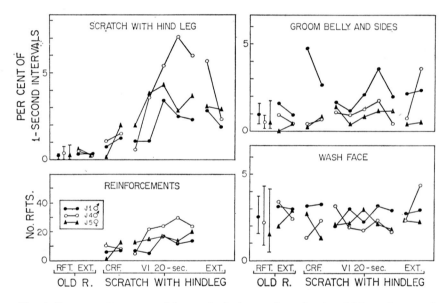

Fig. 4. Per cent of one-second intervals during each session in which each type of grooming movement occurred and number of reinforcements obtained for three hamsters reinforced with food for scratching with a hind leg. Means and ranges for each animal while it was reinforced for another response during previous sessions in the open field and rates of grooming during extinction of that response are also shown.

* Similar results were obtained with two additional animals each given four or five sessions of continuous reinforcement for one of these responses. The results for the other responses have also been corroborated in additional animals with different pre-experimental histories and/or different reinforcement procedures.

to scratch much more than they had before, very minimal scratching bouts, like those of face-washing when that response was reinforced, were not a prominent feature of the reinforced scratching. However, behaviour which can only be described as an abortive attempt to scratch was often seen after the first sessions of reinforcement. This consisted of the hamster going to the part of the box where it customarily scratched itself and, while still on the move, assuming a hunched posture, sometimes half turned as if chasing its tail. This behaviour might be accompanied by one or two little hopping movements in which one back foot was lifted off the ground and sometimes even waved in the air. Then the hamster would usually run back to the feeder. However, once actual scratching (i.e. contact of a back foot with some part of the fur) began, it was rapid and vigorous, and most bouts were long enough to be reinforced. The difference in relative frequency of short bouts between face-washing and scratching with a hind leg deserves more extensive and more quantitative analysis, as well as detailed comparison with the distributions of bout lengths for the other reinforced responses: however, it may represent merely a difference in how these two types of grooming are controlled once they are initiated, and not be specific to the effects of reinforcement.

A more puzzling difference between the two reinforced grooming responses is shown in Fig. 4, which depicts the levels of all types of grooming movements in the hamsters reinforced for scratching with a hind leg. All these animals eventually scratched several times more frequently than they had previously, but they groomed belly and sides only slightly more and showed no tendency at all to face-wash more than they had (compare also Fig. 3). Thus although increasing face-washing with food reinforcement appears to facilitate scratching with a hind leg as well, the reverse does not appear to be the case. This result may tell more about the organization of grooming in golden hamsters than about reinforcement effects *per se*.

Fig. 5 depicts the performance of the two hamsters reinforced for scent marking. Although both animals began to mark consistently above their previous mean levels, the increase in marking was quite small. One animal never exceeded its maximum level in previous sessions in the open field, although its marking was distributed throughout the session so that it received about two thirds of the available reinforcements. Both animals marked more during at least one extinction session than they had while reinforced for marking, but this response also often increased when other responses were extinguished, even when, as in the case of face-washing, it would be difficult to attribute such an increase to an increase in time available for marking. Furthermore, scent marking also tended to increase over sessions in the baseline experiment. Thus these results provide only slight evidence that scent marking is affected at all by reinforcement with

s

food. However, it is clearly necessary to observe more animals reinforced for scent marking and to compare them to a control group selected similarly for relatively high initial levels of marking. It might also be possible to produce more frequent and intense operant-level marking by training animals in an area where another hamster had been living (cf. Ralls, 1971).

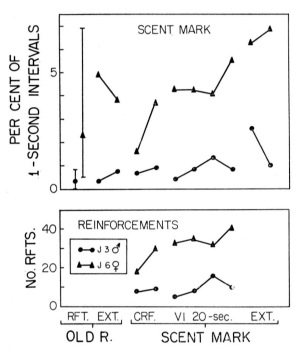

Fig. 5. Per cent of one-second intervals during each session in which scent marking occurred and number of reinforcements earned for two hamsters reinforced with food for scent marking. Mean and range for scent marking while another response was reinforced and its rate during extinction of the previously reinforced response are also shown.

General Discussion and Conclusions

Of course prolonged exposure to some reinforcement contingency might cause face-washing, scent marking, or scratching with a hind leg to be performed as regularly and to take up as much of the time as the other responses that were reinforced in these experiments, but the relatively small effect of food reinforcement on these responses suggests that they are limited by some constraint that bar-pressing, scrabbling, digging, and open rearing are free of. The fact that face-washing and scratching with a hind leg, if not scent marking, do increase somewhat, suggests that this constraint may act on the performance of the response rather than on learning itself.

In the case of face-washing, the constraint could be a rather trivial one; namely, the animal needs a supply of saliva before it will lick its paws and rub them over its face and it cannot secrete enough saliva to support a very high rate of face-washing. One problem with this explanation is that since rats, at least, can be operantly conditioned to salivate (Miller, 1969), one would expect salivation to become part of the whole operant face-washing response. Furthermore, the paws are only licked very briefly if at all in the displacement face-washing in the open field (cf. also Dieterlen, 1959). Reinforcing grooming with water should provide a test of the importance of oral factors. To the extent that hamsters need a wet mouth to groom, the provision of water after each grooming bout should increase grooming more and more.*

A second possible explanation for the constraint on face-washing derives from observations that grooming in many species is easily inhibited by tendencies to perform other behaviour (e.g. Andrew, 1956; Rowell, 1961). Observations like that of the difference between grooming in the home cage and grooming in the open field, and those by Dieterlen (1959) and Daly (1971), suggest that this is the case in hamsters as well. It could be that while food does directly reinforce face-washing, the reinforcement procedure also results in anticipation of food or of approaching the feeder being classically conditioned to the overt, or even unobservable, initiation of face-washing. Such a conditioned anticipation of food might be especially likely to inhibit grooming responses. It is significant in this regard that when face-washing was reinforced the other, unreinforced, forms of grooming did not decrease noticeably in bout length as they became more frequent. The notion that face-washing is inhibited as soon as it begins by an expectation of food that becomes conditioned to it predicts that any form of grooming would be affected by food reinforcement in the same way as face washing. The abortive scratching with the hind leg that developed when that response was reinforced could be taken as evidence that this is so.

Differential effects of interrupting the various behaviours could also have played a role in their apparently different reinforceability. McFarland (in press) has shown that sub-dominant behaviours are less likely to be

---

* Although other species may groom after feeding (cf. Bolles, 1960) and hamsters sometimes do so after a long meal in the home cage, analysis of the session-by-session temporal distribution of grooming for two animals from each group in the baseline experiment showed that grooming in the open field had no particular relationship to eating there.

resumed after a neutral interruption than are dominant behaviours. Selective interruption by reinforcement delivery could tend to mask a facilitatory effect of reinforcement on sub-dominant behaviours, of which grooming and scent marking might be examples. The baseline experiment provides some evidence against this in that the over-all frequencies of the various behaviours in undeprived animals tended to be the same whether or not food pellets and the accompanying tone were presented periodically. Furthermore, in extinction, when the reinforced responses were no longer interrupted by food presentations, the rate of face-washing, scratching, or scent marking remained low (see figures).

The accounts of the present results suggested so far resemble the accounts of Sevenster's and Black and Young's work discussed in the introduction in that they attribute the limited conditioning of certain responses to some inhibitory factor preventing the full effect of reinforcement from manifesting itself. However, associative interpretations of the present findings are also possible. For example the hypothesis, that responses that could not normally function to obtain food are reinforced by food much more weakly than those which could, readily encompasses the differences in the effects of food reinforcement on digging, scrabbling, open rearing, and bar-pressing, on the one hand, and face-washing, scratching with a hind leg, and scent marking, on the other. Bolles (1970) seems to suggest a similar thing for avoidance responses, and, as a more remote example, stimuli that would not normally be relevant to the consequences of feeding are not readily associated with those consequences (Chapter 7). In this case the minimal grooming responses that developed under reinforcement must be interpreted as evidence of a weak effect of reinforcement.

The chief problem with this type of hypothesis for any reinforcer lies in the difficulty of identifying responses that are and are not relevant to the reinforcer. Bolles' suggestion that only species-specific defence reactions are readily acquirable as avoidance responses is relatively free of this criticism because the species-specific defence reactions can be identified as the responses elicited by the aversive stimulus, e.g. freezing to electric shock. Analogously, the responses least affected by food reinforcement might be those decreased by hunger, these might be the same responses that could not normally function in finding food, and the reverse. Similar generalizations might presumably apply to other reinforcers. However, in the present experiments the responses increased to high levels by food reinforcement included some that were not increased by food deprivation, and, in any case, food deprivation does not restrict the range of behaviour nearly so much as do the aversive stimuli used in the sorts of experiments discussed by Bolles.

A further problem with the hypothesis that responses are best reinforceable by functionally related reinforcers is that this possibility may be difficult to distinguish experimentally from the alternative that some responses are just not readily modifiable by reinforcement at all, since it may be difficult to devise experimental consequences appropriate to responses like grooming or scent marking. It must also be kept in mind that different responses can show only limited conditioning for different reasons. For example, grooming in hamsters might be constrained by motivational factors like those suggested previously while scent marking might be refractory to reinforcement *per se*.

Further experiments involving such things as different reinforcers for the same set of responses should help to distinguish among the various mechanisms that could be involved in the constraints on conditioning described here. Detailed sequential analysis of the behaviour of golden hamsters under various conditions might suggest why various behaviours were affected differently by food reinforcement. More precise quantitative information is also needed on the distributions of bout lengths of the various responses both unreinforced and under various reinforcement regimes. Using an "arbitrary operant" which can vary in duration like touching the bar might help to show whether changes in bout length distributions are restricted to certain reinforced action patterns. But it is especially important to inquire how far the cases of limited conditionability described here, whatever their nature, are specific to a free operant situation. In the free operant situation the effect of reinforcement is judged to be stronger the more the animal performs the reinforced response to the exclusion of other behaviour. Since grooming is apparently organized so that it is easily inhibited by other activities, examining its reinforceability in a situation which does not impose this requirement might better allow assessment of the relative contributions of associative and motivational factors to the constraint on its conditioning. For example, in a go- no-go discrimination the measure of learning could be the relative frequency of the reinforced response during the stimulus signalling availability of reinforcement. The ability to withhold the response during the stimulus signalling no reinforcement would also be important here, but the measure of learning would be relatively independent of absolute response rate.

Here I have emphasized the limited operant conditionability of some action patterns of golden hamsters with food reinforcement. In trying to understand how a response's pre-existing role in the animal's behaviour interacts with its acquisition as an operant it may be equally important to focus on why some responses were acquired so rapidly. In these experiments, scrabbling presents some problems because in the baseline experiment it reached its highest levels when food was withdrawn from the hungry hamsters, and dropped almost to zero in the hungry hamsters given food after nine sessions in the open field. Thus in a sense the more a hamster scrabbled for food reinforcement the more it produced the conditions under which it normally would not scrabble. This may just show that we do not understand the motivation of scrabbling very well. The problem could also be resolved by saying that since scrabbling is basically a form of locomotion, thwarted climbing (Daly, 1971), it is likely not to be tied to a fixed function or set of causal factors (cf. Black and Young, 1972). To do so is to underline the fact that our notions about when and how readily responses can be acquired as operants are still very poorly developed. We still know very little about what aspects of responses can predict to what degree their operant conditionability will be limited, or for what reinforcers. And even if a satisfactory account of such constraints can be developed for a single species, its extension to other species will doubtless raise many new problems.

Acknowledgements

I thank Margaret Jackson and Bill Bullock for their invaluable technical help, J. C. Ogilvie and Karen Kaplan for advice and assistance with analyses on the computer, J. A. Hogan and G. E. Macdonald for the loan of equipment, Martin Daly for his translation of Dieterlen and other help with hamsters, and N. Mrosovsky for help in many ways. This research was supported by a grant to the author from the National Research Council of Canada.

References

Andrew, R. J. (1956). Normal and irrelevant toilet behaviour in *Emberiza* spp. *Anim. Behav.* **4**, 85–91.

Azrin, N. H. and Hutchinson, R. R. (1967). Conditioning of the aggressive behavior of pigeons by a fixed-interval schedule of reinforcement. *J. exp. Anal. Behav.* **10**, 395–402.

Black, A. H. and Young, G. A. (1972). Constraints on the operant conditioning of drinking. *In* "Reinforcement: Behavioral Analyses", (R. M. Gilbert and J. R. Millenson, eds.) pp. 35–50. Academic Press, New York.

Bolles, R. C. (1960). Grooming behavior in the rat. *J. comp. physiol. Psychol.* **53**, 306–310.

Bolles, R. C. (1970). Species-specific defense reactions and avoidance learning. *Psychol. Rev.* **77**, 32–48.

Breland, K. and Breland, M. (1966). "Animal Behavior." The Macmillan Company, New York.

Daly, J. M. (1971). Behavioural development, early experience, and maternal behaviour in golden hamsters. (*Mesocricetus auratus*) Ph.D. thesis, University of Toronto.

Dieterlen, F. (1959). Des Verhalten des syrischen Goldhamsters (*Mesocricetus auratus,* Waterhouse). Untersuchen zur Frage seiner Entwicklung und seiner angeborene Anteile durch geruchsisolierte Aufzuchten. *Zeits. fur Tierpsychol.* **16**, 47–103.

Ewer, R. F. (1968). "Ethology of Mammals." Logos Press, London.

Hogan, J. A. (1964). Operant control of preening in pigeons. *J. exp. Anal. Behav.* **7**, 351–354.

Konorski, J. (1967). "Integrative Activity of the Brain." University of Chicago Press, Chicago.

McFarland, D. J. (In press). Time-sharing as a behavioural phenomenon. *Adv. Study Behav.* **5**.

Miller, N. E. (1969). Learning of visceral and glandular responses. *Science* **163**, 434–445.

Mrosovsky, N. (1964). The performance of dormice and other hibernators on tests of hunger motivation. *Anim. Behav.* **12**, 454–469.

Prescott, R. G. W. (1970). Some behavioral effects of variables which influence the "general level of activity" of rats. *Anim. Behav.* **18**, 791–796.

Ralls, K. (1971). Mammalian scent-marking. *Science* **171**, 443–449.

Reynolds, G. S., Catania, A. C. and Skinner, B. F. (1963). Conditioned and unconditioned aggression in pigeons. *J. exp. Anal. Behav.* **6**, 73–74.

Rowell, C. H. F. (1961). Displacement grooming in the chaffinch. *Anim. Behav.* **9**, 38–63.

Sevenster, P. (1968). Motivation and learning in sticklebacks. *In* "The Central Nervous System and Fish Behaviour", (D. Ingle, ed.) pp. 233–245. University of Chicago Press.

Shettleworth, S. J. (1972). Constraints on learning. *Adv. Study Behav.* **4**, pp. 1–68. Academic Press, New York.

Skinner, B. F. (1938). "The Behavior of Organisms." Appleton-Century, New York.

Skinner, B. F. (1959). An experimental analysis of certain emotions. *J. exp. Anal. Behav.* **2**, 264.

Thorndike, E. L. (1911). "Animal Intelligence." The Macmillan Company, New York.

Ulrich, R., Johnston, M., Richardson, J. and Wolff, P. (1963). The operant conditioning of fighting behavior in rats. *Psychol. Rec.* **13**, 465–470.

Vanderwolf, C. H. (1971). Limbic-diencephalic mechanisms of voluntary movement. *Psychol. Rev.* **78**, 83–113.

12

Incompatibility of Response and Reward

by P. Sevenster

In the past, conditioning has been studied as an isolated process. However, if we are to understand the role of conditioning in natural situations and its importance for the development of behaviour, it is time to relate it to the context in which it takes place and to the repertoire of the species concerned. We should focus especially on cases that seem to deviate from the current picture of conditioning as a process able to connect any response to any stimulus by any reinforcement equally readily. Quite understandably, in the past the tendency has been to select for study cases where conditioning was quick and response rate high: possible limitations on conditioning may thus have escaped our attention.

One way to promote our knowledge of such limitations is to try different combinations of responses and rewards in one species and to compare the performance with these various combinations. In the three-spined stickleback (*Gasterosteus aculeatus* L.) I worked with two responses and two rewards, and studied the effect of the four possible combinations on the response rate. It appeared that for three of these combinations the response rates were similar, whereas with the fourth the response rate was conspicuously different. The present analysis aims at an explanation of this difference. More data and details on the experimental methods can be found in Sevenster (1968): here new data will be presented, and only those details relevant to the central theme of this symposium will be discussed. First some descriptive data must be provided.

Descriptions of Courtship and Fighting

Fighting

In the breeding season, the male stickleback is a territorial animal. An extensive account of its territorial behaviour has been given by van den

Assem (1967). Even in a comparatively small tank a male with a nest will attack any conspecific, male or female. Such a male approaches an intruder directly and snaps at it until it flees. If it does not flee, biting is continued, or other forms of agonistic behaviour may develop, but these do not concern us here. The owner of the territory will also attack a rival which is presented in a glass tube or which is enclosed behind a glass screen. In such cases the male will bite persistently at the glass while following the enclosed rival, and a standardized fight may continue for a long period. Typically the nest is not visited during such a fight. Occasionally the male may pause between bouts of biting and just look at its opponent, or there may be a brief spell of threatening.

After-effect

When the rival male is removed, the male's behaviour is still affected by the preceding fight for a few minutes (Sevenster, 1961). Nest visits are rare and sometimes the fish remains immobile for several seconds.

Fighting as a reinforcer

A short spell of this fighting can be used to reinforce certain other behaviour patterns. In each experiment, the experimental male had a nest in a compartment (40 × 35 × 35 cm) of a planted tank with sand on the bottom. At one end this compartment was screened off from a smaller one by an opaque partition, in which a little trapdoor could be moved up electrically to uncover a glass window (15 × 15 cm).

In this second compartment a second male was made to nest or, alternatively, a male was presented in a glass container. With the first method the rival fought back when attacked by the experimental male through the window, whereas a rival in a glass container usually fled or swam up and down the walls. The method chosen did not affect the results that concern us here but since the first method was used most extensively, this will be discussed in more detail.

Both animals were habituated to repeated raising of the trapdoor and would ultimately rush towards the window and start fighting as soon as the door went up. In the experiments presented here the apparatus was constructed so that the trapdoor shut automatically after 10 seconds. As a rule these 10 seconds were spent in biting, interspersed with short pauses of looking at the rival, as described above. This opportunity to fight could be used as a reinforcer in conditioning experiments. The question, why it sometimes seemed to fail as a reinforcer, will not be discussed here. The entire 10-second period will be referred to simply as "a fight" or F.

Courtship

In the stickleback, as in other territorial animals, courtship can be looked upon as a means to allow ripe females into the territory, while at the same time keeping out other conspecifics. In accordance with this view, the stickleback's courtship can be described as essentially an interaction between a tendency to attack the female and a tendency to lead her to the nest. An analysis would carry us too far, but some of the data in support of this interpretation will be mentioned (see ter Pelkwijk and Tinbergen, 1937; van Iersel, 1953; Sevenster, 1961). Usually, a female appearing in the territory is attacked by the male, especially if he has not courted for a while. However, a ripe female ready to spawn does not flee from the aggressive male, even if he bites. Instead she adopts a head-up posture, in which she orients herself towards the attacking male. This adds a new element, namely a tendency in the male to turn and swim off to the nest. Once at the nest certain activities, such as boring, fanning, glueing, creeping through, or pushing, may be performed, before the fish leaves and heads for the female again. If the female still persists in her courtship posture, the male may bite her again or stop just short of her and return to the nest, where the same or other activities may be shown. If the female stays in her position (e.g. because she is prevented from following by a glass tube or screen) the male may go back and forth between her and the nest for a long time. Once this oscillating courtship has started, most of the approaches by the male no longer follow a straight course, as is characteristic of attack, but instead consist of a series of lateral jumps, forming the well-known zigzag dance. These zigzags can be more or less pronounced, that is, the amplitude of their lateral components can be large or small. Also the male's returns to the nest vary: they may be fast or slow, and he may stop before reaching the nest to approach the female again. Finally he may or may not bite the female at the end of an approach, or he may break off the approach and return to the nest while still at a considerable distance from the female. There is some coherence in these variables: the more pronounced his zigzags, the less likely the male is to bite the female at the end of his approach, and the faster and farther he tends to return to the nest afterwards.

On the one hand these variations are controlled by the behaviour of the female. The intensity of her courting, as expressed in the steepness of her head-up posture and in the promptness of her turning (like a wind-vane) with the approaching male, is paralleled by the intensity of the male's tendency to return to the nest and the other features connected with it, notably the likelihood of a bite being delivered. A temporary interruption of the female's head-up posture and even her slightly turning away from the approaching male results immediately in increased biting and a decreased tendency to return to the nest. Summarizing the effects of the female's behaviour, it can be said that the extent to which a courting female differs from all other conspecifics (courtship posture and orientation towards the male), determines the extent to which the male's courtship differs from fighting any other conspecific.

On the other hand, the same coherent variations in the male's courtship may occur without any change in the female's behaviour. This can be demonstrated by recording the courtship behaviour of a male towards a female dummy. Again under these circumstances biting is more likely at the end of a straight approach than after a zigzag dance, and least likely after pronounced zigzags. We can conclude that an intensively courting male is less likely to bite the female or the dummy he is courting. Not infrequently we can observe a male courting a rival male intensively and on such occasions biting is again much reduced or absent. Thus, a strong tendency to court entails a low tendency to bite.

After-effects of courtship

For a long time after the female has been taken away, the male behaves differently from the period before courtship. Several elements of the behaviour are involved in this after-effect (Sevenster, 1961; Nelson, 1965). Quite often the nest is visited immediately on the female's disappearance and some of the activities mentioned previously are performed at the nest. The zigzagging is resumed in the direction of where the female had been, but this at once develops into a wild, darting type of locomotion near the surface. Real zigzags are directed at moving objects, which on other occasions would not elicit this behaviour; they are therefore called vacuum zigzags. (The identification of these vacuum zigzags is somewhat arbitrary, as criteria differ from one observer to another.) The frequency of these vacuum zigzags gradually declines to its previous level; it can thus be used as an index of the waning after-effect. As an example, in Table 1 data are

TABLE 1

Course of vacuum zigzag frequency after courtship.
Data from one session of a BC experiment.

Period Since Disappearance of Female (sec)	Average Frequency of Vacuum Zigzags
0–30	4.96
30–60	2.17
60–90	1.61
90–120	1.45
120–150	1.31
150–180	0.88

summarized which have been collected by one observer. Even when vacuum zigzagging has reverted to its previous level, however, the after-effect is still recognizable in other aspects for a much longer period.

Courtship as a reinforcer

A short opportunity to court a ripe female is a reliable reinforcer in conditioning experiments. The arrangement used was identical to the one described for fighting. In each experiment the female, selected for her readiness to court, was put in a glass container in a screened-off compartment, so as to become visible to the experimental male when the window was uncovered. Again both fish had to become accustomed to the movement of the trapdoor. After a while both would dash to the window as soon as the door was lifted, the female taking up her head-up posture and the male zigzagging. The situation was then fairly standardized, the male's behaviour became relatively stable (though different for each individual, and to some extent for each session with one individual). The 10 seconds were usually spent in two or three approaches and one or two nest visits. Frequently the door was shut during a nest visit, or else a nest visit immediately followed. In either case this nest visit always consisted of the performance of the usual activities. Only then did the after-effects just mentioned ensue. The 10-seconds courtship as a reinforcer will be referred to as C.

Conditioning Experiments

Conditioning of passing through a ring

Both the situations described (F and C) have been used to reinforce passing through a ring. A grey plastic ring with an inner diameter of 50 mm (sometimes 77 mm) was suspended just below the surface. Its position did not seem to affect the results in any fundamental way, but usually the experimental male, if starting from its nest, had to move away from the partition with the trapdoor in order to go through the ring. This reduced spontaneous responding to a minimum, and sometimes necessitated shaping (reinforcing proximity to the ring). In real training the door was lifted as soon as the male had passed the plane of the ring with his eyes, in the direction away from the door. This response will be referred to as R.

The results with courtship as a reinforcer for ring-swimming (in short, RC), have been reported previously (Sevenster, 1968), and will not be presented here in any detail. A high response rate was obtained, as can be seen from the distribution of intervals in the example shown by Fig. 1a, each interval being the time in seconds between the end of C and the next response. Responding stays at this high level for long sessions, and usually

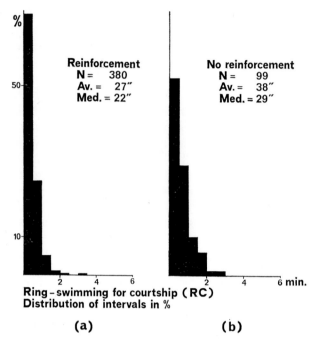

Fig. 1. Swimming through a ring with courtship as a reinforcer. (a) Distribution of intervals between end of courtship and the next response of swimming through the ring when each response was reinforced; (b) Distribution of intervals between successive responses during extinction. In each case the total number of responses, with the average (mean) and median intervals in seconds, are given.

the behaviour during the reinforcement does not change appreciably.

When reinforcement is discontinued, the rate of responding is not altered much initially, and extinction becomes noticeable only later: this is shown on Fig. 1b where an interval is now the time in seconds between successive responses.

The results with fighting as a reinforcer for ring-swimming (RF), are very similar (Fig. 2). The response rate and the behaviour during F show a similar stability within each session.

Both RF and RC experiments exhibit the classical picture of operant conditioning, and will not be discussed any further.

Conditioning of biting a rod

The second response used in the experiments is biting the tip of a rod. A slender transparent rod with a green tip, 5 mm in diameter, was put in the tank. Its position was similar to that of the ring, and appeared to be irrelevant to the results here discussed.

Training the experimental male to bite at the green tip usually required some shaping (for a more detailed account, see Sevenster, 1968), but once a number of bites had occurred, further reinforcement quickly became effective. The response will be called B.

With fighting as a reinforcer for biting (BF), the interval distribution was largely similar to that in the ring experiments. In some cases the distribution shifted even further towards short intervals (e.g. the case presented in Sevenster, 1968). In such cases the animal spent practically all the time for which the window was open in fighting, swimming up and down to strike the rod in between. Nest visits were rare. In other cases there was no obvious difference from the ring experiments (Fig. 3), and this held also for the initial phase of extinction.

With courtship as a reward (BC), however, the interval distribution was conspicuously different (Fig. 4a). Very short intervals were absent, and the range of variation large. The rate of responding, as compared with the ring experiments, was thus low, the average interval being somewhere between 3 and 6 minutes, depending on the individual. Though with each individual there might be variations in response rate from day to day, there was no consistent increase in this rate, no matter how many days the

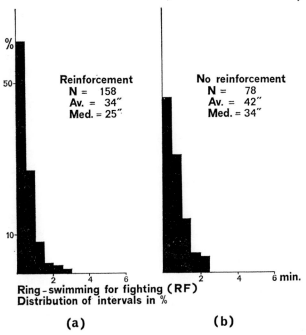

Ring - swimming for fighting (RF)
Distribution of intervals in %

(a)   (b)

Fig. 2. Swimming through a ring with fighting as a reinforcer. Conventions as in Fig. 1.

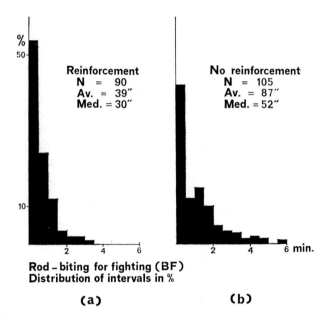

Rod – biting for fighting (BF)
Distribution of intervals in %

(a)   (b)

Fig. 3. Biting a rod with fighting as a reinforcer. Conventions as in Fig. 1.

training was continued. But, as Fig. 4b shows, when reinforcement was abolished, the response rate increased considerably, before the extinction proper became effective: in fact, these response rates were temporarily practically the same as those in BF experiments. Therefore, the response of rod biting as such does not exclude a high rate (as also follows from the results of the BF experiments); nor does the presentation of the female itself exclude a high rate, for with passing through the ring (RC) a high rate was obtained. As I have argued before (1968), the low response rate in these rod-biting experiments with courtship as a reinforcer must be due to the combination of this particular reinforcer with this particular response.

In many experiments a variable ratio schedule of 3 responses for each reinforcement was applied, and in addition the door was lifted by the observer from time to time without the male biting the rod (so-called "exposures"). This enabled one to study the response latencies after unreinforced bites, after presentations of the female contingent upon bites, and after exposures. The average latency after an unreinforced bite appeared to be much shorter, but the average latency after an "exposure" was exactly the same as that after a reinforcement. It was concluded that the mere presentation of the female causes a delay of the next response. It is this delay with which we are here concerned. It reminds one of the after-effect of courtship which was briefly discussed above, and it suggests that rod-biting is inhibited for some time after C. It seems that this inhibition slowly wanes, because in a variable ratio session we can compare the average interval between the first response (if unreinforced) and the next, the average interval between the second response (if unreinforced) and the

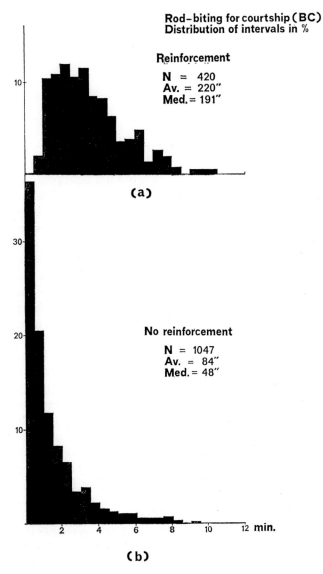

Rod–biting for courtship (BC)
Distribution of intervals in %

Reinforcement

N = 420
Av. = 220″
Med. = 191″

(a)

No reinforcement

N = 1047
Av. = 84″
Med. = 48″

(b)

Fig. 4. Biting a rod with courtship as a reinforcer. Conventions as in Fig. 1.

T

next, and the average interval between responses occurring more than 5 minutes after C (Table 2). It appears that later intervals tend to be shorter

TABLE 2

Average duration of successive response intervals after presentation of the female (C) in one BC experiment with variable ratio schedule

Number of Interval Since C	Average Duration of Interval (sec)	Number of Intervals on which the Average is Based
1st	294	142
2nd	166	69
3rd	132	41
Intervals later than 5 min since C	108	38
First 30 min of extinction	96	26

and gradually approach the interval characteristic of the first phase of extinction. In other words, the inhibition did not disappear after the first bite, and (in the case presented) was still noticeable after 5 minutes.

However, the variation underlying these averages was large. Some of this variation (especially from one session to another) could no doubt be attributed to differences in behaviour during C (possibly as a consequence of a change in the female's performance). However, over shorter periods (within one session) the behaviour of both male and female during C was remarkably stable, and yet the latency of the first response varied over a wide and unpredictable range. In short, we cannot so far predict the length of the interval from the male's behaviour during C or even shortly after C. There are also interesting indications that under these circumstances the occurrence of the first bite does not have much influence on the readiness to bite somewhat later. For example, in one stable sample, we selected 35 cases where a first unreinforced bite had occurred within two minutes after C, and found that the frequency of second bites in the third minute was 0.40 (14/35). This can be compared with 86 cases from the same sample, where no bite occurred within two minutes after C, and where a frequency of 0.42 (36/86) was found for first bites in the third minute. In other words, in this sample the frequency of biting in the third minute was not affected by whether or not a bite had occurred in the preceding two minutes.

If longer periods are considered in this way, discrepancies do occur. For example, of 57 cases where an unreinforced bite occurred in the first three minutes, $50/57 = 0.87$ showed a second bite in the fourth and fifth minute; whereas of 86 cases where no bite occurred in the first three minutes, $55/86 = 0.64$ showed a first bite in the fourth and fifth minute. I am inclined to attribute such deviations to uncontrolled variations in the samples. Further analysis is certainly required, but provisionally it can be assumed on the evidence presented that after each C there is always the same, gradual rise in the probability that the animal will bite the rod. Under this assumption it makes sense to convert the interval distributions to graphs representing the frequency of biting in successive 30-second periods after C. In Fig. 5 the distribution of Fig. 4 is thus converted, but since in this case a variable ratio 3 schedule had been used, unreinforced bites are included in Fig. 5. It will be realized that with successive 30-second periods the sample became progressively smaller and hence less reliable. The graph clearly demonstrates, however, that the likelihood of biting slowly increased until it seemed to fluctuate around a stable level. Fig. 6 shows another example.

To bring out the characteristic feature of the BC experiments more clearly, these data should be contrasted to the corresponding data from BF experiments. In Table 3, the average duration of successive intervals in BF

TABLE 3

Average duration of successive response intervals after presentation of the male (F) in one BF experiment with variable ratio schedule

Number of Interval since F	Average Duration of Interval (sec)	Number of Intervals on which the Average is Based
1st	20	35
2nd	16	35
3rd	13	23
later intervals	21	49

experiments with a variable ratio schedule is given for comparison with Table 2. The intervals are clearly much shorter in BF experiments than in BC. Furthermore it seems that over short periods successive bites in these experiments are also largely independent of one another: for 41 cases where an unreinforced bite occurred in the first half minute, the frequency of biting in the second half was $30/41 = 0.73$, whereas for 29 cases where no bite occurred in the first half minute, the frequency in the second half minute was $20/29 = 0.69$. On this basis the bite frequencies of BF experiments can also be plotted as a function of the time elapsed since F. This has been done for one example in Fig. 7. Obviously the response frequency became high sooner than in Figs. 5 and 6.

Further Analysis of BC Experiments

Rod visits

The observation and recording of the actual behaviour provides a clue

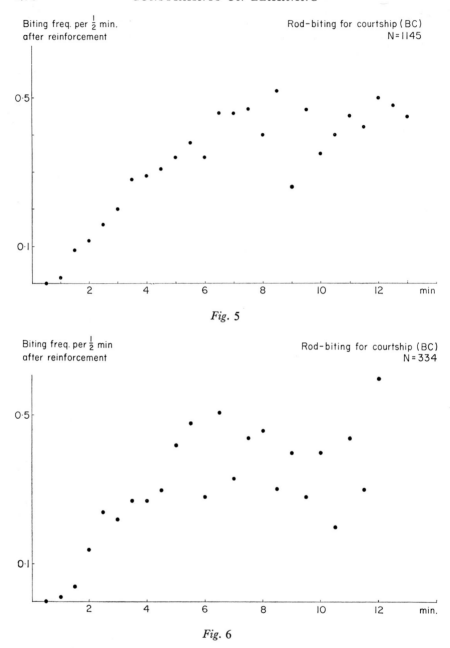

Figs. 5 and 6. Biting a rod with courtship as a reinforcer. Frequency of biting in successive 30-second periods after the end of courtship.

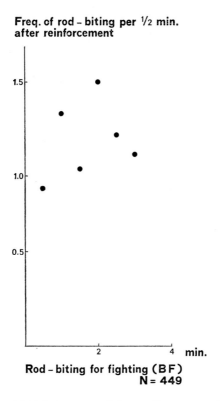

Freq. of rod – biting per ½ min.
after reinforcement

Rod – biting for fighting (BF)
N = 449

Fig. 7. Biting a rod with fighting as a reinforcer. Frequency of biting in successive 30-second periods after the end of fighting.

as to the nature of the delay of the response in BC experiments. During these delays the experimental male approached the rod continually. When these rod visits (defined by the snout of the fish being less than an estimated 2 cm away from the green tip) were plotted in the same way as the bites in Fig. 6, the resulting graph (Fig. 8) was similar to that of the biting frequency in BF experiments (though, of course, many much longer intervals are available for the graph in Fig. 8). In other words, if each rod visit had resulted in a bite, the difference between BC and BF experiments would, as far as rod biting is concerned, largely have disappeared. So in BC experiments the tendency to respond as indicated by the rod visits was there, but the actual biting seems to have been inhibited. This is borne out completely by observational evidence. The fish would approach the rod, and start circling around it with zigzag-like jumps and often with open mouth, sometimes making snapping movements at the tip or softly touching it (cf. Sevenster, 1968). Such rod visits lasted from 1 to 20 seconds, the male pointing at the tip most of the time. He might finally swim off, or he might bite. If this resulted in a reinforcement, he dashed away to the window; but if the bite remained unreinforced (with a variable ratio schedule) he might bite again during the same rod visit (these extra bites have not been counted in the data presented here).

It is obvious from Figs. 5 and 6 that, with the passage of time since C, rod visits were more and more likely to result in a bite, until a certain level was reached. Even then, the overall chance that an individual rod visit would result in a bite remained well below 0.50.

In BF experiments the corresponding data were in sharp contrast. Though here too occasional rod visits did not result in biting, the overall chance that rod visits would result in a bite was about 0.80 in BF experiments, and was even higher for the first few rod visits after F. Below an experiment will be discussed, where the biting frequency on the first rod visits after F was 0.97 (288 cases); the corresponding figure in a BC experiment was 0.00 (91 cases). Further, nearly all the rod visits in BF experiments lasted a few seconds (up to 4) at most, and were never accompanied by the hesitation so characteristic of BC experiments.

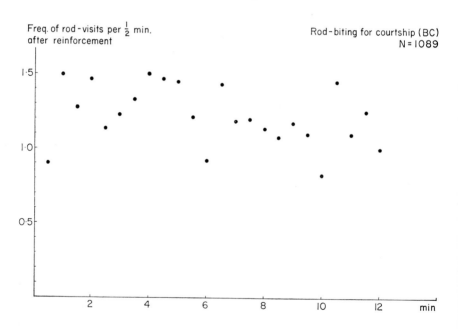

Fig. 8. Biting a rod with courtship as a reinforcer. Frequency of swimming within 2 cm. of tip of rod in successive 30-second periods after the end of fighting.

The nature of the inhibition

The conclusion so far is that in all four response-reward combinations the tendency to respond is high, and roughly equal, but in BC experiments the actual response is more or less inhibited. Should we now assume that the after-effect of courtship simply inhibits the motor-coordination of biting? There seems to be more to it. First, we know that a courting male is able to bite a rival which is suddenly presented. However, it might be argued that in such a case the rival is such a strong stimulus that it overrides a possible inhibition. Secondly, and more convincingly, there were rare but suggestive observations of a trained male in BC experiments interrupting a rod visit to bite a nearby leaf vigorously as if biting the rod was redirected to the leaf. Finally, if the rod with the green tip is put in the tank of an arbitrary male it evokes at most some approaches and investigatory behaviour. However, when we put it in a tank occupied by a male which two months earlier had been used elsewhere for a BC experiment, this male immediately started to court the green tip with a striking intensity.

These and other arguments suggested a second hypothesis: biting the rod is inhibited because the rod has become associated with the female and is now treated like a female dummy. This inhibition is strongest during the period after C.

C-injections

The following tests were carried out to decide between the two hypotheses. Shortly after F in a BF experiment a tube with a ripe female was lowered into the compartment of the experimental male, which was then allowed to court this female for 10 seconds until the tube disappeared again. These presentations will be referred to as "C-injections", indicating their purpose of inducing a motivational change in the experimental male.

According to the first hypothesis in its simplest form, the after-effect of the C-injection should delay the next biting response over the same interval as is found in BC experiments, i.e. an average of between 3 and 6 minutes. According to the second hypothesis in its simplest form, the rod would not be associated with the female, and biting the rod should not be affected by the after-effect of the C-injection.

In carrying out this experiment care was taken that the female could not become associated with the rod in any way. Therefore she was presented in a glass tube instead of behind a trapdoor, and in the corner of the tank farthest removed from the trapdoor behind which the rival was nesting. Moreover presentations were interspersed at random and infrequently in the training schedule. Experiments were begun only after the male had been accustomed thoroughly to the new arrangement, fighting only during F, and courting intensively during the C-injections.

In this experiment, with one male, 288 F reinforcements (without a subsequent C-injection) were available for comparison with 57 C-injections, shortly following F. For the 288 intervals without a C-injection the average latency to the first rod visit was 17 seconds, and the biting frequency on this visit was 0.97. The biting frequency on an arbitrary rod visit was about 0.80, as usual.

After the 57 C-injections there was a response latency of almost one minute. This is less than expected under the first hypothesis, but could still indicate an inhibitory after-effect. However, during this delay of one minute there were practically no rod visits. The average latency of the first rod visit after C-injections was in fact 53 seconds. And, most significantly, the chance that biting occurred on this occasion was 0.75, which is almost the same as the overall frequency of 0.80 per rod visit. Moreover all rod visits lasted only a few seconds and no hesitancy was observed. It should be noted, that a possible inhibitory after-effect of a C-injection on biting within one minute could neither be established, nor discounted, since rod visits did not occur. Instead the male searched near the surface in the way characteristic of the after-effect of courtship (see above), and of BC experiments.

Summarizing this evidence, it can be concluded that the after-effect of a C-injection cancels the tendency to visit the rod for about a minute, but does not affect the biting frequency once rod visiting is resumed. Though a short-lasting inhibitory effect cannot be excluded, the evidence on the whole supports the second hypothesis.

F-injections

As a counterpart to these experiments F-injections were carried out in BC experiments. The arrangement was the same as with the C-injections, but now the tube contained a rival male instead of a courting female. The tube was lowered a short, but somewhat variable interval after C; in every case it had disappeared well within 100 seconds after C. Calculations were therefore made only for response latencies longer than 100 seconds, both after F-injections and in the controls. Since very few responses are found within 100 seconds in BC experiments, this should not have affected the outcome too much. The results were somewhat ambiguous (Table 4). It seems that on most occasions the F-injections had no effect on the response latencies, but that sometimes they reduced them. Although we still await further evidence on these points, it can already be stated that the pattern of behaviour after an F-injection remains characteristic of BC experiments: rod visits are long and are accompanied by the usual hesitancy, and they show a low biting frequency as compared to BF experiments. Again, though the first hypothesis cannot be discarded, the evidence certainly supports the second hypothesis: the behaviour at the rod, including the probability of biting, is determined by the nature of the reinforcement (F or C). The importance of the behaviour it elicits is shown more clearly by the evidence from a few aberrant experiments. In one BF experiment we found an average response latency of more than $5\frac{1}{2}$ minutes, and other features were also characteristic of BC experiments: in this experiment the male had courted the rival intensively instead of fighting it. Conversely, in two BC experiments, response latencies and other features

TABLE 4

Average and median duration of the first interval after C, with and without an F-injection, in BC experiments with three males

F-injections			Controls		
Average Duration (sec)	Median Duration (sec)	Number of Intervals	Average Duration (sec)	Median Duration (sec)	Number of Intervals
206	196	26	213	204	86
249	231	31	255	222	39
137	170	22	241	202	53

were found to be characteristic of BF experiments, and in both these experiments the male had in fact reacted with pure aggression to the female even though she courted intensively. It seems, therefore, that the behaviour at the rod is determined by the mode of reaction to the reinforcing situation, rather than by that situation as such. The terminology becomes therefore more convenient, if F is taken as a situation to which the male reacts with fighting, and C as a situation to which the male reacts with courtship, irrespective of whether a rival or a courting female was offered.

Conclusion

The low response rate in BC experiments which I set out to analyse, can now be interpreted as the result of an interaction of the following factors (represented in the diagram of Fig. 9):

1. *The reinforcing effect* of C, when contingent on B (positive arrow from C to B). This factor increases the probability of the response as in all operant conditioning. It is here reflected in the increase of the response rate above its spontaneous level (which usually is practically zero so that shaping is required), and in the extinction of the response when reinforcement is discontinued.

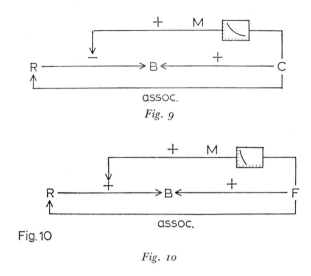

Fig. 9

Fig. 10

Fig. 10

Figs. 9 and 10. C and F: reinforcing situations, courtship and fighting. B: probability of biting at the rod. R: rod. assoc.: association. M: motivation, with a time function to indicate the after-effect, which after F is shorter than after C. ×: facilitatory or enhancing effect. −: inhibitory or lowering effect.

2. *The association* of the rod with C (assoc. in Fig. 9). This factor makes the rod an object which elicits a tendency to court: the rod is treated like a dummy female. This will lower the response rate and thus counteract the reinforcing effect (negative arrow from R to B). It is reflected in the permanently low probability of biting per rod-visit (well below 0.50). Though this factor is clearly related to Pavlovian or classical conditioning, I prefer "association", since the former term currently refers to the conditioned stimulus as a signal for the response, not as its target. The association lasts a considerable time (p. 279).

3. *The motivational after-effect* of C (M in Fig. 9). This factor temporarily enhances the inhibitory effect of the association. During this period (of the order of 5–10 minutes) after C the male is even less likely to bite on a rod-visit, provided the rod is associated with C. Since this period is exactly as long after an exposure (C not contingent on B) as after a contingent presentation, this after-effect must be attributed to the increased tendency to court after C, not to a temporary strengthening of the association.

4. The possible general inhibition of B after C (not in Fig. 9). It should be stressed again that a possible (short-lasting) inhibitory after-effect of C on biting, regardless of the object at which it is aimed, cannot yet be

discarded. This is especially the case since only one experiment with C-injections has been analysed.

The interaction of these factors results in a considerable lowering of the response rate in BC experiments, as compared to RC experiments, where only the first factor, the reinforcing effect of C, seems to be involved.

A similar interpretation may be applied to the high response rate found in BF experiments (see diagram in Fig. 10). However, in these experiments the association of the rod with F facilitates the response and consequently increases the response rate. This facilitatory effect is temporarily enhanced by the motivational after-effect of F, which in the case discussed is reflected in the high probability of biting on the first rod-visit after F (0.97) as compared to the overall probability (0.80). This would also explain why at least in some cases the response rate in BF experiments is definitely higher than in RF experiments, where this facilitation of the response is lacking.

A more general conclusion, in the wider perspective of this symposium, is that response rates may depend strongly on whether the response is or is not compatible with the situation used to reinforce it. Furthermore, since in the case presented here (in BC experiments) no amount of training appeared to increase the response rate, it seems impossible in this species at least, to overcome this incompatibility by learning. The animal cannot learn to use the response in a motivationally neutral way. In this sense the species-characteristic structure of the behaviour puts a definite constraint on learning.

References

Assem, J. van den (1967). Territory in the three-spined stickleback, *Gasterosteus aculeatus* L. *Behaviour Suppl.* **16**, 1–164.

Iersel, J. J. A. van (1953). An analysis of the parental behaviour of the male three-spined stickleback (*Gasterosteus aculeatus* L.) *Behaviour Suppl.* **3**, 1–159.

Nelson, K. (1965). After-effects of courtship in the male three-spined stickleback. *Zeitschr. für vergl. Physiol.* **50**, 569–597.

Pelkwijk, J. J., ter, and Tinbergen, N. (1937). Eine reizbiologische Analyse einiger Verhaltensweisen von *Gasterosteus aculeatus* L. *Z. Tierpsychol.* **1**, 193–200.

Sevenster, P. (1961). A causal analysis of a displacement activity (fanning in *Gasterosteus aculeatus* L.). *Behaviour Suppl.* **9**, 1–170.

Sevenster, P. (1968). Motivation and learning in sticklebacks. *In* "The Central Nervous System and Fish Behaviour", (D. Ingle, ed.), pp. 233–245, University of Chicago Press.

13
Constraints on Reinforcement

by Joan Stevenson-Hinde

The operational definition of a reinforcer proposed by Skinner has survived the test of time against more theoretical competitors. However, along with the apparent safety of the Skinnerian definitions of operant response and reinforcer has come the temptation to generalize beyond the operations actually involved. It has been assumed that all reinforcers should have similar effects on responding, and that the operant chosen can be almost any response in an animal's repertoire. Take for example all the work on schedules of reinforcement. Although it consists largely of experiments in which food was used as a reinforcer for key pecking with pigeons, results are discussed in terms which imply that the effects of any particular schedule can be generalized across a range of reinforcers, operants, and indeed species: "A second step is a description of the performances generated by such schedules. For each schedule in our logical classification, we present the typical performance under standard conditions of a representative organism." (Ferster and Skinner, 1957, p. 2.)

However, as already discussed in Chapter 1, stimuli which are reinforcing to one species are not necessarily reinforcing to another. Contributions to this volume further illustrate that different reinforcers have different effects, and that even if a stimulus is a reinforcer for one response, it may not be for another. This leads one to ask what kinds of limitations on response-reinforcer relations must be considered.

Reinforcers for Chaffinches

The difficulty of arriving at any one formulation for predicting which stimuli will reinforce which responses can be illustrated by comparing one of the traditional reinforcers (food) with a sensory reinforcer (song). First-year, autumn-caught male chaffinches (*Fringilla coelebs*) with high testosterone levels were given the opportunity to peck a vertical key to obtain seed (Kling and Stevenson-Hinde, 1972); to perch on a particular perch to obtain playback of adult song or white noise (Stevenson, 1967; Stevenson-Hinde, 1972); or to peck a vertical key to obtain song (Stevenson-Hinde and Uldal, in prep.).

In the experiments with food as a reinforcer for pecking, the most difficult stage in training involved getting the birds to approach rather than avoid the feeder as soon as it was presented. This took about three sessions. Following this, pecking the key was elicited by taping a grain of seed on the key. Each peck operated the feeder, and after 25 reinforcements were obtained in this way, the grain was removed from the key. Pecking the key continued, with each peck producing a reinforcement (i.e. a 5-second presentation of seed). Thus, after only a few days training, all thirteen of the birds tested came to obtain 100 reinforcements in about an hour's time, with a typical pattern of bouts of pecking and eating interspersed with other activities (for further details, see Kling and Stevenson-Hinde, 1972).

In the experiments with song as a reinforcer for perching, no special training procedure was necessary, since no obvious "consummatory response" was involved, and since perching occurred naturally. However, since perching did occur naturally, it was necessary to alternate periods in which perching on the operant perch produced song with control periods when it did not. Furthermore, since any increase in responding to the operant perch during song periods could simply indicate an arousing effect of song, rather than a reinforcing effect, responding to a second, control perch was also recorded. An index of the reinforcing effect of song for each bird was calculated by considering the frequency of responding to the operant perch weighted by the frequency to both perches, during song as compared with no-song periods. An index greater than 0.50 indicates a positive effect, namely that perching on the operant perch weighted by total perching was greater during song than during no-song periods. An index of 0.50 indicates no reinforcing effect; and less than 0.50 a negative effect, namely that perching to the operant perch weighted by total perching was less during stimulus periods than during control periods (for further details, see Stevenson, 1967 and Stevenson-Hinde, 1972).

Of the twelve birds which were allowed to perch for a playback of one adult song lasting two seconds (Fig. 1), ten produced a reinforcement index greater than 0.50, and for seven it was significantly so ($p < 0.05$, from a two-tailed Sign test on absolute values). A control group treated similarly, except that perching on the operant perch produced a burst of white noise (Fig. 1), failed to show any significantly positive effect (one was significantly negative), and had significantly lower indices than the song group ($p < 0.02$, Mann-Whitney U test, two-tailed). Thus a reinforcing effect of song, but not of white noise, was found. However, the reinforcing effect of song was weaker than the reinforcing effect of food in that individual indices varied over a large range, with not all individuals showing a significant reinforcing effect.

Other birds were allowed to peck a key to produce a playback of adult song. Since the operant level of pecking was zero and since pecking could

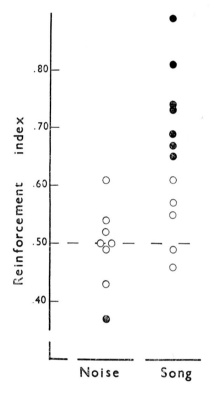

Fig. 1. Reinforcement indices for eight individual chaffinches perching for a burst of white noise, and for twelve individuals perching for adult song. An index greater than 0·50 indicates a positive reinforcing effect, and less than 0·50 a negative reinforcing effect. Filled circles represent indices which differed significantly from the neutral value of 0·50 (from Stevenson, 1967; Stevenson-Hinde, 1972).

not be "shaped", pecking was elicited by taping a grain of seed on the key and introducing food deprivation. All eight birds pecked under these conditions, with each peck producing one song. However, five of the eight birds would not peck unless they were food-deprived. The other three did come to peck the key even when not food-deprived. Fig. 2 shows the results for these three birds, starting from the first session in which more than ten pecks occurred without food-deprivation, and continuing under free-feeding conditions. For all three birds, pecking for song was maintained in the absence of any food deprivation. Furthermore, during extinction sessions (days 27 and 28; 34 and 35), the number of pecks decreased, to increase only again with retraining, in all three birds on the first occasion and two out of three on the second.

In spite of this reinforcing effect of song for pecking, whenever seed was removed from the key (days 4–6; 10–12; 16–18), no pecking occurred.

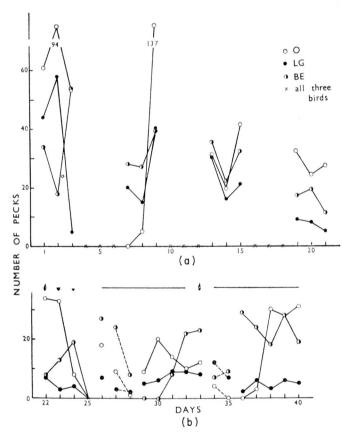

Fig. 2. The number of pecks over daily 40-minute sessions for three chaffinches. On all days, except those connected by dashed lines, each peck produced a playback of one adult song (a CRF schedule). On the days connected by dashed lines (days 27 and 28; 34 and 35), pecking produced no song at all (extinction). In graph (a) two seeds were taped on the response key for the first three days, but not for the next three; and this alternation continued through day 21. In graph (b) the seed on the key is indicated for each day: one seed was on the key on day 22, half a seed on day 23, a quarter of a seed on day 24, and no seed on day 25. From day 26 on, one seed remained on the key (Stevenson-Hinde and Uldal, in prep.).

Even when seed was gradually removed from the key (days 22–24), by going from one seed to $\frac{1}{2}$ seed to $\frac{1}{4}$ seed, pecking dropped to zero with no seed (day 25). Thus, even for the three birds that would peck for song without being food-deprived, seed on the key remained a necessary condition for pecking. This indicates that although song was a reinforcer for pecking, the effect was so weak that song would maintain pecking only if an external stimulus for pecking was present.

Differences in techniques and criteria do not permit any strict ordering of the above response-reinforcer relations from strong to weak. However, the proportion of birds showing a reinforcing effect and the degree of control achieved over the operant response suggest that the relation is strongest with pecking for food, progressively weaker with perching for song and pecking for song, and finally non-existent with perching for noise.

Accepting this ordering of reinforcing effects, what formulation would encompass such an order? One might be the "relevance" of the operant response to the reinforcer. Thus, key pecking is "relevant" to obtaining food, and perching is "relevant" to obtaining song. That is, although extrapolation from an operant situation to a natural situation must be made with the greatest caution, it is conceivable that there is a parallel between a bird perching to turn on song in the present situation and a territory-owning bird approaching the source of an intruder's song in a natural situation (Marler, 1956). A similar parallel of pecking to approach song cannot be found; and artificially-produced white noise is relevant to nothing. However, one could not predict from the "relevance" consideration alone, the stronger reinforcing effect of food for pecking than song for perching.

The best formulation for this difference concerns "causal factors". For song, the antecedent conditions necessary for obtaining reinforcing effects are a combination of early experience in the wild and a high testosterone level (Stevenson-Hinde, 1972). However, these never give hearing song the priority over other types of behaviour that food deprivation gives to feeding. Thus, both of these considerations are necessary to predict the ordering of these reinforcing effects.

Reinforcers within this Volume

As a guide in asking where constraints on reinforcement lie, Table 1 shows a diagram of an operant sequence, and indicates how it may be applied to the particular sequences studied within this volume. In the sequence S^+—R_{op}—S^R—R_{cons}—, the symbols refer respectively to a discriminative stimulus, an operant response, a reinforcing stimulus, and a

U

TABLE 1

Operant sequences, of a discriminative stimulus (S+), an operant response (Rop), a reinforcer (SR), and a consummatory response (Rcons), with constraints placed at numbers (1–5). Solid lines indicate a temporal relation (left to right); and the second line is an alternative, Pavlovian notation, of a conditioned stimulus (CS), a conditioned response (CR), an unconditioned stimulus (US), and an unconditioned response (UR).

causal factors (1) ————

$$S^+ \xrightarrow{(2)} R_{op} \xrightarrow{(3)} S^R \xrightarrow{(4———)} R_{cons} \xrightarrow{(5)}$$
$$CS —— CR —— US —— UR$$

Particular Operant Sequences

Author	Species	S+	Rop	SR	Rcons	Constraint
Bateson	chick	pedal	sit on	flashing light	approach	age (1), early experience (1)
Hogan	chick	food sand	peck peck	food in mouth sand in mouth	ingest ingest	age (1), consequences of SR (4)
McFarland	rats	food	food selection	food-stimuli	ingest	"stimulus relevance" between food-stimuli and post-ingestion con-sequences (4)
McFarland	doves	key key key	peck peck peck	food water temperature	eat drink —	behavioural aspects of homeostasis (1) relevance of Rop to SR (3)
Moore	pigeons pigeons	key key	(eat-) peck (drink-) peck	food water	eat drink	influence of Pavlovian conditioning (2)

	Animal	Manipulandum	Operant response	Reinforcer	Consummatory response	Notes
Jenkins	pigeons	tone	(peck-) interrupt photo-cell	food	eat	influence of Pavlovian conditioning (2)
Glickman	gerbils	bar	press	ICS	post-stimulation foot-thumping, sniffing, locomotion, and oral activities	effect of ICS in eliciting R_{cons} (1)
Shettleworth	hamsters	bar	press	food	eat	effect of hunger and other causal factors on R_{op} (1); relevance of R_{op} to S^R (3)
			dig	food	eat	
			open rear	food	eat	
			scrabble	food	eat	
			scratch with hind leg	food	eat	
			face wash	food	eat	
			scent mark	food	eat	
Sevenster	sticklebacks	ring	swim through	male	attack	influence of Pavlovian conditioning (2); after-effects of R_{cons} (5)
		ring	swim through	female	court	
		rod	bite	male	attack	
		rod	bite	female	court	
Stevenson-Hinde	chaffinches	key	peck	food	eat	causal factors (1), S^+-R_{op} relation (2), relevance of R_{op} to S^R (3)
		perch	hop on	song	—	
		seed on key	peck	song	—	
		perch	hop on	white noise	—	

consummatory response. With a pigeon pecking for food, the particular sequence might be related to the general diagram in terms of key—peck—food—eat—. Of course, the dangers of such an exercise must be avoided. The general diagram should not be taken to imply either theoretical or physiological S—R connexions or associations. It is useful only as a tool for describing diverse experiments. From this it follows that not all experiments will be equally well described in these terms, but hopefully they will not be distorted too much.

Within the general diagram (top of Table 1), constraints on reinforcement operate at a number of locations. Precisely where these lie and how many there are is debatable. Nevertheless five constraints (numbers 1–5) fit many experiments mentioned within this volume (the remainder of Table 1). Although all possible constraints may be operating within each experiment, those listed in the last column are only those which are isolated and discussed by the author.

To begin with, whether or not a stimulus will be reinforcing depends in part on "causal factors". This term is used in a very general sense, to refer to antecedent manipulations, to any condition that holds throughout the period of testing, or in the artificial case to brain stimulation. With the key—peck—food—eat— example, a "causal factor" would be the degree of food deprivation. Other "causal factors" which influence whether a reinforcing effect will be found or not are age (Bateson, Chapter 5; Hogan, Chapter 6) and early experience (Bateson, Chapter 5; Stevenson-Hinde, 1972).

Causal factors may be considered from several angles. McFarland (Chapter 7) points to the successively decreasing role of behaviour in maintaining the three homeostatic systems: food, water and temperature. He suggests that a decrease in the behavioural aspects of homeostasis is correlated with a decrease in the reinforcing effect of the relevant stimulus.

From a second angle, causal factors may affect the probability of an operant and/or a consummatory response. Premack's theory (1965) predicts that a high-probability response should act as a reinforcing event for a lower-probability response: "We assume that any more probable alternative will reinforce any less probable one, and that the reinforcement prediction can be made with no knowledge other than that of the numbers that identify the position of the alternatives on the probability scale." (Premack, 1969, p. 126). A compatible position, but with physiological implications, is taken by Glickman and Schiff (1967): "In our theory the activation of the underlying neural systems is considered the sufficient condition for reinforcement." (p. 85).

Thus it should be possible to predict reinforcing effects from the baseline response probabilities of the operant and consummatory responses, and one way to manipulate response probabilities is by means of causal factors. For example, in Shettleworth's experiments with hamsters (Chapter 11), food deprivation increased the probability of eating, but the baseline rate of bar pressing remained low. The opportunity to eat then acted as a reinforcer for bar pressing. However, food deprivation did affect the baseline probabilities of some of the other operants that Shettleworth used: deprivation increased the baseline rate of open rearing and scrabbling and decreased the rate of face washing and scent marking. Yet these latter two behaviour patterns, although having lower response probabilities than feeding, were among the three that showed at best a minimal reinforcing effect of food. It is difficult to see how a theory based solely on relative response probabilities of operant and consummatory response would predict this weak reinforcing effect. A further difficulty arises with reinforcers which involve no observable consummatory response (e.g. song).

In spite of these limitations, it is true that many stimuli which elicit a "consummatory response" are also reinforcers. In considering the implications of brain stimulation research for a response-oriented view of reinforcement, Glickman (Chapter 10) does find a correlation between the effectiveness of brain stimulation in eliciting certain behaviour patterns of gerbils (post-stimulation foot thumping, sniffing, locomotion, and oral activities) and in acting as a reinforcer. Yet Glickman points out that the correlation is not perfect. This, together with difficulties of interpretation, lead him to a more cautious view than his earlier one (Glickman and Schiff, 1967): "the mere elicitation of some species-characteristic behaviour gives no assurance of concomitant self-stimulation at the same site" (p. 216).

A third issue is whether the operant response shares causal factors with the consummatory response. If it does, it has been suggested that learning should be easier than if it does not (Bolles, 1970). While this view would predict the above results of Shettleworth, it is less easy to reconcile with her finding that, for those responses with baselines unaffected by food deprivation, some showed a strong reinforcing effect of food (bar pressing, digging), while another did not (scratching). To predict this, some evidence is needed that common causal factors are shared by bar pressing, digging, and eating, but not by scratching and eating. Shettleworth discusses some possibilities, which emphasize the need "to understand how a response's pre-existing role in the animal's behaviour interacts with its acquisition as an operant" (p. 261). Such a problem does not arise if one sticks to arbitrary operants. These are "topographically novel responses such as bar-pressing, which can never have had any role in the animal's pre-experimental life" (p. 244). Such arbitrary operants usually have a low operant level, and are little affected by causal factors for the consummatory response. Yet if reinforcement does operate in natural situations, where shaping procedures may not be up to those in the laboratory, reinforcement is more likely to affect those responses which do share causal factors with the consummatory response than those that do not.

A second constraint involves the relation between the stimulus situation (S+) and the operant response (R$_{op}$). The S+ may not be merely an initially neutral stimulus that acquires control over the operant response through differential reinforcement. Even before any testing begins, it may elicit aspects of the operant response, or it may come to do so through Pavlovian conditioning. Siqueland and DeLucia (1969) have capitalized on the former to demonstrate reinforcing effects of visual and auditory stimuli with human infants as young as three weeks. The stimulus was an empty nipple, which elicited sucking. Reinforcement was contingent upon sucking responses that were above a criterion amplitude. Another example is chaffinches key-pecking for song: the three that showed a reinforcing effect pecked only if seed was taped on the key (Fig. 2).

With Pavlovian conditioning (see top of Table 1), involving repeated pairing of a conditioned stimulus (CS) with an unconditioned stimulus (US), the CS may come to elicit a conditioned response (CR) which shares common properties with the unconditioned response (UR). If such conditioning is occurring, then a greater reinforcing effect will be shown when the required operant response can share common properties with the CR, than when it is less compatible, or actually incompatible with, the CR.

A positive influence of Pavlovian conditioning on operant conditioning is suggested in Sevenster's experiments with sticklebacks (Chapter 12), where the consummatory response of attack shared common properties with the operant response of biting a rod. Conversely, when courtship reinforced biting, one fish actually courted the rod instead of biting it. This could be due to Pavlovian conditioning, the rod having become a conditioned stimulus through association with the female or unconditioned stimulus.

The role of Pavlovian conditioning in operant conditioning is elucidated by auto-shaping experiments, as discussed by Moore (Chapter 8) and by Jenkins (Chapter 9). Moore argues that Pavlovian conditioning pervades operant conditioning. Jenkins takes the more cautious view, that "unselected" operants (e.g. key pecking) are susceptible to Pavlovian conditioning, while "selected" operants (e.g. stretching the neck to interrupt a photo-cell beam) are not.

A third constraint concerns the "relevance" of the operant response to the reinforcer—i.e. whether in a natural situation, aspects of the operant response are used in gaining access to the potential reinforcer. Thus, Shettleworth argues that with hamsters food was less of a reinforcer for scratching with a hind leg, face washing, and scent marking because, unlike the other operants she used, they could not be considered as being appetitive responses for food. Finally, Stevenson-Hinde suggests that with male chaffinches song might be a better reinforcer for perching than for key pecking because in a natural situation perching, unlike pecking, can bring the animal closer to song.

The last two constraints are related to the consummatory response. The fourth, applicable to the dietary selection and poison-avoidance work reviewed by McFarland (Chapter 7), refers to the degree to which stimuli correlated with food ingestion (R_{cons}) can become associated with its physiological consequences. That is, if ingestion of a saccharin solution is followed by toxicosis, the "saccharin-flavoured water" is subsequently avoided. If instead of a flavour, external stimuli (flash of light and a click) accompany drinking, then following toxicosis there is no aversion to the "bright, noisy water". Such experiments lead to a stimulus relevance principle, "that the associative strength of a cue with some consequence depends, in part, on the nature of the consequences . . . a flavour has high associative strength relative to a physiological consequence, while an exteroceptive stimulus has low associative strength" (Revusky and Garcia, 1970, p. 21). Mackintosh (Chapter 4) suggests that the "associative strength" may have been acquired early on. McFarland discusses a model in which "stimulus relevance" between food-stimuli and post-ingestion consequences determines the degree of avoidance that will be achieved. The extent to which this learned aversion hypothesis applies also to the post-ingestion effects on chicks' pecking is discussed by Hogan (Chapter 6). Although chicks peck food or sand when confronted with it for the first time, Hogan suggests that pecking is maintained by actually getting the objects into the mouth. Thus the objects in the mouth may be said to reinforce pecking. However, a post-ingestion effects change the reinforcing value, in a positive direction with food, and in a negative direction with sand.

The fifth constraint concerns the degree of compatibility between recent performance of the consummatory response and repetition of the operant response. Such an effect is suggested when a post-reinforcement delay occurs for one operant but not for another. Thus when Sevenster compared the reinforcing effects of courtship on two operants, swimming through a ring and biting a rod, he found that the interval between courtship and the next performance of the operant was much longer with biting a rod than with swimming through a ring. An extensive behavioural analysis supported the view that the delay between courtship and biting was due to a form of behavioural inhibition.

Thus, constraints operating at a number of points have been demonstrated in the preceding chapters. The classification just presented is not absolute: more or fewer varieties might be recognized, depending on the level of analysis. To be able to relate those discussed to a smaller number at a more fundamental level would be more pleasing. Seligman (1970) has attempted to reach such a level directly by defining a continuum of "preparedness", along which an "organism can be either prepared, unprepared, or contraprepared for learning about the events" (p. 408). His approach also carries the message that we can no longer expect a variety of reinforcers to control a variety of operant responses in similar ways. But any such single formulation carries with it the danger of losing some predictive value. The above rather tedious procedure, of asking where constraints on reinforcement lie, is perhaps a better guide to the questions that should be asked when looking for reinforcing effects in particular contexts.

Acknowledgements

I am grateful to the Science Research Council for their support. I should like to thank J. A. Hogan and D. J. McFarland for their helpful comments on the manuscript.

References

Bolles, R. C. (1970). Species-specific defense reactions and avoidance learning. *Psychol. Rev.* **77**, 32–48.

Ferster, C. B. and Skinner, B. F. (1957). "Schedules of Reinforcement." Appleton-Century-Crofts, New York.

Glickman, S. E. and Schiff, B. B. (1967). A biological theory of reinforcement. *Psychol. Rev.* **74**, 81–109.

Kling, J. W. and Stevenson-Hinde, J. (1972). Reinforcement, extinction, and spontaneous recovery of key pecking in chaffinches. *Anim. Behav.* **23**, 424–429.

Marler, P. (1956). The voice of the chaffinch and its function as a language. *Ibis* **98**, 231–261.

Premack, D. (1965). Reinforcement theory. *In* "Nebraska Symposium on Motivation", (D. Levine, ed.). Univ. of Nebraska Press, Lincoln.

Premack, D. (1969). On some boundary conditions of contrast. *In* "Reinforcement and Behavior", (J. T. Tapp, ed.). Academic Press, New York.

Revusky, S. and Garcia, J. (1970). Learned associations over long delays. *In* "The Psychology of Learning and Motivation", Vol. 4, (G. H. Bower, ed.). Academic Press, New York.

Seligman, M. E. P. (1970). On the generality of the laws of learning. *Psychol. Rev.* **77**, 406–418.

Siqueland, E. R. and De Lucia, C. A. (1969). Visual reinforcement of non-nutritive sucking in human infants. *Science* **165**, 1144–1146.

Stevenson, J. G. (1967). Reinforcing effects of chaffinch song. *Anim. Behav.* **15**, 427–432.

Stevenson-Hinde, J. (1972). Effects of early experience and testosterone on song as a reinforcer. *Anim. Behav.* **23**, 430–435.

Stevenson-Hinde, J. and Uldal, C. (In prep.). Song as a reinforcer for key pecking.

Editorial: 4

All the chapters so far have been concerned primarily with sub-human species. Those that follow are concerned for the most part with man. One bridge between the two comes from an evolutionary approach: we must not forget that man, like animals, has been subject to natural selection, and his special learning abilities are themselves the result of adaptation. Humphrey (Chapter 14), focussing on patterns of behaviour that have the consequence of promoting and channelling learning, draws material from every level of complexity touched on in this book, and in doing so shows how the concept of biological adaptation can throw light on studies of learning at all phyletic levels, including man.

That man and animals have been subject to natural selection does not of itself imply similarity of mechanisms in their behaviour. As stressed in Chapter 1, in the past it was too often assumed that principles of learning abstracted from laboratory studies of lower species in carefully controlled (and therefore impoverished) situations would prove of general applicability, and in particular that they would provide a key for understanding human learning. Amongst experimental psychologists, there were a few who stood out against this view—notably Tolman (e.g. 1932) who included "capacity laws" within his system, and Schneirla (e.g. 1959), who gave repeated warnings of the dangers of generalizing across phyletic levels. Schneirla and Rosenblatt's (1961) demonstration, that the ways in which an ant and a rat learn a maze are different in kind, should of course be taken as a warning against the difficulties of extrapolating from rat to man. Bitterman's (e.g. 1960) extensive studies have further demonstrated the need for an appropriate behavioural analysis before cross-phyletic comparisons of performance in learning situations are meaningful. More recently Razran (1971) has attempted a broad synthesis which embraces, in addition to various types of "non-associative" and "associative" learning, "configured" and "symbolic" learning, the latter being almost exclusively a human development, though one that can, at least to some extent, be brought into the laboratory.

It is these so-called "complex processes" with which Foss (Chapter 15) is concerned. In emphasizing the diverse processes that contribute to the modifiability of human behaviour in real-life situations, Foss is careful to point out that they too have their constraints: not only must the processes be described, classified and analysed, but the nature of their limitations must be understood.

Realization of the complexity of human behaviour must not make us swing to the opposite extreme and reject studies of animal learning as irrelevant. Rather our task must be to define precisely where they can be helpful, and where misleading. Not surprisingly, it is with learning in the first few years of life that comparisons with animal studies are most fruitful, and most of the chapters that follow are concerned with that period. It will be apparent that many of the themes already discussed recur in studies of our own species. For instance, we have seen (e.g. Chapters 10, 11 and 12) that a bias has been introduced into experiments on learning through the selection for study of cases in which learning is known to occur easily. If the only situations chosen for study are those in which learning occurs readily, of course learning appears to be ubiquitous. In the next chapter Schaffer makes a related point with respect to human infants: the selection of response systems that are readily modified can blind us to the constraints that may operate on learning in others. However, Schaffer goes farther than this in stressing that only by using a variety of response indices, and by studying the relationships between them and how those relationships change with age, can we begin to understand the development of behavioural organization in the child. If the course of even a simple type of learning, like habituation, varies with a number of pre-experimental variables, such as sex and socio-economic status, as well as with others introduced by the experimenter, such as complexity of the stimulus, it must be subject to multiple constraints. When we find also that there are major differences in the habituation rates of different responses to the same stimulus, and that both the effects of the independent variables and the differences between responses change with age, we realize the magnitude of the task before us.

Schaffer's study is especially concerned with visual fixation and manipulative contact, two responses which are essential constituents of a wide variety of skills. Connolly is concerned with the development of manipulative skills in somewhat older children: some of the constraints he finds are similar to those already discussed in earlier chapters—the development of sensory/perceptual systems and the establishment of sensori-motor relations. In addition, however, skills demand the integration of units—referred to by Connolly as sub-routines: the development of skills thus demands the prior development of these units and the means to mobilize them.

References

Bitterman, M. E. (1960). Toward a comparative psychology of learning. *Amer. Psychologist*, **15**, 704–712.

Razran, G. (1971). "Mind in Evolution: an East-West Synthesis of Learned Behaviour and Cognition." Houghton Mifflin, Boston.

Schneirla, T. C. (1959). An evolutionary and developmental theory of biphasic processes underlying approach and withdrawal. *In* "Nebraska Symposium on Motivation", University of Chicago Press, Lincoln.

Schneirla, T. C. and Rosenblatt, J. S. (1961). Behavioural organisation and genesis of the social bond in insects and mammals. *Amer. J. Orthopsych.*, **31**, 223–253.

Tolman, E. C. (1932). "Purposive Behavior in Animals and Men." Century, New York.

14

Predispositions to Learn

by N. K. Humphrey

One of the aims of this book is to map some of the areas of failure and success in learning. What we make of this map depends which areas we take to be the figure, which the ground. Traditional learning theorists, true to a creed of pan-associationism, may be impressed by the "surprising" failures; but an evolutionary biologist is more likely to be impressed by the successes. The animals we find in nature have not after all been sculpted from a block of uniform potential but have been built up rather like maquettes from clay. It would be odd for a cosmologist to turn his attention to the gaps between the stars, and equally odd for a biologist to make it his task to explain why men can't fly or why horses can't learn mathematics.

I want to make some remarks about a particular kind of biological adaptation—behaviour patterns which help an animal to learn. Much of a child's early schooling is concerned not with acquiring particular knowledge but with learning the means to acquire knowledge. "Learning to learn" has at least two aspects to it: on the one hand learning to want to learn, on the other learning how and what to learn. We have in this book examples which suggest that animals may be *predisposed* to learn in both these ways. The two aspects overlap, but let me for convenience separate them.

Predispositions to Engage in Learning

Learning, it seems, may be its own reward. For man, the point hardly needs making. Most of the games we play, the explorations we make and for that matter much of the research we do is directed towards gaining information which as often as not has no immediate return. Bartlett has called this characteristic hunger for knowledge "effort after meaning". Though the effort may be made for its own sake alone, it is easy to see how, rather like sexual activity, it pays indirectly in terms of biological survival. In other species also, play and exploration form a dominant activity especially in infancy. "Stimulus novelty" is perhaps the most universal reinforcer known: a young monkey will even press a button to look at "abstract paintings"—and may prefer such pictures to pictures of appetising foods (Humphrey, unpublished observations). However we characterize such simple curiosity, one of its consequences is certain to be to promote adaptive learning.

"Imitation" may be a kind of play. By engaging in imitative activity a young animal learns by example from other more experienced members of the community. Aristotle wrote: "From earliest childhood the instinct for imitation is natural to us, as is the universal pleasure in imitations. Man is superior to the other animals in being more imitative, and his first lessons are learned by imitation ... Learning is very agreeable, not only to philosophers but also to other men." (*Poetics* iv). Hogan (Chapter 6) mentions imitation as one of the means by which a chick learns to identify food. A fine example of imitative learning in a sub-human primate is provided by Goodall's (1968) description of how chimpanzees learn to fish for termites by watching others, and later in this book Ryan (Chapter 21) points to the role of imitation in the development of a child's language.

In these and similar cases it is important to recognize the role of the other individual—the "teacher"—who provides the model to be imitated. A human mother deliberately presents her offspring with examples of speech in an easily assimilable form; and a mother hen makes a "demonstration" of her pecking. Teaching, in so far as it too is self-rewarding, shares some of the defining attributes of play. In the case at least of parent-offspring interactions, both sides of the teacher-pupil dyad are likely to come under similar evolutionary selection pressure.

Exploratory behaviour shades from a non-specific interest in the unknown to a more highly organized search for relevant material. Bateson's account (Chapter 5) of stimulus preferences during the course of imprinting provides an important example of the latter, more structured, kind of predisposition to learn. His evidence indicates that a chick seeks out conspicuous stimuli and that once it has become familiar with a particular stimulus it actively searches for stimuli which are slightly different from the original. Thereby it ensures that it exposes itself to the various possible transformations which any real object is likely to undergo, and is enabled to build up an inclusive concept of the object. The chick's approach tendencies serve somewhat the same role that Hebb (1949) assigned to scanning eye-movements in the development of the "phase-sequences" which he considered essential for figural recognition. It would be interesting to examine other exploratory eye- and head-movements during perceptual development in the light of Bateson's evidence. The best way, for instance, for a naïve animal to get to know the possible visual transformations of a solid object would be to examine it actively from different distances and different sides: do animals actually help themselves to learn in such a way? A tendency to seek out "discrepant" visual stimuli would incidentally be an effective way of ensuring the kind of balanced sensory input which Blakemore's experiments (Chapter 3) have shown to be important for the normal development of the visual cortex.

It is possible that the brain in fact has mechanisms specially set aside to guide visual exploration at the crucial early stage when the visual cortex is tuning in to the features of the sensory environment. I have evidence that a monkey which has been deprived of its visual cortex continues to make exploratory eye-movements like those of a very young human child; comparable visual objects attract the operated monkey's and the baby's eye, and psychophysical parameters such as acuity are closely similar in the two cases. It may be that a child's vision is for the first few months of life mediated entirely by the subcortical visual system. Eye-movements guided by this relatively simple system serve to pick out a representative selection of the objects in the environment for the attention (and edification) of the developing visual cortex, acting in effect to introduce the visual cortex to the visual world.

Evidence, at a different level, that human children are attracted to discrepant stimuli comes from the research reviewed by Schaffer (Chapter 16). The tendency is not restricted to children. Grown men too clearly take pleasure in observing *variants* of a particular category, whether their material is postage stamps or birds. A similar tendency lies at the heart of much of the delight we take in what we call aesthetic form. There is hardly any musical composer who does not make use of the device of variation on a theme. He presents us, say, with a simple melody, repeats it several times and then launches into a series of variations, playing it on a different instrument, with different emphasis or in a different key until eventually he returns to the original. Bateson's U-shaped function, showing how a chick initially prefers the standard stimulus, then later prefers variations on that stimulus and then finally prefers the original again, parallels in some ways our own response to classical "sonata form".

Predispositions as to How and What to Learn

Lorenz has argued that the capacity for simple associative learning must itself be an unlearned predisposition. But it remains an open question to what extent an animal may be predisposed towards more complicated "sets" and "strategies" for learning. Research on the acquisition of specific preferences and aversions for foods, described here by Hogan and Mac-Farland (Chapters 6 and 7, respectively), provides examples of what may well be unlearned strategies. It seems (though MacKintosh presents an alternative interpretation in Chapter 4) that rats and chicks come ready equipped with hypotheses about what kinds of stimulus, at what distance in time, are likely to be correlated with subsequent illness. Moreover, rats may simplify the task of establishing such correlations by sampling foods one at a time in "meals"; chicks do not take discrete meals, but the tendency to peck at different foods in "runs" could at least help discriminative learning.

Given the skill to learn, the matter arises of where it should be applied. A child who knows how to read and enjoys doing it still depends for his self-education on what he takes down from the library shelf. Several examples indicate that what an animal learns about may be channelled by initial biases. Bateson has shown how a chick's early perceptual learning is influenced by certain initial stimulus preferences. Blakemore argues that the effects of experience on the differentiation of the visual cortex is probably constrained by a measure of pre-existing selectivity. At the level of language learning, children are guided in what they learn both by their own tendency to be selectively attentive to particular aspects of speech and by the tendency of their mothers to select the speech to which they are exposed (Sinclair, Chapter 19; Ryan, Chapter 21).

Constraints on learning all these predispositions may be but constraints of a peculiarly liberating kind. Freedom, it's said, is the recognition of necessity, and the regretful young man of Maurice Hare's limerick may be offered a soothing rejoinder:

Expostulation

> There was a young man who said "Damn!
> I perceive with regret that I am
> But a creature that moves
> In predestinate grooves,
> I'm not even a bus, I'm a tram".

And reply

> "Young man you should stay your complaint,
> For the grooves that you call a constraint
> Are there to contrive
> That you learn to survive;
> Trams arrive – buses may or they mayn't".

References

Hebb, D. O. (1949). "The Organization of Behavior." Wiley, New York.
Lawick-Goodall, J. van (1968). The behaviour of free-living chimpanzees in the Gombe Stream Reserve. *Anim. Behav. Monogr.* **1**, pt. 3.

15
Human and Animal Learning—A Caution

by B. M. Foss

The evidence presented in the chapters of this book shows that learning is always shaped by constraints and that the constraints vary between species. They may vary also with age, between individuals and with the situation. It is to be expected, then, that the constraints that operate on human learning may be different in kind from those so far discussed.

The most commonly stated difference between man and other animals is that man has language. Pavlov himself considered that this "second signalling system" would involve different principles from those shown in the conditioned responses; but even now it remains a matter of controversy as to whether language is acquired in the way that overt responses are acquired; and very little is known about the way in which language affects other kinds of learning. Obviously it does affect the way in which categories are formed, and it allows information about categories to be transmitted to other individuals. And, at least for some people, language plays a large part in problem solving. However, deaf-mutes, with a minimal vocabulary and language structure, show surprisingly little impairment in solving problems (Furth, 1966). At the other end of the scale, a human's performance in a classical or operant conditioning experiment does vary with the instructions he has been given.

Let us consider now several complex forms of learning which are typically human.

Imitation

This term is used to describe processes differing widely in complexity, and there is no generally accepted classification.

An important distinction lies between imitative performance (of an act already in the individual's repertoire) and imitative learning, in which new responses are acquired. Of particular interest is "observational learning". This term is used to refer to the kind of learning shown when an animal learns more quickly as a result of having watched another animal perform the same task. There is some evidence for this kind of learning in birds and lower mammals, but it is clearly seen in primates. Something like observational learning obviously occurs outside the laboratory setting, as is shown from the records of people who have reared apes in their own homes, and from van Lawick-Goodall's (1965) observations of "termite fishing" by chimpanzees. These illustrate an interesting aspect of this kind of imitation. In the early stages of learning, the act is copied as though in isolation, and not integrated into a total pattern of goal-directed behaviour. This is even more the case for this category of human imitative learning, as noted for instance, by Aronfreed (1969, p. 256).

Humans exhibit many kinds of imitation, some of which are difficult to explain. Putting out the tongue is said to be copied by infants at an age when feed-back matching is impossible (i.e. they have not used mirrors to see if the movement they are making gives a result like that of the actor). Some kinds of human imitation occur at a symbolic level, and are dealt with later under "identification". Other human imitation, though not symbolic, is highly complex. For instance, a good mimic may, at a moment's notice, be able to recreate a real (or imaginary) person as though *in toto*. (Something similar, but not so striking, may be seen when anyone plays a role for the first time, e.g. talking in public or chairing a committee). As Hinde has already noted for song-learning (Chapter 1), and as several writers on imitation believe (e.g. Aronfreed,1969), it seems that a pattern, template, schema, etc., is learnt first, then behaviour is produced to match the pattern. Mowrer (1960) was probably the first to show how a simplified version of such a model might fit with learning theory (though reinforcement may not always be as important as he thought). However, Mowrer's theory depended on the learner being able to match feedback from his own behaviour with the perception of the modeller's behaviour, and it is only in the imitation of sounds that this would be a relatively simple operation.

It is clear, however, that what is imitated may be influenced by a number of factors. One of the most interesting and intangible of these is the extent to which the subject identified with the model. This is discussed below.

Identification

This term is used here, with as little theoretical connotation as possible, to describe the way in which an individual's choice of goals and ways of behaving are related to the group or groups to which he sees himself as belonging. Identification in this sense may be an extension of imitation, but it can occur at a highly symbolic level. For instance, an adolescent may get pleasure from buying and playing a record entirely on his own provided he knows that it is in "the top ten". Or a psychologist may get pleasure from theorizing in a particular way because he knows that other biologically oriented psychologists, with whom he identifies, would be interested.

Such behaviour includes a new mechanism, categorizing (see below), in that the learner categorizes himself along with other members of the group. It need not be a face-to-face group and in some cases (e.g. psychotic) may be imaginary. It is doubtful if it makes much sense to talk of non-human animals as identifying, except that the beginnings of it can be seen in the way primates may appear to choose the individual they imitate (e.g. Hall, 1963).

Most humans identify with a variety of groups, but in some cases where individuals seem to identify with one group only, the consequences (and, to some extent, pre-requisites) of group membership can be seen: uniformity of "taste" (in appearance, talk, food, drink, music, art), attitudes, interests, beliefs. The uniformity applies as much to things and people which are disliked as to those which are liked.

Speculatively, one might suppose that actual group membership was vital 100 generations ago, and that a variety of mechanisms existed to ensure such membership. These would include avoidance of loneliness, and conformity to the group might well be the result of social reinforcers and imitation. However, a new kind of positive reinforcer seems to exist: the intense pleasure resulting from being in a group all liking, or hating, the same thing, person, etc. Perhaps the obvious argument should be reversed. Not, "I belong to a group and therefore I like A and hate B"; but "Liking A and hating B gives me great pleasure if I do it in the company of others. Hence, the existence of A and B is justified because they increase my tendency to belong to a group and it is that which has biological primacy."

While the tendency to identify may have its roots in man's remote past, what determines with whom a given individual identifies is little understood. For some types of identification affection may be a prerequisite, for others, envy, and for yet others similarity of circumstance or goal. In any case, identification is certainly an important influence on what is learned subsequently.

Categorizing

In laboratory studies of conditioning, an animal may respond to all members of a class of stimuli as though they were equivalent, or discriminate between them only in the strength of its response. Experimental studies have usually been concerned with stimuli within one sensory modality, but in real life situations "categories" of equivalent objects may be based on an integration of evidence from several modalities—for instance, for a zebra the category of objects that elicit the fear responses appropriate to a hunting lion has visual, touch, auditory and olfactory components. Such categories must be based on cross-modal integration. At the human level such a category can be given a verbal label, and all sorts of new possibilities for its manipulation arise.

Categorizing occurs in all human perception. Even in the case where one sees something which is quite unrecognizable for the first time, it will nevertheless be categorized as "something I have never seen". Considering how fundamental the process is, it is astonishing that so few people have considered it as a basic mechanism. (It is possible that an equivalent mechanism can be seen on the "motor side" of the organism, in simple form as "response generalization" and in more complex form as "behaviours directed towards a single goal"). The importance for the present chapter lies in the fact that many kinds of human learning (some of them follow) depend on the categorizing process. Also, the process is bound up with certain other basic mechanisms :

(a) *Coding.* When a stimulus object is categorized this normally carries with it a process of coding. One remembers seeing "a dog". Two things follow: there is much less load on memory, as compared with having to remember the total original percept, but this advantage is gained at the expense of discarding much of the original information. The object is remembered as more like a typical instance of the category in which it has been placed. Accuracy of learning/remembering will therefore depend on the number of categories and sub-categories available to the learner. These will have been learnt as a result of previous interaction with the objects.

(b) *Learning supposed facts, classifications, names for things etc.* Much school learning is of these kinds. Some such learning may depend on rote (which is not considered here), but much on categorizing. The most relevant psychological work has been done under the title of remembering, rather than learning, for instance by Bartlett (1932). He used the notion of schema, rather than category, and showed that the material which is retained and reproduced will show distortion resulting from assimilation to schemata (see also Chapters 18 and 19 for a discussion of Piaget's approach to these problems). In the present terminology, the material will have been selectively categorized, so that much information will be lost, as can be seen when the decoding takes place. As might be expected, the selectivity depends heavily on the person's interests; and therefore his identifications.

(c) *Learning of patterns.* Except in cases like eidetic imagery, learning and remembering of patterns (including of course letters, diagrams, pictures, faces etc.) depend on two main processes: autonomous processes, including some of those described by Gestalt psychologists (possibly tendencies to simplicity and symmetry, and fading); and categorizing. The pattern will be recalled as a typical instance of the category in which it has been put.

While the use of labelled categories must depend on processes such as generalization and discrimination which can be studied at much simpler levels, the precise relations between them remain to be defined. Presumably constraints on categorizing may depend on limitations in generalization, discrimination, abstraction and coding.

Concept Formation

I am referring here specifically to the concepts Piaget has studied (see also Chapters 18 and 19). One of the most dramatic and best studied is the concept of conservation of volume. Until the age of seven, say, normal children cannot "see" that the volume of a liquid remains constant when it is poured into containers of different shapes. The problem seems to be not purely semantic. There are ways of "coaching" children so that they form the concept a little earlier, but no remarkable effects of coaching have yet been shown. There are several curious things about the Piagetian concepts. It is difficult to see how they can arise from ordinary processes of abstraction and discrimination learning; and the concepts seem to develop in a more or less fixed sequence. The latter is particularly remarkable, because such a series of developmental stages does not occur in most of the other kinds of learning being talked about here. (An exception perhaps is language learning, though the stages which occur there may be more the result of skill development.) Piaget himself thinks that several factors may be involved, including maturation of the nervous system and the child's interaction with the environment when development between stages occurs.

This kind of development is important in the present context since the stage that a child has reached imposes constraints on the kinds of problems he can learn to solve, and also the kinds of judgement he makes. (For instance, a young child will judge the wickedness of an act in terms of the damage done and not in terms of the intention behind the act.)

Learning Skills and Techniques

This kind of learning is epitomized by motor skill learning, but some symbolic skills may have similar features. Characteristically, in such a skill, complex movements are made to certain environmental or other stimuli. Often the sequence and timing of the movements are crucial; learning is usually highly dependent on feed-back; and limits to the speed of executing the performance, and on the number of features to which the person can react, are fixed by the "channel capacity" of the nervous system. However, as a result of frequent practice, various parts of the skill may become autonomous, or "self-monitoring". They become automatic and do not occupy the attention of the performer. Bryan and Harter (1899) referred to this phenomenon in terms of "lower order habits" (as a result of their experiments on learning morse); Connolly (Chapter 17) uses the term "sub-routine". Most and perhaps all skills have the characteristic of building on previously learned skills (which have become automatic and "habitual"), so that some psychologists have found it useful to regard skills as having an hierarchical structure. It is certainly the case that skilled performance requires previous learning, and usually previous *over*-learning. One cannot write with a pencil until one has learned to hold it, learned to make marks without tearing the paper, etc., and these previously acquired skills must have become automatic in the sense of not requiring attention.

It is interesting to note that motor skills do not need any symbolic processes. A chimpanzee can learn to drive a motor car. As we have said, feed-back is important in skill learning, but may be less important in some much practised self-monitoring skills. For instance, a pianist may play notes in a determined sequence at such a rate that each movement must be initiated some time before the feed-back from the previous movement has occurred (Lashley, 1951).

Some aspects of language learning, especially written language, resemble skill learning, for instance in the way that sub-routines can be run off. This is also true of some thinking skills, for instance, in mathematical thinking. A symbol representing a process (subtraction, squaring, integration) gradually comes to have meaning and eventually is coped with automatically—much as words come to have meaning and may come to be dealt with automatically (articles, conjuctions, etc.).

Learning to Apply Rules

One can ride a bicycle without being able to say how it is done. We can use language without being able to say how it is done (including the experts). It is possible, however, in some cases to formulate rules which give guidance on performing a technique or skill. For instance, being told how to drive a car may help (though it provides no substitute for the active performance with its attendant feedback). For some techniques, being given a rule (or sometimes a complete algorithm) is of great importance—for instance in learning to solve mathematical problems. (The rule may have been arrived at by the learner himself, but for generalization to occur, it must be applied consciously). Learning and applying rules is completely a human phenomenon. It plays a part in much that goes on during socialization, including learning to behave morally and legally.

Some new mechanisms are involved over and above those needed for learning and executing skills. This can be seen by considering the differences between remembering a skill and remembering instructions for doing the skill. In the former case, there is no important difference between acquisition and retention trials. That is, the performer is faced with more or less the same stimuli and is producing the same responses and has roughly the same intentions as when he *learned* the skill. But when he has to recall the rules, which will have been codified, and translate them into actions, then memory for symbols will be involved (which will be prone to the distortions referred to earlier) and also a mechanism of translating from code to action. In a series of experiments, Belbin (1956) showed that sometimes there is no correlation between recall of instructions and putting them into practice.

Problem Solving

The solving of some complex problems may be regarded as the application of a combination of two of the preceding kinds of learning: categorizing and applying rules. This is true of the learning of problem solving but even more obvious in performance. Faced with a problem to solve, one first decides what kind of problem it is and then applies the appropriate steps for its solution. If the categorization turns out to have been inappropriate, then a second categorization may be made, and so on. Such trial and error performance (which may lead to further learning) may look like exploratory behaviour. If the performer arrives at a categorization in which the route to the solution can be clearly seen, he may be said to show insight.

One aspect of so-called creative thinking is the finding of novel solutions. There are several constraints operating against this. Consider having to complete the sentence "I would very much like . . ." A not-novel solution would be "a coffee". It is determined by three main factors. One's state or set; the task (i.e. having to finish the sentence grammatically); the audience. Techniques specially designed to permit novel solutions attempt to relax the control of one or more of these three, by altering the person's set, by stopping him from being dominated by the task (so that he can try "ungrammatic" solutions), by making him be prepared to try "stupid" or socially unexpected solutions, i.e. to make a fool of himself.

The above examples of typically human "complex processes" are illustrative rather than comprehensive; and they obviously overlap extensively. The extent to which any one occurs may be markedly affected by the degree of development of the others. It remains to be seen to what extent these processes can be reduced to those which are inferred from animal learning and performance.

Since this chapter has been concerned with the problems of comparing man's learning with that of other animals, an additional caution must be made. This is that a man's motivation, tasks and goals, in everyday life and in laboratory experiments, may differ so much from those of other animals that new constraints are bound to arise. It is difficult to know what terminology to use. In everyday language, a man may learn or perform in a certain way because of a need to conform, a need to be different, to please the experimenter, because of jealousy, through altruism, or even just to finish a job.

References

Aronfreed, J. (1969). The problem of imitation. *In* "Advances in Child Development and Behavior", IV. (L. P. Lipsitt and H. W. Reese, eds.). Academic Press, New York.

Bartlett, F. C. (1932). "Remembering." Cambridge Univ. Press, London.

Belbin, E. (1956). The effects of propaganda on recall, recognition and behaviour. *Brit. J. Psychol.* **47**, 163–174; 259–270.

Bryan, W. L. and Harter, N. (1899). Studies in the telegraphic language. The acquisition of a hierarchy of habits. *Psychol. Rev.* **6**, 345–75.

Furth, H. G. (1966). "Thinking without Language." Free Press, New York.

Hall, K. R. L. (1963). Observational learning in monkeys and apes. *Brit. J. Psychol.* **54**, 201–226.

Lashley, K. S. (1951). The problem of serial order in behaviour. *In* "Cerebral Mechanisms in Behavior: The Hixon Symposium", (L. A. Jeffress, ed.). Wiley, New York; Chapman & Hall, London.

Mowrer, O. H. (1960). "Learning Theory and Behavior." Appleton-Century-Crofts, New York.

Lawick-Goodall, J. van *see* Goodall, J. (1965). Chimpanzees of the gombe stream reserve. *In* "Primate Behavior", (I. De Vore, ed.). Holt, Rinehart & Winston, New York.

Comment

W. H. Thorpe wrote:

"I suggest that concept formation is a basic and necessary part of problem solving. One can indeed go further and say that categorization is the most fundamental of all because until the animal has decided on his boundaries—so he can say 'this is not that'—he can do nothing; he can make no progress whatever in organizing his experience. So it seems to me that 'perceptual organization' is the topic which is central to the field. This perceptual organization may of course be largely programmed by the hereditary constitution plus the process of embryonic development; or it may be largely the result of sensory experience.

"Secondly 'learning to apply rules' is surely not the sole prerogative of man. It seems to me that Otto Köhler's (e.g. 1950) work on 'counting' shows, at least in its most highly developed examples, something like the adoption of rules. I think too that experiments in which animals learn to make a choice of 'odd' or 'even', or can be trained to a particular rhythm of occurrence or of action, demonstrate a similar thing."

Foss replied:

"I agree that categorizing is a basic process: but it may depend on other processes too. For instance, some perceptual categories probably develop as a result of the learner's own actions, which may in turn have been influenced by reinforcement."

Reference

Köhler, O. (1950). The ability of birds to 'count'. *Bull. Anim. Behav.* **9**, 41–45.

16

The Multivariate Approach to Early Learning

by H. R. Schaffer

Introduction

The choice of a suitable response index to reflect the effects of experimental manipulation is a problem which every investigator of learning must face. My concern in this paper is the extent to which such a choice determines the conclusions drawn from the experiment—in particular, how far the behaviour system from which the response index is derived will dictate the pattern of results obtained.

The issue has generally been treated as a methodological one, in that the investigator naturally wishes to maximize his chances of obtaining reliable results and picking up the effects of his experimental manipulations. He will thus search for the most sensitive index available and discard all others. Yet also involved is the extent to which the very act of discarding has deprived the investigator of the opportunity of making statements not merely about single behaviour systems but about the total psychological organization of the individual. In psychology there has been a tendency to concentrate on isolated response units, from which generalizations may then be made about the organism as a whole. We examine one particular aspect of behaviour, find learning effects reflected in it, and conclude that "the organism" has learned. Yet the very difference in sensitivity to a given experience of a number of response systems simultaneously assessed may in itself be highly informative, leading to statements about the relationships of the various systems to one another and their role within the total organizational pattern. The research strategy thus called for involves a multivariate approach, in which the focus is not so much on the comparison of the effects of different experiences on any one response but rather on the way in which different responses may reflect any one experience.

To examine this problem I shall refer specifically to the study of learning in the human infant. Due to the infant's limited behavioural repertoire, the problem of finding a response index that can be reliably evoked and objectively measured has loomed large in the investigation of early development. A considerable advance has, however, taken place in recent years in the number of techniques available for this purpose, and many of these have now opened the way to an increased understanding of infant functioning. To appreciate the point, one need only consider the body of data that has come into being as a result of Fantz's (1956) visual preference technique, or enumerate the conclusions arrived at by making use of methods developed to record the sucking responses (see Kessen *et al.*, 1970). Yet the very availability of measurement techniques for numerous functions highlights the need to consider one's choice among them; indeed, in infancy research this may be regarded as a particularly important problem, as our knowledge of the inter-relationships between different response systems is especially limited for this time of life. In so far as the pattern of these relationships may well depend on the differential maturity of the systems involved, differences can be expected according to developmental stage. It thus becomes essential to trace the sequences of these relationships if one is to understand the nature of psychological organization at each stage.

Conditioning Studies

Until recently the learning capacities of the infant have been investigated almost exclusively by means of conditioning techniques. Addressed in the first place to the basic problem: "Is learning possible in infancy?" the data leave no doubt that conditioning can indeed be demonstrated even in the neonatal period.

As several recent reviews (Fitzgerald and Porges, 1971; Lipsitt, 1967; Sameroff, 1971) show, however, such learning is hedged in by a number of constraints. Of particular interest is the contention of Soviet investigators such as Kasatkin (see Brackbill and Koltsova, 1967) that the conditionability of any given response in infants is determined primarily by the modality of the conditional stimulus, and that there exists, moreover, an immutable developmental order for CS effectiveness during the infant's first year. This order (proceeding from the earliest effective to the last) involves the vestibular, auditory, tactile-kinaesthetic, olfactory, gustatory, and visual modalities. To this list Brackbill and Koltsova (1967) have further added temporal and thermal stimuli, to be positioned respectively at the lower and upper ends of the continuum. According to this view, therefore, the nature of the response to be conditioned is immaterial and of the components of the classical conditioning paradigm only the CS serves to predict conditionability.

As Fitzgerald and Porges (1971) point out, however, these propositions have not been borne out by research. A lack of systematic investigations precludes a definite conclusion about the assertion of a developmental order in CS effectiveness. Yet Brackbill and Fitzgerald (1969), reviewing the studies carried out in their own laboratory which have applied auditory, tactile, and temporal stimuli to infants in the first few months of life, consider it unlikely that any immutable developmental sequence can be demonstrated. In any case the likelihood of such a progression is weakened by the finding that conditioning does not depend merely on the nature of the CS but also on the nature of the response, with particular reference to its source of nervous system innervation (autonomic or somatic). Auditory and tactile CS's, for instance, have been used successfully to condition such somatic responses as the eyeblink and sucking, yet have failed in the case of autonomically mediated responses like pupillary change. Temporal CS's, on the other hand, have been found to be effective with autonomic but not with somatic responses. It is, in other words, not correct to assert that the outcome of conditioning is predictable on the basis of CS modality alone; the response must also be taken into account. To determine, therefore, which stimuli interact with which responses at specified age points to produce successful conditioning is a task which still requires a considerable amount of parametric work, and not till this is accomplished can a reasonably complete picture of infant conditionability emerge.

Habituation as a Learning Process

In recent years another procedure for the investigation of early learning capacity has come to be employed. This involves a habituation paradigm, i.e. the response decrement that is observed to repeated stimulation when receptor adaptation or effector fatigue are ruled out. Such a procedure, it has been suggested (Kessen *et al*, 1970; Lewis, 1971; Jeffrey and Cohen, 1971), provides one with a useful tool for the study of infants' retentive abilities and enables one to investigate the nature and limits of their information storage capacity. The repeated stimulation, it is argued, leads to something akin to a neuronal model (Sokolov, 1963), with which the stimulus on its next presentation is then compared. When stimulus and central representation are found to match, a decrease in the orienting response occurs, resulting in progressively greater decrements of attention in the course of a trial series. A novel stimulus (preferably weaker in intensity than the original one), when introduced later on in the series and found not to match the model, should then lead to dishabituation and thereby act also as a check for receptor fatigue. Habituation is thus taken to reflect the existence of some form of capactity to retain experience, in that the orienting response facilitates perceptual learning but will diminish upon the acquisition of the learning experience. As such, habituation may well be one of the earliest forms of learning to be found in human development.

The majority of studies employing this paradigm have been based on the assessment of a single reponse, and for this purpose visual fixation has been most frequently employed, yielding measures such as the total amount of fixation, the length of the first fixation, and the number of fixations on each trial. The pattern of findings from these investigations gives considerable support to the belief that a learning process is implicated.

An example is the demonstration that the ability of infants to carry forward information from one trial to the next varies with the length of the inter-trial interval, in that procedures using brief intervals produce response decrement whereas longer intervals result in failure to habituate. Thus Lewis (1969) presented a visual stimulus in a series of 30-second trials to 12-week-old infants and found that both an 0-second and a 5-second interval produced response decrement but not a 15-second interval. "It appears," he concluded, "that response decrement may be related to short-term memory." It also appears, however, that the infant's capacity in this respect increases with age: Pancratz and Cohen (1970) found that 4-month-old male infants did differentiate between a novel and a familiar stimulus after a 15-second interval following familiarization; they did not show this differentiation, however, after a 5-minute interval. Another variable which has been found to affect response decrement is the complexity of the stimulus: Caron and Caron (1968) exposed 2 × 2, 12 × 12, and 24 × 24-square checkerboards to 3½-month-old infants and found more rapid habituation of visual fixation to the simpler patterns. In a study by Ames (1966) infants aged 5 weeks habituated more rapidly to a 2 × 2 than to an 8 × 8 checkerboard, while 11-week-old infants habituated more rapidly to an 8 × 8 than to a 24 × 24 checkerboard.

Of particular interest is the suggestion that, for any given procedure and stimulus, the rate of response decrement to repeated stimulation is a direct function of age. Thus Fantz (1964) presented infants in the age range one to six months with ten pairs of visual patterns, keeping one pattern constant throughout but pairing it with a novel stimulus on each trial. His findings show that the percentage of total fixation to the two stimuli that was devoted to the constant pattern decreased most sharply within the trial series for the oldest of the four age groups examined (4–6 months), whereas no decrement occurred for the youngest group (1–2 months). The older infants, that is, were able to recognize the constant stimulus as familiar and thus appeared capable of successfully spanning the time gaps between presentations; the younger infants, on the other hand, behaved as though they were unable to carry any information forward from one trial to the next and thus treated the reappearance of the constant stimulus as though it were a new event each time.

A number of experiments by Lewis (1969) suggest a similar relationship between response decrement and age. In one study, infants between 2 and 18 months were exposed to a blinking light for four half-minute periods, with half-minute inter-trial intervals. Habituation in the amount of visual fixation was found to be a direct function of age, with younger infants showing less decrement than older infants. This was confirmed by a second study using the same procedure but employing a longitudinal design for the age range 3 to 13 months: an almost perfect ordering between response decrement and age was thereby revealed. A further study extending the age range to 44 months showed, however, that response decrement tends to reach its maximum by 13–18 months.

In view of this age-dependent relationship, Lewis (1969, 1971) has suggested that a measure of a characteristic he terms "cognitive efficiency" may be provided by decremental rate, and quotes a number of lines of evidence in support. For one thing, infants with an Apgar score of 10 at birth (indicating perfect physical condition) were found subsequently to display a significantly greater response decrement in visual attention than infants with lower Apgar ratings. For another, socioeconomic status (known to correlate with intellectual ability) was found to be related to decremental rate, this being greater in infants from upper than from lower class families. Again, a relationship was found in 44-month-old children between decremental rate and success both in a concept formation task and a discrimination learning situation. In another study it was found that the pattern of mothering—specifically, the contingency with which the mother provided stimulation—bore a relationship to response decrement to repeated visual stimulation. And finally, a comparison of response decrement at one year and IQ scores at $3\frac{1}{2}$ years revealed a significant positive relationship between these two measures.

These data seem to indicate that the primitive memory capacity assessed by the habituation procedure is not present in the early weeks of life, that it gradually develops thereafter, and that individual differences in this respect are meaningfully related to a number of antecedent and consequent variables. There are, however, some reservations that must be borne in mind. For one thing, Hinde (1970) has pointed out that differences in methods of assessing decrement can lead to opposite conclusions, and such methodological considerations must clearly be taken into account when comparing different studies. Furthermore, at an empirical level, it may be noted that Schaffer *et al.* (1972), in a longitudinal study to which we shall refer in greater detail below, obtained response decrement of visual fixation at each one of four-weekly tests administered between 6 and 12 months of age. The rate of decrement, however, *decreased* over age when based on the length of the first fixation; total fixation showed little decremental change within this age range. Data given by Kagan (1971) on the first fixation scores by several groups of infants seen at both 4 months and 8 months of age also indicate that the greatest decrement in the course of a 16-trial procedure occurred at the *earlier* age. The relationship between decremental rate and age may thus be more complex than was first thought; one possibility is that the relationship holds for the first half-year of life but that subsequently other variables begin to over-ride this effect.

Some doubt exists, moreover, about the absence of habituation effects in the earliest weeks of life. Friedman *et al.* (1970), for example, claim to have obtained response decrement to visual stimuli as early as the neonatal period. As their procedure did not, however, include checks for fatigue effects, one may well wonder whether the suggestion by Hutt *et al.* (1968), that neonatal habituation in any form is unlikely to be a genuine phenomenon and that the changes in responsiveness so labelled are in fact a function of changes in arousal state, may be applicable to this study. Moreover, as the findings stem from an inexplicable inter-action of stimulus complexity and subjects' sex and do not indicate habituation under all experimental conditions, it is as well to view with some scepticism the authors' conclusion that their results suggest the existence of temporary storage capacity soon after birth.

Nevertheless, neonatal habituation has been reported by other investigators too. Bronshtein and Petrova (1967), for example, found suppression of the sucking response to occur to an auditory stimulus but observed the response to recover after a number of repetitions of the stimulus. Bridger (1961) noted that both startle and heart rate acceleration appeared to habituate to an auditory stimulus. And Engen *et al.* (1963), in an experiment of neonates' responses to olfactory stimuli in which respiration, bodily movement, and heart rate were recorded, obtained response decrement to two of the stimulus substances they used but not to the other two. Once again the possibility of state changes being responsible for these findings cannot be ruled out; it is, however, also significant that the studies just mentioned were all concerned with responses other than visual fixation (and, for that matter, stimuli not presented in the visual modality). The possibility that some response systems may be sensitive to learning effects earlier than others must therefore be considered.

The Use of Multiple Response Indices

The results of a number of investigations which enable one to compare the effects of repeated stimulation on several response systems are now available. The use of multiple response indices has been advocated for a variety of reasons. Kagan *et al.* (1966), for instance, argue that most overt behaviours are ambiguous in meaning, in that a single act may serve more than one need or motive and can be elicited by more than one class of stimuli. Thus prolonged visual fixation may express either an affective "liking" of a familiar stimulus pattern or the individual's efforts to assimilate a strange experience. Without additional information from other response modes one is in no position to determine which of these is eliciting the sustained attention. The measurement of other responses, occurring contiguously with fixation, is thus called for. Inferences about psychological development should not rest on single behavioural assessments but on a sensitive combination of response patterns. And in a subsequent report Kagan (1971) suggests that by recording, say, fixation, vocalization, cardiac deceleration, and smiling, one can obtain four different views of the same attentional process, though each of these reactions may mirror different aspects of this phenomenon with a different degree of fidelity. Similarly Lewis (1967) points out that, by moving merely from the investigation of one response to another, we shall find that the sum of all these investigations of single responses cannot provide us with an accurate picture of the infant as a psychological organism. It is only through the contextual study of responses and their interactions that infant behaviour can be understood.

In a study of habituation in neonates, Moreau *et al.* (1970) adopted such a strategy. These workers compared the effects of two types of stimulation (auditory and somesthetic) on two responses, namely heart rate change and ipsilateral conjugate eye movement. Their rationale for this procedure was to investigate whether habituation is a characteristic of the input system *per se* or whether it is dependent upon particular constellations of input-output relationships. "If habituation were a general phenomenon, we would anticipate that all components of the infant's responsiveness to repeated presentations of the same stimulus would exhibit parallel decay courses, whereas if habituation were specific to given stimulus-response constellations rather than to stimulus processing alone, we would anticipate a different course of decay for different responses." Their results conclusively support the latter alternative: the habituation rates of the two responses differ for both auditory and somesthetic stimulation. "Therefore, changes in the frequency of occurrence of the two types of response cannot be considered as resulting from general and ubiquitous

Y

changes in the infant's 'responsiveness' to stimulation. . . . Habituation, rather than being a unitary phenomenon which affects all response-systems that are activated by a given stimulus, is specific to the particular stimulus-response conjunction examined. The specificity of effect further suggests that different mechanisms may underlie the decrease in frequency with which a stimulus evokes different types of response and cause one to question the validity of the frequently utilized concepts of generalized habituation, generalized responsiveness, and generalized arousal." Again, incidentally, we may note a claim for the existence of neonatal habituation.

If there are indeed differences in habituation rates among different responses, it would be instructive to determine whether such differences would be one way of clarifying the pattern of relationships that prevails show systematic variation from one developmental stage to the next. This among behaviour systems in the course of early development and of providing information about varying sensitivities to learning experiences and the extent to which learning may be regarded as a generalized or specific phenomenon at each stage. Unfortunately the evidence required to spell out the details of this pattern is still sparse and often unclear. Take the two responses that have been most commonly studied in conjunction with one another, namely visual fixation and heart rate. Heart rate changes (accelerative or decelerative) have frequently been described as bearing some form of relationship to an organism's information processing skills: Lacey (1967), for example, has suggested that cardiac deceleration is to be regarded as a biologically adaptive reaction whereby the individual increases his receptivity to external stimuli, and in similar vein Graham and Clifton (1966) consider the deceleration response to be a major component of an orienting reflex—as opposed to cardiac acceleration which is said to be part of a startle-defensive reflex. Although Woodcock (1971) has recently warned investigators of infant behaviour of the potential methodological dangers involved in this measure, its applicability to a wide variety of experimental conditions has tempted many into its use.

In response to repeated stimulation, heart rate changes appear to show some of the same age-related characteristics as visual fixation. In the neonatal period (when acceleration rather than deceleration takes place to stimulation), little habituation of the cardiac response is found that cannot be accounted for by state changes (Graham et al., 1968); by 4 months of age, on the other hand, Clifton and Meyers (1969) observed decrement of cardiac deceleration in the course of familiarization with an auditory stimulus, followed by recovery to a novel stimulus. Yet when one turns to studies that have recorded both visual fixation and heart rate simultaneously in the course of repeated stimulation, a confusing picture emerges. In an investigation of 24-week-old infants, Kagan and Lewis (1965) observed response decrement to occur in the course of repeated exposures of complex visual patterns with regard to both visual fixation and cardiac deceleration; the same infants showed a sharp decrement in fixation scores to a single blinking light during four trials but a very much less marked reduction in cardiac deceleration. In two further studies (McCall and Kagan, 1969; Kagan, 1971) visual fixation declined over trials and recovered to a new stimulus, yet cardiac deceleration showed no systematic variation at any age group between 4 and 13 months. On the other hand, both Meyers and Cantor (1966) and McCall and Melson (1970) obtained just the opposite picture, i.e. no change over trials for visual fixation but habituation of the heart rate response. The pattern of findings is complicated still further by another study by Meyers and Cantor (1967), in which 6-month-old infants were given sixteen 7-second trials with a visual stimulus, followed by a test phase of 8 simultaneous presentations of the familiarized and a novel stimulus. Neither heart rate nor visual fixation showed changes during the initial period (though the brevity of the trials may well account for this); in the test phase male but not female subjects showed a differential response to the unfamiliar as opposed to the familiar stimulus, whereas visual fixation times failed to differ significantly for the two stimuli in both sexes.

A number of studies have examined the sensitivity with which the two kinds of measures reflect varying degrees of stimulus discrepancy after familiarization on a standard. McCall and Kagan (1967), working with 4-month-old infants, found that there was no relationship between amount of recovery of visual fixation and the degree of discrepancy in either boys or girls; the magnitude of dishabituation for cardiac deceleration, on the other hand, was directly related to discrepancy for girls, but not for boys. In a study by McCall and Melson (1969), in which 5-month-old boys were familiarized on a standard visual stimulus and then tested on three degrees of discrepancies, the amount of cardiac deceleration was found to reflect faithfully the difference between the novel and the familiar stimulus; visual fixation did not, however, show this relationship.

It is difficult to bring order to these diverse findings, especially as they are influenced by numerous procedural variables which tend to differ from study to study: variables relating to the nature of the stimuli used, the familiarization technique, and the methods of measuring the infant's response. Whether the patterns of sex differences reported by some workers reflect true variation remains to be established: until confirmation is obtained one must at least entertain the possibility that such differences merely indicate a replication failure. But it does seem apparent that no general pattern emerges in the interrelationship of visual fixation and heart rate changes to repeated stimulation. What is more, when one turns to those studies which have also simultaneously obtained data on such other functions as vocalizing, smiling, and activity, a similar confused picture emerges. As Kagan (1971), at the conclusion of a longitudinal study based on a number of such variables, has put it: "Despite years of serious efforts the relationship of each of these variables to each other and to cognitive process is still ambiguous."

Nevertheless, some suggestions have been put forward to explain the reasons for this ambiguity. McCall (1969), for example, has raised the possibility that individual differences in reaction pattern may obscure more general trends: thus some infants may not display their acquisition of an engram or response to discrepancy in terms of the same response measure as others. It may even be that some subjects react to repeated presentations of a stimulus with one response and to the introduction of a discrepant stimulus with another. Such an interpretation should not be difficult to check with a multivariate approach.

The possibility that autonomic and behavioural measures are differentially sensitive to learning effects has already been raised in relation to conditioning work; it has also been considered in relation to habituation by Meyers and Cantor (1967). In the light of their findings, heart rate must presumably be regarded as more sensitive than visual fixation; as we have just seen, however, not all studies conform to this pattern. On the other hand, there is some evidence that the nature of the response used to index habituation may interact with the modality of the stimulus. The study by Moreau et al. (1970), already referred to, is one example of this possibility. Similarly, Melson and McCall (1970) are driven to conclude that their data for the habituation of fixation and cardiac responses to both visual and auditory stimuli indicates that the acquisition of a central representation for a stimulus may perhaps be more faithfully conveyed by the habituation of different responses for different stimuli. As mentioned previously, students of conditioning have also been led to the conclusion that it is necessary to take into account particular stimulus-response combinations in order to arrive at valid statements about the learning capacities of infants.

Despite the confusing findings reported so far, the notion that differences exist among various response systems in their sensitivity to particular learning experiences and that these differences show orderly changes with age during infancy, remains an attractive one. With regard to two behavioural systems at any rate this notion has now been borne out.

Eye, Hand and Memory

In a series of studies we have recently attempted to explore the inter-relationships of visual fixation, manipulative behaviour, and memory. Specifically, our concern has been to understand the way in which visual and manipulative responses vary to familiar and novel stimuli, and for this purpose we adopted a habituation paradigm, in that we experimentally familiarized infants in a series of trials on one stimulus, then confronted them with an incongruous stimulus, and all along took simultaneous measures of visual and manipulative behaviour.

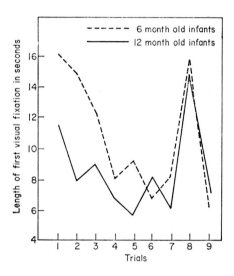

Fig. 1. Length of first visual fixation per trial for six-month-old and twelve-month-old infants. (Schaffer and Parry, 1969).

In our first, and basic, experiment (Schaffer and Parry, 1969), two groups of infants aged 6 and 12 months respectively were presented with a three-dimensional "nonsense" stimulus (a multi-coloured, tapering form seven inches high) in a series of seven 30-second familiarization trials, with 30-second inter-trial intervals. On the eighth trial another (differently coloured) stimulus was substituted, and on the ninth trial the first stimulus was brought back again. As is evident from Fig. 1, visual fixation (as indexed by the length of the first visual fixation) showed marked sensitivity to the familiarization procedure, in that it dropped during the initial seven trials, recovered with the introduction of the new stimulus, and decreased once again on the reappearance of the familiar stimulus. Both age groups showed this pattern. Manipulative measures, on the other hand, provide a different picture (Fig. 2). In the older group latency to contact was also found to be differentially influenced by variations in familiarity, in that relatively prolonged hesitation to approach the initial stimulus gave way to an increasingly greater readiness to make contact as the object became more familiar. It is, however, interesting to note that the second object produced only a slight increase in latency. A very different picture is found in the younger group. Here no sensitivity to variations along the familiarity-unfamiliarity continuum are reflected in the manipulative measure: despite the apparent ability perceptually to categorize the

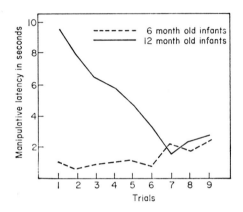

Fig. 2. Manipulative latency per trial for six-month-old and twelve-month-old infants. (Schaffer and Parry, 1969).

stimulus as familiar or strange, the six-month-old infants were indiscriminate in their approach behaviour. Thus they recognized the stimulus as strange on its first encounter yet made contact with it as immediately as after a period of familiarization.

We have been able to confirm this general pattern in other studies. In one, for example, the identical procedure as that for the first experiment was applied longitudinally, in that a group of 20 infants was followed up from 6 to 12 months of age and seen at four-weekly intervals during this period (Schaffer *et al.*, 1972). The results (see Fig. 3) confirm the presence of an indiscriminate approach tendency at the younger age levels—a tendency that was evident until approximately 8 months, after which it was replaced by selective approach-avoidance behaviour. Thus at later ages the unfamiliar stimulus gave rise to differential manipulative as well as visual behaviour, suggesting that manipulation had now also come under

the control of stored experience. From that age on the infants
capable of "wariness"—a term we prefer to avoidance or fear, in
crucial characteristic of the new development appears to relate to the
onset of the ability to check impulsive approach responses and thus
appraise the stimulus first and then select a response (approach *or* avoidance) deemed suitable in terms of the individual's past experience of that
stimulus as well as his present perception of the situation.

The failure of perceptual recognition to control manipulative behaviour at the beginning of the second half-year has also been demonstrated in a simultaneous discrimination situation (Schaffer and Parry,

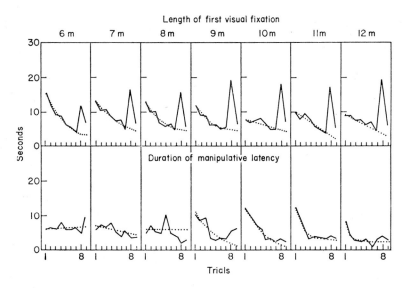

Fig. 3. First visual fixation and manipulative latency data obtained at monthly
intervals between 6 and 12 months of age (the broken lines represent regression
curves based on the observed data obtained on the first seven trials). (Schaffer,
Greenwood and Parry, 1972).

1970), in which infants of 5–7 months were found to be incapable of
distinguishing manipulatively between a novel and a familiar stimulus,
despite being able to make discrimination visually. Co-ordination between
the two functions appeared only in an older age group (8–10 months). Yet
it has also been demonstrated (Schaffer, 1971a) that when two stimuli
differ in terms of their perceptual salience rather than their familiarity,
even the younger infants are able to pay selective manipulative attention.
The absence of such selective behaviour at this age refers thus only to those

situations where the crucial distinguishing feature among stimuli concerns the infant's previous experience of them (Schaffer, 1971b).

Once an infant becomes capable of selective approach-avoidance behaviour to familiar and unfamiliar stimuli, its nature is likely to be determined by a large number of conditions. It has, for instance, been shown that an approaching stimulus will elicit greater wariness on its first appearance than either a stationary or a sideways moving stimulus (Schaffer and Parry, 1972). Even the familiarity of the environment in which the experiment takes place (the infant's home as opposed to a mobile laboratory) will exert an influence (Parry, 1972). It has also been shown (Parry, in preparation) that manipulative latency to the second (incongruous) stimulus introduced after familiarization on another stimulus can be raised by varying the degree of incongruity. It is thus possible to establish gradients of selective manipulative behaviour, though there are indications that these differ in steepness compared with those for visual behaviour.

It appears from these studies that in vision and manipulation we are confronted by two functions which do show a systematic inter-relationship over age. It is a relationship which involves their sensitivity to the effects of stored experience: in one case, from a very early age on, the amount of visual fixation is governed by the extent of the individual's previous experience of that stimulus; in the other case the infant behaves indiscriminately in relation to variations along the familiarity continuum from the time that he first becomes manipulatively capable (at 4–5 months of age) until well on into the second half year of life. A disjunctive effect is thus manifested; the infant "knows" the object is strange yet fails to display the wariness that the older infant will show towards unfamiliar objects. For the time being, action is shielded from the effects of memory in this situation, even though memory can shape the course of visual behaviour. Integration between eye, hand and memory in the infant's response to strange objects becomes a possibility only from approximately 8 months onward.

It is significant that some of these issues arise also from the findings of another recently completed study (Millar and Schaffer, in press), involving this time an operant conditioning situation. In this investigation three groups of infants, aged 6, 9 and 12 months respectively, were exposed to three conditions of spatial displacement of feedback source and manipulation. In the 0° condition, feedback in the form of a brief light and bleep was provided by the manipulandum itself—a cylindrical canister right in front of the infant and within easy reach. Two other identical canisters were fixed out of reach at equal distances from the infant but at 5° and 60° rotation respectively about a line extending from the infant through the manipulandum. In the 5° and in the 60° conditions feedback

was provided respectively by these displaced canisters each time the manipulandum was touched. The procedure consisted of three phases: a one-
minute baseline period, a three-minute conditioning phase (during which
feedback, from the appropriate source, was provided contingent upon
touching the manipulandum), and a three-minute extinction phase. Non-
contingent stimulation was provided to a control group at each age level.

The results, measured in terms of number of discrete manipulations and
illustrated in Fig. 4, indicate that the two older groups demonstrated reliable response acquisition under all three conditions of spatial displacement. The youngest group on the other hand, was able to learn under
the 0° and 5° conditions; yet completely failed to demonstrate any learning under the 60° condition.

It is relevant to our present discussion that, in order to explain these
results, it becomes necessary to go beyond the single response recorded
here, namely manipulation, to another response, i.e. visual behaviour. It is
apparent that the explanation cannot be in terms of spatial discontiguity
per se, for even the youngest infants had no difficulty in coping with the 5°
task, despite the spatial separation of manipulandum and feedback source.
In the 60° condition the two canisters were no further away than in the 5°
condition; what did differentiate the tasks, however, was the relative *visual*
accessibility of the canisters. In the 5° condition manipulandum and feedback source were so close within the infant's visual field that almost simultaneous attention could be paid to them; in the 60° condition, on the other
hand, the extent of displacement was such that an infant, while focusing
on one canister, would no longer directly perceive the other. To solve the
problem, in other words, meant that the subject had to keep in mind a
stimulus that was no longer in his visual field. Incidental observations
made in the course of the study suggest that the older infants successfully
accomplished this task—generally by adopting a strategy of visually
fixating the source of reinforcement and at the same time repeatedly
touching the manipulandum without, however, requiring to attend visually to the latter. This feat the younger infants could not accomplish: they
appeared to be unable systematically to manipulate an object that they
were not directly fixating in order to create a simultaneous visual effect
elsewhere. For them out of sight was out of mind.

We are at present attempting to confirm this interpretation by recording
not only manipulative but also visual responses to the canisters. Preliminary observations, recorded on video tape, support the suggestion that
the learning behaviour of the younger infants (i.e. those around 6 months
of age) breaks down when the task demands that remembered rather than
visually present events control manipulative behaviour. The auditory component of the feedback generally ensures that the subjects at once notice

the reinforcement even at the 60° location, but having fixated it they then appear to become oblivious to the now no longer visually present manipulandum. Events, that is, must be experienced simultaneously at this age if they are to be related to one another, and only after approximately 8 months can an infant hold an event in mind and relate it to an ongoing

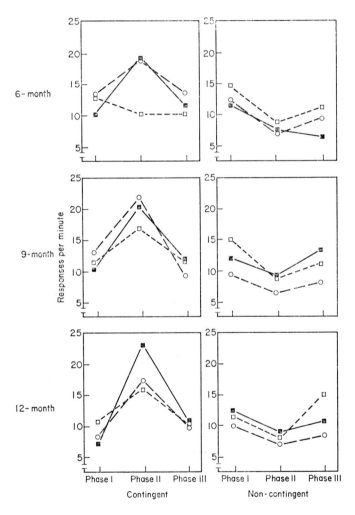

Fig. 4. Mean manipulative responses per minute for 3 age groups under contingent and non-contingent stimulation, presented at 0°——, 5°— —, 60°- - - - spatial displacement, for baseline (Phase I), conditioning (Phase II), and extinction (Phase III). (Millar and Schaffer, in press).

experience. Once again, the consideration of both eye and hand provides a fuller picture of infant functioning than the investigation of either alone.

Conclusions

There are indications that early learning is specific to particular response systems. The evidence, it is true, is not as unequivocal as one would like: nevertheless, the example of visual and manipulative responsiveness does suggest that one must exercise caution in extrapolating from one behaviour system to another. The notion that there is total organismic involvement in the learning of infants certainly cannot be taken for granted: each response must, rather, be examined in its own right. A multivariate approach is thus called for, and when this is applied across the age range it provides the opportunity to uncover lawful developmental changes in the interrelationships of different behaviour patterns. In the case of vision and manipulation at any rate one finds an indication that, with increasing age, a greater degree of coherence among responses may thus be uncovered, in that the extent to which the various response systems are affected by previous experience begins to show a symmetry which was previously lacking.

There is little point in adopting a multivariate approach if results from the different response measures are then merely reported under separate headings and no attempt made to relate them to one another. Indeed the motive of choosing a number of measures may, in the first place, stem simply from a desire to maximize one's chances of obtaining significant results. The learning capacities of the individual will then be assessed solely in terms of those measures that show some degree of sensitivity, the remainder being discarded as uninformative and irrelevant. Yet this goes against the essential spirit of the multivariate approach, which should aim to arrive at statements about the total organizational pattern of psychological functions and according to which differences in sensitivity among response measures should therefore assume central importance. To establish the existence of such lawful differences over age is thus the primary task; to explain them becomes a further problem to which attention will have to be given.

References

Ames, E. W. (1966). Stimulus complexity and age of infants as determinants of the rate of habituation of visual fixation. Paper presented at the meeting of the Western Psychological Society, Long Beach, California, 1966.

Brackbill, T. and Koltsova, M. M. (1967). Conditioning and learning. *In* "Infancy and Early Childhood", (Y. Brackbill, ed.). Free Press, New York.

Brackbill Y. and Fitzgerald, H. E. (1969). Development of the sensory analysers during infancy. *In* "Advances in Child Development and Behaviour", Vol. 4, (L. P. Lipsitt and H. W. Reese, eds.). Academic Press, New York.

Bridger, W. H. (1961). Sensory habituation and discrimination in the human neonate. *Amer. J. Psychiat.* **117**, 991–996.

Bronshtein, A. I. and Petrova, E. P. (1967). The auditory analyser in young infants. *In* "Behaviour in Infancy and Early Childhood", (Y. Brackbill and G. G. Thompson, eds.). Free Press, New York.

Caron, R. F. and Caron, A. J. (1968). The effects of repeated exposure and stimulus complexity on visual fixation in infants. *Psychon. Sci.* **10**, 207–208.

Clifton, R. K. and Meyers, W. J. (1969). The heart rate response of four-month-old infants to auditory stimuli. *J. exp. Child Psychol.* **7**, 122–135.

Engen, T., Lipsitt, L. P. and Kaye, H. (1963). Olfactory responses and adaptation in the human neonate. *J. comp. physiol. Psychol.* **56**, 73–77.

Fantz, R. L. (1956). A method of studying early visual development. *Percept. mot. Skills* **6**, 13–15.

Fantz, R. L. (1964). Visual experience in infants: decreased attention to familiar patterns relative to novel ones. *Science* **146**, 668–670.

Fitzgerald, H. E. and Porges, S. W. (1971). A decade of infant conditioning and learning research. *Merrill-Palmer Quart.* **17**, 79–117.

Friedman, S., Nagy, A. N. and Carpenter, G. C. (1970). Newborn attention: differential decrement to visual stimuli. *J. exper. Child Psychol.* **10**, 44–51.

Graham, F. K. and Clifton, R. K. (1966). Heart rate change as a component of the orienting response. *Psychol. Bull.* **65**, 305–320.

Graham, F. K., Clifton, R. K. and Hatton, H. M. (1968). Habituation of heart rate response to repeated auditory stimulation during the first five days of life. *Child Develop.* **39**, 35–52.

Hinde, R. A. (1970). Behavioural habituation. *In* "Short-term Changes in Neural Activity and Behaviour", (G. Horn, and R. A. Hinde, eds.). Cambridge University Press, Cambridge.

Hutt, C., von Bernuth, H., Lenard, H. G., Hutt, S. J. and Prechtl, H. F. R. (1968). Habituation in relation to state in the human neonate. *Nature* **220**, 618–620.

Jeffrey, W. E. and Cohen, L. B. (1971). Habituation in the human infant. *In* "Advances in Child Development and Behaviour", Vol. 6, (H. W. Reese, ed.). Academic Press, New York.

Kagan, J. (1971). "Change and Continuity in Infancy." Wiley, New York.

Kagan, J., Henker, B. A., Hen-Tov, A., Levine, J. and Lewis, M. (1966). Infants' differential reactions to familiar and distorted faces. *Child Develop.* **37**, 519–532.

Kagan, J. and Lewis, M. (1965). Studies of attention in the human infant. *Merrill-Palmer Quart.* **11**, 95–127.

Kessen, W., Haith, M. M. and Salapatek, P. H. (1970). Human infancy: a bibliography and guide. *In* "Manual of Child Psychology", (P. H. Mussen, ed.). Wiley, New York.

Lacey, J. I. (1967). Somatic response patterning in stress: some revisions of activation theory. *In* "Psychological Stress: Issues in Research", (M. H. Appley and R. Trumbull, eds.). Appleton-Century-Crofts, New York.

Lewis, M. (1967). The meaning of a response, or why researchers in infant behaviour should be oriental metaphysicians. *Merrill-Palmer Quart.* **13**, 7–18.

Lewis, M. (1969). A developmental study of information processing within the first three years of life: response decrement to a redundant signal. *Monogr. Soc. Res. Child. Develop.* **34**, No. 9, (serial No. 133).

Lewis, M. (1971). Individual differences in the measurement of early cognitive growth. *In* "Exceptional Infant", Vol. 2, (J. Hellmuth, ed.). Brunner-Mazel, New York.

Lipsitt, L. P. (1967). Learning in the human infant. *In* "Early Behaviour: Comparative and Developmental Approaches", (H. W. Stevenson, H. L. Reingold, and E. H. Hess, eds.). Wiley, New York.

McCall, R. B. (1969). Magnitude of discrepancy and habituation rate as governors of the attention response of infants to new stimuli. Paper presented at meeting of Society for Research in Child Development, Los Angeles, 1969.

McCall, R. B. and Kagan, J. (1967). Stimulus-schema discrepancy and attention in the infant. *J. exp. Child Psychol.* **5**, 381–390.

McCall, R. B. and Kagan, J. (1969). Individual differences in the infant's distribution of attention to stimulus discrepancy. *Develop. Psychol.* **2**, 90–98.

McCall, R. B. and Melson, W. H. (1969). Attention in infants as a function of magnitude of discrepancy and habituation rate. *Psychon. Sci.* **17**, 317–319.

McCall, R. B. and Melson, W. H. (1970). Complexity, contour and area as determinants of attention in infants. *Develop. Psychol.* **3**, 343–349.

Melson, W. H. and McCall, R. B. (1970). Attentional responses in five-month-old girls to discrepant auditory stimuli. *Child Develop.* **41**, 1159–1171.

Meyers, W. J. and Cantor, G. N. (1966). Infants' observing and heart period responses as related to novelty of visual stimuli. *Psychon. Sci.* **5**, 239–240.

Meyers, W. J. and Cantor, G. N. (1967). Observing and cardiac responses of human infants to visual stimuli. *J. exp. Child Psychol.* **5**, 1–15.

Millar, W. S. and Schaffer, H. R. (In press). The influence of spatially displaced feedback on infant operant conditioning. *J. exp. Child Psychol.*

Moreau, T., Birch, H. G. and Turketwitz, G. (1970). Ease of habituation to repeated auditory and somesthetic stimulation in the human new-born. *J. exp. Child Psychol.* **9**, 193–207.

Pancratz, N. and Cohen, L. B. (1970). Recovery of habituation in infants. *J. exper. Child Psychol.* **9**, 208–216.

Parry, M. H. (1972). Infants' responses to novelty in familiar and unfamiliar settings. *Child Develop.* **43**, 233–237.

Sameroff, A. J. (1971). Can conditioned responses be established in the new-born infant? *Develop. Psychol.* **5**, 1–12.

Schaffer, H. R. (1971a). Cognitive structure and early social behaviour. *In* "The Origins of Human Social Relations". (H. R. Schaffer, ed.). Academic Press, London.

Schaffer, H. R. (1971b). "The Growth of Sociability". Harmondsworth: Penguin Books.

Schaffer, H. R., Greenwood, A. and Parry, M. H. (1972). The onset of wariness. *Child Develop.* **43**, 165–175.

Schaffer, H. R. and Parry, M. H. (1969). Perceptual-motor behaviour in infancy as a function of age and stimulus familiarity. *Brit. J. Psychol.* **60**, 1–9.

Schaffer, H. R. and Parry, M. H. (1970). The effects of short-term familiarization on infants' perceptual-motor co-ordination in a simultaneous discrimination situation. *Brit. J. Psychol.* **61**, 559–569.

Schaffer, H. R. and Parry, M. H. (1972). Effects of stimulus movement on infants' wariness of unfamiliar objects. *Develop. Psychol,* 7, 87.

Sokolov, Y. N. (1963). "Perception and the Conditioned Reflex." MacMillan, New York.

Woodcock, J. M. (1971). Terminology and methodology related to the use of heart rate responsivity in infancy research. *J. exp. Child. Psychol.* **11**, 76–92.

Comments

1. Hutt raised the possibility that the late appearance of the inhibition of grasping could be related to late myelinization of the inhibitory mechanisms. This general issue is considered in his Chapter 23).

2. Bryant asked whether the novel object had ever been novel in shape, since a colour change is only a visual and not a tactual change.

3. Bryant mentioned that the disappearance of the effects of habituation with time could be due to loss of memory or could be due to dishabituation.

4. Schaffer shows that different responses of human infants elicited by the same stimulus may wane at different rates, the differences between the rates changing with age. In particular, visual fixation was found to be governed by previous experience of the stimulus from an early age, while (under the conditions used) manipulation of the same stimulus object was independent of experience. Schaffer comments that "the infant 'knows' the object is strange yet fails to display the wariness that the older infant will show towards unfamiliar objects". This is of course in keeping with the gradual development of fear responses over this age range (e.g. Bronson, 1968). However it is worth noting that differences between the habituation rates of different responses to the same stimulus are also well known in adult animals. For instance, the initial orientation of hunting spiders (Salticidae) towards prey wanes far less rapidly than does approaching or jumping (Precht and Freytag, 1958); and the hunting activities of cats that come early in the sequence wane less rapidly than those that come later (Leyhausen, 1965). Similarly the orientation response to withdrawal-producing stimuli wanes less rapidly than does the withdrawal response itself (e.g. Rodgers, Melzack and Segal, 1963). In these cases the differences could perhaps be related to threshold differences between the several activities: as habituation lowers the effectiveness of the stimulus, high threshold activities would be expected to drop out sooner than ones of lower threshold. Similar threshold differences between different responses to the same stimulus could form a basis for some of the differences in habituation rates found in infants.

References

Bronson, G. W. (1968). The development of fear in man and other animals. *Child Devel.* **39**, 409–430.

Leyhausen, P. (1965). Uber die Funktion der relativen Stimmungshierarchie. *Z. Tierpsychol.* **22**, 412–494.

Precht, H. and Freytag, G. (1958). Uber Ermüdung und Hemmung angeborener Verhaltensweisen bei Springspinnen (Salticidae). Zugleich ein Beitrag zum Triebproblem. *Behaviour.* **13**, 143–211.

Rodgers, W. L., Melzack, R. and Segal, J. R. (1963). "Tail flip response" in goldfish. *J. comp. physiol. Psychol.* **56**, 917–923.

17

Factors Influencing the Learning of Manual Skills by Young Children

by Kevin Connolly

Introduction: The Nature of Skill

"Skill" covers a wide range of performances such as perceptual-motor skills, gross bodily movements, dextrous manipulations, speech production and problem solving. In all of these activities the skilled performer exhibits a greater efficiency in the execution of specific responses and also a greater flexibility in meeting environmental contingencies as they arise than one lacking in skill. Typically, in the study of skill, activities are examined as examples of how an individual processes information and in terms of the problems and limitations which he must meet by the nature of his sensory, effector and central processing systems. These questions are much the same whether we are considering the muscular control involved in grasping an object or the sequential ordering of speech.

The concept most commonly linked with the attainment of skilled performance of whatever kind is practice. In sports, in performing on musical instruments, in typing and in a host of common motor activities the royal road to success is to be found in practice. Learning associated with experience is in some degree cumulative in that each new situation is dealt with in the light of past experience and through the repertoire of means available to the individual to effect change. In considering the constraints to be met by children in the acquisition of motor skills a variety of processes need to be considered. Limitations imposed by any one of these contributing processes at any point in development will be reflected in the level of performance attained.

Paillard (1960) uses the term skill "... to designate among motor activities a particular category of finely co-ordinated voluntary movements, generally engaging certain privileged parts of the musculature in the performance of various technical acts which have as common characteristics the delicacy of their adjustment, the economy of their execution and the accuracy of their achievement". How fine the co-ordination and how delicate the adjustment must be to qualify for the description of "skilled" is difficult to determine, since the term is used to cover what is in fact a continuum of expression. Skilled motor behaviour is however concerned with the patterning and ordering of movements in space and time. To speak of skilled activity implies also that there is a programme of action specifying an objective to be attained. The means-end relationship is a central feature of skilled performance and of its acquisition, because the rules of transformation are of such an order that quite dissimilar movements may be substituted for each other in attaining an objective.

Towards a Model of Skill Development

Piaget's consideration of early motor development assumes a developmental continuity between reflex and non-reflex behavioural sequences. Voluntary prehension is seen as deriving from a primitive subcortically regulated grasping reflex via the mechanisms of "generalized" and "reciprocal" assimilation (Piaget, 1953; Flavell, 1963).

The differentiation of reflex activity which is almost complete at birth should not be confused with the emergence of voluntary behaviour which appears later. Motor development is essentially an outgrowth from non-reflex rather than reflex activity. It is the non-reflexive behaviour of the newborn infant which is the developmental precursor of intentional voluntary action in which the appreciation of means-end relationships plays a significant role. Reflex behaviour is by definition stimulus bound and never acquires intentionality.

The development of a skill involves the construction of a programme of action directed at the attainment of some goal. Intentionality, the deliberate pursuit of a goal by means of instrumental behaviours, is for Piaget one of the hallmarks of intelligence and for Bruner (1969) the *sine qua non* of skilled action. If skill is thought of as a programme of events directed towards achieving a goal, then a fundamental question concerns the units making up the programme and the manner of their organization (Miller *et al.*, 1960). Bruner (1970) and Connolly (1970a) have each suggested that the basic unit of performance may, by analogy with a computer programme, be conceived as a sub-routine. This is an act, the performance of which is a necessary, but not sufficient condition for the execution of some more complex hierarchically organized sequence of sub-routines in which it is embedded. The sequence itself constitutes what is generally thought of as the skill, walking, playing the piano or using a tool such as a spoon.

Welford (1968) views skill as an essentially cognitive or transformational process: the organism is involved in translating a sensory analysis of the problem and the requirements for its solution into an appropriate action pattern which has as its objective the attainment of some particular goal in the environment. Skilled action is thus generative in the sense that language is productive, a minimum set of transformation rules serving to produce a large stock of skilled action patterns used in achieving a wide variety of goals (Bruner and Bruner, 1968).

The sub-routines themselves have two sources of origin; they may be pre-adapted in the genome, or they may be individuated from the undifferentiated expression of an intention through some motor action which is appropriate in the gross sense. Once an action or plan emerges in general terms it can be shaped and refined by practice. An approximately successful outcome of a response has as a consequence the refinement of the sub-routine in a given cognitive strategy. Practice serves to render the sub-routine increasingly predictable in form and less dependent on context. Once modularized such sub-routines may be inserted into new patterns of action and combined according to various rules into new sequences of goal-oriented behaviour. The mastery of more complex tasks thus involves the combining of established (skilled) components of action into appropriate sequences which have a general programmatic property.

In the course of the development of the child's motor skills there is evidence of transfer between different forms of action: for example, the precision grip once mastered and reliably used with a spoon begins to be used in drawing with a pencil or painting with a brush. This may be understood in terms of the recruitment of components of skilled action patterns from a common stock of sub-routines. Once the precision grasp is achieved and modularized it is no longer situation-specific. It may now be employed, according to certain ordering principles which constitute the syntax of skilled action, in a wide range of action programmes—writing, sewing, dissecting, etc.

Skilled behaviour evinces intentionality (i.e. it is goal directed and subject to correction by error signals) and is perfected through practice. In studying the acquisition of skill we are therefore concerned with the manner in which an organism comes to execute a programme of temporally and spatially co-ordinated movements aimed at realizing a specified objective. It is possible to specify the minimal logical components of such a system. The execution of action programmes requires an effector organ which is to be regulated, a control source which provides the specification of the planned action, a receptor which registers the present course of action, some comparator device able to detect any discrepancy between the intended and realized act, and finally a feedback mechanism which can convert any detected discrepancy into correction signals to the effector organ. In other words the execution of the plan needs to be monitored and evaluated. Feedback is thus an essential feature of any control system: it is crucial for the modularization of sub-routines and to the control of any action programmes generated.

Several models of biological control systems embodying the servo-mechanism principle have been described, and a number of them may be linked with the regulation of motor behaviour. Basically two kinds of feedback information available to the organism can be distinguished; feedback proper (sometimes called intrinsic feedback) which arises from the effector system during the execution of an action, and knowledge of results (sometimes labelled reinforcement) which provides consequential information about an action on its termination. A more extensive classification of knowledge of results is given by Holding (1965) and the concept of feedback is reviewed by Bilodeau (1967). One of the most important features in the design of any control system is the feedback loop, that is the means whereby information about the motor output is turned into appropriate instructions to the power supply source. In general terms it is necessary to uncover the appropriate transformation rule or the means of transforming a measure of output into a suitable control signal.

The reafference principle put forward by von Holst and Mittlstaedt (1950; see also von Holst, 1954) is a central construct in considering the regulation of oriented movements. In essence the model specifies a means whereby the nervous system provides information in the form of an action plan and also obtains data about the outcome of the plan in order to produce regulatory feedback. An instruction to the skeletal musculature is conceived of as generating a copy of itself, called the efference copy, which is held in store pending the arrival of afferent information against which it is compared. The afferent information itself is of two kinds; exafference, which is produced by factors external to the organism, and reafference which is intrinsic and produced by muscular activity. The efference copy and the reafferent signal are compared in the central nervous system. If they match exactly movement ceases; but if on the other hand the reafference is too great or too small, correcting signals are despatched to increase or decrease the movement accordingly.

A problem presented by this model concerns the coding of the messages; are they determined by growth processes within the organism or as a result of experience? Held and Hein (1958, 1963) and Held and Blossom (1961) have shown that in man and other mammals the correlations between sources of information are established as a result of experience during self-initiated movements. If the visuo-motor relationships are rearranged experimentally, then readjustment or recalibration can take place provided that the individual has information about the new mapping function. This

can be achieved by his experience of self-initiated and controlled movements of his body in the new conditions. The recalibration is dependent
upon a comparison between the intended movement and the consequential reafferent signal. Hein and Held (1962) accordingly modified the von
Holst and Mittelstaedt model by the addition of a memory component
which they call the correlation store. This is an important addition since it
provides for the fact that combinations of monitored efferent and
reafferent signals have long-term consequences.

Another system capable of controlled voluntary activity has been described by Bernstein (1967) this is based upon his careful descriptions of
the changes in walking which occur as a function of age. The basic logic is
essentially similar, the system requiring the comparison of an intended
action (Sollwert) with feedback from the action so far accomplished (Ist-
wert). These two are then used to generate crucial information concerning discrepancy (Deltawert), which is in turn transformed into the
necessary correction signal.

The stimulus transforms that accompany movement are an important
source of order. This order underlies and is necessary for the organization
and reorganization of plastic sensory-motor systems. They are thus essential data to the young developing organism from which he fashions and
refines the modular sub-routines that are in themselves the building blocks
of skilled action patterns. In other words it is necessary for the development of the smooth, accurate and quite precisely controlled movements
which are for the most part commonplace to our species.

Constraints on Skill Acquisition During Development

On the basis of the theory of skill development sketched out above we
may for convenience identify three classes of constraints or limitations on
the learning of motor skills. These classes of constraints are not mutually
exclusive, indeed their interaction upon each other will be readily appreciated. In learning motor skills the child must come to appreciate the properties of his body (and growth changes in these properties), the properties of
objects, and their inter-relations. The sources of constraint are therefore as
follows.

(i) The functional integrity of the sub-routines, that is their degree of
modularization, and their extent.

(ii) The richness of the motor syntax, the rules which govern the assembly of sub-routines into action patterns or skills. This is essentially a
cognitive limitation.

(iii) The performance capabilities of the sensory-motor system.

In this section I propose to deal with the performance properties of the child's sensory-motor system and return in a subsequent section to establishment and execution of sub-routines and action programmes.

Information processing capacity

An appreciation of the importance of what take place between the reception of signals by the sense organs and the initiation of responses by muscle groups has emerged since the work of Craik (1947, 1948). Craik considered the human operator as a link in a communication channel; receiving, processing and transmitting information. The efficiency with which this information transfer is accomplished is one of the important limiting factors on skilled behaviour. Most skills are characterized by rapid, flexible and fluid movements and not the halting intermittency so evident in the reaction time experiment. The phenomenon of choice reaction times has been usefully considered in terms of information theory, from which it is possible to predict the time required to respond on the basis of the information load or uncertainty inherent in the situation (Hick, 1952). Although there are well documented exceptions to predictions of reaction time based upon the information content of a task (Mowbray and Rhoades, 1959), an analysis in these terms is helpful in evaluating the problem which children have to face.

In the case of choice reaction times we know that the greater the uncertainty the longer the decision time. From the child's point of view the degree of uncertainty inherent in most situations is great, so much is unknown that for him almost anything may happen, and he is therefore compelled to process more information than the adult. For as Kay (1970) has put it, "It (the child) is often facing possibilities which the adult has ruled out of consideration, because on the basis of previous experience he (the adult) can say that some events or classes of events are most unlikely." A child who lacks this experience has to consider more eventualities, and to that extent is having to process more information. The process of modularization discussed above involves a reduction in the amount of information that must be processed in the execution of a given sub-routine. It is following practice that a child is able to identify which of the incoming signals carries the information he requires.

That young children are less efficient information-handling systems than are adults has been demonstrated by Connolly (1970b), who obtained a close correlation between age and information transmission measured as rate of information gain. By ordering and structuring his world the child is able in effect to increase his channel capacity, since in the case of a highly practiced or modularized sub-routine his central processing capacity is freed for use in the evaluation and control of other aspects of the task. Longer action programmes can therefore be constructed and executed.

As responses become modularized, the individual is able to repeat movements with a greater degree of precision. The increased predictability of response reduces the uncertainty, inherent in his own actions, with which the child has to cope. This increasingly permits the monitoring of action by internal signals which precede external ones by a period crucial in the acquisition of skills. An example is provided by certain flight correction movements which I am able to make as I learn the position and movement appropriate to hitting a given typewriter key. Having initiated a movement to depress a key I appreciate that I am making an error, and although my finger still lands on the wrong key I am able to change the force parameters and prevent it from writing a wrong letter on the paper.

Timing and anticipation

Bartlett (1958) argues that the most important feature of expert motor skill is timing and that this timing has little to do with absolute speed. Efficiency he sees as being dependent upon the "regulation of the flow from component to component in such a way that nowhere in the whole series is there any appearance of hurry and nowhere unnecessarily prolonged delay". The secret of this smooth flowing action is anticipation of what is coming next and how this locks in with the overall plan of action. Each component is assessed and adjusted in terms of how well it fits into what Kay (1970) has called the macro-strategy.

A given time is required to respond to a signal, but a person can overcome the intermittency attendant upon this by initiating the response prior to signal onset, so that he anticipates the next move. Anticipation implies that the person knows something of the situation; of the overall programme, and of the feedback information telling him where he is in the programme. It thus implies learning. That children can learn to anticipate there is no doubt, but how well they accomplish such learning and how effectively and reliably they can structure such information is not known. On the basis of what has been argued in the previous section of this essay it follows that the child must learn the sequential probabilities of events linked in a skill, in order that he may adjust their performance in real time.

Input-output relationships

Some theories of learning offer as the basic mechanism the formation of stimulus-response connections. This formulation is open to a number of objections when we consider motor skills. The characteristics of skill could not be easily accounted for in terms of S-R chaining: since flexibility is so important it is clear that a high level of skill does not imply that a person always makes the same response in the same stimulus situation. However, receptor-effector organization is of great importance, as has been demonstrated by studies on stimulus-response compatibility (Fitts and Seeger, 1953). Fitts and Deininger (1953) varied the compatibility of the pairings used in a task which involved a spatial array of stimuli, and found that choice reaction times were inversely related to the degree of compatibility. Leonard (1959) reported that the number of alternatives, from 2 to 8, had no effect on increasing reaction time in a highly compatible situation where the stimulus was a vibration on a finger and the response depressing the stimulated finger. Smith and Smith (1962) have shown effects of practise on a task in which the visual representation of hand movements was reversed. The effects of poor compatibility are persistent and often reappear under stress or high information loads.

The evidence concerning S-R compatibility from studies on adults suggests that particular mappings between stimulus and response are overlearned relationships. They provide a kind of "cognitive geography". The European reads from left to right horizontally, we would expect therefore that he would develop a predominant scanning pattern corresponding to this. In contrast, Chinese is read from top to bottom and right to left, a different spatial array which may well effect stimulus-response compatibility under certain circumstances. Conditions of high stimulus-response compatibility facilitate skilled performance, probably by affecting information processing and hence anticipatory timing. In the case of young children there may be almost no conditions of high S-R compatibility until receptor-effector organization is overlearned by repeated experience of certain stimulus/response mappings. The overall structure of the organism resulting from its evolutionary and developmental history is likely to impose certain dimensions and constraints, bilateral symmetry and awareness of gravity being two obvious ones, on which compatibility is built. The paucity of data relating to these questions is remarkable.

Intersensory integration

In a study of the processes underlying voluntary motor control Birch and Lefford (1967) concluded that, ". . . improved intersensory organization is critical for the development of refined and modulated adaptation to the surrounding environment". The work of Held and his collaborators (loc. cit.) on perceptual-motor behaviour has served to emphasize the intimate connections which exist between sensory processes and the importance of this intersensory liaison for the acquisition of voluntary control. Sensory input is implicit in the notion of skill as a goal-directed programme, not in the S-R sense, but as determining certain kinds of decision regarding action. Such decisions would take the form of a translation between afferent sensory input and efferent motor outflow based upon a motor programme.

Connolly and Jones (1970) examined the ability of children of different ages in intra-modal and cross-modal matching tasks and reported substantial improvements in both as a function of increasing age. A model accounting for the observed changes in afferent-reafferent integration was devised. The model offers a partial explanation of the developmental improvements in skilled performance in terms of an error correcting process which leads to a more veridical representation of the relationship between information from the separate sensory modalities. The degree of interrelationship and equivalence between sources of information available to the child is one of the features which change progressively during development and as such it imposes some limitation on the nature of motor skill learning at any given point in childhood.

Manual Function and Manual Skill

The growth of manual skill is of central concern in studying the psychological development of the child, for as Féré (1887) expressed it, ". . . the hand is simultaneously an agent and interpreter of the growth of mind, it should merit to hold more the attention of physiologists and psychologists who have somewhat neglected it". The hand is used in a variety of ways; for pulling, pushing, poking and lifting. However, it is essentially and primarily a prehensile organ showing a vast range of purposive actions rather than a multiplicity of movements. The fundamental requisite of prehension is that an object should be grasped securely irrespective of its properties or the purpose to which it is to be put. Stability is essential for any subsequent activity no matter what the intention, whether it is to transfer a heavy object from one location to another or to carry out fine, delicate movements with a tool, such as writing with a pen. Stability is not necessarily related to force, and a characteristic of the adult human is that he can grasp securely with his hand a heavy stone or an egg.

Napier (1956) classifies grips into two basic types, distinct in the anatomical and functional sense. These are the power and precision grips, so called because they describe the nature of the functions in which they are used. They are seen by Napier as reflecting contrasting anatomical configurations to which all grip patterns can be assigned. The only exceptions allowed to this are the hook grip, as in carrying a suitcase, and the inter-digital grip, as when smoking a cigarette (Napier, 1971).

In the evolution of primate manual skills the differentiation of the two forms of grip appears late in phylogeny. Prosimians show only a single prehensive pattern, a crude form of grab, irrespective of whether the hand is being used in feeding or locomotion. The New World monkeys, though showing considerable functional advances over the prosimians, still lack any clearly differentiated power and precision grips. Among the Old World monkeys the two forms of grip are differentiated and a greater range of manipulative behaviours has been described (for review see Connolly and Elliott, 1972). In the case of the great apes the anatomical and sensory requirements for manipulative ability (not only truly opposable thumb, fine cutaneous sensory ability, etc., but also the relative size of the thumb and index finger) appear to some extent to have run counter to the requirements for locomotion. In the case of man not only does he have a truly opposable thumb but he also has a proportionately much longer one (opposability index for man is 65 and for the gorilla 47) and according to Napier (1971) selection pressures have operated to produce, ". . . a very high degree of sensory discrimination and nerve-muscle co-ordination, with the result that the central nervous system can call upon the hand to execute manual acts of a delicacy and precision quite impossible for monkeys".

Several important anatomical features of the adult human hand underlie its prehensile abilities. These properties are as follows. (1) The digits may be operated independently, they can be converged or diverged. (2) They may be extended or flexed, either independently or synergistically. (3) The thumb can be truly opposed to the index finger by abduction and rotation. (4) The digits may be moved independently or held in postures involving degrees of flexion, abduction and adduction varying across the digits.

The two grip configurations to which Napier believes all prehension can be reduced are essentially anatomically defined. The power grip involves holding an object in a clamp formed by the partially flexed fingers and the palm of the hand, counter pressure sometimes being applied by the thumb in the plane of the palm. In the precision grip the object is held pinched between the flexor aspect of the finger(s) and the opposed thumb. Only the digits and not the palm of the hand are involved in the precision grip. The nature of the grip employed is almost wholly dependent upon the purpose to which it is to be put, the shape of the object to be grasped and its size (except at extremes) have little or no effect. The posture of the hand in fact is said to bear a constant relationship to the nature of the activity (Napier, 1956).

Connolly and Elliott (1972) described a study in which a series of observations were made on children aged between 34 and 58 months using a tool. The tool in question was a paintbrush, and it was used without restriction on a vertical surface. Some seven different grip patterns were seen and described, though using Napier's criteria exact classification was found to be difficult. On the basis of these observations it appears that prehension in children can be usefully described functionally in terms of the power/precision dichotomy, but the anatomical division defined by Napier did not necessarily reflect the use that the grip would serve. It was concluded that power and precision are appropriately defined independently of the anatomical configuration of the hand by reference to the skill and force employed, and further that in the case of young children the skill and force exhibited are unlikely to correspond exactly to the anatomical configuration described by Napier.

An important and fundamental difference between the power and precision grasps has been pointed out by Landsmeer (1962). This lies in the fact that the power grip provides a means of holding an object immobile with respect to the hand whereas the precision grip permits an object to be moved relative to the hand by means of small independent movements of the digits. In a number of typically human skills, such as writing, movements of both kinds are involved. The nature of the grip is determined by the functional properties of the hand and the requirements imposed by the nature of the task to be performed. Elliott and Connolly (in preparation), following Landsmeer, argue that a grip classification should be based upon whether the configuration permits intrinsic or only extrinsic movements, relative to the hand, of an object held in the hand. This is essential in classifying the grip patterns of children, where the overall anatomical configuration may fall into one class but nevertheless permit manipulation usually reserved to the other.

Manipulation is a skilled motor function which depends not only upon the anatomical properties of the hand but also upon certain postulated psychological structures known usually as schemata. These schemata by the grace of anatomy define the manner of manipulation and the function to which tools may be put. Manipulation itself involves orientation to an object and it will involve what Trevarthen (1968) has called focal vision. Praxic behaviour occurs typically in focal vision and it is here that many skills are elaborated. Indeed the idea of the structure of the immediate extra-body space which we have is probably affected in an important way by the child's manipulation of objects in that space.

In manipulating objects the two hands rarely perform mirror-symmetric roles, and there is usually a polarization favouring one hand or the other. Often one hand performs a supportive role whilst the other carries out certain operations. The hand that manipulates thus becomes temporarily the primary agent for the whole organism. Many manipulative actions can be performed readily by the adult with either hand. This intermanual transfer depends upon an exchange between the hands of the conceptual elements and strategies. Again we return to the practised, modularized sub-routine. In some respects the extent to which a sub-routine has become modularized may be assessed by the readiness with which it is used by either hand.

In bimanual skill, the emergence of which has been studied by Bruner (1970), the two hands, though involved in executing different sub-routines, become integrated into the overall structure of the task. How the child establishes sub-routines and integrates these according to various rules into the overall programme, whilst at the same time coping with limits on his information processing capacity etc., lies at the heart of the problem of learning motor skills. The gradual emergence of lateral dominance, when one hand is used either more frequently than the other, or predominantly in performing certain operations, introduces a special functional assymetry into the acquisition of manual skill. An assymetry of motor strategy will in turn depend upon an orientational or postural control over the relationships between the body, any tool which is held and the proximal environment where it is applied.

In the early stages of motor skill learning, tactile and proprioceptive exploration and manipulation depend largely on visual control, vision serving to define the task and oversee the operations of the hands. Once the nature and mechanics of the operation are learned, once a set of sub-routines are established, pre-patterned movements appear. This now frees visual analysis for transfer to the next functional component in the programme. It is in this way that I believe the smooth performance characteristic of adult skill is assembled in infancy.

Patterns of Prehension in Relation to Task Demands

What constitutes a sub-routine is not immediately clear. It is a hypothetical construct which has been used hitherto as the "quantum" of skill. In order that we may study the growth of a sub-routine and its incorporation into action programmes we must first identify examples of these hypothesized units. It is important to note that the unit is not conceived as a necessarily static entity, for its nature may change as development proceeds. The definition of a sub-routine is essentially functional, not neurological or anatomical. The distinction between function and anatomy has been commented on by Connolly and Elliott (1972), "Anatomy is concerned with both the structure of organs and the operations of which they are capable. In so far as these operations involve movement, however, there is a distinction between movement and function. Function refers to effects, to the operation of the organ in terms of consequences, and thus entails reference to other organs or to the environment." Sub-routines may be postural or they may be movements, such as the power and precision grips or supination and pronation of the forearm employed in turning control knobs (see Elliott and Connolly, in press). These each have their anatomical and physiological substrate, but for our purposes are not defined in such terms. The anatomy and neurology of an organism impose constraints on the nature of the movements that it may make, and these in turn reflect the motor skills that it may learn. Further constraints upon skill acquisition arise from the cognitive structures relating to functional units (sub-routines) and the motor syntax which specifies their operation in action programmes.

The descriptive study reported below was concerned to examine the prehensile patterns exhibited by a group of pre-school children when asked to perform four simple tasks each of which involved grasping objects to execute skilled programmes. The purposes of the study were as follows. (1) To examine how far the grip patterns described by Connolly and Elliott (1972) may be thought of as constituting a "dictionary of grips" used by children in the process of differentiating the adult power and precision varieties. (2) To obtain further material concerning the problem of whether the anatomical configuration of the hand provides the defining characteristics of the grip, rather than the facility for extrinsic and/or intrinsic movements. (3) To explore the effect of size differences in the manipulanda on the grips assumed by young children. (4) To examine any differences in grip pattern between the preferred and non-preferred hand.

Subjects and procedures

The sample studied comprised forty nursery school children, 20 boys and 20 girls. The median age was 4 years 2 months and the age range was from 3 years 5 months to 4 years 11 months: the children all attended the same nursery school. All the tasks were performed on a low table with the child sitting or standing; the observer took up a position at the opposite side of the table. The tasks were as follows.

In task one the child was presented with a collection of 5 plastic tubes, each 8 inches long and having the following diameters; 0.5, 0.75, 1.0, 1.25 and 1.75 inches. The smallest diameter tube weighed 20gms and the largest 80 gms. A second series of rods identical to the first in all respects but of equal weight (made so by packing the tubes with various materials so that they each weighed 80 gms) was also used. The tubes were placed on the table exactly in front of the child and not to either side of his body. They were arranged in no particular series. The child was asked to pick up one tube at a time and locate it in the appropriate hole in a rack placed centrally and just beyond the tubes. A note was made of the hand which the child used and the nature of the grip employed.

In task two the child was presented with 4 wooden dowels all six inches long and having the following diameters; 0.5 0.75, 1.0 and 1.5 inches. The conditions of presentation were as in the previous task but this time the child was asked to push the dowels into a sand tray so that they stood erect. The observer noted which hand was used, the nature of the grip, any changes in grip posture, and where the child grasped the dowel—at one of the ends or centrally.

In task three the children were presented with five plastic hexagonal nuts and bolts of the following sizes: 1.4, 1.2, 1.1, 1.0 and 0.9 inches measured across the flats of the nuts. The bolt heads were of corresponding sizes. The nuts and bolts were spread on the table in front of the child and he was asked to screw them together. Each nut and bolt pair was of a different colour and the observer would ask the child, "now do the green ones please". In this way the order was roughly randomized, i.e. it was not largest to smallest or *vice versa*. The observer recorded which hand the child used to grasp the bolt and which the nut, and the grip assumed on the nut and the bolt. Whether the child turned the nut or the bolt was also recorded.

In task four the child was asked to thread five 1 inch cubes onto a knotted lace, the other end of which was stiffened by a plastic reinforcement extending over about one inch. The observer noted which hand was used to hold the brick and which the lace. Also the grip used on the brick and the lace, both in locating it in the hole and in pulling it through.

If a child used one hand consistently for picking up the tubes (defined by using the same hand for each trial) he was deemed to show a consistent preference for that hand. Such children were then asked to perform the task using the other, non-preferred hand. Children who did not show any consistent preference were asked to repeat the trials, no restraints being imposed. A similar procedure was adopted on the remaining tasks.

Results

Several grip patterns, essentially similar to those described by Connolly and Elliott (1972), were observed, though not all grip patterns were seen in every task. In addition a new grip, the opposed palmar, was described. The grip configurations were as follows:

Adult; a digital grip with the thumb opposed to the tip of the index finger or all fingers, no palmar contact (Figs. 1 and 2).

Transverse Digital; the object lies transversely along the finger tips and is opposed by the thumb. This is a precision grip though the range of intrinsic movements is limited to quite a small amount of lateral rotation by the fingers and thumb (Fig. 3).

Transverse palmar; the object is held in the fist at right angles to the fingers and projects medially. The thumb may be opposed onto the clenched fingers. This grip does not permit any intrinsic movement. It falls into the power grip category (Fig. 4).

Fig. 1. Adult grip on nut (right hand) and bolt head

Fig. 2. Adult grip on brick and lace

Ventral; in this pattern the thumb is opposed to the lateral/ventral surface of the index finger, the index finger is more flexed than is usual in the adult grip and the thumb is not truly opposed. Intrinsic movements are difficult with this grip and were not observed. This grip serves to lock small objects (Fig. 5).

Opposed palmar; this grip was not described by Connolly and Elliott (1972). The overall configuration of the grip shows the thumb opposed to the fingers but the object is supported by and locked into the palm. Intrinsic movements are not possible, it is therefore a power grip (Figs. 6 and 7).

Fig. 3. Transverse digital grip on largest tube.

Fig. 4. Transverse palmar grip.

Fig. 5. Ventral grip on lace.   Fig. 6. Opposed palmar grip.

It is also evident from the bimanual tasks that different grips may be employed by each hand (Figs. 8 and 9).

Fig. 7. Adult grip on nut (right hand)   Fig. 8. Opposed palmar grip on brick,
opposed palmar grip on bolt head.   adult grip on lace.

Tubes in holder. The overall results are shown in Fig. 10. There was a gradual shift in the nature of the grip employed as the diameter of the tube increased. With the smaller diameter tubes the predominant grip was adult, whereas with the largest diameter tube it was transerve digital.

Fig. 9. Adult grip on nut (left hand),
transverse palmar on bolt head.

Weight variation over the range studied showed no systematic effect on the form of the grip used. The observed shift in the nature of the grip employed was not from a precision to a power configuration, but from one form of precision grip to another. Although the transverse digital grip permits some intrinsic movement by lateral rotation of the digits, it is less than that available with the adult grip. The inference drawn from this

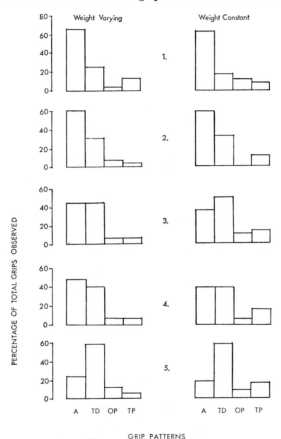

Fig. 10. Effects of increase in diameter of tube and changes in weight on the nature of the grip employed. 1–5 represents size of tube from smallest to largest. A, adult; TD, transverse digital; OP, opposed palmar; TP, transverse palmar.

observation concerns the stability and degree of precision afforded by the two grips. Locating the tubes in their appropriate holes involved the child in making accurate movements not only with the hand but also with the whole upper limb. The change in the form of the grip correlated with the increasing diameter of tubes suggests that the adult grip, whilst providing

AA

the greatest opportunity for precision function, does not allow sufficient stability to be maintained. This trade off between precision possibilities (essentially the opportunity for intrinsic movements) and stability may well be closely related to the size of a child's hand.

When a comparison was made between the preferred (defined in terms of consistent use of one hand for all 5 tubes) and the non-preferred hand an interesting relationship between the use of power and precision grips was apparent (Fig. 11). In the case of the non-preferred hand, although the precision configuration still predominated there was evidence for a greater use of the power grips. It has been argued that there is no qualita-

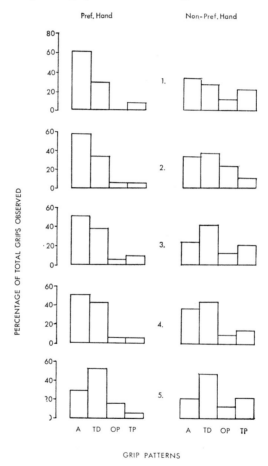

Fig. 11. Comparison of frequency of grip patterns assumed by preferred and non-preferred hands in relation to increase in diameter of the tubes (1–5). Key as in Fig. 10.

tive difference in the performance of motor skills between the hands (Barnsley and Rabinovitch, 1970) but it is known that the two hands consistently tend to assume different roles.

Dowels into sand tray. This task was similar in certain respects to the previous one. Basically it had two components, picking up the dowel and then pushing it into the sand tray. The demands on accuracy were reduced because the dowel did not have to be located in a hole just larger than itself, but force was required to push the dowel into the sand. Most of the children showed two grips in performing the task, one for picking up the

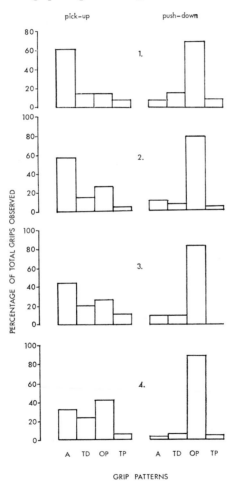

Fig. 12. Grip patterns employed in 'pick-up' and 'push-down' components of dowel into sand task in relation to diameter of dowel. Numbers 1–4 represent smallest to largest diameter. Key as in Fig. 10.

dowel and another for pushing it into the sand. The grip change was accomplished whilst the operation was being executed. The results in relation to the size of the dowels are shown in Fig. 12. The grips employed in picking up the dowels were similar to those used with the tubes and showed essentially the same shift in relation to size. The percentage of precision grips was greater than power grips, though a more marked shift towards a power configuration was observed with the thicker dowels.

To accomplish the second part of the task most children changed their grip on the dowel by realigning their hand in relation to it. The predominant grip used on this component of the task was the opposed palmar, which not only allowed the child to hold the dowel rigid but also to apply force from the shoulder. As the diameter of the dowel increased, so the incidence of the opposed palmar grip increased. In the case of this task and the previous one a note was made of whether the child grasped the tube or dowel at its centre or at the end when picking it up from the table. In the case of the tubes 75 per cent of the initial grasps were in the centre and 25 per cent at one of the ends, whereas with the dowels only 40 per cent of the initial grasps were at the centre of the dowel and 60 per cent at one or other of the ends. This is of interest because it is far easier for the subject to adapt his initial grip to the opposed palmar configuration if the dowel is grasped at one end. The difference suggests that the subjects may have been anticipating the change in grip which they would have to make in order successfully to accomplish the task. This different orientation to the dowel may indeed be evidence for the emergence of a different motor programme.

When the grip patterns used by the children showing a consistant hand preference were compared with those who did not show a consistent preference no differences were found. The dowels were grasped in the same manner and the opposed palmar grip was used predominantly to push down the dowel. When using their non-preferred hand children quite often brought the other hand into use in the pushing operation, and this despite being asked not to. Clearly this was a very natural means of achieving the desired end.

Screwing together nuts and bolts. This task, in distinction to the previous one, required that the child execute a programme involving the reciprocal use of both hands. Although the hands perform together in screwing up a nut and bolt their functions are differentiated. One hand has an essentially passive role of holding whilst the other is active in manipulation. The manipulatory part of the task usually involved locating the nut into the bolt and then rotating it in order to screw it up.

Almost without exception the nut was screwed onto the bolt and the grip assumed was adult. A number of different techniques were used in screwing the nut up to the bolt head. Since the plastic nut was light and fitted very loosely onto the bolt it was possible to effect the screwing up by striking the flats of the nut tangentially in order to "spin" it up. This was rarely seen in the children, though adults asked to assemble the nut and bolt often used this method once the nut was located. The commonest method used by the children consisted in grasping the nut in an adult grip and rotating the hand as far as comfortable by supination of the forearm. The grip on the nut was then released and the hand returned to the original position by pronation of the forearm. The adult grip was again assumed and the cycle repeated. A similar but more efficient procedure used by some of the children took the following form. The nut was grasped in an adult configuration using all four fingers and rotated by the fingers away from the body (by supination). As the rotary action progressed the involvement of the fingers changed. The nut continued to be held by the opposed thumb and index finger but the little finger, followed by the others in radial direction, relinquished their hold thus permitting further rotation. None of the children was observed to do what many adults do, namely to follow this procedure by allowing the contact between the nut and the index finger to revolve round from the ball of the finger to the lateral surface. This technique of progressively varying the grip permits the most efficient performance.

The grip used by the children to hold the bolt varied with the size of the bolt head. With the smallest bolt the grip was predominantly adult whereas with the largest it was predominantly opposed palmar (Fig. 13). The differentiation of power and precision grips between the two hands engaged in this task was quite striking. The manipulating hand made use of a precision grip whereas the "holding" hand used a power grip, thus providing evidence of the integration of two postural sub-routines into quite a complex skill. It was interesting also that the nature of the grips varied with the size of the bolt head.

Some further support for the suggestion that one hand served primarily as the manipulator was obtained by examining whether the nut was always turned in preference to the bolt. Of those children exhibiting a consistent hand preference only 8.5 per cent of their responses entailed turning the bolt. When the children were subsequently asked to use their other hand for the nut and bolt respectively 20.8 per cent of their first responses involved turning the bolt.

A slightly higher percentage of precision grips, 60 as against 45, was found between the preferred and non-preferred hands in the children showing a consistent hand preference (Fig. 14).

Threading bricks. Like the nuts and bolts problem, this task involved the use of both hands: again one hand acted primarily as a "holder" whilst the

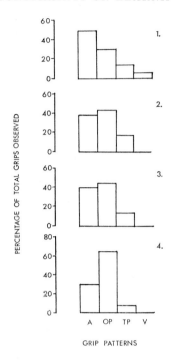

Fig. 13. Grip patterns used in holding bolt head as function of size. 1–4 increase from smallest to largest diameter. Key as Fig. 10 with V, ventral grip.

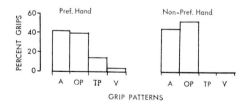

Fig. 14. Comparison of grip patterns between preferred and non-preferred hands of those children showing consistent preference on nut and bolt tasl Key as in previous figures.

other performed the more exacting task of locating the lace in the hole. Efficient performance however demanded that the hands reverse their roles in the course of the task. Once the lace had been inserted into the hole in the brick and pushed through a little way the hands reversed operations. The hand locating the lace took hold of the brick and the other grasped and pulled through the lace.

The results obtained from the observations are presented in Fig. 15. The data for the left and right hands are presented separately for those children showing no consistent preference, for those showing a preference and also for the non-preferred hand. Requiring a child to use his non-preferred hand gave rise to an increase in adult grip with the right hand and an increase in ventral grips with the left. This may reflect the child's manipulatory confidence and dexterity, since the ventral grip serves to lock the lace more firmly but reduces the possibility for intrinsic movements. In the case of the brick, changing to the non-preferred hand resulted in a slight increase in the use of a power grip configuration, an effect thought to reflect the effects of handedness. In the case of the "pull and lace through" component there is a slight increase in the percentage of less dextrous grips with the non-preferred hand. The children who show no hand preference have much the same frequency of grip patterns on all three elements of the task with both hands.

Discussion

It must be stressed that this study is only descriptive: the intention was merely to examine the grip patterns exhibited in carrying out the four relatively simple tasks. Had other dimensions of skill been examined, notably the real time requirements of the tasks, further differences would undoubtedly have emerged. Picking up the tubes and inserting them into their respective holes was quite quickly accomplished, whereas threading the bricks took a good deal of time and gave all indications of being a very demanding task for the children.

It is apparent that by the age of three the power/precision grips are not only differentiated but quite well established and appropriately used. The task demands, however, may well effect a regression to a more primitive configuration: for example, when required to use the non-preferred hand there is a tendency for the child to revert to a less dextrous power grip configuration, whereas for the same task the preferred hand makes use of a precision grip.

The findings lend support to Connolly and Elliott's (1972) conclusion that for young children Napier's power/precision dichotomy is reflected in several grip patterns. For the purposes of further investigations into the development of manual skills the grip patterns described may be usefully

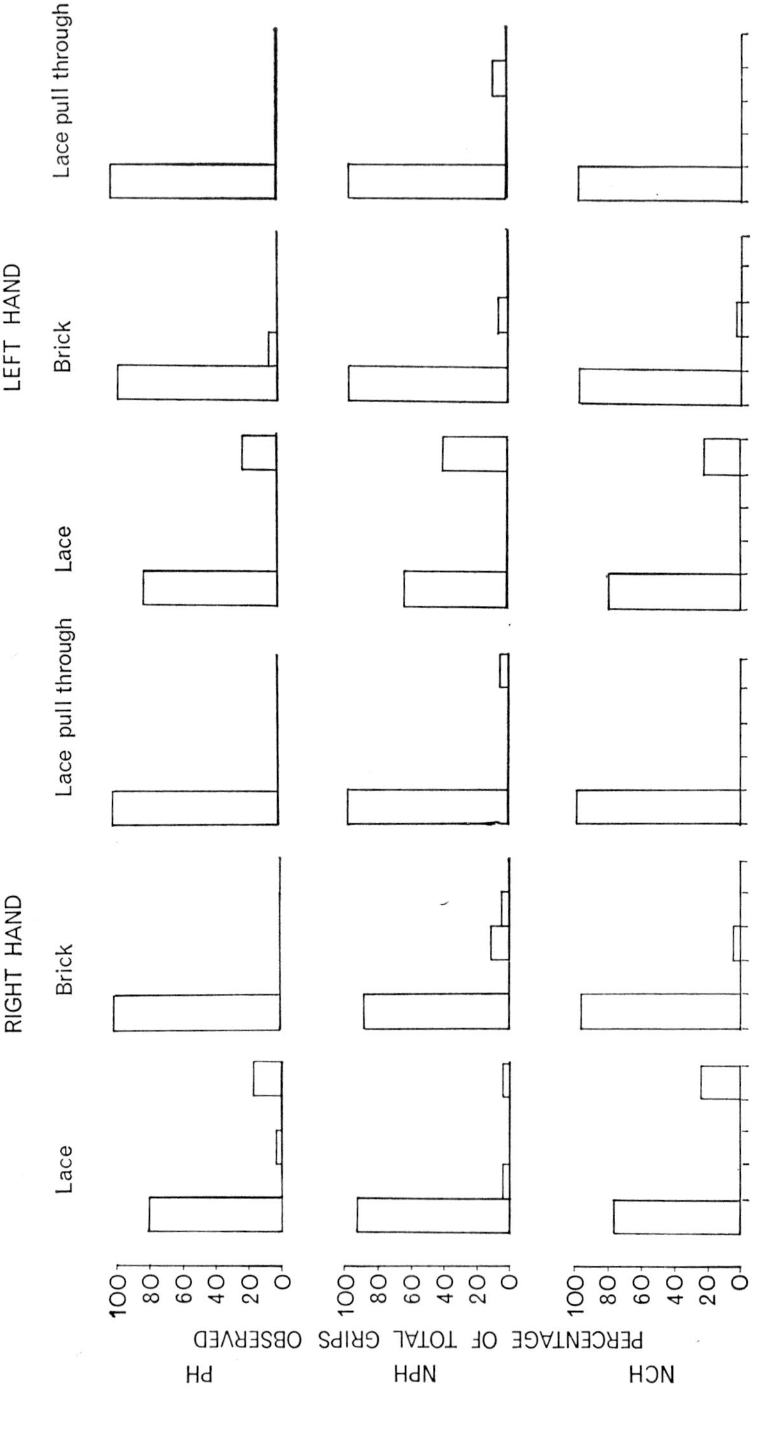

Fig. 15. Grip patterns used by right and left hands in relation to the components of the task, threading bricks onto lace. PH, preferred hand; NPH, non-preferred hand; NCH, no consistently preferred hand. Key to grip patterns as in previous figures.

thought of as a dictionary of grips. Subsequent learning will not increase the range of postural and movement patterns but rather lead to a refinement into the two basic configurations described by Napier. Such refinement reflects the modularization of sub-routines and is evident in the increased predictability with which the young child uses his hands as well as in his increased task success. The manner in which an adult handles a tool reflects not only his knowledge of the tool and the plan of action which he employs but also the "reliability" of the sub-routines available to him. Likewise skilled performance will be a function not only of reliable sub-routines but also of the motor syntax or combinatorial rules applied to them.

Paradoxically development may be seen as a process of reducing the available options, a repertoire of grip patterns being exchanged for the ready availability of a smaller number of reliable ones. Flexibility is not relinquished by this process. It is achieved in other ways, through the efficient use of a small number of postural sub-routines directed by a rich motor syntax into a vast array of action programmes. Physiological, neurological and biomechanical changes also play their part in limiting and providing for the learning and expression of motor skills, but the principle feature in motor skill learning concerns the cognitive rather than physical elements.

Summary and Conclusions

On the basis of the model of skill development outlined several sources of constraint upon motor skill learning may be identified. Such constraints reflect physical growth processes (neurological and mechanical), the establishment through experience of sensory-motor relationships, the assembly of the basic building blocks of skill (sub-routines) and learning the transformation rules by which these units are governed and mobilized in executing action programmes. With respect to patterns of prehension in preschool children it is clear that well-differentiated power and precision grip configurations are present, and also that further refinement and modularization of these sub-routines is continuing. The non-preferred hand tends to revert back to a less flexible grip than that assumed by the preferred hand in the same task.

Acknowledgements

The work reported in this paper has been supported by a research grant from the Spastics Society which is gratefully acknowledged. The model of skill development outlined owes much to the work of Professor

J. S. Bruner, I gladly acknowledge my debt to him. Miss Elizabeth Garrett collected much of the data presented in the final section of the paper. I wish to thank also my colleague Mr. John Elliott for many valuable discussions and much help given in many ways.

References

Barnsley, R. H. and Rabinovitch, M. S. (1970). Handedness: proficiency versus stated preference. *Percept. mot. Skills* **30**, 343–362.

Bartlett, F. (1958). "Thinking: an Experimental and Social Study." George Allen and Unwin, London.

Bernstein, N. A. (1967). "The Co-ordination and Regulation of Movement." Pergamon Press, London.

Bilodeau, I. McD. (1967). Information feedback. *In* "Acquisition of Skill", (E. A. Bilodeau, ed.). Academic Press. London.

Birch, H. G. and Lefford, A. (1967). Visual differentiation, intersensory integration and voluntary motor control. *Monog. Soc. Res. Child Develop.* **32**.

Bruner, J. S. and Bruner, B. M. (1968). On voluntary action and its hierarchical structure. *Internat. J. Psychol.* **3**, 239–255.

Bruner, J. S. (1969). "Processes of Cognitive Growth: Infancy", Vol. III. Heinz Werner Lecture series. Clark Univ. Press, Worcester, Mass.

Bruner, J. S. (1970). The growth and structure of skill. *In* "Mechanisms of Motor Skill Development", (K. Connolly, ed.). Academic Press, London.

Connolly, K. (1970a). Skill development: problems and plans. *In* "Mechanisms of Motor Skill Development", (K. Connolly, ed.). Academic Press, London.

Connolly, K. (1970b). Response speed, temporal sequencing and information processing in children. *In* "Mechanisms of Motor Skill Development", (K. Connolly, ed.). Academic Press, London.

Connolly, K. and Elliott, J. (1972). The evolution and ontogeny of hand function. *In* "Ethological Studies of Child Behaviour", (N. Blurton Jones, ed.). Cambridge Univ. Press, Cambridge.

Connolly, K. and Jones, B. (1970). A developmental study of afferent-reafferent integration. *Brit. J. Psychol.* **61**, 259–266.

Craik, K. J. W. (1947). Theory of the human operator in control systems. I. The operator as an engineering system. *Brit. J. Psychol.* **38**, 56–61.

Craik, K. J. W. (1948). Theory of the human operator in control systems. II. Man as an element in a control system. *Brit. J. Psychol.* **38**, 142–148.

Elliott, J. and Connolly, K. (In press). Hierarchical structure in the development of skill. *In* "The Development of Competence in Childhood", (K. Connolly and J. Bruner, eds.). Academic Press, London.

Elliott, J. and Connolly, K. (In prep.). An analysis of human prehensile patterns.

Féré, C. (1887). "Sensation et Mouvement." Alcan. Paris.

Fitts, P. M. and Deininger, R. L. (1954). S-R compatability: correspondence among paired elements within stimulus and response codes. *J. exp. Psychol.* **48**, 483–492.

Fitts, P. M. and Seeger, C. M. (1953). S-R compatability: spatial characteristics of stimulus and response codes. *J. exp. Psychol.* **46**, 199–210.

Flavell, J. H. (1963). "The Developmental Psychology of Jean Piaget." Van Nostrand, New York.

Hein, A. and Held, R. (1962). A neural model for labile sensorimotor co-ordination. *In* "Biological Prototypes and Synthetic Systems", (E. E. Bernard and M. R. Kare, eds.). Plenum Press, New York.

Held, R. and Bossom, J. (1961). Neonatal deprivation and adult re-arrangement: complimentary techniques for analysing plastic sensory-motor co-ordination. *J. comp. physiol. Psychol.* **54**, 33–37.

Held, R. and Hein, A. (1958). Adaptation of disarranged hand-eye co-ordination contingent upon re-afferent stimulation. *Percept. mot. Skills* **8**, 87–90.

Held, R. and Hein, A. (1963). Movement produced stimulation in the development of visually guided behaviour. *J. comp. physiol. Psychol.* **56**, 872–876.

Hick, W. E. (1952). On the rate of gain of information. *Quart. J. exp. Psychol.* **4**, 11–26.

Holding, D. H. (1965). "Principles of Training." Pergamon Press, London.

Holst, E. v. (1954). Relations between the central nervous system and peripheral organs. *Brit. J. anim. Behav.* **2**, 89–94.

Holst, E. v. and Mittlstaedt, H. (1950). Das Reafferenzprinzip. *Naturwiss.* **37**, 464–476.

Kay, H. (1970). The experimental analysis of skill. *In* "Mechanisms of Motor Skill Development", (K. Connolly, ed.). Academic Press, London.

Landsmeer, J.M.F. (1962). Power and precision handling. *Ann. rheum. Dis.* **21**, 164–170.

Leonard, J. A. (1959). Tactual choice reactions: I. *Quart. J. exp. Psychol.* **11**, 76–83.

Miller, G. A., Galanter, E. and Pribram, K. H. (1960). "Plans and the Structure of Behavior." Holt, Rinehart and Winston, London.

Mowbray, G. H. and Rhoades, M. V. (1959). On the reduction of choice reaction times with practice. *Quart. J. exp. Psychol.* **11**, 16–23.

Napier, J. R. (1956). The prehensile movements of the human hand. *J. Bone Jt. Surg.* **38B**, 902–913.

Napier, J. (1971). "The Roots of Mankind." George Allen and Unwin, London.

Paillard, J. (1960). Patterning of skilled movements. *In* "Handbook of Physiology", Section I, Neurophysiology. Am. Physiol. Soc., Washington.

Piaget, J. (1953). "The Origin of Intelligence in the Child." Routledge and Kegan Paul, London.

Smith, K. U. and Smith, W. M. (1962). "Delayed Sensory Feedback and Behavior." Saunders, Philadelphia.

Trevarthen, C. B. (1968). Two mechanisms of vision in primates. *Psychol. Forsch.* **31**, 299–337.

Welford, A. T. (1968). "Fundamentals of Skill." Methuen, London.

Comments

McFarland commented:

"An important constraint in skill learning is the degree of observability (inference possibility) permitted by feedback from the consequences of the behaviour. In many cases of manual skill, feedback from the consequences of behaviour lacks the richness necessary for improvement of the sub-routine. For example, a bird with a complete plan (or template), of a 'song-to-be-sung', makes a series of vocalizations and uses auditory feedback to compare the vocalizations with the plan. Much depends upon the ability of the bird to utilize the auditory feedback. If it is able only to note that its vocalizations are 'right or wrong', then its ability to modify future vocalizations appropriately will be constrained.

"Similarly, in learning a skill such as that involved in golf, the subject may have a plan appropriate to the play of a particular stroke, but he also needs a sub-routine which enables him to execute the necessary skilled motor movements. Having played his stroke, the subject may have very little information as to what exactly went wrong with his stroke, but he will probably know how 'good or bad' the shot was. I think that it is this poverty of feedback from the consequences of behaviour which makes certain types of skill so difficult to learn.

"In formal terms the difference between high and low observability is a difference in the number of dimensions characterizing the feedback in relation to the number involved in the control of the behaviour. If there are n dimensions involved in the control of the behaviour, and $n-x$ available in the feedback from the consequences of the behaviour, then the degree of observability is inversely related to the value of x — when x is high, the observability of the behaviour consequences is low: in other words, the subject has little information concerning the consequences of the behaviour. The subject then has little information by which to alter the subroutine. As illustrated in the Figure, the sub-routine controls the behaviour by a multi-dimensional vector, but is itself influenced by a vector of low-dimensionality. In formal terms there is low controllability of the sub-routine. Thus a major constraint on skill learning is the degree of controllability of the sub-routine, which in turn depends on the observability of the feedback. In the extreme case of low observability, there is scalar feedback of information, i.e. feedback along one dimension, relating to the degree of nearness of the behaviour. In such a case there can only be scalar control of the sub-routine, such as control of how much the sub-routine should be modified but no indication of how it should be modified."

Connolly replied:

"There are just two points I would like to make. First, I wonder if we are using the term sub-routine in the same way. I used it to describe a component of a skill, in other words to refer directly to behaviour. I should like to be clear that you are using the word in the same way. It seems to me that you may be using it as a hypothetical construct. You refer to a sub-routine which enables the individual to execute skilled motor movements—so it seems to me you are using it to talk of a 'plan'.

"I take your point about quality of feedback. I think there may be a further constraint in the context of development, namely the dimensions of feedback which the organism can process. Of the $n-x$ dimensions available in feedback only a portion of them may be useful to the child (or any other organism) at a given point in development. In other words, to make the most use of some feedback may well require that the organism is able to utilize this information in certain ways. In the case of a child's acquisition of motor skills certain cognitive structures may be necessary to utilize effectively some of the $n-x$ dimensions available in feedback. Maybe another term is required in the formulation you make."

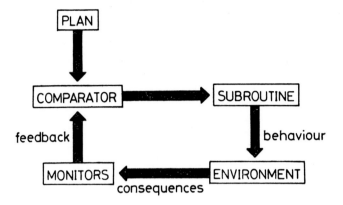

A completely controllable and observable system.

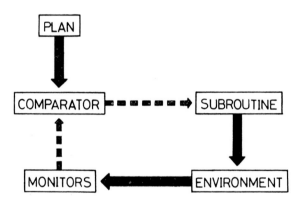

System with low observability and controllability.

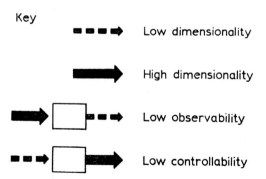

Editorial: 5

The remaining chapters are concerned with more complex functions than those discussed hitherto. Perhaps the most promising approach to their understanding is a developmental one: study of the development of capacities in the growing organism may show us how one form of learning develops from another. A hint that such an approach might prove profitable is present in Connolly's (Chapter 17) citation of Féré's reference to the hand as an agent of the "growth of mind". Piaget has gone further than this: holding that "learning in a strict sense cannot be dissociated from development in general" (Sinclair, Chapter 19), he argues that the only road to its understanding lies through study of the growth of cognitive functions from their simplest beginnings in the young baby. Clearly this is an approach likely to have much to say about the limitations on and predispositions for learning in complex situations.

Piaget's theory is introduced in the next chapter by Etienne (Chapter 18). She first outlines Piaget's general approach, and describes in some detail the stages of cognitive development that the human infant passes through in the first years of life. One achievement during this period is the acquisition of the object concept. During his first few months the human infant seems to behave as if objects had no continued existence: if an object disappears from his field of view, he appears not to search for it. Later, however, he seems to recognize that objects continue to exist if they disappear from his immediate perceptual world. To the biologist the question immediately arises—how far have animals gone in developing the cognitive abilities that human infants show progressively in development? In particular, to what extent can they be said to have an object concept? Etienne shows how this can be tackled experimentally.

In recent years work on the development of language has been stimulated by the work of Chomsky (e.g. 1968) and other structural linguists. In their view human languages have in common, at a rather abstract level of analysis, a certain structure—though they are not in precise agreement as

367

to its nature (Lyons, 1972). Since this deep structure is common to all languages, knowledge of it is presumed to be independent of learning any particular one. Since much of the adult conversation to which a child is exposed provides only "restricted and degenerate evidence" (Chomsky 1968) as to the grammar of its language, it is argued that knowledge of the deep structure of language must be "innate". It is further held that it is this innate knowledge of the deep structure that enables a child to "make sense of" the ungrammatical sentences he hears and to speak grammatically himself.

Now while the available evidence suggests that the higher apes can go only a little way towards acquiring human language (Gardner and Gardner, 1972; Premack, 1972), so that it can properly be said that man *differs* innately from non-man in his ability to acquire language, this is quite a different matter from saying that the ability to acquire language, or the deep structure of language, is innate (Lyons, 1972; Hinde, 1972). Indeed, such a view begs important questions. The ability to acquire language develops gradually, and may depend on all sorts of non-auditory and non-verbal experience. For example, it is almost inconceivable that any form of language could exist in an animal which lacked the object concept. Clearly, therefore, Piaget's approach should have something to contribute to the study of the early stages of language development. The way in which it can contribute is demonstrated in the chapter by Sinclair. She argues that the start of language acquisition is possible only as a result of previous interaction with the environment, and shows how the linguistic abilities of the developing child are constrained by the cognitive abilities that he has developed.

Both Sinclair and Etienne are at pains to emphasize the breadth of Piaget's approach, and Etienne emphasizes the importance of its heuristic impact. But it is in fact the case that the work of Piaget and his followers has been based on the observation of only a limited number of children and on rather primitive experiments. There are many who feel that heuristic appeal must be supported by factual validity. Piaget's stages of development are a case in point. While Etienne is careful to point out that the important issue is that the stages follow each other in succession and not the precise ages at which they appear, it should surely give Piagetians cause for concern if gross differences can be demonstrated between the age at which they state an ability first appears and the age at which it can in fact be demonstrated. The experiments reported by Bryant (Chapter 20) are concerned with such an issue.

The question of language development is continued by Ryan (Chapter 21). As mentioned above, part of the argument used by Chomsky and others that knowledge of the deep structure is innate rests on their view that the language to which the child is exposed is for the most part ungrammatical and unsuitable as a model from which to extract the elements of grammar. Ryan, however, points out that the interaction between mother and infant has special characteristics conducive to the development of language, and that some of these may originate in pre-verbal stages. The development of human language is thus much more subtle than is implied by the hypothesis of innate deep structures.

The inter-relationships between the development of language and other functions is considered from a quite different point of view by Marshall (Chapter 22). Lateralization of brain function is more marked in man than in lower species, is especially conspicuous in relation to language, but develops only gradually in the young child. Is it possible that the complex functions of the human brain, of which language is but one, demand segregation of mechanisms to a degree not found in lower forms? Marshall's discussion leads to further speculation about the relationships between linguistic and other skills.

In a final chapter which draws together a number of matters from the preceding ones, Hutt takes issue with the concept of developmental stages. He also emphasizes some other types of constraint, including neurophysiological ones, that he feels have been underestimated elsewhere.

References

Chomsky, N. (1968). "Language and Mind." Harcourt, Brace, World, New York.
Gardner, B. T. and Gardner, R. A. (1972). Two-way communication with an infant chimpanzee. In "Behaviour of Nonhuman Primates", Vol. 4, (A. M. Schrier and F. Stollnitz, eds.) Academic Press, New York.
Hinde, R. A. (ed.) (1972). "Non-verbal Communication." Cambridge Univ. Press. London.
Lyons, J. (1972). Human language. In Hinde, R. A. (ed.) 1972.
Premack, D. (1972). On the assessment of language competence in the chimpanzee. In "Behaviour of Nonhuman Primates", Vol. 4, (A. M. Schrier and F. Stollnitz, eds.). Academic Press, New York.

18

Developmental Stages and Cognitive Structures as Determinants of What is Learned

by Ariane S. Etienne

We may start to study behaviour with close observation of one well-determined component, and analyse it as empirically as possible, basing each step of the research on the results obtained previously. On the other hand, we may attempt to embrace wider aspects of behaviour in a more theoretical framework, and thus try to understand behaviour as a whole. This may require giving unifying concepts priority over the plurality of empirical facts. The value of this second approach is therefore expressed mainly in its heuristic impact.

Jean Piaget's work on the cognitive development of the child attempts to understand the nature of human intelligence and its product, knowledge. His approach to developmental psychology is therefore guided by theoretical interests which go beyond the study of behaviour itself. Through the study of behaviour he intends not only to reveal the principles of cognitive development, but also to apply his empirical results to epistemological questions concerning the degree of adequacy of human knowledge and the laws of its progression. At the same time, however, Piaget's approach to behaviour is based on ethological methods, namely the observation of the child in his familial and social environment.

Piaget's views on cognitive development during the child's preverbal or sensori-motor period—which may be of special interest for the student of animal behaviour—will be presented here in relation to their implications about learning. Thus the first part of this paper summarizes his theory of the development of behaviour through the sequence of sensori-motor stages, the structure or general organization of which determines the nature of the learning processes and the range of what the young infant can learn. The analysis of the infant's construction of object permanence—one of the fundamental categories of cognitive behaviour and thinking—will then illustrate how the structures that characterize different developmental stages express themselves not just in the functioning of cognitive mechanisms, but also in their product, i.e. knowledge. Finally, we will discuss the problem of object permanence in animals, where it can be considered from the points of view both of the cognitive structures that characterize the species and of the development of these structures.

Stages in Cognitive Development

Early in his empirical studies in child psychology, Piaget was struck by systematical differences between the infant's and the adult's way of reasoning. Following up this first impression, he found that children of various ages have their own way of interpreting their environment and acting upon it, and that these differences are due not solely to particular deficiencies in experience or information: at any given age the child's cognitive processes reflect a total structure or organization (Piaget, 1968a), which permits certain kinds of adaptive behaviour to occur, but not others. However, this does not mean that the organization that underlies the observed behaviour is controlled only by endogenous growth processes. Maturation of the nervous system certainly plays an important role; but we shall see that cognitive development is based on a continuous interaction between the subject and the environment.

Prechtl (1969) describes the development of the central nervous system in a similar way: "The infant's brain is by no means a miniature model of the adult brain, but a relatively simple nervous system which has very particular properties at each phase in its development. These properties are determined both by genetically fixed programmes of growth and by environmental factors which influence the function and sometimes even the structure."

Cognitive development can be divided into a series of stages which follow each other in a strict order. The structure of each stage leads to the next stage and is then integrated into it (Inhelder, 1956; Piaget, 1967). Cognitive development thus proceeds continuously, whatever the differences between its initial and final states may be. The structure of each stage involves maturational factors; however, cognitive stages have to be interpreted as successive phases of the child's interaction with his physical and social environment. Therefore, the notion of stage implies a temporal order of development and not specific age criteria: children from various backgrounds may show considerable differences in their cognitive behaviour, but they will go through the same general sequences of stages.

The notion of developmental stages is sometimes criticized. It can be argued that the imposition of stages on the continuity of development can imply discontinuities where none exist (Hinde, 1971): this is especially the case with behaviour, where development involves more diverse components and is more open to environmental influence than organic growth. Also, some investigators have found that certain behaviour patterns or cognitive operations appear sooner than Piaget asserted (Bower, 1967; Bower *et al.*, 1970a, b; Mehler and Bever, 1967; Bryant and Trabasso, 1971), or that they can be accelerated by training (Bruner, 1964). These findings could be used as arguments against the existence of stages or against the developmental sequences proposed by Piaget. The methodology and interpretation of these studies have been criticized and further evidence is needed (Inhelder *et al.*, 1966; Piaget, 1968b; Lunzer, 1972). But in any case we cannot expect a theory as comprehensive as Piaget's to be empirically perfect; as stressed already, its value rests not only on the validity of its predictions, but also on its heuristic impact.

The Main Stages

The following is a brief outline of the main stages in cognitive growth—Piaget calls them "periods"—and the types of learning they determine. As elsewhere in this paper, the age-ranges indicated for each period are only indications of the rate at which cognitive development occurs and not rigid limitations.

The sensori-motor period (from birth to about 2 years)

The term "sensori-motor" is used to describe preverbal behaviour, which does not yet involve internal representation. During this period the infant progresses from a few elementary activities to a wide range of well-adapted behaviour. This progress involves a constant interaction with the environment, in which the infant tries to apply his pre-existing action-patterns to persons and objects, and changes these patterns if they do not lead to the desired results. The range of possible experience and of learning is thus at any moment closely determined by the sensori-motor patterns already developed.

The preoperational (or prelogical) period (from 2 to 7 years)

The appearance of several new types of behaviour, one of which is language, indicates that the infant is now capable of internalized behaviour. Representative and conceptual thinking—i.e. internalized action—must, however, become progressively organized, as was the case for sensori-motor behaviour in the preceding period.

Progressive internalization proceeds from a state of unco-ordination and confusion at the present stage towards the point where actions can be mentally cancelled, i.e. they can be seen to be reversible, as when a ball of clay is stretched out into a sausage shape, and the sausage can be retransformed into a ball. This is accompanied by a capacity to conceive of quantitative constants, i.e. to understand that certain transforming actions leave intact certain quantitative properties of the external world, just as the amount and weight of clay do not change when the shape of clay is transformed. This "mental reversibility" will provide the child with the means to reconcile apparently contradictory data, such as the increased length but reduced thickness of the clay that has been transformed from a ball into a sausage.

Learning in this period is mainly concerned with the outcome of actions on objects, many of which the child cannot yet foresee or coordinate. It is the elaboration of an underlying logical framework that will make possible, in the next period, the coordination of isolated previsions and the elimination of contradiction.

The period of concrete operations (from 7 to 11 years)

The child reaches the stage of logical statements and understands their character of necessity, whatever perceptual elements may suggest to him. Concepts are used correctly with regard to their extension and definition, principles of physical invariance (substance, weight, volume) are constructed and mathematical operations can be developed. All this shows that the child has now achieved an internal co-ordination of mental operations that allows him to resolve apparent contradictions by comparing and by co-ordinating the conflicting aspects of external reality. Limitations are set by the fact that the infant can use logical operations only with regard to concrete elements; he is, for instance, unable to reason on the formal level of merely possible events.

The period of formal operations (from 11 years onwards)

In his reasoning, the adolescent adopts logical strategies that are independent from their content. Thinking can occur on a hypothetico-deductive level, mental operations can be combined together in all possible ways (combinatorial) and are applied to much wider units than before (propositional logics). This progress is no longer realized under the direct influence of external experience; it is based on a further internal co-ordination of all logical operations, which now become organized into an integrated system. From now on learning is concerned with the acquisition of information, which enriches the content, but does not change the form of knowledge.

Development and Learning in the Sensori-motor Period

Learning as a function of sensori-motor schemes

The infant is born with a set of elementary action-patterns, which are relatively unconnected with each other. These include sucking and swallowing, crying, grasping, visual fixation and tracking movements and gross bodily movements. Certain of these action-patterns remain stationary or regress; others, such as sucking, grasping or visual tracking—are exercised through repetition and applied to a variety of different objects. The underlying structure of these patterns, i.e. their repeatable and generalizable features, can therefore be considered as the first consistent units in the baby's behavioural repertoire. Piaget (1935) calls these units "schemes" (schème), which must not be confused with a figurative schema (Piaget and Inhelder, 1969). In his theory, all further development in behaviour is based on the differentiation, generalization and mutual co-ordination of the first reflex-like schemes just mentioned.

A baby who sucks the nipple of a bottle or the corner of his blanket incorporates or *assimilates* these external elements into his sucking-scheme; in other words, he applies a pre-existing general action-pattern to these objects. In the same sense, he assimilates a toy he grasps into his grasping scheme, and a moving configuration he fixates into his visual tracking scheme.

Elements from the external world (and also parts of the child's own body) have no other meaning for the infant than that given to them through assimilation into schemes. The nipple and the blanket are something that can be sucked and grasped, the moving configuration something that can be visually followed. But behaviour that is not controlled by an underlying scheme occurs randomly, is non-adaptive and cannot lead to any further development.

The notion of "scheme" is therefore central to Piaget's theory. Schemes are the underlying organizers of adaptive behaviour *and* of knowledge about the external world in which behaviour occurs. The structure of behaviour and the knowledge about the external world remain limited and partial so long as particular schemes are used in an unconnected way. This is the case at the beginning of the sensori-motor period, where grasping or sucking occurs without looking (cf. Schaffer, this volume), so that objects are simply things that can be touched, sucked or looked at. During development, schemes become progressively co-ordinated and can thus be applied either simultaneously (grasping an object and examining it visually) or in ordered temporal sequences (observing an object as it disappears behind an obstacle, removing the obstacle and grasping the object). At a more advanced stage, the schemes become integrated into a coherent structure or system and can then lead to behaviour both coherent in itself and adaptive with respect to the environment.

The adaptation of sensori-motor behaviour is brought about mainly by the process of *accommodation*, which involves the adjustment of schemes to the elements to which they are applied. A scheme is in fact accommodated whenever it is used in a concrete context. For instance, the baby opens his hand to a different degree when seizing his blanket or a toy, and he tends to adapt the movements of his head and eyes to the displacement of the external element he is following visually. Accommodation may thus be just a temporary feature of a single act. However, if the baby is motivated to actualize a scheme on a completely new object or in an unfamiliar situation, the necessary adjustment of the scheme may lead to its more permanent enrichment or differentiation. This modification of the scheme can concern its motor co-ordination (the baby may develop a new way of seizing small objects, between his thumb and index finger, for example; see Connolly, this volume); but it may also concern the identification of the objects (or situations) to which the scheme can be applied (the baby will give up his efforts to grasp the moon and he will only look at it). Thus the notion of scheme, which at first is limited to the motor components of a general action-pattern, extends in meaning, during the sensori-motor development, to include external elements, in the presence of which the pattern can be successfully performed.

In brief, the development of cognitive behaviour is based on the mutual interrelation of schemes and on the differentiation and enrichment they undergo by being constantly adjusted to the external world. This is achieved through maturation of the nervous system as well as through the child's long-lasting interaction with his environment. Furthermore, the outcome of both these factors is under the control of a fundamental internal tendency to realize a general structure which is in itself coherent and in agreement with the phenomenal world. Piaget designates this tendency with terms like "equilibration" or "autoregulation", which are more descriptive than explanatory. Throughout his work he gives many examples to show how this equilibration occurs. However, much has to be done to determine the exact mechanisms through which the child's cognitive behaviour changes from more elementary structures to more differentiated ones.

Piaget (1959) himself seldom speaks of learning, but uses the term "cognitive development", thus insisting on the fact that the three factors maturation, interaction with the environment and equilibration always act conjointly. One may, however, define learning in the framework of his theory in the following terms: 'Learning is the process through which experience with the environment leads to a permanent (or at least long-lasting) adaptive change in the structure or mutual co-ordination of schemes." This definition insists that the modification of schemes can occur only on the basis of their previous structure and interrelation. Furthermore, learning refers not just to the acquisition of particular information or skills, but mainly to the transformation of the learning mechanisms themselves; this transformation is mainly achieved by the mutual organization of schemes.

Schemes, assimilation and accommodation (as complementary aspects of their functioning), and regulation or equilibration as a developmental vector that controls the schemes' adjustment to the environment and their co-ordination into a general structure, form the basic concepts in Piaget's theory. They describe the continuity of cognitive development, though they do not yet provide us with a precise description of the mechanisms that control structural changes. The notion of a scheme is advantageous in that it refers to meaningful and complete units in the subject's behavioural repertoire at a given developmental level. In contrast to the ethological concept of "fixed action-pattern", a scheme combines perceptual and motor components and is, furthermore, open to developmental changes. This concept may well be extremely useful in defining the nature of cognitive development in a more detailed way.

The sensori-motor stages

Stage one (from birth to 1 month). During the first stage the reflex-schemes with which the baby was born are repeated frequently and applied to various objects. Through this functional exercise their motor co-ordination is strengthened, and they become adjusted to the shape, size, position, etc., of certain objects (e.g. sucking the mother's breast is performed differently from sucking the thumb). The baby thus learns to recognize different sucking-objects, not only because of their sensory qualities and the reinforcement they provide (Lipsitt, 1969), but also through their incorporation (assimilation) into the sucking scheme and the different kinds of adjustment (accommodation) they require.

Piaget observed that the newborn infant does not reach for an object visually presented to him (see, however, p. 379), nor does he bring an object put into his hand under visual control. Similarly, he does not usually look in the direction of a sound. More recent studies, however, have shown that where the newborn infant does change the orientation of his eyes upon the perception of a sound, he looks in the correct direction (Wertheimer, 1961; Moreau *et al.*, 1970). It thus appears that the newborn infant shows either no co-ordination at all, or a weak co-ordination between his different reflex-schemes and sensory modalities: this co-ordination will need to be exercised at a later developmental stage. Learning in stage one would therefore concern only very limited components of behaviour, and not yet its general organization.

Stage two (from 2 to 4.5 months). A second stage leads to "habit formation", i.e. the first stable and systematically produced assimilations of certain objects or parts of the child's own body into a given scheme. The baby, for instance, sucks his thumb more often than other objects and performs the components of this activity, such as bringing the thumb to the mouth and adjusting the sucking movements to the thumb, with more and more ease. The scheme "sucking anything that can be brought into the mouth" gets thus differentiated into a more closely determined scheme, "thumb-sucking". Furthermore, the infant starts to show anticipatory reactions to signals that precede a rewarding (or frustrating) situation, such as feeding. This can be considered as classical conditioning. In the framework of Piaget's theory the establishment of a conditioned response is, however, based on an active integration or assimilation of the conditioned stimulus into a scheme. In this view the stimuli that precede the feeding situation do not lead to an anticipatory attitude to feeding through a direct S-R association; rather are they absorbed as a new sensory component of the pre-existing scheme of sucking the mother's breast, and it is only through their incorporation into this scheme that they become relevant for the subject.

Stage three (from 4.5 to 9 months). According to Piaget, the third stage is initiated by the co-ordination of vision and prehension consequent upon nervous maturation (Piaget, 1935) and, as is suggested by the work on young mammals, by the possibility, first, of relating changes in the visual input to active motion (Held and Hein, 1963), and, second, of integrating visuo-motor control of head movements with non-visual control of limb movements (Held and Bauer, 1967). This co-ordination leads to important developmental progress: merely visually or tactile-kinesthetically guided schemes can now be combined with each other into schemes that are under the control of both sensory modalities, as for instance when the baby seizes his blanket and pulls it while simultaneously watching the external results of his action. Under the influence of visual control, the baby will try to reproduce the manipulations that led accidentally to an interesting result, such as pulling a string that makes an object shake. Such an action will be repeated over and over again, not only in its original context, but also in new situations: for example, a new object that catches the baby's attention may elicit string-pulling even though it is far away and not connected to the string. At the same time, the baby observes the whole sequence of external events, i.e. how his hands grasp the string, pull it, and how the object subsequently moves. This new aspect of his behaviour will lead to further developments in stage four.

In stage three the infant possesses more complex schemes. These allow him to act on a greater number of things and to become more aware of their properties than previously. Learning about these properties continues, however, to be limited, as the structure of the new schemes is still non-articulated and cannot lead to fine adjustments. This is expressed by the baby's lack of awareness of geometrical and causal relationships between objects and events, as when he pulls a string on seeing a distant, unconnected object.

It must be mentioned here that Bower *et al.* (1970a, b) elicited reaching towards objects and virtual images in newborn infants. Anticipatory reaching began when the visual stimulus came within a distance of 20 cm (Bower *et al.*, 1970a) and thus entered the zone of clear vision of the newborn infant's optical system (Haynes *et al.*, 1965). However, none of Bower's subjects looked at an object held in its hand before the age of three months (Bower *et al.*, 1970b). Given the ingenious techniques used by Bower, these findings—which also imply that vision precedes touch ontogenetically—must be given due consideration. It may be, for instance, that visually controlled reaching occurs only under optimal conditions at a very early age, and that generalized visually controlled reaching needs further maturation (of the visual system in itself and of the hand-eye co-ordinating mechanisms) as well as exercise.

Stage four (from 9 to 12 months). At this stage the particular schemes, constructed but not yet co-ordinated with each other during the previous stage, become integrated into goal-directed sequences. For instance, the baby will move a screen in order to reach an object hidden behind it. In other words, the infant learns to use certain schemes (removing the obstacle) as a means of actualizing a second scheme (taking the desired object). So objective relationships—for example, the position of objects in relation to each other—must be correctly observed and can guide behaviour.

At this stage the child will use as means only those schemes in his behavioural repertoire that are firmly established—such as seizing and removing a screen, lifting a cushion or a blanket, or pushing the adult's hand towards a desired object. Furthermore, adjustments in the actions are no longer made if the external situation becomes too complicated. For instance, having watched the displacement of an object from screen A to screen B, the child may still expect to find it behind screen A. With systematic training procedures the child could probably learn to orient his searching towards the correct screen. The relevant question here, however, is whether the infant is able to generalize from what he has learned in one situation to new and different ones. In Piaget's view, such generalization would be improbable at this developmental level. Particular reactions can be improved through particular learning acts at any given stage; what cannot be rapidly acquired, but only progressively developed through a continuous interaction with the environment, is the understanding of general spatial, temporal and causal relationships.

Stage five (from 12 to 18 months). The novelty of this stage lies in the child's interest in new events. Schemes are no longer carried on in a conservative way; rather they are actualized in various ways and thus produce variations in their outcome. Having, for instance, observed how a toy falls to the ground, the child drops it from different heights and at different angles, carefully watching what happens to it. This tendency can lead to the invention of new means to a goal. Having tried in vain to obtain an object that is out of reach on a carpet, the infant may by chance pull a corner of the carpet; observing that there is a relation between the displacement of the carpet and that of the object, he may progressively pull the carpet towards him in order to reach the object. In the same way the infant may use a stick and apply it in many different ways to a remote object until he has displaced the latter sufficiently to grasp it. Another feature of stage five is the imitation of gestures and vocalizations that do not belong to the child's spontaneous repertoire.

The interest in novelty greatly extends the child's potentialities for learning about his physical and social environment. The efficient use of new techniques means their adjustment to more and more aspects of the external situation. When it comes to the imitation of language, the infant can conform his vocalizations to the external model. Limitations do, however, arise from the child's strategies of learning. These are still restricted to trial-and-error procedures, allowing the goal to be reached only step by step. This limitation will be overcome in the next stage, where the child starts to co-ordinate his schemes on an internal level before applying them to the external situation, thus bypassing concrete correction procedures.

Stage six (from 18 to 24 months). The infant's sensori-motor schemes are developed sufficiently to become integrated into coherent structures. At the same time, the child progressively internalizes his behaviour, i.e. co-ordinates schemes by applying them to signifiers, such as symbols or signs that refer to external things, rather than to the things themselves.

The integration of particular schemes into a total structure or system is best illustrated by the child's orientation in space. Using Klein's *Vierergruppe* as model of the child's capacity to orientate himself in space, Piaget shows how any particular displacement the infant undertakes is controlled by the general properties of this group structure. While the spatial adjustment of behaviour was previously regulated through feedback processes, it can now be guided by an anticipatory control. For instance, the infant will expect to arrive back to A from B when he reverses his initial itinerary, which started from A and ended in B, or he will know that he can reach a certain place either directly or indirectly by taking an alternative route.

The occurrence of anticipatory control is shown also by the instances of "insight" behaviour, where a new solution is found without a preliminary phase of trial-and-error learning. Piaget regards insight not as the product of a sudden inspiration, nor of a learning process which would by definition be guided by external relationships, but rather as the result of an internalized, and thus more rapid, co-ordination of schemes.

The transition to internalized behaviour is likely to involve a phase of semi-internalization, in which the child mimics with his own body the external objects and the transformations he wants to apply to these objects. Piaget (1945) observed, for instance, how one child suddenly stopped his unsuccessful attempts to open a matchbox, imitated the opening of the box by opening and closing his own mouth, and then opened the matchbox without further hesitation. The imitation apparently led to a better analysis of the relations involved in the external situation and to the adjustment and mutual co-ordination of schemes before they were actually carried out.

Such behaviour has rarely been observed. It coincides, however, with the appearance of a delayed imitation and symbolic play, two activities in which the infant imitates objects or events not in the actual context of action. It seems, therefore, that imitation occurring in the absence of the model serves as a substitute for it. A further implication is that these imitative activities lead to the construction of signifiers such as mental images and language: objects and events can then be represented without external imitation.

The formation of the semiotic (or symbolic) function, as Piaget calls the infant's new faculty for creating autonomous signifiers and for operating on them instead of on the practical reality, leads to important changes in learning. The acquisition of language extends and transforms the possibilities of communication between the infant and his social environment: information, which is essential for learning, can now be exchanged more quickly, while embracing a wider range of new elements. Similar progress occurs in the use of information. More and more the infant compares new information with what he already knows by internal representation. He no longer needs to try out all new knowledge by concrete action—action that would limit the extension of new associations as well as the speed at which they are performed. Furthermore, internalized acting or representative thinking allows the reconstruction of the past and the anticipation of future actions, whereas sensori-motor behaviour was limited by the present context of action.

As previously mentioned, the development of conceptual or representative thinking takes time. From the age of two to six or seven, the child's conceptual understanding of things lags behind certain types of sensori-motor behaviour, which form a consistent system. In spite of the fact that he is now exposed to models, such as language, which reflect certain logical structures, he cannot learn these through simple verbal transmission. According to Piaget, concepts correspond to internalized sensori-motor schemes and they will evolve like these schemes: starting from an undifferentiated state and lacking interconnection they are used in more precise contexts and become increasingly co-ordinated with each other, thus ending up as well defined units of a coherent system.

The Child's Construction of Object Permanence

We have already seen that the infant gives meaning to elements of his environment by integrating them into his sensori-motor schemes or, at a later stage, into his mental schemes, i.e. concepts. Therefore, the infant's knowledge of the external world reflects the structure and interrelation of his schemes at any stage of his cognitive development. Piaget (1937) illustrated this by deducing from the child's behaviour in many different situations his conception of basic categories, such as space, time, causality and the object-notion. He gives special importance to the object-concept, as its construction reflects the development of all the other categories and can be analysed through relatively simple experiments.

The main aspects of the object-notion are its principles of invariance. Among these, object permanence (which is also called object conservation or existence constancy) is the most prominent one, as it refers to the whole object and not just to certain of its properties: as adults we believe things to keep their identity and to have a continuous existence, whatever their relation to our perceptual field may be. An object may be seen at different distances or from different angles and will still be recognized as such. And if we can no longer perceive it, we continue to believe in its existence and expect to find it localized somewhere in space, according to its previous displacements.

This seems to be common sense. The whole object-notion, with its aspects of identity, consistency, and autonomous and permanent existence, represents, however, a strongly debated epistemological question; and, for Piaget, the child takes two years, i.e. the whole length of the sensori-motor period, to reach it. Thereby he attributes permanence to his mother at an earlier age than he does to inanimate objects (Gouin-Décarie, 1965; Bell, 1970).

According to Bower (1967), seven-week-old babies believed in the possible reappearance of an interesting object if it underwent a gradual perspective disappearance. But in more recent research, Bower *et al.* (1971) observed the infant's visual tracking response towards moving, disappearing and reappearing objects, and his new results cast doubt on his earlier interpretation, i.e. that young babies believed in the continued existence of an object as such.

The ontogeny of object and person permanence embraces a wide range of developmental processes and is still far from understood. It is briefly presented here as Piaget describes it, without relating it to its perceptual basis (such as the constancy of size, form and colour), which in itself represents a field of deep controversy (compare, for instance, von Holst, 1957, and Piaget, 1961).

Stages one and two (from birth to 4.5 months). During the first two sensori-motor stages the infant seems to recognize certain external elements on which he acts repeatedly; he also forms his earliest habits by associating certain actions with some objects rather than with others. For Piaget, this means that the baby recognizes a global situation defined by his own actions, postures and sensations pertaining to the object. With regard to the object in itself, the baby does not yet isolate it as an autonomous element of the external world, independent from his own actions and perceptions and which has a continuous existence. Thus, if the experimenter distracts the child while he is playing with a toy, he will not return to the toy; similarly, if an object he touched and wanted to grasp moves accidentally beyond his reach, he does not search for it.

In general, the young infant seems to live in a world of moving pictures, unrelated to each other; they disappear and reappear as if by magic. This impression is strengthened by the poor co-ordination between actions that are controlled through different sensory modalities, even though they may concern the same objects. The infant seems in fact not to live in a homogeneous space, but in a plurality of heterogeneous spaces, corresponding to the unco-ordinated perceptual fields of his sensory modalities.

Stage three (from 4.5 to 9 months). At this stage objects become more coherent, as they are now consistently grasped and manipulated under visual control. Furthermore, a series of new types of behaviour appear; and these lead to object permanence in stage four. The infant now follows rapidly moving objects with his eyes and, in certain cases, anticipates their position (for instance, when objects fall, the child anticipates their landing). After a momentary distraction he returns to the object he was manipulating or trying to grasp before the distraction. Yet, in this and other cases, the relative permanence thus attributed to the object depends on the infant's motivation to resume or to continue an action, and the mechanisms of this permanence are often based on the continuation of the adjustment or accommodation of an action to its object. Things are not yet perceived and handled as autonomous objects, consistent in their duration in time and localized in relation to other objects. Thus the infant will free his field of vision by removing a cloth from his eyes, yet he will not remove a screen covering an object. And, even in a state of great hunger and thirst, he will not attempt to get hold of the milk-bottle which the experimenter hides in his hands or under the child's blanket.

Stages four and five (from 9 to 18 months). During these stages the infant searches for a completely hidden object: the criterion Piaget uses consistently for assessing the child's understanding of object permanence. In stage four, adequate searching behaviour occurs in simple situations, where the object is placed behind an obstacle and remains there. In stage five, the baby can comprehend a succession of visible displacements, thus searching for a hidden object in the last hiding place. He no longer expects, as in stage four, to find the object in a familiar place, and he is no longer satisfied by looking for it in its first hiding-place. In fact the infant now becomes capable of focusing attention on the external reality. Objectivity is thus achieved for spatial, temporal and causal relationships. This progress is revealed in the increasing coherence of the object-concept. Reciprocally, the development of the previously mentioned categories—spatial, temporal and causal—depends on the object being a consistent element of the outside world.

Stage six (from 18 months to 2 years). Finally, the infant finds objects in cases where their previous displacement could not have been watched. For instance, the experimenter may take a coin, close his hand and move it under several objects. If he then shows an empty hand to the child, the infant will search under all objects until he has found the coin. Objects have thus reached such a degree of permanence that their disappearance can no longer mystify the child, even if their location has to be inferred from previous events. This is possible only because the child has organized space into a group-structure, which interrelates all positions and displacements of the child's own body and of external elements with each other. But, at the same time, this "group of displacements" is absolutely dependent on the object as its fundamental invariant.

The infant now becomes capable of delayed imitation and symbolic play: through these two activities absent objects are represented and must therefore necessarily be conceived as permanent. This brings us back to the formation of the symbolic or semiotic function, which we have defined as the capacity to create and to use signifiers that are dissociated from the thing they refer to. Object permanence represents thus a necessary condition for all cognitive progress to be achieved on a representative and conceptual level, and in particular for the acquisition of language.

Object Permanence Among Animals

The fully developed object-notion, leading to the construction of autonomous signifiers and forming a coherent system with other cognitive categories, is a particularly human achievement. Animals, however, live in the same physical world, and any practical understanding of the general principles according to which this world is organized may provide them with some adaptive advantage.

As Lorenz has pointed out, species differ in the way they deal with spatial, temporal and causal relationships (Lorenz, 1941) and with the fact that objects or individuals remain identical (Lorenz, 1935). With regard to object-notion, we may therefore expect to find adaptive behaviours reflecting the phylogenetical history of the species. Furthermore, animals may show some degree of object permanence where this is of special selective advantage, but no permanence at all in other areas of their interaction with the environment. In a broad classification, based on the animal's reactions to the disappearance of an object, a prey or another member of the same species, we may distinguish three kinds or degrees of object permanence:

(1) Predatory species of various phyla have developed special devices to increase the chance of further contact with a prey that has disappeared. On an elementary level—insects, spiders, and some lower vertebrates—the animals may adopt stereotyped searching postures or movements when they lose sight of the prey. Experiments on the dragonfly larva (*Aeschna cyanea* M.) have shown that the duration of these after-reactions depends on the intensity of the prey stimulus and on the animal's locomotor behaviour during its presentation (Etienne, 1972). It seems probable, therefore, that the larva's search for a hidden prey is determined by physiological after-effects, following upon the activation of the systems controlling the predatory behaviour.

In the dragonfly larva, a kind of elementary permanence thus exists in a merely physiological dimension. This permanence lasts for a limited time span and concerns only objects that have a specific survival value: it is therefore unrelated to any general cognitive structure within the animal.

(2) In many species, appetitive and aversive behaviours seem to be totally controlled by perceptual cues. These cues may either form part of the desired or avoided element, or they may have been associated with it in the animal's earlier experience. The species concerned—which include birds such as the pigeon and the domestic chicken, and mammals such as the rabbit (Krushinskii, 1962)—show no sign of object permanence. However, they apparently can learn delayed responses, and can be trained to search successfully for an object that repeatedly disappears in standardized

spatial and temporal conditions. It may well be that the development of real object permanence in the human infant starts in this way, namely with the formation of delayed searching responses; this response would involve familiar objects only and would not yet be guided by any general understanding of spatial or temporal relationships.

(3) The European jay (*Garrulus G. Glandarius L.*) (Bossema, 1968 and pers. comm.), crows and other *corvidae* (Krushinskii, 1962), as well as certain mammalian carnivores (Krushinskii, 1962; Thompson and Heron, 1954), monkeys (Tinklepaugh, 1928); Vaughter *et al.*, 1972) and apes (Köhler, 1922) spontaneously search for hidden objects. These species seem to have a good spatial orientation, to be able to tolerate temporal delays and to show plasticity and adaptibility in their behaviour. The development of their behaviour is relatively slow and very open to environmental influences; it is not unlikely that it passes through a series of stages that could be characterized in terms of their overall structure or organization.

Two studies dealing with object permanence in the growing animal are summarized below. The first is concerned with the formation of delayed response in the domestic chick. We will see that the acquisition of this response occurs step by step, but is unrelated to any general stage of cognitive development. The second relates to the domestic cat, which attains an elementary form of genuine object permanence, the continuous development of which is expressed through a variety of behaviour patterns.

The domestic chick

Fig. 1 shows one of the situations in which I attempted to train young chicks to search for a prey-object that had disappeared. In each trial the chick was placed between the two screens, facing a worm inside a glass tube. The worm was then pulled through the tube—the chick following it —until it disappeared behind a screen. The chick was then left for one minute in the test box. It could get the worm either by going directly behind the correct screen, or by circling first round the wrong screen and then finding its way behind the correct screen. Individual chicks were trained for one day in three separate sessions, and on each occasion the procedure was repeated ten times.

Chicks of the age of three, six and fourteen days developed qualitatively the same searching pattern (Etienne, in prep.b). In the first trials, they pecked a few times against the screen behind which the worm had disappeared, and then showed behaviour the orientation of which seemed unrelated to the worm. Sooner or later—generally during one of the first three trials—they walked fortuitously behind the correct screen and found the worm. From that time onwards, birds of all age-groups learned rather rapidly to go behind the screens after the disappearance of the worm (Fig. 2a). It was, however, apparent during the first two training sessions that the chicks did not observe the direction in which the worm had

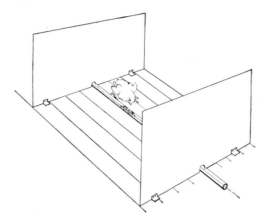

Fig. 1. The double-screen test. The chicks were placed between two screens (40 × 25 cm), 32 cm apart. A mealworm, which was protected by a glass tube, was then pulled in one direction and disappeared behind a screen. The bird was left one minute in the text box (60 × 60 cm) and could eat the worm if it went behind the right screen.

disappeared; they started by going behind the wrong screen so often as the correct one (Fig. 2b). The percentage of trials in which the chicks immediately chose the correct screen became higher than chance only during the third training session, and many birds never learned to adjust their initial search to the directional cue. This was especially so with the six-day-old chicks, which learned to take into account the directional clue significantly less than the three-day-old birds. Indeed, the youngest chicks were most successful in this respect.

Differences in the rearing conditions and in the preliminary experience with moving and disappearing cues influenced the two aspects of the chicks' searching strategies (Etienne, in prep.a). One experiment gave particularly unexpected results. On days three, four and five, chicks were presented with mealworms, which they followed along a glass tube with an opaque section (tunnel) in its centre. When tested on day six in the standardized double-screen situation, they learned significantly better than their naïve controls to take the directional cue into account. A series of control experiments were carried out to determine what the tunnel-experienced birds had learned to use in the totally different double-screen situation. Birds that could follow worms travelling through a completely transparent tube learned even more quickly to choose the correct initial direction than tunnel-experienced birds. It this seems that the tunnel-experienced group had not learned anything that was relevant to the disappearance and reappearance of the worm. Instead, they had simply learned to follow the worm more intensively and continuously so long as it was visible. This interpretation was confirmed by further controls and observations.

A last step in this research consisted in studying how the preliminary opportunity to follow visible moving cues affected the chick's behaviour in the double-screen situation at two different ages. During the three days that preceded their testing in the double-screen situation, both age-groups were presented with worms that were pulled through a totally transparent glass tube. Fig. 3 shows that this preliminary experience significantly im-

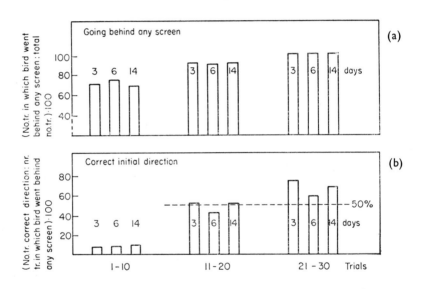

Fig. 2. Results of double-screen test. Chicks of 3, 6, and 14 days ($N = 59$) were trained in three sessions, each of 10 trials, to search for a worm which had disappeared behind one of two screens. (a) percentage of trials in which the animals went behind either of the two screens, for each of the three training sessions. (b) number of trials in which the chicks went directly (within 8 sec after the disappearance of the worm) behind the correct screen, as a percentage of the total number of trials in which the birds went behind either screen.

proved the capacity of six-day-old chicks to go immediately behind the right screen, but not that of thirteen-day-old ones. Thus the preliminary exposure to visible moving cues improved the birds' performance significantly only in the age-group that normally showed a deficiency of attention in following the partially visible cue.

These experiments indicate that very young chicks readily learned searching behaviour in relation to a hidden prey in a constant situation. Their searching strategies were mainly based on a simple association between a given place (the space behind the screens) and the presence of a reward. This association was at first independent of the direction in which the worm had been moved. Some chicks—not more than 50% in any age-

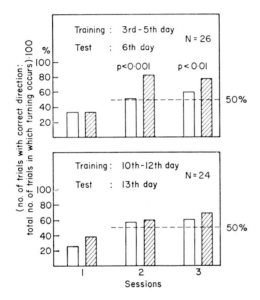

Fig. 3. Effects of pre-training 3–5 and 10–12 day old chicks with worms pulled through a glass tube on double screen test. Both chicks which had preliminary experience with moving worms (hatched bars) and naïve controls (open bars) were given three test sessions, each of 10 trials. Number of trials (in each of the three test sessions) in which the birds chose the right screen (within 8 sec after the disappearance of the worm) as percentage of the total number of trials in which the birds went behind any screen.

group—learned the additional step of adjusting their search to the previously perceived directional cue. The hidden prey then elicited correctly oriented searching behaviour in the chicks, one of the main criteria for object permanence. However, this progress represented a differentiation of the stereotyped delayed response the birds had so far established. The chicks did not, for instance, look just for the one worm that had disappeared in a given direction; rather, after having eaten it, they continued to circle around the screens as before.

Any progress in the adjustment of behaviour to such general aspects of the phenomenal world as object permanence should increase with age and experience. Yet the youngest chicks in these experiments developed the most adequate searching behaviour, and there was an unexpected drop in the performance of naïve birds at the age of six days. On the other hand, the effect of experience with moving and disappearing objects depended on the birds' increased attention to a moving cue; it did not involve learning that an object that disappeared in one direction was likely to be localized in the same direction.

As previously mentioned, it is possible that, at a very early stage, the human infant extends his reactions from perceptible to imperceptible elements of his environment in the same way as the chick learns to look for a hidden worm in these experiments. The child's expectation to see the mother reappear through a certain door, or the repeated discovery of a missing toy under his blanket, may involve a precursory level of object permanence. The factors that guide the baby's search at this stage cannot yet be related to the knowledge of objective spatial and temporal relationships between things and events. In the child, such an initial conditioning to the permanence of certain privileged objects is then integrated by his cognitive structure and thus generalized to all objects. The chick, on the contrary, seems not to go beyond the association between certain stimuli and certain responses to these stimuli, and such associations remain limited to a standardized situation. The bird's experience leads to the construction of certain adaptive responses, but it is not absorbed into a general cognitive structure, and thus does not change this structure. On the basis of what we know so far, we can assume that the chicken at three days learns to search for a hidden object as well as, or perhaps in certain respects even better than a fully-grown bird (Révész, 1924; Krushinskii, 1962).

The domestic cat

Gruber et al. (1971) studied the development of object permanence in the kitten, using animals between six days and 110 weeks. The majority of them were laboratory-raised, but a few were house-reared. The research was carried out in a Piaget-like style, namely by exposing the animals to several situations, to investigate behaviour typical of various aspects of object permanence.

Gruber et al. came to the conclusion that the domestic cat reaches at about 20 weeks a degree of object permanence that the child reaches at nine months. Its development follows a series of steps that closely resemble the first four stages Piaget has described for the construction of the object-notion.

Stage one (from birth to 4 weeks). The kitten does not respond to a distinct auditory click made laterally to the animal or to a visual stimulus presented in front of him. It seems that at this age the animal is still predominantly responsive to olfactory and tactual stimuli relevant to feeding—feeding being nearly always initiated by the mother approaching the litter (Schneirla *et al.*, 1963). Learning in the newborn kitten concerns mainly gradual progress in his feeding adjustment to the mother.

Stage two (from 4 to 7 weeks). From the twentieth day, the kitten will approach the mother for feeding (Schneirla *et al.*, 1963). Approximately one week later, when the animal has achieved basic aspects of sensorimotor co-ordination (Hein and Held, 1967), he will turn his head towards a sound and track visible objects. He now orientates his behaviour to certain distinct objects, such as a soft cloth object, which he plays with and follows visually when it is moved about. Yet the kitten arrests his tracking movements at the point of disappearance of an object swinging in a circular orbit around him and shows a startle response when the object reappears on his other side. Furthermore, if a kitten plays with a soft object on a chair and accidentally knocks it down, thus temporarily losing sight of it, he does not follow it to the floor. Similarly he does not return to a play-object after being distracted by the momentary presentation of a visual or auditory stimulus. And in situations where the animal is left undistracted with an interesting object, he plays with it for something between 15 seconds and a few minutes. At a later stage, this time span will be increased to 15 minutes.

Stage three (from 7 to 16 weeks). The kitten will follow a soft cloth object after pushing it off the chair. Similarly, he anticipates the direction in which an object that swings around his head will reappear. The play-object thus continues to control the kitten's behaviour after having left his immediate field of action and perception. But if the animal is distracted by the experimenter while he is playing, so that the continuity of his behaviour is more strongly interrupted, he does not reorientate his behaviour to the object. If the experimenter covers an object with a cloth just as the kitten reaches for it, the animal will paw the cloth for a few seconds, and then wander off.

Stage four (from 16 weeks onwards). This stage is characterized by the appearance of true searching behaviour for a play-object that has been covered by the experimenter. The animal now paws at the cloth much more vigorously than before, until he recovers the object. If the cloth is difficult to remove, the animal persists for one or two minutes.

Stage five. A further development of object permanence would be shown by moving an object through a series of visible displacements in order to see if the animal goes directly to the last hiding-place. Because of the great speed at which kittens react, this stage could not be tested.

Stage six. The main criterion of this stage is the subject's search for a hidden object whose displacement could not be seen. The two oldest house-reared kittens of this study were seven months old. If the play-object was hidden under a cloth while they were distracted by the experimenter, they gave some signs of search. They started wandering about the area where the object had last been seen, emitting sharp cries. But they did not search in the specific place where they had last encountered it. Laboratory-reared kittens of the age of 20 months did not recover the object. This level of object permanence may thus not be reached by the domestic cat.

Finally, object permanence was reached somewhat sooner by house-reared than by laboratory-reared kittens. This result, too, expresses the similarity between the development of the subject-object relationship in the kitten and in the human infant: in both species the establishment of this relationship depends on the opportunity of achieving sensori-motor co-ordination through correlating active movement with changes in sensory input (Held, 1965) and on the amount and variety of general physical and social experience.

Final Remarks

We have distinguished three basically different ways in which animals may react to the disappearance of an object, thus conforming in various degrees to the principle of object permanence. The types of behaviours mentioned or described in three different species express different kinds of cognitive organization. These are characterized, among other things, by the learning processes they allow to occur.

Dragonfly larvae recognize their prey by a few fixed characteristics, they show stereotyped predatory behaviour and are probably not able to extend their learning capacities beyond the formation of elementary associations between the presence of food and other stimuli in their environment. They react to the disappearance of prey by exhibiting equally stereotyped movements or postures: it is unlikely that an extended experience with vanishing and reappearing prey could modify the form or orientation of their searching responses.

The domestic chick acquires much information about its environment at the very beginning of its life, as when, for instance, it becomes imprinted on its mother or learns to recognize food. At a very early age this nidifugous bird is equipped with highly developed learning mechanisms, allowing it to associate certain responses with stimuli that are in its perceptual field or have been presented shortly before the onset of the response. The animal will normally not make use of such previously perceived cues. The mere capacity to perform delayed responses may, however, represent a necessary step in evolution towards behaviour not solely controlled by immediately perceived external elements. Indeed, we have considered the possibility that the chick's conditioned search and the young infant's first searching responses towards hidden objects may be acquired through similar processes. From a phylogenetical as well as on-togenetical point of view, specific delayed responses may thus represent a precursor to object permanence.

In order to show spontaneously adaptive behaviour which conforms to object permanence, an animal must have experienced the temporal and spatial aspects of this principle under many different conditions and gen-eralized this experience from one situation to another. The achievement of object permanence would therefore require a slowly developing cognitive system, which is very open to external influences and can thus change its own structure through the integration of this experience. We have seen that the development of object permanence in the kitten and in the infant proceeds on the same lines, with the difference that it progresses more quickly and stops at an earlier stage in the kitten than in the infant. It may be that any kind of cognitive organization that allows the animal to behave in accordance with very general aspects of the external world develops according to identical principles. It would be worthwhile to test this hy-pothesis through ontogenetical studies in other species, and especially in primates.

Acknowledgements

I want to thank Professor R. A. Hinde for criticizing the manuscript, Miss E. Ellem and Miss M. Luft for translating my English into English, and Miss J. Hanby and Mr. D. Bygott for drawing Fig. 1.

References

Bell, S. M. (1970). The development of the concept of object as related to infant-mother attachment. *Child Dev.* **41**, 291–311.

Bower, T. G. R. (1967). The development of object-permanence: some studies of existence constancy. *Perception and Psychophysics* **2**, 411–418.

Bower, T. G. R., Broughton, J. M. and Moore, M. K. (1970a). Demonstration of intention in the reaching behaviour of neonate humans. *Nature* **228**, 679–681.

Bower, T. G. R., Broughton, J. M. and Moore, M. K. (1970b). The co-ordination of visual and tactual input in infants. *Perception and Psychophysics* **8**, 51–53.

Bower, T. G. R., Broughton, J. M. and Moore, M. K. (1971). Development of the object concept as manifested in changes in the tracking behaviour of infants between 7 and 20 weeks of age. *J. exp. Child Psychol.* **11**, 182–193.

Bossema, I. (1968). Recovery of acorns in the European jay. *Koninkl. Nederl. Akad. v. Wetenschappen.* Proceeding Series C, **71**, 1–5.

Bruner, J. S. (1964). The course of cognitive development. *Am. Psychol.* **19**, 1–16.

Bryant, P. E. and Trabasso, T. (1971). Transitive inferences and memory in young children. *Nature* **232**, 456–458.

Etienne, A. S. (1972). The behaviour of the dragonfly larva *Aeschna cyanea* M. after a short presentation of a prey. *J. Animal Behav.* **20**, 724–731.

Etienne, A. S. (In prep.a). Searching towards a disappearing prey in the domestic chick as affected by preliminary experience.

Etienne, A. S. (In prep.b). Searching towards a disappearing prey in domestic chicks of different ages.

Gouin-Décarie, T. (1965). "Intelligence and Affectivity in Early Childhood; an Experimental Study of Jean Piaget's Object Concept and Object relations." International Universities Press, New York.

Gruber, H. E., Girgus, J. S. and Banuazizi, A. (1971). The development of object permanence in the cat. *Devl. Psychol.* **4**, 9–15.

Haynes, H., White, B. L. and Held, R. (1965). Visual accommodation in human infants. *Science* **148**, 528–530.

Hein, A. and Held, R. (1967). Dissociation of the visual response into elicited and guided components. *Science* **158**, 390–392.

Held, R. and Hein, A. (1963). Movement-produced stimulation in the development of visually guided behaviour. *J. comp. physiol. Psychol.* **56**, 872–876.

Held, R. (1965). Plasticity in sensory-motor systems. *Sci. Am.* **213**, 84–94.

Held, R. and Bauer, J. (1967). Visually guided reaching in infant monkeys after restricted rearing. *Science* **155**, 718–720.

Hinde, R. A. (1971). Some problems in the study of the development of social behaviour. *In* "The Psychobiology of Development", (E. Tobach, L. R. Aronson and E. Shaw, eds.) pp. 411–432. Academic Press, New York.

Holst, E. von (1957). Aktive Leistungen menschlicher Gesichtswahrnehmung. *Studium Generale* **4**, 213–243.

Inhelder, B. (1956). Criteria of the stages of mental development. *In* "Discussions on Child Development", Vol. I (J. M. Tanner and B. Inhelder, eds.) pp. 75–107. Tavistock, London.

Inhelder, B., Bovet, M., Sinclair, H. and Smock, C. D. (1966). On cognitive development. *Am. Psychol.* **21**, 160–164.

Köhler, W. (1922). Uber eine neue Methode zur psychologischen Untersuchung von Menschenaffen. *Psychol. Forschung* **1**, 390–397.

Kruschinskii, L. V. (1962). "Animal Behaviour: its Normal and Abnormal Development." Consultants Bureau, New York.

Lorenz, K. (1935). Der Kumpan in der Umwelt des Vogels. *J. Ornithol.* **83**, 137–213, 289–413.

Lorenz, K. (1941). Kant's Lehre vom Apriorischen im Lichte der gegenwärtigen Biologie. *Blätter f. dts. Philos.* **15**, 94–125.

Lipsitt, L. P. (1969). Learning capacities in the human infant. *In* "Brain and Early Behaviour", (R. J. Robinson, ed.) pp. 227–245. Academic Press, New York.

Lunzer, E. A. (1972). The Piaget controversy. *Times Educational Suppl.* **2960**, 18, 71.

Mehler, J. and Bever, T. G. (1967). Cognitive capacity of very young children. *Science* **159**, 141–142.

Moreau, T., Birch, H. C. and Turkewitz, G. (1970). Ease of habituation to repeated auditory and somesthetic stimulation in the human newborn. *J. exp. Child Psychol.* **3**, 193–207.

Piaget, J. (1935). "La Naissance de l'Intelligence chez l'Enfant." Delachaux et Niestlé, Neuchâtel.

Piaget, J. (1937). "La Construction du Réel chez l'Enfant." Delachaux et Niestlé, Neuchâtel.

Piaget, J. (1945). "La Formation du Symbol chez l'Enfant." Delachaux et Niestlé, Neuchâtel.

Piaget, J. (1959). Apprentissage et Connaissance. In "Etudes d'épistémologie genetique", Vol. VII. (J. Piaget, ed.) pp. 21–67. P.U.F., Paris.

Piaget, J. (1961). "Les Mécanismes Perceptifs." P.U.F., Paris.

Piaget, J. (1967). "Biologie et Connaissance." Gallimard, Paris.

Piaget, J. (1968a). "Le Structuralisme." P.U.F., Paris.

Piaget, J. (1968b). Quantification, Conservation and Nativism, Science 162, 976–979.

Piaget, J. and Inhelder, B. (1969). The gaps in empiricism. In "Beyond Reductionism". (A. Koestler and J. R. Smythies, eds.) pp. 118–160. Hutchinson, London.

Prechtl, H. F. R. (1969). The problems for study. In "Brain and Early Behaviour", (Robinson, R. J., ed.). Hutchinson, London.

Révész, G. (1924). Experiments on animal space perception. Brit. J. Psychol. 14, 387–414.

Schneirla, T. C., Rosenblatt, J. S. and Tobach, E. (1963). Maternal behaviour in the cat. In "Maternal Behaviour in Mammals", (H. C. Rheingold, ed.), pp. 122–168. Wiley & Sons, New York.

Thompson, W. R. and Heron, W. (1954). The effect of restricting early experience on the problem solving capacity in dogs. Canad. J. Psychol. 8, 17–31.

Tinklepaugh, C. R. (1928). An experimental study of representative factors in monkeys. J. comp. Psychol. 8, 197–236.

Vaughter, R. M., Smotherman, W. and Ordy, J. M. (1972). Development of object permanence in the infant squirrel monkey. Devl. Psychol. 7, 34–38.

Wertheimer, M. (1961). Psychomotor coordination of auditory and visual space at birth. Science 134, 1692.

19

Some Remarks on the Genevan Point of View on Learning with Special Reference to Language Learning

by H. Sinclair

During the period which Hinde (Chapter 1, this volume) referred to as a period of heroic optimism, many psychologists published works on "laws of learning", "learning theories", etc. It is certainly no accident that among the rare notable deviationists from this trend were the developmental psychologists, Baldwin and Werner, to name two, and, of course, Piaget, on whose theory this paper is based.

In Piaget's work the term "learning" hardly occurs until the publication of volume VII of the Etudes d'Epistémologie Génétique, entitled "Apprentissage et connaissance" (1959) followed in the same year by "La logique des apprentissages". Most of his works have titles such as "The growth of logical thinking" (1956), "The child's construction of reality" (1937), etc. In Piaget's view, learning in a strict sense cannot be dissociated from *development* in general. Moreover, as an epistemologist, Piaget is interested in the acquisition of knowledge by human beings, and therefore in concept formation in a rather special sense: i.e. the acquisition of basic notions which form a consistent conceptual framework inside which different pieces of information and various discoveries can be organized. In this sense, the central question concerning learning is whether this framework of thought is built up by means of a mosaic of bits of learning acquired haphazardly, or whether on the contrary all learning, i.e. the assimilation of external data, is dependent upon, and varies with, internal organizational levels (developmental stages). The latter answer is the one given by Piaget, based on many years of experimental work and theoretical elaboration. It may be useful, in this paper to clarify, in the Piaget

sense, certain terms, e.g. "basic concepts", "learning", "cognitive development", with the aid of some examples.

Basic Concepts

There are different kinds of basic concepts; roughly they may be divided into logico-mathematical concepts on the one hand, and concepts
belonging to physics on the other hand. Though not acquired in exactly
the same way, both kinds of knowledge depend on the subject's interaction
with his environment, the accent being on *action*; the experiences resulting
from this interaction are constructed by the child according to his level of
development.

An example of a logico-mathematical concept is the concept of natural
numbers, with all that goes with it—ordinality, cardinality, commutativity,
additivity, etc. Suppose that a child of four (well below the age at which
the concept of number is normally established) is given five blocks, and is
told by an adult that he can count them, using his fingers: "see", the adult
says, "one, two, three, four, five, five blocks". What kind of learning may
take place? Exceptionally, the child may simply and passively learn a trick,
which will bring him praise. Normally, however, he will think, and *act*. He
will put the blocks in a row, or build a tower, and he will notice that the
row gets larger or the tower higher with every block added; he will arrange
the blocks in different ways, and find that four go nicely together in a
square, but that the last one does not fit; in short, he will be learning from
his actions. These actions will later become mental operations on numbers,
such as knowing that adding one and substracting one comes to the same as
doing nothing at all, that putting two and three together is equivalent to
adding one and four, etc. Being told the names of the numbers he will
somehow or other link this information (well before he has acquired these
operations) to what are as yet pre-operations on and pre-concepts of dis-
continuous quantities. He may, for example, regard the numbers almost as
if they were names for the individual blocks; or he may link the number
five to the last block in the row, but not to the total collection, and treat
"five" rather like an older child would treat "the fifth". Unless he is a
genius, he will not, at that age, and by such training, acquire the full-
fledged concept of number.

An example of a concept in physics is the notion of inertia (or rather,
conservation of movement). A six-year-old may be shown how to build a
slope with some bricks and a plank, and to have a toy car running down it.
Again, he will not simply copy this situation without reflecting and acting
on it; he will vary the angle of the slope, he may take other objects to roll
down the slope, and he may learn something about gravity, make remarks

and ask questions on weight, but we should not expect him to derive the concept of inertia, as Galileo did, from such a situation. Learning is neither passive copying, nor the emergence of pre-established ideas.

According to Piaget, psychologically and epistemologically important learning consists of active construction of a gradually widening and at the same time more solid framework of logical thinking and of a progressively more ordered world of physical objects. Though these acquisitions require discussion with other people and a stimulating environment in general, they do not need external reinforcement, and they are never lost, except in pathological cases. Much, if not most, of this important learning or cognitive development (in this sense there is no difference between the two terms) takes place so to say subterraneously, without any direct change in behaviour being observable. Piaget's famous tasks tap this basic knowledge, and allow us to observe behavioural changes due to a progress in cognitive structure, often in subtle detail thanks to the exploratory dialogue the experimenter conducts with the subjects. The interviewing method is extensively adapted to each individual child, but the tests are not meant to provide the investigator with a diagnosis of individual intellectual capacities or achievements; on the contrary, Piaget is interested in the acquisition of knowledge in general, in the development of The Subject. The knowledge acquired is neither an externally imposed link between events, to which the subject passively submits (as extreme empiricists would maintain), nor an emergence of latent, inborn concepts released by an experience which acts only as a catalyst (as extreme rationalists would maintain).

Cognitive Development and Learning

Piaget's formalizations of successive stages in cognitive development have to be seen as structural models of the output of the knowing subject. At the same time, however, Piaget is concerned with the process itself; and though on this point he has gone less far in the construction of a formal model, it is clear from many works that his process model will be of a biological type, based on regulatory mechanisms. Such mechanisms link human beings to other organisms through a functional continuity. Just as lower organisms compensate for variations in the environment (causing a disequilibrium or a disturbance) by a recombination of already existing elements, so that a new adaptive complex results, so new patterns of thought grow out of the combinations of already existing patterns (with the possible difference that it is the growing thought patterns themselves that create the disturbance). By assimilating more and more varied contents a certain pattern of thought or action will encounter an obstacle to which it cannot accommodate; the subject will then search for a different but allied pattern which is already established and will find a new combination to deal with the situation, thereby creating a new, more powerful, pattern. In this way, each new acquisition opens up possibilities for conflicts, whose resolution leads to new structures of thought.

This theory provides us with a succession of general stages, which can be subdivided into smaller steps, and whose formalization makes it possible to discover connections between many different behavioural changes that might otherwise seem to to be unconnected results of atomistic "learning" in the classical sense. The regulatory mechanisms by which transition from one sub-stage to another takes place are rooted in the biology of all living organisms, but the stages and sub-stages themselves are species-specific. Since the regulatory mechanisms are closely linked to the underlying structures, they acquire a different significance in the context of human knowledge. Evidently, children do not only acquire basic concepts; they also learn many types of behaviour which may seem to find a simpler explanation in the classical "laws of learning"; e.g. brushing one's teeth, eating with a spoon, reciting the names of all the villages in the Canton of Geneva, crossing the street when the light goes green, etc. However, when examined closely, even these achievements have, to a greater or lesser extent, something to do with general cognitive structures: they imply spatial or temporal coordinations, and some kind of hierarchical organization. It may well be that the limited learning situations which were thought to reveal universal rules of learning are in fact very special cases of much more profound and general processes.

Speaking in terms of constraints, or, as Piaget prefers, factors of development, the establishment of cognitive structure can be said to depend on the following:

(1) maturation (of the CNS, of motoric and perceptual abilities),

(2) stimulation through interaction with the environment, using "environment" in the broadest sense,

(3) equilibration or regulation mechanisms.

The second factor, i.e. environmental stimulation, has traditionally been stressed by empiricists, whereas the third factor, equilibration, has been introduced by Piaget into psychology and has fundamental significance. Development is obviously dependent on external stimulation, but apparently very little on specific situations. Likeable and reliable people have to be around, food and cover have to be provided, etc. But it doesn't seem to make any difference what particular kinds of objects are available. Whether young children live in New York, in a tropical forest or in a snow-covered region does not seem to alter their basic cognitive development in any important way. Many inter-cultural studies (e.g. Mosheni, 1966; Opper, 1970; Bovet, 1968; Dasen, 1970) have shown this universality. Babies playing with educational toys, or with sticks and stones, or even only with their mother's hair and their own fingers if they are carried on their mother's back, seem to pass through the same succession of developmental stages and, at least up till the age of two years, with the same speed (Dasen, personal communication).

According to Piaget's theory, it is less the external circumstances than the internal equilibration factor (the recombination of patterns into new structures) that sets limits to what can be learned; but it is also this same factor that opens up new possibilities at every step forward. An experiment designed by Bovet (Inhelder *et al.*, in press) illustrates how what may be a limitation or an obstacle to learning at one stage, may be an incitement to new acquisitions at another, and can be treated as an already structured complex element at still another stage.

The procedure is the following: both the experimenter and the subject have a number of matchsticks at their disposal; but the child's matches are shorter than those of the experimenter, and of a different colour (7 of the subject's red matches add up to the same length as 5 of the experimenter's green matches). The experimenter constructs a model road (either in a straight or in a broken line) and the child is asked to construct a straight road of equal length ("just as long a road", "just as far to walk"). Three situations are presented (see Figs. a, b and c). Situation (a) is the first one presented, though situation (c) is the easiest and the one that suggests the correct solution to (b) and (a). All three situations remain on view to the subject after he has made his first construction, and he is led to reconsider his initial solutions, encouraged by the experimenter to compare the different situations.

The most primitive solution to situation (a) is the construction of a line whose extremities are congruent with the extremities of the model line; with 4 small matches a straight road is constructed with the same points of departure and arrival. Despite the zig-zags of the model, the child asserts that "the roads are just as long, you have just as far to walk". In situation (b) the elementary solution is to count the matches, regardless of the fact that the subject's matches are shorter than those of the model road. Since the child is asked to construct his road away from the model, he cannot use the ordinal reference-points of points of arrival and departure. In situation (c) the ordinal reference gives the correct solution: 7 short matches in a straight line. According to their level of cognitive development, the subjects (5 and 6 year olds) showed four distinct behaviour patterns. At the earliest level, no suggestion by the experimenter that they should compare the situations has any effect: the children give the primitive solutions to situations (a) and (b), and the correct solution to (c), and they are totally satisfied with their answers. At a slightly more advanced level, situation

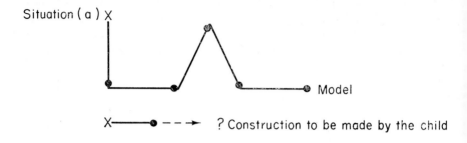

Situation (a) X   Model

X————● – – →   ? Construction to be made by the child

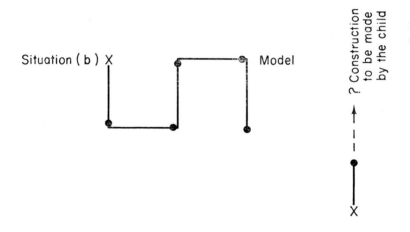

Situation (b) X   Model

? Construction to be made by the child

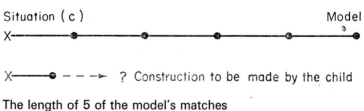

Situation (c)   Model
X

X————● – – –→   ? Construction to be made by the child

The length of 5 of the model's matches
= that of 7 of the child's matches

Fig. 1. Length-construction experiment situations (a), (b) and (c).

(b), where they build their road with the same number of matches as the experimenter's road, creates perplexity in situations (a) and (c); in situation (a), using 5 matches results in a straight road that "goes further" (as the children say) than the model road, in situation (c) it results in a road that "goes less far" than the model road. The efforts made by these children to link the situations result in a contradiction that cannot be resolved: they conclude that a road of equal length cannot be constructed with their matches, only with the experimenter's matches. At a more advanced stage the effort to link the originally isolated patterns of solution results in interesting compromises. For example, returning to situation (a) after the numerical equivalence solution had been given for (b), the children would break one of their matchsticks in two, constructing a road with the same number of "bits" (5), which still did not go beyond the model road. In certain cases, a return to situation (c) leads to an understanding of the fact that the difference in length of the matches has to be compensated for by using more of them; a return to (b) will then result in a correct solution. No conflict arises with the child's idea of "going just as far" since in this case the two lines are not directly one beneath the other, and the child does not get the impression that his road "goes further" than the model road. At this stage, he may apply his newly found solution to situation (a) and, after an initial surprise, grasp the fact that though his road may seem to go further, this does not mean that it is longer. These subjects have achieved a new theoretical construct by recombining isolated patterns that in themselves were inadequate for the solution of the problem. At a yet higher level of development, situation (c) will immediately be taken as the key to problems (a) and (b).

Experiments such as these show that the same information presented to children at different levels of development is absorbed in quite different ways. At first, the information does not act as a disturbing factor, and the isolated modes of reasoning provide the child with satisfactory solutions. Later, this primitive equilibrium is destroyed, a conflict arises, regulatory mechanisms are activated, and a solution is found – not by totally discarding the original, isolated, thought patterns, but by coordinating and recombining them.

Piaget's aim is to arrive at an explanation of human knowledge. His principle is that this can only be achieved through the study of development, since the functioning of already constituted structures can only be understood by knowing how they have been built up. His method is the construction of abstract models, of a logical type for the structural aspect and of a biological type for the process aspect. Such models leave the possibility open of finding a "material" basis in future neurological research.

The Application of Piaget's Theory to Language Acquisition

Is it possible to apply this theory about human knowledge to other fields? Etienne (Chapter 18) has already given an example of how Piaget's theory can be heuristically fruitful for the study of animal behaviour. There would thus seem to be no obstacle to transposing the theory to the acquisition by human beings of language. Without doubt, ability to talk implies mastery of a highly complex system. Yet the difference in kind between knowledge of a language and knowledge of logic or physics should not be overlooked, if only because language is, on the one hand, a means of communicating and representing what one knows, and, on the other hand, an object to be known.

Language is only one of the manifestations of the symbolic or representative function, without which intelligence could not progress beyond the sensori-motor stage, others being mental imagery, symbolic play, gestures and drawing. This representative function has its roots in imitation (which starts during the sensori-motor period) and progresses under the influence of general cognitive development. Language, however, has a place apart. Firstly, it is a conventional system, resulting from a long series of historical changes. In other symbolic activities the subject can invent his own symbols and make his own rules, but to communicate verbally, he has to adopt the language of his environment. Secondly, language is a highly structured system with intricate rules. Other symbolic activities may imply certain techniques (drawing) and creative behaviour inside a common framework (dramatic play, games) but no knowledge comparable to that of grammar (though a special position is occupied by games such as chess—de Saussure's favourite analogy with language).

Language as a Conventional System

Comparisons between animal communication patterns and human language are hazardous; no animal species seems to have anything approaching a generative grammar. Despite the hazards, the following comparison may elucidate some points.

Certain birds do not seem to be able to change the vocalization of their species no matter to what vocal experience they may be submitted. Others, almost all the song-birds, can adopt the pattern of foster-parents, and some can even be trained to imitate human beings. Thorpe (1969) has shown that if chaffinches are reared in a sound-proofed room, or deafened at birth, they develop "what you might call the most elementary schema of what is normally regarded as the song of the species". With deaf-born infants, no such schema emerges; vocalizations, indicating distress, discontent and pleasure or contentment appear during the first months, but disappear afterwards; nothing is produced except the sounds that are the most deeply anchored in the physiological system. Obviously, experiments with infants in sound-proofed rooms are impossible for moral reasons, though they would be more conclusive. If we can believe Herodotus, a related experiment was actually carried out by putting twins in the care of a shepherd, with the understanding that he would leave them with his sheep, never talk to them, but only see to it that they were fed and otherwise cared for physically. When the shepherd observed their "first word" he was to report. This experiment was intended to determine the original form of human language. The first word reported was pronounced by the twins when the shepherd one day arrived to bring them bread and was greeted with "bèkos", meaning bread in Phrygian. Leaving aside speculation about why the word for bread should resemble the sound made by sheep, the experiment indicates rather the imitation of sheep bleating by the children than the fundamentality of Phrygian. Admittedly, no proof exists that human infants if left alone together would not elaborate something resembling a natural language—in prehistoric times something like that must have happened—but this does not detract from the fact that language acquisition is demonstrably more dependent on a specific model than cognitive development in general.

Language as a Means of Representing Knowledge

It could be supposed that language acquisition is only tied to cognitive development in general in so far as it serves to represent and to communicate what is known, and that therefore certain expressions are neither understood, nor used by young children in the way adults use them. In a trivial sense this is certainly true: children will hardly talk about Gaussian curves or electrical charges without knowing at least something about them, nor will adults belonging to cultures that are not familiar with these "objects". In a less trivial sense it has been shown that expressions such as *all, some, more, less* and the difference in acceptability between "dogs and animals" and "animals are dogs" are not apprehended in the same way by children below five as by children of seven or eight (Donaldson and Wales, 1970; Sinclair, 1967). Mental operations have to progress to a point where concepts such as comparison of quantities, class inclusion, etc., become possible, for the corresponding expressions to acquire their generally accepted sense. On the other hand, to be able to say "I want the red cherries" does not at all mean that the speaker has mastered such concepts as intersection or inclusion; in fact, from that utterance it is impossible to deduce whether the situation comprised yellow, green and red cherries, or red cherries and red apples, or just red cherries, or any other collection (though emphatic intonation would help). While it is therefore justifiable to affirm that language as a respresentation and communication of what is known is dependent upon cognitive development, this appears to be true in the sense of a direct dependence on corresponding concepts only in the case of a certain class of lexical items, of certain operator-like expressions, and certain sentence-patterns. Moreover, the fact that children use *more, all*, etc. in a different way from adults tells us something about the relation between certain aspects of language and logical thinking, and about logical thinking itself, but not very much about language acquisition. In fact, it is a rather tricky question to decide *what* has not been acquired by the child who asserts that in a bunch of 7 roses and 3 tulips there are more roses than flowers . . .

Language as a Highly Structured System to be Known

Since language is a conventional system it could be supposed (and many psychologists have thought so) that, since it depends on an explicit external model, language learning is simply a result of associative, imitative learning, and that cognitive development only intervenes in the use the subject makes of what he has learned. Since Chomsky's critique of this view, no serious psychologist can continue to defend it. Moreover, any parent or teacher knows only too well that children actively construct their language; *he goed, I taked it, my foots*, are not mere imitations of adult language heard but examples of creative, rule-governed behaviour. How does the very young child acquire such rules as plural or past-tense formation to the point that he applies them even in cases where the adult does not? How does it happen that young children the world over, whatever language they hear spoken around them, seem to go about their language acquisition task in the same manner? They all start their careers as communicators by conventional language with holophrastic utterances such as *aplu, all gone, alle alle, 'nito* (all indicating absence or disappearance); they then progress to two and three word utterances such as *Kathryn no sock, Papa non assiè* (assiette), and at least in the very early period one gets the impression (confirmed by many observations in many different languages, cf. Slobin, in press) that they go about their language acquisition in the same way: paying attention to, and producing, certain characteristics of the speech they hear around them, but not all; creating rules that have something to do with adult sentence patterns, but whose results are far from a parrot-like imitation.

Linguistic Universals and Language Acquisition

Except for Piaget and a few others, psychologists have mainly been concerned with differences among individuals or groups of individuals; similarly, linguists have been concerned with differences between languages. Language acquisition, however, reminds us forcibly of the fact that all languages are the creation of the human mind, and that they must have certain features in common. Traditional grammarians were interested in linguistic universals, but this interest was frowned upon until Chomsky revived the question. Language learning and the form it takes in the early stages would be impossible unless the child approached the learning of his mother tongue with some idea of what the structure of human language is like—some way of treating the quite heterogenous samples of speech he hears around him. As Chomsky puts it (1965): "What are the initial assumptions concerning the nature of language the child brings to language learning, and how detailed and specific is the innate schema . . . that gradually becomes more explicit and differentiated as the child learns the language?" Except for the word "innate", the Genevan school agrees that this is the important question to ask. In our view, it is precisely the fact that this initial schema is not innate in the obvious sense (though it may be so in the sense of a predisposition) that can provide hypotheses about the child's assumptions. Children do not learn to talk in the sense of communicating something about reality by conventional "words" before they are in their second year. By that time they have reached a certain level of practical intelligence that shows structural properties which Piaget has brought to light. This intelligence-in-action is the basis of all later cognitive constructs, which elaborate on different levels this initial structure that, like higher level structures, resembles a mathematical group. We would like to suggest that this group of action-patterns also serves as a heuristic model for language learning; that it is precisely what the child has learned (every child!) during his first 18 months or so which provides him with the necessary assumptions to start language acquisition. That these assumptions are adequate for doing so is due to the fact that all languages have been created by humans. The constraints on the form natural languages can take relate to characteristics of the human mind; and these constraints are precisely what makes it possible for children to start talking during their second year, and to go about language acquisition in the way they do. In a certain sense, something like a basic schema of human language does exist, and so does a set of basic assumptions permitting an oriented approach to the input—both derive from fundamental properties of the human mind, and therefore, at another level, from neurological coordinations (McNeill, 1971). Natural languages, however, have undergone a long process of historical change, and they have moved far away from a hypothetical basic form. After the first period of language acquisition the differences in the learning of different mother tongues become more marked than the similarities—though we have observed quite striking correspondences in several experiments dealing with various languages (Sinclair and Ferreiro, 1970; Sinclair and al. 1971).

Though the problems of language elaboration, once the first, structurally universal, stages have been accomplished, are fascinating, the questions of the beginnings of acquisition are more fundamental—just as much from the psychological as from the linguistic point of view. As Chomsky has argued, any linguistic theory that aims for explanatory adequacy has to include an account of linguistic universals—and this is equivalent to constructing a theory of language acquisition (Chomsky, 1965).

Clearly we are very far from a detailed hypothesis about the way structural properties of sensori-motor intelligence provide assumptions about structural properties of language; nor do we know anything about how the process model that accounts for the construction of this practical intelligence can be converted into a heuristic model lending itself to the basic strategies of language learning. Similarly, though Chomsky (1965) has made suggestions about linguistic universals, we are as yet incapable of describing these universal features in any precise way. It should be realized, however, that universals can be of different types: i.e. phonological, semantic or syntactic. Recent work in developmental psycholinguistics, using mainly observational methods, is often directed by a theoretical choice regarding which type of fundamental categories appears the most important. Some investigators analyze the early semantic relationships (such as possession, localization) that can be inferred from early child speech (Bloom, 1970); others are interested in the pre-language, babbling period, during which phonological categories are elaborated (Braine, 1971). Genevan psycholinguists are mainly interested in syntactic structures.

From many accounts and analyses of early language behaviour it appears that something very like the progressive integration and differentiation of action and thought patterns as described by Piaget also takes place in language learning. Ervin (1964), for example, has noticed how irregular plurals such as *feet* appear at first as isolated forms, apparently without connection to the rest of the plural system which is being elaborated. Subsequently, these forms are absorbed into the system, and appear as *foots, feets* and even *feetses*. A little later they will reappear in their correct form, but this time, one supposes, they are exceptions to a system rather than isolated items. Similar phenomena are observed in Klima-Bellugi's (1966) account of negation formation: *can't* and *won't* appear as unanalysed entities before the appearance of *can* and *will*; the auxiliary system takes a long time to construct.

Though such analyses confirm the hypothesis of an active construction, subjected to constraints as to what the structure can absorb and what has to be temporarily left aside, they cannot tell us directly about the basic strategies for language acquisition.

An Experimental Approach

To devise experimental methods capable of giving us at least some hints about these basic strategies and assumptions, we considered the possibility of presenting very young children with grammatically incorrect utterances, resembling what one-and-a-half and two-year-olds produce themselves, hoping that, as Chomsky (1961) says, they would "attempt to impose an interpretation [on them], exploiting whatever feature of grammatical structure is preserved", and supposing that the basic strategies would be reapplied, even if the subjects were no longer at the very first beginnings of language acquisition (they were between 2 years and 10 months, and 6 years old). We presented these children utterances such as "boy girl push", "girl boy push", "push boy girl", etc., in all possible word-orders, and "box boy open", "boy box open", etc., and we asked them to guess what was meant, and to show with toys the meaning they guessed at (Sinclair and Bronckart, in press). A succession of strategies emerged from this experiment. The two earliest types take the following form: either the children take the boy doll and the girl doll and make them walk on the table, saying, "they take a walk together"; or they put the two dolls one next to the other and then proceed to give them a push, remarking, "I push them down, they both fall." At this level, word order does not seem to influence solutions. Subsequently, one of the nouns is taken as acting on the other: that is, the boy pushes the girl or vice versa. In the case of the word order noun-verb-noun, and especially for "boy open box" the sequence is interpreted very early on as subject-verb-object; but in the case of two animate nouns either following or preceding the verb we notice the following strategies: firstly, the noun nearest to the verb is interpreted as the subject (whether it precedes or follows the verb); then, the noun nearest to the verb is interpreted as the object. In a final stage, this proximity link between verb and noun loses its importance, and the first noun is always taken to be the subject, the second the object, whatever the position of the verb (cf. Bever, 1970).

From these results we would like to propose a tentative reconstruction of the earliest segmentation and functional interpretation procedures. A first rule can be formulated as follows: take each utterance as consisting of two parts. An utterance is either the description of a state of an object or a person (examples in spontaneous speech of 2-year-olds would be: *truck broke, birdie there*), or it is the expression of an action on an object or a person (this action being desired by the child himself, or being performed by him in the present). Examples in spontaneous speech would be: *hit ball, coat off,* etc. Secondly, a system of rules elaborates the structure of utterances describing actions on objects or persons; at this level such utterances are considered as consisting of three parts. One rule would be: look for the action word and for semantic properties. According to syntactic and semantic properties of the verb, choose either one of the two following rules: establish an agent-action proximity link, add whatever is left as the patient; or, establish a patient-action proximity link, add whatever is left as the agent.

It is only in a third stage that a new system of rules becomes established: a sentence consists of two parts, a subject and a predicate. Both parts, but especially the predicate, may be composed of sub-parts; in the case of a "transitive" action, the verb phrase consists of the verb itself and its object.

We were especially interested by the first two types of solutions which seem to re-occur, at different ages, and in different experiments, whenever sentences proposed for interpretation involve a difficulty which at the age in question has not yet been mastered. For example, most children between two and a half and three have no difficulty in correctly acting out sentences such as "the boy plays with the ball" or "the girl pets the dog" (though a long introductory play-period is necessary to make them understand the instruction). They can even act out the two sentences if they have to wait till the experimenter has said both. However, if we join two sentences by a pronoun, the difficulty of finding the word to which the pronoun refers, or maybe even the general difficulty of understanding that the third person pronouns may refer to words previously said, seems to re-activate the two primitive strategies we described. The sentence "the boy plays with the ball and then he puts the ball in the basket' is acted in the following manner by our youngest subjects: the boy doll is made to kick the ball and then the child himself puts the ball into the basket; or, alternatively, the boy doll is made to jump into the basket. The second part of the sentence is thus interpreted either as an action performed by the child, but on the correct object, or as an "intransitive" action performed by what grammatically is the object of the verb.

These behaviour patterns cannot be explained by manipulatory difficulties, since they only occur in sentences with pronouns, and since the same sentence, but with the subject expressed by a noun, is correctly understood. Nor can the action-performed-by-the-child pattern be explained in the sense that boys would take the pronoun *he* to refer to themselves (and girls *she*) since we presented both sentences with *boy-he* and sentences with *girl-she*, and in each case an equal number of boys and girls chose the solution of taking the pronoun to refer to themselves. If we make the sentences more difficult, e.g. by using reversible sentences such as "the girl pushes the boy", instead of irreversible ones such as "the boy plays with the ball", we find that these interpretation patterns (the child himself performing the action or the verb being interpreted as an intransitive verb) occur even beyond the age of three.

We therefore feel justified in considering these patterns not as accidental solutions that may occur from time to time when the children are distracted or tired, but as genuine strategies they use when confronted with an utterance they have difficulty in understanding. Some of the first rules for producing and understanding utterances might therefore be the following : (1) An utterance consists of two parts. It expresses the description of a state, and names a person or object and a property thereof; (2) An utterance consists of two parts. It indicates a desired or presently being performed action; it names the action and the object thereof.

If we suppose these rules to be a part of the basic assumptions young children have about the nature of human language, we can look for the way they may be derived from the heuristic model provided by sensori-motor intelligence. Speaking in general terms, the very young baby does not differentiate between action, object and agent; an action or reflex pattern during the first months constitutes an unanalysable entity. It is only gradually, by performing the same action on a number of different objects (e.g. shaking rattles, spoons, dolls, etc.) and different actions on the same object (e.g. shaking, licking, throwing a rattle), that action and object become differentiated. Similarly, only gradually does the baby realize that not only he himself is an actor, but that other people, too, can perform the same actions as he does. It would appear that, at a different level, language patterns follow this development. Holophrases form unanalysable entities. They are followed by two-and three-word utterances such as we observed experimentally. These patterns for producing and understanding utterances can be seen as indicative of two differentiations: between action and object, and between the child himself as actor and another acting subject. A further step in grammar construction follows from the combination of these two patterns and leads to the differentiation of three elements: actor, patient and action.

In the present state of our linguistic and psycholinguistic knowledge the attempt to link the child's construction of grammar to his previous construction of practical intelligence may appear highly speculative. Whatever the ultimate explanation of such behaviour patterns as we observed may be, their occurrence in different experimental situations allows us to identify them as the expression of a very general underlying competence-structure.

References

Bever, T. G. (1970). The cognitive basis for linguistic structures. *In* "Cognition and the Development of Language", (J. R. Hayes, ed.). Wiley, New York.

Bloom, L. (1970). "Language Development: Form and Function in Emerging Grammars." Cambridge, Mass., M.I.T. Press, Cambridge, Mass.

Bovet, M. (1968). Etudes interculturelles du développement intellectuel et processus d'apprentissage. *R. suisse psychol. pure appl.*, **27**, No. 3–4, 189–200.

Braine, M. (1971). An inquiry into the nature of the morphophoneme in preliterate children. Linguistic institute symposium on psycholinguistics. Buffalo.

Chomsky, N. (1961). Some methodological remarks on generative grammar. *Word*, **17**, 219–239.

Chomsky, N. (1965). "Aspects of the Theory of Syntax." M.I.T. Press, Cambridge, Mass.

Dasen, P. (1970). Cognitive development in Aborigines of Central Australia. Doctoral thesis, Australian National University, Canberra.

Donaldson, M. and Wales, R. (1970). The acquisition of some relational terms. *In* "Cognition and the Development of Language", (J. R. Hayes, ed.). Wiley, New York.

Ervin, S. M. (1964). Imitation and structural change in children's language. *In* "New Directions in the Study of Language", (E. H. Lenneberg, ed.). M.I.T. Press, Cambridge, Mass.

Greco, P. and Piaget, J. (1959). Apprentissage et connaissance. *Etudes d'épistémologie génétique*, Vol. 7. P.U.F., Paris.

Goustard, M., Greco, P., Matalon, B. and Piaget, J. (1959). La logique des apprentissages. *Etudes d'épistémologie génétique*, Vol. 10. P.U.F., Paris.

Inhelder, B., Bovet, M. and Sinclair, H. (In press). "L'Apprentissage des Structures Cognitives". P.U.F., Paris.

Klima, E. S. and Bellugi, U. (1966). Syntactic regularities in the speech of children. *In* "Psycholinguistics Papers". (J. Lyons and R. Wales, eds.). Edinburgh University Press, Edinburgh.

McNeill, D. (1971). Sentences as biological processes. Paper presented at the C.N.R.S. Conference, Paris.

Mosheni, N. (1966). La comparaison des réactions aux épreuves d'intelligence en Iran et en Europe. Thèse de doctorat. Paris, Université de Paris. (Unpublished).

Opper, S. (1970). Intellectual development in Thailand. Unpublished doctoral thesis. Cornell, university.

Piaget, J. (1937). "La Construction du Réel chez l'Enfant." Delachaux and Niestlé, Neuchâtel.

Piaget, J. and Inhelder, B. (1956). "La Genèse des Structures Logiques Elémentaires." Delachaux and Niestlé, Neuchâtel et Paris.

Saussure, F. de (1916). "Cours de Linguistique générale." Payot, Paris. English edn. *"Course in General Linguistics"*. Translated by W. Baskin. Philosophical Library, New York.

Sinclair, H. and Ferreiro, E. (1970). Etude génétique de la compréhension, production et répétition des phrases au mode passif. *Archives de psychologie*, Vol. XL, **160**, 1–42.

Sinclair, A., Sinclair, H. and Marcellus, O. de (1971). Young children's comprehension and production of passive sentences. *Archives de psychologie*, XLI, **161**.

Sinclair, H. Bronckart, J. P. (In press). S.O.V., a linguistic universal? *J. exper. child psychol.*

Slobin, D. (In press). Cognitive prerequisties for the development of grammar. *Linguistic research*, Edmonton.

Thorpe, W. H. (1969). *In* "Beyond Reductionism", (A. Koestler and J. R. Smythies, eds.), p. 186. Hutchinson, London.

Piaget, J. and Inhelder, B. (1969). The gaps in empiricism. *In* "Beyond Reductionism", (A. Koestler and J. R. Smythies, eds.). Hutchinson, London.

Comments

1. Bryant pointed out that there appeared to be a direct clash between the Bovet experiment described by Sinclair and one by Gelman (1969). Gelman trained children to use numbers without the sort of failures that occurred in Bovet's experiment.

Sinclair replied:
    "There is no direct clash:
    (a) Gelman did not train children 'to use numbers'. She trained simultaneously for number and length problems using *oddity training* and *learning set training*—half the training situations were concerned with number, half with length. 'Number cues', says Gelman, 'occurred only in the number problems'. In fact, she found better results for length conservation than for number: 'This result is understandable if one analyses the two problems in terms of cues contained therein. Length cues were present in both problems, while number cues occurred in only the number problems. Thus in length problems the Ss were reinforced for responding to the relevant length cues. This tendency probably transferred and produced negative transfer to the irrelevant length cues in the number problem'.
    (b) Gelman could not have found 'the sort of failures' that occurred in Bovet's experiment, since Gelman only tested for judgements (equal or not equal) and trained on such judgements, whereas Bovet asked for constructions. Moreover the behaviours observed by Bovet occurred during the training sessions, and are not interpreted by her as types of failures but as steps on the way to understanding. In fact, the majority of her subjects (of the same age as Gelman's) succeeded on the post-test."

2. Chantrey wondered how rule-governed behaviour (see p. 406 of this chapter) and the appearance of isolated word forms (p. 408) fitted into ideas about the development of visual classsifications. For instance, Gibson *et al.*

(1962) showed that 4-year-old children had difficulty in discriminating 180-degree rotations of letter-like forms. As the children became older, they made fewer errors in this task. However McGurk (1970) has shown that very young infants can distinguish quite well between 180-degree rotations of two-dimensional forms. He concludes that his results : ". . . indicate that infants between 6 and 26 weeks perceive a difference between an otherwise identical pair of objects when the orientation of one of the objects differs from that of the other by 180-degrees."

Gibson (1969, p. 415), referring to Gibson *et al.*, 1962, says : "Transformations of rotation and reversal ... do not serve as distinctive features of objects. An object is seen to remain the same object if it is turned over or walked around, and what the child learns (if learning is necessary) is to perceive its permanence despite change in position. It is not surprising, therefore, that reversed and rotated forms are so often matched as identical by young children. But when children are exposed to our writing system, they suddenly discover that a number of letters are rotations or reversals of others and yet are actually unique."

The implication is that between 6 weeks and 4 years the child forms rules about the visual world and, specifically, learns that if an object falls over, it does *not* become a different object. When it comes to learn to read, it has to learn that sometimes an inversion or reflection *is* important and must therefore provide itself with an exception to the rule which it has built up. This situation seems to parallel that observed by Ervin (1964) and discussed by Dr. Sinclair (p. 408).

3. There was some discussion about children brought up with little or no experience of adult conversation. After the conference, Baerends contributed the following:

"My daughter Martina Baerends, who is a human psychologist and speech therapist, found in 1970 a case of 'secret language' used by twins in the Dutch province of Drenthe. The non-identical twins (two girls), when arriving for the first time in school at the age of six years, talked a language characterized by the presence of all vowels and vowel combinations normally used in Dutch, but by the replacement of all consonants by *t*. *S* was used only as a final *s* in some plurals and diminutives. The children could also say 'mamma' and 'papa', but these were the only words in which *m* and *p* were used. They appeared to have a knowledge of the structure of words, and their sentence construction seemed not much retarded.

"The inability to pronounce consonants disappeared rapidly during speech therapy. After three months the initial consonant- (and double consonant-) vowel connections were correctly made and after one year their speech was almost normal.

"The 'secret language' was identical in the twins. It was roughly understood by the mother and the only sister (four years older). The twins, their sister and their parents were of normal intelligence. The parents had a farm and both took a very active part in running it. The older sister was regularly attending school after the twins had reached the age of two. The situation of the farm was isolated; the family had very little contact with other families. The twins got along very well with each other and this further promoted a lack of communication with other people."

4. The work of White and his colleagues (1964), indicating that the ages at which various sensori-motor skills develop depends on the toys and other amenities available to the children, suggest a necessity for some reservations in Sinclair's view that development through the early stages is not influenced by wide differences in experience.

References

Ervin, S. M. (1964). Imitation and structural change in children's language. *In* "New Directions in the Study of Language", (E. H. Lenneberg, ed.). M.I.T. Press, Cambridge, Mass.

Gelman, R. (1969). Conservation acquisition: a problem of learning to attend to relevant attributes. *J. exp. Child Psychol.* **7**, 167–187.

Gibson, E. J. (1969). "Principles of perceptual learning and development." Appleton-Century-Crofts, New York.

Gibson, E. J., Gibson, J. J., Pick, A. D. and Osser, H. (1962). A developmental study of the discrimination of letter-like forms. *J. comp. physiol. Psychol.* **55**, 897–906.

McGurk, H. (1970). The role of object orientation in infant perception. *J. exp. Child Psychol.* **9**, 363–373.

White, B. L., Castle, P. and Held, R. (1964). Observations on the development of visually directed reaching. *Child Developm.* **35**, 349–364.

20
What the Young Child has to Learn about Logic

by P. E. Bryant

The Inference Problem

If a child is going to make any sense out of the experiences he has, he must be able to order and rearrange the information derived from them in a systematic logical manner. It is quite a reasonable assumption that a child's chances of learning about his world must depend very heavily on his ability to be logical. Thus, anyone who is interested in the role of learning in development must take quite seriously any suggestion that children are in some way or other illogical.

There have, in fact, been some suggestions that young children lack some pretty basic logical abilities. One common claim is that children cannot make logical inferences until they reach the age of about seven or eight years (Piaget and Inhelder 1941; Piaget, 1970; Kendler and Kendler, 1967; Smedslund, 1969). The hypothesis is that children younger than this cannot combine separate experiences in order to produce a new inferential solution.

This is indeed an important hypothesis, and it has serious implications for our notions of the way a child learns. For, if the child cannot co-ordinate his different experiences, if these must remain separate as far as he is concerned, there must be a very severe limit to the knowledge that he can pick up about the rules which govern his environment. There must be very few rules which can be satisfactorily acquired by a child (or an animal), who cannot combine what he learns in one situation with what he learns in another. This is a point which has long been recognized by learning theorists (Maier, 1929, 1936; Kendler and Kendler, 1967).

The most explicit claim that children younger than seven years are unable to make logical inferences comes from Piaget and his colleagues. They have repeatedly suggested that the young child cannot understand that $A > C$ when he is given the two separate items of information that $A > B$ and that $B > C$. Piaget's central tenet about children at this age is that they are dominated by their immediate perceptual input, and cannot do anything about re-organizing this input once it arrives. One result is that they cannot co-ordinate separate perceptual items, and this means that they cannot put the separate AB and BC inputs together inferentially. Moreover they do not understand that B can be simultaneously smaller than one thing and bigger than another. Thus the theory is that perceptual domination effectively stops the child making inferences about quantity, and thus prevents him understanding even the simplest principles of measurement. So the inference question takes on an added importance. Any test of young children's ability to make inferences will also be a test of one of Piaget's central ideas about young children, namely that perceptual domination leads to severe logical constraints.

The suggestion that children cannot make inferences about quantity until the age of about seven years is based on the results of experiments in which the task is to combine the information that $A > B$ and that $B > C$ to reach the conclusion that $A > C$. The experiments were introduced by Piaget (Piaget and Inhelder, 1941, Chs. 10 and 11; Piaget et al., 1960, Chs. 2 and 5) and taken up by Smedslund (1963, 1966). Typically what happens in such an experiment, when, for example, the quantity is length, is that the subject sees that A is longer than B, and then that B is longer than C, and then, without being able to make a direct comparison, is asked which is the greater, A or C. Piaget and Smedslund both found that children younger than seven were not able to answer the AC question satisfactorily in this situation, and we have repeated this observation ourselves with our own subjects. Children older than seven years, however, do quite consistently conclude that $A > C$.

The most important question raised by these experiments is whether they really do demonstrate that young children lack the mechanisms that are needed to put separate experiences together inferentially. I wish to argue that they do not, and that young children are really quite adept at making inferences. I shall also try to demonstrate that the most important developmental question in this area is not whether young children have an inferential ability but rather how and when they use this ability in their normal life. This argument will be based first on the way in which traditional inference experiments were designed, and secondly on the results of some more recent and rather different experiments on inferences in very young children.

Take first of all the design of the traditional inference experiments. Two assumptions are usually made in such experiments, the first that the child who succeeds can make inferences, the second that the child who fails cannot. Both assumptions are questionable. Failures may be caused simply by memory lapses. The inference task must always be a successive one, and thus when the child is asked the AC question he must do two things: he must remember the AB and BC comparisons, and he must co-ordinate them to yield the correct ABC order. Therefore a failure may be caused either because the child forgets the initial comparisons or because he cannot combine them inferentially. So failures in the traditional inference task do not have a clear meaning.

Nor is it even certain that the child who succeeds does so by making a genuine inference. He may do so simply by repeating a verbal label picked up in the initial comparisons. In the two initial comparisons, the correct response to A is "larger", and to C "smaller". Yet these are the correct responses to A and to C in the inferential AC question. If he repeats the label which was correct before, he will again be correct in the inferential problem. Thus a child who says that A is larger than C may do so in a manner which essentially is not inferential.

These two criticisms of the inference experiment have been made before (Smedslund, 1969; Youniss and Murray, 1970), but until recently there do not seem to have been any attempts to control for both factors in any one experiment. I wish to describe some experiments in which we attempted to rule out the effects both of memory failures and of the repetition of verbal labels remembered from the initial comparisons.

First Experiment: With Visual and Verbal Feedback

The first two experiments were carried out by Tom Trabasso and myself (Bryant and Trabasso, 1971), and in these experiments we tried to find out whether young children aged four, five and six years can make inferences about sticks of different lengths.

Our basic material consisted of five sticks of different colours, whose lengths were 7, 6, 5, 4 and 3 inches. We had five rather than three sticks in order to make the inferential problem genuinely inferential. If you have five lengths, four initial comparisons are possible, $A > B, B > C, C > D$ and $D > E$. This means that three lengths, B, C and D, crop up in two comparisons each, and that each length is the smaller in one comparison and the greater in the other. Thus B, C and D will have been equally often larger and smaller, for any child who has been given all four initial comparisons. It will easily be seen that only one new inferential comparison can be based on these three values, and that is the BD comparison. All the other new comparisons involve either A or E: they are AC, AD, AE, BE and CE. Since A was always the larger and E always the smaller in the initial comparisons, these latter five comparisons cannot be regarded as genuinely inferential. Thus by increasing the number of lengths from three to five we were able to introduce one crucial and genuine test of inferential ability, the *BD* comparison.

We also had to take precautions that errors on this *BD* comparison were not caused by forgetting of the initial comparisons, and to do this we took two steps. The first was to make the children very familiar with the initial comparisons, so that they would be unlikely to forget them. The second step was to test how well the children remembered the initial comparisons at the time they were asked the inferential question.

In order to do this we divided the experiment into two phases, a training phase in which we made sure the children learned the four initial comparisons, and a test phase in which we tested their ability to make new judgements and also to remember the old judgements.

In the training phase we actually taught the children the four initial comparisons. For every child a particular colour represented a particular length. Thus the child had to learn initially that the red stick was longer than the blue stick, that the blue stick was longer than the green one, that the green stick was longer than the white one and so on. This phase, therefore consisted of a considerable number of trials. In each trial we first showed the child two of the sticks, both sticking out an equal amount from the top of a box so that the child could not judge their relative size from their physical appearance. We asked the child sometimes which was the taller and sometimes which was the shorter, and when he replied we told him whether he was right or not and actually showed him the full lengths of the sticks by taking them out of the box. Thus we gave visual, as well as verbal, feedback on every trial and we continued these trials until the young children were quite proficient on each of the four comparisons.

Then the second phase of the experiment, the test phase, began. Here we asked the children about all ten possible pairs. Four of these pairs (*AB, BC, CD, DE*) were the original comparisons, six (*AC, AD, AE, BD, BE, CE*) were new. Of these six, as I have argued, only *BD* can be regarded as genuinely inferential. We presented each of the ten pairs four times and never at any time in the test phase did we give any verbal or visual feedback. The child simply saw the two sticks sticking out an equal amount from the top of the box and had to say which of the two was the taller or shorter. He was not told or shown whether his choice was the right one.

Thus the children first learned the initial four comparisons and then were tested both for their recall of these comparisons and for their ability to combine them inferentially. In particular we wanted to see whether they could put together the data that $B > C$ and $C > D$ to realize that $B > D$.

The results of this experiment were very clear. The four, five and six year olds were able to learn the four initial comparisons, though they sometimes took two sessions to do so. Moreover they could recall these initial comparisons in the test phase pretty well. But most important, they were able to make the crucial *BD* inferential comparison. Without ever being able to compare *B* and *D* directly all three age groups were able reliably to give the reply that $B > D$.

TABLE 1

Probability of correct choices on tests for inference
(*BD*) and for retention of initial comparisons (*BD*
and *CD*)

A. 1st Experiment (Visual and Verbal Feedback)

	BD	BC	CD
4 years	0.78	0.92	0.90
5 years	0.88	0.86	0.92
6 years	0.92	0.94	0.98

B. 2nd Experiment (Verbal Feedback)

	BD	BC	CD
4 years	0.82	0.89	0.87
5 years	0.85	0.87	0.97

The scores for this inferential comparison and for memory of *BC* and *CD* comparisons in the test phase are given in Table 1, which shows that all three age groups are reliably above chance level on all three scores in the first experiment.

Our preliminary conclusion was that young children can, under some circumstances, make inferences. They can combine separate judgements to produce a new and genuinely inferential comparison.

Second Experiment: With only Verbal Feedback

We decided, however, to repeat the experiment with one modification. This was to carry out the training phase without any visual feedback. On each training trial the child was shown two rods of different colours protruding equal amounts from the top of a box, and was asked which was the longer (or shorter). When he had made his choice we only told him whether he was right or wrong. He never actually saw the full lengths of any of the rods. Throughout the experiment he only saw each rod sticking out of the top of the box by 1 inch.

This step was taken to ensure that the children did not solve the BD problem by remembering the absolute lengths of the sticks. They could have solved the BD problem in the first experiment simply by remembering that *B* was 6 inches and *D* 4 inches. We actually thought this type of absolute memory extremely unlikely, since in another experiment we had demonstrated how very difficult it is for four and six year old children to solve a size discrimination by remembering absolute sizes (Lawrenson and Bryant, 1972). However, the control was certainly necessary.

There were two age groups in this experiment, four and five year olds. Their results were very much the same. In general the training phase took longer. However the scores on the crucial BD comparison in the test phase, as Table 1 shows, were just as good as before, and, of course well above chance.

This surely is conclusive proof that even four year old children can make inferences. They could not have solved the *BD* problem merely by repeating a verbal label, nor by remembering the absolute lengths of the sticks. To solve this problem they must have made an inference.

One may now ask why such young children produced an inferential judgement in our experiment, but not in other experiments. The obvious answer is that we made sure that the children remembered the information which they were later required to co-ordinate. However, this does not necessarily mean that a child has only to remember data to be able to put them together inferentially. It only means that, at some stage, young children can both remember the initial comparisons and combine them. What is needed is an experiment in which the child's memory for the initial data is related directly and continuously to his success with an inferential question.

Third Experiment: On Memory and Inferences

Gill Perkins and I (Bryant and Perkins, unpublished data) have recently been conducting such an experiment with five year old children. In this experiment we adopt a purely verbal technique. We tell the child a story about how we visited a house in which there were rather a lot of brothers and sisters, and how we met on different occasions pairs of these children and see in each case that one child is taller than the other. Thus we tell them that Jane (*A*) was taller than Tom (*B*) and Tom (*B*) taller than Susan (*C*), and so on. Having told this story once, we immediately test the child's memory for these four pairs and at the same time ask him the inferential question, who is taller *B* or *D*. This procedure constitutes one trial and immediately it is over the child is given another trial consisting again of a presentation followed by a test, and then another trial and so on. Thus trial by trial we plot a direct relationship between the child's memory for the initial comparisons and his ability to make an inference on the basis of these comparisons. The answer is very clear. The child can make the *BD* inference as soon as he is able to remember the *BC* and *CD* comparisons consistently. All he has to do is to remember the direct comparisons correctly in order to be able to put them together.

Inferences and Behaviour

It seems therefore that young children can combine information inferentially when they have access to the data on which the inference must be based. This leaves us with the question of how their ability to make inferences affects their actual everyday behaviour.

There is, as far as I can see, no basis yet for an answer to this question, probably because the prevailing view has been that young children cannot, and therefore do not, make inferences. One can only then suggest lines for future research. One possibility might be to look at a distinction between passive and active inference problems. The situations that I have been discussing are essentially passive in the sense that the child is handed all the necessary information on a plate, and does not have to collect it for himself. We have seen that in such a passive task young children can make inferences.

One can, on the other hand, give the child a more active situation in which he is simply told that he has to compare *A* and *C*, although *A* and *C* are, for one reason or another, not directly comparable. Here the child has to produce for himself the idea of using *B* as a common measure, as well as going through the *AB, BC* process. Piaget (1953) very effectively demonstrated that children younger than seven simply do not set about looking for a *B:* they do not spontaneously seek a common measure. We (Bryant: unpublished data) have recently repeated this observation with five year old children, and the striking thing about our experience was that all the children had previously done very well in a passive inference task. Yet they were plainly at a loss in our active test.

Here then is an example of children having the relevant logical mechanisms, but not using them as fully as they might. There is a gap between what they can do and what they actually do do. It may be that the difference between younger and older children is that the size of this gap between potential and performance diminishes with age, although it probably never entirely disappears.

What possibly happens is that the child gradually acquires effective strategies for putting his inferential ability into practice. His task, at any rate above the age of four years, is not to acquire the inferential mechanisms, but to learn when and where and with what material to use these mechanisms. Nor need there be any mystery about how this learning occurs. A lot of it probably happens at school where children are taught, after all, such basic strategies as how to use a ruler. Yet the way children do learn how to use their basic logical abilities may turn out to be the central question in the field of logical development.

Acknowledgements

Most of the argument in this paper is based on a project which the author conceived and carried out jointly with Dr. T. Trabasso.

The work was made possible by a grant from the S.S.R.C.

References

Bryant, P. E. and Trabasso, T. (1971). Transitive inferences and memory in young children. *Nature* **232**, 456–458.

Kendler, T. S. and Kendler, H. H. (1967). Inferential behaviour in young children. *In Advances in Child Development and Behaviour*, Vol. III. (L. P. Lipsitt and C. C. Spiker, eds.). Academic Press, New York.

Lawrenson, W. and Bryant, P. E. (1972). Absolute and relative codes in young children. *J. child Psychol. and Psychiat.* **13**, 25–35.

Maier, N. R. F. (1929). Reasoning in the white rat. *Comp. Psychol. Monogr.* No. 29.

Maier, N. R. F. (1936). Reasoning in children. *Journ. Comp. Psychol.* **21**, 357–366.

Piaget, J. (1953). How children form mathematical concepts. *Scientific American*, (November).

Piaget, J. (1970). "Genetic Epistemology." Columbia University Press, New York.

Piaget, J. and Inhelder (1941). "La Developement des Quantites Physiques chez l'Enfant." Delachaux and Niestlé, Paris.

Piaget, J., Inhelder, B. and Szeminska, A. (1960). The child's conception of Geometry. Routledge and Kegan Paul, London.

Smedslund, J. (1963). The development of concrete transitivity of length in children. *Child Dev.* **34**, 389–405.

Smedslund, J. (1966). Performance on measurement and pseudomeasurement tasks by 5–7 year old children. *Scand. J. Psychol.* **7**, 81–92.

Smedslund, J. (1969). Psychological Diagnostics. *Psychol. Bull.* **71**, 237–248.

Youniss, J. and Murray, J. P. (1970). Transitive inferences with non-transitive solutions controlled. *Dev. Psychol.* **2**, 169–175.

Comments

1. There was considerable discussion concerning the relation between Bryant's data and Piaget's theory. Sinclair was inclined to argue that the essential issue was the succession of stages, the precise ages at which they occurred being of only secondary importance. Many others of those present, however, felt that here were well-designed experiments yielding hard data, of which the theoreticians were obliged to take notice.

2. *Chantrey commented*:

"I wonder whether the confusion/disagreement between you and the Piagetians does not arise because you are both using absolute measures of ability. Is it not possible that this is all a question of relativability in terms of a continuum. For a Piagetian to say that a child cannot make inferences implies that an older child can. Would you therefore agree with a view which says that inference is an ability which develops slowly and a child of 7–8 years is unable to perform a relatively difficult inference task? If this is the case, then a developmental (longitudinal) study of the number of presentations of the $A > B, B > C, A$? C problem would show a decrease in the number of trials with age. The 'mechanism' of this would need to be investigated, but may have to do with the fact that older children have come across such problems in every day life anyway which might facilitate the setting up of any spatio-temporal scheme."

Bryant was inclined to agree with this, suggesting that development may however involve putting a capacity to function rather than the development of a new capacity.

21

Interpretation and Imitation in Early Language Development

by Joanna Ryan

Introduction

One fashionable approach to language development contains an argument about the constraints which must operate on the means whereby children learn to talk and understand their native language. From the nature of what is acquired it is argued that certain mechanisms of acquisition must operate and others are precluded. Specifically, Chomsky (1965), in giving an account of syntactic structure, claims that its nature is such that no child could possibly learn it from the speech he hears. To quote: "We have a certain amount of evidence about the character of the generative grammars that must be the 'output' of an acquisition model for language. This evidence shows clearly that taxonomic views of linguistic structure are inadequate and that knowledge of grammatical structure cannot arise by application of step-by-step inductive operations (segmentation, classification, substitution procedures, filling of slots in frames, association, etc.), of any sort that have yet been developed within linguistics, psychology or philosophy" (Chomsky, 1965). Because of this apparent impossibility of a child acquiring the rules of language by means of any known learning process, the existence of certain innate forms of knowledge has been postulated.

This argument has by now many facets to it. Different and further aspects of language development have been emphasized by various proponents of this view, and an assorted range of evidence has been advanced in its support. The logical argument, about the nature of language, is however the central issue, and the one of most relevance to this conference since it postulates a source of constraint on learning in the nature of the material to be acquired. It is not the purpose of this chapter to attempt to evaluate this argument on its own terms, that is to examine in detail the processes of inference and kinds of knowledge needed to derive rules of base structure from those of surface structure. Rather, the aim is to broaden the framework somewhat and examine some of the assumptions, contained in this general approach to language development, that make such an argument seem as plausible as it does to many people (e.g. to McNeill, 1970; Slobin, 1971).

The following additional features of language development have been variously supposed to either prove or illustrate its innate basis: its species-specificity and alleged independence of intelligence level (Chomsky, 1968); its "biological basis" and maturational characteristics, such as an apparent critical period (Lenneberg, 1967); the alleged universality of the developmental stages (Lenneberg, *l.c.*), the supposed linguistic poverty and relative unimportance of the environment (Fodor, 1966; Chomsky, 1968; Lenneberg, 1967); the surprising (to McNeill, 1966) speed with which children acquire language; their "creativity" in doing so (McNeill, 1966); and the absence of mistakes in the acquisition of some grammatical rules (McNeill, 1966).

Not all of this evidence is as well-established or as clear in its implications as its proponents make out. Thus, the judgement of what is "speed" in developmental matters requires a metric of relative difficulty for different skills: this we do not possess. McNeill's argument, that the apparent speed with which children acquire language is evidence of its innate basis, is open to the *reductio ad absurdum* that if they acquired it more slowly then it would be less innately determined, and more the result of experience. The alleged universality of the developmental stages is based on extremely crude indices, that do not do justice to the complexity of the processes involved. Bloom's (1970) work, for example, using much more detailed descriptive categories, shows considerable and significant variation in developmental patterns between three children. The supposed linguistic poverty and unhelpfulness of the environment has been emphasized on the basis of no data at all; as will be argued below this insistence belittles the complexity and richness of much mother-infant interaction.

These misrepresentations apart, it is not at all obvious that some of the other considerations, although important facts in themselves, do constitute evidence for the innate basis of language. The fact that language in its natural occurrence is species-specific and universal within the species, does not necessarily imply anything about its mode of development in individuals. Neither does its species-specificity imply that other species, if suitably trained, could not acquire similar essential skills. Further, facts concerning the "biological basis" of language development (e.g. the relevant neurology), whilst providing information about some of the necessary conditions for development to occur, say nothing about other necessary ones, nor about the processes whereby all the necessary conditions become sufficient. Lastly, the absence, or otherwise, of errors in speech production during development has many possible interpretations other than McNeill's one of innateness.

These various arguments rest on an extremely simplistic view of developmental change, and also on a confusion about the word "innate". Most importantly however, this whole approach contains a very narrow characterization of what it is that is acquired, and therefore has to be explained, during language development. The acquisition of the rules of syntax is seen as the major part of language development, and this is viewed in almost total isolation from any other aspects of language. Language is regarded as something to be studied as the object of the child's knowledge, rather than as a means, for the child, of either communication or knowledge. Aspects of language use, such as participation in mutual dialogues, timing of utterances, appropriateness of utterances to the context, to the listener, and to the listener's reactions, are all neglected. It is not just that the development of such necessary communicational skills is ignored; more importantly, their relevance to other more formal aspects of language acquisition is denied. It is thus not surprising that language acquisition appears the "mystery" that it does to McNeill (1970) and others, since the child is viewed as mastering the rules of syntax out of nothing, without the use of any previously established skills. In fact, during the two years before the onset of marked syntax, the child is acquiring many other skills that are at least as essential to speaking and understanding a language as the mastery of grammar is supposed to be. The so-called "one-word stage" cannot be regarded as the mere accumulation of a vocabulary, in preparation only for its subsequent incorporation into sentences. Although much is learnt during this period about the sounds and conventional meanings of words, so also are various non-linguistic conventions about the appropriate utterance of words, about relations between speakers, and about participation in mutual dialogues. The child learns how to use words to communicate with others, as well as the meanings of words.

The question arises as to how different claims about the characterization of what is acquired during development, and therefore about what has to be explained, are to be settled. This question involves issues in linguistic theory, particularly about accounts of meaning, that are beyond the scope of this chapter. What features of language and language use are regarded as central to a theory of meaning will determine what is seen as the major task facing the child in acquiring language. However, apart from the considerations about the communicative functions of language, there are also some further general considerations about development which militate against studying children's language as an isolated phenomenon, in the way that much current psycholinguistics does. Whilst it is not clear what a general developmental theory, or an explanation of developmental change, would be like, it is clear that interaction between an organism and the environment is a *sine qua non* for development to occur at all. Interaction and change are the primary phenomena that we have to study in development. Any account of developmental phenomena that is more than narrowly descriptive of what changes take place, that has any explanatory force at all, must attempt to relate the observed changes to the interaction of the organism and environment. Current psycholinguistic work is not alone in ignoring the effective linguistic environment in which the child develops, and the kinds of interaction that occur. Earlier work on language development also neglected this—and did so in spite of its concentration on the presyntactic period when certain special features of linguistic interaction between adults and children might appear particularly striking to the investigator. Studies of other aspects of mother-infant interaction, such as feeding, attachment and control, have also tended to ignore the details of verbal interchanges. Despite this neglect, there is by now some scattered evidence about the kinds of processes that occur. In the rest of this chapter some of those that are unique to interaction between adults and children (as opposed to other adults) will be discussed. These are the active interpretive responses of adults, and the imitative responses of children.

Interpretive Responses of Adults

Adult speech to young children is characterized by the fact that it is systematically simpler in some respects than that between adults, and also that much of it is interpretive of what the child has said.

Brown and Bellugi (1964) observed that the adults in their study used relatively short sentences when speaking to children. Further, their speech was on the whole grammatically correct, unlike much adult conversation: this fact about adult conversation has been made much of (by e.g. Fodor) when emphasizing the unhelpful nature of the environment. In a more detailed investigation, Phillips (in press) compared mothers speech to 8, 18 and 28 month children with that to an adult interviewer. Speech to the adult differed from that to any of the groups of children in the following ways, amongst others: the adult-directed speech contained longer utterances, more verbs and more verb forms, more modifiers, more function words, fewer "concrete" nouns, and was less repetitious. Further, intonation to children was more exaggerated, and articulation more deliberate. It was also found that speech to the 28-month children was more complex than that to 18-month children on most of the measures that distinguished adult-directed speech from that to children generally. Similar results were found by Bingham (in preparation) in comparing speech to differently aged children. It is interesting to note that, in both these studies, the mothers' speech to the youngest pre-verbal infants was not systematically simpler than that to the slightly older groups. In Bingham's study it was more complex in several respects. It is apparently only when infants provide their mothers with some indication of their developing linguistic abilities that mothers systematically adapt their speech in the direction of greater simplicity.

Such findings concerning greater simplicity are hardly surprising, but they emphasize how, in adjusting their speech to the abilities of their offspring, mothers provide a more helpful linguistic input than has been assumed.

Brown and Bellugi (1964) also observed that mothers frequently responded to their children by expanding the child's utterance—that is, by reproducing it and also adding something to it or otherwise changing it. Two of the mothers did this about 30% of the time, the third rather less frequently. Such expansion was primarily interpretive of the child's utterance, delimiting its meaning more precisely, rather than corrective. Explicit corrections were extremely rare, a result since replicated by Lieven (personal communication) with younger children. Expansions cannot be regarded simply as the provision of obligatory grammatical features that the child has omitted since they also involve judgements of the relation between the utterance and the context. Brown and Bellugi suggest that they act as a kind of "communication check" for the mother, establishing what the child may have meant by his utterance. More recent work with younger children, before the beginnings of syntax, indicates that many of them experience extensive verbal interchanges during which mothers actively try to engage them in dialogue. They do this both by direct questioning, but also by picking up, repeating, commenting on, expanding or otherwise interpreting what the child has said. For example, in Lieven's single case study the mother responded to 80% of the child's analysable utterances in some way or other, and about 39% of her sentences contained questions, many more than to adults. Approximately 65% of her responses in some way extended the child's utterance, either grammatically or semantically.

What are the functions of such interpretive responses? One consequence may be to provide the child with readily assimilable syntactic and semantic information, but the exact causal role of this remains to be established. The function for the mother may be related to the ambiguity of the child's utterance. There are many different sources of ambiguity in child speech, as well as of unintelligibility, and a consideration of these is helpful in elucidating some aspects of what it is that a child has to learn about speech, and therefore in characterizing the skills that a child has to master. This topic is treated at greater length in Ryan (1973), but briefly, adults can experience the following kinds of difficulty in trying to understand the speech of very young children at the earliest stages of language development:

(1) Difficulty due to the fact that the child makes noises with no speech-like characteristics at all, such that adults would not readily say he was even trying to speak.

(2) Difficulty due to the fact that the child's noises are not recognizably part of the adult vocabulary, but that he makes them in such a way that he would be described as trying to speak. Whether or not it is true that the child is "trying to say something", and whether or not this is something that is in principle verifiable, it is an important fact about adults that they do behave towards children in this way—as though the child was trying to say something. Adults use other features of the child's behaviour, to credit him with "saying" something, and in interpreting what he is "saying". These features include aspects of the utterance, such as intonation patterns; accompaniments of the utterance, such as pointing or playing with particular objects by the child; and circumstances of the utterance, such as the presence or absence of particular objects or people, and any preceding events. One interesting phenomenon, sometimes reported in the literature (Leopold, 1939; Bloom, 1971), is that non-standard sounds, used in certain ways, are often described as the "child's word" for something. This may be related to adult interpretive processes. It also implies that the child has learned something general about speech, independent of specific forms learned from adult vocabulary.

(3) Difficulty due to the fact that a child utters a recognizable word but it is unclear what he means by uttering it, or why he has said it—that is, what sort of an utterance it is. For example the child may say "dog", and it may be unclear whether this is a request for the dog, a request for the dog's removal, a comment on the dog's presence, on some feature of the dog's current behaviour, or on some feature of the behaviour of others towards the dog, or whether the child is simply naming the animal. In such cases of ambiguity the same clues to interpretation as listed above under (2) may be used in understanding what the child meant. This source of ambiguity is considered at greater length below.

(4) Difficulty due to the fact that a child may use standard and recognizable words with unconventional reference. Such unconventional reference takes two forms: extension to objects, etc., not usually covered by the words

in question, and restriction to a subclass of the objects, etc., usually referred to. Extension seems to be an extremely common phenomenon, especially at the initial stages of language development, as it is described in most of the literature. Associated with extension is variability in reference; children's words change in their reference from early idiosyncratic usage to more conventional adult usage. The basis of extended reference is not usually failure to distinguish the referents, since the child's non-verbal behaviour often shows discrimination. Extension appears to have a basis, related either to objective characteristics of objects, or to the child's needs and perspectives. Extension can be seen as a partial consequence of the child's lack of particular words. It also illustrates how, even at the very early stages, children's use of words is not derived in any simple way from that of adults. Extension suggests a generalization, in a systematic if idiosyncratic way, of something that may have initially been imitated from adult speech.

This categorization, (1)–(4), differs from the more traditional descriptions of what a child has to learn prior to syntax, namely (1) the sounds (phonology) and (4) the meanings (semantics) of words. What it adds are various features pertaining to the intentionality of the act of speaking: whether the utterance of a particular noise is to count as an act of communication at all, (2), and what kind of an utterance it is to count as, (3). (2) suggests that a child can be counted as speaking in the sense of meaning something, even though the noises he makes do not have any conventional meaning, and (3) that even when words with conventional meaning are used, there can still be a question as to what the child meant by uttering those words. Recent philosophy of language, particularly the work of Grice (1957), Austin (1962) and Strawson (1964), contains a useful discussion of the distinction, implicit in this categorization of infant speech, between linguistic conventions, i.e. what words and sentences mean, and what people mean by uttering words and sentences. Traditionally, accounts of language development have concentrated on the first aspect of meaning, although this distinction has not been explicitly recognized in such work. This neglect of what Grice (1957) calls "utter's meaning" has contributed to the acommunicational view of language development implicit in most psychological work. A fuller account of this argument is to be found in Ryan (1973).

The ambiguity described under (3), which is due to the fact that a child may utter a recognizable word but that it can be unclear as to what he meant by uttering it, is of interest both from the point of view of the active interpretive role of adults, and in connection with accounts of early child speech that have occurred frequently in the literature. There are two recurrent themes in the various accounts: firstly, that young children use the same word with a variety of meanings on different occasions (e.g. Stern, 1923; Leopold, 1939), and secondly, that children's one-word utterances are "really" sentences. Thus Stern claims that "children's utterances are really whole sentences, because one and the same unit is used with a multitude of meanings", Leopold that "one-word sentences constitute for the child a complete expression of thought and feeling", and McNeill (1970) that "single-word utterances express complex ideas and are thus equivalent to the full sentences of adults".

Rather than describing the child as using the same word with a variety of meanings, it would be more accurate to describe the child as using the same word to make several different utterances, on different occasions. There is nothing strange about this in that adults use similar or identical sentences to make different kinds of utterances—the difference depending on the ways in which speakers intend their utterances, and on features of the utterance and its context. Nor are children special in the variety of interpretations that can be given to their utterances of the same single words. However, there is much more scope for ambiguity than with adults, partly for the obvious reason that the form of single- or two-word utterances conveys less information than does the form of longer and more complex utterances. There is a further reason for this ambiguity, namely that we do not know much about what kind of utterances children are capable of making, what concepts they can express, nor the ways in which their utterances are related by them to other linguistic or non-linguistic aspects of the total situation. There is clearly considerable scope for detailed empirical observation here. As Bloom (1970) points out, in order to understand the speech of young children, we usually have to know what they are doing. Any empirical study, however, requires that we have explicit criteria for the metalinguistic terms we use in describing a child's speech. How, for example, do we decide whether or not a child is using words to name, to comment on, to describe, to assert the existence of something, to refuse, to request, to point out related features for which the words are not known, to greet—plus all the other plausible functions that a child's utterance can be interpreted as having?

The claim that a child's one-word utterance is really a sentence, that a child is somehow expressing "more" than the simple form of his utterance would suggest, seems to be a claim about how adults interpret children's utterances—namely, as having some of the same potential functions that more complex utterances have. Taking a narrowly grammatical definition of a sentence, as something having constituent parts and internal structure, these claims are clearly false of one-word utterances. These views of early child speech should be seen as descriptions of how adults understand (or fail to understand) child speech, rather than of the nature of the speech itself. This is because they have tended to conflate the means (mentioned above) by which adults interpret children's utterances with the devices it is assumed the child uses to express himself, given his limitation to the one-word form. They assume that a child uses the same devices to convey his meaning as adults use in interpreting his utterance. The question arises as to whether or not we can in principle tell if such an assumption is correct. In some cases we can tell if we are wrong in our interpretations (e.g. if we do something we think is appropriate, and the child screams); however very often we cannot. It is possible that what is most important for the child, especially at the earliest stages, is not whether he is correctly understood by adults, but that his utterances are interpreted at all. The context of rich interpretation provided by many mothers, combined with the considerable ambiguity of one-word utterances, provides an extremely informative situation for the child as regards what he is taken to mean. We cannot assume when a child starts to produce one-word utterances, that the possible meanings of his utterances are as clearly delimited for him as they are for adults who interpret them.

This section has described some of the special ways in which adults speak to children, and respond to children's speech. The next section concerns one special feature of how children respond to adult speech.

Imitation in Children's Speech

Children's speech, in interaction with adults, is often characterized by immediate repetition of part or all of the adult's utterance. Imitation, along with other forms of verbal interaction, has been much neglected. It has also, however, been the focus of extreme attitudes as regards its possible functions in language acquisition. To judge from all the available sources, overt imitation of adult speech is an extremely common phenomenon, especially during the "one-word stage". Exactly how common it is, and whether or not it occurs in all children is difficult to assess, partly because of the way in which it has been ignored, and partly because of the varying definitions it has received. For example, Bloom (1970) drops all imitated utterances from her analyses, assuming without question that they are not of central interest. The neglect of imitation in earlier works is probably due in part to a practical cause. Before the advent of tape-recorders it was impossible to obtain a full record, in any natural situation, of what both child and adult said. The definitions of imitation vary according to how exact a replica an utterance has to be to count as an imitation, and how immediate. There is no consistency about this in the literature.

The reported estimates of imitation vary from none in Leopold's (1939) and Bloom's (1972) single cases, through a range of 5–20% of all utterances in Ervin's (1964) study, an average of 10% in Slobin's (1968) account of Brown's data, a range of 16–52% in Rodd and Braine's (1970) study, to 51% in Lieven's (personal communication) case. All these studies involved children under three years. This wide range is partly explicable in terms of the different definitions used. However it must also reflect substantial individual differences, since the variation within single studies is considerable. It also seems generally agreed that the frequency of imitation decreases with age, although only two of the above studies contain longitudinal information on the same child. Thus Rodd and Braine found that the amount of imitation for one child between 23 and 25 months decreased from 34% to 19%. Lieven found a decrease from 51% of all analysable utterances at 17 months, to 40% at 19 months and 35% at 21 months.

Imitation has been dismissed as of no relevance at all to grammatical skills (McNeill, 1966; Fodor, 1966). This is mostly because of the general considerations, advanced by Chomsky, about possible mechanisms of acquisition. It is also dismissed on the grounds that mastery of a language does not consist in the ability to produce memorized sentences, but rather in the ability to produce (and understand) indefinitely many new ones, not previously heard. On the other hand, some behaviourist accounts elevate imitation to an importance that it could not possibly have. Such accounts (e.g. Mowrer, 1960; Jenkins, 1969) are entirely speculative, not being based on any of the available data as to the occurrence and nature of imitation. In particular they fail to take into account the complex and selective nature of the imitation that does occur (see below). Piaget (1951) provides what is currently the fullest account of the possible role of imitation, both non-verbal and verbal, in language development and in the beginnings of representational thought generally. His concern is primarily with the development of imitation as a necessary precursor to language development, and with its role at the very beginnings of language. As such it will be considered separately from the function of imitation as part of linguistic interaction during subsequent language development.

The main evidence cited as proof that imitation is not helpful is that of Ervin (1964). She compared the grammatical structure of imitated and spontaneous (non-imitated) utterances, of five children aged 22–35 months. Utterances which were partial imitations but which also contained substitutions were excluded from the definition of imitation, but those containing omissions or changes in order were included. The imitated utterances did not differ from the spontaneous ones in the kinds of grammatical structures present, and it was concluded from this that imitation could not be progressive, in the sense of leading to knowledge of new grammatical rules. Rodd and Braine's (1970) study, on children aged 21–28 months, using a more liberal definition of imitation, also showed that there was no difference between the grammatical structures present in the imitated and spontaneous utterances.

However, these studies do not constitute exhaustive explorations of the function of imitation. It is well known from memory experiments that children will only repeat correctly those sentences beyond their memory span that they can understand and spontaneously produce themselves. Those sentences containing rules or forms they do not use themselves, they tend to change into their own constructions. It is not therefore surprising that the two studies cited found the results they did. What should have been investigated is not the possible difference between spontenous and imitated utterances on the part of the child, but rather what kind of adult utterances the child was trying to imitate. There is some evidence from other studies (cited below) that children tend to imitate unfamiliar utterances more often than familiar ones. It is possible that the children in the two studies mentioned above were tending to imitate forms that were beyond their current productive capacities, but that in imitating them they could only reproduce them using forms present in their spontaneous speech. This reconstructive ability implies that at the very least children can recognise some equivalence in meaning between adult forms and their own. That they cannot reproduce some adult forms exactly does not mean they cannot learn something from trying to imitate them, since it is possible (although unproven) that they may notice the mismatch between the adult and their own utterances.

There is some additional indirect evidence of the function of imitation in grammatical acquisition. Cazden (1968) has shown how new noun and verb inflections entered a child's speech completely correctly but with a very restricted range of application. After this period of invariably correct but occasional production, there was a period of markedly increased production, during which many errors of commission and overgeneralization were made. Finally, the inflections were used widely and correctly, according to the criteria employed. Brown (1968), examining the development of Wh-questions, found similar although more complex trends. In particular he found an initial period when Wh-questions were used as unanalysed routines, in a restricted and unproductive way. These examples illustrate both the possible functions and the limitations of imitation. Imitation may allow new forms to enter a child's speech and the child may learn much about the use and meaning of each form, as well as its phonology, from its initial restricted application. Imitation cannot account for the errors of overgeneralization described by Cazden, nor for the gradual development of the Wh-question transformation through several constructions never found in adult speech.

Slobin (1968) also observed that children often imitate their mother's expansions of their previous utterances, incorporating some of the changes made by the mother.

The role of imitation in the development of one child, at earlier stages has been investigated in some detail by Lieven (personal communication), using tape-recordings made in the home. Her definition of imitation was "an utterance of the child contained in the previous two utterances of the mother, and not in the previous utterance of the child". Most of the child's analysable utterances consisted of single words or phrases. The imitated items were compared with those uttered spontaneously (i.e. those not contained in the previous utterances of the mother, nor in the child's own previous utterance). The category of imitations included many more different words than did that of spontaneous utterances. Thus, over three sessions, 85% of all imitated words were discrete items (i.e. occurred only once in the sessions), but only 49% of the spontaneous ones were. There was also little overlap in the content of the two categories. An analysis for grammatical class was also carried out, using adult categories, and also a class of "ready-mades". "Ready-mades" are defined by Lyons (1968) as "expressions which are learned as unanalysed wholes, and employed on particular occasions by native speakers". Examples in this case included "please", "hello", "allgone", "alright". It was found that the category of spontaneous words contained many more "ready-mades" (31%) than did the imitations (7%). This was despite their frequent occurrence in the mother's speech, both to the child and to adults, and thus their availability for imitation.

These figures suggest that in this case imitation is progressive in the sense that the child's imitated words included a greater number of different lexical items, and fewer clichéd or routine phrases, than did her spontaneously produced words. Such findings do not prove that imitation plays a causal role in language development, in that they do not show that new words in fact enter a child's spontaneous speech repertoire via its imitated productions. Such findings only show that imitation could play such a role, whereas the reverse findings, that the category of imitated words was similar to, or less diverse and more conventionalized than, that of spontenous words, would exclude such a role. Further substantiating evidence comes from the fact that this child seldom imitated words that she used spontaneously, and also from a similar result of Shipley et al.'s (1969) study. They found that children between the ages of 18–33 months were more likely to imitate unfamiliar than familiar utterances. Here the unfamiliar utterances contained nonsense words, but were constructed to sound like English.

Lieven also found that, despite the decline with age in single-word imitations, when multiple-word utterances first appeared in the child's speech a very high proportion of these were either complete or partial imitations of the mother's previous utterances. In one script 55% of all the child's two-word utterances were preceded by the mother using both words, and 87% by the mother using at least one of the words. There is in the literature considerable discussion of the extent to which children's two-word combinations can be regarded as reductions of adult utterances, or as original combinations of the child, and thus evidence of "creativity" (McNeill, 1966). Lieven's findings suggest that, at least for one child, the first two-word combinations are very closely tied to adult models in their actual production. It is very likely that with increasing age more spontaneous two-word utterances will be produced, thus allowing greater scope for novel combinations.

All this evidence taken together suggests that imitation is important in allowing new lexical items and new grammatical constructions to enter a child's speech repertoire. It does not however tell us more precisely exactly what the child is learning about a new form in imitating it. There are many possibilities here, since the mother's utterances provide a rich source of information about both the linguistic and non-linguistic contexts for the use of a particular word or combination of words, as well as about its phonology. Much more detailed longitudinal information is needed in this respect, tracing the changing use of specific items.

Two further questions about imitation arise: Why, given its function suggested above and the fact that children's vocabulary grows continuously, does imitation gradually decrease in frequency? And how do children learn to imitate initially? Imitation does not ordinarily constitute a means of communication, or of imparting information, although there are some rather specialized functions that it sometimes serves in adult dialogue. For example, repetition of part or all of someone's utterance, with a certain intonation, can indicate lack of comprehension, and function as a request for clarification. Imitation can also function as an emphatic form of agreement, or as an expression of reciprocated feeling. There are also certain conventional forms of greeting and parting where it is appropriate to repeat what has just been said, e.g. "hello", "how are you", "good-bye".

However in most dialogues imitation is a communicational dead end. A vivid illustration of this is the difficulty and frustration experienced in trying to converse with a pathologically echolalic child—that is an older child, whose speech is mainly characterized by immediate imitations and frequent repetitions of previously heard utterances. It is not at present clear what causes such pathological persistence of imitation. It is often, although not invariably, found in children diagnosed as autistic and as psychotic (Cunningham, 1968), and occasionally in subnormal children.

In view of the mainly dysfunctional nature of imitation as regards communication, it would be of interest to know how mothers respond to their children's imitations, as opposed to their spontaneous productions, and whether their responses change with increasing age. Lieven in her case study found that the mother tended to respond with a subsequent utterance less often to imitations than to spontaneous words. When she did respond to imitations, her utterances tended to be simpler grammatically, to extend the child's utterance less often, and more often to be a simple repeat of the mother's own previous utterance, than with responses to spontaneous words. These differences are particularly striking in view of the finding, mentioned above, that at this age imitated words are more diverse and less often "ready-mades" than are spontaneous ones—and thus in their content of possibly greater interest to the mother. The mother's responses are thus likely to discourage imitation, and to provide relatively little information for the child about his utterance.

The Origins of Imitation

The question of the origins of imitation is an extremely complex one that cannot be fully considered here. Piaget's (1951) account is of relevance in two respects: firstly, as providing a description of the various developmental substages of imitation of all kinds during the sensory-motor period, and secondly, as regards the function of imitation in the beginnings of language. Very little subsequent work has been done on the development of imitation, so it is not clear whether Piaget's account is empirically correct or not. As regards the function of imitation, there are several obscurities in Piaget's theory that make it difficult to evaluate.

Imitation develops so that by the final stage of the sensory-motor period the child is allegedly able to reproduce, without prior practice, unfamiliar models and actions in their absence. This is called "deferred imitation". Such ability must involve some system of internal representation on which the deferred imitation is based, and Piaget suggests mental images for this role. Thus, "imitation is no longer dependent on the actual action, and the child becomes capable of imitating internally a series of models in the form of images or suggestions of actions" (ibid. p. 62). The mental image is "the symbol", or "interior copy or reproduction of the object", and "the product of the interiorization of imitation" (ibid. p. 70). Piaget maintains that such images and memories are essentially individual and idiosyncratic, ". . . a translation of personal experiences" (ibid. p. 71).

The function of deferred imitation, in the development of language and representation generally, is that it "*provides*" differentiation and co-ordination between "signifiers" (in this case mental images) and what is "signified" (the absent model). What however is the nature of this provision? Piaget draws a distinction between the representative relationships involved in deferred imitation and in language. He contrasts the individual nature of mental images with the externally and socially determined nature of words, as regards the form of representation. Otherwise, there are important similarities between the two in their representative functions, with imitation providing the earlier and less social form. This would seem to imply that the development of deferred imitation in other areas is necessary before language can appear, and one might look for empirical relationships on this account. However this inference is rendered invalid by Piaget's further claim that the first words are not "true signs", but intermediate in their nature between such signs and the idiosyncratic images (symbols) of imitation. This intermediate status is seen in the changing and subjective meaning that the first words have, and also in their allegedly imitative nature: they are held to be either onomatopaeic, and thus direct imitations of the objects so designated, or else isolated imitations of words used by adults. It is thus not clear from Piaget's writings whether the development of deferred imitation is necessary before this earliest use of words can appear, or only before the subsequent development of "true" verbal signs. If the latter is the case, then what other relationship is being posited between the representative abilities involved in deferred imitation and those in the first use of words, other than that of parallel and simultaneous development? How does the ability developed in one sphere transfer to another? Piaget at one point (ibid. p. 3) says they "interact" but he never elaborates on this.

Whilst imitation is supposed to supply the child with the ability to copy absent models, play is supposed to supply what Piaget calls the "meanings of symbols" (ibid. p. 3). By the end of the sensory-motor period pretence or make-believe play develops. In this the child chooses objects to stand for other objects, in their absence, and out of the context in which they occur normally. The object or activity which is chosen as a play substitute may have little or no natural connection with what they represent; rather the connection is what Piaget calls "motivated", being the product of individual imagination and needs. Pretence play resembles imitation in its "representational element whose existence is proved by the deferred character of the reaction" (ibid. p. 98). They differ from each other in that in play there is no accommodation to objective reality, but instead there is "subjective assimilation" and a distortion of reality. In imitation, by contrast, the child's activity is predominantly determined by the external reality he is copying. Whilst in extreme cases Piaget's distinction between imitation and play, between copies and distortions of reality, is clear, there are many intermediate cases where there appears to be an element of both. However "distorted" the symbolization involved in play is, there is always some element of copying of an earlier or absent model; in some of the examples Piaget quotes there is an obvious element of imitation.

Piaget maintains that ludic assimilation and imitative accommodation eventually became closely co-ordinated, having been differentiated during the sensory-motor period. This progressive integration appears to take the form of the same objects being involved in simultaneous accommodation and assimilation of this kind (ibid. p. 21). Once again Piaget only makes passing and scanty reference to what this process of integration and co-ordination consists in; maintaining however that the "constitution of the symbolic function is only possible as a result of this union" (ibid. p. 3).

This account of the non-verbal origins of language, and of the simultaneous development of the "representative function" in many aspects of behaviour, solves several internal problems, as far as Piaget's general theory of development is concerned. His postulation of the essential continuity between sensory-motor and representative modes of thought, particularly his account of the origins of language in the non-verbal sensory-motor developments of play and imitation, allows him to preserve his overall thesis of functional continuity but structural discontinuity that he sees in all development. However, as this critique has emphasized, Piaget's theory seems to be least testable at the most crucial points, i.e. at the links between the various allegedly related areas of development. In many places, his account is so overdetermined, in the sense of everything being different from but essentially similar to or related to everything else, that it is difficult to see what empirical substance it has.

These difficulties should not, however, detract from the possible importance of imitation as a precursor to particular aspects of language development. What is needed is some way of linking Piaget's account of imitation as one necessary prerequisite of language development, to the observations, cited above, of verbal imitation in the course of language development.

Acknowledgements

I should like to thank Elena Lieven for much helpful discussion, and for permission to quote her unpublished data.

References

Austin, J. L. (1962). "How to do Things with Words." O.U.P., London.

Bingham, N. E. (In prep.). Maternal speech to pre-linguistic infants.

Bloom, L. (1970). "Language Development." Cambridge Mass., M.I.T.

Bloom, L. (1972). One word at a time. Paper to Ling. Soc. Amer., Univ. of Buffalo.

Brown, R. (1968). The Development of Wh-Questions in Child Speech. *J. verb. learn. verb. behav.* **7**, 279–290.

Brown, R. and Bellugi, V. (1964). Three Processes in the child's acquisition of syntax. *In* "New Directions in the Study of Language," (E. Lenneberg, ed.). M.I.T. Press, Cambridge, Mass.

Cazden, C. B. (1968). The acquisition of noun and verb inflections. *Child Dev.* **39**, 433–448.

Chomsky, N. (1965). "Aspects of the Theory of Syntax." M.I.T. Press, Cambridge, Mass.

Chomsky, N. (1968). "Language and Mind," Harcourt, Brace and World Inc. New York.

Cunningham, M. A. (1968). A comparison of the language of psychotic and non-psychotic children who are mentally retarded. *J. child Psychol. Psychiat.* **9**, 229–244.

Ervin, S. (1964). Imitation and structural change in children's language. *In* "New Directions in the Study of Language", (E. Lenneberg, ed.). M.I.T. Press, Cambridge, Mass.

Fodor, J. (1966). How to learn to talk: some simple ways. *In* "The Genesis of Language", (F. Smith and G. A. Miller, eds.). M.I.T. Press, Cambridge, Mass.

Grice, H. P. (1957). Meaning. *Phil. Rev.* **68**, 377–388.

Jenkins, J. (1969). "Handbook of Socialisation", (Goslin, ed.). Chicago.

Lenneberg, E. (1967). "The Biological Foundations of Language." Wiley, New York.

Leopold, W. F. (1939). "Speech Development of a Bilingual Child." Northwestern University, Evanston.

Lyons, J. (1968). "Introduction to Theoretical Linguistics." C.U.P., London.

McNeill, D. (1966). Developmental Psycholinguistics. *In* "The Genesis of Language", (F. Smith and G. A. Miller, eds.). M.I.T. Press, Cambridge, Mass.

McNeill, D. (1970). "The acquisition of Language." Harper and Row, New York.

Mowrer, O. H. (1960). "Learning Theory and the Symbolic Process." Wiley, New York.

Phillips, J. R. (In press). Syntax and vocabulary of mothers' speech to young children. *Child Dev.*

Piaget, J. (1951). "Play, Dreams and Imitation in Childhood." Routledge and Kegan Paul, London.

Rodd, L. J. and Braine, M. D. S. (1970). Children's imitations of syntactic constructions as a measure of linguistic competence. *J. verb. learn. verb. Behav.* **10**, 430–443.

Ryan, J. F. (forthcoming, 1973). Early language development. *In* "The Integration of the Child in the Social World", (M. P. M. Richards, ed.). C.U.P., London.

Shipley, E., Smith, C. and Gleitman, L. P. (1969). A study in the acquisition of language. *Lang.* **35**, 322–344.

Slobin, D. A. (1968). Imitation and grammatical development in children. *In* "Contemporary Issues in Developmental Psychology", (N. S.Endler, L. R. Boulter and H. Osser, eds.). Holt, Rinehart and Winston, New York.

Slobin, D. A. (1971). "Psycholinguistics." M.I.T. Press, Cambridge, Mass.

Stern, W. A. (1923). "The Psychology of Early Childhood." Allen and Unwin, London.

Strawson, P. F. (1964). Intention and convention in speech acts. *Phil. Rev.* **4**, 4–60.

22

Language, Learning and Laterality

by John C. Marshall

Introduction

The constraints on language-acquisition discussed in this paper are drawn in the main from neuropsychological studies of language development and dissolution. I shall be particularly concerned with the hypothesis that there is a correlation between level of performance attained and the degree of specialization of function in the brain-mechanisms subserving that performance. "Specialization" is taken to include both hemispheric lateralization and focalization of function within a hemisphere.

The hypothesis is not new: Goethe is reputed to have remarked that "the absence of symmetry is evidence of the progress of evolution" (see Hécaen and Ajuriaguerra, 1963); more recently Henschen (1926) claimed: "In nature there seems to be a law that in order to attain full development of higher faculties originally distributed over two organs, a concentration of the capacity in only one of them is necessary."

Specialization of function manifests itself most strikingly in man, yet we now have reason to deny that "animals below man have two 'right' hemispheres, one on each side" (Teuber, 1967). To take just two recent examples, Webster (1972) has reported in split-brain cats that the "non-dominant" hemisphere (the hemisphere ipsilateral to the preferred paw) is more skilled in solving certain visual discrimination problems; and Nottebohm (1971, 1972) has shown that in the adult chaffinch "full song" is mediated via the left hypoglossal nerves.

Relationships between learning and specialization of neural function can also be demonstrated in non-human species. Thus, the principles of mass action and equipotentiality may be true for rats reared in restricted environments, but for free-environment rats smaller (non-striate) posterior lesions produce a greater deficit in maze-learning than larger anterior lesions (Smith, 1959). Similarly, Nottebohm's work (1971, 1972) indicates that if the left hypoglossus is sectioned in the young chaffinch, before vocal

445

learning has taken place, normal song develops under the control of the right. Although such homologues are notoriously misleading, we may eventually hope to discover general biological constraints which lead complex organisms in the direction of lateralization and focalization of function (see Corballis and Beale, 1970).

An important neurological aspect of the language-learning problem can be phrased thus: studies of adult subjects with focal brain-injuries "show that there is a high degree of cerebral organization of psychological functions" (Warrington, 1970). This is particularly notable with respect to lesions which disrupt language and speech. Although he is far from being a *tabula rasa*, a similar degree of specialization is not seen in the child. We may therefore ask: How and Why is this plasticity lost as the child, between birth and puberty, acquires command of a language-system? What difference would it make if sub-components of the language-faculty were not represented in (at least partially) distinct locales? In Lashley's words (1937): "The fundamental problem for the student of localization is to discover what functions are served by this grouping and arrangement? What functions does it permit that could not be carried out if the cells were uniformly distributed throughout the system?" Lashley considered two extreme and opposed ways of interpreting the facts.

1. "Some part of the structural diversity of the nervous system may well be an accidental product of the mechanism of embryonic development. By the general principles of neurobiotaxis, neuroblasts developing simultaneously in a given region are subject to the same developmental forces and will send their axons to a common field. Thus local groups of cells having similar functional connections will arise; yet the fact of their aggregation and the consequent 'localization of function' may be entirely without significance for the integrative processes in which they participate."

That the embryonic development in question is "accidental" seems *a priori* highly unlikely. In the absence of positive reasons for it, one might expect hemispheric (and inter-hemispheric) specialization for complex cognitive skills in the human adult to be maladaptive. Injury to one hemisphere produces a functional disability which cannot be fully compensated for by the other hemisphere. Why should the "safety factor" of partial equipotentiality which characterizes other duplicated organs, the brains of (some) non-human primates, and the cerebral hemispheres of the human child be lost to the adult? (Campbell, 1960). Whilst brain-injury is more common in the early years of childhood, tumours, direct trauma, and cerebro-vascular accidents occur only too frequently in adolescence and adulthood.

Lashley's second proposal sounds more reasonable . . . and much more interesting.

2. ". . . separate localization of functions is determined by the existence of diverse kinds of integrative mechanism which cannot function in the same nerve field without interference. (. . .) If temporal order is determined by space factors in the nervous system, the fields in which this type of organization is dominant cannot also serve other space systems. There is thus some reason to believe that the utilization of the spatial arrangement of excitations in the timing functions determines an additional group of isolated cerebral areas."

Before investigating Lashley's hypothesis, I shall begin at the end and review, briefly, some of the data which relates to linguistic specialization in the normal adult brain.

Linguistic Specialization and its Development

Evidence that the left-hemisphere is dominant for linguistic functions in the vast majority of right-handed subjects (without familial sinistrality or early brain damage) comes from a wide variety of sources. These include:

(1) Studies of the incidence of dysphasia following left- or right-sided injury to the brain (Zangwill, 1967).

(2) Studies of the sequelae of surgical intervention, e.g. left and right hemispherectomy (Smith, 1966), and commissurotomy (Sperry et al., 1969).

(3) Studies of direct electrical or pharmacological intervention, e.g. cortical (Penfield and Roberts, 1959) and subcortical stimulation (Ojemann et al., 1968), and the intracarotid injection of amytal (Milner et al., 1964).

(4) Electrical recording of the immediate precursors of speech—cortical command potentials (McAdam and Whitaker, 1971)—and of the central correlates of linguistic perception and analysis—evoked cortical potentials (Wood et al., 1971).

(5) Psychological studies of the "right ear advantage" for speech stimuli in dichotic listening (Kimura, 1967), and the "right visual field effect" for letters and words (Kimura, 1966).

A number of the above data-sources provide, in addition, evidence for intra-hemispheric specialization. Thus study of aphasia-producing lesions (Broca, 1863), electrical stimulation (Penfield and Roberts, 1959), and cortical command potentials (McAdam and Whitaker, 1971) suggests that the left frontal lobe, especially the inferior portion of the pre-central gyrus, plays an important role in controlling the vocal tract in syllable-sized units. One can think, then, of Broca's area as effecting the "translation" of language-elements into their articulatory signs, under the constraint of the phonemic regularities of the language in question.

Aphasia-studies (Wernicke, 1874), the sequelae of temporal lobectomy (Milner, 1967), and evoked cortical potential recordings (Morrell and Salamy, 1971; Matsumiya *et al.*, 1972) implicate association cortex of the left temporal lobe, especially the middle zone of the upper temporal convolution, in many linguistic functions, including lexical selection and the decoding of phonological patterns from primary acoustic stimulation.

Aphasia-studies also suggest that the left infero-parietal region—secondary association areas of the angular and supra-marginal gyri—is involved in lexical selection. Some accounts of the formation and integration of (non-limbic) cross-modal associations (Geschwind, 1969) regard the region as providing the speech areas with non-vocal inputs in a form appropriate for linguistic elaboration.

Accounts of "conduction" aphasia (Konorski, 1970) suggest that the arcuate fasciculus acts as a relay-line connecting Wernicke's with Broca's area. Its function may thus be to provide one means of linking the internal representation of linguistic objects with their articulatory signs.

Penfield and Roberts (1959) postulated that the functions of Broca's area, the supplementary motor area, and of Wernicke's area "are coordinated by projections of each to parts of the thalamus . . ." Recent work has been consistent with this speculation. Thus dysarthric and perhaps other expressive symptoms have been observed after lesion of the nucleus ventralis lateralis and the pulvinar (Bell, 1968; Samra *et al.*, 1969; Van Buren and Borke, 1969). These deficits are both more common and more profound following left lesions. Similar results, including object-naming difficulties, have been obtained following electrical stimulation of the pulvinar (Ojemann *et al.*, 1968) and portions of the ventrolateral thalamic nucleus (Ojemann and Ward, 1971).

There is, of course, no question but that many sub-cortical areas are vitally implicated in the control of articulate speech. However, there is still disagreement over whether some of the main symptom-complexes of aphasia are best interpreted as resulting from damage to cortical "centres" and cortico-cortical connections (Geschwind, 1965), or as disconnections and disturbances of timing relationships in cortico-thalamic circuits (Penfield, 1969; Pribram, 1971). Whitaker (1971) provides a discussion of this controversy.

Let us now contrast this specialization with the "plasticity" and absence of focalization which characterizes the child's brain. In early childhood, loss, disturbance, or retardation of language may result from injury to either hemisphere (Freud, 1897). When lesions have occurred before the onset of speech, Basser (1962) reports "no significant differences between the mean age of onset of speech for cases with left or right hemisphere lesion". Compared with similar adult lesions, the prognosis for rapid recovery in the cases is very favourable. For lesions sustained after the onset of speech but before age 10, the proportion of children showing aphasic symptoms following right hemisphere injury is still substantial (Basser, 1962), although not as high as in left-hemisphere cases (Gutmann, 1942). (According to Kimura, 1963, normal children show a "right ear advantage" in dichotic speech-perception tasks from age 4 onwards.) The likelihood of eventual remission of symptoms is still far greater than in adult subjects (see Lennenberg, 1967, for discussion).

The nature of the aphasic deficit and its pattern of remission also differ as a function of age. Ford (1937) notes that lesions sustained by children between the age of two and three "in whom speech function is not fully developed usually result in complete loss of speech, not fractional loss of speech as in older children. In time the child will usually begin to talk just as an infant first learning to speak. First inarticulate sounds are made, then single words, later phrases, and finally short sentences". "It seems impossible," Ford claims, "to reconcile the speech disturbances resulting from cerebral lesion in infants with any type of aphasia as seen in adults."

Between the ages of 4 and 10, Gutmann's data (1942) show a uniform pattern of dramatic reduction in spontaneous speech, sometimes amounting to mutism, with dysarthria and telegrammatic speech during the recovery period. Gutmann reports that this is "equally true of cases with frontal and temporal lesions", although in the latter case receptive disturbances—auditory and visual comprehension—may also be in evidence. Observations by Alajouanine and Lhermitte (1965) are consistent with these claims. The latter also stress the absence or rarity of logorrhoea, phonemic and semantic paraphasias, and comprehension disorders in the child with temporal lobe damage. These symptoms are common after similar injuries in the adult.

There is still considerable disagreement both about the extent of linguistic specialization in the adult brain, and about the potential for recovery and re-organization in the immature brain. Nonetheless the general progression is not in doubt. The significance of such a pattern of development is perhaps best viewed in the light of departures from the adult norm.

Normal and Pathological Departure from the Norm

There are at least two groups of "normal" adult subjects (i.e. who have not sustained early brain damage) for whom claims of "bilateral" language-representation have been made: left (and perhaps "mixed") handers, especially those in whom the trait is familial, and right-handers with close left-handed family. This suggestion was originally made on the basis of the following putative facts: subjects belonging to these groups may show aphasia after lesions to either hemisphere; and compared with "pure" right-handed subjects, the aphasic symptoms are relatively less profound to begin with and have a greater likelihood of complete (or almost complete) remission (Chesher, 1936; Luria, 1947; Conrad, 1949; Subirana, 1952) irrespective of the side of the injury. Ettlinger et al. (1956) present evidence that this is not true of all left-handers—"unilateral representation in left or mixed handers without early left brain damage. lent form of cerebral organization in sinistrals"—but they do not rule out the probability that " 'cerebral ambilaterality' may well occur in a certain proportion of cases". The data of Milner et al. (1964), obtained from amytal testing, suggest that this proportion is 16% bilateral speech representation in left or mixed handers without early left brain damage. (Milner et al.'s estimates for left and right representation in this group are 64% and 20% respectively). Studies of dichotic listening and visual field performance (Curry, 1967; Zurif and Bryden, 1969) are likewise consistent with the claim that at least a substantial proportion of left-handers have relatively ambilateral hemispheres for language reception. If, for the moment, then, we accept the validity of the above observations, can deleterious results, in terms of Lashley's second hypothesis, be shown to follow?

Developmental delay (or failure) of hemispheric specialization has often been hypothesized to be correlated with many kinds of learning-deficit—Orton's theory (1937) of developmental language problems, especially reading and writing failures, provides the classic example. The existence of correlations of the above type is not in question although their significance is debatable. Thus it would be possible to argue that such factors as poverty of environment (Geffner and Hochberg, 1971), sex differences in rate of maturation (Kimura, 1963), and mild (but probably bilateral) brain-damage (Dreifuss, 1963; Richlin et al., 1971) are correlated with both rate of learning and rate of development of brain-specialization without holding that these two parameters stand in a causal relationship. That is, such data does not unambiguously favour Lashley's second hypothesis to the exclusion of the first.

Levy (1969) provides a better line of argument. She suggests that there may be a "competitive antagonism" between the mechanisms for "Gestalt apprehension" (characteristic of right hemisphere performance) and analytic perception and production strategies (characteristic of left-hemisphere performance). Levy speculates that "during the evolution of the hominids Gestalt perception may have lateralized into the mute hemisphere as a consequence of an antagonism between functions of language and perception". Although there is no direct evidence for such antagonism, Levy and others (Miller, 1971) have provided strong circumstantial support for the claim. Assuming that the cerebral hemispheres of left-handed subjects are less clearly differentiated in terms of linguistic ability than those of "pure" right-handers, Levy predicted, and found, that whilst the verbal I.Q.'s of right and left-handers did *not* differ significantly, the left-handers had a dramatically lower performance (visuo-spatial) I.Q. Language capacity in the right-hemisphere "drives out", as it were, the abilities for which that hemisphere should be dominant. Both Levy's (1969) and Miller's (1971) subjects were normal university students. There is however, evidence from pathological populations which is also consistent with the hypothesis. Thus Lansdell (1969) took a group of subjects with left-hemisphere damage which had resulted in right-hemisphere speech-representation as assessed by the amytal test. He found that "the earlier the indication of brain damage the better was their verbal development and the poorer was their non-verbal performance". Studies of hemispherectomy for infantile hemiplegia similarly suggest the existence of a "developmental hierarchy" in which the acquisition of language "takes precedence over nonlanguage and verbal reasoning functions" (Smith, 1970).

What then is language that a formal incompatibility might exist between the structures necessary for its acquisition and maintenance and the structures which mediate complex visuo-spatial skills?

Concerning the Nature of Specialization

Animal studies suggest that the neurological results of learning (and overlearning) differ as a function of the hierarchical structure of what is learned. Thus overlearning of a simple, single habit may render the behaviour relatively immune from the effects of focal injury. "Learning-sets", however, are not rendered similarly immune. It has thus been suggested that the effect of learning is to "diffuse" the neurological substrate of simple habits, but to "focalize" the substrate for high-level skills whose range of appropriate application is correspondingly larger (See Piercy, 1964, for references and discussion). With respect to language-performance, Piercy (1964) notes that "in patients with a severe aphasia it is the overlearned verbal habits, such as automatic word series and conventional greetings, which are most likely to be spared, whereas the more general and versatile aspects of verbal skill are more vulnerable to a focal lesion". Hughlings Jackson (1879) regarded such forms of "non-propositional" language as "right-hemisphere" speech.

We might speculate, then, that individual tokens of linguistic and visuo-spatial stimuli are laid down in both hemispheres with a "degree of diffusion" proportional to some kind of frequency-principle. The higher-order codings of tokens into structurally-significant types then takes place in a single hemisphere—the left for natural classes of linguistic objects, the right for visuo-spatial objects. Jane Holmes and I have recently obtained evidence consistent with such speculation: in a tachistoscope experiment with normal, right-handed subjects, we demonstrated that the left-hemisphere (Right Visual Field presentation) is primarily responsive to the syntactic properties of words, recognizing nouns more easily than verbs, whereas the right-hemisphere (Left Visual Field presentation) is primarily responsive to 1st order probabilities, recognizing high-frequency words more readily than low-frequency words.

Let us now consider some general properties of linguistic and visuo-spatial structures. The most striking aspect of linguistic objects is that the relationship between their "superficial" and their "real" structure is code-like, not cypher-like. Thus, although of necessity speech-stimuli are linearly-ordered in time, the relationship between the phonological concatenations in terms of which speech is perceived, and the temporal segments of the acoustic wave which exemplify phonological sequences, is not one-to-one. A similar point can be made concerning English orthography. In a word such as *bite*, the long vowel is conditioned by a later element, *e* (compare *bit—bite*). Similarly, in syntax, the conceptual status of a lexical element is conditioned by structures which can be temporally far removed from the element in question. In a sentence such as "The man who I saw yesterday . . . robbed the bank", *man* is the logical subject (or agent) of the matrix sentence; in "The man who I saw yesterday . . . was robbed by the bank", *man* is the logical object of the matrix sentence. That is, the deep structure of the latter sentence is "The bank robbed the man." (see Liberman, 1970, for discussion).

The neurological substrate of language, then, must be highly responsive to serial order on a number of different levels, and must have the capacity to decode from one serial order to another. (Adequate performance of complex manual skills is likewise critically dependent upon correct programming of serial order, a fact which is presumably not unrelated to the association between the language-hemisphere and the preferred hand.)

By contrast, structures based upon proximal and hierarchical relationships, irrespective of order, are more characteristic of visual objects. If "followed by" is the crucial predicate of linguistic grammars, "coincident with" might be claimed as the fundamental notion of a picture-grammar (Clowes, 1969, 1971). To illustrate, in a grammar having a classical, Chomskian level of deep structure, the analysis of "John received the book" may be explicated in a notation which exhibits the relationship between that sentence and "Someone gave the book to John." In the first sentence *John* is NP_1 ($NP_1 + V + NP_2$); in the second, *John* is NP_3 ($NP_1 + V + NP_2 + NP_3$); the status of *John* as indirect object is determined by its place and labelling in the full phrase structure of this latter string. Consider now an elementary part of a pictorial description of the following figure:

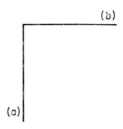

If the North End of Line (a) and the West End of Line (b) are coincident then the region of their coincidence is a *corner*. But the status of (a) as a vertical line is not affected by this further labelling. There are, of course, examples where the status of an element is determined by the configuration as a whole. The slanted line is the East Edge of (c) but the West Edge of (d). It is, however, not without interest that right-left disorientation is

a sign of left-hemisphere pathology (Benton, 1959).

The above illustrations are too trivial to count as an explanation of hemispheric specialization. But they do, I hope, show why one might consider study of the formal properties of language- and picture-grammars to be a promising approach to the validation of Lashley's second hypothesis.

References

Alajouanine, T. and Lhermitte, F. (1965). Acquired aphasia in childhood. *Brain* **88**, 653–662.

Basser, L. S. (1962). Hemiplegia of early onset and the faculty of speech with special reference to the effects of hemispherectomy. *Brain* **85**, 427–460.

Bell, D. S. (1968). Speech functions of the thalamus inferred from the effects of thalamotomy. *Brain* **91**, 619–638.

Benton, A. L. (1959). "Right-left Discrimination and Finger Localization." Hoeber, New York.

Broca, P. (1863). Localisation des fonctions cérébrales. Siege de la faculté du langage articule. *Bull. Soc. d'Anth.* **4**, 200–208.

Campbell, B. (1960). The factor of safety in the nervous system. *Bull. Los Angeles Neurological Society* **25**, 109–117.

Chesher, E. C. (1936). Some observations concerning the relation of handedness to the language mechanism. *Bull. Neurol. Inst. New York* **4**, 556–562.

Clowes, M. B. (1969). Transformational grammars and the organization of pictures. *In* "Automatic Interpretation and Classification of Images", (A. Graselli, ed.). Academic Press, New York.

Clowes, M. B. (1971). On seeing things. *Artificial Intelligence* **2**, 79–116.

Conrad, K. (1949). Uber aphasische Sprachstorungen bei hirnverlezten Linkshander. *Nervenartz* **20**, 148–154.

Corballis, M. C. and Beale, I. L. (1970). Bilateral symmetry and behavior. *Psych. Rev.* **77**, 451–464.

Curry, F. K. W. (1967). A comparison of left-handed and right-handed subjects on verbal and nonverbal dichotic listening tasks. *Cortex* **3**, 343–352.

Dreifuss, F. E. (1963). Delayed development of hemisphere dominance. *Arch. Neurol. (Chicago)* **8**, 510–514.

Ettlinger, G., Jackson, C. V. and Zangwill, O. L. (1956). Cerebral dominance in sinistrals. *Brain* **79**, 569–588.

Ford, F. R. (1937). "Diseases of the Nervous System in Infancy Childhood and Adolescence." Thomas, Springfield, Ill.

Freud, S. (1897). "Die infantile Cerebrallahmung." Hölder, Vienna.

Geffner, D. S. and Hochberg, I. (1971). Ear laterality performance of children from low and middle socioeconomic levels on a verbal dichotic listening task. *Cortex* **7**, 193–203.

Geschwind, N. (1965). Disconnexion syndromes in animals and man. *Brain* **88**, 237–294.

Geschwind, N. (1969). Problems in the anatomical understanding of the aphasias. *In* "Contributions to Clinical Neuro-Psychology", (A. L. Benton, ed.). Aldine Chicago.

Gutmann, E. (1942). Aphasia in children. *Brain* **65**, 205–219.

Hécaen, H. and Ajuriaguerra, J. de (1963). *Les Gauchers: Prévalence Manuelle et Dominance Cérébrale*. Presses Universitaires de France, Paris.

Henschen, S. E. (1926). On the function of the right hemisphere of the brain in relation to the left in speech, music and calculation. *Brain* **49**, 110–123.

Jackson, H. J. (1879). On affections of speech from disease of the brain. *Brain* **2**, 203–222.

Kimura, D. (1963). Speech lateralization in young children as determined by an auditory test. *J. comp. physiol. Psychol.* **56**, 899–902.

Kimura, D. (1966). Dual functional asymmetry of the brain in visual perception. *Neuropsychologia*, **4**, 275–285.

Kimura, D. (1967). Functional asymmetry of the brain in dichotic listening. *Cortex* **3**, 163–178.

Konorski, J. (1970). Pathophysiological mechanisms of speech on the basis of studies of aphasia. *Acta Neurobiologiae Experimentalis* **30**, 189–210.

Lansdell, H. (1969). Verbal and nonverbal factors in right-hemisphere speech. *J. comp. physiol. Psychol.* **69**, 734–738.

Lashley, K. S. (1937). Functional determinants of cerebral localization. *Arch. Neurol. Psychiat. (Chicago)* **38**, 371–387.

Lenneberg, E. H. (1967). "Biological Foundations of Language." Wiley, New York.

Levy, J. (1969). Possible basis for the evolution of lateral specialization of the human brain. *Nature* **224**, 614–615.

Liberman, A. M. (1970). The grammars of speech and language. *Cognitive Psychology* **1**, 301–323.

Luria, A. R. (1947). *Traumatic Aphasia*. State Publishing House, Moscow.

Matsumiya, Y., Tagliasco, V., Lombroso, C. T. and Goodglass, H. (1972). Auditory evoked response: Meaningfulness of stimuli and interhemispheric asymmetry. *Science* **175**, 790–792.

McAdam, D. W. and Whitaker, H. A. (1971). Language production: Electroencephalographic localization in the normal human brain. *Science* **172**, 499–502.

Miller, E. (1971). Handedness and the pattern of human ability. *Br. J. Psychol.* **62**, 111–112.

Milner, B. (1967). Brain mechanisms suggested by studies of temporal lobes. *In* "Brain Mechanisms Underlying Speech and Language", (C. H. Millikan and F. L. Darley, eds.). Grune and Stratton, New York.

Milner, B., Branch, C. and Rasmussen, T. (1964). Observations on cerebral dominance. *In* "Disorders of Language", (A. V. S. de Rueck and M. O'Connor, eds.). Little, Brown and Co., Boston.

Morrell, L. K. and Salamy, J. G. (1971). Hemispheric asymmetry of electrocortical responses to speech stimuli. *Science* **174**, 164–166.

Nottebohm, F. (1971). Neural lateralization of vocal control in a passerine bird: 1. Song. *J. exp. Zool.* **177**, 229–262.

Nottebohm, F. (1972). Neural lateralization of vocal control in a passerine bird: 2. Subsong, calls and a theory of vocal learning. *J. exp. Zool.* **179**, 35–50.

Ojemann, G. A., Fedio, P. and Van Buren, J. M. (1968). Anomia from pulvinar and subcortical parietal stimulation. *Brain* **91**, 99–116.

Ojemann, G. A. and Ward, A. A. (1971). Speech representation in ventrolateral thalamus. *Brain* **94**, 669–680.

Orton, S. T. (1937). "Reading, writing and speech problems in children." Chapman and Hall, London.

Penfield, W. (1969). Consciousness, memory and man's conditioned reflexes. *In* "On the Biology of Learning", (K. H. Pribram, ed.). Harcourt, Brace and World, New York.

Penfield, W. and Roberts, L. (1959). "Speech and Brain-Mechanisms." Princeton University Press, New Jersey.

Piercy, M. (1964). The effects of cerebral lesions on intellectual function: a review of current research trends. *Br. J. Psychiat.* **110**, 310–352.

Pribram, K. H. (1971). "What makes man human?" American Museum of Natural History, New York.

Richlin, M., Weisinger, M., Weinstein, S., Giannini, M. and Morgenstern, M. (1971). Interhemispheric asymmetries of evoked cortical responses in retarded and normal children. *Cortex* **7**, 98–105.

Samra, K., Riklan, M., Levita, E., Zimmerman, J., Waltz, J. M., Bergmann, L. and Cooper, I. S. (1969). Language and speech correlates of anatomically verified lesions in thalamic surgery for parkinsonism. *J. Speech Hear. Res.* **12**, 510–540.

Smith, A. (1966). Speech and other functions after left (dominant) hemispherectomy. *J. Neurol. Neurosurg. Psychiat.* **29**, 467–471.

Smith, A. (1970). Dominant and nondominant hemispherectomy. Paper presented to the *Second Annual Cerebral Function Symposium*, Denver, Colorado.

Smith, C. J. (1959). Mass action and early environment in the rat. *J. comp. physiol. Psychol.* **52**, 154–156.

Sperry, R. W., Gazzaniga, M. S. and Bogen, J. E. (1969). Interhemispheric relationships. *In* "Handbook of Clinical Neurology", Vol. 4, (P. J. Vinken and G. W. Bruyn, eds.). Wiley, New York.

Subirana, A. (1952). La Droiterie. *Arch. Suisses Neurol. Psychiat.* **69**, 321–359.

Teuber, H-L. (1967). Lacunae and research approaches to them. *In* "Brain Mechanisms Underlying Speech and Language", (C. H. Millikan and F. L. Darley, eds.). Grune and Stratton, New York.

Van Buren, J. M. and Borke, R. C. (1969). Alterations in speech and the pulvinar. *Brain* **92**, 255–284.

Warrington, E. K. (1970). Neurological deficits. *In* "The Psychological Assessment of Mental and Physical Handicaps", (P. Mittler, ed.). Methuen, London.

Webster, W. G. (1972). Functional asymmetry between the cerebral hemispheres of the cat. *Neuropsychologia* **10**, 75–87.

Wernicke, C. (1874). *"Der Aphasische Symptomencomplex."* Cohn and Weigert, Breslau.

Whitaker, H. A. (1971). On the representation of language in the human brain. Linguistic Research Inc., Edmonton.

Wood, C. C., Goff, W. R. and Day, R. S. (1971). Auditory evoked potentials during speech perception. *Science* **173**, 1248–1251.

Zangwill, O. L. (1967). Speech and the minor hemisphere. *Acta Neurologica et Psychiatrica Belgica* **67**, 1013–1020.

Zurif, E. B. and Bryden, M. P. (1969). Familial handedness and left-right differences in auditory and visual perception. *Neuropsychologia* **7**, 179–188.

23

Constraints upon Learning: Some Developmental Considerations

by S. J. Hutt

Developmental Stage: A Constraint upon Learning

A concept prominent in several of the later chapters is that of "developmental stage", particularly as it is employed in the writings of Piaget. The notion of a stage in human development has much in common with that of sensitive period in the development of animals, i.e. a period of enhanced sensitivity to particular stimuli, affecting the learning of particular behaviour patterns, and supposedly having long-term effects. Although work on stages of development and on sensitive periods has progressed independently since the 1930s, they have been subject to much the same criticisms and have given rise to surprisingly similar controversies.

Developmental stage as a descriptive term

Earlier pronouncements about stages of "readiness" to learn in humans, and about critical periods for learning in animals, have each had to be modified in the light to recent evidence seriously questioning the immutability of such stages and periods. Work by early developmental psychologists such as Gesell and Thompson (1929), McGraw (1935) and Dennis (1941) seemed to point to the inevitability of appearance of certain motor patterns in infants, suggesting that within wide limits of environmental experience, these behaviours were the direct result of maturational processes. This led some workers, such as Gates (1937), to postulate that readiness to acquire even cognitive skills such as reading must await the arrival of a particular developmental stage (in this case a mental age of $6\frac{1}{2}$ years) before children could reasonably profit from the teaching of reading. We now know that what a child can and what he cannot learn at a particular age depends upon how he is taught. Fowler (1965), employing an experimental reading programme, and Moore (1966), using a "talking typewriter", have each had considerable success in teaching reading to children of 3 years. The talking typewriter has also been used with success in remedial programmes for educationally backward children.

The "readiness" doctrine had also been supported by evidence on children's attention span. Van Alstyne (1932) showed that with increasing age the attention span of young children increased from 7 minutes at age 2 to 13. 6 minutes at age 5. Thus, it seemed futile to try to teach a child to read when his attention span was only about 10 minutes long. However, as Moyer and Gilmer (1955) have subsequently shown, how long a child attends depends upon what he has to attend to: with objects especially constructed to provide visual and manipulative stimulation, these authors obtained attention spans varying from 26.5 minutes to 35.0 minutes over the same age range. In similar vein, the long-standing claim by Piaget that children cannot combine information inferentially until 8 years of age could be shown to be false, once it was understood that the task comprises at least two components and not one. Bryant (Chapter 20) has elegantly shown that children can combine information inferentially, several years earlier than Piaget had supposed, provided they have access to the data upon which the inference must be based. Thus, just as the apparent immutability of critical periods for learning has been questioned by ethologists, so psychologists have come to realize that whether there are developmental stages for learning depends upon what has to be learned, how the material is taught and how we test for learning.

With so many qualifications, we may perhaps question whether "developmental stage" is either a necessary or a useful concept. Is it not sufficient, as Bijou and Baer (1963) have suggested, simply to give the child's age in relation to a particular measure of performance? Indeed, this is probably sufficient if we are considering a simple perceptual-motor task such as card-sorting (Connolly, 1970) or serial-choice reaction time (Fairweather and Hutt, 1972) where changes with chronological age are gradual and monotonic. However, what the concept of developmental stage connotes, which age of subject does not, is that some developmental changes appear to be qualitative rather than quantitative. A new skill (or, usually, a set of skills) appears in the child's behavioural repertoire, rather than an incremental change in a previously existing skill. Perhaps the most striking examples of such step-function changes in behaviour are seen in the area of language acquisition. For example, few children starting at infant school (4–5 years old) are able to form grammatically correct tag-phrases ("Isn't it?, won't we?"), yet most will have acquired the rule for performing these transformations some months later. Even more interesting is the sudden appearance of grammatically incorrect utterances, which appear to be exceedingly refractory to correction, for example, double negatives, such as "Nobody don't like me" at the age of 3 years.

Developmental stage as an explanatory concept

In cases like this, which do not appear to fit any obvious learning paradigm and which have more the appearance of a qualitative than of a quantitative change in behaviour, it is tempting to use developmental stage as an explanatory concept. Kessen (1962) has made the same point: we are tempted to explain the occurrence of a small child's negativistic behaviour by the pronouncement that he has reached the negativistic stage. Although, as Kessen points out, there is a non-trivial use for such statements—it suggests a group of explanations which do not work—this kind of thinking is as stultifying to further investigation as labelling a behaviour pattern "innate", (Lehrman, 1970). Ryan's lambasting of current thinking (Chapter 21) in developmental psycholinguistics is therefore particularly timely. As she points out explanations in terms of developmental stages underestimate the sheer complexity of the processes underlying language acquisition. Language is acquired in a social situation to perform a social function: communication. It would be very peculiar indeed, from a biological point of view, if the only important variable was the hearing of grammatically correct utterances. To be fair to Brown and his co-workers, they have never underestimated the helpfulness of the social environment in language acquisition, but have been much more concerned to show *what* environmental influences are unhelpful to acquiring *what* aspects of language (Cazden, 1965). Moreover, many of the important points raised by Ryan—the inferences made by parents in expanding infants' sentences, the frequency of misinterpreting his utterances—are all fully acknowledged by Brown *et al.* (1969). The point nevertheless is well taken: much more research is needed on the natural history of language in parent-child interaction, including the role of imitation. The fact that certain infant utterances could not have been the result of imitation (e.g. double negatives) does not mean that imitation plays no role in language acquisition. The question is: what is the functional relationship between utterances which clearly are the result of imitation and those which are not? In other words, *what* is learned by imitation?

The tendency to use developmental stage as an explanatory concept is not confined to the development of language. Several of the chapters are framed within the context of what Sinclair calls "Piaget's theory". I have always been unclear in what sense Piaget's theory is a theory. It seems to me that it might more accurately be described as a taxonomy of behaviour. I am not arguing, as have some psychologists (e.g. Bijou and Baer, 1963) that classification of behaviour by developmental stages is neither necessary nor useful. I simply want to point out a possible danger of confusing a taxonomy with an explanatory system. This is illustrated by Etienne's Chapter 18, in which she suggests that what can be learned at a particular developmental stage is limited by the cognitive structure extant at that time. But what are the features by which the cognitive structure is defined? At least in part, by what is learned. Implicit in the very title of Etienne's paper is a tautology which I believe characterizes a good deal of Piagetian psychology. (It is perhaps no accident that some child psychiatrists, such as Wolff (1960), have been so impressed by the similarities of the developmental psychologies of Piaget and Freud: both have a prodigous capacity for *post hoc* explanation.) It may be that in principle a cognitive structure could be defined in such a way as to provide for any particular age a working model of intellectual processes, but we must be clear what expectations we may have of such a model. The components of a model should each specify one set of the behavioural data to be accounted for; the model should state precisely what are the inter-relationships amongst the component parts; and preferably, though not essentially, it should provide a hint as to what kind of underlying mechanisms might give rise to such inter-relationships. Thus, a model should do more than provide vivid labels from one area of discourse for attachment to the phenomena of another.

This is where I have some reservations about Connolly's contribution (Chapter 17). Connolly's study of the natural history of manipulative skill is both interesting and important, but I am unclear as to how it is illuminated by his proposed model of skill development. The model provides some neat descriptive labels, but it tells us very little either about how the component parts are organized or about possible underlying mechanisms; nor can I see what testable predictions arise from it. Similarly, although Etienne has described some of the components of behaviour which would have to be accounted for in a model of each developmental stage, she gives little indication of how the components are thought to be interconnected. If Piaget's cognitive structures are not merely a behavioural taxonomy, but models of intellectual processes (as I do not doubt Etienne and Sinclair would maintain) then I would like to know what predictions can be made from them and what results could in principle refute them. Or are we to argue that for a model of biological processes, prediction and refutation are not important criteria of its utility? Curiously enough, whilst Bryant (Chapter 20) makes no pretention of model making, his experiments on how logical inferences in children are made are readily assimilated to existing models of human performance (e.g. Broadbent, 1971; Norman, 1969), and at least indicate what may be some of the links between presentation of a logical inference problem and its solution. At the same time, I am reluctant to accept, what seems to be one implication of

Bryant's analysis, that recall of the individual paired comparisons is not only a necessary, but a sufficient, condition for making logical inferences. I would be interested to see how autistic children perform on this test. They are often reported as having normal short-term memory whilst manifesting very poor conceptual skill (Hermelin and O'Connor, 1971). My guess is that whilst recalling the individual comparisons they would be unable to solve the $B > D$ comparison.

Developmental stage as a maturational concept

Sinclair has reminded us that inherent in Piaget's theory of development—we should perhaps remember that Piaget is a biologist by training—is the importance of maturation of the central nervous system as a constraint upon learning. It is perhaps surprising that only two chapters in this book have discussed the role of neurological development, those by Blakemore and Marshall. On the other hand, some psychologists might maintain that on the basis of proportional representation of usefulness to psychologists, two mentions of neurology out of nineteen is about right. My own belief is that, although it may be slightly less treacherous to build a house upon quicksand than a psychology upon neurological foundations, what Hebb has called "neurophysiologizing" may be both a legitimate and an instructive exercise for comparative and developmental psychologists. Whilst it is a truism that there can be no function without structure, the puzzle of why an animal responds to this stimulus and not that at one age, why this response to a stimulus is superseded by that at another, can sometimes be unlocked by considering what neural machinery is available to the animal at a particular age. Two examples are provided by Sackett's (1963) work on the chicken retina and Anokhin's (1964) work on the cochlea of the baby crow, which we have already mentioned (Comments on Chapter 2). Sackett's studies suggest that the developmental stage for maximum imprinting in newly-hatched chickens is determined by maturation of movement-sensitive ganglion cells. Similarly, Anokhin's studies show that the specificity of the food-begging response of the baby crow is determined by the selective neuroanatomical maturation of the basilar membrane: the only cells which are functionally mature at hatching are the ones that resonate to the adults' "caw" sound.

Perhaps the only systematic attempt to provide a neurological framework for sensitive periods in learning in animals is provided by Fox (1966). Fox observes that the early social behaviour of non-precocial animals may be divided into a number of functional stages, whose sequence is remarkably similar, even though their exact chronology differs from species to species. From consideration of various structural and functional parameters of the CNS and of the organization of reflex pattern—which may not themselves be implicated in the social behaviour in question—Fox suggests that each behavioural stage is associated with a particular pattern of neurological development which is strikingly similar in each of several species. Dealing with early socialization in human infants, Bronson (1965) has also identified three developmental stages which may be defined in neurological terms: the first month of life when the infant is effectively a brain stem preparation; the second to fifth month, when subcortical forebrain and limbic structures are approaching maturity; and the sixth month onwards, when the visual neocortex is beginning to show rapid maturation. Bronson argues that the successive maturation of short-axon networks at each of these three functional levels is associated with changes in specific responsiveness to stimuli and in learning mechanisms, and that it is these selective mechanisms which determine what is learned when in early development. Thus, when we question how a child or other animal comes to perform this behaviour pattern rather than that at a particular stage in ontogeny, one quite proper answer might be: because this structure, but not that, is mature. In other words, our answer would be in terms of a "hidden mechanism" (Harré, 1960).

A few examples of interesting correspondences between brain maturation and behavioural development will be informative. Recent work by Wall (1970) suggests that information about a manipulated object may have a specific route to the brain via the dorsal roots, whose myelination is completed at $3\frac{1}{2}$ months. Both Piaget and White and Held (1966) have identified a stage in sensori-motor development when the infant begins to show visually-guided reaching; the mean age for the onset of this behaviour is $3\frac{1}{2}$ months. Ambrose (1961) has shown that the maximum generalization of smiling to a human face in babies occurs at about 3 months, suggesting that by this age babies can code the brightness features of the human face. This corresponds with the attainment of full myelination of the visual system as far as the lateral geniculate. The optic radiation only attains its full complement of myelin during the fifth month of life and it is during this period that the visual cortex also shows a major increase in maturation. It is therefore of interest that the onset of "sobering" to strangers—which would presuppose the finer pattern discrimination usually associated with cortical processes—begins at about this time (Bronson, personal communication). In marked contrast to the subcortical visual pathways, the acoustic tectum and tegmentum and the cochlea are already mature before birth. This suggests that some sound discrimination may already be possible in the human neonate. A series of experiments by Hutt et al. (1968) have led to the hypothesis that the peripheral auditory apparatus of the baby is specifically adapted to ensure response to the most important biological stimulus in his environment, his mother. Here is an example of how a question about the function of a neural structure may lead unexpectedly to behavioural experiments. A surprising finding of Yakovlev and Lecours (1967) is that the myelination of the reticular activating system (RAS) is not completed until the second decade of life. However, if we recall that the RAS is primarily a structure concerned with the integration of motor behaviour (Jung and Hassler, 1960), it may be somewhat less surprising that the stage of optimal performance of perceptual-motor and athletic skills, late in the second decade of life, is also the time when maximum conductive efficiency is attained. We may thus begin to see how closely behaviour and learning are related to differential maturation of brain structures in early development. Whilst developmental stages in behaviour cannot be defined in neurological terms, consideration of neural development may help to assess their validity.

Other Variables Affecting Learning

Any conference whose topic is as fundamental as the present one will inevitably leave a number of relevant issues unexplored. In conclusion, therefore, it may be appropriate to remind ourselves of a number of variables which have not been treated in this conference but which may exert important constraints upon learning. I will mention just three.

(1) *Sex of subject*. It is surprising how infrequently the sex of animal subjects is specified in psychological research reports. Even at a human level, it seems to have been assumed until quite recently that sex differences in non-sexual behaviour are the result of cultural expectations and therefore of little significance. However as several authors have recently argued, psychological sex differences may have common biological roots in both animals and in man, as the result of either early sexual differentiation of the brain (Gray, 1971; Hutt, 1972a, b) or hormonal effects upon the mature brain (Broverman *et al.*, 1968). Watson (1969) has shown that the nature of reinforcement effective in an operant situation is very different for boys and girls as young as 10 weeks of age. The problem-solving strategies too of older boys and girls differ characteristically (see review by Hutt 1972a). Very clear sex differences have been demonstrated in the acquisition of a simple perceptual-motor skill—a serial choice response task—in children between the ages of 5 and 12 years. Not only do girls show consistently shorter choice reaction times than boys, but there are spurts in the performance of both sexes at those ages when it has been shown that the pre-pubertal secretion of sex hormones is beginning to take place (Fairweather and Hutt, 1970, 1972a, b). It was these findings which led us to consider the next variable.

(2) *Hormonal state*. Using the same task, we have been stydying the effects

of endogenous changes of hormones during the menstrual cycle and of exogenous hormones administered to a small group of women being treated for various endocrinological abnormalities. Although we were looking specifically for possible effects of oestrogen—which recent investigators have implicated as a causal factor in psychological sex differences—we are wondering whether progesetrone might play a role which is at least as important. Certainly there appears to be increasing variability of performance in perceptual-motor skill just prior to menstruation (Hutt, 1971). The effects of androgens on attentional processes (Andrew and Rogers, 1972; Klaiber *et al.*, 1971) suggests that learning of particular kinds may be considerably affected by hormonal factors. Whilst in some cases hormones may influence behaviour through their effects upon the autonomic system, there is also evidence that they have indirect effects upon central processes. For this reason, we have included in our studies one index of cerebral state—cortical evoked potentials. Moreover, in other studies with children, one of the most important variations affecting skill has been shown to be:

(3) *Electro-cortical state*. Both level of performance and rate of learning of our serial choice response task is affected by the type of activity found in the EEG. The most dramatic examples of this are provided by so-called spike-wave activity which produces a marked reduction in the child's "channel capacity" (Fairweather and Hutt, 1969). These studies again suggest that consideration of neurophysiological and neuro-endocrinological variables may be a further important source of information about constraints upon learning.

References

Ambrose, J. A. (1961). The development of the smiling response. *In* "Determinants of Infant Behaviour", (B. M. Foss, ed.). Methuen, London.

Andrew, R. J. and Rogers, L. (1972). Testosterone, search behaviour and persistence. *Nature* **237**, 343–346.

Anokhin, P. K. (1964). Systemogenesis as a general regulator of brain development. *In* "The Developing Brain, Progress in Brain Research", Vol. 9. (W. A. Himwich and H. E. Himwich, eds.). Elsevier, Amsterdam.

Bijou, W., and Baer, D. M. (1963). "Child Development." Appleton-Century-Crofts, New York.

Broadbent, D. E. (1971). "Decision and Stress." Academic Press, London.

Bronson, G. (1965). Hierarchical organisation of the central nervous system in early life. *Behav. Sci.* **10**, 7–25.

Broverman, D. M., Klaiber, E. L., Kobayashi, Y. and Vogel, W. (1968). Roles of activation and inhibition in sex differences in cognitive abilities. *Psychol. Rev.* **75**, 23–50.

Brown, R., Cazden, C. and Bellugi-Klima, U. (1969). The child's grammar from I to III. *In* "Minnesota Symposia on Child Psychology", Vol. 2. (J. P. Hill, ed.). University of Minnesota Press, Minneapolis.

Cazden, C. B. (1965). Environmental assistance to the child's acquisition of grammar. Ph.D. thesis, Harvard University.

Connolly, K. J. (1970). Response speed, temporal sequencing and information processing in children. *In* "Mechanisms of Motor Skill Development." K. J. (Connolly, ed.). Academic Press, London.

Dennis, W. (1941). Infant development under conditions of restricted practice and of minimal social stimulation. *Genet. Psychol. Mon.* **23**, 143–189.

Fairweather, H. and Hutt, S. J. (1969). Inter-relationships of EEG activity and information processing in paced and self-paced tasks in epileptic children. *EEG. clin. Neurophysiol.* Suppl. **27**, 432.

Fairweather, H. and Hutt, S. J. (1970). The development of information processing and reaction times in normal schoolchildren. *Bull. Brit. Psychol. Soc.* **23**, 61.

Fairweather, H. and Hutt, S. J. (1972a). Sex differences in a perceptual-motor skill. *In* "Gender Differences: their Ontogeny and Significance", (C. Ounsted and D. C. Taylor, eds.). Churchill, London.

Fairweather, H. and Hutt, S. J. (1972b). Development of choice reaction times in children. Unpublished report.

Fowler, W. (1965). A study of process and method in three year old twins and triplets learning to read. *Genet. Psychol. Monogr.* **72**, 3–90.

Fox, M. W. (1966). Neuro-behavioral ontogeny. A synthesis of ethological and neurophysiological concepts. *Brain Res.* **2**, 3–20.

Gates, A. I. (1937). The necessary mental age for beginning reading. *Elementary School J.* **37**, 497–508.

Gesell, A. and Thompson, H. (1929). Learning and growth in identical infant twins. *Genet. Psychol. Monogr.* **6**, 1–24.

Gray, J. A. (1971). Sex differences in emotional behaviour in mammals including man: endocrine bases. *Acta Psychologica* **35**, 29–46.

Harré, R. (1960). "Introduction to the Logic of Science". Macmillan, London.

Hermelin, B. and O'Connor, N. (1971). "Psychological Experiments with Autistic Children." Pergamon, Oxford.

Hutt, C. (1972a). "Males and Females." Harmondsworth, Penguin Books.

Hutt, C. (1972b). Neuroendocrinological, behavioural and intellectual aspects of sexual differentiation in human development. *In* "Gender Differences: their Ontogeny and Significance", (C. Ounsted and D. C. Taylor, eds.), Churchill, London.

Hutt, S. J. (1971). Some hormonal effects upon perceptual-motor skill. *Bull. Brit. Psychol. Soc.* **24**, 240–241.

Hutt, S. J., Hutt, C., Lenard, H. G., von Bernuth, H. and Muntjewerff, W. J. (1968). Auditory responsivity in the human neonate. *Nature* **218**, 888–890.

Jung, R. and Hassler, R. (1960). The extra-pyramidal system. *In* "Handbook of Physiology", Vol. 2, Sect. 1, Neurophysiology, (F. Field, ed.). *Amer. Physiol. Soc.*, Washington D.C.

Kessen, W. (1962). "Stage" and "structure" in the study of children. *Monogr. Soc. Res. Child. Devel.* 55–72.

Klaiber, E. L., Broverman, D. M., Vogel, W., Abraham, G. E. and Cone, F. L. (1971). Effects of infused testosterone on mental performances and serum L.H. *J. clin. endocr. Metab.* **32**, 341–9.

Lehrman, D. S. (1970). Semantic and conceptual issues in the nature-nurture problem. *In* "Development and Evolution of Behavior", (L. R. Aronson, E. Tobach, D. S. Lehrman and J. S. Rosenblatt, eds.). Freeman, San Francisco.

McGraw, M. B. (1935). "Growth: a Study of Johnny and Jimmy". Appleton, New York.

Moore, O. K. (1966). Autotelic responsive environments and exceptional children. *In* "Experience, Structure and Adaptability", (O. J. Harvey, ed.). Springer, New York.

Moyer, K. E. and von Gilmer, B. H. (1955). Attention spans of children for experimentally designed toys. *J. Genet. Psychol.* **87**, 187–201.

Norman, D. A. (1969). "Memory and Attention." Wiley, New York.

Sackett, G. P. (1963). A neural mechanism underlying unlearned, critical period, and developmental aspects of visually controlled behavior. *Psychol. Rev.* **70**, 40–50.

Van Alstyne, D. (1932). Play Behavior and Choice of Play Materials of Preschool Children. University of Chicago Press, Chicago.

Wall, P. D. (1970). The sensory and motor role of impulses travelling in the dorsal columns towards cerebral cortex. *Brain* **93**, 505–524.

Watson, J. S. (1969). Operant conditioning of visual fixation in infants under visual and auditory reinforcement. *Devel. Psychol.* **1**, 508–516.

White, B. L. and Held, R. (1966). Plasticity of sensori-motor development in the human infant. *In* "Causes of Behavior", Vol. 2 (J. F. Rosenblith and W. Allinsmith, eds.). Allyn & Bacon, Boston.

Wolff, P. H. (1960). "The Developmental Psychologies of Jean Piaget and Psychoanalysis." International Universities Press, New York.

Yakovlev, P. I., and Lecours, A-R. (1967). The myologenetic cycles of regional maturation of the brain. *In* "Regional Maturation of the Brain in Early Life", (A. Minkowski, ed.). Blackwell, Oxford.

Comments

1. Humphrey asked if Hutt would deduce, from Yakovlev and Lecours' findings on rate of myelination, that babies do not establish sleep-dream cycles until adulthood (since the reticular formation does not complete its myelination until then).

Hutt replied:

"This question challenges my contention that myelination is an important determinant of behavioural change. The question rests on what Jung and Hassler (1960) described as 'the fashionable belief amongst psychologists that the ARAS controls arousal,' whereas the weight of evidence points to its being a motor centre. Both Magoun's synchronizing centre (n. tractus solitarius) and Jouvet's dream centre (n.r. pontis caudalis) are lower down the brain stem than the classical Moruzzi-Magoun ARAS. Thus, whilst changes in vigilance may be mediated by changes in motor output, it is unlikely that the ARAS controls sleeping and dreaming. The fact that our peak age for athletic skills and concentration correspond with the completion of myelination of the ARAS is surely suggestive that there is some link?"

2. Hutt (p. 461–3) emphasizes the role of "maturation" of the central nervous system, presumably referring to tissue growth and differentiation within it. Of course maturation itself poses a further developmental problem. Processes of maturation by definition occur in, and depend on, the intraorganismic environment: they are not influenced by extraorganismic factors only because the environment relevant to them is maintained constant by homeostatic mechanisms. In addition, it is not always easy to separate the consequences of tissue differentiation *per se* from those of experience : even when maturation has led to the development of an eye, that eye may not be functional until it has been exposed to light (e.g. Knoll, 1953; Riesen, 1966).

References

Jung, R. and Hassler, R. (1960). The extra-pyramidal system. *In* "Handbook of Physiology," Vol. 2, Sect. 1, Neurophysiology. (F. Field, ed.). *Amer. Physiol. Soc.* Washington D.C.

Knoll, M. (1953). Uber das Tages—und Dämmerungssehen des Grasfrosches (*Rana temporaria* L.) nach Aufzucht in veränderten Lichtbedingungen. *Z. vergl. Physiol.* **35**, 42–70.

Riesen, A. H. (1966). Sensory deprivation. *In* "Progress in Physiological Psychology", (E. Stellar and J. M. Sprague, eds.), **1**, 117–147. Academic Press, New York.

Epilogue

That generalizations about learning must be hedged about by reservations relating to species, task and context is amply established in the preceding chapters. The constraints described do not include all possible ones, but perhaps their collection into one volume will stimulate the description of others. We would not wish to suggest any absolute guide lines as to how they will be found. Certainly some of the chapters in this book demonstrate that the sophisticated use of conventional techniques can still bring remarkable insights. But we must feel a need for the study of learning in a wider range of situations, and especially a need for comparative study: detailed comparisons between the learning performances of the same species in different contexts, and between those of different species in the same context, seem especially likely to throw light on the constraints that determine the course of learning.

As the different ways in which learning is constrained are described, the problem of the classification of constraints arises. This is hardly touched on in this volume. One possible start lies in our sub-title – Limitations and Predispositions. Another arises from the question of whether the constraint is basically one of capacity or not. Most of the earlier chapters are concerned with constraints that are not: knowledge about them comes either from a close examination of the way in which the course of learning is determined in one situation, or from comparative studies between learning performances of the same or closely related species. A preliminary classification of sub-types within this category is given in Chapter 13. Constraints involving capacity may be studied by comparing the behaviour of distantly related species in similar situations (e.g. Chapter 18) or by comparing different individuals (perhaps of different age) of the same species. In either case, and especially when distantly related species are compared, it is necessary to bear in mind the danger that the identification of constraints of capacity will be confused by constraints of other types. And when comparative studies are made, studies of constraints must involve asking how it comes about that learning does occur as well as why it does not. Whether, when we have a classification of constraints, it will still appear profitable to think in terms of general laws hedged about by constraints, or whether some quite new formulation will seem more profitable, is an open issue.

Whether we are concerned with limitations or predispositions, the question of adaptedness arises. Are we concerned with a constraint that has been evolved as a consequence of natural selection, or not? And if so, has natural selection operated directly to produce that constraint, or is the constraint itself a consequence of natural selection operating on some other function? These are questions which have been discussed too little in this volume, largely because studies of adaptive differences in learning performance between species have hardly started. But evidence of the type discussed in Chapter 1 indicate that they exist. If they do, then surely man himself is no exception. The difficulty with the human case is that there is no closely related species with similar capacities with whom he can be compared: an important tool for revealing constraints is therefore missing. One method, touched on in Chapter 23, involves the controversial area of sex differences. Another, intrinsic to the developmental approach, is the study of the nature of the differences between age groups. That we do find the means to come to terms with the limitations and predispositions for learning of the human organism is, as Tinbergen has stressed in his 1972 Croonian Lecture, a matter of the greatest importance. If children are adapted to learn in certain ways, if girls learn some things more quickly than do boys, if city living requires men to learn ways of behaving for which they have no natural bent, these are things of which we should surely be aware.

Reference

Tinbergen, N. (1972). Functional ethology and the human sciences. The Croonian Lecture 1972. *Proc. Roy. Soc. Lond. B*, **182**, 385–410.

Author Index

Subject Index